AF600249

Collected Works of Northrop Frye

VOLUME 18

The Secular Scripture
and Other Writings on Critical Theory
1976–1991

The Collected Edition of the Works of Northrop Frye has been planned and is being directed by an editorial committee under the aegis of Victoria University, through its Northrop Frye Centre. The purpose of the edition is to make available authoritative texts of both published and unpublished works, based on an analysis and comparison of all available materials, and supported by scholarly apparatus, including annotation and introductions. The Northrop Frye Centre gratefully acknowledges financial support, through McMaster University, from the Michael G. DeGroote family.

The Secular Scripture and Other Writings on Critical Theory 1976–1991

VOLUME 18

Edited by Joseph Adamson and Jean Wilson

UNIVERSITY OF TORONTO PRESS
Toronto Buffalo London

Toronto Buffalo London

ISBN 0-8020-3945-6

Library and Archives Canada Cataloguing in Publication

Frye, Northrop, 1912–1991.
The secular scripture and other writings on critical theory, 1976–1991 / Northrop Frye ; edited by Joseph Adamson and Jean Wilson

(Collected works of Northrop Frye ; v. 18)
Includes bibliographical references and index.
ISBN 0-8020-3945-6

1. Criticism. 2. Literature – History and criticism.
I. Adamson, Joseph, 1950– II. Wilson, Jean III. Title. IV. Series.

PN56.R6F72 2006 801′.95 C2005-906636-9

This volume has been published with the assitance of a grant from Victoria University.

University of Toronto Press acknowledges the financial assistance to its publishing program of the Canada Council for the Arts and the Ontario Arts Council.

University of Toronto Press acknowledges the financial support for its publishing activities of the Government of Canada through the Book Publishing Industry Development Program (BPIDP).

For our children—Lois and Murray—
and for Roy and Lois Wilson

Contents

Preface

This volume contains thirty-one items pertaining to literary theory and criticism from the last fifteen years of Northrop Frye's life. The first dates from April 1975, when Frye delivered the Charles Eliot Norton Lectures at Harvard, while the last, a response to essays on *Anatomy of Criticism*, was presented in April 1990 to the American Society for Eighteenth-Century Studies. The Harvard lectures, six in all, were published in 1976 as *The Secular Scripture: A Study of the Structure of Romance*, one of Frye's most popular and influential books. The remaining writings are on a variety of topics and stem from a number of different occasions and contexts. Most of the essays were first presented orally; indeed, apart from miscellaneous pieces such as letters to the editor (nos. 3 and 21), a brief comment or introduction (nos. 5, 7, and 15), and anthology or handbook entries (nos. 8 and 20), only three items (nos. 13, 16, and 22) were produced solely in view of publication. The writings are arranged in chronological order, with items that were first delivered as lectures ordered according to the date of original presentation rather than to the date of publication, and those with a year date only preceding those with a specific day or month.

Headnotes to the individual items specify the copy-text, which, unless otherwise indicated, is the first published edition. All known reprintings in English are also listed. We have noted the existence of typescripts and where they can be found in the Northrop Frye Fonds (abbreviated as NFF) in the Victoria University Library. A full listing is contained in the *Guide to the Northrop Frye Papers* (Toronto: Victoria University Library, 1993), compiled by Dolores A. Signori. All authoritative versions of individual items have been collated, and variants of particular interest are given in endnotes. Substantive changes to the copy-text are included in the list of editorial emendations at the end of the volume. References to Frye's notebooks follow the system explained in detail in Robert D. Denham's preface to vols. 5 and 6 of the Collected Works; in particular, "Notebook" (abbreviated as NB) refers to holograph material, and "Notes" to typed material (see *LN*, x).

We have followed the general practice of the Collected Works in handling published material from a variety of sources. Since the conventions of spelling, typography, and punctuation derive from the different publishers' house styles rather than from Frye, we have regularized them silently throughout the volume. For instance, Canadian spellings ending in "-our" have been substituted for American "-or" ones, commas have been added before the "and" in sequences of three, and titles of poems and short stories have been italicized. We have silently corrected obvious misspellings and typographical errors, as well as minor grammatical infelicities. Occasionally we have combined two short paragraphs to form a single, longer one. All editorial additions have been placed in square brackets. Page numbers from the original edition of *The Secular Scripture* have been inserted into the text of no. 1 for convenience of reference.

Frye's allusions and sources are identified in endnotes or in square brackets within the text. The relatively rare references provided by Frye himself are given in braces when they appear in the text and are indicated by "[NF]" in the case of endnotes. Frye frequently modernizes spelling and orthography, and as a rule we have retained his modernization, but occasionally accidentals have been changed silently within a quotation in accordance with a specific source. All references to the Bible are to the King James or Authorized Version, and we have consistently used the Loeb edition for Classical works; *The Riverside Chaucer*; and *The Riverside Shakespeare*. Endnotes often indicate the existence of an annotated copy of the work in question in Frye's own collection, now the Northrop Frye Library (abbreviated as NFL) in the Victoria University Library. Such a notation is not repeated in subsequent references to the same text, and for the most part this information is not provided in the case of standard works of literature and philosophy. In accordance with the general practice of the Collected Works, full bibliographical references are given only once; where necessary, subsequent notes direct readers to the note in which such information is provided.

Authors mentioned in passing are generally not annotated, but life dates are provided in the index, as is the date of first publication of individual works. Where a title alone appears, the author's last name is inserted in square brackets to facilitate effective use of the index. This is sometimes done even in the case of well-known titles, not only for consistency, but with the needs of a wide and diverse readership in mind. "For many years now," says Frye at the end of no. 28, "Auguries of Experience," "I have been addressing myself primarily not to other critics, but to students and a nonspecialist public, realizing that whatever new directions can come to my discipline will come from their needs and their intense if unfocused vision" (450). The annotations reflect to some degree our recognition of the inclusiveness of Frye's work in another sense as well. Trained in Comparative Literature, we are both particularly mindful of the international range of Frye's reading, and, accordingly, offer our various notes of identification and explanation in an avowedly comparatist spirit. Finally, we would highlight a passage from the last item in the present volume, which comments wryly on a common practice in the 1940s: "many scholars made their reputation by editing texts in whatever way would best represent their original appearance and make them most forbidding for the modern reader" (479). Bearing in mind Frye's very different approach, we have endeavoured to provide a practical edition of his writings, which we hope will reflect the author's own evident concern for his audience and will be helpful to readers from a variety of backgrounds and orientations.

Acknowledgments

For their invaluable support and encouragement, we wish to thank Alvin Lee, the General Editor of the Collected Works of Northrop Frye; Jean O'Grady, the Associate Editor; and Ward McBurney, the Editorial Assistant. All three have shared their expertise with unfailing patience and generosity, and it has been a pleasure to work with them. We are grateful to James Carscallen and Konrad Eisenbichler for their translation of various documents, and to Jean O'Grady, who recovered the original English preface to the Italian edition of *The Secular Scripture*; we also appreciate the kind cooperation of the publisher, Il Mulino. Miranda Purves expertly typed or scanned the items originally, and Michael Happy, Michael Lutz, and Helen Smith provided excellent research assistance. Special thanks to Ward McBurney for preparing the index and for helping out in so many other ways; his assistance has made all the difference.

To the anonymous readers who reported to the University of Toronto Press, we owe a particular word of appreciation. They took great care with the manuscript and offered both detailed and inspired suggestions for its improvement, as did, subsequently, Margaret Burgess, whom we were exceedingly fortunate to have as copy-editor. Finally, we would like to express our sincere gratitude to the following, who provided essential information incorporated into the annotations: Alan A. Adamson, David Blewett, Margaret Burgess, Clayton Chrusch, Sean Davidson, Robert Denham, Michael Dolzani, Walter Englert, John Ferns, Glen Gill, Donald Goellnicht, Ron Granofsky, Nicholas Halmi, Brian John, Howard Jones, Peter Kingston, Alvin Lee, Geert Lernout, Duncan Lucas, Graeme MacQueen, Ward McBurney, Richard Morton, Susie O'Brien, Helen Ostovich, John Robertson, Eileen Schuller, Ian Singer, Peter Walmsley, Lois Wilson, and Roy Wilson.

Credits and Sources

We wish to acknowledge the following sources for permission to reprint works previously published by them. We have not been able to determine the copyright status of all the works included in this volume, and welcome notice from any copyright holders who have been inadvertently omitted from these acknowledgments.

Addison Wesley Longman for "Preface," "On Fiction," "On Poetry," and "On Drama," from *The Practical Imagination*, ed. Northrop Frye, Sheridan Baker, and George Perkins (1980); and for "Preface," "Allegory," "Archetype," "Bible as Literature," "Bible, Translations of," "Comedy," "Epic," "Freudian Criticism," "Genre," "Jungian Criticism," "Lyric," "Mimesis," "Myth," "Plot," "Romance," "Satire," "Structure," "Symbol," and "Tragedy," from Northrop Frye, Sheridan Baker, and George Perkins, *The Harper Handbook to Literature* (1985).

Prof. Shay Cohen, Brown University, for "Vision and Cosmos," from *Biblical Patterns in Modern Literature*, ed. David H. Hirsch and Nehama Aschkenasy, Brown Judaic Studies, 77 (1984).

Cornell University Press for "The Survival of Eros in Poetry," from *Romanticism and Contemporary Criticism*, ed. Morris Eaves and Michael Fischer. © 1986 by Cornell University. Reprinted by permission of the publisher.

Prof. Robert D. Denham for "Literature as Therapy," from *Northrop Frye Newsletter*, 3, no. 2 (1991); and for "Auguries of Experience," from *Visionary Poetics: Essays on Northrop Frye's Criticism*, ed. Robert D. Denham and Thomas Willard (1991).

Harvard University Press for *The Secular Scripture: A Study of the Structure of Romance* (1976). © 1976 by the President and Fellows of Harvard College. Reprinted by permission of the publisher.

Indiana University Press for "Romance as Masque," from Northrop Frye, *Spiritus Mundi: Essays on Literature, Myth, and Society* (1976).

The Johns Hopkins University Press for "The Responsibilities of the Critic," from *Modern Language Notes*, 91 (1976), © The Johns Hopkins University Press; and for "Response," from *Eighteenth-Century Studies*, 24 (1990–91). © American Society for Eighteenth-Century Studies. Reprinted by permission of the publisher.

Midwest Modern Language Association for "Literature, History, and Language," from the *Bulletin of the Midwest Modern Language Association*, 12 (1979).

Modern Language Association of America for "Literary and Linguistic Scholarship in a Postliterate World," from *PMLA*, 99 (1984); and for "Letter to the Editor," from *PMLA*, 100 (1985).

Oxford University Press for "The Expanding World of Metaphor," from *Journal of the American Academy of Religion*, 53 (1985).

University of Georgia Press for "Lacan and the Full Word," from *Criticism and Lacan: Essays and Dialogue on Language, Structure and the Unconscious*, ed. Patrick Colm Hogan and Lalita Pandit (1990).

Prof. Paolo Valesio, member of the editorial board of *Yale Italian Studies* (1977–78), for "Comment on Peter Hughes's Essay," from *Yale Italian Studies*, 1 (1977).

With the exception of those listed above, all works are printed by courtesy of the Estate of Northrop Frye/Victoria University.

Abbreviations

NOTE: Books are by Frye unless otherwise indicated.

AC	*Anatomy of Criticism: Four Essays*. Princeton: Princeton University Press, 1957.
AV	Authorized Version
BG	*The Bush Garden: Essays on the Canadian Imagination*. Toronto: Anansi, 1971.
Bronson	Samuel Johnson. *Rasselas, Poems, and Selected Prose*. Ed. Bertrand H. Bronson. New York: Rinehart, 1958.
C	*Northrop Frye on Canada*. Ed. Jean O'Grady and David Staines. CW, 12. Toronto: University of Toronto Press, 2003.
Caws	Stéphane Mallarmé. *Selected Poetry and Prose*. Ed. Mary Ann Caws. New York: New Directions, 1982.
CP	*The Critical Path: An Essay on the Social Context of Literary Criticism*. Bloomington: Indiana University Press, 1971.
CW	Collected Works of Northrop Frye
DV	*The Double Vision: Language and Meaning in Religion*. Toronto: University of Toronto Press, 1991.
EAC	*The Eternal Act of Creation: Essays, 1979–1990*. Ed. Robert D. Denham. Bloomington: Indiana University Press, 1993.
ENC	*Northrop Frye's Writings on the Eighteenth and Nineteenth Centuries*. Ed. Imre Salusinszky. CW, 17. Toronto: University of Toronto Press, 2005.
Erdman	*The Complete Poetry and Prose of William Blake*. Rev. ed. Ed. David V. Erdman. Berkeley: University of California Press, 1982.

FI	*Fables of Identity: Studies in Poetic Mythology*. New York: Harcourt, Brace & World, 1963.
FS	*Fearful Symmetry: A Study of William Blake*. Princeton: Princeton University Press, 1947.
FS2	*Fearful Symmetry: A Study of William Blake*. Ed. Nicholas Halmi, with an Introduction by Ian Singer. CW, 14. Toronto: University of Toronto Press, 2004.
GC	*The Great Code: The Bible and Literature*. New York: Harcourt Brace Jovanovich, 1982.
Herford	*Ben Jonson*. Ed. C.H. Herford, Percy and Evelyn Simpson. 11 vols. Oxford: Clarendon Press, 1925–52.
Kermode	*Selected Prose of T.S. Eliot*. Ed. Frank Kermode. London: Faber & Faber, 1975.
Keynes	Sir Thomas Browne. *Selected Writings*. Ed. Geoffrey Keynes. London: Faber & Faber, 1968.
LN	*The Late Notebooks of Northrop Frye, 1982–1990: Architecture of the Spiritual World*. Ed. Robert D. Denham. CW, 5–6. Toronto: University of Toronto Press, 2000.
M&B	*Northrop Frye on Milton and Blake*. Ed Angela Esterhammer. CW, 16. Toronto: University of Toronto Press, 2005.
MD	*The Myth of Deliverance: Reflections on Shakespeare's Problem Comedies*. Toronto: University of Toronto Press, 1983.
MLA	Modern Language Association of America
MM	*Myth and Metaphor: Selected Essays, 1974–1988*. Ed. Robert D. Denham. Charlottesville: University Press of Virginia, 1990.
NB	Notebook
NF	Northrop Frye
NFC	*Northrop Frye in Conversation*. Ed. David Cayley. Concord, Ont.: Anansi, 1992.
NFF	Northrop Frye Fonds, Victoria University Library
NFL	Northrop Frye Library (the annotated books in Frye's personal library, now in the Victoria University Library)
NFR	*Northrop Frye on Religion: Excluding "The Great Code" and "Words with Power."* Ed. Alvin A. Lee and Jean O'Grady. CW, 4. Toronto: University of Toronto Press, 1999.
NFS	*Northrop Frye on Shakespeare*. Ed. Robert Sandler. Markham, Ont.: Fitzhenry & Whiteside, 1986.
NP	*A Natural Perspective: The Development of Shakespearean*

	Comedy and Romance. New York: Columbia University Press, 1965.
NR	*Northrop Frye's Notebooks on Romance*. Ed. Michael Dolzani. CW, 15. Toronto: University of Toronto Press, 2004.
RE	*The Return of Eden: Five Essays on Milton's Epics*. Toronto: University of Toronto Press, 1965.
SeS	*The Secular Scripture: A Study of the Structure of Romance*. Cambridge, Mass.: Harvard University Press, 1976.
SM	*Spiritus Mundi: Essays on Literature, Myth, and Society*. Bloomington: Indiana University Press, 1976.
SR	*A Study of English Romanticism*. Chicago: University of Chicago Press, 1968.
StS	*The Stubborn Structure: Essays on Criticism and Society*. Ithaca, N.Y.: Cornell University Press, 1970.
TS	Typescript
TSE	*T.S. Eliot*. Chicago: University of Chicago Press, 1963.
WGS	*A World in a Grain of Sand: Twenty-Two Interviews with Northrop Frye*. Ed. Robert D. Denham. New York: Peter Lang, 1991.
WP	*Words with Power: Being a Second Study of "The Bible and Literature."* New York: Harcourt Brace Jovanovich, 1990.
WTC	*The Well-Tempered Critic*. Bloomington: Indiana University Press, 1963.

Introduction

I

The first part of this volume is taken up by one of Northrop Frye's most remarkable literary studies, *The Secular Scripture,* a work that has not yet received the readership it deserves. Its original publication in 1976 partly explains this neglect: it appeared at the very moment that Frye's influence[1] was beginning to ebb, as the contestatory criticism of poststructuralism, deconstruction, and New Historicism took wing and began to overshadow the entire discipline. Moreover, its subject matter did not seem to suggest the weight and wisdom that were to be associated with the two Bible books (*GC* and *WP*), though its argument anticipates and develops significant parts of *Words with Power.* Its publication now in the Collected Works offers an opportunity for readers to discover—or rediscover—one of Frye's most important studies.

The other material in this volume, representative of the last stage of Frye's career, reflects his sense at the time that he was working "toward some kind of final statement," albeit not necessarily "a single unified" one (*LN,* 189). This statement eventually saw the light of day, only months before his death in January 1991, as *Words with Power* (1990). Like *The Secular Scripture,* many of the papers assembled in the present volume contributed significantly to the development of that book. In the same paragraph in Notebook 44, Frye mentions "over twenty unpublished, or rather unreprinted, essays" (*LN,* 189), several of which are included here: "the Vico" (no. 4, "The Responsibilities of the Critic"), "the Wiegand lecture" (no. 10, "Literature as a Critique of Pure Reason"), "the short lyric introduction" (no. 11, "Approaching the Lyric"), "the Royal Society symbols paper" (no. 18, "The Symbol as a Medium of

Exchange"), "the Smith paper" (no. 25, "Framework and Assumption"), as well as, among "the various religion papers," the "Chicago" (no. 19, "The Expanding World of Metaphor") and the "Way" (no. 24, "The Journey as Metaphor"). In a related note, he cites the Wiegand, the Royal Society, and the Smith papers for inclusion in a volume of twelve essays, which he hoped to complete in addition to *Words with Power* (*LN*, 197). The volume never materialized as such, though the particular essays intended for it found their way into two collections edited by Robert D. Denham: *Myth and Metaphor: Selected Essays, 1974–1988* (1990) and *The Eternal Act of Creation: Essays, 1979–1990* (1993). Contributions described as "winding-up symbols"—"the Italian conference" and "the San Francisco meeting" (*LN*, 197)—are included in the present volume as nos. 26 and 27, "Maps and Territories" and "Epilogo," presented in 1987 at a conference in Rome dedicated to Frye's work, and no. 28, "Auguries of Experience," delivered the same year at the first of two special sessions on Northrop Frye at the annual convention of the Modern Language Association of America (MLA).

Some of the papers collected here were originally presented at conferences, some at meetings organized by scholarly associations or research centres, some in conjunction with special lecture series. In accordance with the variety of occasions on which they were delivered, the essays cover a range of topics, from the more specialized scholarly subject matter of no. 2, "Romance as Masque," to the interdisciplinary discussions of no. 23, "Literature and the Visual Arts," no. 25, "Framework and Assumption" (the role of convention in knowledge), and no. 29, "Literary and Mechanical Models" (computing in the humanities). A number of lectures focus on issues of serious interest to a wider public, both within and beyond the academy; a recurrent theme, for instance, is that of the social authority of the writer. Two of the talks (nos. 28 and 31) concern the significance of Frye's own life's work. The miscellaneous pieces—introductions, letters to the editors of journals, handbook entries, responses, etc.—reflect the same diversity of context. The style varies according to the type of presentation, but the studies all show the distinctive hallmarks of Frye's power as a writer: the clarity of exposition, the dialectical elegance, the sense of verbal deftness and ease of address, the sharp wit, and the arresting absence of jargon and pedantry. They reflect Frye's desire to formulate his thoughts in broadly intelligible language and, increasingly, to address himself "not," as he says in "Auguries of Experience," "primarily . . . to other critics, but to students and a nonspecialist public, realizing that whatever new directions can come to my discipline will come from their needs and their intense if unfocused vision" (450).

We might offer, in this regard, our personal memory of "Literature as a Critique of Pure Reason," which Frye delivered as the Wiegand lecture at the University of Toronto. The talk was presented in the evening to an overflowing audience in one of the largest auditoriums on campus. There was a buzz in the room, the electric feeling that an important event was unfolding. It was a typical "performance" by Frye in his later years: an aging, seemingly fragile man, occasionally sipping from a glass of water at his side, speaking deliberately but without much inflection, his eyes and wit sparkling, apparently unintimidated by the intense glare of attention focused on him. Thus he assumed, in his eminence, the role of spokesperson for imaginative culture, for as broad a literate audience as possible, in a society swept up by more "realistic" pursuits.

And yet, in these writings, it is the *realism* of Frye's concerns that stands out, his sense of the urgent need to articulate the actual authority of literature and criticism in contemporary society. This in part explains the impression of a formulaic quality in his writing: themes and examples recur, the same authors keep cropping up, passages are repeated in a standard form, and many readers will recognize much that is familiar from his other works.[2] There is Valéry's definition of cosmology as a poetic art, the "stock example," as he himself calls it in no. 17 (312) of Gibbon's *Decline and Fall*, Hopkins's "overthought" and "underthought," the reiterated definitions of metaphor and myth, and the discussion of primary and secondary concerns. The discussion of *Henry V* appears in several pieces, where it serves to bring home the distinction in literature between ideology and myth. This formulaic quality is not a symptom of something mechanical in Frye's thinking. It is an aphoristic element characteristic of his style, and a reflection of his constant struggle to *formulate* his insights effectively and for maximum resonance. In no. 22, "Lacan and the Full Word," he remarks on the French psychoanalyst's predilection for the oracular. This "discontinuous style," he observes, can provoke two different responses. One is to organize the "oracles into an interlocking system, even though . . . Lacan is the sort of writer who keeps suggesting the systematic in order to be free to break out of system" (392). The other possibility—one that also applies just as clearly to Frye's work—is to treat the sayings as fragmentary, to respond to their suggestiveness and recognize their possible application in very different areas. The aphoristic tendency in Frye, even more, perhaps, than in Lacan, is the force that complements the encompassing and interpenetrative power of his work. Between these two poles, the fragmentary and the diagrammatic, singular insight expands into a unity of such insights, in the warp and woof of a unique dialectical movement.

II

The Secular Scripture: A Study of the Structure of Romance was originally delivered in April 1975 as a series of lectures during Frye's term as Charles Eliot Norton Professor of Poetry at Harvard University. The occasion spurred Frye to develop more extensively his thoughts about romance as a literary form, a subject already central to the four essays in *Anatomy of Criticism*. At the end of his discussion of archetypal criticism in the Second Essay of that book, he observes that "archetypes are most easily studied in highly conventionalized literature: that is, for the most part, naive, primitive, and popular literature," and he suggests "the possibility of extending the kind of comparative and morphological study now made of folk tales and ballads into the rest of literature" (104). In Notes 56a, one of the *Secular Scripture* notebooks, he remarks that after searching for some time for "a unified theme," he now has "the main structure of a book [he has] been ambitious to write for at least twenty years, without understanding what it was, except in bits and pieces" (*NR*, 199–200). His hope is to "make it the subject of [the lectures] at Harvard. After all, it's fundamentally an expansion of the paper I did for the Harvard myth conference." The latter paper, "Myth, Fiction, and Displacement" (*FI*, 21–38), first published in 1961, outlines and develops a "central principle about 'myth criticism': that myth is a structural element in literature because literature as a whole is a 'displaced' mythology" (*FI*, 1).[3]

The specific subject of *The Secular Scripture* is the study of sentimental romance, the literary development of the formulas found in the oral culture of the folk tale. It first appears in European literature in the Greek and Latin romances of the early Common Era. As a central form, it surfaces again in the medieval romances and in the Elizabethan reworkings of the conventions of Greek romance, reemerging in the Gothic novels of the eighteenth century, and forming the structural basis of a great variety of nineteenth-century prose fiction, most explicitly in writers such as Walter Scott and William Morris. In the twentieth century it appears again, most unabashedly in fantasy and science fiction. The recurrent appeal of romance can be seen recently in the long-term success of the *Star Wars* films, in the spectacular popularity of J.K. Rowling's *Harry Potter* series and the cinematic version of J.R.R. Tolkien's *The Lord of the Rings*, as well as in the ongoing attraction of genres such as detective fiction and "thrillers."

Frye observes that the forms of storytelling peculiar to saga, legend, and folk tale do not differ essentially from those of the Bible and certain other texts—the "epic of the creator" (13–14)—which have had a sacred circle drawn around them by religious and cultural authority. The distinction between sacred and secular scriptures, as far as Frye is concerned, is primarily one of social context. Sentimental romance—the "epic of the creature" (14)—has been vilified for centuries by the established cultural tradition, and the disapproval of such "proletarian" or popular forms holds even today. Even when they become privileged objects of study, as is currently the case in cultural and film studies, the interest is often largely confined to their hidden ideological imperatives—what they tell us to do. The term "popular culture," despite its widespread currency, remains undefined, but Frye offers what appears to be a very simple definition, at least of its literary form. It is that area of verbal culture which requires for its appreciation minimal expertise and education, and is therefore available to the widest possible audience. At the same time, by virtue of its wide-ranging appeal, popular literature often points the way to future literary developments, for with the exhaustion of a literary tradition there is often a return to primitive formulas, as was the case with Greek romance and the Gothic novel. Frye does not imply any value judgment in distinguishing popular from elite culture. He maintains, instead, that they are both ultimately two aspects of the same "human compulsion to create in the face of chaos" (25).

The second chapter deals with the "context" of romance, the literary elements of abstract design that distinguish romance from more realistic and descriptive forms. In the last two centuries, the realist novel has had a privileged position, partly because of its causal logic and its perceived role as offering detailed insight into the objective world. The opposing view of art is the romantic one. Here we find a much freer employment of mythological and metaphorical imagery, along with the prominence of a "moral dialectic," as Frye puts it in *Anatomy of Criticism*, "a dialectic of desire and repugnance" (106). Of all forms of literature, romance is the most clearly shaped by ritual and desire, by patterns of both integration and expulsion, and by "both the wish-fulfilment dream and the anxiety or nightmare dream of repugnance" (*AC*, 106). Concerned with "universal" actions that express human wishes and fears, romance is made up of a sequence of archetypes, the individual psychology of which has been explored in detail, as Frye notes, by Freud and Jung. Its plotting and imagery thus bring into play the entire field of intertextuality, the vast echo chamber of literary conventions, archetypes, and mythological themes of the imaginative universe.

Chapter 3 explores the conventional basis of characterization in romance, and through it the central structural principle of a moral dialectic or polarity. From the Greek romances on, the genre typically features female protagonists whose loyalty and quick-wittedness enable them to survive and eventually triumph in the face of threats of rape and death. The predominance of poetic justice in romance is, in Frye's view, primarily a structural matter. The principle of polarity assumes a vertically shaped imaginative universe and an up-and-down, or, rather, down-and-up movement between different orders of experience, four in all. An encapsulated version of the journey through that mythological world is first outlined in an essay from 1960, "New Directions from Old" (*FI*, 52–66), while the two basic patterns, the cyclical and the dialectical, are simply and clearly articulated in "Myth, Fiction, and Displacement" (*FI*, 21–38), the paper mentioned above as the one Frye identifies as the starting point for *The Secular Scripture*:

> The structural principles of a mythology, built up from analogy and identity, become in due course the structural principles of literature. The absorption of the natural cycle into mythology provides myth with two of these structures; the rising movement that we find in myths of spring or the dawn, of birth, marriage, and resurrection, and the falling movement in myths of death, metamorphosis, or sacrifice. These movements reappear as the structural principles of comedy and tragedy in literature. Again, the dialectic in myth that projects a paradise or heaven above our world and a hell or place of shades below it reappears in literature as the idealized world of pastoral and romance and the absurd, suffering, or frustrated world of irony and satire. (*FI*, 33–4).

These descending and rising movements are the subject of the next three chapters of the book.

The opening paragraph of chapter 4 speaks of "four primary narrative movements in literature. These are, first, the descent from a higher world; second, the descent to a lower world; third, the ascent from a lower world; and, fourth, the ascent to a higher world. All stories in literature are complications of, or metaphorical derivations from, these four narrative radicals" (64). They correspond, at least in a general way, to the four *mythoi* of *Anatomy of Criticism*—tragedy, irony, comedy, romance—which are organized in the same way around the movements of ascent and descent. Chapter 4 begins with a brief examination of the four levels of the imaginative topocosm, which comprises "heaven" or "the place of the presence of God"; "the earthly paradise or Garden of Eden, where man lived before the fall"; "the world of ordinary experience we now live in"; and "the demonic world or hell" (64). This scheme—a constant in Frye's work—looks ahead to the four symbolic variations of *Words with Power*, similarly organized on the basis of a vertical axis and four levels, each identified with an archetypal image: mountain, garden, cave, and furnace. Several of the essays in the present volume explore the same type of imagery; in particular, no. 12, "The Survival of Eros in Poetry," no. 17, "The *Koiné* of Myth," and no. 24, "The Journey as Metaphor," offer differently focused discussions of the imagery addressed in the last four chapters of *Words with Power*.

After a brief discussion of descents from above, chapter 4 turns to a detailed description of the journey to the world below our earth. This is without doubt one of the most popular thematic areas of romance. The structural core is invariable, beginning with a break in the continuity of identity analogous to the entering of a dreamlike world. As we descend, there are the themes of Ovidian metamorphosis—the transformation of humans into animals and other parts of nature—and of double identity, often linked to the Narcissus theme and to the idea of a world of reduced dimensions. In the lower reaches of descent there is, among other things, an increase in sinister, objectifying imagery, such as mirrors (objectification of the self) and clocks (objectification of time). At the very bottom of the night world loom the themes of human sacrifice and the cannibal feast, where the identification of human and animal worlds is complete. What follows is the point of "nothingness" that Frye discusses later in *Words with Power* (288–91), beyond which emerges the first stage of ascent, often through the counter-absurdity of an act of the creative imagination that defeats death.

Chapters 5 and 6, devoted to ascent themes, show how, in the higher stages of ascent, the predominantly social context of comedy makes way for the pastoral world of romance. The cyclical imagery of nature and human life now points to a world of recovered identity above that of ordinary experience. In contrast with stories of descent, where the individual is an objectified and estranged unit in an increasingly inhuman order, ascent narratives are marked by progressive individualization and an increasing participation in the world outside the self, the not-me of nature and the surrounding universe. Ultimately, the individual renounces the projections that have estranged him or her from the world of identity.

The closing chapter concludes with the important theme of recreation, to which Frye will turn again in *Creation and Recreation*, in "Typology II" of *The Great Code*, and in the last two chapters of *Words with Power*. In the context of literature, one that may be extended to the entire realm of human activity, creation requires both the creative work and the response to it, so that the responsibility for recovering the world of identity through an act of recognition now shifts to the reader. The ultimate goal of reading and criticism is, thus, the individual's recreation in his or her imagination of the interpenetrating mythological universe. Frye argues that the conception of a model creation is essentially emancipatory. As a paradigm of a world that makes human sense and that is imposed on and transforms the natural world, it plants a social vision in the human mind that, breaking once and for all with the state of nature, also breaks with any social order that rationalizes as "natural" a hierarchy of oppression and injustice. Such a model world is often conceived as coming from elsewhere, from a divinity or a world above.

Significantly, chapters 2, 3, and 5 of *The Secular Scripture* all end by circling around and focusing on precisely this paradoxical necessity of maintaining an interdependency between a human and a transcendental creative power. The universe of romance, Frye concludes, discloses two aspects: the revelation of man to man through the human creation of stories—the so-called "secular scripture"—and revelation through the Word, God's revelation to man, though God here may be more like a resisting otherness, such as reality or nature, against which the imagination struggles and tests itself. Our sense of the mythological universe as a human creation and our opposing sense of revelation as coming from something uncreated and transcendentally other, are, Frye insists, indispensable complementary poles of our mental evolution. For without the "sense that the mythological universe is a human creation," as we see at the end of chapter 2, "man can never get free of servile anxieties and superstitions, never surpass himself, in Nietzsche's phrase." On the other hand, "if there is no sense that it is also something uncreated, something coming from elsewhere, man remains a Narcissus staring at his own reflection, equally unable to surpass himself." We must, Frye argues, maintain this "struggle" between "the created scripture and the revealed scripture," for it is through "the suspension of belief between the spiritually real and the humanly imaginative that our own mental evolution grows" (43).

Chapter 5 closes on a similar note, with an account of the *Hymn of the Soul* from the apocryphal Acts of Thomas. Adapting from that poem the figure of twins who descend from above with the soul's lost garment and the message of its identity, Frye calls us back to the theme of *de te fabula*—"the story is about you" (122)—and concludes with a reiteration of one of his central concerns: the wisdom of seeing the two scriptures, sacred and secular, those "great twins of divine creation and human recreation" (104), not as conflicting but as complementary visions of the human quest for identity. Without the push and pull between the two, Frye suggests, the mirror of human narcissism can never be broken. For the same reason, the recovery of myth, the articulate form of that transcendental power in human culture, is imperative, for without it we will find ourselves without the "models for human creation" (121). The idea that we can dispense with such models, or that they can be deconstructed endlessly, is the most naive illusion—"disillusion as the last illusion," in Wallace Stevens's words.[4] Since Romanticism, creativity has been identified with a world of repressed innocence and visionary power, both part of us and other, an ambivalent creative energy associated, in *Words with Power*, with the myth of titanism: Prometheus, the thief of fire, wrested from the gods the means with which to transform an oppressive order into a more fully human one. What begins, then, as a discussion of the literary structure of romance ends with an exploration of the ways in which imaginative culture and social vision are profoundly connected. Romance is the place where human beings dream, and Frye's study points to the indispensability of such dreaming for the creative life of a society and its capacity for transformation.

III

The Secular Scripture explores three related areas of thought that continue to preoccupy Frye: the dialectical polarization of imagery into desirable and abhorrent worlds; the recovery of myth in the act of literary recreation; and the struggle and complementarity between secular and sacred scriptures. A number of the other writings collected here develop these same central themes. No. 2, "Romance as Masque," published the same year as *The Secular Scripture*, is a continuation of Frye's earlier studies of Shakespearean comedy and romance, a lifelong project that began with "The Argument of Comedy" in 1948.[5] "Romance as Masque" begins with a discussion of Old and New Comedy, and comes to focus on the two structural principles highlighted in *The Secular Scripture*: cyclical movement and polarity. As a theatrical form, the masque was a highly contrived spectacle for an aristocratic elite. For this very reason, it serves to illustrate Frye's paradoxical claim about the revolutionary potential of the structure of romance: despite being a rhetorical mirror for the ideology of a ruling class, the poetic imagery of the masque offers at a more imaginative level an emancipatory vision of human life. The essay thus brings us back to the concluding insights of *The Secular Scripture*; it too emphasizes that the ultimate dimension of human reality is, in the end, not an objective condition from which we are estranged, but a state of mind informed by the creative imagination.

Frye's interest in the thought of the eighteenth-century Italian philosopher Giambattista Vico is well known.[6] The latter's grandly conceived recursive conception of history was one of the sources of the theory of modes in *Anatomy of Criticism*. A number of the writings here are also indebted to Vico's study of myth as the primary form of our verbal apprehension of the world. In no. 5, "Comment on Peter Hughes's Essay," and then more fully in no. 6, "Literature, History, and Language," Frye addresses Vico's three phases of language—hieroglyphic, hieratic, and demotic—and adapts them to a historical scheme of verbal culture that appears in its final form in chapter 1 of *The Great Code*. The hieroglyphic, as Frye defines it, corresponds to the *metaphor* "A is B," and is an imaginative or poetic form of language that opens up a channel of energy between subjective and objective worlds. The hieratic mode, which dominates the next historical stage, is the *metonymic* "A put for B," a "Platonic" conception of language. This is also the verbal form of ideology, which substitutes an inferior state of human reality for a more desirable one, the latter being for the moment, so we are led to believe, well out of reach. Finally, in the post-Renaissance, scientific epoch, which ushers in the demotic phase of language, words are primarily thought of as *descriptive* ("A is like B"), analogues of an objectified physical reality against which they can be verified by observation and experiment. Frye hints here at a fourth level of language, the "rhetorical" address found in the Bible and other religious texts, which he eventually decided to call the *kerygmatic* (from the Greek *kerygma* or "proclamation").

The two remaining essays on Vico (no. 4, "The Responsibilities of the Critic," and no. 9, "Vision and Cosmos") focus on the role of literature in such a verbal framework. Vico's explicit argument—very much, as Frye points out, in the spirit of Michelet and Marx—is that myth or poetic wisdom must be demythologized and read as an allegory of human structures of authority, which are its "real meaning." His thought, however, according to Frye, contains something more. The underlying force of myth is not primarily a projection of political authority and class structure, but an "inner imaginative structure" (no. 4, 159), which literature and art recreate at each historical phase. This concept of recreation takes on, for Frye, new meaning in Vico's final stage of culture, the age of "the people": human beings are now able to assume responsibility for the world they themselves imagine and create, in the form of the institutions and laws shaping their society. One of the lessons to be drawn from Vico, then, is that literature and criticism should make us more fully conscious of the "created world" (167–8), the world we have created and are creating. This world can be largely identified with the arts and sciences, the mental and imaginative source of the ways in which we transform the natural and social environment. Here lies the importance of Vico's pivotal principle that all we can really know with any certainty is the world we ourselves have created. Explicitly challenged is the Cartesian ideal of a detached and isolated ego confronting objective reality with the transparency of its reason. "We can never," Frye maintains, "understand the poet's authority without Vico's principle of *verum factum*, that reality is in the world we make and not in the world we stare at" (no. 19, 356).

In Vico's ironic cycle, this entry into the created world seems to be a stage that cannot be sustained and soon deteriorates, ending with the projection of a new tyrannical order and the bringing on of a new *ricorso*—another "failed spiral" (no. 6, 175). Part of Frye's argument in the concluding chapter of *The Secular Scripture* concerns the possibility of avoiding precisely such a failure, and of entering into what he calls "a third imaginative order," one possessing affinities with the expanded vision that we attain in the higher reaches of romance. Earlier in the same work, at the end of chapter 3, he refers to Yeats—a poet who shared an interest in Vico as well as in Spengler, that other cyclical thinker—and to his mythological view of cultural history:

> The dove-and-virgin cycle is comedy-centred, it is true, but it is not simply the antithesis of its predecessor, as Yeats's scheme would have it. It is in some respects a more expanded world, and we sometimes have the feeling in a romance or comedy of moving from one world into a larger one. . . . When the action passes from one level to the other through the recognition scene, we have a feeling of going through some sort of gyre or vortex, to use another Yeats image, a feeling we express in the phrase we so inevitably use when summarizing a romantic plot: "it turns out that . . ." (62)

The entry into a genuinely new imaginative order would show no sign of simply returning to the tragic phases of history as outlined in Yeats's *A Vision*. Indeed, "in our day every genuine issue, in the arts as outside them, is connected with getting clear of all such notions of cyclical historical fatality" (63).

In no. 23, "Literature and the Visual Arts," and no. 24, "The Journey as Metaphor," Frye returns to the question, observing that "the end of a cycle does not compel us to repeat the same cycle, but gives us a chance to transfer to another level" (407), and that "the genuine quest cycle is of the type in which the conclusion is the starting point renewed and transformed by the quest itself" (410). In a Hegelian manner, the cycle may conceal a potential dialectical movement out of the cycle and onto a more comprehensive level of understanding. The response to Peter Hughes's paper speaks of the "return to myth and romance in contemporary literature" as a return that "could also form part of a counter-*ricorso*," a recovery of myth and metaphor "within a total demotic context." The "cyclical return" would thus be transformed "into something more like a spiral expansion" (171), a movement evoked by the title of no. 19, "The Expanding World of Metaphor," as well as by the title of an earlier version of the same paper, "Expanding the Boundaries of Literature." Human consciousness as it expresses itself in literature is bounded by limits that are to be progressively transcended and absorbed, not returned to again and again in a fruitless repetition.

All such failures to transcend the cycle, in Frye's view, are relapses into some form or another of what the Bible denounces as idolatry: the alienation of one's own creative power and responsibility, and their projection onto a naturalized tyrannical order. We return to the point of

Frye's insistence, in *The Secular Scripture*, on the recognition of a necessary complementarity of human words and the creative word or Logos, the paradox of an otherness, an ultimate dimension or reality that both transcends and expresses itself through human beings. The latter is not a being that can be objectified—"God" is neither an object nor a being—but is to be thought of as "some kind of force or power or will that is not ourselves, an otherness of spirit" (43), which at the same time is identifiable with human creative power. As Frye puts it in Notebook 44: "God must be thought of as the inconceivably transcendent: all thoughts of that psychotic ape homo sapiens being divine have to be dismissed" (*LN*, 195). Without such a conception, human beings will keep on turning the wheel of history by projecting the source of their own creative power onto objects or figures outside themselves.

IV

The essays pertaining to Vico largely reflect Frye's concerns as they appear in *Creation and Recreation* and *The Great Code*. With "Vision and Cosmos," there is a detectable shift to matters fully developed in *Words with Power*. As he does at the beginning of *The Secular Scripture*, Frye starts by establishing the context of the mythological universe, emphasizing that even when its social authority has long since disappeared, cosmology continues to flourish as a poetic space. Drawing many of its examples from the Renaissance, "Vision and Cosmos" focuses on Eros as an example of a creative "power" that flourished thanks to a rich poetic tradition, despite its suppression by official medieval authority, until it openly began to reassert itself in the Romantic revolution. The example of sexual love is more fully treated in "The Survival of Eros in Poetry." In the eighteenth century, Frye argues, as the old cosmology is turned on its head and attention shifts to a new conception of nature as *natura naturans*, human sexuality is clearly recognized and accepted as a source of creative initiative. This cosmological framework is one of the important organizing principles in *Words with Power*, where, broadly speaking, the first two symbolic modes are based on the old cosmology, in which the creative initiative comes from above, and the last two on the new one that begins to emerge with Romanticism, in which the initiative now rises, like Shelley's Demogorgon, from below. The end of "The Survival of Eros in Poetry" suggests the importance of such "speculative cosmologies" for creative writers: "Such a world is dominated by forces that were originally gods—Eros, Prometheus, Cybele . . . and others. . . . But it is only a nervous habit that keeps us calling such forces gods: they are states of the human mind with metaphorical identities in nature. More important, they are the shaping powers of poetry, the authentic muses" (266–7). By the time *Words with Power* is published, these "states of the human mind" or "shaping powers of poetry" finally have settled into what the *Late Notebooks* call HEAP, the mythic figures of Hermes, Eros, Adonis, and Prometheus, and their respective areas of symbolism: mountain, garden, cave, and furnace.

Unlike *The Great Code*, which is primarily engaged with the internal structure of the Bible, many of the later essays here, written at the time Frye was working on *Words with Power*, focus more on the relationship of the Bible to the "secular scripture" of literature. Thus, the main areas of Biblical symbolism are linked to a secular imaginative tradition by the use of tutelary divinities from Greek mythology. At the same time, Frye argues that the existence of the Bible in Western culture makes possible a unique perspective that both informs and transcends literature and its purely hypothetical language. The study of the latter, with its ironic detachment from both assertion and experience, was, according to "The Expanding World of Metaphor," as far as he got in the *Anatomy*. Beyond the hypothetical use of metaphor is the ecstatic identification, also discussed in "The *Koiné* of Myth," that defines both erotic and religious imagery, in which worshippers or lovers identify with something outside themselves. Frye traces this impulse back to the earliest stages of human history, to the cave drawings, for example, of animals in Altamira or Lascaux, which, if we keep in mind "the fantastically difficult conditions of lighting and positioning in which they were done," give us "some sense of the titanic will to identify that they represent" (no. 19, 346). While literature reabsorbs and individualizes this original form of metaphor, the language of the Bible takes us a step further, assimilating the imaginative language of the poet to the ecstatic and existential language of proclamation. Despite there being almost nothing in the Bible that is not myth or metaphor, it is not composed in the literary language of "as if," but extends the meaning of literary metaphors into the individual's life. In "Literature, History, and Language," when he describes this transformative capacity, Frye uses, perhaps for the first time, a phrase that alludes to Luke 4:32, the source of the title of his last major work:[7] "The operations of the human mind are also controlled by words of power, formulas of the type called mantras in Indian religion. Prose in this phase is discontinuous, a series of gnarled epigrammatic statements which are not to be argued about but must be accepted and pondered, transformed into words of power" (174).

"Auguries of Experience" tells us that, after toying for a time with the words "prophetic" and "apocalyptic" for this mode of language, Frye finally retained the theological term *kerygma*—"proclamation" or "revelation"—"even though that meant opposing the formidable authority of Rudolf Bultmann, for whom *kerygma* and myth are mutually exclusive" (448). In the *Harper Handbook* entry on the "Bible as Literature," Frye explains that the language of the Bible shares important features with rhetorical address, which "is an intermediate form between the imaginative or literary and the discursive or direct-address use of words." The "element of persuasion bound up with the figurative use of language" (364) in rhetoric is existential or situational, like the language of the Bible, which aims at imparting an imperative message and transforming the reader or listener. At the same time, Biblical language is highly metaphorical and mythological, employing the same kind of imagery and narrative forms that we find in literary texts. In Bultmann's understanding of the term, the *kerygmatic* message must be clarified and carefully separated from its often obfuscating containment by myth. Frye's understanding is the reverse. "The two dragons I want to kill," he declares in Notebook 44, "are Bultmann's 'demythologize' and Derrida's 'logocentric.' The Bible is myth from Genesis to Revelation, & to demythologize it is to obliterate it" (*LN*, 157). "Auguries of Experience" reiterates that myth and metaphor, "the central elements of literature," remain "hypothetical" in literature itself, whereas in the Bible, they are "existential, incorporating the reader with a completeness that literature cannot attempt" (448).

Taken as an imaginative whole, the Bible offers a unique metaliterary perspective that shows literature and the secular imagination as something finite and contained by a larger, comprehensive vision, the Word of God. This metaliterary conception of the relationship between the Bible and literature explains Frye's attention in several of the essays to the work of Stéphane Mallarmé. The most influential of the French symbolist poets, Mallarmé envisioned the world of the verbal imagination enfolded, as it is in the Bible, within a single book. Where the Bible is concerned with human existence in its most ultimate and comprehensive terms, Mallarmé takes the hypothetical condition of the literary imagination, its nothingness or condition of pure possibility—"la fleur absente de tout bouquet"—to its furthest extreme, to a point where the hypothetical and the existential, at their most approximate, all but touch.

When Frye highlights the difference between this hypothetical language of literature and the existential language of the Bible, he is obviously not denying the prophetic authority of imaginative literature in human society. The opposite is true: his preoccupation with the *kerygmatic* coincides, as we have seen, with his growing interest in the role of the imagination as an expanding form of authoritative consciousness in a secular context as well. This prophetic concern is a natural development of his insistence, from the beginning of his career, that literature is not an object to be contemplated, but "a power to be possessed" (*StS*, 85).[8] "The Journey as Metaphor" concludes with the "essential point . . . that literary metaphor, which is purely hypothetical, grows out of an existential type of metaphor, as we might call it, where a subject does identify himself with something not himself, in an experience that has no further need for language, although it has also fulfilled the entire function of language" (421–2).

V

In the last fifteen years of his career, the period of the writings gathered here, Frye was acutely aware of the preoccupations of a new generation of literary critics. The spectres of deconstruction, poststructuralism, and New Historicism drift in and out of several of the later papers; he alludes in more than one to Jacques Derrida's concepts of *écriture* and *différance*, and, indeed, devotes a short essay (no. 22) to some of the main theoretical concepts of Jacques Lacan. In "Literary and Linguistic Scholarship in a Postliterate World," his address to the MLA Convention in 1983, at the very apex of the rise of deconstruction, Frye's attitude is gracious and remarkably undefensive. Earlier that year, the same tone prevails in his replies to questions during the discussion of his paper "The Survival of Eros in Poetry." Expressing his disappointment "that there is still so much clutter and confusion in critical theory," he makes it clear nonetheless that he is "interested and even exhilarated by the variety of things that do appear, and by the number of approaches to the study of literary documents that would have been inconceivable half a century ago" (273).

At the same time, however, Frye's writings are tinged with the irony of a certain bemusement and sense of *déja vu*, as the old critical fallacies keep returning in new attire. The MLA address articulates a genuine concern about the "great variety of social groups—Christian, Marxist, Moslem, anarchist, liberal, conservative—all of them full of hardliners who simply deny, in the interests of their own dogmas, that poets have any authority except what they might derive from whatever ideology the dogmatists themselves want to advance. Their confident and self-hypnotized assurance has influenced many of the more timid critics to believe or assume that if there is any value in the study of literature, it cannot inhere in literature itself" (292). *The Secular Scripture* expresses the same caution about critics who degrade literature "into the anxieties of the kind of social concern that has been called, very accurately, the treason of the clerks" (42). Such warnings leave Frye open to the hasty disapproval of those who would dismiss him as a "formalist," indifferent to the importance of sociopolitical factors in literature—this in spite of his publishing in mid-career *The Stubborn Structure* (1970) and *The Critical Path* (1971), the former, as subtitled, a collection of "Essays on Criticism and Society," and the latter, even more specifically, "An Essay on the Social Context of Literary Criticism."

Frye's view of the social role of literature most certainly differs from that of critics primarily interested in literature as a form of ideological expression, even when they clearly assume that literature also serves as a critical and prophetic voice in society.[9] Such ideological criticism he regards as deficient, for just as ideological critics cannot explain the peculiar authority of literature, so they are unable to account for the normative basis of their own judgments. The final piece in this collection notes the growth of "the spirit of irony" in contemporary criticism, a spirit as undeniably shaped by cultural myths as that of any other period, and therefore as historically limited. Frye uses the word "irony" here in the modal sense that he employs in the First Essay of *Anatomy of Criticism*. There he speaks of the reader as having "the sense of looking down on a scene of bondage, frustration, or absurdity" and implicitly judging the action by "the norms of a greater freedom" (34). Irony, as Frye's "Response" to the Eighteenth-Century Studies papers makes clear, "cannot really make its point as irony unless it is bounced off an attitude on the part of the reader which contains a standard of normality. That is, irony is not irony unless it is a divergence from something that the ironist is implicitly appealing to in the reader" (482). Even in a scholarly discipline dominated by so much contestation, this "sense of normality on the part of the audience," as he puts it in "Literature as Therapy"—this recognition that "a certain action [is] grotesque or absurd or evil or futile or whatever" (471)—is the basis for more than just a modicum of consensus. The same point is reformulated in *Words with Power*, where Frye speaks of the "real opposite of the dystopia" as being not a Utopia, but rather "the sense of a social norm. . . . An audience watching a comedy recognizes the absurdity and grotesqueness of the characters who usually dominate the action, because it already possesses a vision of a more sensible society" (309). This norm, on its highest level, Frye describes as an unbounded "vision of fulfilled primary concerns, freedom, health, equality, happiness, love" (310).

In the essays following the publication of *The Great Code*, beginning with "Vision and Cosmos" in 1982, the conception of myth and literature as directly engaged with the expression of primary human concerns moves to the foreground of Frye's preoccupations, finally to assume a central place in *Words with Power*. The definitions of primary and secondary concerns appear in many of the later essays, and are first mentioned in the 1983 MLA address:

> Primary concern is based on the most primitive of platitudes: the conviction that life is better than death, happiness better than misery, freedom better than bondage. Secondary concern includes loyalty to one's own society, to one's religious or political beliefs, to one's place in the class structure, and in short to everything that comes under the general heading of ideology. All through history secondary concerns have had the greater prestige and power. We prefer to live, but we go to war; we prefer to be free, but we keep many people in a second-class status, and so on. (293)

Primary concerns deal with the basic urgencies of human life, both the physical ones and the emotional and spiritual extension of these concerns, which, however different in their forms, are common to all societies and cultures. God may not be a primary concern *per se*—one of the needs we share with other creatures—nor may be art or the quest for beauty, and yet in the end such "conscious and creative concerns," as they are termed in "Framework and Assumption," are so closely tied to the most fundamental ones as to be almost indistinguishable from them: "When a society comes close to the level of bare subsistence . . . the arts, including the literary arts, do not disappear: they leap into the foreground among the essentials of survival" (432). Citing the opening sentence of Aristotle's *Metaphysics*, "all men by nature desire to know," Frye remarks that it is hard to exclude the desire for knowledge and wisdom from the primary concerns of human beings.

Secondary concerns, on the other hand, pertain to the social contract. They are ethnocentric, having to do with the identities and loyalties of particular groups, such as one's tribe, nation, religion, class, gender, or political party. Displacements or projections of genuine human necessities, they are the elements of belief that make up a social mythology or an ideology. In "Framework and Assumption," Frye maintains that "what human societies do first is make up stories. I think, in other words, that an ideology always derives from a mythology, as a myth to me means a *mythos*, a story or narrative" (431). Ideology "is thus an applied mythology, and its adaptations of myths are the ones that, when we are inside an ideological structure, we must believe, or say we believe" (*WP*, 23). Whereas ideology is the assertion and prescription of something as a matter of belief, in literature, basic human concerns are presented in the context of an imaginative and ironic expansiveness. However strident the expression of a writer's declared beliefs may be, it is this primary level of myth and story, of metaphor and imagery, that draws the novelist, playwright, or poet, whose ultimate aim is to write a successful novel, play, or poem. Primary concern has always been the responsibility of literature, but perhaps more than ever, Frye suggests, the creative writer has become the major "spokesman" for "the human preoccupation with such things as food, sex, happiness, and freedom" and our "anxieties and frustrations about not getting such things" (no. 26, 438). A central assumption here is that the goal and purpose of social community is to provide individuals with the means to thrive in every way possible, to flourish in the particular and abundant fulfilment of primary concerns. Thus, a radically progressive liberalism[10] intersects with Frye's understanding of *kerygma* as the spiritual means by which human beings might have "life more abundantly," as he expresses it in the Biblical phrase taken from John 10:10 (*WP*, 42).

With the ascendancy of a myth of freedom, literature gains in prophetic significance, for it provides us with a vision of the world we have failed to make, and of the more fully human world that is possible. "Framework and Assumption" concludes with the reminder that the mirror of art enables us to "see ourselves capable of creation as well as destruction, with reason a means to an end of ultimate consensus, however distant" (435). In a similar vein, in "Literature as a Critique of Pure Reason," Frye distinguishes the purely rational from the full range of the creative mind, which would include that imaginative element that produces the arts. At the end of the essay, he speaks eloquently of the "essential role" the arts have to play "in the liberating of the human mind." The work of literature creates a world that is entirely playful and yet somehow more real and intense than ordinary experience. As such, it creates "a focus for a community" that reflects the latter's concerns, but remains "detached from immediate action." If we place and maintain "the works of the human imagination in the centre of the community," they will enable us in time "to see that community itself as the total form of what human beings can bring forth, their own larger life that continues to live and move and possess its inward being" (243–4).

In "Literary and Linguistic Scholarship in a Postliterate World," Frye observes "that all creative impulses, including the literary one, begin in the sense of the unreality of time and space in ordinary experience." It is this persistent dissatisfaction that drives the writer, through myth and metaphor, to attempt "to establish or reconstitute a sense of a present moment and a spatial presence as the basis of whatever significance the verbal imagination can find in life" (296). Without this imaginative perspective, with only the myopia of ideology to guide it, reason is "simply a faculty that intensifies [human] viciousness" (no. 25, 435). Throughout history, primary concerns have been supplanted by secondary or ideological anxieties and obsessions: survival by the compulsion to war, sex by the imposition of moral taboos, property by the justification of systems that enrich a few while dispossessing the many, freedom by political systems that put the claims of vested interests before the needs of the human beings they govern. Today more than ever we see the starkness of this dispensation; it has become "obvious," Frye declares in "Maps and Territories," "that primary concerns must become primary, or else. This fact ought to give a new social importance to the writer" (439). Consciously or not, as he argues in his letter to the editor of *PMLA*, writers turn to myth to keep alive "a social imagination of a different order from what any conceivable political action can attain to by itself" (391).

Several of the essays refer to Shakespeare's *Henry V* to illustrate the nature of the authority of literature. On one level, the play is simply propaganda for the English king, but on another level, as Frye points out in "Literary and Linguistic Scholarship in a Postliterate World," the "realities" of this carefully crafted world of "historical destiny" and causality are swept aside, as "the total annihilation of everything they bring before us shows that they are also illusions." What comes into the foreground in their place is "first, the immense power of counter-logic in the metaphorical structure, and, second, the equally powerful counter-historical movement in the myth, the total story being told." In the end, we recognize that the myth of the play is not "follow[ing]" history; instead, it "absorbs the historical movement and then confronts it" (295–6). Literature thus works at two levels: a horizontal or historical level, where the writer struggles with his or her contemporary ideological reality, and a vertical or mythological level, which connects the vision of the work to the total framework of literature as an ever expanding word or myth. It is at the level of metaphorical verticality, where an imaginative structure is recovered, that literature is "mimetic": it imitates itself, and, paradoxically, only in this way can the writer find something original to say. As Frye explains in "Framework and Assumption," "the new, though certainly new, is also deeply traditional." There exists "a discontinuous quality in the larger historical tradition. Something that has disappeared for years or centuries may suddenly reappear; conventions long ignored or forgotten suddenly materialize again, like the angels who traditionally do not move in time or space but simply become visible somewhere else" (429–30).

The distinction between the horizontal and the vertical bar in Frye's scheme corresponds to the differing experiences of reading and *seeing* a work. We follow a work linearly when we read it, in time—with the ear, hearing it, as it were—until we reach the end and "make an effort to understand what the body of words conveys, in a simultaneous or comprehensive act that we metaphorically call 'seeing'" (no. 23, 397). What we see is the "underthought," a term that Frye borrows from Hopkins: that is, the counterlogical and counterhistorical structure of mythological and metaphorical meaning. In his discussion of Vico in "The Responsibilities of the Critic," Frye emphasizes that genuine criticism leads not to an act of judgment of the work—the evaluative fallacy attacked in the opening pages of *Anatomy,* and still prevalent today in the form of a politically prescriptive criticism—but to an act of *recognition,* Aristotle's *anagnorisis.* Just as the "difficulties" in the use of metaphor, as he contends in "The *Koiné* of Myth," "begin with projecting it, thinking of it as something with an independent being" (323), so the critic *cum* judge keeps us imprisoned in our acts of projection, entrapped at the level of the anxieties of our institutions and social mythologies. In "Literary and Linguistic Scholarship in a Postliterate World," harkening back to the last chapter of *The Secular Scripture,* Frye insists that "in the full critical operation there must always be a catharsis of belief," which separates the counterforces of myth and metaphor from the confines of ideology, and frees them to "open up to us . . . a world of recovered identity, both as ourselves and with something not ourselves" (298).

Frye does not mean to denigrate either logic or history. He does wish, however, to oppose the unquestioned authority of historical approaches in literary scholarship, old and new, by establishing as an essential critical principle the unique and specific authority of literature and imaginative experience. The recreation of a society's mythological structure—its revitalization in each new context—keeps alive a vision in which history is both absorbed and confronted. Or rather, myth takes history and "twists it around so that it *confronts us* in the present" (no. 17, 316, emphasis added). In this way, the audience "is compelled to respond to a dimension of time that is no longer purely sequential" (no. 19, 351). "The Journey as Metaphor" offers the example of a confronting statement such as Jesus' "I am the way." Here, the temporal movement of the journey becomes an arresting of the eye and a stretching out in space. The *mythos* of story becomes the space—or place—of recognition and vision. For what the work of literature confronts us with is not a rational or descriptive statement but, like God's revelation to Job after the comforters are silenced, a vision of something: a recreation of myth, an imaginative vision informed by human concern.

This confrontational aspect of literature is often thematized, as, for example, in the play-within-a-play that Hamlet produces to "catch the conscience of the King" (*Hamlet*, 2.2.605). "Literature as Therapy" uses the example of *The Taming of the Shrew*, which turns on the dramatic device of Petruchio confronting Katherina with a mirror image of her shrewishness, "and so shows her exactly what it looks like when she can see it objectively" (472). An illustration Frye turns to more than once is the story of the Crucifixion of Jesus. What has the power to confront us today is not the historicity but the *myth* or story of the Crucifixion, which raises and absorbs the suffering and deaths of countless human beings into a "higher dimension of time" than that of the historical; it "confronts us with our own moral bankruptcy," and compels us "to stop and think of what [we] do with this" (no. 15, 299). "Myth as the Matrix of Literature" points to the Biblical account of the Exodus as another example of such stories or "words with power": "The black spiritual 'Go down, Moses: let my people go' indicates what power a myth can have long after its connection with history has disappeared" (309). This capacity to confront us is what makes the arts a counter-environment that is "antipathetic to the civilization in which it exists" (no. 30, 475). The prophetic role of literature can be explicit even in the most disturbing writers, for, as Frye observes, behind their violent prejudices and pathologies often lies a "fundamentally anti-political attitude, an anarchism tending to break down all social mythologies devoted to promoting special social interests" (no. 23, 407). Literature enables us to see things with "a kind of intensity with which they are not seen in ordinary experience"; it is perhaps the most salutary "means of concentrating and intensifying the mind and of bringing it into a state of energy" (no. 30, 475–6).

In "The Symbol as a Medium of Exchange," Frye remarks on the ecstatic or "peak" experiences that literature and poetry make possible. He observes that such experiences "are symbolic, and reflect our two traditional meanings of 'symbol': they are portents or auguries of what life could be, and it is worth any amount of commonplace life to purchase one of them" (336). The function of literature is to be a portent or symbol of life's genuine possibility, a foretelling of an unborn world of human life and experience. It is "a kind of model-thinking," which presents "an infinite set of possibilities of experience to expand and intensify our actual experience" (no. 19, 348–9). These "peak" experiences—a term that Frye borrows from Abraham Maslow—erupt as "the frozen or simultaneously grasped aspects of a *mythos* or continuous narrative" (no. 17, 325). As we know, Frye's own career as a thinker was punctuated by a handful of just such discontinuous ecstatic experiences, beginning with the famous Blake breakthough in 1934, which he described in an interview as an explosive "feeling of an enormous number of things making sense that had been scattered and unrelated before . . . a vision of coherence" (*NFC*, 47, 48). The quest for "a more intense mode of life and experience" (no. 18, 337) becomes, in symbolist poets such as Mallarmé and Rilke, the central end of literary activity. There is little doubt that such expansion and intensity were the ultimate goal of Frye's critical thinking as well. He embraced the Romantic conception of the imagination as "a constructive, unifying, and fully conscious faculty that excludes no aspect of consciousness, whether rational or emotional" (no. 10, 241). This is perhaps the most important and recurrent theme in the present volume. The writings gathered here recall us again and again, by myriad pathways, to the indispensable place of literature in human societies and to the emancipatory capacity of the human imagination in its function as the "primary activity of human consciousness" (241).

The Secular Scripture and Other Writings on Critical Theory 1976–1991

1

The Secular Scripture: A Study of the Structure of Romance

April 1975

From the book (Cambridge, Mass.: Harvard University Press, 1976). Originally presented as the Charles Eliot Norton Lectures at Harvard University, where Frye had spent the year as Charles Eliot Norton Professor of Poetry. The dedication reads, "To my Harvard-Radcliffe students, 1974–75." Included are both Frye's original preface, from July 1975, and the preface he wrote on 1 February 1978 for the Italian translation of the book, La scrittura secolare *(Bologna: Il Mulino,* 1978). *Typescripts and drafts of* The Secular Scripture *are in the NFF, 1992, box 1, files 2–3 and 5–7, and proofs are in the NFF, 1988, box 25, files 1–3.*

Extensive notes produced by Frye in preparation for the Harvard lectures, as well as several shorter sets of notes, have been published in Michael Dolzani's edition of Northrop Frye's Notebooks on Romance (CW, 15). *Of these, Notebook 10* (NR, 275–94) *consists of several outlines and a sketching out of many of the central insights developed in* The Secular Scripture. *Notes 56, much longer, contains for the most part discussions and synopses, often quite detailed, of a number of the authors and works featured in the book. For convenience of reference, the sections that include Frye's personal reflections have been published as "Notes 56a"* (NR, *182–210). The remaining unpublished synopses, designated "Notes 56b," are located in the NFF, 1991, box 28, files 5–6. A list of the works discussed in both Notes 56a and Notes 56b is provided in an appendix at the end of the* Notebooks on Romance *(NR, 375–6).*

Preface

There is not much to say about this book except that it contains the lectures which I gave as Charles Eliot Norton Professor of Poetry at Harvard University in April 1975. This came at the end of an exhilarating and most profitable year in residence at Harvard. To record the personal obligations of my wife and myself to the kindness and hospitality of my Harvard colleagues would swell this preface into a long, and for them embarrassing, catalogue. So I have simply dedicated the book to my students: the fact that there were several hundred of them indicates another aspect of Harvard's friendliness to a visitor.

Those familiar with my other work will find many echoes of it here, from the Schiller reference at the beginning to the Hippolyta one at the end. However, the book has its own place in my writing as a very brief and summary geography lesson in what I call the mythological or imaginative universe. Most of my scholarly interests at present revolve around the thesis that the structure of the Bible provided the outline of such a universe for European literature. The present book is based on that thesis, though concerned with secular literature, and there are many references in it, including its title, to this aspect of its argument. [*viii*]

A book based on public lectures can hardly be organized on a basis of documentation: there are practically no notes, and only two or three examples are given out of many hundreds of possible ones. Many readers will readily think of better examples; but if they are interested in the general idea, they may use this book as a kind of figured bass on which to develop their own progressions. Even if there is ultimately only one mythological universe, every reader sees it differently.

Victoria College
Massey College
University of Toronto
July 1975

Preface to the Italian Translation

This book is a study of the literary genre known as romance in its two main forms. These two forms I call, using terms from Schiller, naive and sentimental. Naive romance includes folk tales of the kind collected in Grimm's *Fairy Tales*. Sentimental romance is the literary tradition starting with late Classical literature, including Heliodorus and Apuleius, and continuing to our own day. My references are mainly to Spenser, Scott, William Morris, and contemporary science fiction.

The thesis of the book is, first, that the formulas of romance show very little change over the centuries. Second, that this is evidence, not only of a stable and continuously popular genre, but of a kind of unconscious human epic. The Bible is the kind of book in which God himself is the hero: romance is a "secular scripture," where the hero represents humanity and the quest he achieves the possibility of human existence. This in turn expands into a survey of the landscape of romance, in which there are themes of descent and of ascent. Descent takes the hero into lower and lower steps of consciousness, ending with death: ascent takes him up again to his original identity. The final chapter attempts to show how this coordinated view of romance passes from stories in books into a vision of human action.

February 1978

I The Word and World of Man

This book is concerned with some principles of storytelling. The discussion revolves around fiction, and especially around what I am going to call naïve and sentimental romance, using two critical terms derived from Schiller's essay *On Naive and Sentimental Poetry*.[1] I am not using these words precisely as Schiller uses them—I could not bring myself to call Goethe a naive poet, as he does—but they are not used in quite their ordinary English senses either. By naive romance I mean the kind of story that is found in collections of folk tales and *Märchen* like Grimm's *Fairy Tales*. By sentimental romance I mean a more extended and literary development of the formulas of naive romance. Most of this, in early and modern times, has been in prose narrative.

Sentimental romance begins, for my purposes, in the late Classical period. There is Greek romance in Heliodorus, Achilles Tatius, Longus, Xenophon of Ephesus, and others.[2] There is Latin romance in Apuleius and (probably) the Apollonius story, used twice by Shakespeare.[3] And there is early Christian romance in the *Clementine Recognitions*,[4] in the story of Barlaam and Josaphat,[5] and the more legendary lives of the saints. This literature covers a period of many centuries, and none of it except Apuleius's [4] *Golden Ass* is generally familiar, but I have to refer to it occasionally because it shows the stock themes and images of romance with special clarity, as early works in a genre so often do.

Medieval romance presents different structural problems, which I shall have to touch very lightly. But in sixteenth-century England, with Sidney's *Arcadia* and similar works, the late Classical conventions reappear. When the novel developed, romance continued along with it in the "Gothic" stories of "Monk" Lewis and his Victorian successors. William Morris[6] is to me the most interesting figure in this tradition for many reasons, one of them being his encyclopedic approach to romance, his ambition to collect every major story in literature and retell or translate it. In the twentieth century romance got a new lease of fashion after the mid-1950s, with the success of Tolkien and the rise of what is generally called science fiction.

No genre stands alone, and in dealing with romance I have to allude to every other aspect of literature as well. Still, the conventions of prose romance show little change over the course of centuries, and conservatism of this kind is the mark of a stable genre. In the Greek romances we find stories of mysterious birth, oracular prophecies about the future contortions of the plot, foster parents, adventures which involve capture by pirates, narrow escapes from death, recognition of the true identity of the hero and his eventual marriage with the heroine. We open, let us say, [Sir Walter Scott's] *Guy Mannering*, written fifteen centuries later, and we find that, although there are slight changes in the setting, the kind of story being told, a story of mysterious birth, oracular prophecies, capture by pirates, and the like, is very much the same. In Greek romance the characters are Levantine, the setting is the Mediterranean world, and the normal means of transportation is by shipwreck. [5] In science fiction the characters may be earthlings, the setting the intergalactic spaces, and what gets wrecked in hostile territory a spaceship, but the tactics of the storyteller generally conform to much the same outlines.

One of the roots from which these chapters grew was an abandoned essay on the Waverley novels of Scott. The home I was brought up in possessed a good edition of the Waverley novels, and I had, I think, read them all in early life, with utter fascination. Some years later, at college, *Guy Mannering* was on a course and I reread it, but I had entered the age of intolerance by then, and *Guy Mannering* now seemed to me only a clumsy and faked narrative with wooden characters and an abominable style. I read Scott as little as possible through my earlier professional life, but about twenty years ago I was talking to a late friend whose name it is a pleasure to mention here, Richard Blackmur,[7] about the amount of tedium in modern life caused by plane journeys and waiting in airports. He remarked that he had got through a long and exhausting trip himself with the aid of Scott. "I love Scott," he said. I tried the recipe. Richard was right, as he so often was: when one is travelling by jet plane it is deeply reassuring to have a stagecoach style for a travelling companion.[8]

By this time I was ready to become fascinated once more by Scott's formulaic techniques. The same building blocks appeared every time: light and dark heroines, outlawed or secret societies, wild women chanting prophecies, heroes of mysterious and ultimately fortunate birth; but the variety with which they were disposed was what now impressed me. I noticed that much of the criticism of Scott attempted to assimilate him to standards that were not his. It was said that his characterization was what was important and that his plots were of secondary interest: this is nonsense, of course, but was said about him because it is [*6*] believed to be true of more fashionable writers. After I began to glimpse something of the uniformity of romance formulas over the centuries, I understood that my interest in Scott belonged in a larger context.

Meanwhile, an early absorption in Blake had expanded in two directions. One direction took me into the Bible by way of Milton: this is to be explored in another book.[9] The other direction was one that connected Blake with two other writers in particular, Spenser and William Morris, both writers of sentimental romance. So Spenser, Scott, and Morris appeared as three major centres of romance in a continuous tradition, and, these once identified, other centres, like the tales of Chaucer and the late comedies of Shakespeare, soon fell into place. This left me with a sense of a double tradition, one Biblical and the other romantic, growing out of an interest in Blake which seemed to have contained them both. The title of this book, *The Secular Scripture,* suggests something of its relation to a study of the Bible. The distinction underlying this relation is our first step.

Every human society, we may assume, has some form of verbal culture, in which fictions, or stories, have a prominent place. Some of these stories may seem more important than others: they illustrate what primarily concerns their society. They help to explain certain features in that society's religion, laws, social structure, environment, history, or cosmology. Other stories seem to be less important, and of some at least of these stories we say that they are told to entertain or amuse. This means that they are told to meet the imaginative needs of the community, so far as structures in words can meet those needs. The more important stories are also imaginative, but incidentally so: they are intended to convey something more like special knowledge, something of what in religion is called revelation [7]. Hence they are not thought of as imaginative or even of human origin, for a long time.

The more important group of stories in the middle of a society's verbal culture I shall call myths, using that word in a rather specific way which would not apply without modification outside the present argument. The more peripheral group, regarded by its own society, if not necessarily by us, as less important, I shall connect chiefly with the words "folk tale," though other words, such as "legend," also belong to it. It is difficult to make an adjective out of the words "folk tale," so I shall speak of my two types of verbal experience as the mythical and the fabulous.

In European literature, down to the last couple of centuries, the myths of the Bible have formed a special category, as a body of stories with a distinctive authority. Poets who attach themselves to this central mythical area, like Dante or Milton, have been thought of as possessing a special kind of seriousness conferred on them by their subject matter. Such poems were recognized, in their own day, to be what we should now call imaginative productions; but their content was assumed to be real, if at one remove, and not only real but about what most deeply concerned their readers.

When we turn to the tales of Chaucer or the comedies of Shakespeare, the primary motive of the author seems to be entertainment, in the sense of the word just used. Here we notice an influence from folk tale, so pervasive as to make it clear that folk tale is their direct literary ancestor. There are hardly any comedies of Shakespeare, and few tales told on the Canterbury pilgrimage, that do not have some common folk tale theme prominently featured in them. In Greek literature, the central mythical area is provided mainly by the Homeric epics and the tragic poets. The comic writers are allowed to be more inventive, and tell [*8*] stories that have no connection with the Greek equivalent of revelation, though, as in *The Birds* and *The Frogs*,[10] they often parody it. Again we notice, as we go from New Comedy[11] to the later prose romances, an increasingly close connection with folk tale.

Most myths are stories about or concerning the gods, and so the distinction between the mythical and the fabulous overlaps a good deal with the distinction between the sacred and the secular. But it is not identical with it, since many stories may be mythical, in the present sense, without being sacred. The largest and most important group of these are the national stories, which as a rule shade insensibly from the legendary to the historical. "In addition to the Bible," says George

MacDonald, "each nation possesses *a* Bible . . . in its history."[12] Thus the legends of the dynasties of Argos and Thebes were mythical for the Greeks in our sense, but were not strictly sacred even in the Greek sense. In Western literature, the overlapping of mythical and sacred is much closer, but even there national history has a particular seriousness. The alternative title of Shakespeare's *Henry VIII,* "All is True," perhaps indicates a seriousness of this kind, and one that the audience would not have expected from *The Tempest,* even though *The Tempest* has held the stage so much better.

The difference between the mythical and the fabulous is a difference in authority and social function, not in structure. If we were concerned only with structural features we should hardly be able to distinguish them at all. Most of the stories about the accepted divine beings are myths rather than folk tales, but structurally this distinction is more one of content than of actual shape. The parallelism in structure between myth and folk tale meets us everywhere in literature: an example is the exposed-infant theme of Greek New Comedy, which is not necessarily "derived" [9] from myth[13] but is obviously similar to some myths. There are only so many effective ways of telling a story, and myths and folk tales share them without dividing them.

But as a distinctive tendency in the social development of literature, myths have two characteristics that folk tales, at least in their earlier stages, do not show, or show much less clearly. First, myths stick together to form a mythology, a large interconnected body of narrative that covers all the religious and historical revelation that its society is concerned with, or concerned about. Second, as part of this sticking-together process, myths take root in a specific culture, and it is one of their functions to tell that culture what it is and how it came to be, in their own mythical terms. Thus they transmit a legacy of shared allusion to that culture. Folk tales by themselves, at least at first, lead a more nomadic existence. They travel over the world through all the barriers of language: they do not expand into larger structures, but interchange their themes and motifs at random, like the principles of chaos in Milton. But as literature develops, "secular" stories also begin to take root in the culture and contribute to the shared heritage of allusion.

The mythical poet, then, has his material handed him by tradition, whereas the fabulous poet may, up to a point, choose his own plots and characters. Aristophanes produced a distinctive "gimmick" for each of his comedies, and was expected to do so; Sophocles was expected to tell the mythical stories that had been made relevant to the Dionysus cult. Otherwise, the audience could ask, and feel that it had a right to ask, "What has all this to do with Dionysus?"[14] The characters and plots of mythical poets have the resonance of social acceptance about them, and they carry an authority that no writer can command who is merely being what we call "creative." The transmission of tradition [*10*] is explicit and conscious for the mythical writer and his audience: the fabulous writer may seem to be making up his stories out of his own head, but this never happens in literature, even if the illusion of its happening is a necessary illusion for some writers. His material comes from traditions behind him which may have no recognized or understood social status, and may not be consciously known to the writer or to his public.

The fact that myths stick together to form a mythology is clearly shown in an explicitly Christian story, such as the Barlaam and Josaphat romance, which comes from about the eighth century. This is said to be a Christianized version of the story of the Buddha, though there is hardly enough story for many specific parallels to emerge. Prince Josaphat is kept in seclusion by his father, who hates Christianity: the hermit Barlaam gets through to see him on the pretext that he has a precious jewel to show him. The jewel turns out to be an interminable sermon in which Barlaam sets forth the entire structure of Christian mythology from creation to last judgment, with appendices on the ascetic life, the use of images in ritual, the necessity of baptism, and the doctrine of the two natures of Christ. What makes so long a harangue possible—its plausibility is another matter—is simply the interconnection of the individual myths in the total Christian mythology: every concept or doctrine involves all the others. This was similarly the reason for the proverbial length of Puritan sermons, many centuries later. Such sermons were not necessarily digressive or shapeless, but, as in other forms of oral literature, there were certain mnemonic hooks or couplings leading from one point to the next until everything that God had in his mind for man had been expounded.

According to the Venerable Bede, this was how English literature got started with Caedmon. When the harp was [*11*] passed around at a feast and guests were expected to take their turns chanting or improvising poetry, Caedmon had to retire to the stable in humiliation. On one such occasion an angel appeared before him and commanded him to sing. The theme suggested to him was the creation, that is, page one of the Bible.

Once started on that, there was no stopping Caedmon until he had sung his way through the entire mythological corpus:

> He sang of the creation of the world, the origin of the human race, and the whole story of Genesis. He sang of Israel's departure from Egypt, their entry into the land of promise, and many other events of scriptural history. He sang of the Lord's incarnation, passion, resurrection and ascension into heaven, the coming of the Holy Spirit, and the teaching of the apostles. He also made many poems on the terrors of the last judgement, the horrible pains of hell, and the joys of the kingdom of heaven. In addition to these, he composed several others on the blessings and judgements of God, by which he sought to turn his hearers from delight in wickedness and to inspire them to love and do good.[15]

Caedmon was thus doing what the medieval miracle plays were later to do, in huge cyclical sequences that took several days to get through.

But while the difference in social function between myth and fable makes for these differences in characteristics, the identity in structure pulls in the opposite direction. Secular literature, even in the oral stage, also builds up an interconnecting body of stories. Thus *Beowulf*, which is close in its conventions to oral literature, refers parenthetically to other stories about Siegmund [ll. 874–900], Offa [ll. 1925–62], and Ingeld [ll. 2023–69], and most of the Icelandic Sagas contain allusions or cross-references to other Sagas. Given a slightly different direction [*12*] of social development, such a body of legend might easily have become mythical in our present sense of the term. Myths stick together because of cultural forces impelling them to do so: these forces are not primarily literary, and mythologies are mainly accepted as structures of belief or social concern rather than imagination. But it is the structure of myths that makes the process possible, and since folk tales possess the same kind of structure they can stick together too.

In secular literature, before copyright laws and individual claims to stories are set up, a standard relating to completeness in telling traditional stories seems often to be implied. Others have told this story before, the author gives us to understand, but I'm going to tell it better and more fully, so you won't have to refer to anyone else for missing features. In certain social contexts, such completeness might well become a qualification for passing over from the fabulous to the mythical category, as doubtless happened with the two Homeric poems. The standard of completeness shows the encyclopedic tendency of myth at work in what we are now calling folk tale or fable.

The *Beowulf* poet alludes to the story of Offa to identify a contrasting pattern of story: Hygd, the good queen the poet is talking about, reminds him by contrast of Thryth, the wife of Offa, who was a bad one. Similarly, an eighteenth-century novelist will tell an inset tale, like the story of the Man on the Hill in [Fielding's] *Tom Jones* [bk. 8, chaps. 11–14], which has a narrative movement opposite to that of the main story. The effect of such an inset tale is to establish the main story as one of a category of stories, giving it a broader significance than it would have as an isolated story. As a body of myths expands, it absorbs other stories, especially the stories connected with specific local places and people that are called legends. Thus the great Hebraic myths of the creation [*13*], deluge, and exodus expanded to include the legends of the Judges and the prophets Elijah and Elisha. A later process of expansion took in the folk tales of Jonah, Ruth, Tobit, Esther, Judith, and Susanna. Christian mythology similarly expanded to include a large body of romance, including many saints' lives and such apocryphal stories as the Harrowing of Hell.[16] Such an absorption of legend marks the political and social ascendancy of a society with a central mythology, as it takes over other areas, and this mythical imperialism is possible because of the structural similarities among all forms of story.

The literature of a polytheistic mythology can emphasize certain cults or even absorb or promote new ones, just as Christianity could use legend to enhance the prestige of a specific saint or shrine. Some of the Greek romancers say that they intend their stories to be an offering to Eros, or a demonstration of that god's power. The conclusion to *The Golden Ass* of Apuleius was evidently among other things a plug for the cult of Isis.[17] The same structural principle may still be used where there is no longer any question of cult. Greene's story *Pandosto*, the main source of Shakespeare's *Winter's Tale*, treats Apollo's oracle at Delphi in a way which would tempt us to assume, if it had been written two thousand years earlier, that it was trying to promote the prestige of that oracle. We are touching here on the relation of imaginative structures to belief or worship: the general principle is that imaginative structures as such are independent of belief, and it makes no difference to the structure whether the implied beliefs are real, pretended, or denounced as demonic, like the religion of the Trojans in Chaucer's *Troilus and Criseyde*.[18]

Just as a mythology may absorb new legendary material, so it may itself cease to carry the sense of superior importance or authority. This happens whenever one culture [14] supersedes another. Classical mythology became fabulous, a branch of secular literature, in Christian times, and Biblical mythology, as such, is rapidly becoming fabulous now. Very ancient Near Eastern stories of the creation as the killing of a dragon whose body supplied the material for it, originally mythical, have become fabulous in the Old Testament. Such a use of them, naturally, does not destroy their structural outlines. Similarly, Classical mythology still could, long after it had become fable, be used as a counterpoint to Christian mythology.

The Bible is the supreme example of the way that myths can, under certain social pressures, stick together to make up a mythology. A second look at this mythology shows us that it actually became, for medieval and later centuries, a vast mythological universe, stretching in time from creation to apocalypse, and in metaphorical space from heaven to hell. A mythological universe is a vision of reality in terms of human concerns and hopes and anxieties: it is not a primitive form of science. Unfortunately, human nature being what it is, man first acquires a mythological universe and then pretends as long as he can that it is also the actual universe. All mythological universes are by definition centred on man, therefore the actual universe was also assumed to be centred on man. Some Greek thinkers had realized that the earth went around the sun, but the medieval world ignored them because the geocentric model was more reassuring, at least from the point of view of those who controlled the culture.

The secession of science from the mythological universe is a familiar story. The separating of scientific and mythological space began theoretically with Copernicus, and effectively with Galileo. By the nineteenth century scientific time had been emancipated from mythological time. But in proportion as the mythological universe becomes [15] more obviously a construct, another question arises. We saw that there is no structural principle to prevent the fables of secular literature from also forming a mythology, or even a mythological universe. Is it possible, then, to look at secular stories as a whole, and as forming a single integrated vision of the world, parallel to the Christian and Biblical vision? This is the question implied in the "secular scripture" of my title. In the chapters that follow I should like to look at fiction as a total verbal order, with the outlines of an imaginative universe also in it. The Bible is the epic of the creator, with God as its hero. Romance is the structural core of all fiction: being directly descended from folk tale, it brings us closer than any other aspect of literature to the sense of fiction, considered as a whole, as the epic of the creature, man's vision of his own life as a quest.

One of my predecessors in the Norton Lectures, J.L. Borges, says, in a little story called *The Gospel according to Mark*: "generations of men, throughout recorded time, have always told and retold two stories—that of a lost ship which searches the Mediterranean seas for a dearly loved island, and that of a god who is crucified on Golgotha."[19] The Crucifixion is an episode in the Biblical epic: Borges is clearly suggesting that romance, as a whole, provides a parallel epic in which the themes of shipwreck, pirates, enchanted islands, magic, recognition, the loss and regaining of identity, occur constantly, as they do in the last four romances of Shakespeare. Borges is referring to different episodes of the two complete stories, but he puts his finger on an essential structural problem of criticism.

We notice that mythical poets, including Dante and Milton, do not themselves acquire the authority of the myths they treat, unless by accident, or unless, like Homer, they come at the very beginning of a cultural development. The [*16*] Devil in Bernard Shaw's *Man and Superman* remarks contemptuously of *Paradise Lost* that to this day every Englishman believes that the whole of Milton's "silly story" is in the Bible.[20] But it is clear that the belief is founded on a cultural misunderstanding, "Englishmen" being more ignorant of what is in the Bible than the Devil can afford to be. If one actually does know the Bible or the teachings of a religion based on it, he has probably not derived his knowledge from the poets. The distinction of mythical and fabulous, in other words, overlaps not only with the distinction of sacred and secular, but with the distinction of true and false, or of what is believed to be true or false.

Myths are usually assumed to be true, stories about what really happened. But truth is not the central basis for distinguishing the mythical from the fabulous: it is a certain quality of importance or authority for the community that marks the myth, not truth as such. The anxiety of society, when it urges the authority of a myth and the necessity of believing it, seems to be less to proclaim its truth than to prevent anyone from questioning it. It aims at consent, including the consent of silence, rather than conviction. Thus the Christian myth of providence, after a battle, is often invoked by the winning side in a way which makes its truth of secondary importance. The storm that wrecked the Spanish Armada was a providential event to the English, but a natural event to the Spaniards. Elizabeth I issued a medal quoting the Psalms, "God breathed with his winds, and they were scattered"; Philip of Spain said to the survivors: "I sent you forth to fight with men, not with the elements."

Shakespeare's Henry V makes it a capital offence to give credit for the victory of Agincourt to anyone but God.[21] The French, whose opinion did not count, would have ascribed it rather to the bitch-goddess Fortune, and some even in [*17*] the English army—Fluellen, for example—might have agreed with them. But such dissenting voices have to be silenced as long as the excitement of the victory lasts. Similarly, while the battle was going on, it would have been highly injudicious to question the assumption that St. George was supporting the English or, on the other side, St. Denis the French, much less suggest that one saint originated in a pagan folk tale and the other in a pious fraud. Yet the first doubt at least might have been defensible theologically, even in the fifteenth century.

Greek critics distinguished verbal structures as true, false, and plastic, or more accurately plasmatic, the presenting of things as they conceivably could be.[22] Truth and falsehood are not literary categories, and are only approximately even verbal ones. For the literary critic, at all events, everything in words is plasmatic, and truth and falsehood represent the directions or tendencies in which verbal structures go, or are thought to go. This leads to a general distinction between serious and responsible literature on the one hand, and the trifling and fantastic on the other. Again, these are not literary categories, or qualities inherent in literary works themselves. They are the primary elements of the social acceptance of or response to literature. Hence what is accepted as serious or dismissed as trifling may vary from one age to another, depending on currents of fashion or cultural attitudes operating for the most part outside literature.

The original criterion of truth is personal: a thing is true because a tradition of sufficient authority, or a person representing that tradition, says or endorses it. Here truth is identified, not so much with the verifiable statement, as with the "existential" statement of supreme importance for the community. This personal standard of truth is normally established under the social conditions of an oral [*18*] culture, and we notice how the great religious teachers tend to disclaim all connection with writing and confine themselves to the spoken word. Later on, truth tends to be thought of rather as truth of correspondence. A verbal structure describes something, and is called true if it is a satisfactory set of verbal symbols for what it describes. The development of writing throws a heavy emphasis on the descriptive aspect of words, and consequently a writing culture tends to identify truth more and more completely with truth of verbal correspondence.

In proportion as this more rational conception of truth develops, the fabulous acquires the quality of the imaginary, of something admitted not to be true. And because of the structural identity of fable and myth, the word "myth," like the words "fable" and "fiction," also takes on a connotation of "not really true." The New Testament uses the word *mythos* in this sense, and urges us to avoid *bebelous mythous*, profane stories [1 Timothy 4:7]. *Mythoi*, or just stories, were what other religions had: what Christians had were *logoi*, true stories. Confronted with this distinction, a literary critic can say only that the structural principles of the two appear to be identical. But if one story is true and another one of the same shape false, the difference between them can only be established by attaching a body of discursive writing to the true story, designed to verify or rationalize its truth.

The same point had struck Plato much earlier. It horrified Plato that the accredited teachers of religion in his day were poets employing myths instead of philosophers employing dialectic. Plato used myths himself a good deal, of course, as has been often enough said since his time. But there appear to be different levels of myth in Plato. On the highest level, myths are illustrations of principles established by dialectic, the instrument of knowledge about the [*19*] intelligible world. From that knowledge we move up to a myth showing this knowledge in a state of union, the wise man's untroubled vision of reality. We cannot enter into the great myths of creation, reincarnation, or the history of Atlantis which Socrates and Timaeus expound [Plato, *Timaeus*] without a preliminary training in philosophy. Such myths are as far as possible removed from the obstacle myths or silly stories which offend our sense of reality and moral decorum, and yet have gained a special authority by tradition. Plutarch says that the gods of whom indecent stories can be told are no gods [*Moralia*, 417e–f]: it follows that such stories are not true myths. Thus Plato, if I am right about him, makes the distinction between myth and fable as wide as he can get it, one being at the top and the other at the bottom of his vision of reality.

But for Plato knowledge about the intelligible world is also to be used for controlling the masses of people below it, who live by trust in authority. For them, whatever can be formulated as a doctrine, a history, a law, an argument, or a moral principle, and so belongs outside literature, can be illustrated by a story. The story is popular, addresses itself to untutored minds, and so helps to overcome the gap between the rulers who know and the ruled who must believe. The latter, if they do not know what truth is, may have to be lied to. But a myth on this lower level may be a lie and still represent true indoctrination, and true indoctrination is the real social function of literature. Much of what the poets give us, however, is lower-level myth without any relation to true indoctrination, still less to dialectic: this is part of the shadow knowledge which has no function in Plato's republic.

Similarly, Christianity possessed a body of true myth or revelation, most of it in the Bible. This was distinguished from unauthorized myth by having a large body of conceptual [20] writing attached to it, the doctrinal system of Christian theology. As with Plato, the Christian has to pass through this doctrinal system before he can understand the myths of the Bible. In the nineteenth century Cardinal Newman remarked that the function of scripture was not to teach doctrine but to prove it:[23] this axiom shows how completely the structure of the Bible had been translated into a conceptual system which both replaced and enclosed it. Even the fact that the original data were for the most part stories, as far as their structure is concerned, often came to be resented or even denied. Whatever resisted the translating operation had to be bracketed as a mystery of faith, into which it was as well not to look too closely.

When Christianity came to northern Europe, one of its first tasks was to destroy non-Christian mythology, along with the heroic poetry that could serve as a rallying point for a cultural tradition outside Christianity. Such poetry flourished with great persistence, and as late as A.D. 800 Alcuin could warn against listening to it, asking *Quid Hinieldus cum Christo?*—What has the northern hero Ingeld to do with Christ? He was paraphrasing St. Paul, but also echoing the protest of the conservative Athenians: "What has all this to do with Dionysus?"[24] Alcuin spoke for the great majority of those who controlled the art of writing, and they saw to it that we today have only the most fragmentary knowledge of what must have been a very great oral tradition. In doing so they set up, for a new cycle of civilization, much the same model of social response to literature that Plato had used, and passed it on to us. The similarity between Biblical myths and the fables of the heathen could be accounted for by the fact that the devil, like man, is a clever mimic.

The Platonic revolution, as transmitted through Christianity [21], has given us a hierarchy of verbal structures with four main levels in it. On top is the level of high myth, Biblical or Platonic, which is not only not literary but cannot be really understood except by those who have passed beyond the need for literature. Next come the serious verbal structures, the nonliterary ones that tell the truth by correspondence about history, religion, ethics, or social life. Below this is the relatively serious literature that reflects their truths and communicates them to the populace in the more agreeable forms of story or rhetorical embellishment. This is the middle ground of myth, in Plato the level where poets may operate by writing hymns to the gods and encomia on virtuous men. Below this is the literature designed only to entertain or amuse, which is out of sight of truth, and should be avoided altogether by serious people.

There are two results of this situation, one positive and constructive, the other negative and obstructive. The positive result was only possible because the rigorously hard line of this attitude did not maintain itself. There were many mitigating factors, like Aristotle's more liberal conception of mimesis, and because of them literature did succeed in gaining a real place in the Christian social order. As its place was essentially secular, the imaginative standards came to be set by the fabulous writers, and the mythical ones had to meet those standards. They got no special advantage, except by accident, from choosing themes to which their society attached special importance. There is said to be an illustration in an early edition of *The Pilgrim's Progress* showing the plays of John Dryden being advertised in Vanity Fair. Bunyan would certainly have thought that his theme, the imitation of Christ in the Christian life, gave his book, whatever its aesthetic merits, a fundamental seriousness that no play of Dryden's could [22] possibly match. Samuel Johnson, Coleridge, perhaps Matthew Arnold, would have agreed with the general principle, without being able to take Bunyan as seriously as Dryden within the category of literature itself. Samuel Johnson says that Pope's *Messiah* is greatly superior to Virgil's *Fourth Eclogue*, but that this is no credit to Pope, because Pope has derived his poem from an immeasurably superior source, the Book of Isaiah.[25] This statement is nonsense as far as literary criticism is concerned, and Johnson knows that it is nonsense: he is making the statement simply to emphasize the priority of his religious commitments to his literary standards.

The negative results of the Platonic and Christian view, however, are more obvious and important for the subject of romance. Serious literature, according to that view, is addressed to those who have a natural hankering for pleasure, and really want to read just for fun, but can be persuaded to read for instruction as well. It is for this group, according to a principle generally accepted in Elizabethan times, that Classical mythology is intended. The fables of the gods are pleasant enough to entice the more light-minded reader, but when he digests them he will find that they are really wholesome food, that is, moral platitudes. Thus Adlington, in the preface to his translation of Apuleius:

> And therefore the poets feigned not their fables in vain, considering that children in time of their first studies are very much allured thereby to proceed to more grave and deep studies. . . . By the fable of Actaeon, where it is feigned that when he saw Diana washing herself in a well, he was immediately turned into an hart, and so was slain of his own dogs, may be meant, that when a man casteth his eyes on the vain and soon fading beauty of the world . . . he seemeth to be turned into a brute beast. . . . The fall [23] of Icarus is an example to proud and arrogant persons, that weeneth to climb up to the heavens. . . . By Phaeton, that unskilfully took in hand to rule the chariot of the sun, are represented those persons which attempt things passing their power and capacity.[26]

We finally come, at the bottom of the hierarchy, to popular literature, or what people read without guidance from their betters. Popular literature has been the object of a constant bombardment of social anxieties for over two thousand years, and nearly the whole of the established critical tradition has stood out against it. The greater part of the reading and listening public has ignored the critics and censors for exactly the same length of time. This is an issue which we shall have to look into, because the bulk of popular literature consists of what I have been calling sentimental romance.

Any serious discussion of romance has to take into account its curiously proletarian status as a form generally disapproved of, in most ages, by the guardians of taste and learning, except when they use it for their own purposes. The close connection of the romantic and the popular runs all through literature. The formulas of New Comedy and Greek romance were demotic and popular formulas, like their counterparts now, treated with condescension by the highbrows, one form of condescension being the writing of such tales themselves, as academics write detective stories today. A similar situation, according to Arthur Waley,[27] appeared in classical China, which produced some excellent romances although romance was never accepted as a valid form of literature.

Popular literature, the guardians of taste feel, is designed only to entertain: consequently reading it is a waste of time. More closely regarded by anxiety, it turns [24] out to be something far worse than a waste of time. Romance in particular is, we say, "sensational": it likes violent stimulus, and the sources of that stimulus soon become clear to the shuddering censor. The central element of romance is a love story, and the exciting adventures are normally a foreplay leading up to a sexual union. Hence romance appears to be designed mainly to encourage irregular or excessive sexual activity. This may be masturbation, which is the usual model in the minds of those who speak with contempt of "escape" reading, or it may be a form of voyeurism. Most denunciations of popular romance on such grounds, we notice, assume that the pornographic and the erotic are the same thing: this overlooks the important principle that it is the function of pornography to stun and numb the reader, and the function of erotic writing to wake him up.

Throughout the history of culture, not many people have really questioned this Platonic and traditionally Christian framework. In every age it has been generally assumed that the function of serious literature is to produce illustrations of the higher truths conveyed by expository prose. The real social function of literature, in this view, is to persuade the emotions to align themselves with the reason, and so act on the "heart," which perhaps means not so much the pump in the chest as the primary or primitive brain. The disputes are mainly, not about the status of literature, but about how efficient the serious aspect of serious literature is in separating itself from the moral turpitude of mere entertainment.

Every so often a particularly bloody-minded censor denies that there is any separation. In Elizabethan times there was Stephen Gosson, an able and acute writer given his premises, who wrote *The Schoole of Abuse* largely to attack the new threat that popular literature was posing in [25] the theatre.[28] Gosson demonstrates that Classical myths were not stories told for the sake of their morals: whether the morals are inserted by the poets themselves or by their readers, the stories in themselves are not instructive but delightful, and therefore detestable. An example of a more liberal view founded on similar premises is the implication in Judge Woolsey's court decision on *Ulysses*, which held that *Ulysses* was serious rather than obscene because its attitude to sex was more nauseating ("emetic") than enticing.[29]

Many literary critics today still have Platonic minds, in the sense that they attach what for them are the real values of literature to something outside literature which literature reflects. This may be scholastic theology or Senecan ethics in one age, Marxist economics or Freudian psychology in another, sociolinguistics or phenomenology in another. Freudian and Marxist critics, of the more orthodox kinds at least, generally subscribe to the Platonic view of literature, and I have been amused to notice, in discussions of my own work, how my proposal to take literature itself as the area of critical investigation, without granting anything else priority to it, causes Freudian and Marxist anxieties to go up like barrage balloons.

In bourgeois society, a good deal of anxiety about popular literature has had a vestigial class motivation. Prohibition was clearly part of an effort to impose a middle-class ethic on a working class who might be alcoholically stimulated to do less work. Similarly, sexual prudery has often been a middle-class reaction to the fact that the pleasures of sex are available to ordinary people, and are therefore, as the proverbial lady says, "much too good for them." Phrases emphasizing the cheapness of popular literature, such as "dime novel," or "penny dreadful," lingered long after inflation had made them archaic, and it was a common [*26*] assumption, sometimes reflected in legislation, that very expensive books were automatically serious. Such anxieties are no longer much with us, except sporadically, but some of the habits of mind they engendered still are, and account for much of our confusion today about the social function of the humanities. I am aware, of course, that popular literature of various types has recently come in for a good deal of academic processing. I am trying to suggest a literary perspective on it which may help to bring it into the area of literary criticism instead of confining it to linguistics or to the less fashionable suburbs of sociology.

There seem to me to be two ways of looking at popular literature. If by popular literature we mean what a great many people want or think they want to read when they are compelled to read, or stare at on television when they are not, then we are talking about a packaged commodity which an overproductive economy, whether capitalist or socialist, distributes as it distributes food and medicines, in varying degrees of adulteration. Much of it, in our society, is quite as prurient and brutal as its worst enemy could assert, not because it has to be, but because those who write and sell it think of their readers as a mob rather than a community. In such a social context the two chief elements of romance, love and adventure, become simply lust and bloodlust. As in most melodrama, there is often a certain self-righteous rationalization of the tone: this is what we're all involved in, whether we like it or not, etc. But the fact that sex and violence emerge whenever they get a chance does mean that sexuality and violence are central to romance: this is an important cultural fact about it which we shall have to return to.

Popular literature could also mean, however, the literature that demands the minimum of previous verbal experience and special education from the reader. In poetry, this [27] would include, say, the songs of Burns and Blake, the Lucy lyrics of Wordsworth, ballads and folk songs, and other simple forms ranging from some of the songs and sonnets of Shakespeare to Emily Dickinson. Much if not most of this would be very unpopular in the bestseller sense, but it is the kind of material that should be central in the literary education of children and others of limited contact with words. When we apply this conception of the popular to stories in prose, we find ourselves again close to folk tale, and begin to understand more clearly what the real connection between romance and popular literature is.

The central mythical area is an area of special authority, which means that people in authority take it over. It becomes the centre also of education, and the literature based on it thus becomes highly allusive and erudite, these qualities increasing as the mythology expands into other cultural areas. *Paradise Lost* is "elite" literature, if it is understood that I am not using the word in its cliché sense. It is elite not because it is Biblical in its choice of subject, but because the whole structure of humanist learning, with Biblical and Classical mythology radiating out from it, has to be brought to bear on the reading and study of the poem. By contrast, *The Pilgrim's Progress* is, or was, popular literature, because it assumes only the kind of understanding of the Christian myth that every English family with any books or education at all would have possessed in Bunyan's day and for two centuries thereafter. Pope's *Dunciad* is "elite" literature of a more secular kind, with its echoes from Classical epic and its dense texture of personal allusion and of what we call in-jokes. Defoe's *Robinson Crusoe* is popular because it demands only the kind of awareness of the world that, again, an eighteenth-century Englishman likely to read any book would normally have.

If there is anything to be said for this conception of popular [28] literature, we should be careful not to idealize it as a virtuous resistance to elitism, the poor but honest hero of bourgeois romance who triumphs over his wealthier rival. Popular literature, so defined, is neither better nor worse than elite literature, nor is it really a different kind of literature: it simply represents a different social development of it. The same writer may feel the pull of elite and popular tendencies within himself. The popular helps to diversify our literary experience and prevent any type of literary education from getting a monopoly of it; but as time goes on, popular writers without exception survive by being included in the literary "establishment." Thus Spenser has acquired a reputation as a poet's poet and a storehouse of recondite allusion and allegory; but in his day *The Faerie Queene* was regarded as pandering to a middlebrow appetite for stories about fearless knights and beauteous maidens and hideous ogres and dragons, instead of following the more sober Classical models.

As a rule, popular literature in this sense indicates where the next literary developments are most likely to come from. It was the popular theatre, not humanist neo-Classical drama, that pointed the way to Marlowe and Shakespeare; it was the popular Deloney,[30] not the courtly and aristocratic Sidney, who showed what the major future forms of prose fiction were going to be like; it was the popular ballad and broadside and keepsake-book doggerel of the eighteenth century that anticipated the *Songs of Innocence* and the *Lyrical Ballads*. In prose, the popular literature signalizing such new developments has usually taken the form of a rediscovery of the formulas of romance.

The history of literature seems to break down into a series of cultural periods of varying length, each dominated by certain conventions. During these periods, what one distinguished scholar of this university has called the [29] burden of the past[31] increases rapidly in weight and oppressiveness. Writers improve and refine on their predecessors until it seems that no further improvement is possible. Then the conventions wear out, and literature enters a transitional phase where some of the burden of the past is thrown off and popular literature, with romance at its centre, comes again into the foreground. This happened with Greek literature after New Comedy, when Greek romance emerged; it happened at the end of the eighteenth century in Britain, when the Gothic romances emerged, and it is happening now after the decline of realistic fiction, as I shall try to explain more fully in the next chapter.

We should note that, if we accept my second definition of popular, the words "popular" and "primitive" mean essentially the same thing, except that "popular" has its context in class structure and "primitive" in history. If we define popular literature as what ignorant and vicious people read, the prejudice implied will make it impossible to understand what is going on in literature. Similarly, if we define the primitive only as the chronologically early, we create an illusion of literature gradually improving itself from naked savagery to the decent clothing of accepted cultural values. But actually the primitive is a quality in literature which emerges recurrently as an aspect of the popular, and as indicating also that certain conventions have been exhausted. The Greek romancers, for all their coyness, are more primitive in this sense than Homer or Aeschylus; the Gothic romancers, like many of the poets contemporary with them, are primitive in a way that Pope and Swift are not, and so are the folk singers and science fiction writers of our own day as compared with Eliot or Joyce.

In every period of history certain ascendant values are accepted by society and are embodied in its serious literature. Usually this process includes some form of kidnapped [30] romance, that is, romance formulas used to reflect certain ascendant religious or social ideals. Spenser knew very well what he was doing with his ogres and dragons: he was trying to get imaginative support for the Protestant revolution of his time, both in its insurgent phase, the main subject of book 1 of *The Faerie Queene*, and in its authoritarian phase, the main subject of book 5. At other times popular enjoyment of sexuality or violence is simply gratified or exploited. But something forever excluded from accepted values always gets away, never wholly absorbed even by the greatest literature.

Of Borges's two retold stories, the Biblical and the romantic, the Biblical story finally ends with the Book of Revelation, in a fairytale atmosphere of gallant angels fighting dragons, a wicked witch, and a wonderful gingerbread city glittering with gold and jewels. But the other story, the ship searching the Mediterranean for a lost island, never seems to come to an end. It may go into the Atlantic looking for happy islands here, or into the Pacific, as in Melville's *Mardi*, or into outer space, journeying to planets so remote that light itself is too slow a vehicle. When we study the great classics of literature, from Homer on, we are following the dictates of common sense, as embodied in the author of Ecclesiastes: "Better is the sight of the eyes than the wandering of the desire" [Ecclesiastes 6:9]. Great literature is what the eye can see: it is the genuine infinite as opposed to the phony infinite, the endless adventures and endless sexual stimulation of the wandering of desire. But I have a notion that if the wandering of desire did not exist, great literature would not exist either.

There is a line of Pope's which exists in two versions: "A mighty maze of walks without a plan," and "A mighty maze, but not without a plan."[32] The first version recognizes the human situation; the second refers to the constructs of [31] religion, art, and science that man throws up because he finds the recognition intolerable. Literature is an aspect of the human compulsion to create in the face of chaos. Romance, I think, is not only central to literature as a whole, but the area where we can see most clearly that the maze without a plan and the maze not without a plan are two aspects of the same thing.

II The Context of Romance

Literary critics have inherited from Aristotle two principles: one, the conception of art as imitating nature; the other, the distinction of form and content. In nonliterary writing, the verbal structure imitates what it describes in the way that a copy imitates an external model. In literature, however, the art is the form, and the nature which the art imitates is the content, so in literature art imitates nature by containing it internally. This principle is a practical one, and still very useful: one limitation of it is that it relates only to the work of art as product, as finished and done with. It is perhaps more natural for us today to think in terms of continuous process or creative activity, and for that we need two other conceptions parallel to form and content.

In the context of process, the form becomes something more like the shaping spirit, the power of ordering which seems so mysterious to the poet himself, because it often acts as though it were an identity separate from him. What corresponds to content is the sense of otherness, the resistance of the material, the feeling that there is something to be overcome, or at least struggled with. Wallace Stevens calls these two elements imagination and reality: as often with Stevens's terminology, the words are used much more [36] precisely than they appear to be, and I shall adopt them here.[33]

The imagination, then, is the constructive power of the mind, the power of building unities out of units. In literature the unity is the *mythos* or narrative; the units are metaphors, that is, images connected primarily with each other rather than separately with the outer world. "Reality," for Stevens, is whatever the imagination works with that is not itself. Left to itself, the imagination can achieve only a facile pseudo-conquest of its own formulas, meeting no resistance from reality. The long-standing association between the words "imagination" and "fancy" may suggest that the imaginative, by itself, tends to be fantastic or fanciful. But actually, what the imagination, left to itself, produces is the rigidly conventionalized. In folk tales, plot themes and motifs are predictable enough to be counted and indexed; improvised drama, from *commedia dell'arte* to guerrilla theatre, is based on formulas with a minimum of variables. Anyone recording, or reading about, reveries, daydreams, or conscious sexual fantasies must be struck by the total absence in such things of anything like real fantasy. They are formulaic, and the formulaic unit, of phrase or story, is the cornerstone of the creative imagination, the simplest form of what I call an archetype.

In the course of struggling with a world which is separate from itself, the imagination has to adapt its formulaic units to the demands of that world, to produce what Aristotle calls the probable impossibility [*Poetics*, chap. 25]. The fundamental technique used is what I call displacement, the adjusting of formulaic structures to a roughly credible context. A friend of mine, at the beginning of his teaching career, was faced with teaching a "creative writing" course to students of very limited literary experience. One of his devices was to give them a Grimm fairy tale and tell them to displace it, [37] turning it into a plausible story in which every detail of the original would be accounted for. A literary example of such a technique is Ibsen's *Vikings at Helgeland*, a displacement of the Sigurd saga.[34] Here Fafnir the dragon has become a tame bear, the changing of shapes in the original is accounted for by the heroine's being slightly drunk, and so on. Artificial displacements of this kind are useful mainly for practice pieces; but it is clear even from this example that realistic displacement is closely related to parody.

In the fiction writing of the last four or five centuries there has been a kind of reversible shuttle moving between imagination and reality, as Stevens uses those words. One direction is called "romantic," the other "realistic." The realistic tendency moves in the direction of the representational and the displaced, the romantic tendency in the opposite direction, concentrating on the formulaic units of myth and metaphor. At the extreme of imagination we find the themes and motifs of folk tale, elements of the process that Coleridge distinguished as fancy, and described as "a mode of memory" playing with "fixities and definites."[35] At the extreme of realism comes what is often called "naturalism," and at the extreme of that the shaping spirit wanders among documentary, expository, or reminiscent material, unable to find a clear narrative line from a beginning to an end.

Problems of design, of composition and balance and contrast, are obviously as central in the verbal arts as they are in music or painting. They appear in the rhetorical texture, an obvious example being the antithetical structure that we find in Hebrew parallelism, the Latin elegiac, and the English heroic couplet. They appear in the ballet-like couplings and intertwinings of characters in Goethe's *Elective Affinities* or Henry James's *Golden Bowl*: and they [38] appear in contrapuntal plots like the story of Gloucester in *King Lear*. Characters occupy the *designed* time and space of their creators; they may as logically end their fictional lives at marriage as at death; their paths may cross in sheer "coincidence." The more undisplaced the story, the more sharply the design stands out. Later on we shall refer to Carlo Gozzi, the eighteenth-century Italian dramatist who is useful to a study of romance because he writes undisplaced fairy tales full of magic and metamorphosis. We are not surprised to find that it was Gozzi who maintained that the entire range of dramatic possibilities could be reduced to thirty-six basic situations.[36] The inference for us is that even the most contrived and naive romantic plot, even the most impossibly black-and-white characterization, may still give us some technical insight into the way that stories get told.

The romantic tendency is anti-representational, and so is parallel to the development of abstract or primitive movements in painting. Critics of painting have learned to examine such pictures on their own terms; critics of fiction have to learn to look at romances, with all their nonrepresentational plots and characters, equally on their own terms. Many Victorian critics of painting demanded anecdotal pictures, because their frame of reference was literary, and so they felt that if a picture were just a picture there would be nothing to say about it. Many literary critics, even yet, are in the same position when confronted with a romance which is "just a story."

When the novel was established in the eighteenth century, it came to a reading public familiar with the formulas of prose romance. It is clear that the novel was a realistic displacement of romance, and had few structural features peculiar to itself. *Robinson Crusoe, Pamela, Tom Jones,* use much the same general structure as romance, but adapt [39] that structure to a demand for greater conformity to ordinary experience. This displacement gave the novel's relation to romance, as I suggested a moment ago, a strong element of parody. It would hardly be too much to say that realistic fiction, from Defoe to Henry James, is, when we look at it as a form of narrative technique, essentially parody-romance. Characters confused by romantic assumptions about reality, who emphasize the same kind of parody, are central to the novel: random examples include Emma Bovary, Anna Karenina, Lord Jim, and Isabel Archer.[37]

The supreme example of the realistic parody of romance is of course *Don Quixote,* which signalized the death of one kind of fiction and the birth of another kind. But the tradition of parody can be traced all through the history of the novel, up to and beyond *Ulysses,* and extends to many novelists who have been thought to be still too close to romance. Thus Fielding's *Joseph Andrews* began as a parody of [Richardson's] *Pamela,* and Jane Austen's *Northanger Abbey* is a parody of Gothic romance. The sketches that Jane Austen produced in her teens are nearly all burlesques of popular romantic formulas. And yet, if we read *Pride and Prejudice* or *Emma* and ask the first question about it, which is, What is Jane Austen doing? What is it that drives her pen from one corner of the page to the other? the answer is of course that she is telling a story. The story is the soul of her writing, to use Aristotle's metaphor [*Poetics,* chap. 6], the end for which all the words are put down. But if we concentrate on the shape of her stories, we are studying something that brings her much closer to her romantic colleagues, even to the writers of the horrid mysteries she parodied. Her characters are believable, yet every so often we become aware of the tension between them and the outlines of the story into which they are obliged to fit. This [40] is particularly true of the endings, where the right men get married to the right women, although the inherent unlikelihood of these unions has been the main theme of the story. All the adjustments are made with great skill, but the very skill shows that form and content are not quite the same thing: they are two things that have to be unified.

The Waverley novels of Scott mark the absorption of realistic displacement into romance itself. Scott begins his preface to *Waverley* by outlining a number of facile romance formulas that he is *not* going to follow, and then stresses the degree of reality that his story is to have. His hero Waverley is a romantic hero, proud of his good looks and education, but, like a small-scale Don Quixote, his romantic attitude is one that confirms the supremacy of real life. He is overimpressionable, and his loves and loyalties are alike immature. If not really what Scott later called him, "a sneaking piece of imbecility,"[38] he is certainly in the central parody-romance tradition of characterization. Parody enters the structure of many other semi-romantic novels, though sometimes, as in the later novels of Dickens, it appears to be largely unconscious. In *Little Dorrit* and *Our Mutual Friend* the romantic element, a sprawling octopus of a plot involving disguise, conspiracy, mystery, suspense, and violence, which we can hardly follow at the time and cannot remember afterwards, seems to be almost an anti-narrative. Some features of *Ulysses*, such as the parody of popular female fiction in the "Nausicaa" episode, are similar, and indicate that the real affinities of *Ulysses* are with the past, the tradition stretching from Defoe of which it seems a kind of swan song.

The association of parody and displacement is particularly clear in the many stories, from Mrs. Radcliffe in the eighteenth century to certain types of detective fiction in our day, in which the reader's interest in some fantastic or supernatural situation is worked up, only to be deflated [41] again with a commonplace explanation. In Scott's *Anne of Geierstein* the heroine engages in a certain amount of moonlight flitting, and it is suggested that she is descended from a fairy or elemental spirit, and has acquired by this heredity the ability to transport herself through space without the usual physical movements. A long inset tale is told about her grandmother to lend emotional weight to this suggestion; but eventually everything she does is explained on more or less plausible grounds. The implication in such a device is that fairy tales are for children: the mature reader will want and expect a more matter-of-fact account. The fantasy here is introduced because the action of *Anne of Geierstein* takes place in the fifteenth century, and such fantasy illustrates the kind of superstitions that people at that time had. However, the real effect of the device is to put the undisplaced and displaced versions of the same event side by side. Its significance, then, is not in any child-and-adult value judgment about beliefs, but in the fact that undisplaced versions present the narrative structure more abstractly, just as a cubist or primitive painting would present the geometrical forms of its images more directly than straight representation would do.

As soon as the novel established itself as a respectable literary medium, critics promptly assimilated it to the old Platonic-Christian framework, as described in the previous chapter. The serious literary artists who tell stories in prose, according to this view, also tell us something about the life of their times, and about human nature as it appears in that context, while doing so. Below them comes romance, where the story is told primarily for the sake of the story. This kind of writing is assumed to be much more of a commercial product, and the romancer is considered to have compromised too far with popular literature. Popular literature itself is obviously still in the doghouse.

This means that what gives a novelist moral dignity is [42] not the story he tells, but a wisdom and insight brought to bear on the world outside literature, and which he has managed to capture within literature. This is what distinguishes George Eliot from Marie Corelli, Joseph Conrad from John Buchan, D.H. Lawrence from Elinor Glyn.[39] All through the nineteenth century and our own there had also been a flourishing development of romance and fantasy, in Wilkie Collins, Bulwer-Lytton, Lewis Carroll, William Morris, and others.[40] Some of these writers were immensely popular in their day, and a few, like Lewis Carroll, have never lost their popularity. But they do not seem to fit the history of fiction as defined by the great realists: they are simply other writers. On the boundary of serious fiction and romance are Scott and Dickens, whose reputations have oscillated a good deal between the two ranks. The setting of *Waverley*, we notice, is a genuine historical event, the 1745 rebellion, and the book is equipped with footnotes indicating an essential mark of literary seriousness, the ability to read nonliterary documents. But Scott came finally to be regarded as too much of a romancer to be worthy of close study. Dickens fared rather better: he too was darkly suspected of being a mere entertainer, but he had obvious social concerns, and besides, he wrote *Hard Times*, a novel so dull that he must surely have had some worthy nonliterary motive for producing it.

The prevailing conception of serious fiction is enshrined[41] in the title of F.R. Leavis's book *The Great Tradition*, a study of George Eliot, Henry James, and Joseph Conrad which assumes that these writers are central in a hierarchy of realistic novelists extending roughly from Defoe to D.H. Lawrence. The assumption seems reasonable, yet when empires start building walls around themselves it is a sign that their power is declining, and the very appearance of such a title indicates a coming change of fashion on the part of both writers and readers. As soon as a defensive [43] wall is in place, the movements of the barbarians on the frontiers, in this case the readers of romance, Westerns, murder mysteries, and science fiction, begin to take on greater historical importance. These movements assumed a more definite shape after the appearance of Tolkien's *Lord of the Rings* in the mid-1950s. On the T.S. Eliot principle that every writer creates his own tradition, the success of Tolkien's book helped to show that the tradition behind it, of George MacDonald and Lewis Carroll and William Morris, was, if not "the great" tradition, a tradition nonetheless.[42] It is a tradition which interests me rather more than Tolkien himself ever did, but for a long time I was in a minority in my tastes. Over twenty years ago, in the remotest corner of a secondhand bookshop, I picked up a cheap reprint of William Morris's *The Roots of the Mountains*. The bookseller remarked that the two little green volumes had been sitting on his shelves since the day he opened his shop in 1913. Fortunately he had some other stock that moved faster, but if the shop is still there it is probably featuring paperback reprints of William Morris romances in a series which, though still cautiously labelled "adult fantasy," seems to be finding its public.

The change of taste in favour of romance raises a good many questions about the validity of some common critical assumptions about fiction which have been fostered by the prestige of a displaced and realistic tradition. There is still a strong tendency to avoid problems of technique and design and structure in fiction, and to concentrate on what the book talks about rather than on what it actually presents. It is still not generally understood either that "reality" in literature cannot be presented at all except within the conventions of literary structure, and that those conventions must be understood first. To give an example of what I mean:

Pirandello's *Six Characters in Search of an Author* [44] claims to be, at least in its closing scene, a parable of the relation of fiction to reality. Now we notice that one recurring theme in romance is the theme of incest, very often of father and daughter. In the Apollonius story, retold by Gower and the basis of Shakespeare's *Pericles*,[43] we are first introduced to the wicked king Antiochus, who is sexually connected with his daughter. Apollonius himself, or Pericles, the hero of the story, also acquires a daughter whom he loses, who is sold to a brothel, who meets him when he does not know who she is. In short, father–daughter incest keeps hanging over the story as a possibility until nearly the end. This part of the Apollonius story is said to be derived from a lost play of Euripides in which a father unknowingly buys his daughter as a slave, and in which the threat of incest must have been more imminent. In Pirandello the inner play of the six characters, representing reality, is a gloomy melodrama in which at the crucial scene a man enters a brothel and becomes involved with a girl who turns out to be—guess what—his own daughter. The play shows us nothing at all about the relation of fiction to reality: what it shows us is that some conventions of storytelling are more obsessive than others.

In the general area of romance we find highly stylized patterns like the detective story, which are so conventionalized as to resemble games. We expect each game of chess to be different, but we do not want the conventions of the game itself to alter, or to see a chess game in which the bishops move in straight lines and the rooks diagonally. Whether we consider detective stories worth reading or not depends on our willingness to accept the convention. Edmund Wilson, for example, refused to accept the convention, and remarked that readers of detective stories were obviously neurotics trying to attach an inflated importance to a pointless activity.[44] Now if we do find wit, [45] lively plotting, vivid characterization, or cogent social comment in detective stories—and it is not so difficult to find such things—we should appreciate the author's ingenuity in getting good writing into so ritualistic a form. The right next step for criticism, it seems to me, is not to assume that there is a difference in value between detective fiction and other types of fiction, but to realize that all fiction is conventionalized, and that it is equally a *tour de force* of ingenuity to get good characterization and social insight into a story as complicated as *Tom Jones* or *Emma*, both of which also contain mysteries impelling us to continue reading until we reach the "solution."

It will have occurred to you already that this "romantic" and "realistic" contrast is a nineteenth-century one, and that even in the nineteenth century it will not always work: it will not work with Balzac, for instance. But the prestige of "realism" in the nineteenth century reflected the prevailing fashions of that culture, nearly all of which emphasized some form of correspondence, the paralleling of mental structures with something in the outer world. It was an age of representational painting and realistic fiction, and of analogical, or, as I generally call it, allegorical criticism, approaching works of literature as historical or psychological documents. The reason for such an emphasis in criticism is that the more displaced a work of fiction is, the easier it is to see it in terms of its social function rather than its structure. When we start to read Zola or Dreiser, our first impulse is to ask, not what kind of a story is being told, but what is being said about the society that the story is "reflecting."

The beginning of a new kind of criticism is marked by Oscar Wilde's

"The Decay of Lying," which explains very lucidly that, as life has no shape and literature has, literature is throwing away its one distinctive quality when it [*46*] tries to imitate life. It follows for Wilde that what is called realism does not create but can only record things on a subcreative level: "M. Zola sits down to give us a picture of the Second Empire. Who cares for the Second Empire now? It is out of date. Life goes faster than Realism, but Romanticism is always in front of Life."[45] Wilde was clearly the herald of a new age in literature, which would take another century or so to penetrate the awareness of critics. He is looking forward to a culture which would use mythical and romantic formulas in its literature with great explicitness, making once more the essential discovery about the human imagination, that it is always a form of "lying," that is, of turning away from the descriptive use of language and the correspondence form of truth. The nineteenth century was also an age that threw up such philosophical schools as "idealism" and (in a different context) "realism," which may be described as two sets of reasons for feeling confident about the adequacy of words to represent external reality. Twentieth-century literature and painting are part of the same cultural movement that in philosophy has shifted the centre of interest back to the linguistic structure itself, after destroying much of our old naive confidence that words have an unlimited ability to represent things outside themselves.

Nineteenth-century writers of romance, or of fiction which is close to romance in its technique, sometimes speak in their prefaces and elsewhere of the greater "liberty" that they feel entitled to take. By liberty they mean a greater designing power, especially in their plot structures. Some time back I dropped the word "coincidence" [p. 27], and the word is worth pausing a moment on. In displaced or realistic [*47*] fiction the author tries to avoid coincidence. That is, he tries to conceal his design, pretending that things are happening out of inherent probability. The convention of avoiding coincidence is so strong that we often say such things as "if this happened in a book, nobody would believe it." In *Jane Eyre* the heroine, in flight from Rochester's proposal to make her his mistress, wanders into the world at random, and is eventually taken in by the only family in England with which she has a previous connection unknown to herself. The odds against the inherent probability of this are so vast that we say, mildly, that it is a far-fetched coincidence. In ordinary life a coincidence is a piece of design for which we can find no practical use. Hence, though coincidences certainly happen in ordinary life, they have no point there except to suggest that life at times is capable of forming rudimentary literary designs, thereby seeming to be almost on the point of making sense. Those disposed to believe in providence, that is, a power that shapes our rough-hewn ends into more symmetrical forms, generally comic ones, are often inspired by such a coincidence to express their belief. "Seems like it was sort of meant, like," to quote an example I once overheard. Doubtless Charlotte Brontë had her views about providence too, even if we can see no providence in this case except her desire to tell her story without inhibitions.

In realism the attempt is normally to keep the action horizontal, using a technique of causality in which the characters are prior to the plot, in which the problem is normally, Given these characters, what will happen? Romance is more usually "sensational," that is, it moves from one discontinuous episode to another, describing things that happen to characters, for the most part, externally. We may speak of these two types of narrative as the "hence" narrative and the "and then" narrative. Most realistic [*48*] fiction, down to about the middle of the nineteenth century, achieved some compromise between the two, but after the rise of a more ironic type of naturalism the "hence" narrative gained greatly in prestige, much of which it still retains.

The question of how far any real logic or causality is involved in a "hence" narrative is doubtless very complicated, but fortunately does not concern us. We often use the word "logic" to mean the continuity of an emotional drive, as when a man despairing of justice in this life is forced by "logic" to believe in another one. The literary critic deals only with rhetoric, and one of the functions of rhetoric is to present an *illusion* of logic and causality. On the other side, a very clear example of an "and then" narrative is the Apollonius story, which I have already referred to. Apollonius is a suitor to the daughter of king Antiochus, who, we remember, lives in incest with her. Antiochus presents him with a riddle setting forth the situation. If Apollonius fails to solve it he must die, according to the conventions in such matters; if he succeeds he must die anyway because the secret will be out. Not very logical, that is, not very rhetorically convincing as an illusion of logic, but, as Coleridge remarks about the *Arabian Nights*, the abandoning of such logic has its own fascination, and in any case all we want to know is what will happen next.[46] Well, Apollonius does solve it, whereupon Antiochus, for unstated reasons, not impossibly connected with the need to have something to come next, gives him a respite of thirty days.

Apollonius goes to Tarsus, where he is warned of the danger to his life by a friend he meets there. In a displaced or probable story this would mean that the guilty secret of Antiochus was already well known throughout his world. Apollonius learns that the Tarsians cannot protect him [49] against Antiochus because they are starving to death in a famine, whereupon he goes back to his own domain, the city of Tyre, and returns with a hundred thousand pecks of grain to feed Tarsus. However, he still has to avoid the vengeance of Antiochus. Antiochus then dies, and Apollonius, along with the reader, is told for the first time that Apollonius is the heir to Antiochus's kingdom. Instead of entering on his inheritance, however, Apollonius goes to Egypt, where he stays fourteen years. He loses his daughter, who after a very rough time is eventually reunited with him. He has also lost his wife at sea, and is finally told in a dream, doubtless sent by a god who is getting tired of the story, to go to Ephesus and expound his adventures to the chief priestess in the temple of Diana there. She being his lost wife, that fixes that up. Some of the gaps in this story, including the credibility gaps, may be the result of trying to keep the action moving at all costs; but there are other places, such as the journey to Egypt, where the storyteller seems to abandon, even to avoid, the line of direct action.

In any case the Apollonius story is not just a series of "and thens": it drives us on toward a conclusion which restates the theme of the opening. At the beginning Apollonius encounters a king who is living in incest with his daughter, so that his daughter is also his wife: at the end Apollonius himself is a prince united with his lost wife and daughter. The story proceeds toward an end which echoes the beginning, but echoes it in a different world. The beginning is the demonic parody of the end, and the action takes place on two levels of experience. This principle of action on two levels, neither of them corresponding very closely to the ordinary world of experience, is essential to romance, and shows us that romance presents a *vertical* perspective which realism, left to itself, would find it very [50] difficult to achieve. The realist, with his sense of logical and horizontal continuity, leads us to the end of his story; the romancer, scrambling over a series of disconnected episodes, seems to be trying to get us to the top of it.

This vertical perspective partly accounts for the curious polarized characterization of romance, its tendency to split into heroes and villains. Romance avoids the ambiguities of ordinary life, where everything is a mixture of good and bad, and where it is difficult to take sides or believe that people are consistent patterns of virtue or vice. The popularity of romance, it is obvious, has much to do with its simplifying of moral facts. It relieves us from the strain of trying to be fair-minded, as we see particularly in melodrama, where we not only have outright heroism and villainy but are expected to take sides, applauding one and hissing the other. In the context of play, of which more in a moment, this moral polarizing provides the same kind of emotional release that a war does, when we are encouraged to believe in our own virtue and the viciousness of the enemy. In the university disturbances of a few years ago, the exuberance in creating simple melodramas out of very mixed-up situations reminded many people, with some justification from a critic's point of view, of similar romance conventions on television.

If we ask why such a story as the Apollonius romance was so popular, one answer is that a sequence of archetypes, traditional fictional formulas or building blocks, has an interest in itself, however poor the logic or "hence" narrative connecting them may be. Thus in the Tarsus episode, where Apollonius finds the city starving, returns to Tyre, and comes back with ships loaded with grain, the archetype is that of the young hero coming over the sea as an image of fertility and the renewal of the food supply, the same one that lies behind the St. George story. The [51] lack of plausibility does not matter, because the formula holds the attention like a bright light or colour.

If we further ask why Shakespeare used the Apollonius romance, not only for an early and experimental comedy, but for one of his final plays,[47] we are up against a more central problem of criticism. Ben Jonson called *Pericles* a "mouldy tale,"[48] and his view has been often echoed by others, including by implication Shakespeare himself, who almost goes out of his way in *The Winter's Tale* to emphasize the naive and corny nature of his plot. In most traditional tales that are reworked by great writers, what is traditional is the "and then" sequence of events, and the writer himself supplies his own "hence" connective tissue. *Pericles*, however, seems to be a deliberate experiment in presenting a traditional archetypal sequence as nakedly and baldly as possible. Perhaps literature as a whole, like so many works of literature, ends in much the same place that it begins. The profoundest kind of literary experience, the kind that we return to after we have, so to speak, seen everything, may be very close to the experience of a child listening to a story, too spellbound to question the narrative logic.

There are other dramas—Goethe's *Faust*, for example—which have been criticized for lack of "unity," meaning continuity or "hence" narrative, but might display a good deal more coherence to critics able to see them as archetypal sequences. Another fiction writer who specializes in setting down the traditional formulas of storytelling without bothering with much narrative logic is Edgar Allan Poe. This fact, along with the ascendancy of realism, accounts for the curiously schizophrenic quality of Poe's critical reception. There have been no lack of people to say that Poe is fit only for immature minds; yet Poe was the major influence on one of the subtlest schools of poetry [52] that literature has ever seen. Similarly, it is clear that of all Shakespeare's plays, one that affected T.S. Eliot very powerfully was the "mouldy tale" of *Pericles*. This is explicit in *Marina*, but I think the influence of Shakespeare's Phoenician sailor goes far beyond that poem.[49] The episodic structure of *Pericles* may remind us of the theme of time in *Four Quartets*, the conception of human life itself as much more a series of "and thens" than a continuous narrative, and where reality is more in the up-and-down perspective than in the horizontal one.

In *Pericles* the discontinuity of the action forces us to see the vertical shape of the whole story, but the same shape is still there in more continuous actions. Very highly concentrated romance, say, *The Tempest* or the third book of *The Faerie Queene*, often shows us a carefully arranged hierarchy of characters, which in *The Tempest* ranges from Prospero at the top to the "three men of sin" [3.3.53] at the bottom. One might rank these three in a sub-hierarchy with Antonio as low man, as Auden appears to be doing in *The Sea and the Mirror*.[50] Such stage directions as "Prospero on the top, invisible" [act 3, scene 3], may even suggest some incorporating of this hierarchy into the staging of the play. The general principle is that the higher up we are, the more clearly we can see the bottom of the action as a demonic parody of the top. Thus in Dante's *Purgatorio* [canto 32, ll. 148–60], after Dante has climbed the whole of the mountain and got rid of all his sins, he sees the consolidated demonic vision of the *Inferno*, in its Biblical form of Beast and Whore. Similarly, Gower tells the Apollonius story because the theme of incest makes it an illustration of the seventh deadly sin of lechery, the one that medieval writers and preachers left to the end as the most interesting. Doubtless for Gower it would be the reading of the whole story through to the end that would enable the reader to see incest as sinful rather than merely entertaining. [53]

The characterization of romance is really a feature of its mental landscape. Its heroes and villains exist primarily to symbolize a contrast between two worlds, one above the level of ordinary experience, the other below it. There is, first, a world associated with happiness, security, and peace; the emphasis is often thrown on childhood or on an "innocent" or pregenital period of youth, and the images are those of spring and summer, flowers and sunshine. I shall call this world the idyllic world. The other is a world of exciting adventures, but adventures which involve separation, loneliness, humiliation, pain, and the threat of more pain. I shall call this world the demonic or night world. Because of the powerful polarizing tendency in romance, we are usually carried directly from one to the other.

It looks, therefore, as though romance were simply replacing the world of ordinary experience by a dream world, in which the narrative movement keeps rising into wish fulfilment or sinking into anxiety and nightmare. To some extent this is true. The realistic tendency seeks for its material, or, more accurately, for analogies to its material, in the world of waking consciousness; the up-and-down movement of romance is an indication that the romancer is finding analogies to his material also in a world where we "fall" asleep and wake "up." In many works of fiction reality is equated with the waking world and illusion with dreaming or madness or excessive subjectivity. Examples range from *Don Quixote* to Jane Austen, but, as these examples make clear, such a standard marks the ascendancy of realism. The romancer, *qua* romancer, does not accept these categories of reality and illusion. Both his idyllic and his demonic worlds are a mixture of the two, and no commonsense assumptions that waking is real and dreaming unreal will work for romance. The passengers on the wrecked ship in *The Tempest*, though never at any [54] moment quite sure whether they are waking or dreaming, go on with their habitual reactions. When Antonio and Sebastian plot to murder Alonso, they are following the directives of *Realpolitik*: this is the kind of thing you do in the "real" world if you want to get ahead. Ferdinand, watching the masque of spirits enacting Prospero's fancies, assumes that what he is seeing is an illusion, however delightful. Both are right in a way, but not in the play's way: the standards of reality and illusion that the play presents are the opposite of these.

What there does seem to be is some connection between illusion and anxiety or apprehension, and between reality and serenity; between illusion and tyranny and between reality and freedom; between illusion and the absence of identity, "When no man was his own," as Gonzalo says [*The Tempest*, 5.1.213], and between reality and the possession or recovery of it. Reality for romance is an order of existence most readily associated with the word "identity." Identity means a good many things, but all its meanings in romance have some connection with a state of existence in which there is nothing to write about. It is existence before "once upon a time," and subsequent to "and they lived happily ever after." What happens in between are adventures, or collisions with external circumstances, and the return to identity is a release from the tyranny of these circumstances. Illusion for romance, then, is an order of existence that is best called alienation. Most romances end happily, with a return to the state of identity, and begin with a departure from it. Even in the most realistic stories there is usually some trace of a plunge downward at the beginning and a bounce upward at the end. This means that most romances exhibit a cyclical movement of descent into a night world and a return to the idyllic world, or to some symbol of it like a marriage: this cyclical movement is what the remainder of this book will try to explore in more detail. [55]

According to Aristotle (expanding the very elliptical argument slightly), two types of human actions are imitated in words [*Poetics*, chap. 9]. The historian imitates human actions or *praxeis* as such: everything "practical" that man does, from kings planning wars to peasants digging their fields, may be material for history. There are other types of action which are symbolic and representative of human life in a more universal perspective, and which the poet is more interested in. For these actions the best term is ritual. Religious services, weddings and funerals, convocations and Norton lectures, parades and tournaments, parties and balls and receptions, games and sporting events of all kinds, centennial celebrations, are rituals in this sense. Rituals, like myths, begin in the stage of society described by the term *religio*: they are symbolic acts of social cohesion in which the acts that we think of as specifically "religious" are not yet clearly differentiated from others.[51] We said that in romance as a whole neither the waking world nor the dream world is the real one, but that reality and illusion are both mixtures of the two. Similarly, ritual is a conscious waking act, but there is always something sleepwalking about it: something consciously being done, and something else unconsciously meant by what is being done.

One of the major nonliterary social functions of myth is to explain or rationalize or provide the source of authority for rituals. We do this now, the myth says, because once upon a time, etc. The ritual is, so to speak, the epiphany of the myth, the manifestation or showing forth of it in action. In literature itself the *mythos* or narrative of fiction, more especially of romance, is essentially a verbal imitation of ritual or symbolic human action. This is clearest in drama, where the presentation of the play is itself ritualistic, and still clearer in highly romantic forms of drama, such as Peele's *Old Wives' Tale* or *Mucedorus*, or, [56] once again, the last plays of Shakespeare or Ibsen.[52] The decline of realism in our day has gone along with the rise of the film, with its unprecedented power of presenting symbolic action.

A drama is described as a play: play is normally the opposite of work, and Ben Jonson was subjected to some ridicule when he published his plays under the title of *The Works of Ben Jonson*.[53] The difference between the practical actions studied by historians and the ritual actions expressed in literature might be called, perhaps, actions of work and actions of play, keeping in mind the fact that play, as Huizinga points out in *Homo Ludens*, is not necessarily either enjoyable or free from the sense of obligation.[54] Work is purposeful, directed to an external end; ritual, except for its connection with magic, is self-contained and expressive. Work is done in the actual environment; ritual is enacted within what I have called a mythological universe.

Narrative forms have to depend more than drama does on descriptions of rituals: hence the long accounts of tournaments in chivalric romance, singing matches in pastorals like Sidney's *Arcadia*,[55] the highly stylized scenes of courtship in love stories, and the like. The same punctuating of the narrative by social ritual occurs in realistic fiction too, ranging from the court scenes in *War and Peace* to the reception that triggers off the tremendous meditative explosion in the last volume of Proust.[56] But in romance, essentially the whole human action depicted in the plot is ritualized action. The ritualizing of action is what makes possible the technique of summarized narrative that we find in the "and then" stories of romance, which can move much more quickly than realism can from one episode to another.

In a medieval chivalric romance the jousts and tournaments [57], the centripetal movement of knights to Arthur's or Charlemagne's court and their dispersal out from it into separate quests, the rescued damsels and beloved ladies, the giants and helpful or perilous beasts, all form a ritualized action expressing the ascendancy of a horse-riding aristocracy. They also express that aristocracy's dreams of its own social function, and the idealized acts of protection and responsibility that it invokes to justify that function. The same thing is true of all ages of romance, from the Cinderella and industrious-apprentice romances of bourgeois aggressiveness to the adventure stories of Rider Haggard and John Buchan and Rudyard Kipling which incorporate the dreams of British imperialism.[57] This is the process of what we called "kidnapping" romance, the absorbing of it into the ideology of an ascendant class.

When we look at social acts as rituals, we become at once aware of their close relation to a good deal of what goes on within the mind. Anyone reading, say, William James's *Varieties of Religious Experience* must be impressed by the extraordinary skill with which many people arrange their lives in the form of romantic or dramatic ritual, in a way which is neither wholly conscious nor wholly unconscious, but a working alliance of the two. William James takes us into psychology, and with Freud and Jung we move into an area where the analogy to quest romance is even more obvious. In a later development, Eric Berne's "transactional" therapy, we are told that we take over "scripts" from our parents which it is our normal tendency to act out as prescribed and invariable rituals, and that all possible forms of such scripts can be found in any good collection of folk tales.[58] Romance often deliberately descends into a world obviously related to the human unconscious, and we are not surprised to find that some romances, George MacDonald's *Phantastes*, for example, are [*58*] psychological quests carried out in inner space. Such inner space is just as much of a "reality," in Wallace Stevens's use of the word, as the Vanity Fair of Thackeray: Vanity Fair itself, after all, is simply a social product of the illusions thrown up by the conflicts within this inner consciousness. When we look back at the Cistercian developments of Arthurian legend, with their stories of Galahad the pure and his quest for the Holy Grail, we see that an identity between individual and social quests has always been latent in romance.

When psychology enters this area, it is concerned mainly with the defensive devices that people use in trying to strengthen the barriers between the waking consciousness and other parts of the mind. That is, it is concerned with the individual counterpart of what I have just called kidnapped romance, the constant effort to keep the romantic thrust of sexuality and wish fulfilment under the control of the status quo. In relation to the actual world, Freud's picture of the ego as a sort of Poor Tom, fighting for its life against an id and a superego and any number of other foul fiends biting it in the behind is perhaps as good as any.[59] For the actual world, as such, keeps dreaming and waking, play and work, in a continuous antithesis: each takes its turn in dominating our interests, yet remains separate from the other. But man lives in two worlds, the world of nature and the world of art that he is trying to build out of nature. The world of art, of human culture and civilization, is a creative process informed by a vision. The focus of this vision is indicated by the polarizing in romance between the world we want and the world we don't want. The process goes on in the actual world, but the vision which informs it is clear of that world, and must be kept unspotted from it. If it is not, ritual is degraded into compulsive magic and the creative energy of the poet [59] into the anxieties of the kind of social concern that has been called, very accurately, the treason of the clerks.[60]

In English literature, perhaps the purest evocations of the idyllic world are Milton's *L'Allegro* and *Il Penseroso*, where the alternating rhythm of ritual and dream, the need to experience as part of a community and the need to experience as a withdrawn individual, have been transformed into complementary creative moods. We notice that L'Allegro spends a good deal of his time listening to the tales of naive romance, and Il Penseroso a corresponding amount of time reading sentimental romance, "where more is meant than meets the ear" [l. 120]. The phrase expresses the haunting sense of what is often called allegory in romance, but it seems to me that the word "allegory" here is misleading: I should prefer some such phrase as "symbolic spread," the sense that a work of literature is expanding into insights and experiences beyond itself. The symbolic spread of realism tends to go from the individual work of fiction into the life around it which it reflects: this can be accurately called allegorical. The symbolic spread of a romance tends rather to go into its literary context, to other romances that are most like it in the conventions adopted. The sense that more is meant than meets the ear in romance comes very largely from the reverberations that its familiar conventions set up within our literary experience, like a shell that contains the sound of the sea.

The critical method suggested by realism begins by detaching the literary work being studied from its context in literature. After that, the work may be discussed in relation to its historical, social, biographical, and other nonliterary affinities. Such a method, inadequate as it is, is often rationalized as a proper emphasis on the "uniqueness" of the work. At this point, perhaps, we can see the weak spot in the traditional form–content distinction: what is called [*60*] content is the structure of the particular or individual work. With romance it is much harder to avoid the feeling of convention, that the story is one of a family of similar stories. Hence in the criticism of romance we are led very quickly from what the individual work says to what the entire convention it belongs to is saying through the work. This way of putting it may be critically somewhat illiterate, but, like other illiterate statements, it may have its own simple eloquence. The reading of an individual romance, say a detective story or a Western, may be in itself a trivial enough imaginative experience. But a study of the whole convention of Westerns or detective stories would tell us a good deal about the shape of stories as a whole, and that, in its turn, would begin to give us some glimpse of still larger verbal structures, eventually of the mythological universe itself.

The mythological universe has two aspects. In one aspect it is the verbal part of man's own creation, what I call a secular scripture; there is no difficulty about that aspect. The other is, traditionally, a revelation given to man by God or other powers beyond himself. These two aspects take us back to Wallace Stevens's imagination and reality. Reality, we remember, is otherness, the sense of something not ourselves. We naturally think of the other as nature, or man's actual environment, and in the divided world of work and ego-control it is nature. But for the imagination it is rather some kind of force or power or will that is not ourselves, an otherness of spirit. Not all of us will be satisfied with calling the central part of our mythological inheritance a revelation from God, and, though each chapter in this book closes on much the same cadence, I cannot claim to have found a more acceptable formulation. It is quite true that if there is no sense that the mythological universe is a human creation, man can never [*61*] get free of servile anxieties and superstitions, never surpass himself, in Nietzsche's phrase. But if there is no sense that it is also something uncreated, something coming from elsewhere, man remains a Narcissus staring at his own reflection, equally unable to surpass himself. Somehow or other, the created scripture and the revealed scripture, or whatever we call the latter, have to keep fighting each other like Jacob and the angel, and it is through the maintaining of this struggle, the suspension of belief between the spiritually real and the humanly imaginative, that our own mental evolution grows. Meanwhile we have one principle to go on with. The improbable, desiring, erotic, and violent world of romance reminds us that we are not awake when we have abolished the dream world: we are awake only when we have absorbed it again.

III Our Lady of Pain: Heroes and Heroines of Romance

In the ethical scheme of Dante's *Inferno,* there are two modes of sin, *forza* and *froda,* violence and fraud, and every sin is committed under one or other of these aspects.[61] Ethically, *froda* ranks lower than *forza,* because its use of disguise and concealment makes it more difficult to recognize as vice. Hence there is a greater imaginative appeal in *forza*. *Forza* and *froda* also organize the demonic part of *Paradise Lost*. They are contrasted in the speeches of Moloch and Belial respectively in book 2, where Moloch wants an all-out assault on heaven and Belial suggests concealment. The Limbo of Vanities, or Paradise of Fools, in book 3 consists of souls who have tried to take the kingdom of heaven either by violence, through suicide, or by fraud, through hypocrisy.

For the study of literature we need a principle which is that of Mandeville's *Fable of the Bees* in reverse: public vices become private benefits.[62] *Forza* and *froda* being the two essential elements of sin, it follows that they must be the two cardinal virtues of human life as such. Machiavelli personified them as the lion and the fox, the force and cunning which together make up the strong prince.[63] So it is not surprising that European literature should begin with the celebration of these two mighty powers of humanity, of [*66*] *forza* in the *Iliad,* the story of the wrath (*menis*) of Achilles, of *froda* in the *Odyssey,* the story of the guile (*dolos*) of Ulysses.[64]

When violence and fraud enter literature, they help to create the forms of tragedy and comedy respectively. The tragic hero is normally a person capable of being an agent and not merely a victim of violence, but tragedy is mainly a form in which an actual or potential agent of violence becomes a victim of it. As *forza* is open violence, tragedy seldom conceals anything essential from audience or reader. We know who murdered Duncan and Hamlet senior; we know what Iago's honesty amounts to; we know that Goneril and Regan are evil before they quite realize it themselves. And when we ask what it is that brings the tragic hero to grief, we find that it is often a deficiency in dealing with fraud. Othello is violent, but cannot see through the fraud of Iago; Macbeth is violent and attempts fraud, but his conscience makes the fraud very unconvincing; in Hamlet, violence and guile are spasmodic, as he plunges into each in turn. To have murdered Claudius in cold blood with his back turned would have been the act of Machiavelli's strong prince, violence and cunning united in perfect heroic integrity. Such a resolution to the play would still have been tragic, but tragic with a strong reassuring major chord of deliverance from a nightmare, such as we have at the end of *Macbeth*.

Peacock's well-known essay on the four ages of poetry says that poetry begins in the flattery of barbarian rulers, the poets being hired to eulogize their robberies and cruelties.[65] Certainly one can find evidence that this has been an important social function of poets. In the Scandinavian Saga of Harold Hardradi (the name means "hard ruler," or ruthless), a poet is quoted who bursts into song like this: [*67*]

> No poet can with justice
> Describe the royal vengeance
> That left the Uplands farmsteads
> Derelict and empty.
> In eighteen months, King Harold
> Earned himself renown;
> His acts will be remembered
> Until the end of time.[66]

The corresponding pattern in romance is the story of the hero who goes through a series of adventures and combats in which he always wins. Marlowe's Tamburlaine, for instance, appears to have been uniformly successful up to the moment of his death. But even death is a defeat of sorts, hence there is an inner dialectic in the eulogy of power which tends to make all heroes of action ultimately tragic heroes. Often a hero seems to be trying to achieve some kind of liberation for himself through his physical strength. Such liberation may be symbolized by invulnerability, as in the stories of Achilles, Samson, Hercules, and Grettir the Strong.[67] But sooner or later some chink in the armour opens up and the hero is destroyed.

The success of the hero derives from a current of energy which is partly from him and partly outside him. It depends partly on the merit of his courage, partly on certain things given him: unusual strength, noble blood, or a destiny prophesied by an oracle. The most basic term for this current of energy is luck (Icelandic *gaefa*). Luck is highly infectious: the lucky man can always form a *comitatus* or group of devoted followers around him. Once he has lost his luck, he finds that bad luck is equally infectious: the unlucky man must be avoided like the plague, because in a sense he is the plague. When Ulysses in Homer returns to [*68*] Aeolus to explain that through no fault of his own he has run into misfortune, Aeolus tells him to clear out, that an unlucky man is hated by the gods, and he will have nothing more to do with him [*Odyssey*, bk. 10, ll. 70–5].

A hero may lose his luck in various ways: sometimes through a self-destructive quality in himself, expressed by such words as "fey" or "hybris," sometimes through the kind of accident that is clearly not quite an accident, such as the death of Achilles through a wound in his vulnerable heel. Most commonly, however, the hero is brought down by some form of *froda*, usually some magical or other power which may be physically weak but is strong in other areas that the hero cannot control. Such a power is often wielded, or symbolized, by a treacherous woman. Shakespeare's Mark Antony, caught in the toils of Cleopatra, finds that he has lost his luck even in the simplest sense of not being able to win games of chance with Caesar [*Antony and Cleopatra*, 2.3.26–39].

The comic story is more particularly the story of guile and craft, the triumph of *froda*. Its themes often feature disguise and concealment of identity, both from other characters and from the audience, and its plot normally moves toward an end acceptable to the audience but unlikely under the conditions of the action, so that some surprising or unexpected event is needed to resolve the conclusion. Its literary model is the *Odyssey*. It is Ulysses who devises the stratagems of the Trojan horse and the escape from Polyphemus, and who according to Lucian is the model of literary liars.[68] Such qualities arouse the unstinted admiration of the goddess Athene, who feels a deep kinship with a mortal who, despite his limited human area of activity, is so superbly crooked. He is, she says, very like her: [*69*]

> Cunning must he be and knavish, who would go beyond thee in all manner of guile, aye, though it were a god that met thee. Bold man, crafty in counsel, insatiate in deceit, not even in thine own land, it seems, wast thou to cease from guile and deceitful tales, which thou lovest from the bottom of thine heart. But come, let us no longer talk of this, being both well versed in craft, since thou art far the best of all men in counsel and in speech, and I among all the gods am famed for wisdom and craft.[69]

There are several things to notice in this speech. One is that there are obviously trickster gods: one thinks, among many examples, of the infant Hermes in the Homeric Hymn, who grew up to be the patron of thieves.[70]

It is clear that the goddess of wisdom (*metis*) is also a goddess of guile (*kerdosyne*). Athene, Ulysses, and probably Homer as well, have no notion of disinterested or contemplative wisdom: wisdom for them means practical sense, and includes, on the human plane, the ability to get out of a tight spot. Then again, Athene is a female deity. In Homeric conditions of life—that is, the conditions assumed in the literary conventions adopted by the Homeric poems—the physical weakness of woman makes craft and guile her chief weapons, and when women in the heroic code are violent, like Clytemnestra or Medea, they normally operate by magic or through male proxies.

Ulysses himself, of course, is a genuine hero, on the titanic scale of all Homer's warriors. It is he alone who can string the great bow, and, except in the cave of Polyphemus, he turns to craft, as Athene implies, not out of weakness, but out of sheer exuberance. Considering this, there seems to be something very curious about the second half of the poem. The situation looks like the ancient story type in which a heroine is besieged by a number of suitors, proposes [70] some ordeal to them, and chooses the one who passes the ordeal, while the others lose their lives. Examples of the theme range from the Greek Atalanta to the eighteenth-century story of Turandot; Grimm is full of it, and we also found it at the beginning of the Apollonius romance.[71] In the *Odyssey* Penelope is not strong enough to set up the traditional situation in which her suitors can get eliminated by ordeals or tests: her weakness forces her to resort to fraud, in the form of weaving and unweaving her web as a device for stalling them off. But one wonders whether Homer is not giving us a rationalized version of a matriarchal story which was Penelope-centred and not Ulysses-centred, in which Penelope's right to choose her suitor was unconditioned by any previous commitment. This would bring the *Odyssey* into line with Robert Graves's "white goddess" type of story.[72] Samuel Butler, reflecting a more Victorian attitude, suggests that Penelope, or some votary of hers, wrote the *Odyssey* herself, taking care to whitewash her own morality in the process.[73]

A Penelope-centred *Odyssey* would be a more "primitive" version of Homer's story, but, remembering the account we gave earlier of the word "primitive," a more primitive version of Homer is not necessarily one that existed before Homer, but one that comes into existence whenever literature adopts "primitive" conventions, which it does every so often throughout its history. Such primitive periods usually begin with what is called "decadence," a moralized term of which the structural meaning is an exhaustion of possibilities in a previous development. In Greek heroic literature, this point is first reached with the tragic structure of Euripides.

Women in Greek tragedy are more frequently victims than agents of a tragic situation, and hence they intensify the tragic mood rather than the tragic action. In such a play as *The Trojan Women* the tragic mood is so strong [71] that it drives us into a moral resistance to tragedy, into a feeling that the whole Trojan enterprise was wrong or silly rather than heroic, or even inevitable. Euripides, by using his women in this way, increases the tragic emotion, which may be why Aristotle calls him the most tragic of poets [*Poetics*, chap. 13], and at the same time weakens the ethos that put tragedy into the centre of Greek literature. His contemporary Aristophanes applies a parallel principle to comedy: in a society still male-dominated, female initiative is an effective comic device, as in the sexual strike organized by Lysistrata. Aristophanes also frequently puts Euripides into his plays, at least once (in *Thesmophoriazusae*) in a way which significantly relates him to his female characters.

Euripides and Aristophanes were succeeded by the writers of New Comedy.[74] The audience for this was closer to what we should call a petit-bourgeois audience, one that wanted some reflection in its plays of its own primarily mercantile ethos. Hence New Comedy developed a form which regularly portrays the victory of the weak over the strong, of the young over the old, of women over their lords, of slaves over masters. The young man wants his girl, and normally gets her, with the aid of a tricky slave. The slave may confront a situation in which failure could mean crucifixion, but he invariably triumphs. New Comedy thus features a plot in which the driving force is what we have been calling fraud. It may take the form of disguise or deliberate deception, of the concealment of the identity of the main characters from other characters and the audience, of overhearing conversations, of telling cock-and-bull stories with hypocritically simulated emotions. Whatever it is, it wins. What loses is *forza* or violence: the *senex* may rave in fury and utter the most frightful threats, backed with the power to carry them out, but he is finally rendered helpless.

After New Comedy we come to the romances, of which [72] the most elaborate and best written is the *Ethiopica* of Heliodorus, and the simplest and most familiar the *Pastoralia*, or *Daphnis and Chloe*, of Longus.[75] In Heliodorus particularly we can see how the story is constructed around the heroine Chariclea, not the hero Theagenes, and how everything depends on a seventeen-year-old girl's craft and wiliness. Theagenes is descended from Achilles, and every so often he puts on some kind of heroic stunt, like capturing a runaway bull. But the author has to remind himself that he has a hero, whereas Chariclea never long disappears from the centre of the action. We first see them with Chariclea bending tenderly over her wounded lover: we later discover that there has been a battle, that Theagenes has fought gallantly, but that Chariclea, sniping from a concealed position, has picked off most of the enemy with bow and arrow.

In *Daphnis and Chloe* exposed infants are discovered and adopted by rustics, and the children grow up among the lambs and kids—one almost wonders whether this kind of pastoral imagery is the origin of our word "kids." They get sexually interested in each other, mainly as a result of taking baths together, but nothing comes of it, and the illustrations supplied by the animals do not seem helpful. Daphnis is then taken firmly in hand by a married woman: she adds, however, a footnote on the difference between married women and virgins, and the thought of making his Chloe bleed throws Daphnis into such a panic that his lovemaking promptly goes back to square one. Eventually the plot thins, the secret of the two births is cleared up, Daphnis and Chloe are wedded, and, in the last sentence of the story, bedded.

It looks as though there were some structural principle in this type of story which makes it natural to postpone the first sexual act of the heroine, at least, until after the birth [73] mystery in the plot has been solved. Certainly this is the view of Heliodorus's Chariclea. Throughout the ten books of her adventures, which are spent mainly with pirates, soldiers, and other nonvirginal types, Chariclea pursues, unremittingly, three objectives. The first is to marry Theagenes; the second is to solve the mystery of her origin and find out who she is; the third is to defend her virginity from everyone, including Theagenes, until after that mystery is dispelled. Or, as she says: "I may be sure by Theagenes' oath, that he shall not fleshly have to do with me, until I have recovered my country, and parents, or if the gods be not content herewith, at least until I by mine own free will be content he shall marry me. Otherwise never."[76] One can, of course, understand an emphasis on virginity in romance on social grounds. In the social conditions assumed, virginity is to a woman what honour is to a man, the symbol of the fact that she is not a slave. Behind all the "fate worse than death" situations that romance delights in, there runs the sense that a woman deprived of her virginity, by any means except a marriage she has at least consented to, is, to put it vulgarly, in an impossible bargaining position. But the social reasons for the emphasis on virginity, however obvious, are still not enough for understanding the structure of romance.

We notice that, just as a man may defend his honour without necessarily having any virtue except the courage to do so, so Chariclea's dedication to virginity is not part of a general commitment to moral integrity. It certainly does not imply that she is also truthful or straightforward; in fact a more devious little twister would be hard to find among heroines of romance. Whenever she is approached [74] by a man unsympathetic to her virginal ambitions, which includes practically every man she meets in anything like her own age group, she adopts some ruse which enables her to avoid the threat without open resistance. When she comes upon a sorceress animating the corpse of a dead son on a battlefield, her protector and guardian tells her that this is an unlawful rite and gets her away, but not without a strong desire on her part to turn the situation to her own advantage. At the end of the story she remarks resignedly, in a soliloquy, that as nobody believes her anyway she should perhaps try telling the truth, but she is relieved of this burden by the arrival of the recognition scene.

Yet of course her policy of lying is advantageous to the author, because it causes some of the complications that lengthen his book. This is part of what I mean by saying that craft or fraud is the animating spirit of the comic form. When hero and heroine go through one adventure after another, always threatened with disaster and yet somehow escaping, the plot acquires a wriggling, serpentine quality reminding one of the labyrinthine caves which so often occur in the setting. It also reflects the kind of delaying tactics that the heroine engages in. Marvell writes a poem to a "coy" mistress, fending her lover off to the end of time, in which he speaks of her "quaint honour" [*To His Coy Mistress*, l. 29]. The etymology of the words "coy" and "quaint," from *quietus* and *cognitus* respectively, and implying something both concealed and knowledgeable, is significant. We may compare the etymology of a word often attached to females in our day, the word "cute."

Secrecy, including disguise, is a necessary part of the heroine's tactics, partly because she is so often in a position where the hero must be convinced that he is acting on his own initiative. In Terence's *Andria*,[77] the action, as is usual in Roman comedy, takes place on the street, much of it [75] outside the heroine's house. A group of males, a young man, his friend, his slave, his father, the friend's father, a stranger bearing the *cognitio*, run around busily, plotting, scheming, lying, eavesdropping, threatening, resolving, revealing, misunderstanding, and exclaiming. Inside, the heroine, who has no speaking part in the action, beyond one lugubrious wail offstage as her labour pains come on, is giving birth to the hero's son. If we turn the action inside out, so to speak, we find ourselves in this silent and darkened room, where the heroine is quietly gathering all the threads of the action into her hands. Somehow or other she is going to establish her pedigree, marry the hero, present him with a male heir, and force her prospective father-in-law to like the situation. This side of the action is never alluded to, unless the fact that the play is named after her constitutes such an allusion. The heroine works under cover, in disguise or in secret until it is time for her identity to be recognized.

In such New Comedy plots as that of *Andria*, where the action is suddenly reversed near the end, the reversal includes a discovery about the heroine's identity, normally one which makes her a free citizen instead of a prostitute or slave, by virtue of having been stolen by pirates in infancy or what not. This device of the heroine's being both slave and free has had an amazing vitality in romantic comedy, and persists almost unchanged at least through the eighteenth century, despite the altered social conditions. In Goldsmith's *She Stoops to Conquer* the heroine disguises herself as a maid to attract the attention of an immature hero, who can see serving maids, through the haze of class prejudice, as things to be fondled and flirted with, but cannot endure the sight of a woman on his own social level. The word "conquer" in the title perhaps suggests that he will continue to be something of an emotionally [76] dependent inferior. The opposite situation appears in Richardson's *Pamela*, where the heroine first appears as a symbol of class aggression to the hero, that is, essentially, as a slave. She refuses to play this role, and resists until the hero is compelled to marry her on her own terms. *Pamela* is subtitled "Virtue Rewarded," but "Virginity Rewarded" would give a clearer idea of the structure. Here again virginity is female honour, the symbol of the heroine's sturdy middle-class independence. In both stories the heroine's life is lived on two social levels: we have already seen why this movement of the action from one level to another is so important in romantic narrative.

The Fanny Price of Jane Austen's *Mansfield Park* also has a double social identity, being a poor relation brought up in a wealthy home. She has, in typical heroine fashion, decided on her cousin, Edmund Bertram, but she has to cope with a most flattering proposal favoured by everybody except her. Fanny appears to be a humble, acquiescent, even passive young woman, but while she blushes and weeps and agonizes and is overwhelmed with confusion, she is also directed by a steely inflexible will that is determined to have Edmund or nobody.[78] As her guardian Sir Thomas Bertram says, with the exasperation of a man who discovers that his society is less male-dominated than he had been assuming: "But you have now shewn me that you can be wilful and perverse, that you can and will decide for yourself."[79]

Fanny clearly has Jane Austen's own sympathy, as is obvious from the way that the story is worked out. At the same time it is also clear that the kind of authority Sir Thomas represents seems to Jane Austen a right and natural authority. It is not that Jane Austen is a woman novelist expressing a woman's resistance to social conditions governing the place of women in her time. She accepts [77] those conditions, on the whole: it is the romantic convention she is using that expresses the resistance. This principle that an element of social protest is inherent in romance is one that we can only suggest now, and will return to later. Meanwhile we may note that in *Emma* the hero has a moral ascendancy over the heroine which is fully justified by his greater maturity and common sense. Yet what actually happens at the end of the book is that the heroine takes on a matriarchal role, and compels him to move from his house into hers, in order not to disturb her father's dedication to inertia.

Most of Shakespeare's comedies are dominated by a similar type of heroine, and Shakespeare drew many of his comic plots from contemporary romances which are more uninhibited than he is in their treatment of the conventions. Thus in Barnabe Riche's story *Apolonius and Silla*, a source of *Twelfth Night*, the heroine, finding that the lover she has determined on has left the country without paying any attention to her, gets into a ship in pursuit of him. The captain goes into his rape-or-else routine almost before he has pulled up his anchor; the heroine prays to whatever god looks after heroines in these situations; a storm smashes the ship, and she floats to shore on the captain's chest, which is full of money and clothes, thereby enabling her both to dress up as a boy and to support herself while running her chosen man to earth. Shakespeare's heroines are usually in more complex situations, and have to be more ingenious. Rosalind in *As You Like It* keeps inventing fictions up to the very end of the action. Her remark at the end of the fourth act might be a motto for such heroines: "I shall devise something; but I pray you commend my counterfeiting to him" [4.3.181–2]. Helena in *All's Well* is also a deviser and a counterfeiter: the opposite situation occurs in *Measure for Measure*, where the heroine is determined [78] on virginity, with the dramatic action, much of it undertaken by herself, pulling her in the opposite direction. These plays turn on the folk tale device of the bed trick, a drastic but effective way of getting the hero into his predestined bed.

In such romances the heroine's role is primarily concerned with her relation to the man whom she, or her creator, is determined she shall marry, come hell or high water, both of which do come with remarkable frequency in romance. In this role she is a potential bride, and if her virginity is emphasized, it is so merely as part of the extension of the story. This principle may not apply primarily to the heroine at all. My one-volume edition of *Tom Jones* runs to 886 pages, and it is not until page 883 that we finally read about "that happy hour which had surrendered the charming Sophia to the eager arms of her enraptured Jones."[80] Sophia has doubtless remained virginal up to that point, but Jones certainly has not; yet it is he who must be satisfied that his series of amorous conquests has not included his own mother before he can achieve a properly quiet consummation for his reader.

It may be thought that I am considerably labouring what is after all a fairly rudimentary principle of dramatic structure in various fields, the principle that the G-string comes off last. But it is precisely the elementary facts of structure that we are so inclined to overlook, and the social facts that we are inclined to exaggerate. One of the social facts is that in a male-dominated society a man often assumes that he ought to get a virgin at marriage, otherwise he may feel that he has acquired a secondhand possession. Yet it seems clear that romance, even when it comes to terms with this notion, is talking about something else in its emphasis on virginity.

It reflects another social fact of male-oriented conventions [79] that the heroine of romance is supposed to carry out her tactics in low profile, that is, behave with due modesty. It follows that the conventions may look more realistic and iconoclastic if she is given a more active role. *All's Well That Ends Well* has the reputation of being more realistic than some of Shakespeare's other plays, mainly because the heroine makes it so clear from the beginning what she wants. This conventional iconoclasm is the central principle of many of the comedies of Bernard Shaw, where a busy, bustling, managing heroine so often dominates the stage. She is usually the spokesman of revolutionary common sense, with the males around her spouting various forms of reactionary ideology. In *Too True To Be Good* the action, or what passes for action, ends with a haunting and eloquent speech by a character first introduced as a burglar. Shaw, however, notes that the audience is left hanging on the ideological rhetoric of a male speaker, and adds a note to the printed text explaining that such talk is all very well, but of course what is really important is what the heroine does. "His own favourite is the woman of action," he says of himself.[81] The note sounds a trifle senile in its context, and yet, of course, it is true that the heroine's activity is the mainspring not only of this comedy (the action of which is really her own wish-fulfilment dream), but of a great deal of comedy in general. The normal motive for the Shavian heroine is given by the heroine of the same play, when she says, "I have the instincts of a good housekeeper: I want to clean up this filthy world and keep it clean."[82] Shaw's heroines have only an incidental interest in marriage, often none at all: their role is primarily maternal, and they are psychologically virgin mothers. This situation comes into its sharpest focus in *Saint Joan*, which raises issues that take us into another area.

There are two major structural principles in fiction: one [*80*] is the polarization of ideal and abhorrent worlds, which we have seen is central to romance; the other is the cycle of nature, in which the solar and seasonal cycles are associated in imagery with the cycle of human life. The heroine who becomes a bride, and eventually, one assumes, a mother, on the last page of a romance, has accommodated herself to the cyclical movement: by her marriage, or whatever it is, she completes the cycle and passes out of the story. We are usually given to understand that a happy and well-adjusted sexual life does not concern us as readers. The heroine's virginity, on the other hand, is associated with the stresses and complications she has to go through before marriage, and which constitute the story proper. She may of course be married, as she is in the *Odyssey* or in Chaucer's *Franklin's Tale*, but there her loyalty to her husband puts her symbolically in the same situation. Virginity or married loyalty is her normal state during the endurance, suffering, suspense, and terror which precede her real life after the story. The two poles of her career in the story, therefore, are her eventual triumph, which usually includes both marriage and the recovery of her identity, and, opposite, the point of her lowest fortunes, when she is often a sacrificial victim or near victim, threatened with rape or death, if not both.

At the end of Heliodorus's story, Chariclea discovers that she is the daughter of the Queen of Ethiopia, although she is white and the Ethiopians are black. The explanation is that when she was conceived her mother had her eyes fixed on a picture of Andromeda during the orgasm, and the result of this was a white baby. The queen suspects that her fellow Ethiopians may find this explanation less plausible than the author apparently does, and smuggles the infant out of the country. Chariclea arrives back in Ethiopia as a captive taken in war, to be sacrificed according to [*81*] custom. The role played by Andromeda's picture in her conception indicates that she herself, in one aspect, is an Andromeda figure, a heroine exposed for a sacrifice which she narrowly avoids. The human sacrifice, usually of a virginal female, is astonishingly persistent as the crucial episode of romance: we meet it in the sixth book of *The Faerie Queene*,[83] and it is still going strong in the late prose romances of William Morris.

As a rule the heroine avoids this fate, and so has the role of a snatched-away sacrificial victim. The virgin as sacrificial victim takes us back to Jephthah's daughter in the Bible [Judges 11:29–40] and to Iphigeneia in Euripides, and Euripides gives us the snatched-away version of it. Iphigeneia is rescued by Artemis and taken off to Tauris on the Black Sea, where she becomes, not unnaturally, the priestess of a cult of human sacrifice. Her father Agamemnon is portrayed by Euripides as a rather weak figure, and the theme of a heroine exposed to a sacrificial situation by a foolish or inattentive father has run all through fiction. Sheridan LeFanu's *Uncle Silas* has a heroine whose father, a somewhat dithery Swedenborgian, is obsessed by the notion that his brother Silas, who is a thoroughly bad lot, has been gravely misunderstood, and sends his daughter to Silas's house, where she very nearly gets murdered. In Meredith's *The Egoist* the heroine is pushed toward marriage with the "egoist" anti-hero, largely through her father's utter inability to understand anything that goes on outside the range of his own comfort. This novel is technically more displaced than *Uncle Silas*, but the imagery linking the heroine to the Iphigeneia situation is more explicit. The same theme appears in Shakespeare. Portia, undergoing the ordeal of the caskets, which has been arranged by her father for unstated reasons, and in danger of being married to two undesirable suitors, says "I stand for sacrifice" [*The Merchant of Venice*, 3.2.57], [*82*] with a reference to Hesione, another female sacrificial victim who was rescued by Hercules.[84]

Sometimes, of course, the heroine has to go through with her sacrificial role. Jephthah's daughter does, and so do a number of others down to the heroine of the eighteenth-century French romance *Paul et Virginie*.[85] The somewhat inevitably named Virginie goes back from an idyllic island in the Indian Ocean to civilization and petticoats, then sets out again for the island and arrives within sight of it as a result of the usual shipwreck. Urged to remove her petticoats and save herself from drowning, she elects to drown with one hand on her heart and the other on her clothes: a triumph of propriety over self-preservation somewhat unusual even in this quixotic genre. Yet it is in keeping with the conventions of romance, where even a purely symbolic rape may still be, or represent, a fate worse than death.

Shaw's *Saint Joan* is again a play about the sacrifice of a virgin. Joan is hated even by those she redeems from English tyranny, not because of her skill and courage, but because she cannot help telling the brusque truths of common sense to those who must live on lies and illusions. The play ends with an epilogue showing that if Joan returned to earth in Shaw's own time she would get much the same rejection, if less brutal treatment. It may be significant that in the main action of the play Shaw portrays her as belonging, not so much to a higher world as to a future one, a world of nationalism and Protestantism. This seems to me a pedantic and misleading treatment of her, and one that indicates a final unconscious irony in the play. Shaw himself, apparently, cannot accommodate Joan or Joan's "voices" into his twentieth-century world without a process of rationalization which, in a very real sense, explains her away. This is an example of how a writer whose actual [*83*] structures are close to romance can be misled by what he thinks of as realism.

The virgin who marries at the end of the story, we saw, represents the structural principle of the cycle and of accommodation to it. The virgin who is sacrificed, or escapes sacrifice and remains a virgin, similarly symbolizes the other principle, the separation or polarizing of the action into two worlds, one desirable and the other detestable. This is one reason why we often get two heroines in romantic literature, one associated with virginity and the other with love and marriage. Thus Spenser, in the third book of *The Faerie Queene*, portrays the virtue of chastity through Belphoebe, a Diana figure vowed to virginity, and also through Britomart, who is equally virginal for the action of the poem, but who is in love and fully intends to marry. Belphoebe is more explicitly associated with Queen Elizabeth, because Elizabeth was a virgin queen, but as long as there was a possibility of her changing her status the poet had to keep Britomart in reserve. It is obvious that in a romance, which is almost by definition a love story, there is a technical difficulty of what one does with a permanently virginal figure, even if not immobilized by allegorical association with a queen. Belphoebe stays in her wood hunting stags: it is Britomart who goes out on adventures disguised as a man, like Shakespeare's heroines.

Milton's *L'Allegro* and *Il Penseroso*, which contain almost everything essential to an understanding of romance, also give us a clue to the significance of these two heroine figures. In *Il Penseroso* the poet's mistress is a personified "Melancholy" [l. 12], who is a nun, a vestal virgin rather than a Christian nun. (To the extent that she could be a Christian nun she would represent a purely aesthetic approach to Christianity, like the cloisters, stained glass [84] windows, organ music, and hermitage of the closing lines.) Such a melancholy mistress forms a contrast to the "heart-easing Mirth" [l. 13] of *L'Allegro*, who is presumably more liberal, though the poet is cautious about defining the extent of her favours. However, it seems clear that Mirth represents the normal idyllic conclusion, and Melancholy a withdrawal from it into solitude: this contrast of cadences in romance will be a recurrent theme from here on. We begin to see the possibility of a further development of the theme of virginity, one which represents a lifelong sublimation expressing itself as a commitment, or spiritual marriage, to something impersonal, such as religious devotion or a political cause. Such a figure would represent, or at least point to, a world above that of the main action of the story.

In Scott's *Waverley* there are two heroines, Rose Bradwardine and Flora MacIvor. Waverley is more attracted to Flora at first, but she refuses him outright. She is wholly committed to the Jacobite cause, and she realizes that Waverley has only blundered into his Jacobitism. When the cause collapses, she retires to a convent on the Continent. Meanwhile the hero goes through various adventures about which there is a good deal of mystery, with a female shape fluttering in and out of his quarters. Eventually this proves to be Rose Bradwardine, arranging the plot in typical heroine fashion, until the hero is ready to know which woman he ought to be marrying. Flora is a quixotic figure like Waverley himself, though a considerably more impressive one, and to some extent she does reflect the mores of Scott's society, in which, as a rule, a successful female career consists of a good marriage and retirement to a convent is a sign of maladjustment. Nevertheless, Flora is much the more memorable of the two heroines: in fact, she and her brother, with his tragic fate, upstage the whole cast. [85]

In Scott's later novel *The Pirate* we have two sisters, Minna and Brenda Troil, who are explicitly contrasted along Miltonic lines as grave and gay, penseroso and allegro types. The melancholy sister Minna is a romantic devoted to a cause of a type that a Canadian reader would call separatism. When a pirate named Cleveland appears in the story she feels strongly attracted to him because she regards pirates as symbols of the kind of romantic rebelliousness she favours. The heroines are then abducted: Cleveland, however, makes something of a habit of forgoing his sexual demands, having previously saved the honour of two Spanish ladies in earlier forays. As the Spanish ladies were really "persons of quality,"[86] his record of abstinence saves him from being hanged. However, there is enough heavy breathing to convince Minna that she has been wrong about pirates, and the penalty for her mistake in judgment is perpetual virginity.

In *Ivanhoe* there are again two heroines, the Saxon Rowena and the Jewish Rebecca. Rowena is determined to marry the man of her choice, but has otherwise few distinguishing characteristics except her blonde hair. Rebecca is menaced in the usual style by a Norman noble, Brian de Bois-Guilbert, and she also nearly becomes a sacrificial victim, because Brian's superior in the Templar order is an obsessed bigot who wants to convict her of sorcery. With the figure of Rebecca, the innocent victim of a venomous bigotry who remains steadfast in her faith, we begin to see that romance, in its stress on the theme of virginity, may be talking about something more than the condition of the hymen membrane.

At the lowest point of such a heroine's career, when her innocence and gentleness are most strongly contrasted with the malignancy of the powers arrayed against her, she gives the impression of someone living in a world below the one that she ought to be living in. Hence she is, mythically [*86*], in the position of a goddess in a lower world. When we come to this mythical core of a common, even a hackneyed situation, we come back to the problem I mentioned before, of having to distinguish what the individual story is saying from what the convention the story belongs to is saying through the story.

In another Greek romance by Achilles Tatius, *Leucippe and Clitophon*,[87] which is, by and large, a rather silly story, the heroine is separated from her lover, is kidnapped and reduced to slavery, is threatened with torture and lashes; yet she still defies her tormentors and talks about the freedom of her soul. We can distinguish between the preposterous and contrived melodrama of this particular romance, and the convention expressed by it, where some kind of genuine human dignity does come through. Deep within the stock convention of virgin-baiting is a vision of human integrity imprisoned in a world it is in but not of, often forced by weakness into all kinds of ruses and stratagems, yet always managing to avoid the one fate which really is worse than death, the annihilation of one's identity. In Achilles Tatius we are a very long way, in power and splendour, from anything like "I am Duchess of Malfi still."[88] But we are in the same imaginative area for all that. If we want an image, or objective correlative, for this kind of integrity, there is an exquisite one in Sidney's *Arcadia*, where the heroine wears a diamond set in a black horn, with the motto attached "yet still myself."[89] What is symbolized as a virgin is actually a human conviction, however expressed, that there is something at the core of one's infinitely fragile being which is not only immortal but has discovered the secret of invulnerability that eludes the tragic hero.

The simplest way out of the sacrificial situation, for the storyteller, is the Proserpine solution. When Proserpine is [87] seized by a demon lover and carried off into a world of death, she touches the food of death, to the extent of eating some pomegranate seeds. Here the communion image of food replaces the sexual one: eating the seeds is a sacrificial act in which what is sacrificed is symbolically her virginity. As a result she has to spend half of each year in the lower world and half above, revolving with the cycle of nature. She is the archetype of all romantic virgins who marry and live "happily" ever after. It is possible that some of these heroines, if their happy postnarrative lives were more fully investigated, would be found, like Proserpine, to be spending at least half their time in hell. But occasionally we realize that this is not the whole area of romance, and that some heroines may symbolize not only a descent from a higher world but a permanent return to it.

We notice that Rebecca in *Ivanhoe* has near-miraculous powers of healing: this theme often recurs in romance, attached mainly to virtuous females like the Helena of *All's Well*, and sometimes dependent on the physical preservation of virginity. The bigotry in Rebecca's society is so perverted that it is precisely her life-giving powers that bring her under suspicion of sorcery. This suggests that the beleaguered virgin may be more than simply a representative of human integrity: she may also exert a certain redemptive quality by her innocence and goodness, or, in other contexts, by her astuteness in management and intrigue.

At the heart of all literature is what I have called the cycle of *forza* and *froda*, where violence and guile are coiled up within each other like the yin-and-yang emblem of Oriental symbolism. Here the imaginative centre is clearly in tragedy, the heroic dimension being the one that makes the greatest emotional impression on us. The heroic is associated with an often invulnerable strength, yet the [*88*] heroism ends in death and the strength is not after all invulnerable. The comic side of this, the victory of guile, often takes the form of a triumph of a slave or maltreated heroine, or other figure associated with physical weakness. With the rise of the romantic ethos, heroism comes increasingly to be thought of in terms of suffering, endurance, and patience, which can coexist with such weakness, whatever other kinds of strength it may require. This is also the ethos of the Christian myth, where the heroism of Christ takes the form of enduring the Passion. Such a change in the conception of heroism largely accounts for the prominence of female figures in romance. But, as secular literature is not bound by any doctrinal inhibitions, the romantic heroine can take on a redemptive role as well, like her divine counterpart in the Christian story.

This means that the myth of romance, though closely related to the myth of Christianity, and for centuries contemporary with it, should not be thought of as derived from it. As soon as we think of redemptive female descents to a lower world we think of Euripides' Alcestis, who is pre-Christian. Alcestis prolongs her husband's life by her journey to the world of the dead to offer herself as a substitute, but she is not a redeemer herself, and has to be rescued from Death in her turn by Hercules. Her redemptive effort is achieved by sacrifice, and she is snatched from the ultimate sacrifice like Iphigeneia. She does this for a man whose general attitude to the situation is, "Well, perhaps my father should have gone instead, but certainly somebody should." As in the Christian myth, we often wonder in romance whether the people for whom the heroine's efforts are made are always worth it. Is getting the Bertram of *All's Well* worth the skill, devotion, and elaborate deceptions of Helena? Richardson's Pamela, again, contemplates [*89*] with the greatest enthusiasm and affection her approaching marriage to the man who had done his level best to ruin her life.

Much older than Alcestis is the mysterious figure of Inanna, or Ishtar, who in very ancient Mesopotamian poems is shown descending into the world of the dead in full regalia, passing seven gates, at each of which some of her regalia is removed, until she arrives naked and helpless in the presence of the shades of death.[90] Why she descends we do not know, and certainly the scene makes far more of an impact without a motive. But questions of substitutes demanded by the powers of death seem to be involved, as they are in the descent of Christ also. Keeping in mind the Christian parallel, it is as though there were two aspects to the symbolism of the sacrificial victim, one in which she is a hostage for death, and so exposed to death herself, and another in which she is what has come instead of death. In the latter aspect she is, potentially, the conqueror of death and the redeemer of its captives. One of the most fundamental of human realizations is that passing from death to rebirth is impossible for the same individual; hence the theme of substitution for death runs all through literature, religion, and ritual. Redemption is one form of substitution, though one more satisfying to theology than to romance.

In any case there are escapes and ascents as well as descents, both for the heroine herself and for those she helps. We have the Ariadne who guides Theseus out of the labyrinth, the Isis who restores Lucius to his human shape in Apuleius, the Lucia and Beatrice whose love and care get Dante through Purgatory, and other forms of *das Ewig-Weibliche*[91] that draw us upward to our more deeply desired goals. Here again we have what looks like a counterpart to [90] the Christian schema, and the one that underlies the great Eros myth in which the lover is raised to a higher world by his mistress.

The poet Yeats developed, or had suggested to him, a theory of history in which two contrasting types of civilization dominate the Western world in turn. Classical culture, in this view, was essentially a heroic culture, aristocratic and violent, its central myth being the story of Oedipus, who kills his father and lives in incest with his mother. It was succeeded by the Christian culture, which is democratic and altruistic, based on the myth of Christ, who appeases and reconciles his father, crowns his virginal mother, and rescues his bride the Church. The coming of each culture is symbolized by the conjunction of a bird and a woman, the bird being the manifestation of a god. Classical culture is heralded by the sexual union of Leda and the swan, Christian culture by the nonsexual union of the Dove and the Virgin. Tragedy is at the heart of Classical civilization, comedy at the heart of the Christian one. The progeny of Leda and the swan represent Eros and Ares, sexual love and war; the Virgin's son is divine love and a prince of peace. After the Christian cycle is ended, Yeats says, we shall return to a heroic and violent culture of the Classical type.[92]

I do not think much of this as a general view of history; but the modulation I have been dealing with, the change from Greek tragedy through Euripides to New Comedy and thence to prose romance, is well symbolized by it. It is true that literature after Euripides, or at least the romantic literature which forms the bulk of it, is mainly under the sign of the Dove and the Virgin. But this applies whether the literature itself is pagan or Christian: it is still under the Dove and the Virgin when the dove is Venus's dove and the virgin Diana. Heliodorus and Achilles Tatius are said to [*91*] have been Christian bishops, and Heliodorus, according to a legend transmitted by Montaigne on being compelled to choose between his bishopric and acknowledging the authorship of his romance, made the only choice that any self-respecting author could make, and ceased to be a bishop.[93] But whether these writers were Christian or not, the fictional devices employed are common to Christian and pagan romance.

I think that what I have been calling the *forza–froda* cycle is essentially Yeats's Leda and swan cycle. It was not destroyed by Christianity, but survived intact: we have the same tragic structures and heroic ethos in Shakespeare, and the old comic formulas are still working in Dickens. But the growth of what we have been calling sentimental romance takes us into a second imaginative universe. One pole of this is an idyllic world where human desires and ideals can find more scope, and where violence and fraud can occasionally be seen in the form of their corresponding virtues, fortitude and prudence. The other pole is a night world symbolized by human sacrifice, a world which is more an object of moral abhorrence than strictly a tragic one. The dove-and-virgin cycle is comedy-centred, it is true, but it is not simply the antithesis of its predecessor, as Yeats's scheme would have it. It is in some respects a more expanded world, and we sometimes have the feeling in a romance or comedy of moving from one world into a larger one. In speaking of Terence's *Andria* I said that the action seems to move simultaneously on two levels, one of the foreground action, the other inside the heroine's mind. When the action passes from one level to the other through the recognition scene, we have a feeling of going through some sort of gyre or vortex, to use another Yeats image, a feeling we express in the phrase we so inevitably use when summarizing a romantic plot: "it turns out that . . ." [*92*]

Where tragedy arises in this dove-and-virgin type of literature, its effect is quite different from tragedy in Aeschylus or the *Iliad* or the mature period of Shakespeare. A romance is normally comic, in the sense that usually the heroine's wiles or whatever are successful and the story ends with marriage or some kind of deliverance. Tragedy or pathos comes from some obstacle or accident which frustrates this conclusion. A heroine may meet disaster through being betrayed or deserted by her lover, or, like Richardson's Clarissa, may fail to stick to the tried and true virginal tactics. Such romantic tragedies as *Romeo and Juliet* or [Scott's] *The Bride of Lammermoor* seem more like a comedy gone wrong: for all Romeo's talk about the stars, his tragedy is not built into the scheme of things as the tragedy of Lear is, or that of Oedipus before him.

Certainly there are close connections between the imaginative universe of romance and that of Christianity: the myth of Christianity is also a divine comedy which contains a tragedy, and thinks of that tragedy as an episode within a larger comic structure. But they are not the same thing, and should not be confused. My last chapter will suggest that we may be moving into a third imaginative order, but I cannot see that this third order shows any sign whatever of simply returning to the first one. Not only Yeats, but several other writers, most of them insane, have believed in or proposed such a return, and in politics a parallel notion has produced the black cloud of illusion that we know as fascism. But in our day every genuine issue, in the arts as outside them, is connected with getting clear of all such notions of cyclical historical fatality.

In Blake's poem *Earth's Answer* a female Earth, called upon by the poet to stop turning in cycles and enter the world of eternal light, complains that she cannot do so because "Starry Jealousy does keep my den" [l. 7]. This starry [93] jealousy in Blake is the "Covering Cherub," the cosmic peacock whose eyes are the stars, and who keeps us bound to fate because he also keeps the Earth under the tyranny of unending space and time.[94] The Covering Cherub is winged, like other angels, and the overtones of "covering" are sexual, the Earth being his *femme couverte*.[95] The poem heralds an age when the cyclical conjunctions of divine birds and human women are finally broken, and the human imagination has passed beyond the empty heavens into its original earth.

IV The Bottomless Dream: Themes of Descent

From the beginning the poetic imagination has inhabited a middle earth. Above it is the sky with whatever it reveals or conceals: below it is a mysterious place of birth and death from whence animals and plants proceed, and to which they return. There are therefore four primary narrative movements in literature. These are, first, the descent from a higher world; second, the descent to a lower world; third, the ascent from a lower world; and, fourth, the ascent to a higher world. All stories in literature are complications of, or metaphorical derivations from, these four narrative radicals.

Explicitly for the first eighteen centuries of the Christian era, and implicitly after and long before that, these patterns of ascent and descent have been spread over a mythological universe consisting of four main levels, two above our own, one below it. The highest level is heaven, the place of the presence of God: this world is strictly beyond space, but may be symbolized, as in Dante's *Paradiso*, by the spatial metaphor of heaven in the sense of the sky, the world of sun, moon, and stars. The world above the moon is traditionally thought of as the world that escaped the fall, and is consequently what is left of the order of nature as God originally made it. Level two is the [*98*] earthly paradise or Garden of Eden, where man lived before the fall. The associations of the word "fall" suggest that Eden is to be thought of as the highest point in the world, as it is geographically in Dante. Level three is the world of ordinary experience we now live in. Animals and plants seem to be well adjusted to this world, but man, though born in it, is not of it: his natural home is level two, where God intended him to live. Level four is the demonic world or hell, in Christianity not part of the order of nature but an autonomous growth, usually placed below ground.[96]

All four of these levels are symbolically ambivalent, and these ambivalences are of great importance in the structure of romance. In Chaucer, for example, the disasters and tragedies wrought by the conjunctions of the stars in *The Knight's Tale* and *Troilus and Criseyde* make it clear that the heavens are for him, as for most science fiction writers today, much more a symbol of alienation than of divine presence. Chaucer is careful to explain this in Christian terms: stars would not have met in "synod unbenign," in Milton's phrase (*Paradise Lost*, bk. 10, l. 661), if there had been no fall, and only pagans are completely subject to their malign influence. But the emotional ambivalence remains. As for the earthly paradise, according to Christian doctrine it was, but it cannot now be; consequently in romance the paradisal is frequently a deceitful illusion that turns out to be demonic, or a destructive vision. The fourth level, though purely demonic in Christianity, is in romance often a world where great rewards, of wisdom or wealth, may await the explorer.

The ambivalence in the third level of ordinary experience is of a different kind. This world seems to be hard to incorporate into the great Christian epics: Dante and Milton place their settings in heaven, hell, and Eden, but thirteenth-century [*99*] Italy, and seventeenth-century England, enter only through external allusion. In Spenser's *Faerie Queene*, which is more typical of romance, the world of experience is introduced through allegory, by means of the fact that the main setting of the poem, "faerie," a purgatorial world of moral realization like Dante's, is nevertheless one that occupies the same time and space as our world. But the level of ordinary experience is also represented in Spenser as a sexual world, symbolized by satyrs. These satyrs, though not quite human, are not quite evil either: they represent perhaps what human life would be like if human beings were as completely adjusted to the "fallen" level of nature as animals and plants are. Their lives consist, in Eliot's phrase, of birth and copulation and death,[97] but they regard copulation as the only sensible way of putting in the time between birth and death. They remind us of the half of ordinary experience that is often, except in romance, ignored: the dreaming experience of the night, with its erotic resonance.

At present we are concerned with descent themes, and these fall into two groups: those that suggest descent from the sky or, more precisely, one of the two higher worlds, heaven and Eden, and those that suggest descent to a subterranean or submarine world beneath this one. In the latter, the normal road of descent is through dream or something strongly suggestive of a dream atmosphere. In the former, we meet first of all the familiar motifs of the birth of the quasi-divine hero, who really has two fathers, his real father, who is a god, and his assumed father, who is normally the husband of his human mother. His birth often arouses the jealousy of the assumed father; hence the common romance theme of the calumniated mother, who is sentenced to death with her infant but escapes, or is put out to sea in an empty boat or raft, or has her child exposed [*100*]. Shrouding and concealment are natural consequences of a threatened birth, and the infant hidden by a terrified mother or nurse occurs in the myths of Zeus and Dionysus as well as the Biblical stories of Moses and Jesus.[98] In later literature the theme of descent from a higher world enters the poems that speak of birth as coming down from a state of innocence or freedom into a "prison-house," as Wordsworth calls it,[99] of corruption or confusion. In Victorian romance there are many stories about delicate children, who, like Blake's Thel, find this world too much for them and return to their place of innocence. One of the freshest and most attractive of these is George MacDonald's *At the Back of the North Wind*, the story of an imaginative little boy who makes a friend of the north wind, then discovers and returns to a place of serenity and peace which is "back of" the north wind, a place explicitly identified with the Garden of Eden in Dante's *Purgatorio*.[100]

Closely linked with stories of this type is the standard theme of the infant exposed on a hillside and picked up by shepherds, so common in New Comedy and Classical romance. In the Christian myth Christ, of course, comes to this world from above (*descendit de coelis*, as the creed says), but the Nativity stories in the Gospels show a good many analogues to the New Comedy themes. Christ is actually of royal descent, acknowledged by three kings (as they later become), yet born in obscurity, besides having his life threatened by a usurper king. His birth takes place in a semi-pastoral setting, a manger flanked by an ox and an ass, surrounded with shepherds, and watched over by the quasi-pastoral figure of Joseph, who is really his foster father. It is not so far from this vision of peace to *Daphnis and Chloe*, where what there is of both action and passion is contained by an idyllic world, a pastoral setting of sexual innocence constructed out of the imagery of various [*101*] pastoral poets, including Theocritus and Sappho. The imagery of *Daphnis and Chloe* revolves around the seasonal cycle, represented in myth by the death of Adonis. Thus Daphnis's foster father has a beautiful garden, and a spiteful rival of Daphnis gets into it and tramples down all the flowers "like a boar."[101] The climax of the story, as noted earlier, is a sexual union which is part of a spring fertility rite. There are also hints of more sinister things like wars and attacks from pirates, though none of them come to much—*Daphnis and Chloe* is a very placid story.

But for all the innocence, the idyllic pastoral world is still a second world, a world of derived identity, with a higher world above it which enters only symbolically, in the form of the discovery of the true parentage. When the two infants were exposed on the hillside, birth tokens indicating a higher social rank were put beside them: these are produced to establish their identity at the end. The fact that they simply sit there throughout the story indicates something about the nature of suspense in this type of narrative that we shall have to return to. The father who originally exposed Daphnis says that he expected Daphnis to die, and consequently the birth tokens were really intended to be death tokens. We may compare the gifts presented to the infant Jesus by the wise men, which are also, especially myrrh, emblems of the Passion (cf. Mark 15:23; John 19:39).

There are said to be customs and rituals in ancient Greece that explain the child-exposing convention; but they do not explain why Victorian writers, fifteen centuries later, should be as preoccupied with it as ever. With the archetype, at least: the actual exposure and adoption procedure is found only in stories with a strong folk tale feeling about them, like [George Eliot's] *Silas Marner*. Scott and Dickens would often be helpless for plot interest without the motif of mysterious birth: in Dickens a hero's parents, like those of [*102*] Oliver Twist, may be triumphantly produced at the end of the story even though they are mere names, playing no part in the story itself. In his autobiography, Trollope notes the fact that *Doctor Thorne* sold better than some of his other novels, adding the realist's customary protest: "The plot of *Doctor Thorne* is good, and I am led therefore to suppose that a good plot,—which to my own feeling, is the most insignificant part of a tale,—is that which will most raise it or most condemn it in the public judgement."[102] In *Doctor Thorne* the heroine is not Thorne's daughter but the daughter of somebody much wealthier, so that the obstacles to her marriage with the hero are removed. After a glance at Scott and Dickens, we may say that what *Doctor Thorne* had was not *a* good plot but *the* good plot.

Whether romance begins with a hero whose birth is, as Wordsworth says, a sleep and a forgetting,[103] or whether it begins with a sinking from a waking world into a dream world, it is logical for it to begin its series of adventures with some kind of break in consciousness, one which often involves actual forgetfulness of the previous state. We may call this the motif of amnesia. Such a catastrophe, which is what it normally is, may be internalized as a break in memory, or externalized as a change in fortunes or social context. The change in mind may be brought about by the wrath of a god, usually at the kind of errors most apt to make gods nervous, such as boastfulness. The themes of rash promise and of fatal curiosity, as when Pandora or Psyche open boxes that they should have left shut, are closely connected, implying as they do the collapse of the rightful order in the mind and the separation of consciousness from the proper rhythm of action.

The break in consciousness may also be induced by drugs, a love potion like the ones in the Tristram and Sigurd legends, or a disease like Silas Marner's catalepsy. It [*103*] may be externalized as a disaster like capture by pirates, or a wandering into the land of the fairies, involving a change so drastic as to give the sense of becoming someone else altogether. Thus Alice, pressed to recount her adventures by the Mock Turtle and Gryphon, says she can tell them her adventures of that day, "but it's no use going back to yesterday, because I was a different person then."[104] In *The Winter's Tale* a mood of jealousy explodes without warning in Leontes' mind and takes it over, replacing his former feelings about his wife with a malignant psychosis. It is really an obliteration of memory, and in another type of story it could be the result of a curse or demonic possession. In the Indian play *Sakuntala*,[105] the prince who is the hero is betrothed to the heroine, but as a result of a curse inflicted by an irritable hermit his memory of her is destroyed. The mystery in Wilkie Collins's *The Moonstone* is about the stealing of a diamond: the solution is that it was stolen by the hero himself as a result of an anxiety dream inspired by opium, given him without his knowledge by a malicious physician.

One of the early burlesques of Jane Austen bears the title *Henry and Eliza*. Eliza is discovered under a haycock at the age of three months by Sir George and Lady Harcourt. They are delighted with the precocious infant's conversation, and take her into their home as their daughter. She remains there until the age of eighteen, when, being detected in stealing a banknote of fifty pounds, "she was turned out of doors by her inhuman Benefactors." After a page or two of adventures, Eliza resolves to go back to her foster parents to see if she can hit them up for anything more. Lady Harcourt receives her with "transports of Joy," exclaiming that Eliza is not their adopted daughter but their real child. Pressed for an explanation, she says that she was left "breeding" by her husband when he went [*104*] to America, that he had wanted a boy, and finding that she had produced a girl, she set the infant under a haycock and promptly forgot she had had her.[106] The author shows a regrettable tendency to humour, which might have been of some disadvantage to her if she had continued with this genre; but she certainly knows what the genre is. Seldom has the role of amnesia in getting a story started been more clearly set forth.

At the beginning of a romance there is often a sharp descent in social status, from riches to poverty, from privilege to a struggle to survive, or even slavery. Families are separated and the hero may, like the hero of Scott's *Redgauntlet*, find himself falling in love with his sister. But the structural core is the individual loss or confusion or break in the continuity of identity, and this has analogies to falling asleep and entering a dream world. The latter is a world of increased erotic intensity, as is obvious from the imagery of romance alone, without reference to psychology. We are often reminded of this type of descent by the imagery of the hunt. A knight rides off into a forest in pursuit of an animal, and as he disappears the dream atmosphere closes around him. Sometimes he finds himself in a forest so dense that the sky is invisible. In this threshold symbol of entering a world of sleep all images begin to take on an erotic quality, so that the surrounding forest becomes a sexual personality.

The hunt is normally an image of the masculine erotic, a movement of pursuit and linear thrust, in which there are sexual overtones to the object being hunted. These overtones lead, in English, to many puns on "deer" and "hart." As we sink deeper into the dream, the quasi-sexual object of pursuit becomes the surrounding forest itself. There seems to be an increasing identity between the forest and a shrouding female body, of a rather sinister kind. This [*105*] comes out vividly in the story of Actaeon, changed to a stag and hunted by his own hounds at the prompting of an elusive virginal forest goddess who is not to be seen naked.[107] Behind various incest and Oedipal taboos is the suggestion that the hunter is seeking a false identity which is the same thing as his own destruction. The consummation of the hunt is the death of the animal, which for Actaeon is the turning of the pursuer into the victim. We are reminded of the song in *As You Like it*: "What shall he have that kill'd the deer? / His leather skin and horns to wear" [4.2.10–11]. The song goes on to make the inevitable joke about cuckolds, but of course the cuckold with his horns is a displaced version of Actaeon, the victim of his own pursuit.

The image of the hunter pursuing an animal is never very far from metamorphosis, or the actual changing of the hunter into an animal. If it is true, as the structuralists tell us, that every structural system includes a set of transformations,[108] metamorphoses are the normal transformations of the structure of myth. Every aspect of fall or descent is linked to a change in form in some way, usually by associating or identifying a human or humanized figure with something animal or vegetable. Daphne becomes a laurel and Syrinx a reed;[109] Adam and Eve in Genesis, on losing their original preternatural gifts, become the rational animals symbolized by the "coats of skins" [3:21] they receive from God. Even Daphnis and Chloe are almost assimilated to the animals they are brought up with. The story of Apuleius about a man metamorphosed into an ass includes an outward and social as well as a dreaming aspect of the motif. The ass is *par excellence* the proletarian animal, whose lot is slavery and incessant beating, with no [*106*] chance to participate in noble life such as at least some horses have.

We get a fairly undisplaced version of hunting, metamorphosis, and exchanged identity motifs in a play of Carlo Gozzi, *Il Re Cervo* (*The King Stag*).[110] Here the king is turned into a stag by an enchantment he has brought about himself, and is hunted by his own hounds. His treacherous minister takes advantage of this to enter the king's body, thus becoming a demonic double of the king, who is forced to enter the body of a beggar. We also have a bird-catcher who seems to be identified to some degree with his birds, and is a comic and lower-class version of the royal hunter. The bird he is particularly associated with is the parrot, a bird that has a natural connection with this world—we shall see why in a moment. A better-known example of the bird-catcher figure appears in a very similar type of play, *The Magic Flute*, where his name, Papageno, again points to the parrot, and where the sinister shrouding female influence is represented by the Queen of the Night.[111]

Changes in identity do not have to go all the way into metamorphosis: they may stop at sexual disguise, such as a heroine putting on boys' clothes or vice versa. Shakespeare, with his boy actors, prefers the former, but the reverse is also common: even Huckleberry Finn, in the middle of the latency period of boyhood, puts on female clothes twice. Change of name is a still simpler device, often used without any apparent motive in romance. The two heroes of Sidney's *Arcadia* have three names apiece, and one, disguised as an Amazon, is referred to as "she" as long as the disguise lasts.

If I dream about myself, I have two identities, myself as dreamer and myself as character in my dream. The dreamer is, so to speak, a god in relation to his dreamed self: he created him but remains in the background watching [*107*]. The dreamer may be concerned for the fate of his double in the unknown world that the latter ventures into, but his power of rescue may vary. Sometimes the story is so told that the hero remains aware of what he was at the beginning. Rasselas and his sister, in Samuel Johnson's story, descending from their prison-paradise in Abyssinia to the lower world of Egypt, take a long time to realize that they are no longer considered of royal parentage in this lower world, but, Rasselas says, "my birth has given me at least one advantage over others, by enabling me to determine for myself."[112] Few remarks in romance explain more clearly the essential point about the device of concealed original identity.

There is often a god behind the action of a romance, who expresses his will by some kind of oracle or prophecy which speaks of the ultimate outcome as predetermined. Such oracles are common in Greek romance, are still going strong in Elizabethan times, and survive in various forms later, the astrological predictions in *Guy Mannering* being an example. A god of this type is clearly a projection of the author himself, and as such he is placed outside the action. He becomes an alienation figure in Brecht's sense of the term,[113] reminding us that the show is only a show after all. In some plays, including Gozzi's play just mentioned and *The Tempest*, the constructor of the action is a magician, who renounces his magic as a sign that the play is over. We have also a producer or stage manager at the beginning of *Sakuntala* and Goethe's *Faust*. A slightly different type of alienation figure is the jester, like the Touchstone who accompanies the two heroines of *As You Like It* into the forest. This jester type is clearly of some structural significance, as he appears also in the totally unrelated Sanskrit drama: he seems to be a kind of one-man chorus, speaking for the audience's desire to be entertained by the story. [*108*] Autolycus in *The Winter's Tale* is parallel: his outrageously unlikely ballads still have a curiously close relationship to the kind of story being told in the play itself. The fact that there is no trace of a Touchstone or Autolycus figure in Shakespeare's main sources indicates that drama, with its immediacy of impact, needs such a focus in a way that narrative does not. In a written narrative the sense of derived identity is already contained, so to speak, in the mode of presentation.

In the Christian story of Barlaam and Josaphat, which I mentioned earlier, we are told that there are two natures in Christ: without leaving his father's throne in heaven he entered the virgin's womb: he suffered on the cross as a man, but not as God. Whatever one thinks of this theologically, it gives us the myth of the redemptive quest of Christ in the standard romance pattern of a double identity, one only being involved in the descent. On the other hand Adam, after his fall, changes his identity, and the later one may be said to be the shadow or dreaming counterpart of the one he had before. The Classical parallel to the Adam story, as several Renaissance mythographers noted, is the story of Narcissus, where we also have a real man and a shadow. The mistress of Narcissus, Echo, reminds us of the parrot or echo bird that we have already met. What Narcissus really does is exchange his original self for the reflection that he falls in love with, becoming, as Blake says, "idolatrous to his own shadow."[114] In Ovid's story he simply drowns,[115] but drowning could also be seen as passing into a lower or submarine world. The reflecting pool is a mirror, and disappearing into one's own mirror image, or entering a world of reversed or reduced dimensions, is a central symbol of descent. A study of mirror worlds in romance might range from the Chinese novel best known in the West by the title *The Dream of the Red* [*109*] *Chamber*[116] to some remarkable treatments of the theme in science fiction, such as Arthur Clarke's *The City and the Stars* and Stanislaw Lem's *Solaris*. That narcissistic hero Peer Gynt also begins his adventures with a tale of jumping off a precipice on the back of a reindeer into the water, where a mirror image of the reindeer comes up to meet him.[117]

Modulations of the mirror image bring us to the pictures, tapestries, and statues which so often turn up near the beginning of a romance to indicate the threshold of the romance world. Some of the Classical romances are presented to us as commentaries on pictures, which means that they attempt to recapture, or at least invoke, in words, that quality of naive and involving stare that pictures can appeal to more effectively. In Scott's *The Antiquary* the hero is put to bed in the antiquary's house in a "Green Chamber" said to be haunted and full of tapestries. "The subject was a hunting-piece . . . branches of the woven forest were crowded with fowls." The hero has metamorphosis dreams in this chamber: "He was a bird, he was a fish, or he flew like the one, and swam like the other . . . wild and wonderful metamorphosis."[118] There is a good deal of mystery about the hero's parentage, as usual, and eventually we discover that the motto for these tapestries was supplied by his mother. According to his biographer Mackail, this passage had a strong influence on William Morris, whose own romances are clearly linked to his other activities as a designer of textile patterns.[119] The closest analogy to such picture arts in contemporary popular culture is the television commercial, which presents its products as magical objects. On a more complex level, a similar technique appears in novels with a symbolic visual emblem, after which the novel is often named, as in *The Scarlet Letter* and *The Golden Bowl*. Even Jane Eyre produces [*110*] a curious set of surrealistic pictures at the beginning of her involvement with Rochester.[120]

Closely related is the use of special language, often with a large amount of the antiquated in it, which helps to enclose a romance like a glass case in a verbal museum. The invented languages of Tolkien come at the end of a long tradition which includes the synthetic Gothic of *Ivanhoe* and the yea-verily-and-forsooth lingo in which William Morris wrote his later prose romances and translations. Yet synthetic languages, however absurd they often sound, do seem to belong to romantic decorum: two very different contemporary examples are the Nigerian story of *The Palm Wine*

Drinkard and Anthony Burgess's *A Clockwork Orange*.[121] Sometimes the special language has a specifically dreamlike quality. There is a brutal sneer at Lady Gregory's "drivel" in *Ulysses*, but anyone listening to Joyce's own recording of the end of the ALP chapter may wonder if her "Kiltartan" idiom was not one of the central influences on the dream language of *Finnegans Wake*.[122] Such phenomena are related to the general theme of "charm," the use of words for emotional purposes derived from the magical casting of a binding spell. This in turn is appropriate for a world where one progressively loses one's freedom of action, the lowest stage of which is imprisonment or paralysis or death itself.[123]

The Narcissus theme helps to explain why the confusion of identity in romance is so often associated with the theme of twins. A knockabout comedy of Plautus about twins [*The Brothers Menaechmus*] is the main source of Shakespeare's *Comedy of Errors*, which draws on the Apollonius romance for its conclusion.[124] Critics usually note this resignedly, feeling that Shakespeare is utterly unaccountable and haphazard in his use of sources. What we should note, I think, is the profundity of Shakespeare's insight into romance structure which enabled [*111*] him to see that Plautus's comedy and the recognition scene in the Apollonius romance were the beginning and the end of the same kind of story. The connecting links, which Shakespeare was clearly aware of, are, first, Plautus's *Amphitryon*, where the doubles are created by the magical power of gods, and, second, Apuleius, which seems to be glanced at in one remark in the dialogue: "If thou art chang'd to aught, 'tis to an ass" [2.2.199]. In the dark haunted forest of *A Midsummer Night's Dream*, the two heroes are not twins, but are as confused in their identity as though they were, and in this play again the metamorphosis into an ass recurs.

Shakespeare, like many other writers of comedy, often comes close to the *commedia dell'arte* convention, at the centre of which is Harlequin.[125] Of the various things Harlequin does, one is to divide himself into two people and hold dialogues with himself. He also sometimes dresses up as a woman, and sometimes plays a mute part—we shall come back to this mute figure in a moment. Another modulation of the twin theme, which also suggests a dreamer and the self he is dreaming about, occurs in the folk tale of *The Two Brothers*, which is in Grimm, and its literary developments. The latter include the medieval story of Amis and Amiloun. In this type of story one brother goes out on a quest or in search of adventure, the other remaining home, though able to tell from some sign how his brother is faring, and going into action when help is needed. This structural device is still useful in displaced stories where the look-alike twins are replaced by close friends, as in Scott's *Redgauntlet*.

On the lower reaches of descent we find the night world, often a dark and labyrinthine world of caves and shadows where the forest has turned subterranean, and where we are surrounded by the shapes of animals. If the meander-[*112*]and-descent patterns of Palaeolithic caves, along with the paintings on their walls, have anything like the same kind of significance, we are here retracing what are, so far as we know, the oldest imaginative steps of humanity.[126]

Mythologies begin with creation myths, and creation myths are of two main types, depending on whether man is looking up or down from his middle earth when he is constructing it. If we look down, we see the cycle of animal and plant life, and creation myths suggested by this would most naturally be sexual ones, focusing eventually on some kind of earth-mother, the womb and tomb of all living things. If we look up, we see, not different forms of life emerging, but the same sun rising in the east. The cycle of the same, in Plato's phrase (*Timaeus*, 35), suggests rather an artificial creation myth, a world made, not born, and made by a conscious and planning intelligence. Such a myth tends to be associated with a sky-father, who goes about his mysterious business without nursing his children. In sexual and earth-mother creation myths death does not have to be explained: death is built in to the whole process. But an intelligently made world could not have had any death or evil originally in it, so that a myth of fall is needed to complement it.

It is often assumed that the sexual and maternal myths are older, being more appropriate for an agricultural society, as their rivals were for the patriarchal, tool-using, urban society that came later. Certainly in Hesiod we gather that the sky-god we now have is a latecoming usurper and tyrant, the earth having sullenly retired below with her defeated titans.[127] These subterranean titans, as that or as giants, persist all through romance. The artificial myth won out in our tradition, and the lower [*113*] world became demonized, the usual fate of mythological losers. But many echoes of a very different feeling about the lower world linger in romance. Even in Grimm a lowerworld ogre may have a wife or mother who is willing to deceive him to help the hero.

Most of what goes on in the night world of romance is cruelty and horror, yet what is essential is not cruelty as such but the presence of some kind of ritual. In another Greek romance, *Ephesiaca*, by Xenophon of Ephesus, where the hero and heroine are called Habrocomes and

Antheia, there is a series of demonic ordeals with a strong resemblance to those in the descent myths of the Bible, including the stories of Joseph and Daniel and the Passion of Christ. Many centuries later Chaucer, putting his heroine Constance, in *The Man of Law's Tale*, through similar tribulations, deliberately inserts the Biblical parallels.[128] There is no birth mystery in Xenophon's story, except that the junior leads are unreasonably beautiful: this makes the hero proud and boastful, and so he incurs the resentment of Eros. They are married at the beginning of the tale, and their future woes are summarized by an oracle. They take passage in a ship to try to avoid the forewarnings, but any reader of romances could have told them that that was a silly idea. The sailors get drunk, and the ship is captured by pirates. The drunkenness is a projection of the theme of the break in consciousness, and outlawed societies similar to these pirates are performing the same function in the smugglers of *Guy Mannering*, the Highland clans of Rob Roy, the bravos of Manzoni's *I promessi sposi* [*The Betrothed*], the terrorist conspirators of Bulwer-Lytton's *Zanoni* and Wilkie Collins's *The Woman in White*, along with their twentieth-century successors. In Xenophon the captain is homosexually attracted to the hero and the first mate to the heroine, so that we are at no loss for the usual type of romantic suspense.

Habrocomes and Antheia are both sentenced to be [*114*] crucified; Antheia's sentence is commuted to being shut up in a pit with two mastiffs, whereupon the guard, who has the usual interest in her, feeds the mastiffs so that she comes to no harm. The resemblance to the story of Daniel in the lion's den is clear, and so is a parallel with the story of Absalom [2 Samuel 18] in a following episode, where Antheia is captured by a band of robbers who have a custom of hanging a victim from a tree and throwing javelins at him (in this case her). Antheia is strung up for this ordeal, but is rescued by a law-and-order group. Finally, weary of these amusements and of getting so many immodest proposals besides, Antheia asks a physician to give her a drug that will kill her. He gives her one that merely puts her to sleep, and as a result she is buried alive, with the traditional rituals of sacrificed victims and burned garments. She wakes up when liberated by grave robbers. This theme also occurs in the Apollonius story, and, with modifications, in Heliodorus: the archetype of death and rebirth, along with that of a descent to a lower world of graves and caves, is here present in one of its primary forms.

In the theme of the apparently dead and buried heroine who comes to life again, one of the themes of Shakespeare's *Cymbeline*, we seem to be getting a more undisplaced glimpse of the earth-mother at the bottom of the world. In later romance there is another glimpse of such a figure in Rider Haggard's *She*, a beautiful and sinister female ruler, buried in the depths of a dark continent, who is much involved with various archetypes of death and rebirth.[129] In Xenophon of Ephesus the hero meets an old man who continues to love and live with his wife even though she has been embalmed as a mummy: similar themes are also in Haggard's story. Embalmed mummies suggest Egypt, which is preeminently the land of death and burial, and, largely because of its Biblical role, of descent to a lower world. [*115*]

This lower world is a world of increasing alienation and loneliness: the hero is not only separated from the heroine or his friends, but is often further isolated by being falsely accused of major crimes. The calumny of the hero is parallel to that of the calumniated mother or accused queen, but usually comes at a different stage of the total story. The hero is often a victim of what used to be called the badger game: an unscrupulous female tries to seduce him, and when he refuses sets up a cry that he has tried to rape her. This ordeal is part of Joseph's descent to Egypt in the Bible [Genesis 39], and figures prominently in Heliodorus. Variations of it are still functional in *Tom Jones*, *The Moonstone*, and elsewhere, but it recedes in twentieth-century romance, in response to a convention that a male hero who would refuse sexual intercourse would be neither believable nor admirable.

Animal companions are frequent in descent themes, as part of the pattern of metamorphosis. Metamorphosis of the Ovidian type, where something that has been human or quasi-human becomes an object in the world of nature, represents the falling silent of the world in its paradisal or humanly intelligible phase. In our world man can no longer, in Blake's phrase, converse with animal forms of wisdom night and day.[130] Sometimes the silent companion of the hero's descent is a ghost, the grateful dead man of a common folk tale motif. One of the Biblical descent stories, that of the Book of Tobit, has Tobias accompanied by a dog and by the angel Raphael, who is closely related structurally to the grateful dead man.[131] The dog is a common lowerworld symbol:[132] the hounds of the hunt, also, often represent the fact that animals may have more useful senses than human beings in this world. Human beings of the same structural type are often mute or inarticulate. Scott especially is fond of such figures: we have Lutin in *The Fortunes of Nigel*, the dumb dwarf who is Norna's servant [*116*] in *The Pirate*, the dumb (or at any rate silent) girl in *Peveril of the Peak*, and Dominie Sampson in *Guy Mannering*, who knows all the standard Classical and modern languages even though he can barely speak himself. Ghosts and banshees attached to aristocratic families, like the White Lady in *The Monastery*, also belong to this oracular world. In naive romance, we have the folk tale theme of the "bear's son," often portrayed as a lazy, powerful, awkward hero who may be driven from human society to seek solitude like a bear hibernating in a cave. The Icelandic hero Grettir the Strong is a hero of this type: he kills a bear in a cave behind a waterfall with the help of a companion named Björn (bear), whom he also kills a few pages further on.[133] Parallels have been noted between Grettir's story and that of the much earlier *Beowulf*, in which the isolation of the hero is strongly marked. Beowulf descends to a mysterious submarine world in pursuit of Grendel's mother: his companions wait for him until noon,[134] then disperse with no further inquiry.

Some of the Palaeolithic cave paintings mentioned earlier represent not only animals but what appear to be human beings in animal masks. In literature "such deliberate disguises," in Eliot's phrase [*The Hollow Men*, l. 32], extend from the Homeric story of Circe [*Odyssey*, bk. 10] to the beast-headed rout of Milton's *Comus* and beyond. In their total significance these figures are fertility spirits, part of the death-and-rebirth pattern of the lower world, but in the present context of descent they represent chiefly Ovidian metamorphosis, the reducing of humanized beings to something subintelligent and subarticulate. In the Jonsonian masque they form the "antimasque" which begins the action, symbolizing the kind of chaos and disorder that is contrasted with the courtly occasion for the masque itself. A related motif of freezing into some [*117*] kind of invariable pattern appears in many forms, including the paralysis which besets the Lady in *Comus*, as it did, much earlier, Theseus and Pirithous in Greek myth.

At lower levels the Narcissus or twin image darkens into a sinister *Doppelgänger* figure, the hero's shadow and the portent of his own death or isolation. In ordinary life there are two central data of experience that we cannot see without external assistance: our own faces and our own existence in time. To see the first we have to look in a mirror, and to see the second we have to look at the dial of a clock. The night world progressively becomes, as we sink deeper into it, a world where everything is an object, including ourselves, and consequently mirrors and clocks take on a good deal of importance as objectifying images. The

Classical romancers had to make do with doubles only, as the clock had not been invented. In more recent times, Poe is one of the hardiest explorers of this underworld region, and his fascination with clocks and pendulums and dial faces needs no elaboration. The mirror and twin themes in Poe branch out into various *Doppelgänger* formulas, as in *William Wilson* and *The Imp of the Perverse.*

The reflection of one's personality may take the form of a container where the hero's soul or life is kept, and of such objects the closest to the central Narcissus theme is the portrait, as we have it in Oscar Wilde's *Picture of Dorian Gray* and elsewhere. Doubles in time are, of course, much more complicated than doubles in space: the great pioneer work here is Henry James's unfinished *The Sense of the Past,* and the doubles produced by some kind of "time machine" have been extensively explored in science fiction. We can also have such mirror devices as that of Gide's *The Counterfeiters,* a book about a man who is writing a book called *The Counterfeiters.* We may note that this device is [*118*] already present in *Paradise Lost,* where the final fall of Adam includes his being absorbed into, and told the story of, the book which is later on to start with him.

At the bottom of the night world we find the cannibal feast, the serving up of a child or lover as food, which we have in the Greek stories of Thyestes and Tereus, and later Provençal legends incorporated into Pound's *Cantos.* Such a theme is important not for its horrific *frisson,* but as the image which causes that *frisson,* the identifying of human and animal natures in a world where animals are food for man. Such a theme merges readily with the theme of human sacrifice in its most undisplaced form, which is the swallowing of a youth or maiden by a subterranean or submarine monster. St. George, Perseus, Rogero in Ariosto [*Orlando Furioso,* canto 10], and many other heroes save virgins from this fate; Theseus puts an end to the offering of young Athenians to the Minotaur in the underground labyrinth of Crete; the brothers of Bluebeard's last wife put an end to the series of slaughtered brides. In most versions of the Bluebeard story, and elsewhere, the victims are allowed to escape or revive: this happens even to the fifty children swallowed by the subterranean demon in William Beckford's *Vathek.*

The birth of the divine hero, we remember from Yeats, is often symbolized by the conjunction of a divine bird and a human woman. At the furthest remove from this we find a demonic parody of the same image, the bestial conjunction, usually, of a male animal and a human female.

Thus the Minotaur was the result of the impregnating of Pasiphae by a bull. In Apuleius the nadir, so to speak, of the main action of the story comes at a point where a woman is condemned as a whore, and, as her judges have discovered unusual aptitudes in the ass who is the transformed Lucius, the ass is ordered to have public intercourse with her. It is the peculiarity of this scene that its fantastic setting [*119*] is what gives it its essential horror. Granted that asses cannot be trained to do this sort of thing, still, if they could be so trained, that is undoubtedly what the human race would be most interested in training them to do.

If we may now pull together these descent motifs and see what their undisplaced form is, the descending hero or heroine is going down into a dark and labyrinthine world of caves and shadows which is also either the bowels and belly of an earth-monster, or the womb of an earth-mother, or both. A female monster of this type appears in a Mesopotamian myth as Tiamat, the primeval creature whose body formed the creation.[135] The same motif is slightly displaced in stories where a hero kills a dragon who guards a treasure hoard, like Fafnir in the Sigurd saga. The undisplaced, or death-and-rebirth, form of the dragon quest is a descent through his open mouth into his belly and back out again, the theme that appears in the Biblical story of Jonah and is later applied to Christ's descent to hell. In the interests of general decorum, Christ and Jonah are assumed to be returning by the same route: we may however compare Dante, who also enters the "mouth" of hell, and reaches the end of it at the Satanic rectum. A very slightly more undisplaced version of this would identify hell with the body of Satan, so that Dante would not only enter his mouth but be excreted from the other end, becoming as a result what Carlyle would call a Diogenes Teufelsdröckh, a god-born devil's dung.[136]

I mention this because the mythological universe is, in one of its aspects, a gigantic or macrocosmic body, with analogies to the human body. The stars, sun, and moon present an analogy to a human brain, especially when they are taken to be images of the intelligence of a creating god. At the bottom of this macrocosmic world we find the organs of generation and of excretion, which are emphasized [*120*] in proportion as this part of the mythical universe is made demonic. Devils are associated with blackness, soot, and sulphurous smell, besides having the horns, hoofs, and tails of the sort of fertility spirit that is close to the sexual instinct.

The radical of satire, as Lucian established long ago,[137] is a descent narrative, where we enter a lower world which reveals the sources of human absurdity and folly. Most great satirists, including Swift, Rabelais, and Joyce, have understood very well that most of these sources are to be located in the abdominal, genital, and excretory regions, a fact emphasized in modern psychology but not discovered by it, as the etymology of such words as hypochondria and hysteria makes clear. *Gulliver's Travels* reminds us that we recurrently find in this lower world very little people and very big people. The latter include the giants who are related to the titans in Hesiod's story of the defeated earth-mother: they are usually stupid and easily deceived giants, but sometimes, notably in Rabelais, we are reminded of the exuberant strength that lies suppressed, for the most part, in our lower bodily areas. The little people appear as gnomes, dwarfs, and similar types of earth spirit. Sometimes the same identity changes from one to the other: thus the immense devils of the first book of *Paradise Lost* shrink into tiny fairies at the end of the book.

As winter turns to spring, nature shows a power of regaining her youth that does not exist for individual human life. Robert Graves tells us that his earth-mother, whom he calls the white goddess, originally renewed her virginity every spring: the impossibility of this in human experience is one reason for the emphasis on preserving virginity in romance. A great deal of literary and religious imagination is concerned with the effort to assimilate and identify individual [*121*] human life with natural rebirth. Explorers of the New World were often more interested in fountains of youth than in anything they actually found, and the search for prolonged youth is still a theme of romance in, for example, Bulwer-Lytton's *A Strange Story*. The buried treasure hoard guarded by a dragon, full of gold and jewels (which are of subterranean origin in any case), affords an obvious motive for a descent quest. But much more important in early societies is the quest for renewed fertility, and sometimes, as in Ruskin's thoroughly traditional fairy tale, *The King of the Golden River*, we realize that the release of the life-giving powers that come with the spring and the rain is the authentic form of the treasure hoard. The Fafnir figure, the dragon guarding the hoard, is in that case lineally descended from the sea monster of many myths who has swallowed all the water in the world, and continues to devour all the youth and beauty it can get.

The fertility of the land and the virility of the king who rules it have an ancient magical connection, and the link between natural and sexual vitality appears in such images as the lance and grail of the Percival legend, which, according to Jessie Weston, were originally magical food providers.[138] Lance and grail, at least in the Grail's developed form as a chalice or cup, have an analogy to male and female genital organs. Milton's *Comus* gives us a Christian and demonized view of this aspect of the descent: Comus is the son of Circe; he attempts a sexual seduction designed to break the Lady's connection with the higher world of chastity, and his chief emblems are a wand and a cup. Similarly, the replacing of an aged and impotent king by a youthful successor is really a displacement of the theme of renewing the old king's youth. Hence many descent themes, from the Harrowing of Hell to the psychological quests of [*122*] Freud and his successors, centre on the theme of the release, revival, or reemergence of parental figures buried in a world of amnesia or suppressed memory. In romance the descent theme often has a great deal to do with one's descent in the genealogical sense, where the crucial event is the discovery of the real relation between the chief characters and their parents. Sometimes we simply have a death and revival of parental figures, as at the conclusion of Sidney's *Arcadia*, where the king has been given a sleeping potion by his queen, and comes to life in the middle of a trial of the two young heroes on the charge of having murdered him. We may compare the oracle scene in *Cymbeline* [act 5, scene 4], and the appearance of parental figures there.

When it is wisdom that is sought in the lower world, it is almost always wisdom connected with the anxiety of death in some form or other, along with the desire to know what lies beyond. Such wisdom, however displaced, is usually communicated in some kind of dark saying, and riddles and ciphers and oracular utterances of all kinds proliferate around the end of the descending journey. They are naturally prominent in Poe, with his fondness for this area, and one appears at the end of the wanderings of Arthur Gordon Pym. It is not very helpful: Keats's Endymion is more fortunate, and gets fairly specific advice about how the poet's imagination should put together the world he has been traversing [*Endymion*, bk. 3, ll. 689–711].

Here again we go back to very ancient imaginative patterns, such as the Egyptian myth of the underworld judgment, with its weighing of the heart, its negative confessions of the "I am not a crook" type, and its separation of souls into those who pass into the world of Osiris and those who are devoured by a crocodile.[139] This lowerworld judgment is in marked contrast to the upperworld apocalypses in Christianity and elsewhere: institutional Christianity [*123*] gets them mixed up, but the poetic imagination knows the difference. The upperworld is essentially a form of revelation or full knowledge: in the underworld the central figure is not only a prisoner and accused, but he himself knows nothing and yet is known.

The horror of being totally known is so great that most romances evade it by the device of a trial founded on an unjust, malicious, or mistaken charge, which the hero or heroine avoids by the revelation of his or her real identity. This means that the trial presupposes a wrong identity. But occasionally, as in Kafka's *The Trial*, the primitive fear returns. Even in the most displaced and farcical forms of the theme, such as the ordeal of the blindfolded Parolles in *All's Well* [act 4, scene 3], we glimpse something about an involuntarily acquired self-knowledge that is more terrible than death itself. The symbol of this hostile knowledge is generally some form of scales or balance, the emblem of the law, and a sinister emblem because it quantifies, so to speak, all the elements of life that we feel cannot or ought not to be weighed or measured. Most romances keep well out of the way of such emblems, and provide instead various superficial modulations of it which assist the escape of the chief characters. One peculiarly silly example, which I am forced to mention because it occurs so often in romance, is the virgin-detecting gadget, the machine which proves that the heroine really is one in spite of everything, and which appears at the end of Heliodorus and Achilles Tatius. It survives in the girdle of Florimell in Spenser's *Faerie Queene* [bk. 4, canto 5, st. 3, ll. 1–5] and elsewhere.

It is possible never to get out of this lower world, and some may not even want to. For it may also assume the form of a false paradise, like Spenser's Bower of Bliss. Of those turned into animals by Circe, some might refuse to return to human shape—this theme was a popular Renaissance [*124*] paradox. Or there may even be genuine paradises in the lower world, descending from the Classical Elysium, or at least places of contentment, like the underworld community that we meet in the last part of Herbert Read's *The Green Child*. Sometimes, too, the descent imagery is merely playful, as in many children's stories.

Yet even in *Alice in Wonderland* the tone is curiously ambiguous. Alice descends in pursuit of a rabbit preoccupied with the dial of his watch: she is not, like Dante in the *Inferno*, traversing a cone from base to apex, but a spiral-shaped poem, ending in the word "death," appears later in the story.[140] There is a good deal of alienation in Alice's world: she is never quite sure of her own identity, and the continuity with her previous life is broken when her carefully memorized poems turn into grotesque parodies. Giants and dwarfs, we saw, inhabit the lower world: Alice is always either too big or too small, hence often a nuisance or an unwanted guest. She feels estranged from her body by her changes of size, and falls into a pool of what a post-Victorian reader would simply call her liquid excretions. A sinister beheading queen makes her appearance, and the theme of metamorphosis is introduced in the witches' kitchen of the ugly duchess, where a little boy turns into a pig, not that Lewis Carroll would have considered that much of a metamorphosis. The story ends in a trial in which all the characters present turn on the heroine. We notice the prominence of cards in the story: cards and dice are common in descent narratives, because of their overtones of fatality and chance.

The only companion who accompanies us to the end of the descent is the demonic accuser, who takes the form of the accusing memory. The memory is demonic here because it has forgotten only one thing, the original identity of what it accompanies. It conveys to us the darkest knowledge [*125*] at the bottom of the world, the vision of the absurd, the realization that only death is certain, and that nothing before or after death makes sense. The white goddess may sweep on to a renewed life, take another lover, and forget her past, but man can neither forget nor renew. But although in a world of death nothing is more absurd than life, life is the counter-absurdity that finally defeats death. And in a life that is a pure continuum, beginning with a birth that is a random beginning, ending with a death that is a random ending, nothing is more absurd than telling stories that do begin and end. Yet this is part of the counter-absurdity of human creation, the vision that comes, like the vision of the *Bhagavadgita*, to alienated figures on a battlefield of dying men, and ends with finding one's identity in the body of the god of gods who also contains the universe.

In William Morris's *The Earthly Paradise*, a group of lonely old men from Classical and Northern worlds gather on an island and exchange the traditional tales that they have known from childhood. It seems the most futile of activities, the work of disillusionment, weariness, and exhaustion, almost of senility. Even the designer of the whole enterprise calls himself "the idle singer of an empty day."[141] And yet, we read in the epilogue that they are not simply putting in the time until they die: they are fighting a battle against death, with some dim understanding that the telling and retelling of the great stories, in the face of the accusing memory, is a central part of the only battle that there is any point in fighting:

> And these folk—these poor tale-tellers, who strove
> In their wild way the heart of Death to move,
> E'en as we singers, and failed, e'en as we,—
> Surely on their side I at least will be, [*126*]
> And deem that when at last, their fear worn out,
> They fell asleep, all that old shame and doubt
> Shamed them not now, nor did they doubt it good,
> That they in arms against that Death had stood. [6:329]

One thinks of one of the greatest figures of romance, Scheherezade, telling her thousand and one tales so that the suspense of each tale may keep her alive for one more night.[142] Perhaps even the storytellers in Boccaccio's *Decameron* are not simply running away from the plague that rages outside their walls. "Once upon a time": the formula invokes, out of a world where nothing remains, something older than history, younger than the present moment, always willing and able to descend again once more.

V *Quis Hic Locus?* Themes of Ascent

We identified two types of descent themes: those that descend from a higher world to this one and those that descend from this world to a lower one. The general theme of descent, we saw, was that of a growing confusion of identity and of restrictions on action. There is a break in consciousness at the beginning, with analogies to falling asleep, followed by a descent to a lower world which is sometimes a world of cruelty and imprisonment, sometimes an oracular cave. In the descent there is a growing isolation and immobility: charms and spells hold one motionless; human beings are turned into subhuman creatures, and made more mechanical in behaviour; hero or heroine is trapped in labyrinths or prisons. The narrative themes and images of ascent are much the same in reverse, and the chief conceptions are those of escape, remembrance, or discovery of one's real identity, growing freedom, and the breaking of enchantment. Again there are two major narrative divisions: the ascent from a lower world and the ascent to a higher world.

As the hero or heroine enters the labyrinthine lower world, the prevailing moods are those of terror or uncritical awe. At a certain point, perhaps when the strain, as the storyteller doubtless hopes, is becoming unbearable, there [*130*] may be a revolt of the mind, a recovered detachment, the typical expression of which is laughter. The ambiguity of the oracle becomes the ambiguity of wit, something addressed to a verbal understanding that shakes the mind free. This point is also marked by generic changes from the tragic and ironic to the comic and satiric. Thus in Rabelais the huge giants, the search for an oracle, and other lowerworld themes that in different contexts would be frightening or awe-inspiring, are presented as farce. *Finnegans Wake* in our day also submerges us in a dream world of mysterious oracles, but when we start to read the atmosphere changes, and we find ourselves surrounded by jokes and puns. Centuries earlier, the story was told of how Demeter wandered over the world in fruitless search of her lost daughter Proserpine, and sat lonely and miserable in a shepherd's hut until the obscene jests and raillery of the servant girl Iambe and the old nurse Baubo finally persuaded her to smile.[143] The Eleusinian mysteries which Demeter established were solemn and awful rites of initiation connected with the renewal of the fertility cycle; but Iambe and Baubo helped to ensure that there would also be comic parodies of them, like Aristophanes' *Frogs*. According to Plutarch, those who descended to the gloomy cave of the oracle of Trophonius might, after three days, recover the power of laughter.[144]

In an atmosphere of tragic irony the emphasis is on spellbinding, linked to a steady advance of paralysis or death; in an atmosphere of comedy, we break through this inevitable advance by a device related to the riddle, an explanation of a mystery. Such an explanation, which usually takes the form of a recognition scene, transforms a story into a kind of game. That is, the story becomes a puzzle, of which the recognition scene is the solution. The fact that it is usually a rather easy, not to say transparent, puzzle does [*131*] not affect this. The ideal is a reversal of movement which is both a surprise to the reader and yet seems to him an inevitable development of events up to that point. This ideal has never been attained by any work of literature, and even if it were, it would seem to us at best only a triumph of ingenuity. The reason for this melancholy situation is that a completely successful comic resolution depends upon an ideal reader or listener, which means one who has never encountered a comedy or romance before, and has no idea of literary convention. We notice that where complex explanations are required in Shakespearean comedy, they are sometimes postponed until *after* the end of the play, when the audience, who knows more about such things than the characters, will not be there to hear them. What is really recognized is simply the cyclical movement of the story, down through the threatening complications and up again through the escape from them, not the particular mystery by which this movement may be operated.

We can see this more clearly in comic stories where there is no effort at surprise, and where the recognition has been visible throughout. In *The Earthly Paradise* Morris tells the story of *The Man Born To Be King*, the theme of which is summarized in the argument: "It was foretold to a great king, that he who should reign after him should be lowborn and poor; which thing came to pass in the end, for all that the king could do" [3:107]. The old king makes the most desperate efforts to exterminate the coming new one, who relentlessly grows from infant to youth to man, turning up at intervals to remind the king of the uselessness of his efforts. In such a story there is no "suspense"; we know from the beginning that the infant's survival is predestined, and we simply watch its progress. The progress is rationalized in the story by appeals to fate, to the prophecy of an [*132*] oracular wise man, and to the conjunctions of the stars. Morris is unlikely to have "believed" in fate or prophecy or astrology, nor need the reader. What entertains us is the archetype of death and rebirth, where the growing new life takes over the feelings of the irresistible and inevitable which are normally attached to death. The same principle operates in rescue scenes, in impossible tasks, which we know will somehow be accomplished, in unanswerable riddles which we know will somehow be answered. The feeling that death is inevitable comes to us from ordinary experience; the feeling that new life is inevitable comes to us from myth and fable. The latter is therefore both more true and more important.

Such themes in romance are often linked with the providential framework of the Christian universe which is contemporary with so much of it. Thus Sidney, at the beginning of the fourth book of the *Arcadia*:

> The almighty wisdom evermore delighting to show the world, that by unlikeliest means greatest matters may come to conclusion: that human reason may be the more humbled, and more willingly give place to divine providence: as at the first it brought in *Damaetas* to play a part in this royal pageant, so having continued him still an actor, now that all things were

> grown ripe for an end, made his folly the instrument of revealing that, which far greater cunning had sought to conceal.[145]

Damaetas is a ridiculous clown, and we are reminded of the comment about the blundering Dogberry and his cohorts in *Much Ado*: "What your wisdoms could not discover, these shallow fools have brought to light" (5.1.232–4; cf. Matthew 11:25). The echo from the New Testament emphasizes the parallel between comic and Christian myths. In the earlier version of Sidney's story generally known as the Old Arcadia, the passage [*133*] corresponding to the one quoted contains the words: "So evil a ground doth evil stand upon, and so manifest it is, that nothing remains strongly, but that which hath the good foundation of goodness."[146] Such passages remind us that the technical devices of storytelling are not simply responses to popular demand, which hardly existed for Sidney in any case, but the result of working within a certain kind of mythological framework.

There is a little more narrative suspense in the Houdini motif, where hero or heroine wriggle out of their prisons by themselves. The great exemplar here is the escape of Ulysses from the cave of Polyphemus [*Odyssey*, bk. 9], which contains most of the archetypes of this episode. The prison is often controlled by one of the giants who inhabit the lower reaches of the night world, and in less displaced romances he is often a cannibal giant. Front-de-Boeuf in *Ivanhoe*, to whose castle we shall come in a moment, is often referred to as gigantic. In the Polyphemus story Ulysses gets out by being mistaken for a sheep, more or less: in other words the assimilation of human and animal forms is still present. In more displaced fiction a similar Polyphemus figure could be a Dickensian grotesque threatening to devour or pollute the heroine, like Gride in *Nicholas Nickleby* or Uriah Heep in *David Copperfield*. The word "grotesque," incidentally, always carries with it something of its "grotto" or lowerworld connections. More often the displaced imprisoning giant is a jealous father, who locks up the heroine.

The ingenuity shown by the escaping character represents very often a triumph of what we have been calling *froda*, wiliness or craft. When it is purely that, we are being shown a triumph of evil, as in the escape of Medea in Euripides. More usually, deception and theft and disguise are enlisted in a good cause. In the progress from darkness [*134*] to light, which is the area covered by this phase, we find the myths of the origin of fire, which are usually myths of stealing it. Similarly, blindness, or living in the dark, is often associated with the world of the giant which is being escaped from, as again in the Polyphemus story. In the Book of Genesis blindness and animal disguise themes are combined in the story of the deception of the blind Isaac by Jacob, who covers his smooth hands with the skin of an animal to pass as the rough and hairy Esau. In Chaucer's *Merchant's Tale* the cuckolded husband has his sight restored by an outraged deity, but his wife manages to persuade him that he really is blind after all. In a more genial setting, even Jane Eyre's Rochester has something of the blind giant about him at the end of the story: the restoring of his sight is a symbol of his evolution from pursuing lover to Victorian husband. Because of the frequency of the convention of escape, we may sometimes feel that there is something illusory about the dungeon or whatever: however dark and thick-walled, it seems bound to turn into a womb of rebirth sooner or later. This theme is clearest when the romance has allegorical overtones, as in the prison of Orgoglio in *The Faerie Queene* or of Giant Despair in *The Pilgrim's Progress*. There is also in this case some connection with the atmosphere of a nightmare, from which one can always escape by waking up.

The conventional happy ending of romance may seem to us faked, manipulated, or thrown in as a contemptuous concession to a weak-minded reader. In our day ironic modes are the preferred ones for serious fiction, and of course if the real conception of a work of fiction is ironic, a conventionally happy ending would be forced, or, in extreme cases, dishonest. But if the conception is genuinely romantic and comic, the traditional happy ending is usually the one that fits. It is obvious however both that the [*135*] happy ending exists only for readers who finish the book, and, within the book, only for characters who survive to the end of the story. Such characters are apt to expound a good deal on the benevolence of whatever power got them out of their predicaments, and we may sometimes feel that this shows some insensitivity to the fates of the subordinate characters who perished on the way.

In *Ivanhoe* much of the action takes place in Front-de-Boeuf's castle, where terrible things almost go on. A Jew is going to be tortured to make him give up his money; his daughter and another heroine are being threatened with rape. They all escape relatively unharmed, but in the actual Middle Ages there were many people who went through such ordeals without escaping. Scott even interrupts his narrative to show how true this was, by quoting a passage from the Anglo-Saxon Chronicle. He also provides foils for his two heroines. Rowena gets out of the castle, but another Saxon woman previously abducted did not; Rebecca escapes a trial for sorcery on the ground that her medical skill is witchcraft, but another Jewess, from whom she had learned her skill, was actually martyred on the same pretext. It seems clear that appeals to God, by virtuous characters threatened with evil, may be of little use unless God has a secretary to handle such calls in the form of a good-natured novelist, backed by a sentimental public.

The happy endings of life, as of literature, exist only for survivors. When confronted with something profoundly evil in life like the Nazi regime in Germany, we may say that after all it did collapse in a few years. This fact was of no help to the millions of people it tortured and murdered before it fell, and yet it is true, however smug it may sound, that the survivors have the more complete perspective. Hence the modern world may accept comic mythologies [*136*], such as the progress myth in the democracies and the classless society myth of Marxism, although the benefits of such happy endings are only for those living in a remote future. One of the things that comedy and romance as a whole are about, clearly, is the unending, irrational, absurd persistence of the human impulse to struggle, survive, and where possible escape. It is perhaps worth noting how intense is the desire of most readers of romances for the happy ending. In *Ivanhoe*, once more, a subordinate character named Athelstane, whom most readers would hardly care much about, is killed off, but was brought to life again because of objections made to Scott by a reader. Scott's complaisance in this matter strikes us, in our ironic age, as a trifle meretricious, but, again, we may be judging by the wrong conventions. Even the desire to be reborn in a happier future may be more deep-seated than we think. In Morris's *News from Nowhere* the calmness with which the inhabitants of that happy future world accept their nineteenth-century "Guest" perhaps suggests that, like the inhabitants of the Christian heaven, they would expect people from an earlier and sadder time to be reborn into it.

The standard escape device of romance is that of escape through a shift of identity, the normal basis of the recognition scene. As a rule the recognition scene involves producing some equivalent of a birth certificate, which causes the action to return to the point of the hero's or heroine's birth. As this is usually a time many years before the story begins, we have two interlocking rhythms of time, one the time of the narrative action, the other a much more deliberate and creative time in which hidden truths are eventually brought to light. Certain folk tale themes, such as the hare-and-tortoise race in Aesop and the similar race of Atalanta, who loses to her suitor because he throws golden balls in front of her to distract her attention,[147] remind us [*137*] that in the conventions of comedy and comic romance, at least, the slower and more leisurely rhythms of time are the ones that win out in the end.

Such a discovery about birth is usually accompanied or followed by a marriage. Tragedy or threatening tragic complications in romance often involve stresses within families, such as a father's overbearing will or the threat of incestuous relationship. In the love-and-honour conflicts so frequent in romantic stories, the imperatives of honour usually have to do with attachments to family, tribal, or class loyalties. Tragedy often results from the inability to break with these. Even Mark Antony's primary "duty" is to remain a Roman in the family of Caesar, as Cleopatra sardonically notes [*Antony and Cleopatra*, act 1, scene 1]. It seems intolerably simplistic to explain all forms of nightmare by the fear of incest, as some Freudians do,[148] yet incest is certainly a central theme in night-world imagery, and the transfer of energies and affections from one's family to the new family of a marriage is the easiest kind of comic resolution. A comic resolution, in fact, could almost be defined as an action that breaks out of the Oedipus ring, the destruction of a family or other close-knit social group by the tensions and jealousies of its members.

The next stage of ascent is the separation between the lower world and those who are destined to escape from it. Again we start with an act of conscious detachment, one that takes the form of recognizing the demonic as demonic. The detective story is a genre directed toward this kind of recognition. The detective story is, in a comic context, an epiphany of law, a balancing and neutralizing activity in society, the murderer discovered at the end balancing the corpse that we normally find at the beginning. Devotees of detective stories tell me that there is usually a sense of anticlimax when the murderer is identified, an anticlimax only [*138*] resolved by reaching for another story. One implication of this is that law is not justice, though at its best it may point in the direction of justice. In literature, as in life, the only real justice is poetic justice, and the story of the triumph of law does not quite achieve this.

In any case the detective story operates, for the most part, in a deeply conservative social area, where the emphasis is on reintegrating the existing order. Its vogue was contemporary with realism. Fiction in the last generation or so has turned increasingly from realism to fantasy, partly because fantasy is the normal technique for fiction writers who do not believe in the permanence or continuity of the society they belong to. Similarly, the detective story, as a ritual game which the powers of law and order always win, has modulated to a type of thriller with much more anarchic social overtones. The usual conservative tendency in comedy is to move from subjective illusion to an acceptance of the standards of society, as a superior norm. Thus in Jane Austen's *Emma,* the novel in which her early burlesques of romance forms paid off, Emma imposes a romance pattern on her friend Harriet, whose parentage is unknown, and who therefore, by all the rules of romance, must be of some quite exceptional birth. Emma's discovery that Harriet is, in parentage as well as character, pretty well what she appears to be is the discovery that liberates her from illusion.

In *Sense and Sensibility* we have a more somber study of a progress toward social reality in the mind of Marianne, who is, at least structurally, the central figure of the story. Marianne's sensibility is of a polarizing kind that divides people into those like herself, who cannot and should not try to control their emotions, and those who, like her sister Elinor, are so calm as to have no emotions. Following a disappointment in love, her sensibility drives her into an [*139*] illness which it has directly created. She recognizes this when she recovers from it, and remarks that if she had died she would have been guilty of self-destruction. After her recovery she adopts the genuine form of the same polarization, the contrast between the sensibility she had indulged and the sense which Elinor had shown all along. I mention this book here because it illustrates so clearly the contrast we have already spoken of, between what an individual story may present and what the convention it belongs to may present. Every so often we have had glimpses of an inherently revolutionary quality in romance, however conservative the individual stories may be, and the polarizing element in Marianne's mind indicates a place where we may pick up a clue to it.

We noticed that the trial scene which is common at or near the end of a romance is usually an unjust trial, one that proceeds on false assumptions. Or, as in the Chinese play *The Chalk Circle,* we may have two trial scenes, one before a foolish judge and one before a wiser one, to represent the progress from illusion to reality. In such stories illusion is an attribute of society as a whole rather than of an individual. Such a society sets up a perverted order, sometimes, as in the *Odyssey,* during the absence of a genuine ruler whose return puts an end to it. The process of escaping from such a society may involve a complete social *culbute* or overturn, separating and opposing the liberated forces from the enslaving ones. Revolutionary attitudes are dialectical and polarizing attitudes, and this involves, in romance, the identifying of the demonic or regressive and its clear separation from whatever is progressive in the story. In romance it is much more frequently the individual, the hero or heroine, who has the vision of liberation, and the society they are involved with that wants to remain in a blind and gigantic darkness. In [*140*] the *Odyssey*, the containing form is still a conservative one, but even there we notice how the gradual emergence of the disguised Ulysses in the household tends to polarize the characters, those who have to be destroyed at the end having already condemned themselves by their attitudes.

We found that in descent narratives the central image is that of metamorphosis, the freezing of something human and conscious into an animal or plant or inanimate object. Ascent themes introduce us to the opposite kind of metamorphosis, the growing of identity through the casting off of whatever conceals or frustrates it. The simplest form of such ascending metamorphosis is the removal of enchantment, in which an animal disguise or something parallel is replaced by the original human form. The frog becomes the prince; Lucius the ass, in Apuleius, becomes Lucius the initiate of Isis; the Wife of Bath's loathly lady, having got what she wanted, becomes a beautiful lady. Closely related is the comic theme of release from a humour, where a character with a mechanical pattern of behaviour is able to become free of it.

We are now coming, by the same reverse movement, into the area of the twins or *Doppelgänger* figures who are so prominent in descent imagery. The theme now before us is that of the separating of the demonic principle from its opposite, when the two closely resemble each other. An early Christian romance known as the *Clementine Recognitions* features a hero named Clement, identified with a famous early Christian apostle and writer, who attaches himself to the more famous St. Peter, and follows him in his evangelical wanderings.[149] Clement is the son of parents who have become separated through a slandered-mother situation: Clement's uncle had designs on his mother, who left home, taking her twin sons with her. Clement, the third son, remained at home with the father until the father [*141*] left in search of the mother and also disappeared. The mother, of course, was shipwrecked and separated from the twins. In the course of the story, or what there is of a story, the family is picked up in stages. First, a beggar woman living in the greatest poverty and misery is discovered by Peter, and is identified as the mother. He has to supply hands for her by a miracle first, because she has gnawed them off for hunger. Students of folk tale say that the accused-mother motif is closely related to another known as "the maiden without hands," an association which may be the original reason for this bizarre detail.[150]

Peter and his entourage then go to Antioch, where there are two prominent Christians who "turn out to be" the twins. They were captured by pirates, no less, at the time of the shipwreck and were sold to a Jewess who was a Christian proselyte. In the neighbourhood is an old man who is an astrologer and believes in fate and the origin of everything in natural causes. Peter cures him of these theological errors and he is shown to be the long lost father, whose name is Faustus. Evidently this story of a reuniting family is intended as some sort of allegory of the Last Judgment, which for the author and his readers, members of the family of God, will be one vast recognition scene.

We notice that the mother has twin sons: they have changed their names, just to make it harder, but nothing is otherwise made of this feature, which is doubtless taken over from an earlier story. On the other hand, there is a strong emphasis on the theme of the demonic double. Peter's great opponent all through the story is Simon Magus the enchanter, and in connection with him Peter remarks that God has appointed for this world certain pairs, the one coming first being evil and the second good. He gives ten examples of these pairs, beginning with Cain and Abel and ending with Antichrist and Christ. One of [*142*] these ten pairs is Simon Magus and Simon Peter. At the end of the story Simon Magus, through his enchantments, implants his own face on Faustus. Peter promises to remove this false face if Faustus will go to the market-place in his Simon Magus appearance and make a speech renouncing the latter's point of view and defending the Christian one. Faustus does and Peter does, and all ends happily.

This rather childish conclusion seems to be again an allegory of the annihilation of error through consolidating and defining it as the opposite or parody of the truth. In short, the *Clementine Recognitions*, as its title implies, passes over the theme of confused identity in the twins, who are not confusing anybody in spite of the change of names, and focuses on the opposite theme of demonic resemblance. The story of Barlaam and Josaphat, mentioned earlier, also introduces the theme of a demonic double, an antagonist of Christianity who looks exactly like a defender of it, and employs it with an equally earnest clumsiness. Such devices in

Christian stories reflect the revolutionary and dialectical element in Christian belief, which is constantly polarizing its truth against the falsehoods of the heathen, but, like other revolutionary doctrines, feels most secure when the dark side takes the form of a heresy that closely resembles itself. In secular literature the theme of the separating of a character from a demonic shadow or double may be as rudimentary as these examples or as subtle and complex as Conrad's *Secret Sharer*.

We have already come across the device of the doubled heroine, sometimes represented by a dark and a fair girl, sometimes linked to a grave-and-gay contrast of temperament. Often we have two sisters, the older one dark and haughty, the younger one fair and milder. The two heroines of the *Arcadia* follow this pattern, which is a commonplace [*143*] in Victorian fiction: it even occurs in *Huckleberry Finn*, with the Grangerford sisters. We saw that in this arrangement one girl is sometimes heading for the choice of one of her suitors and marriage to him, the other for virginity or devotion to a cause, and that this device helps to produce the two major cadences of romance, the allegro one and the penseroso one. Sometimes the dark heroine has a suggestion of the demonic about her, as in the Miriam of Hawthorne's *Marble Faun*; sometimes, as with the Cora of *The Last of the Mohicans*, one girl is killed off mainly to clear her out of the way so that the hero can marry the other in a monogamous society. In *The Castle of Otranto* the more interesting of two heroines is similarly eliminated to fulfil a prophecy about the extinction of her father's line. In such situations there may be a slight suggestion that one girl is a displaced sacrificial object whose death prolongs or renews the other's life. In Dickens we have, in a male setting, an explicit use of this theme in the martyrdom of Sydney Carton at the end of *A Tale of Two Cities*.

This device has a long ancestry in romances where the heroine is doubled with another figure who has so much less of the reader's sympathy that he does not mind much if she gets killed. In Heliodorus there is a treacherous go-between named Thisbe, who appears in the story when the heroine Chariclea is hidden in a cave by an Egyptian robber named Thyamis. Thyamis, seeing that his fortunes are apparently lost, goes into the cave to murder Chariclea. Heliodorus explains, in a comment alluded to by Shakespeare (*Twelfth Night*, 5.1.118–19), that it is the custom of "barbarians," in desperate straits, to kill the person they most love in order to have company in the next world: similar themes have met us earlier. Thyamis enters the cave, finds Thisbe there with her back turned to him, and stabs her, thinking her to [*144*] be Chariclea. The hero

Theagenes then enters, finds Thisbe lying on her face, also assumes her to be Chariclea, and utters a long lament about the cruelty of fortune. Being a hero in a romance, he completes the lament before he turns her over. The fact that Thisbe resembles Chariclea so closely, at least from behind (later on Chariclea's voice is mistaken for Thisbe's), makes her a shadow or demonic double of the heroine. Whatever barbarians may do, it is often convenient for a romancer to have such a figure to kill off, to provide a death-and-rebirth displacement for the heroine.

We often have too, in softer lighting, contrasted groupings of progressive and regressive characters, who forward or retard the festive conclusion. In Scott there are quite elaborate constructions of this kind, generally of female figures. In *The Pirate* there is a sibyl named Norna, who believes that she can control the weather and predict the future. She has doubts about her abilities, but she is sane enough, not merely to ask herself whether she is sane, but to decide to stay mad, on the ground that it's more fun that way. She is, of course, "cured" in the last chapter, because in romance all magicians, whatever the reality of their powers, have to renounce their magic at the end. Norna is the mother of the pirate: she thinks, however, that she is the mother of the hero, and is anxious for the latter to marry Minna, the wrong or regressive heroine, because she herself represents that function in the plot. Thus she has the displaced role of a magician who constructs, not the total action, like Prospero in *The Tempest*, but the regressive part of the action, like Archimago in *The Faerie Queene*, an enchantment that the surviving characters must break free from.

This polarizing of action is obvious enough in romance; but the test of every revolutionary movement, however [*145*] romantic, comes when it must establish continuity with what has preceded it. We remember that a romance often begins with a break in consciousness or loss of memory: in ascent imagery, then, we should expect a third stage, following the recognition of the demonic and its separation from the progressive or surviving elements, which would be the restoring of the broken current of memory. The theme of restoring the memory is, naturally, often an element in the recognition scene itself, as the action then normally returns to the beginning of the story and interprets it more truly than the previous account has done. The favourite device employed is what I call a talisman of recognition, some emblem or object, a birthmark on the body, tokens put beside an exposed infant, and the like, which symbolizes the original identity.

In the nineteenth century, theories about an unconscious mind that never really forgets anything were starting to be developed, and such a mind supplies a possible setting for the recovery of a lost memory. In several Victorian romances a situation recurs in which the key to the recognition is held in the memory of someone who does not know that he or she possesses it. Thus a good deal of the action of Wilkie Collins's *The Woman in White* turns on a secret concealed in the damaged brain of a madwoman, one which relates to the social origin of the villain who has married the heroine. In Sheridan LeFanu's *House by the Churchyard*, which is closer to the conventional detective story, the mystery about the identity of the villain is locked inside the unconscious brain of the man the villain had nearly murdered, and a trepanning operation is attempted to dig out the memory.

In Wilkie Collins's story there is a dog who has taken a strong dislike to the plausible villain, according to a common principle of romance which may be called "dog [*146*] knows." After great efforts it is finally established that the mystery surrounding the villain is the fact that he was not a gentleman by birth, as the dog had perceived all along. Collins's detective dog belongs on the opposite side of animal imagery from what we met in the previous chapter, the hunt in a forest that begins to enclose the hunter in a dream world, and where there is often, as in the story of Actaeon, an identification of hunter and victim. The clearest example of a direct contrast to this theme is the fox hunt, where a band of red-coated sportsmen ride across open country, in late fall after the crops are reaped, in pursuit of the animal whom Jorrocks, the great hero of Robert Smith Surtees' fox-hunting novels, calls "the thief of the world." The fox hunt from this point of view is a symbolic ritual aimed at the discovery of the demonic, and the fox is never killed by the hunter but is torn to pieces by the hounds, an Actaeon in reverse. Yet the fox is also the wily and resourceful hero of the beast epics who wriggles out of one tight corner after another, symbolically identical with the guileful Ulysses and his picaresque descendants.

The total social context of this is a little difficult to grasp, even though Surtees is remarkably incisive about it. The fox hunt is carried on by a horse-riding aristocracy of "barbarians," in Matthew Arnold's phrase,[151] dominating a countryside of farmers. Jorrocks, a London Cockney merchant, is a convert to their cause, and the incongruity of his class origin and his hobby is the main source of Surtees' humour. At the end of *Handley Cross*, one of the best of these stories, Jorrocks is put on trial for his sanity.[152] The prosecutor keeps referring to fox hunts as fêtes or festivals, and to Jorrocks as a lord of misrule. He speaks in the spirit of nineteenth-century realism, and for a middle-class revolutionary movement in which the aristocracy's privileges are steadily being curtailed by a mercantile ethos which symbolizes [*147*] something of the calculating wariness of a fox *redivivus*. To Jorrocks, of course, his society is equally perverted: the implication is that Jorrocks stands for a kind of romantic violence which may be postbourgeois as well as prebourgeois. This is a point we must drop here and come back to later.

In more realistic stories, the theme of breaking and restoring the current of memory, or the kind of continuous action which is parallel to the memory, may be expressed in quieter ways. In Jane Austen's *Mansfield Park* the private theatricals set up in Sir Thomas Bertram's household constitute, in the author's eyes, a reversal of all normal social and moral standards, with only the heroine Fanny holding out against it. The hero's capitulation to this rebellion greatly weakens Fanny's resistance, and Fanny also finally surrenders, a sentence or two before the return of Sir Thomas puts a dramatic end both to the theatricals and to part 1. A few pages later Fanny, in a speech of a type unprecedented in Jane Austen, is uttering a eulogy on the noble faculty of the memory.[153]

With the restoration of memory, and the continuity of action that goes with it, we have reached, so to speak, the surface of the earth, and are well on the way toward the higher themes of ascent, which take us toward the recovery of original identity. This is suggested whenever a talisman of recognition also restores the memory of the crucial character. One of the most complete and haunting examples of such a progression is the ring in the Indian play *Sakuntala*. The ring is given to Sakuntala, the heroine, by King Dushyanta, who has fallen in love with her. A curse is put on the king which makes him forget all about Sakuntala and his life with her, and in the meantime Sakuntala loses her ring. The ring falls into the sea; a fish swallows it, a fisherman catches the fish, takes it to the [*148*] palace, where it is opened and the ring discovered; the ring is brought to the king's attention, and as soon as he sees it his memory is restored. Here all the elements of a total cycle of recognition are present: the descent into the lower world; the fish as a denizen of that world; the ring, symbolizing the current of memory, disappearing and returning, the period of its return being the signal for reunion.

We noted that the lower world may be submarine as well as subterranean: the sea is particularly the image of an unconscious which seems paradoxically to forget everything and yet potentially to remember everything. In any case similar complexes of objects fallen into the sea and recovered, of fish and fishermen, of the whole sense of a past life restored, inhabit a variety of comedies and romances, including *Pericles*. The Biblical myth has parallels in the Jonah story and in the elaborate fishing imagery of the Gospels, where the descent of Christ to a lower world is given a submarine dimension as he and his disciples become "fishers of men" [Mark 1:17]. The same theme may be treated ironically, as it is in Herodotus's story of the ring of Polycrates, which that king threw into the sea to try to put a check on his good luck, but was swallowed by a fish and came back to him, indicating that the gods were still determined to be jealous of him [*History*, bk. 3, secs. 40–4].

In stories about the birth of a hero, a frequent opening theme is that of putting him into a chest or ark which is sent floating on the water. In one of the *Gesta Romanorum* stories[154] this happens to an infant born of a union of brother and sister. The brother is killed in battle; the sister, a princess, rejects a more powerful suitor and is dispossessed from her kingdom, reduced to a single castle. The infant is rescued from the water by fishermen, and grows up in an abbey, where, on discovering the secret of his birth, he decides to become a crusader, the normal remedy for [*149*] neurosis in medieval romance. His ship is driven by a storm to his mother's castle; he lands, defeats the usurper, and marries his mother. After the discovery of the second incest, another fisherman takes him to an isolated rock, from which he can only be released (this part is not clear in detail) by keys, which he throws into the sea. The keys are swallowed by a fish and extracted by a search party who are following a divine directive to make the hero the next pope. This story, which might be called the apotheosis of Oedipus, and is the basis of Thomas Mann's *The Holy Sinner*, follows logically the descent-and-return sequence in the submarine tonality.

So far the themes of romance have also been those of comedy, but now we are at a point where comedy and romance begin to diverge. We notice that utopias or ideal communities have a very restricted role in literature. Even in Plato the real form of the community is ultimately not the Republic, but the symposium of free speech and thought which contains it. The festive societies which appear at the ends of comedies are usually anti-utopian, based on the kind of pragmatic common sense or good will that transcends all social planning. But even so the theme of comedy remains predominantly social. In literature, however, the pastoral, the Arcadia, the simplified life of a handful of shepherds who are also lovers and poets, seems to represent something that carries us into a higher state of identity than the social and comic world does. The closer romance comes to a world of original identity, the more clearly something of the symbolism of the Garden of Eden reappears, with the social setting reduced to the love of individual men and women within an order of nature which has been reconciled to humanity.

In *As You Like It* the melancholy Jaques is a character who feels some affinity with the jester Touchstone. Like [*150*] Touchstone, he is a kind of Brechtian alienation figure, and even tries to be a jester himself; like Touchstone, he makes a set speech turning on the number seven; and, as with Touchstone, there is no trace of him in Shakespeare's main source. At the end of the play he withdraws from the eight happily marrying characters to consult with a hermit and live in a cave. *As You Like It* is more comedy than romance: our sympathies remain with the festive group, and Jaques's withdrawal is puzzling, even ridiculous. But we have no time to wonder about him, because Rosalind comes out to speak the epilogue and ask for our applause. In *The Tempest*, which is more romance than comedy, Prospero speaks the epilogue and again asks for our applause, but the reason for the applause is to set him free for a more meditative life.

This does not mean that the world of recovered identity in romance is always a world "annihilated," in Marvell's term,[155] to a single individual: that is merely the penseroso conclusion that leaves us with the figure of the hermit. Romance has its own conception of an ideal society, but that society is in a higher world than that of ordinary experience. We remember the two great structural principles of narrative: the polarizing and separating of a world above and a world below, and the movement through the cycles of nature and human life. We use cyclical images of spring and youth and dawn to symbolize the idyllic world, and those of winter and night and death for the lower world, but they are symbols pointing beyond themselves, and there is a considerable difference, in romance and elsewhere, between a polarization which transcends the cycle of nature and a polarization which accommodates itself to it. Thus in Christianity, although resurrection, a movement upward to a higher world, is in a sense the opposite of rebirth, we celebrate it in the images of the fertility cycle, including eggs and rabbits. [*151*]

D.H. Lawrence's *The Man Who Died* is an account of the Resurrection in which Christianity, with its artificial creation myth and its hero who is the son of a sky-father, has been absorbed into a mythological universe centred on an earth-mother and perpetual renewal. The risen Christ becomes the lover of a priestess of Isis who has been taught to "wait for the reborn man,"[156] and at the end of the story he leaves her, promising to return when the cycle comes round again. Two things are notable here. One is that a female-centred mythology is likely to be even more male-dominated than its rival: when the female is at the centre, the male is a comet passing her who may or may not, at his pleasure, go into a revolving orbit. The vagrant or casual wanderer, the bee pollinating the flower who could just as well have been another bee, is a central rebirth image. The other is that there is a considerable ironic element in any polarizing situation assimilated to cyclical movement, as we realize in early January when our New Year's resolutions have collapsed into habitual routine. A closer association of romance, irony, cycle, and the casual wanderer is in Joseph Conrad's *Chance*. The two parts into which this story is divided, "Damsel" and "Knight," suggest a parody of romance, and we find the damsel's life polarized between a regressive father, who is jealousy incarnate, and a lover who is generosity incarnate, which is nearly as hard on her. At the end, with father and lover dead, the character whose central place in the story was the result of sheer "chance" marries her.

Romance, in any case, eventually takes us into the great Eros theme in which a lover is driven by his love to ascend to a higher world. This ascent is full of images of climbing or flying, of mountains, towers, ladders, spiral staircases, the shooting of arrows, or coming out of the sea on to an island. The great exemplar of the theme is Dante's *Purgatorio*, where Dante is inspired by his love of Beatrice to [*152*] climb a mountain leading to the Garden of Eden. In making this climb Dante is returning to his own original state as a child of Adam. This means that he is moving toward a self-recognition scene. That is, he finds and becomes his real self as it would have been if Adam had not fallen and man's original identity had been preserved. This movement upward toward self-recognition is central to romance, and is in fact what all recognition scenes really point to; but it is seldom treated so explicitly. T.S. Eliot, a devoted student of Dante, is fascinated by the theme: perhaps his most eloquent treatment of it is in the poem *Marina*, a mixture of motifs from the *Purgatorio* and *Pericles*, the motto to which, beginning "*Quis hic locus?*"—"What place is this?"—has given me my title. Self-recognition, or attaining one's original identity, reverses all the Narcissus and twin and *Doppelgänger* themes that occur in the descent.

When Dante reaches Eden on top of the mountain, he meets a young girl named Matilda, but is separated from her by a river. Here the theme of virginity appears in another context, where it is associated with the magical preservation of the idyllic world. This association appears as late as William Morris's *The Wood beyond the World*, where the marriage of the heroine dissolves the magical world: "all wizardry left her since the day of her wedding."[157] In *The Tempest*, as soon as Miranda is ready to marry Ferdinand and descend into her brave new world, the magical connection between man and nature is broken, and Ariel is released. Prospero's fussing over preserving Miranda's virginity to the last moment is not morality but magic. Here again we see that there are two forms of the upward quest, one a sublimated quest ending in virginity, the other a sexual quest ending in marriage. The former usually focuses on a sister or daughter figure, as in the fourteenth-century [*153*] *Pearl*[158] and any number of similar visions down to *Marina*. The traditional symbolic basis of the sexual quest, which goes back to the Song of Songs in the Bible, is the identification of the mistress's body with the paradisal garden.[159] The great medieval quest of sexual union, paralleling the sublimated quest of the *Purgatorio*, is *The Romaunt of the Rose*, where the garden modulates to a tower.[160]

Apart from the idealizing of the presexual state, there is a sense in which virginity is an appropriate image for attaining original identity: what is objectively untouched symbolizes what is subjectively contained, so to speak. More important is the sense of virginity perpetually renewed, or life in a world where every experience is fresh and unique, with the sun reborn every day, in the image of Dylan Thomas's *Fern Hill*.[161] In such a world the primary categories of experience, time and space, begin to lose the large amount of alienation they have in our experience. Time becomes less an image of fatality and destruction, and becomes rather an expression of energy, exuberance, and the kind of genuine freedom which is the same thing as discipline. The traditional symbol for this experience of time is the dance, and the original identity of the order of nature is often presented in literature as a dance. One of the most attractive of such presentations in English literature is Sir John Davies' *Orchestra*, which is of particular interest to us here because it takes us back again to the figure of the chaste Penelope. The poem is a love song sung to Penelope by the chief of her suitors, Antinous, and at the end Penelope sees in the dance of the elements of nature an image of the same kind as that of her own web, though a fuller image because it involves her feet and not merely her hands. The implication is that Penelope's weaving and unweaving is an image of the order of nature, as it must be so long as its real master remains absent from it. [*154*] Similarly, space is a world of an alienated "out there" in ordinary experience, but in the middle of it is a tiny "here," which we possess and call our home. In the upper world the Garden of Eden suggests a life in which nature itself has become home, its animals and plants a rejoined part of our society.

But, of course, in the world of Eros we can also have tragedy or frustration, of the kind expressed in all the poems deploring the cruelty of a mistress. The disdainful mistress is, in this phase at least, the incarnation of Robert Graves's white goddess or triple will, the Diana of heaven, earth, and hell whose virginity means only the elusiveness of a nature that remains unreconciled to man. As we contemplate this Diana, the symbol of nature as a closed cycle that man is trapped in, she turns into Venus flanked by her lover Mars and her child Cupid, the presiding deity of the red and white world of sexual love, the hungry desire satisfied only by death, the Eros fulfilled in Thanatos. This is the world of *The Knight's Tale* in Chaucer, where Theseus builds an amphitheatre of altars to Mars, Diana, and Venus, where Arcite fights in red under Mars and Palamon in white under Venus. The red Arcite wins the battle but dies, the spilled-blood sacrifice for the marriage of Palamon and Emily.

Here again the tragic or frustrated is seen as an incomplete form of the total picture. The love for a mistress who does not need or much want such love, where the lover gives everything and the mistress gives only by a rare acceptance of a gift, is a childlike and emotionally dependent relationship which, if it is not to end in frustration, must develop into something else. The development is illustrated in the lovely story of Cupid and Psyche that floats like a soap bubble up from Apuleius's tale of Lucius transformed to an ass. Psyche, the soul who is the bride of [*155*] an invisible Love, falls under the wrath of Venus, who takes toward her the role of the conventional cruel or bullying stepmother of ballad and folk tale, the latter being, as Blake's *Mental Traveller* indicates, an image of the hostility of nature in our world. Psyche is assigned impossible tasks, one of them including a journey to the world of the dead. The tasks are accomplished by spirits of nature, so that her final reconciliation with Venus is also a reconciliation of nature with the human soul, as again in the Biblical theme of the regaining of Eden.

We remember that a central image of descent was that of being involved with pictures or tapestries or statues or mirrors in a way that suggested the exchange of original identity for its shadow or reflection. On the opposite side we have statues coming to life, as in the concluding scene of *The Winter's Tale*; we have stories of snow maidens thawed out and sleeping beauties awakened. The familiar Classical version is the story of Pygmalion, which is appropriately slipped in near the end of *The Romaunt of the Rose*.[162] One very significant image of this type is the conclusion of a masque, where, as in *Comus*, the actors come out of their dramatic frame and revert to the people they actually are.

We saw that *Alice in Wonderland*, for all its lightness and humour, preserved some of the traditional imagery of a lowerworld descent. Alice passing through the looking-glass into a reversed world of dream language is also going through a descent; the incidents are largely suggested by nursery rhymes, but we may note the twin theme in Tweedledum and Tweedledee. Before long, however, we realize that the journey is turning upwards, in a direction symbolized by the eighth square of a chessboard, where Alice becomes a Psyche figure, a virginal queen flanked by two older queens, one red and one white, who bully her [*156*] and set her impossible tasks in the form of nonsensical questions. Cards and dice, we said, have a natural connection with themes of descent into a world of fatality; chess and other board games, despite *The Waste Land*, appear more frequently in romance and in Eros contexts, as *The Tempest* again reminds us. As Alice begins to move upward out of her submarine mirror world she notes that all the poems she had heard have to do with fish, and as she wakes she reviews the metamorphoses that the figures around her had turned into.

There is no Biblical counterpart to the Psyche story in Apuleius, but there is a series of apocryphal writings, of Gnostic or Manichean origin, which include "acts" of various apostles, where Philip, Thomas, John, and others go through the world performing miracles and breaking up marriages. The miracles are easy enough: their real triumphs come when they have persuaded someone of prominent social position to live apart from his wife, on the Manichean principle that humanity can only be saved by self-extermination. Suddenly, in the middle of these dreary anxieties, there comes a great trumpet call from a very different imaginative world, the *Hymn of the Soul* in the Acts of Thomas.[163]

The Soul says that when he was a child in the palace of his father, his parents provided him with money and jewels and sent him down to Egypt, where he was to find a pearl in the sea guarded by a serpent, and come back to his original state again. He also has a brother who remained in the upper world. The Soul disguises himself and descends, but his disguise is penetrated and he is persuaded to eat the food of the lower world, like Proserpine before him. This causes him to forget both his origin and his mission, and fall into a deep sleep. His parents send a "letter" to him, the lowerworld oracle that we have met before; the Soul reads [*157*] it, and as he reads his memory comes back. He puts the serpent to sleep, seizes the pearl, and starts back again. At the beginning of his quest he had been clothed in a garment which is clearly the form of his original identity. He meets this garment again and realizes that it is, in fact, his real self. He sees it "as it had been in a mirror," and it is brought him by twins: "Two, yet one shape was upon both."[164] Putting it on, he makes his way back to his own world. Like Apuleius's story, this is a story of the "Soul"; in other words, it is the story of ourselves. Crucial to it is the role of the letter or message, which not only awakens him but is what draws him upward to his self-recognition. It seems that one becomes the ultimate hero of the great quest of man, not so much by virtue of what one does, as by virtue of what and how one reads.

In traditional romance, including Dante, the upward journey is the journey of a creature returning to its creator. In most modern writers, from Blake on, it is the creative power in man that is returning to its original awareness. The secular scripture tells us that we are the creators; other scriptures tell us that we are actors in a drama of divine creation and redemption. Even Alice is troubled by the thought that her dream may not have been hers but the Red King's.[165] Identity and self-recognition begin when we realize that this is not an either/or question, when the great twins of divine creation and human recreation have merged into one, and we can see that the same shape is upon both.

VI The Recovery of Myth

One very obvious feature of romance is its pervasive social snobbery. Naive romance confines itself largely to royal families; sentimental romance gives us patterns of aristocratic courage and courtesy, and much of it adopts a "blood will tell" convention, the association of moral virtue and social rank implied in the word "noble." A hero may appear to be of low social origin, but if he is a real hero he is likely to be revealed at the end of the story as belonging to the gentry. Even in Shakespearean romance distinctions of rank are rigidly maintained at the end. Bourgeois heroes tend to be on the industrious-apprentice model, shown in its most primitive form in the boys who arrive at the last pages of Horatio Alger working for five dollars a week with a good chance of a raise.[166] Detective stories often feature an elegant upper-class amateur who is ever so much smarter than the merely professional police; the movies and fiction magazines of two generations ago dealt a good deal with the fabulously rich, the sex novels of our day with lovers capable of prodigies of synchronized orgasm. Here again genuine realism finds its function in parody, as, for instance, *The Great Gatsby* parodies the "success story," the romantic convention contemporary with it. [*161*]

We all know, or feel that we know, why romance does this kind of thing: the reader is expected to "identify with" at least the idealized characters. And we all know, too, that this identifying process is something to be outgrown: sooner or later we recognize something immature in it. For poets and critics this is not much of a danger, but what most of them have to pass through, at some time and in some form, is identification with an author, usually as an intense form of discipleship. We often find in literature metaphors suggesting a kind of poetic reincarnation, such as Blake employs about Milton or Spenser about Chaucer, when Spenser speaks of "Thine own spirit, which doth in me survive" [*The Faerie Queene*, bk. 4, canto 2, st. 34, l. 7]. Sometimes, as with Chaucer's "Lollius," the master may be purely fictional, a symbol of the literary tradition.[167] Middleton Murry saw Keats as struggling between a good and an evil angel of identification, one named Shakespeare and the other Milton.[168] When Keats wrote *To Autumn*, says Murry, "Shakespeare had triumphed in Keats's soul,"[169] because *To Autumn* is such a good poem.

This attitude has recently revived as a form of existential criticism. Its method is brilliantly satirized in Borges's story of Pierre Menard, whose life's work it was to rewrite a couple of chapters of *Don Quixote*, not by copying them, but by total identification with Cervantes.[170] Borges quotes a passage from Cervantes and a passage from Menard which is identical with it to the letter, and urges us to see how much more historical resonance there is in the Menard copy. The satire shows us clearly that nothing will get around the fact that writer and reader are different entities in time and space, that whenever we read anything, even a letter from a friend, we are translating it into something else. Dante tells us that he could never have got through hell and purgatory without the instruction of Virgil [*Purgatorio*, canto 23, ll. 118–29]. Virgil, [*163*] many centuries later, when interviewed by Anatole France in Elysium, complained that Dante had totally misunderstood him.[171] Without going in quite the same direction that some critics have done, I think it is true that this is how the recreating of the literary tradition often has to proceed: through a process of absorption followed by misunderstanding, that is, establishing a new context. Thus an alleged misunderstanding of Ovid produced a major development in medieval poetry, and some later romance is bound up with such phrases as "Gothic revival" and "Celtic twilight," misunderstandings of earlier ages that never existed.

But if romance so often appears as a kind of naive social snobbery, what becomes of the revolutionary quality in it that we mentioned earlier, the proletarian element rejected by every cultural establishment? We remember that we found the focus of this revolutionary quality near the end of a romantic story, usually at the recognition scene. It appears in the polarizing between two worlds, one desirable and the other hateful, the triumphant upward movement of the living hero rising from the dead dragon, the point that expresses the reader's identity with a power of life strong enough to smash through any kind of barrier or danger. In Christianity the archetype of the completed romance is Christ rising from the dragon of death and hell with his redeemed captives; but the central figure need not take on such portentous overtones. The heroine who is saved from rape or sacrifice, even if she merely avoids Mr. Wrong and marries Mr. Right, is reenacting the ancient ritual which in Greek religion is called the anabasis of Kore,[172] the rising of a maiden, Psyche or Cinderella or Richardson's Pamela or Aristophanes' Peace, from a lower to a higher world.

Spenser, though speaking for an establishment, understood [*164*] this very well, and in the first book of *The Faerie Queene* he described the victory of the Protestant revolution in England under the ancient myth of St. George killing his dragon. The Waverley novels were written by a Tory, yet the defeated insurgent forces, the Jacobite Highlanders in *Waverley*, the supporters of Queen Mary in *The Abbot*, the Saxons in *Ivanhoe*, express the greatest social passion and power in those novels. The fact that Scott was a Tory is connected with his being also a historical novelist. The struggles he describes are within the cycle of history, and never suggest any ultimate transcending of history. In this respect he is a contrast with William Morris, who raises the opposite problem. How, we wonder, could a writer who was a radical socialist, very politically involved with revolutionary activities, spend so much of his time writing what often seem like very self-indulgent romances? The same question was asked, much less sympathetically, by Morris's anarchist comrades, who eventually forced him out of the party. Their attitude foreshadowed a very similar issue which appeared in the Soviet Union during the Stalin regime in the 1930s.

There is a strongly conservative element at the core of realism, an acceptance of society in its present structure, an attitude of mind that helps to make Balzac typical of realism, just as the opposite revolutionary attitude helps to make Victor Hugo typical of romanticism. The Stalinist bureaucracy adopted a doctrine of "socialist realism" as part of the authoritarian aspect of its rule, rationalized by the dogma that romanticism is a form of bourgeois ideology, and that Marxism represents the only possible combination of the revolutionary with the realistic. The essential idea of this version of "socialist realism" was protest before revolution, panegyric afterward. Genuine realism, in certain contexts, does have a revolutionary social function: [*165*] this function consists mainly in opposing, by parody, the kidnapping of romance, and of literature and culture in general, by an ascendant class. Napoleon patronized such painters as [Jacques-Louis] David, but it is Goya's *Disasters of War* that tell the truth about the kind of thing that Napoleon is and does in the world. According to the Stalinist scheme, writers outside the Soviet Union would follow this tradition of realism: writers inside it would set up a new kind of kidnapped romanticism, celebrating the glories of the *de facto* power, slightly disguised by harmless criticism and by talk about a continuing process of building socialism. Maxim Gorky gave his support to this program, though it was Gorky, in an earlier and more genuinely creative period, who clearly saw the real link between the revolutionary and the romantic.[173] It is possible that social, political, or religious revolution always, and necessarily, betrays a revolutionary ideal of which the imagination alone preserves the secret.

Similar phenomena may be observed in our own culture. The soap operas of radio and television are addressed primarily to a female audience, and feature a heroine plunged into the woes typical of so many forms of romance. But while she continually struggles against a swarm of complications, the decisive polarizing of romance does not take place. She never quite reaches what I have been calling the night world, a life so intolerable that it must end either in tragedy or in a permanent escape. This is partly so that the story, along with the financial support of its sponsors, can last indefinitely, but there is another social dimension involved.

In speaking of figures of identification I mixed up two general types. Both are in a larger sense romantic; but the princes and knights of naive romance are romantic in a way that bourgeois heroes and industrious apprentices are [*166*] not. These latter are presented under a guise of realism, often as models we could conceivably follow. The models sometimes have real-life prototypes, such as Benjamin Franklin;[174] consequently some sense of society must appear in the background, however simplified. Similarly with the soap operas just mentioned, which in some isolated areas, like Newfoundland outports, are eagerly discussed in detail over party-line telephones whenever a new instalment comes out. What is identified with here is the society being portrayed in the story, to the extent that a society is present, and such identification is a sign of a fairly thoroughgoing conservatism.

This brings us to the problem of criticism represented by Don Quixote at the puppet show or Huckleberry Finn at the circus or small children with a department-store Santa Claus.[175] What the naive, uninstructed, childlike or illusion-ridden viewer accepts as "real" a more knowledgeable and emancipated one sees to be a carefully planned show, and planned within the framework of a literary convention. It follows that the journey toward one's own identity, which literature does so much to help with, has a great deal to do with escaping from the alleged "reality" of what one is reading or looking at, and recognizing the convention behind it. The same process exists in the elementary teaching of literature, or should. The child should not "believe" the story he is told; he should not disbelieve it either, but send out imaginative roots into that mysterious world between the "is" and the "is not" which is where his own ultimate freedom lies.

Society, we said, makes a special and nonliterary use of myth, which causes it to form a mythology and eventually a mythological universe. Such a mythology surrounds us on all sides, and on several levels. The lowest level is that of the cliché mythology that soaks into us from early childhood [*167*], from parents, teachers, classmates, news media, popular culture, and the judicious mixture of flattery and threats in advertising. On this level social mythology is adjustment mythology, designed to produce the docile and obedient citizen. It "indoctrinates," as we say; not because anyone, at least in our society, wants it to or plans it that way, but because the whole enterprise is automatic and mindless, an expression not of social unity but of gregariousness. Professional educators, in North America at least, appear to be dedicated to the proposition that school children should learn as much as possible of this adjustment mythology, and as little as possible of anything else. The demand for "relevance" is a hoarse echo of the same axiom.

Every teacher of literature should realize that literary experience is only the visible tip of the verbal iceberg: below it is a subliminal area of rhetorical response, addressed by advertising, social assumptions, and casual conversation, that literature as such, on however popular a level of movie or television or comic book, can hardly reach. What confronts the teacher of literature is the student's whole verbal experience, including this subliterary nine-tenths of it. One of the things that the study of literature should do is to help the student become aware of his own mythological conditioning, especially on the more passive and critically unexamined levels. It is, of course, unlikely to do this as long as the teachers are unconscious victims of the same conditioning.

Popular romance, in whatever media it may come, is often an expression of a frivolous or silly social mythology, and a value judgment on the social mythology is likely to be more relevant to criticism than a value judgment on the literary merit. This principle increases in importance when the mythology is not merely silly but [*168*] actively vicious or evil. Take the following passage from a story in O. Henry's *The Gentle Grafter*:

> "Two months ago," says Buckingham Skinner, "I was doing well down in Texas with a patent instantaneous fire kindler, made of compressed wood ashes and benzine. I sold loads of 'em in towns where they like to burn niggers quick, without having to ask somebody for a light. And just when I was doing the best they strikes oil down there and puts me out of business. 'Your machine's too slow now, pardner,' they tells me. 'We can have a coon in hell with this here petroleum before your old flint-and-tinder truck can get him warm enough to perfess religion.'"
>
> {The narrator comments} I liked Buckingham Skinner from the start, for as good a man as ever stood over the axles and breathed gasoline smoke.[176]

This passage will illustrate, first, what such a word as "obscene" really means, and, second, that real obscenity is not neutralized by a serious literary intention, as is assumed in the futile anxieties of censorship, but is a quality of the social mythology that the writer accepts.

What we have called kidnapped romance is usually romance that expresses a social mythology of this more uncritical kind, which may be intense but is not deep, and is founded on prejudice and unexamined assumptions. R.M. Ballantyne's *The Coral Island*, a story for boys written in the nineteenth century, features three English lads who have been shipwrecked on a South Sea island. They live a happy life there for some months, but when "natives" turn up they show that they belong to an officer caste as well. It is common knowledge that William Golding's *Lord of the Flies* is in part a parody of *The Coral Island*. But it is significant that *Lord of the Flies*, appearing after the decline of [*169*] realism, is not strictly a realistic parody. It uses the same paradisal archetype as its predecessor, but develops it in a more comprehensive way, bringing out the corruption of human nature that has always been an essential part of the archetype. *The Coral Island* is by no means a stupid book, but it is, to use Robert Frost's image about realism, a somewhat overscrubbed potato: the effect of all that clean living is to produce a superficial reflex response, like the gleaming smiles of a toothpaste ad.

Rider Haggard remarked that a series of adventures was easy enough to write, but that a real story had to have a "heart," that is, a focus or centre implying a total shape with a beginning and an end. The series of adventures that he said was easy appears in the more rudimentary forms of romance represented by continuous comic strips and the interminable radio and television serials just mentioned. These in turn have a long tradition, much older than the "vast French romances" of *The Rape of the Lock* [canto 2, l. 38], of stories in which we seldom get a clear sight of progress toward a conclusion. Such stories do not end: they stop, and very frequently they can be easily started again. They are designed to provide a kind of idealized shadow of the continuum of our lives, an endless dream world in which we can keep losing ourselves.

A modulation of the endless romance is the linking together of a series of stories by a frame providing a unified setting. The root of this in human life is, possibly, the child's bedtime story: the Arabian Nights setting also preserves the sense of a threshold to a dream world. *The Canterbury Tales*, *The Faerie Queene*, Dickens's *Master Humphrey's Clock*, and Morris's *Earthly Paradise* are examples showing how powerful the impulse is to derive a sequence of romances from a setting providing some unity of place. This unity of place has been technologically achieved by [*170*] the television tube, which provides, at least in centres where there is a round-the-clock supply of programs, a shadow counterpart for the whole continuum of existence, dreaming as well as waking. The impact of television had a good deal to do with the drug cults and social hysteria of the late 1960s, which showed symptoms both of a withdrawal from waking reality and of an irritability of the sort produced by dream deprivation. More important, it made the impact of cliché mythology so intolerable that it provoked a frenzied rejection of it, followed, as such outbreaks must be, by a kind of stupor.

Unconsciously acquired social mythology, the mythology of prejudice and conditioning, is clearly also something to be outgrown: it is therapeutic to recognize and reject it, as with other repressed material. Lying beyond it is the next level of social mythology, or, roughly speaking, the area of serious belief. A belief, in this sense, is essentially a statement of a desire to attach oneself to, or live in or among, a specific kind of community. America has a genuine social mythology in which beliefs in personal liberty, democracy, and equality before law have a central place. Every major American writer will be found to have struck his roots deeply into this serious social mythology, even if he advocates civil disobedience or makes speeches in a country with which America is at war. Genuine social mythology, whether religious or secular, is also to be transcended, but transcendence here does not mean repudiating or getting rid of it, except in special cases. It means rather an individual recreation of the mythology, a transforming of it from accepted social values into the axioms of one's own activity.

The traditional attitude of society is that its concern must always be primary, and that all individual action should move within its orbit. In historical Christianity, as [*171*] in Marxism today, an intense indoctrinating process begins in childhood: the individual may be allowed to rediscover and recreate these doctrines, but without altering them to a degree that would alarm social concern. A conservative, mystical strain of social or religious acceptance runs all through romance, from the Grail stories of the Middle Ages through Novalis and George MacDonald in the nineteenth century to C.S. Lewis and Charles Williams a generation ago. For the poet, an intense commitment to certain beliefs is often a necessity: we see this particularly in religious belief, which to so many poets of the last century seemed the only possible basis on which the creative imagination could operate. But of course when beliefs are presented within literature, the impact on the reader is purely imaginative, and it is unnecessary for him to share or even sympathize with those beliefs to respond appropriately. Imaginative response transcends belief of all kinds, and this takes us back to the divergence of romance from comedy that I mentioned in the previous chapter.

Comedy ends with a festive society: it is contained by social assumptions. Belief, I am saying, is essentially a form of attachment to a community: in other words belief is also primarily social in reference, which is why the Christian myth is a comedy rather than a romance. Virgil leaves Dante at the summit of Purgatory, crowning and mitring him, making him Pope and Emperor over himself, as a man who has attained free will.[177] Then a stern and scolding Beatrice appears, Dante is reduced to a whimpering and tearful child, and the comic-providential universe closes around us again as Dante prepares to enter the City of God. But for one instant we have had a glimpse of the secular scripture, of what Wallace Stevens means when he says that the great poems of heaven and hell have been written but the great poem of earth has still to be written.[178] [*172*] All societies, including the City of God, are free only to the extent that they arrange the conditions of freedom for the individual, because the individual alone can experience freedom. This principle is, of course, as true of democracy and Marxism as it is of Christianity.

Romance has no continuing city as its final resting place. In folk tales and fairy tales the chief characters live in a kind of atomized society: there is only the most shadowy sense of a community, and their kings and princesses are individuals given the maximum of leisure, privacy, and freedom of action. In real life, of course, royal figures have even less of such things than other people: it is different in stories. The same disintegrated society reappears in the cells of hermits, the caves of ogres, the cottages hidden in forests; in the shepherds of pastoral, the knights errant who wander far from courts and castles, the nomadic ranchers and rustlers of Western stories, which are a later form of pastoral, and their descendants in the easy-riding school founded by Jack Kerouac.[179] The Bible is a divine comedy, with society gathered into one body at the end; the secular scripture is a human romance, and its ideals seem to be different.

These ideals, we saw, are commonly symbolized by some kind of paradise or park like the Biblical Eden, a world in which a humanity greatly reduced in numbers has become reconciled to nature. Such an ideal represents an attitude to nature which is the opposite of that of the cycle of violence and cunning that begins with Homer. In this cycle man is enclosed within nature, nature being something that renews but inexorably destroys again, and seems to be controlled by mysterious and capricious gods. This vision has revived in Yeats and in Robert Graves, the latter telling his son Juan that in a woman's world dominated by the white goddess of nature, man can only keep [*173*] warm in December by remembering what it was like in June.[180] But in our day we have passed through and inherited the Biblical view that there are no gods or numinous forces in nature, and that man has to find the clues to his destiny within his own institutions. The dragon-killing and giant-quelling of chivalric romance suggests a civilizing force gradually increasing its control of a turbulent natural order. The myth of Eden, similarly, suggests a final reconciliation with nature as something to be attained after the human community has been reordered. We reach the ideal of romance through a progressive bursting of closed circles, first of social mythology, whether frivolous or serious, then of nature, and finally of the comic-providential universe of Christianity and other religions, including Marxism, which contains them both.

Revolutionary social ideals are traditionally those of liberty, equality, and fraternity, and the first two seem to be particularly the concern of comedy, whose tendency it is to gather all its characters together in the final scene and assign certain rights and functions to each one. After exhausting these images, romance's last vision seems to be that of fraternity, Kant's kingdom of ends where, as in fairy tales, we are all kings and princesses.[181] The principle of the aristocracies of the past was respect for birth; the principle of fraternity in the ideal world of romance is respect rather for those who have been born, and because they have been born.

We have been using the word "cycle" to describe the total story of romance, and the simplest form of a story with Rider Haggard's "heart" or quest in it is the closed circle or *nostos* form of the *Odyssey*, where Ulysses, after massacring the suitors and hanging the servant maids, climbs back into bed with Penelope—the point at which, according to tradition, the *Odyssey* originally ended.[182] The [*174*] emotional overtones of such a closed circle may be ironic, suggesting that there is nothing worth doing that does not have to be done over again, as in E.R. Eddison's story *The Worm Ouroboros*. Sometimes, however, the irony is only half the story, and the cycle in that case becomes the only possible way of suggesting what is beyond the cycle. This is what Eliot's *East Coker* is saying in its circular motto, "In my beginning is my end"; it is what Camus means when he says that we have to think of Sisyphus as a happy man,[183] and it may be what *Finnegans Wake* is saying on its final page, in such phrases as "Till thousendsthee," just before we swing back to the beginning again. *Ulysses* concludes with the monologue of Molly Bloom, who seems a pure White Goddess figure, the incarnation of a cyclical nature who embraces and abandons one lover after another. And yet she too is an embodiment of the chaste Penelope, and at the end of her ruminations she goes back to something very like the dawn of a first love.

More frequently, the quest romance takes on a spiral form, an open circle where the end is the beginning transformed and renewed by the heroic quest. Dante's *Inferno* is a descending spiral, taking us into narrowing and unchangeable closed circles; the *Purgatorio* spiral gives us the opposite creative movement. When Dante reaches the presence of God at the end of the *Paradiso,* the universe turns inside out, becoming God-centred instead of earth-centred, an end that reverses the beginning of all things. Dante is within the orbit of the sacred scripture, where God is the creator, but the same principle of reversed movement can be associated with human creativity. Such a reversal occurs at the end of Proust, where an experience of repetition transforms Marcel's memory of his life into a potential imaginative vision, so that the narrator comes to the beginning of his book at the point where the reader [175] comes to the end of it. Time being irreversible, a return to a starting point, even in a theory of recurrence as naive as Nietzsche's, can only be a symbol for something else. The past is not returned to; it is recreated, and when time in Proust is found again (*retrouvé*), the return to the beginning is a metaphor for creative repetition.

Creative repetition is of course one of the central principles of all criticism, which has held for many centuries that poetry presents a kind of controlled hallucination: something in the past, normally accessible only to the memory, is brought into the present by the imagination. Hence, as Hobbes explains, the Greek tradition that the mother of the muses is Mnemosyne, memory. This conception of the creative function of memory is violently attacked by William Blake, who insists that "imagination has nothing to do with memory,"[184] and yet Blake is really expounding a different aspect of the same principle. For Blake the imagination brings to life the spectres of the dead, as he calls them,[185] who inhabit the memory, creation thus being to memory what resurrection is to death. The notion of a world of pure memory, where everything forever continues to be as it has been, is the core of the religious conception of hell, which is why Blake dislikes it. But of course nobody's memory is like this: all memory is selective, and the fact that it is selective is the starting point of creation. Plato's doctrine of *anamnesis* or recollection, that we can know only what we *re*-cognize or re-experience,[186] is a projection of the fact that a memory can be objectified in a conscious being, hence repeated, hence recreated.

I spoke of the end of canto 27 of the *Purgatorio*, where Virgil makes Dante his own Pope and Emperor before taking leave of him. In Yeats's *Dialogue of Self and Soul* the poet arrives at much the same place, but then splits in two. The "soul" wants to keep climbing, as Dante does, to [*176*] seek ultimate forgiveness and atonement in a world still further up. The "self," representing the creative power of the poet, looks down from the top of the world into his own memory of his past life, and sees that for him there is nothing for it but to go back into the world of love and war, of suffering and humiliation, of nausea and self-contempt, so that he may finally come back up again possessing the vision of innocence and the holiness of all things with which the poem concludes. Yeats's poem is not about reincarnation, even if Yeats thought it was: it is about the fact that creation is essentially a recreating of memory. In turning away from what the "soul" thinks of as God's world, the "self" or poet in his creation is also imitating the creative activity of God. This has been a central principle of criticism at least since Elizabethan times. Mallarmé tells us that a dice throw does not abolish chance, meaning, roughly, that human creation does not deliver us from death, though it is all that we have to fight death with. But the context of this conclusion is a work called *Igitur*, the title of which refers to the verse in Genesis about the end of the original creation: "Thus (*igitur*) the heavens and the earth were finished, and all the host of them."[187]

The frequent association of romance with the historical, such as we see in the Waverley novels, is based, I should think, on the principle that there is a peculiar emotional intensity in contemplating something, including our own earlier lives, that we know we have survived. But there is beyond this a special kind of transformation of the past which is distinctive of romance. Our descending and ascending themes showed us two contrasting organizations of human life. Themes of ascent are pervaded by struggles to escape and survive: the other side, of descent and disappearing identity, takes place in a world of violent and cunning leaders. This is the [*177*] world of order and degree, the world that tragedy and tragic irony present from the inside, the world celebrated in the famous speech about degree by Ulysses in *Troilus and Cressida* [1.3.75–137], Shakespeare's most ironic play.

Romance usually presents us with a hierarchical social order, and in what we have called kidnapped romance, this order is rationalized. Thus chivalric romance rationalizes the social structure of the feudal system, in which few medieval barons resembled the knights of the Round Table. Later writers of romance fall into a kind of sliding scale of projection and recovery in their attitude to the past. The projecting writers fall in love with the hierarchical structures that they find in earlier history, and present them as ideals to be recreated in their past forms. There is a good deal of this in Carlyle, with his oversimplified work ethic which leads him to a dream of a reactivated aristocracy. There is a good deal of it in Yeats, with his carpet-knight adulation of some very dubious leaders and his fatalistic "vision" of history, and a good deal of it in such writers as G.K. Chesterton who think within a mythology of decline from earlier standards of authority, and identify recreation with their revival. Here again I am not speaking of literary merit, but of the quality of social mythology accepted. In projected romance the past becomes the mirror of the future, and we remember from our survey of descent themes that remaining imprisoned within a mirror world keeps us in the basement of reality.

William Morris is an example of a writer whose attitude to the past is one of creative repetition rather than of return. Morris admired the Middle Ages to the point of fixation, and yet the social reference of his medievalism is quite different from that of Carlyle, or even Ruskin, who so strongly influenced him. According to Morris, the Middle Ages appears right side up, so to speak, when we see it [*178*] as a creation of artists, not in its reflected or projected form as a hierarchy; when we realize that the genuine creators of medieval culture were the builders and painters and romancers, not the warriors or the priests. For him the fourteenth century was the time when, with the Peasants' Revolt, something like a genuine proletariat appeared on the social scene, its political attitude expressed in John Ball's question, where were the "gentlemen" in the working society of Adam and Eve?[188] In *News from Nowhere*, the "dream of John Ball" (the title of another work of Morris) comes true: the people in that happy future world are an equal society of creative workers. They have not returned to the fourteenth century: they have turned it inside out.

As we make the first great move from projection to the recovery of myth, from return to recreation, the focus of interest shifts from heroes and other elements of narrative toward the process of creating them. The real hero becomes the poet, not the agent of force or cunning whom the poet may celebrate. In proportion as this happens, the inherently revolutionary quality in romance begins to emerge from all the nostalgia about a vanished past. Even for Yeats the same thing happens in his less occulted moments: in his early play *The King's Threshold*, for instance, where we are shown that kings would have no motivation to act like kings if poets did not provide the imaginative conception of kingship.

Don Quixote sounds like an unlikely source for such a romantic revolutionary vision, but there is one there nonetheless. The Quixote who tries to actualize in his life the romances he has been reading is a psychotic, though a psychotic of unusual literary interest. I suppose psychosis, or certain forms of it at least, could almost be defined as an attempt to identify one's life "literally" with an imaginative projection. But in the second part of the book, Sancho Panza is given an island to rule, and rules it very well: [*179*] while he is doing so, Don Quixote offers him advice which is surprisingly sensible.[189] Earlier I quoted Borges as describing the story we are calling the secular scripture as a search for some dearly loved Mediterranean island. I suspect that Borges's island has a good deal to do with Cervantes' island, a society where Sancho Panza, who is not a Machiavellian prince but one of us, is ruler, and where Don Quixote, possibly the greatest figure in the history of romance, has recovered his proper function as a social visionary.

We are perhaps beginning to see at this point that to recreate the past and bring it into the present is only half the operation. The other half consists of bringing something into the present which is potential or possible, and in that sense belongs to the future. This recreation of the possible or future or ideal constitutes the wish-fulfilment element in romance, which is the normal containing form, as archaism or the presentation of the past is the normal content. Thus the recreation of romance brings us into a present where past and future are gathered, in Eliot's phrase [*Burnt Norton*, pt. 2, l. 19]. It is also Eliot who shows us that the starting point of creation is the impinging of wish-thinking on the memory, the intrusion of "it might have been" into "it was" that we encounter at the opening of *Burnt Norton*. Eliot's rose garden, which is created out of this intrusion, seems very remote from Morris's vision in which the preindustrial craftsmanship of the Middle Ages provides a model for a postindustrial Arcadia, but they are symbolic first cousins for all that, Adam and Eve being their common grandparents. Such a union of past and future in a present vision of a pastoral, paradisal, and radically simplified form of life obviously takes on a new kind of urgency in an age of pollution and energy crisis, and helps to explain why romance seems so contemporary a form of literary experience.

Technology, for capitalism and still more for Communism [*180*], seemed at one time to promise the kind of human ascendancy over nature that would accompany the final recovery of myth, but the poets have dragged their feet in its celebration. Blake, D.H. Lawrence, Morris, Yeats, Pound, are only a few of those who have shown marked hostility to technology and have refused to believe that its peaceful and destructive aspects can be separated. The poets see nothing imaginative in a domination of nature which expresses no love for it, in an activity founded on will, which always overreacts, in a way of life marked by a constant increase in speed, which means also an increase in introversion and the breaking down of genuine personal relationships. The great exception, the literary movement that was expected to seize on technology as its central theme, was assumed to be science fiction. But the way in which science fiction, as it has developed from hardware fantasy into software philosophical romance, has fallen into precisely the conventions of romance as outlined here is so extraordinary that I wish I had the time and the erudition to give it a separate treatment. Visions of utopias, or properly running communities, belong in its general area; but, in modern science fiction, anti-utopias, visions of regression or the nightmarish insect states of imaginative death, must outnumber the positive utopias by at least fifty to one.

The guides who supervise tourists in developing countries, especially Marxist ones, always want to take them to the collective farms, engineering projects, and other monuments of the existing regime, and are often puzzled or annoyed when the tourists want to see the works of art that were produced in the old exploiting days. The reason for this takes us further into the theory of criticism than we might suppose. Such words as "classic" or "masterpiece" tell us nothing about the structure of literary works: they [*181*] refer to social acceptance, and there are no inherent formal qualities that classics or masterpieces have that other works do not have. If there were, criticism would be a much easier occupation, if a less rewarding one. It is very different with the sense of formal design in, say, the cultural products in a museum, which may range from Benin bronzes to Viking ships, from Chinese pottery to Peruvian textiles. We know that all the cruelty and folly of which man is capable was all around these artefacts when they were produced, and that some of that cruelty and folly may be reflected from the art itself. Nevertheless there is something in the energy of design and the purity of outline that lifts them clear of all this. Whatever the culture was, its designed products belong in the state of innocence,[190] as remote from the evils of that culture as Marina was from the brothel in *Pericles*. I have not given this example at random: Marina in the brothel represents a corresponding power of formal design in the literary arts, and is therefore, like all highly concentrated art, in one sense art talking about itself.

We started this argument with a distinction between myth and fable in which myth has priority in social importance. This in our tradition has given the Bible, as the epic of which God is the hero, the central place. We said that a sexual creation myth, which has a natural focus on an earth-mother figure, was superseded, in our tradition, by an artificial creation myth in which the world was made by a sky-father. So far as such myths condition our sense of external reality, the change seems to have been a retrograde step. It is impossible to reconcile a story of God making things in roughly their present forms with the real story of nature, where an evolution of complex organisms out of simpler ones gives a much more satisfactory vision of "genesis," however many gaps there may still be in our [*182*] knowledge. The artificial myth won out, obviously, because it made reality humanly intelligible, giving us a world that begins and ends in time, that has a top and a bottom in at least metaphorical space. It looks at the moment as though these human limitations make the artificial creation myth only a projection of the fact that man creates and makes things. But it still has a powerful grip on the human imagination, and one wonders if there are other factors suggesting that it may be something more than that.

We noticed that in this myth God makes only a model world, and that the difference between it and the world we are in now has to be accounted for by supplying the alienation myth of a "fall" to complete the story of creation. In the great cycle of descent and ascent that we have been studying in romance, themes of descent are connected with the establishing of order, authority, and hierarchy, and the artificial creation myth is the first narrative unit of that descent. The creation-fall is thus the starting point of the whole complex of social acceptance, in which laws, rituals, customs, and the authority of warriors and priests and kings are all manifestations of the otherness of the spirit I mentioned earlier. Everything man has that seems most profoundly himself is thought of as coming to him from outside, descending from the most ancient days in time, coming down from the remotest heights in space. We belong to something before we are anything, and, just as an infant's world has an order of parents already in it, so man's first impulse is to project figures of authority, or precedence in time and space, stretching in an iron chain of command back to God.

Where we came from is the main subject of the myths that carry the primary authority of social concern, and play so large a part in rationalizing our acceptance of such [*183*] authority. The imagination, as it reflects on this world, sees it as a world of violence and cunning, *forza* and *froda*. The typical agent of cunning is a woman, whose main instrument of will is her bed: in the *Iliad* even the greatest of goddesses, Hera, decoys Zeus in this way in an effort to aid the Greeks [bk. 14]. Thus the *forza-froda* cycle is also that of Ares and Eros, both of which, for human beings, end in Thanatos or death. Ares and Eros are functionaries of Venus, whose alternative form is Diana of the triple will, the white goddess who always kills, and whose rebirth is only for herself.

Romance, the kernel of fable, begins an upward journey toward man's recovery of what he projects as sacred myth. At the bottom of the mythological universe is a death and rebirth process which cares nothing for the individual; at the top is the individual's regained identity. At the bottom is a memory which can only be returned to, a closed circle of recurrence: at the top is the recreation of memory. In romance violence and sexuality are used as rocket propulsions, so to speak, in an ascending movement. Violence becomes melodrama, the separating of heroes from villains, angels of light from giants of the dark. Sexuality becomes a driving force with a great deal of sublimation in it. In the traditional romance, where the heroine is so often a virgin reaching her first sexual contact on the last page, the erotic feeling is sublimated for the action of the story. The much more thoroughgoing sublimation in our two greatest Eros poets, Plato and Dante, needs no further elaboration here.

As we go up, we find ourselves surrounded by images of increased participation: with human society, in the festive endings of comedy; with nature, in pastoral and Arcadian imagery; with aspects of divinity, in myths of redemption. The conception of evolution is an ascending metamorphosis [*184*] myth of this kind, attaching us to the whole family of living things. Goethe's essays on the metamorphoses of plants link the conception of evolution to that of the secular scripture, and introduce some of the traditional ascent motifs, connecting straight-line ascent with the symbolically "male" and spiral ascent with the symbolically "female."[191] The end of fable, as the total body of verbal imagination that man constructs, brings us back to the beginning of myth, the model world associated with divine creation in Genesis.

The model world seems to us now, however, not like a past state to return to, but an inner model or social vision to be recreated out of our "lower" world of experience, the real creative power, as we see it, being something that comes from below. What the artificial creation myth appears to be telling us is that, somehow or other, models for human creation have been implanted in the human mind. However they got there, and whoever gave them to us (and the traditional metaphors are of course expendable), in developing the forms of culture and civilization we seem to be recreating something that we did not get from nature. Whether this is true or not, the artificial creation myth still has an essential function for us: it emphasizes the uniqueness, the once-for-all quality, in the creative act, and helps to deliver us, if not from death or Mallarmé's "chance," at least from the facile ironies of an endlessly turning cycle.

In the descending hierarchical order, where the individual is primarily a unit of his society, there is a sense of growing isolation that intensifies as we reach a place in which we feel that, as Sartre says, hell is other people.[192] The creative act is an individualizing act, hence, for all the sense of participation, we are also returning to a second kind of isolation. As Goethe also notes about the ascending [*185*] metamorphosis of plants, there is a process of renunciation in the ascent as well, a cutting off of everything from the liberated individual. The cells of the hermits who so often appear in high romance have real-life prototypes in Thoreau's Walden retreat, and in Indian yoga, with its conception of identity as something to be gained by suppressing the metamorphoses of the mind. We have already found expressions of this in the "penseroso" cadences of romance: it also comes into the theme of the renounced quest, the story for example of Shelley's Prometheus, who becomes free as soon as he stops trying to fight the tyrannical Jupiter whom he has created himself, and keeps in business by resisting. The same theme dominates the story told by Wagner and retold by Tolkien, of a stolen ring that has to be given back, a return that achieves its recreation by a creatively negative act, a cancelling out of a wrong action.

The artificial creation story in Genesis culminates in the Sabbath vision, in which God contemplates what he has made. In human life creation and contemplation need two people, a poet and a reader, a creative action that produces and a creative response that possesses. We may recall that the Dante who achieved freedom of will at the top of Purgatory was not merely Dante the poet, but Dante the student of

Virgil. The first step in the recovery of myth is the transfer of the centre of interest from hero to poet. The second, and perhaps final, stage is reached when the poet entrusts his work to his reader, as Joyce, after spending seventeen years on the great dream of Finnegan, handed it over to what he called the "ideal reader suffering from an ideal insomnia."[193]

Such a reader of *Finnegans Wake* clearly would need some heroic qualities, but even with less difficult works it is still true that there is a perspective from which the [*186*] reader, the mental traveller, is the hero of literature, or at least of what he has read. As we have seen, the message of all romance is *de te fabula:* the story is about you; and it is the reader who is responsible for the way literature functions, both socially and individually. His duty may not constitute what a once famous pious work called the whole duty of man,[194] but there is no whole duty without it. One's reading thus becomes an essential part of a process of self creation and self-identity that passes beyond all the attached identifications, with society or belief or nature, that we have been tracing. Such a reader, contemplating the cycle of descent into subjects and objects, where we die each other's lives, as Heraclitus says,[195] and of ascent to identity where we live each other's deaths, is a Moses who can see the Promised Land [Deuteronomy 3:27–8, 34:1–4], in contrast to the Joshua who merely conquers Canaan, and so begins another cycle of descent.

Moses' vision was the climax of his career as the leader of a wandering people. The normal form of romance is the quest story that reflects the cyclical movement we have been tracing; but we also found continuous or "endless" forms in various types of popular literature. There is always something of the nomadic in romance, something that recalls its heritage of travelling folk tales and ballads. Recurrently, from Surtees' fox-hunting stories to the Biblical vision of two people in a garden that stretched from Egypt to (according to Josephus) India, we have seen romance associating itself with an imaginative uprooting, a drive over and across everything settled and planted and built. It is perhaps easiest to see this "endless" form in the great Oriental romances, such as the Japanese tale of Genji,[196] where it is congenial to religious and other perspectives in the culture; but it is inherent in romance, and is returning in our own literature today. [*187*]

In the last scene of *A Midsummer Night's Dream* that very shrewd critic Hippolyta remarks that Peter Quince's play is the silliest stuff she has ever heard. But, says Theseus, whose conception of the imagination is confused because he is preoccupied with his own "image" as a gracious prince, the worst plays are no worse than the best, "if imagination amend them" [5.1.212]. It must be your imagination, then, says Hippolyta, and not theirs. For Theseus the one thing good in Peter Quince's play is the fact that it is offered to him, and he confers merit on it by accepting it. Such an attitude would be more appropriate for God, perhaps, than a Duke of Athens, but then Theseus thinks of himself as in some degree a human representative of God. It is Hippolyta who has, however unconsciously, expressed the real goal of humanism. In the world of order and hierarchy there are literary hierarchies too, the order of "classics" and "masterpieces." Genuine humanism is not a return to this order, but an imaginative recreation of it: we admire them and do something else, as Hopkins says.[197] Homer and Shakespeare, both of whom have minstrels and *jongleurs* among their characters, do not lose their importance in our experience when the wandering tribes of folk tale and anecdote, of popular story and ballad and nursery rhyme, find a home there too. The mythological universe is not an ordered hierarchy but an interpenetrating world, where every unit of verbal experience is a monad reflecting all the others. This is the human counterpart of the vision symbolized in Genesis as the Sabbath vision: it is how the world looks after the ego has collapsed. The "outside" world disappears, but it does not disappear into the "inside": that kind of metaphor has been left far behind.

The greatest romance in English literature, and one of the supreme romances of the world, is Spenser's *Faerie* [*188*] *Queene*. The six books of this epic end with the quest of courtesy, the word of man, as the integrating force of the human community. This sixth book is full of the pastoral imagery which belongs to the higher reaches of romance; the poet himself appears near the end of it, and the enemy of courtesy, the Blatant Beast, slander or bad words, escapes again at the end. His escape suggests an ironic closed-circle containing form for the whole epic. Then, after his six efforts of creation, Spenser gives us an epilogue or Sabbath vision, in the great poem called the *Mutabilitie Cantos*. At the end of this poem the poet identifies himself with God's contemplative vision of the model created world, and the last line reads: "O that great Sabbaoth God graunt me that Sabaoths sight!" There is a pun on Sabbath and Sabaoth, "hosts," as the liberated subject, no longer a subject, contemplates the objects, no longer objects, in all their infinite variety. Spenser thus passes on to his reader the crowning act of self-identity as the contemplating of what has been made, including what one has recreated by possessing the canon of man's word as well as God's. As Wittgenstein said a generation ago, in a much misunderstood aphorism, in such an act of possession there are no more words, only the silence that marks the possession of words.[198] A good deal has been said since then about the relation of language and silence, but real silence is the end of speech, not the stopping of it, and it is not until we have shared something of this last Sabbath vision in our greatest romance that we may begin to say that we have earned the right to silence.

2

Romance as Masque

16 October 1975

Originally presented at the Second Alabama Symposium on English and American Literature, which was devoted to Shakespearean romances, held at the University of Alabama, 16–18 October 1975. From SM, *148–78, where it was first published together with (as pt. 1) "Old and New Comedy," a paper originally given as a lecture in Stratford, England and revised for publication in* Shakespeare Survey, *22 (1969): 1–5. The entire essay was reprinted, with minor changes, in* Shakespeare's Romances Reconsidered, *ed. Carol McGinnis Kay and Henry E. Jacobs (Lincoln: University of Nebraska Press, 1978), 11–39. The typescripts are in the NFF, 1988, box 5, files hh–kk, and preliminary notes are in the NFF, 1991, box 36, file 11.*

I

Let us start with the two comic genres of Old Comedy and New Comedy, familiar from Greek literature.[1] The distinguishing feature of New Comedy, the form predominant from Roman times to the nineteenth century, is the teleological plot, in which, as a rule, an alienated lover moves toward sexual fulfilment. New Comedy reaches its *telos* in the final scene, which is superficially marriage, and, more profoundly, a rebirth. A new society is created on the stage in the last moments of a typical New Comedy, and is often expanded by a recognition scene and a restoring of a birthright. The recognition is connected with the secret of somebody's birth in the common device of the foundling plot. Simpler and equally popular is the comedy in which a hero, after many setbacks, succeeds in doing something that wins him the heroine and a new sense of identity.

In such a structure the characters are essentially functions of the plot. However fully realized they may be, they are always organically related to the roles on which the plot turns, whether senex, parasite, buffoon, or bragging rival. The *commedia dell'arte* indicates with great clarity how a group of stock characters, related to a stock plot, is the basis of the comic structures of Shakespeare and Molière, as both of these dramatists show many affinities with the *commedia dell'arte*. In Ben Jonson's "humour" theory the New Comedy conception of character as a plot function is rationalized in a most ingenious way.[2] A character who is, by definition, essentially what his context in the plot makes him to be obviously has something predictable at his basis. The humour is also, by definition, a character dominated by a predictable reaction. But predictability of response is also one of the main sources of the comic mood, as has been noted by a number of theorists of comedy down to Bergson. Therefore, in a "comedy of humours," comic structure, comic characterization, and comic mood are rigorously unified. A similar unity forms the basis for the "well-made play" of Scribe and Sardou in the nineteenth century, a type of drama well within the New Comedy tradition. Many of Jonson's plays, unhappily, especially the later ones, were so "well made" that they failed on the stage through overelaborateness.

New Comedy developed two main forms: the romantic form of Shakespeare and the more realistic and displaced form of the neo-Classical tradition, in which the greatest name is Molière. The more realistic such comedy becomes, the more it is in danger of becoming a sentimental domestic comedy, like the *comédie larmoyante* of the eighteenth century. A combination of realistic treatment and New Comedy structure has a tendency to sentimentality inherent in it, as its theme approximates very closely the favourite rubric of the agony column: "Come home; all is forgiven." Molière focuses nearly all the dramatic interest on a central "humour" or blocking figure, whose particular folly, whether avarice or snobbery or hypochondria, helps to keep the tone well away from the sentimental. In Sheridan and Goldsmith the effort to achieve a dry and witty texture is more of a strain. The domestic virtues do not appear to have attracted the loyalty of a major dramatic genius, unless we wish to call Beethoven a major dramatic genius: *Fidelio* is a bachelor's tribute to domestic felicity, but the extraordinary unevenness of the music perhaps indicates some doubt in his mind.[3]

Eventually the New Comedy structure deserted the stage for the domestic novel, where a sentimental tone is easier to accommodate. The foundling plot reappears in [Fielding's] *Tom Jones* and is a standard feature of Dickens. The conception of characterization in Dickens is very close to that of the Jonsonian humour, except that the looser fictional form can find room for a great number of peripheral characters who are not directly concerned in the central plot.[4] But when English drama revived towards the end of the nineteenth century, the formulas of New Comedy were used mainly for purposes of parody, parody being the usual sign in literature that some conventions are getting worn out. We begin with mysterious-heir parodies in Gilbert and Sullivan, notably in *H.M.S. Pinafore* and *The Gondoliers*; then we have Wilde's urbane spoof of the foundling plot in *The Importance of Being Earnest*.

Wilde's contemporary, Bernard Shaw, was well aware of the extent to which some standard New Comedy devices had already been parodied by Ibsen. Shaw's parodies of New Comedy recognition scenes include the ingenious device that enables Undershaft to adopt his son-in-law as his successor in *Major Barbara*, and the discovery in *Arms and the Man* that Captain Bluntschli is of the highest social rank possible in his country, being an ordinary Swiss citizen, besides being made rich enough, by inheriting a hotel business, to upstage his rival Sergius. A more conventional type of New Comedy concealed-parentage plot is parodied in *You Never Can Tell*. In the next generation, the writer who most closely followed the New Comedy structure as laid down by Plautus and Terence was P.G. Wodehouse.[5] In other words, the teleological New Comedy structure seems to have dropped out of the centre of "serious" literature in the twentieth century.

In this situation writers of comedy clearly have to do something else, and what they are doing may be easier to understand if we think of Old Comedy not simply as a form used by Aristophanes which died with him—in fact before him—but as in a larger structural sense a permanent genus of comedy, open in any age to writers bored or inhibited by other conventions, or suspecting that their audiences are. When we look at Old Comedy in this way, it begins to expand into *the* alternative genus to New Comedy.

The structure of Old Comedy is dialectical rather than teleological, and its distinguishing feature is the contest or *agon*. This feature makes for a processional or sequential form, in which characters may appear without introduction and disappear without explanation. In this form, characters are not functions of a plot, but vehicles or embodiments of a contest. The dramatic contest of Old Comedy is as a rule not simply between personalities as such, but between personalities as representatives of larger social forces. These forces may be those of some form of class struggle, as in Brecht, or they may be specific crises like a war or an election, or psychological drives or attitudes of mind. In Aristophanes they are often the forces associated with demagogues in Athens, like Cleon, who were obsessed with prosecuting the war against Sparta. Such a form is an appropriate one for introducing historical or contemporary figures. We recall how Socrates and Euripides appear in Aristophanes;[6] in Bernard Shaw, who shows the transition to Old Comedy conventions very clearly, we have the caricatures of Asquith and Lloyd George in *Back to Methusaleh*; and this prepares the way for more recent plays about Churchill, the Pope, and various analogues of Hitler. Such characters may also come from literature: I think, as a random example, of Tennessee Williams's *Camino Real*, which begins with Don Quixote and Sancho Panza entering from the audience in a way curiously reminiscent of *The Frogs*.

We notice in Aristophanes that while the *agon* may conclude with the victory of something the dramatist approves of, it may equally well be a victory of something patently absurd, as in *The Birds* or *Ecclesiazusae*. A comic structure based on a contest in which absurdity is the victor is clearly anti-teleological, and the greatest possible contrast to the more idealistic New Comedy. So, although Aristophanes himself is a high-spirited writer, full of jokes and slapstick, the form he uses, in its larger context, is also an appropriate form for black or absurd comedy. Even in him the hostile personal attacks, while they may have been permitted for what were in origin religious reasons, are not simply all in good fun. We may rationalize the guying of Socrates and Euripides on this basis, but there is still Cleon. The darker tone latent in Old Comedy was recognized in Elizabethan times: Puttenham says, for example: "this bitter poem called the old *Comedy* being disused and taken away, the new *Comedy* came in place, more civil and pleasant a great deal."[7] It was doubtless the sardonic mood of *Every Man out of his Humour* that made Jonson speak of it as close to Old Comedy, though it is still within the conventions of New Comedy in its structure. In our day the black comedy is normal, but half a century ago, when Chekhov showed characters slowly freezing in the grip of a dying class, many audiences found it difficult to believe that *The Cherry Orchard* or *The Three Sisters* were comedies at all.

New Comedy may go either in a romantic or in a realistic direction: one typical development of Old Comedy is towards fantasy, which now seems to us a peculiarly modern technique. Where characters are embodiments of social or psychological conflicts, the conception of the individual as defined mainly by the "sane" or waking consciousness of ordinary experience is only one of many possible points of view. In New Comedy we are continually aware of the predominance of the sense of experience: we notice this, for example, in the rigid social hierarchy of Shakespearean comedy, which the action of the play never essentially disturbs. Old Comedy, by contrast, may be called the drama of unchained being. In Aristophanes some of the characters may be gods, as in *The Birds*, or the dead, as in *The Frogs*, or allegories, as in *Peace*. A similar tendency to introduce characters who are not coterminous with the bodies of individuals is marked in the theatre of the absurd, especially in Ionesco. One direction of this tendency is the archetypal characterization that we find, for instance, in [Beckett's] *Waiting for Godot*, where the two main characters identify themselves with a number of representative figures, such as the two thieves crucified with Christ.

Waiting for Godot is also, in one of its aspects, a parody of the vaudeville dialogues, the long shapeless rigmaroles which used to be packed around the "feature film" in my youth. Such verbal filler occasionally appears in legitimate drama, as in the first scene of Shaw's *The Apple Cart*, which dimly recalls the "well-made play" convention of introducing the story and atmosphere through such devices as a heroine–confidante conversation at the beginning. In fact a good deal of the texture of many Shaw plays consists of a type of cross-talk dialogue which bears much the relation to Old Comedy that the *commedia dell'arte* does to New Comedy. In more sophisticated versions of such dialogue, as we have it in certain forms of night club entertainment (e.g., Nichols and May),[8] it becomes more clearly a verbal *agon*. When the contest is one of incident rather than words, we may have the loose sequential structure of some of the early Chaplin films, where there is a series of collisions between the hero and a number of unsympathetic antagonists, very similar in form to, for example, the last part of Aristophanes' *The Acharnians*.

In New Comedy the essential meaning of the play, or what Aristotle calls its *dianoia* [*Poetics*, chap. 6], is bound up with the revelation of the plot, but such a meaning may be crystallized in a number of sententious axioms that express reflections arising from the various stages of the plot. These sententious maxims are one of the best-known features of New Comedy rhetoric. Old Comedy is less sententious and more argumentative than New Comedy, hence it can find a place for the long harangue or monologue, which tends to disrupt the action of a New Comedy, and appears in it only as a technical *tour de force*, like the speech of Jaques on the seven ages of man [*As You Like It*, 2.7.139–66]. In Aristophanes we sometimes have a direct address to the audience, technically called *parabasis*; in Shaw the parabasis is transferred to a preface which the audience is expected to read along with the play; and many recent comedies not only include but are based on monologue, as in several plays of Beckett and in Albee's *Zoo Story*.

As we can see from Aristophanes' use of a chorus, Old Comedy, because of its looser processional form, can be more spectacular than New Comedy. In New Comedy, once we go beyond the incidental songs that we find in Shakespeare, music and spectacle tend to caricature the complications of the plot, as in [Beaumarchais's] *The Marriage of Figaro*. But Old Comedy is in its nature closer to musical comedy; and we notice how the plays of Shaw, despite their intensely verbal texture, often make surprisingly good musical comedies. Again, the fact that Old Comedy is less preoccupied with the game of love and the rituals of upper- or middle-class courtship make it a better medium for a franker and more explicit treatment of the workings of the sexual instinct. Even the scurrility which is so conspicuous in Aristophanes recurs in *MacBird*[9] and similar forms of undercover drama.

Of modern dramatists, perhaps T.S. Eliot shows most clearly the conflict between the two types of comedy. Eliot begins his dramatic efforts with the exuberant and superbly original *Sweeney Agonistes*, subtitled *Fragment of an Agon*, where, besides the obvious and avowed influence of Aristophanes, many of the features noted above appear, such as the assimilation to musical comedy and vaudeville forms. When he settles down to write seriously for the stage, however, we get such confections as *The Confidential Clerk*, where the main influence is Euripides' *Ion*, usually taken as the starting point of New Comedy. But *The Confidential Clerk* seems, in comparison with *Sweeney Agonistes*, a somewhat pedantic joke, an attempt to do over again what Oscar Wilde (and, for that matter, Gilbert) had already done with more freshness.

Shakespeare's comedies conform for the most part to a romantic development of New Comedy. But Shakespeare was a versatile experimenter, and there is at least one play which comes close to the genus of Old Comedy as we have been dealing with it here. This play is *Troilus and Cressida*. Here the characters are well-known figures from history or literature; the structure is a simple sequential one, built up on the background movement of Helen from Greece to Troy and the foreground movement of Cressida in the reverse direction; the characters are both embodiments and prisoners of the social codes they adopt, and so far as the action of the play itself is concerned, the only clear victor of the contest is absurdity. There is no fantasy in the play, except in the sense in which the Trojan chivalric code is fantasy, but the characterization is archetypal, with a strong sense that the Trojan War, the beginning of secular history, is establishing the pattern for all the history that follows. We find this in the two tremendous speeches of Ulysses on degree and on time, the two primary categories of life in this world, and in Pandarus's remark: "let all pitiful goers-between be call'd to the world's end after my name; call them all Pandars" [3.3.200–2]. The reasons why this play seems a peculiarly "modern" one, and is often performed in contemporary dress, should be clear by now.

New Comedy, especially in its more romantic or Shakespearean form, tends to be an ideal structure with strong analogies to religion. The sense in which Christianity is a divine comedy is a New Comedy sense: the hero of the Christian comedy is Christ, and the heroine who becomes his bride is the reborn society of the Christian Church. Similar affinities between romantic New Comedy and religious myth may occur outside Christianity, as we see in Sanskrit plays, notably [Kalidasa's] *Sakuntala*. Old Comedy is a more existential form in which a central theme is mockery, which may include mockery of the gods, above or below. The presiding genius of New Comedy is Eros, but the presiding genius of Old Comedy is more like Prometheus, a titanic power involved by his contempt for the gods in a chaotic world of absurdity and anguish.

There are two major structural principles in literature: the principle of cyclical movement, from life to death to rebirth, usually symbolized by the solar and seasonal cycles of nature, and the principle of polarity, where an ideal or attractive world, described or implied, is contrasted with an absurd, repulsive, or evil one. In New Comedy the containing form is cyclical: the teleological action moves toward the new life or reborn society of the final scene. The principle of polarity exists within this, as, say, the opposition of a father to his son's desire to marry the heroine. In Old Comedy, where the contest between two contrasting sets of values is usually very prominent, polarity is as a rule the containing form. That is, Old Comedy suggests some kind of social norm implicitly contrasting with its main action in the audience's mind, something in the light of which the absurdity of that action appears properly absurd.

There are glimpses of this in Aristophanes, as in the festival of Dionysus in *The Archarnians*, but there is no consistently idealized picture of life presented in his plays. Similarly in New Comedy, idealized life occurs not so much in the action as in the kind of "lived happily ever after" life that is often assumed to begin at the end of the action.

The comedy of the English Renaissance was confined to New Comedy for many reasons, of which perhaps the simplest and most obvious is censorship, combined with the clerical, and more particularly puritan, disapproval of theatres generally. An age in which *Mucedorus* could be denounced as morally corrupting and Sir Thomas More['s *Utopia*] treated like a revolutionary manifesto was clearly not an age for an Aristophanes.[10] We notice that *Troilus and Cressida* was one of the least popular plays of an otherwise quite popular dramatist. Yet the rigid New Comedy frame was also a hampering one, and although romance is equally rigid in its conventions, and masque far more so, romance and masque both represent to some extent two directions of dramatic experiment away from the established form.

II

In the masque the organizing principle is that of polarity, the contrast between the two orders symbolized by the two parts into which it was divided, the antimasque and the masque proper. The antimasque normally came first (Middleton even spells it "antemasque"), and it often depicted the grotesque, the ribald, or whatever the audience was ready to accept as socially substandard. Bacon, in his brilliant little essay on masques and triumphs, lists antimasque figures as "fools, satyrs, baboons, wild-men, antics, beasts, sprites, witches, Ethiops, pigmies, turquets, nymphs, rustics, Cupids, statua's moving, and the like."[11] The masque proper was a stately and elaborate ceremonial in honour of a distinguished person, frequently royal. The theme was usually allegorical or Classical, of a kind that often required a good deal of explanation when printed, especially when Ben Jonson was the author. Such a theme was appropriate to the elitism of the setting, the Classical deities clearly having been originally created on the analogy of an aristocracy. The actors of the later and more elaborate antimasques were often professionals; those in the masque proper more likely to be lords and ladies whose names were proudly listed in the printed versions. Highbrow anxieties about mingling upper and lower classes in the plays of the popular theatre were seldom ruffled by a masque, which tended to make social distinctions an essential theme in the spectacle. In Jonson especially the general idea is that the antimasque represents a parody or burlesque of something of which the real form is presented later in direct association with the king, or the most eminent figure present.

The masque thus held up an idealizing mirror to its audience, and not only dramatized its stratified social structure, but also in its imagery reflected the whole religious and philosophical cosmology which rationalized that structure. In this cosmology the world began with an act of creation in which a divine power imposed an order on the turbulence of chaos. The order is often called a harmony and is symbolized by music; the creative power is also the power of love, love being, on the purely automatic level of "attraction," the force that enables the warring principles of chaos to separate into the four elements, each of which keeps to its own place. Creation takes the form of a hierarchy or chain of being, and the hierarchy of Jacobean society, the chain of authority depending from the king, continues the natural order of things in its social and political aspects. At every point there is a political and a cosmological parallel: at the bottom of the chain of being is chaos; at the bottom of society are the corresponding elements of anarchy and unrest.

The king, therefore, not only rules by divine right but is a visible emblem of the authority of God. Considering that Jonson remarked to Drummond of Hawthornden that Donne's *Anniversaries* were blasphemous because he said things about Elizabeth Drury that should only have been said about the Virgin Mary,[12] it may seem strange that Jonson sometimes speaks of King James in terms that would be more appropriate to Christ. In *Love Freed from Ignorance and Folly*, the action turns on guessing riddles of which the right answers are Britain and King James: the riddles themselves come from some paradoxes of Nicholas of Cusa, where the right answer is God.[13] Similarly in *Oberon*:

> 'Tis he, that stays the time from turning old,
> And keeps the age up in a head of gold.
> That in his own true circle still doth run;
> And holds his course as certain as the sun.
> He makes it ever day, and ever spring,
> Where he doth shine, and quickens every thing
> Like a new nature: so that true to call
> Him by his title, is to say, He's all. [ll. 350–7]

But what seems like a rather brutal flattery is consistent with the genre that Jonson was working in and did so much to create. We may find it hard to realize what a strain these masques must have been on the people in whose honour they were held, not least the king. He, when present, was always at the centre of the whole show, being, like Ariel, an actor in it, however passive, as well as an auditor. It is understandable that the few remarks recorded of James at masques should betray an exasperated weariness at being dragged out to so many such entertainments. It is clear that sometimes he would have given his crown to possess the equivalent of that bastion of democratic liberties, the television button, which can turn the whole foolish noise into silence and darkness, leaving not a rack behind.

Prospero's speech after the masque in *The Tempest* [4.1.156], just echoed, expresses with definitive eloquence another characteristic of the masque: its transience. Like a miniature World's Fair, where a whole city is set up and torn down, the masque was an enormously expensive and variegated performance which glittered for a night and disappeared. Some of the printed texts give a sense of trying desperately to salvage something of the intense experience of the original production. "These things are but toys" is Bacon's opening remark in his essay ["Of Masques and Triumphs," 416], and the masque does have something of the cultural quality that Fabergé symbolized in a later age, of elaborate "devices" or playthings for a leisure class.[14] The flickering light of candles and torches must have greatly increased the sense of unreality, almost to a point of hallucination. The masque, in short, irresistibly suggests the imagery of magic or summoned-up illusion.

This was the aspect of the masque that got Jonson down: it seems ironic that an author with so strong a sense of the permanence of literature, who was unique in his day for his anxiety to get his plays into print, should have been associated with a fragile and highly specialized dramatic development that had so little significance outside its immediate setting and occasion. Jonson was proud of his ability to write masques, naturally, but the feeling that Inigo Jones,[15] with his endlessly resourceful stage effects, was the real magician and stole the show from him every time, was hard on his self-respect. To preserve that self-respect he clung to the cosmology which the masque dramatized. For him the masque consisted of a perishable body, created by Inigo Jones, and an immortal soul, the poetry that he could supply. The body was also represented by the antimasque, the epiphany of temporary disorder or confusion obliterated by the real masque, which comes to a focus in the figure in front. The *de jure* monarch in particular, who represents the continuity of order in society, is a visible emblem of permanence, including the permanence of Jonson's fame. Thus in the preface to *Hymenaei*: "So short-lived are the bodies of all things, in comparison of their souls. And, though bodies oft-times have the ill luck to be sensually preferred, they find afterwards the good fortune (when souls live) to be utterly forgotten. This it is hath made the most royal Princes, and greatest persons . . . not only studious of riches and magnificence in the outward celebration of show . . . but curious after the most high and hearty inventions, to furnish the inward parts" [ll. 6–15]. Unfortunately for this pious hope, the antimasques, along with the elaborate settings, proved to be more popular in appeal to the audience than the highly allusive allegories, buttressed with documentation and footnotes, which Jonson regarded as the soul of the genre. The audience in general, including King James, preferred dancing to talking, and the principle that the dance was the real soul of the masque had much more authority. In a later masque of Shirley's[16] there is an opening announcement that there is to be no antimasque: this provokes protest from one of the characters, who says that the audience will never stand for such a thing, and something like thirteen antimasques follow. Jonson saw in the proliferation of antimasques the degeneration of the form, and in this he was clearly right. Again, the breakdown of the form presaged the fall of the social structure which supported it: one of many examples of the socially prophetic role of the arts.

To return to the cosmology which the masque reflects: we have a descending movement of order and harmony on chaos, which is the original creative act of God, perpetuated in human society by the structure of authority. God could have created only a perfect world, and this original creation formed a second or ideal level of reality. It included the Garden of Eden, and all myths of a Golden Age or an earthly paradise are reminiscent of it. All that is now left of it is, or is symbolized by, the heavenly bodies. The fall of man established a third level, and the fall of Satan a fourth one, which now has the third in its grip. In the original creation the Son of God descended to the second level, walking in the Garden of Eden; at the Incarnation he descended to the third, and, after his death on the cross, to the fourth. These descents were followed by a rising movement, through the Harrowing of Hell, the Resurrection, and the Ascension. This rising movement is redemptive, bringing man back from his alienated or fallen state to a condition nearer his original one.

Writers of masques, apart from Milton, are so concerned with the secular occasion that there is little explicit reminder of this cosmology. But the cosmology itself was so firmly fixed in the Jacobean mind that such a form as a masque, where the presence of nobility and royalty suggested in itself a secular analogy to spiritual authority, had to fall into a similar shape. Jacobean Christianity, Jacobean drama, Jacobean masque, all inhabited the same mythological universe. Besides, royalty and nobility were not merely an analogy: they represented, to a very considerable degree, the continuing visible form of spiritual authority, especially in Protestant England, where the Church itself had been put under the headship of the temporal sovereign.

In the cosmology, authority descends from above: any descending movement which is not that of authority represents evil, following its own law of moral gravitation, and sinking through our world towards the demonic level and the bottom of the chain of being. The central symbol for this kind of descent is metamorphosis, in the sense of transformation into a lower state of existence, such as we have in Ovid's *Metamorphoses*, in Apuleius, and in the stories about Circe in the *Odyssey* and elsewhere. This theme often appears in the antimasque, and when it does, the movement to the masque proper thus incorporates a cyclical progression from chaos to cosmos, unorganized energy to new life, into the polarized structure. The main thrust of the movement to and through the masque proper is therefore upward, in the reverse direction from Circean metamorphosis, and to higher levels of the chain of being.

Both antimasque and masque present unreal worlds, but the masque has at least the reality of an ideal, a dream of a happy island or paradisal garden of perpetual spring, with its providential parental figures of king and queen inhabiting it like the presences in the rose-garden of Eliot's *Burnt Norton*. It is significant how often Jonson associates Britain with the legend of the floating island—Delos in Classical myth—which has been caught and fixed for a moment. The magically evoked instant is real for that instant, however quickly it fades. And in that instant Britain is seen as what, according to Christian teaching, it originally was: a green and pleasant land,[17] part of the Garden of Eden or Golden Age of unfallen man. In Jonson the magic which calls this state of innocence into a moment of being is symbolized, in particular, by Mercury and Proteus, gods of magic and metamorphosis, and in *The Fortunate Isles* Proteus says of Britain:

> There is no sickness, nor no old age known
> To man, nor any grief that he dares own.
> There is no hunger there, nor envy of state,
> Nor least ambition in the Magistrate.
> But all are even-hearted, open, free,
> And what one is, another strives to be. [ll. 508–13]

We have to keep the vertical metaphor of the chain of being in our minds to understand the consistency of masque imagery. The descending movement is from the divine through the angelical, human, animal, vegetable, and mineral worlds down to chaos, and the movement itself, when not voluntary or authoritative, is associated with sinister enchantments and the lowering of intelligence and freedom of movement. Human beings turned into animals, statues, or flowers, like Narcissus, are typical images of such enchantment. In masques this kind of movement is often reversed, going through the corresponding disenchantments. In Jonson's *Lovers Made Men*, a simplified form in which antimasque and masque have the same characters, we begin with the lovers in the world of the dead, led there by Mercury in his role as psychopomp. They are not actually dead, but think they have died for love. They drink of the river Lethe or forgetfulness, but what they forget is their death, and they come to life again. Thus the main movement is that of a freeing from enchantment or metamorphosis and a restoration of the original identity. In Campion's *Lords' Masque* we are introduced to Prometheus making women: Jupiter, furious, turns them to statues, but after the proper invocations the statues are brought to life. We recall that "statua's moving" was a common masque theme for Bacon, though he associates it with the antimasque. An anonymous *Masque of Flowers* shows flowers turning into men, in a reversal of the Narcissus theme.

Most of the imagery of the masque, then, is strung along what we may call an *axis mundi*, the centre of the vertical line of images held together by the chain of being, and going in an upward direction. This upward movement of *axis mundi* imagery connects the masque with a very similar family of image sequences that appears in alchemical symbolism, where the alchemical processes symbolize the transformation of the soul from the state of original sin, the *prima materia*, to the state of original identity, the *lapis*. Closely linked, also, is the immensely long tradition in ritual and literature of ziggurat imagery, where the theme is the climbing of a tower or a mountain representing the hierarchies of being. This latter is as old an archetype as civilization affords: it is the basis of Dante's *Purgatorio* and is going as strong as ever in Yeats, Eliot, and Ezra Pound, whose "Dioce"[18] goes back to Herodotus and his description of the original towers of Ecbatana and Babylon.[19] Its ancient forms have been studied by Gertrude Rachel Levy in *The Gate of Horn* and *The Sword from the Rock*. In narrative poetry the sequence usually goes up some kind of spiral climb, but this is not very dramatic, and would be difficult to stage even for Inigo Jones. What is symbolically a going up on the *axis mundi* is often represented in drama as a going within. The masque is naturally a proscenium drama, and in the usual arrangement the audience was seated at one end of a hall, the other end displaying a curtain on which the antimasque scene was painted. The scene normally portrayed something low down on the chain of being, just above chaos, such as the slope of a mountain, or simply rocks, rocks being common enough to be recognized at the time as something of a cliché. Afterwards the curtain parted to exhibit one or two inner scenes, spatially thought of as within the mountain or rocks, but symbolically representing an order superior to or on top of them.

Thus in Jonson's *Oberon* we first meet satyrs, then an inner scene shows us two "sylvans" asleep in front of a palace, sylvans being evidently higher in rank than satyrs; then the palace opens to disclose "Fays" or knights, and the masque ends in panegyric of Prince Henry, in whose honour it was held. In Jonson's *Pleasure Reconciled to Virtue* the scene is a mountain (Atlas), beginning with a "grove of ivy" at the bottom, from which Comus, here the genius of gluttony, comes with an antimasque of tuns or bottles. Hercules in this masque has to choose between Vice (Comus) and Virtue; he chooses Virtue and gets Pleasure as well, both of whom are much higher up on the mountain, along with Mercury and the masque dancers. In Campion's *Lords' Masque* we begin with the "lower part" of a divided scene, with Mania, the goddess of madness, in a cave, and from there we move up to the sphere of fixed stars.

The ascending imagery is accompanied by reversals of the stock symbols of descent. Antimasque scenes often begin in a thick mazy wood, a labyrinth where there is no certain direction. In Jonson's *Masque of Augurs* an antimasque dance is said to be "a perplexed Dance of straying and deformed Pilgrims, taking several paths" [ll. 271–2]. A symbol of lost direction, the echo song, becomes a standard feature of masques. But there is also a higher labyrinth, the controlled and ordered movements of the stars, and *Pleasure Reconciled to Virtue* introduces a dance imitating these movements, of which the coryphaeus is Daedalus. When a man appears on the stage as an actor he has already undergone a form of metamorphosis: in the junctions of actors and audience in the masque, such as the dance in which the masquers "take out the ladies," the actors come back to their original identity.

What we have called ziggurat imagery often features two things on the top: an idealized landscape or garden, and the body of a bride who is united with her lover at this point, and whose body is often identified with the garden, as in the Song of Songs [4:12] in the Bible. In Jonson's *Hymenaei*, perhaps the most elaborate of wedding masques, where Juno symbolizes the marriage union, the masquers' dance is compared to "the Golden Chain let down from Heaven" [l. 320] by Jupiter, and the masque is introduced by the figure of Reason, described as "seated in the top of the Globe (as in the brain, or highest part of Man)" [ll. 129–30], indicating that the upward movement through the *axis mundi* has an analogy to the human body also. Then again, the strong association of the masque with magic, and perhaps also the link in imagery with alchemy, help to make occult themes prominent in Jonson—perhaps it is not an accident that Jonson's greatest play is about an alchemist, however much of a scoundrel. In *Mercury Vindicated from the Alchemists* we move from an alchemist's laboratory presided over by Vulcan to "a glorious bower, wherein Nature was placed, with Prometheus at her feet" [ll. 196–7]. In *The Masque of Augurs* we move from an antimasque said to have no connection with the main theme to the gods Apollo and Jupiter, the true augurs in the service of the king: again there is a sense of lower and higher mysteries. The Ovidian and Chaucerian image of the House of Fame or Rumour is employed as a symbol of the confusions of the lower states of being: we may compare the dialogue of Truth and Opinion in *Hymenaei*. In *The Fortunate Isles* we are introduced to a credulous Rosicrucian, teased by an "aery spirit" who reminds us of Ariel, and who promises him visions of "gardens in the depth of winter" [l. 168] and a journey from the depths of the sea to the height of the Empyrean. Eventually he is declared to be a gull, but his dreams of an earthly paradise are satisfied by the Britain of King James.

We noted that occasionally the rising on the chain of being is expressed in a cyclical movement from darkness to dawn, winter to spring, age to youth. The fact that Britain is an island in the far west, a land of the region of sunset, enables the action of some masques to begin in a dark world, as in *Love Freed from Ignorance and Folly*. Here the antimasque presents a sphinx who has kidnapped the "daughters of the Morn," journeying from east to west, and also holds Love a prisoner. As mentioned, Love has to guess riddles of which the answers are Britain and King James. The antimasque is danced by "twelve she-fools," and ends with the recognition of James the sun-king, the rising dawn that puts ignorance and folly to flight. A somewhat similar imagery is employed in *The Masque of Blackness*, with its sequel *The Masque of Queens*.

Milton's *Comus* is, of course, not typical of the court masque, but for that very reason it indicates the kind of thing that could have been done with the form to make it a solid and durable dramatic genre. For one thing, Milton is much less preoccupied by the secular occasion and more aware of the cosmological structure of masque symbolism. It has often been noted that the descent of Peace in the *Nativity Ode* is reminiscent of masque devices, and the *Nativity Ode* is based on the same Christianized cosmology that informs the masque, its theme being the descent of a principle of order and control, of divine origin and repeating the creation, which is symbolized by the harmony of music. The Incarnation opens up a polarizing contrast between the paradisal model world of God's original creation, now entering the third level of human life for the first time since the fall of Adam, and the world of the dark demons infesting that fallen order, who represent what corresponds to the antimasque in the poem. The Christ child is the rising sun that puts these demons to flight, like King James in Jonson. I have spoken elsewhere of the masque-like arrangement of the opening books of *Paradise Lost*, with the vision of hell followed by the blaze of light in heaven [*RE*, 17–18; *M&B*, 46]. In *Arcades* we have a Classical version of the paradisal order that God originally created, its protection symbolized by the Genius of the Wood, the objective counterpart of the lady in whose honour the masque is given.

In *Comus* we begin with the same protected order, symbolized by the Attendant Spirit, who belongs to a world above our own and directly beneath heaven, like the Garden of Eden. *Comus*, however, like *Arcades*, is written in a Classical tonality, and the Attendant Spirit's home is associated rather with the Gardens of Adonis (in the background is the easygoing etymology that derives "Adon" from "Eden"). The fact that the Lady's chastity is identified with virginity means that she is less explicitly Christian than a vestal or pagan saint like the nun in *Il Penseroso* or the ideal poet in the Sixth Elegy, just as the "divine philosophy" [l. 476] of the two brothers is less Christian than Neoplatonic.

The Lady and her brothers descend into a labyrinthine forest symbolizing the lower world, where they lose their way and the Lady sings an echo song, after which we are introduced to the antimasque of Comus and his rout. Comus is the son of Circe, and is consequently not Jonson's fat slob but the presiding genius of the world of descending metamorphosis. He and his followers are demonic fire-spirits like the *ignis fatuus*, parodies of the circling heavenly bodies which they profess to imitate, and which symbolize the higher labyrinth of heavenly order. Comus and his band are connected, like the false gods of the *Nativity Ode*, with everything "fallen" that we associate with the word "natural," on its lower or physical level, the level of animals and plants. The Lady's chastity is what is natural to her on the upper, paradisal and originally human level of nature. The emblems of Comus, the cup and the wand, are sexual symbols representing the aspect of the natural in which man tends to lose his human identity. The argument is hardly intelligible without some understanding of the hierarchic cosmology, both Christian and Neoplatonic, in which there are two contexts for the word "nature."

At the end the Lady returns to her own stage of higher nature, and is presented, along with her brothers, to her parents. Here we have the junction of audience and actors that is characteristic of the masque form, except that the symbolism is more concrete. The Lady and her brothers are the only human beings in the play: everyone else is a spirit of the elements of the nature into which the Lady has descended. The action of her descent, like that of Christ in the *Nativity Ode*, polarizes them into the good and the bad, the Attendant Spirit and Sabrina being benevolent spirits of air and water like the Genius of the Wood in *Arcades*, the fire-spirits Comus and his followers (along with some earth-spirits, parenthetically referred to in the text) remaining demonic. We notice too the symbolism of a night world in the far west which we met in Jonson: the setting, near the Welsh border, reminds us also of the sunset world of the Irish Ocean and the mouth of the Dee in *Lycidas*. The release of the Lady by Sabrina, the spirit of the Severn river, belongs to the archaic cyclical symbolism of the dead waters of winter succeeding to the living waters of spring, for even after the Lady has been rescued from Comus she is still "frozen."

The familiar features of Old Comedy, as we have it in Aristophanes, the ribaldry, the sense of an unstructured or substandard society, the fantasy, the dancing, are all features reappearing in the antimasque. The antimasque, as Enid Welsford has noted,[20] goes back to something far older than the masque itself—in fact older than Aristophanes, and an ancestor of his form also. It has affinities with the satyr play which was the embryo of tragedy, and in Elizabethan tragedy, when the mood turns fantastic or grotesque, we get scenes reminding us of antimasques, especially when the theme includes magic. The witches in *Macbeth* are an obvious instance, and in *Macbeth* we also have other illusions, like the moving wood, which were common masque features. For all the obvious differences, the structural affinities of the masque are closer to Old Comedy, being polarized and based on spectacle, than to New Comedy, which is cyclical and based on plot.

III

In Shakespeare's romantic comic form the structure is taken from New Comedy, but the presence of what I have elsewhere called a green world[21] makes the polarizing element in his comedy much more prominent, being a collision and eventual reconciliation of two opposed worlds or orders of experience rather than of groups of characters. We make a distinction between Shakespeare's comedies and the romances of his final period, implying that this distinction is generic, or has a generic aspect. In terms of what we have been saying, it seems to me that the "comedies" are plays in which the New Comedy scheme maintains itself to the end, though in its own distinctively romantic way. In Terence or Molière the hero and heroine wriggle out of the obstacles and prohibitions of the blocking figures and arrive at marriage and a festive ending within the social order that the blocking figures have set up. In the romantic comedy of Shakespeare and of some of his contemporaries and predecessors, the central characters approaching marriage, who have the audience's sympathy, are placed in a different symbolic setting, or what we might call, in this strange world of the 1970s, a separate reality,[22] usually represented as a forest, which permeates and finally transforms the more "realistic" world of the blocking figures. There the two worlds have an approximate relation to the worlds of wish-fulfilment dream and of waking consciousness, the former being strong enough to mould the latter into something like its own shape, which implies that it is ultimately more real.

In the romances the two worlds are more sharply opposed: the blocking worlds are an intense contrast to the comic spirit, often forming tragic actions in themselves, as in *The Winter's Tale* particularly. Something in these worlds has to be condemned and annihilated before the festive conclusion can take place, not simply reconciled or won over. What is annihilated is the state of mind, the jealousy of Posthumus or Leontes, the intrigues of Cymbeline's Queen or the Court Party in *The Tempest*, rather than the people in those states, though some of the people get eliminated too, at least in *Pericles* and *Cymbeline*. The structure of the romances thus approximates the complete polarity of the antimasque and masque. The dramatic romances of Shakespeare and his contemporaries, whatever the circumstances of their original performance, have their roots in the popular theatre with its unselected audience. The masque, driven by a steadily narrowing class consciousness into a brittle spectacle as ephemeral as a firework display, nevertheless has features that make it possible for us to think of romantic comedy as a kind of democratized version of the same form, a people's masque, as it were.

In Shirley's *Love's Cruelty* there is a frequently quoted passage about masques: "in the instant as if the sea had swallowed up the earth, to see waves capering about tall ships, Arion upon a rock, playing to the dolphins . . . a tempest so artificial and sudden in the clouds, with a general darkness and thunder . . . that you would cry out with the mariners in the work, you cannot 'scape drowning."[23] The explicit reference is to Jonson, but the modern reader will think of *The Tempest* or *Pericles*. In fact Shakespeare, who, as far as we know, never looked at a Quarto proof and left his plays to be gathered up after his death, may have been temperamentally closer to the masque than Jonson was. In any case the romances show an ascending movement from chaos and absurdity to peace and order very like that of the masque, and an actual masque, or masque-like scene, the epiphany of Diana in *Pericles*, the dream of Posthumus in *Cymbeline*, the sheepshearing festival in *The Winter's Tale*, and the wedding masque in *The Tempest*, appears at the peripety of the action. In drama later than Shakespeare, the most ambitious dramatic romance dealing with themes of redemption and the recovery of original identity, along with a good many alchemical themes, is perhaps the second part of [Goethe's] *Faust*, and we can see how that poem flowers out of the two gigantic masques, which dramatically are rather antimasques, of the scene at the Emperor Maximilian's court and the Classical Walpurgis Night.

As I see it, there are six romances in the last period of Shakespeare's production: *Pericles, Cymbeline, The Winter's Tale, The Tempest, Henry VIII,* and *The Two Noble Kinsmen.* The first and last are clearly works of collaboration, and are not in the Folio, but collaboration does not mean that the plays lack unity. Shakespeare in any case would have been the senior collaborator, more likely to be responsible for the general design and scheme of the play. We may look first at *Henry VIII,* now an unpopular and rarely performed play, so often said to be largely the work of Fletcher that the statement has come to have the force of an established fact, though it is not one. If we look at it objectively, without worrying about whether it was really the right sort of play for Shakespeare to be ending his career with, we can see how different generically it is from the other histories. It is, in the first place, a pageant: tremendous parades of nobility take place, to such an extent that one contemporary complained that it made greatness too familiar. The coronation of Anne Boleyn in the fourth act is the spectacular climax. When the play was performed at Stratford, Ontario, some years ago, the production was gorgeously costumed, with many resources beyond anything that Shakespeare himself could have commanded; but even Stratford gave up on this scene, and had it simply described as taking place offstage. The spectacular nature of the play is perhaps the reason for the low-keyed quality of the writing. The greater the extent to which spectacle is visually provided, the greater the violation of decorum in having obtrusively magnificent poetry in the text accompanying such spectacle.

The hero of *Henry VIII* is not so much the king as the wheel of fortune. The first turn of the wheel brings down Buckingham, the second turn Wolsey, the third Queen Katherine and others. If we like, we can see a rough justice or even a providence operating: Wolsey's fall is the nemesis for his treatment of Buckingham, and Queen Katherine, though innocent, has to go in order to get Elizabeth born. For this reason it is unnecessary to apply moral standards to King Henry: whether we think him resolute or merely ferocious, we cannot be sure if he turns the wheel of fortune or has simply become a part of its machinery. Certainly in the crucial event of the final scene, the birth of Elizabeth, there is a factor independent of his will, even though he takes the credit for it, as befits a king. In this final scene there is a "prophecy" by Cranmer about the future greatness of England under Elizabeth and her successors, which generically is a very masque-like scene, a panegyric of the sort that would have normally accompanied the presence of a reigning monarch in the audience.

The only difficulty is that this scene shows the final triumph of Cranmer and of Anne Boleyn, and the audience knows what soon happened to Anne, as well as to three of her successors, and eventually to Cranmer. It also knows that the reign of Elizabeth was preceded by that of Queen Katherine's daughter, whose existence Henry appears to have forgotten: "Never before / This happy child, did I get any thing," he says [5.4.64–5]. The parade of dignity and nobility, the exhibition of power and greatness controlled by a king who is not in the audience but confronting us on the stage, has few of the conventional elements of the masque, but it does leave us with a sense of transience, a world of "shadows, not substantial things," to quote another skilful masque writer,[24] that soon disappears and gives way to what is in its future and the audience's present. Another episode in the play that suggests the masque is the dance of spirits around the dying Katherine, where there seems to be a glimpse of something transcending history. What impresses us most strongly about the play is the reversal of the ordinary standards of reality and illusion. Nothing could be more immediately real than the ups and downs of fortune in King Henry's court; nothing more illusory than a prophecy of a future three reigns away, or the sick fancies of a dying woman. But what the play presents is a sense of reality and illusion quite the opposite of this.

The prologue insists on the seriousness of the play and the suppression of all buffoonery in it. Nothing of the very little that we know or can guess of Shakespeare's own political attitudes would lead us to believe that those attitudes were revolutionary or even liberal: there is no reason to suppose that he would have shrunk from Jonson's flattery of royalty if that had been part of his job. It is the integrity of the dramatic spectacle itself—and *Henry VIII* has, I think, far more integrity than it is usually given credit for having—that turns the whole solemn parade into a gigantic perversion of real social life, no less of one than Shelley's *Masque of Anarchy*. What Shakespeare was aware of as a dramatic craftsman, on the other hand, his sense of what the play needed, is sometimes shown by the incidents and characters he adds to his sources, and in *Henry VIII* this consists mainly of the two episodes, Queen Katherine's vision and Cranmer's prophecy, that have some standard features of the masque.

What emerges from a deeply serious, even tragic, play is an irony so corrosive that it has almost a comic dimension. The higher one is in social rank, the more one becomes bound to a formalized upper-class ritual. With a ruthless king as master of ceremonies, this ritual becomes a kind of sinister sacrificial dance, in which the most conspicuous figure becomes the designated next victim. In *The Two Noble Kinsmen* the sense of ritual compulsion is carried a step further. This play begins with the ritual of Theseus's wedding, and Theseus himself is possessed by the anxiety of ritual: "Forward to th' temple. Leave not out a job / O' th' sacred ceremony" [1.1.129–30]. There are two similar commands later in the same scene. The ritual, however, is interrupted by a counter-ritual: three queens in black, one kneeling in front of each of the three chief figures, urge Theseus to war instead of love. The theme of death taking precedence over marriage is repeated in the climax of the play, when Arcite wins the battle with Palamon but dies. And just as death takes precedence of marriage, so a destructive and enslaving passion destroys the freedom of friendship. This is true not only of Palamon and Arcite, but also of Emily. Emily's emotional life revolves around an early friendship with another woman: she has no interest in marriage, much less in marriage to the survivor of a fight to the death over her, but the rigid class code leaves her no choice. The source of the play is Chaucer's *Knight's Tale*, and Chaucer also has a clear sense of the compulsive and mechanical quality of these deadly ritual games. But *The Two Noble Kinsmen* exhibits a kind of sleepwalking commitment to them that seems almost Aztec, as in the emphasis on the fact that all those who have volunteered to assist Palamon and Arcite will lose their lives if their principal does. The action of the play is dominated by Venus, who is not Homer's laughter-loving Aphrodite but a goddess as menacing as the Indian Kali, flanked by her lover Mars, the god of war, and her child Cupid, the Eros who is fulfilled only by Thanatos or death.

In two of the earlier comedies that most closely resemble masques, *Love's Labour's Lost* and *A Midsummer Night's Dream*, there is a burlesque interlude that corresponds to the antimasque: the pageant of worthies in the former and Peter Quince's play in the latter. In both plays, however, the effect of the burlesque is not to bring out the superior dignity of the upper-class figures, but to throw an ironic light on their lack of self-knowledge. The gentlemen in *Love's Labour's Lost* are "worthies" who have dedicated themselves to a heroic cause which they abandon at the first distracting stimulus; Theseus in *A Midsummer Night's Dream* has had his own will and his conception of his duty quietly overruled by fairies in whose existence he does not believe. A much grimmer and starker burlesque appears in *The Two Noble Kinsmen*, in the form of a morris dance, an actual antimasque imported from a masque of Beaumont's, where the leading figure is a madwoman, "the jailer's daughter." This is a girl who

fell in love with Palamon when he was her father's prisoner and set him free. It is the only "natural," spontaneous, and apparently free-willed action in the play, and a totally disastrous one for her: her humiliation is so complete that she does not even have a name. After looking at this Venus-ruled play, we can perhaps understand why the action of *The Tempest,* which goes in the opposite direction, should culminate in a masque in which, although it is a wedding masque, one of the main themes is the exclusion of Venus.

I spoke of *Troilus and Cressida* as Shakespeare's closest approach to the dialectical and processional structure of Old Comedy. This again shows us the Trojans as victims of the heroic ritual code to which they have bound themselves. In such a situation someone more "realistic," like the ruthless Achilles or the wily Ulysses, comes out on top. In *The Two Noble Kinsmen* there is nothing corresponding to the Greeks of the earlier play, and in *Henry VIII* nothing corresponding to the Trojans, but the two plays taken together illustrate different aspects of the self-imprisoning human will to live in a world of illusion and call it reality. In the four better-known romances the movement of the action is more conventionally comic, but it is a movement towards a separating of the two orders of reality and illusion, the orders which for Wilson Knight are symbolized by music and the tempest.[25] This takes us back to masque cosmology, as music and tempest are the two poles of the chain of being, the tempest the chaos at the bottom of existence and music the order and harmony imposed from above.

I spoke of *The Two Noble Kinsmen* as a play dominated by Venus: in the comic romances the god or goddess who acts as a providence for the action corresponds to the figure in the audience of the masque for whom the action takes place. Thus *Pericles* is the play of Diana, *Cymbeline* of Jupiter, *The Winter's Tale* of Apollo. The providence of *The Tempest* is a human magician, but his magic creates a wedding masque in which Juno appears, Juno being especially the patron of marriage, as in Jonson's *Hymenaei*. These deities are, so to speak, on the opposite side of the stage from the audience, but in the epilogue to *The Tempest* there is a strong hint that the magic and illusion of the play is in large part the creation of the audience. The audience has to release Prospero just as Prospero has to release Ariel, and for the same reason: he has been working for them, and now he wants his liberty. Similarly the gods who direct the action of *Pericles*, *Cymbeline*, and *The Winter's Tale* to a serene conclusion are working for the audience who recognize this conclusion as "right."

In the fine craftsmanship of Ben Jonson's verse there is something almost plastic, something that makes his own metaphor appropriate when he speaks of "the well joining, cementing, and coagmentation of words; when as it is smooth, gentle, and sweet, like a table upon which you may run your finger without rubs, and your nail cannot find a joint."[26] Such solidity of technical skill goes with the directing of the masque towards the central figure in the audience: all the illusion points to the waking and conscious reality in the recognition of that figure. But Shakespeare's verse is continually approaching the boundaries of conscious verbal expression, the area where conventional language begins to merge into the rhythms and sounds of a realm of experience we know nothing about, though magicians may claim some knowledge of it. This is the kind of verbal music that takes us beyond drama, with its antithesis of actors and spectators, beyond masque, where the actors sometimes rejoin the spectators, into a world where the distinction of actor and spectator no longer holds, where reality is what the word itself creates, and after creating, sees to be good.

In New Comedy the normal action is the victory of a younger generation and its erotic ambitions over the older people who block them. Older people block younger ones, normally, because they want to keep on possessing them, and they want to possess them because the illusion of possession is the only way of concealing from themselves the fact that they are possessed. When they are baffled or reconciled we have a sense of rebirth, as the palsied grip of the elders on the comic society is relaxed and new energies take over. This New Comedy structure is incorporated into the romances: Imogen marries Posthumus and Perdita Florizel despite parental opposition, and Marina and Miranda are also joined with their lovers. There is also a cyclical pattern of renewal as the "winter's tale" of Leontes' jealousy gives place to a new spring, or as Imogen (whose story is closely related to another "winter's tale," the Snow White story familiar from Grimm) waits out her winter until her stepmother dies and her obsessed father and, later, her lover can be brought to see the light. But the main theme in all plays is the reintegrating of the older generation, Pericles with Thaisa, Cymbeline with Caesar, Leontes with Hermione, Prospero with the King of Naples and his own Milan inheritance. It is a fully mature life that becomes transformed, and such a theme is symbolically connected not with rebirth but with resurrection, which in a sense is the opposite of rebirth, a vertical thrust upward from death to a life which is no longer subject to cyclical rotation. Thaisa and Hermione are in effect raised from the dead, a power Prospero also claims, and the prayers said by Leontes over Hermione's grave are paralleled in the great song over the grave of "Fidele" in *Cymbeline* and in the false epitaph set up for Marina in *Pericles*.

This theme of illusory death and genuine resurrection is parallel to what we described in connection with the vertical movement up the *axis mundi* or chain of being in the masque. Changing a person into a statue would be an image of metamorphosis, or descent to a lower state of being; the "statua's moving" that Bacon mentions as frequent in masques, and which we found in Campion's *Lords' Masque*, is an image of restored identity. The crisis of *The Winter's Tale* is the changing of the alleged "statue" of Hermione into the real Hermione; a similar image of resurrection is employed when Pericles is roused from his stupor by Marina, and when Imogen recovers from the narcotic drug. We also noticed that in the masque what is higher on the chain of being is often represented by what is inside the antimasque curtain. Without going into the complicated question of the Elizabethan inner stage, we notice how frequently the "higher" place in the romances is represented by an inner one: the cave of Belarius in *Cymbeline*, Paulina's chapel in *The Winter's Tale*, Prospero's cell in *The Tempest*.

Music is the symbol of the higher or paradisal world for many reasons. It represents the original order and harmony that are being regained, as in the traditional "music of the spheres."[27] Its rhythm, again, symbolizes the higher quality of time in the regained world, a world where time is an expression of inward energy and not of objective fatality. This aspect of renewed time is often represented by the dance, as in Sir John Davies' poem *Orchestra*, and though Jonson spoke contemptuously of the "concupiscence of jigs" in Shakespeare's romances,[28] the dances are there for structurally much the same reason that they are in Jonson's masques. The text is emphatic that music plays the decisive role in bringing Thaisa and Hermione to life, and supernatural harmonies surround Belarius and Prospero. There is also a different function of music, represented by the songs of the rascally Autolycus and the mischievous Ariel, in which it has a hypnotic effect, riveting the attention but putting the consciousness to sleep. Here it is working in the opposite direction of charm or paralysing of action. We may compare the aubade "Hark, hark, the lark," sung to Imogen [*Cymbeline*, 2.3.20–6], after she has spent a night with Iachimo in her room, by order of the degenerate Cloten, whose obscene comments on the lovely song form one of the most extraordinary passages of bitonal counterpoint to be found even in Shakespeare. We take the song to be appropriate to the innocence of Imogen and her remoteness from the kind of thing represented by Iachimo on the one hand and Cloten on the other, but Cloten intends the song to be an aphrodisiac stimulant propelling her in his direction.

The fact that music is found on both sides of the polarizing action reminds us that the obvious genre in which to continue these romance and masque features is the opera, especially such an opera as [Mozart's] *The Magic Flute*, with its fairy-tale setting (in what Gurdjieff would call "pre-sand Egypt"[29]) and its polarizing action, in which hero and heroine are pulled upwards from a dark realm to a light one. It is a rare soprano who can bring out the curiously inhuman quality of the Queen of Night's first great aria, which sounds as though written for a flute solo rather than a voice. The reason is that the Queen of Night is a magic flute too, and she has her own kind of music, though a kind in harmony with the songs of sirens, not the music of the spheres. There are many similar contrasts in Wagner and elsewhere, but they would take us too far afield.

The romance differs from comedy in that the concluding scene of a comedy is intensely social. The emphasis is thrown on the reintegrated community; there are multiple marriages, and the blocking characters are reconciled or have been, like Shylock, previously excluded. In the four comic romances there are glimpses of something beyond this, something closer to the imagery of pastoral, a vision of a reconciliation of man with nature, in which the characters are individualized against nature, like Adam and Eve in the solitary society of Eden. In *The Winter's Tale* the sense of "great creating nature" [4.4.88] as an integral part of what man's life ought to be comes to a focus in the sheepshearing festival, a masque scene in which the dance of the twelve satyrs forms the antimasque. In *The Tempest* the corresponding focus is in the masque of Prospero, where we meet the goddesses of earth, sky, and rainbow in a world from which the deluge of the tempest has receded, where the rainbow, as in the Biblical deluge story, is the sign that the curse has been lifted from the ground.

The virginity of Perdita and Miranda, which is central to both scenes, is a state traditionally associated both with innocence, the primal state of man, and with magic. It is a state not expected to last: both girls are eager for marriage. Prospero's fussing about preserving Miranda's virginity to the last moment is not morality but magic: all magic, like all music, depends on timing, and it must be the right time when Ariel is released, when the world of magical illusion is dissolved, and when Miranda enters her brave new world. Perdita's dislike of grafted plants is not a hereditary nervousness about bastards, but a sense of the virginity of nature, of nature as a virgin mother who needs no fathering art. Both masques are interrupted, one by Prospero's speaking and the other by the "whoobub," as Autolycus calls it [4.4.616], of Polixenes, churning up the illusions of the lower world. The interruption is a part of the sense of the transient quality of the masque, but that transience gives us an insight into what, perhaps, all dramatic and ritual spectacles are about. Human kind, as Eliot says, cannot bear very much reality [*Burnt Norton*, ll. 44–5]: what it can bear, if it is skilfully enough prepared for it, is an instant of illusion which is the gateway to reality.

3

Letter to the Editor of *Parabola*

1976

From Parabola, *1 (Winter 1976): 4. The letter appeared in "Full Circle: A Readers' Forum," which contained a number of letters welcoming the new magazine.*

I am very pleased that you are setting up a new periodical connected with "Myth and the Quest for Meaning." This is about as central an area in the contemporary intellectual scene as one could find, but it cuts across so many of the conventional disciplines that it is absolutely essential to have something specifically designed to bring together scholars in literature, comparative religion, popular culture, and other related fields.

I understand that your opening issues will be featuring Mircea Eliade and Joseph Campbell, which indicates that you know where the central people are and are able to count on their support and interest. I wish you all the best for your efforts, and will take the keenest interest in the periodical as it develops.

4

The Responsibilities of the Critic

20 February 1976

Originally presented as a lecture at Johns Hopkins University. From Modern Language Notes, *91 (October 1976): 797–813. Reprinted in* MM, *124–40. The typescripts are in the NFF, 1988, box 5, files ff–gg, 1991, box 36, file 3 (annotated), and 1991, box 39, file 4.*

Many nineteenth-century writers, including Burke, Carlyle, and Arnold, were badly shaken by all the revolutionary talk about the "rights of man" following the French Revolution, and were fond of insisting that men have no rights, only duties.[1] Similarly, the academic critic represents the practical arts, notably literature, within the university, and it is safer for him to talk about his responsibilities than about his privileges. Many poets and novelists wonder why, if he must thrust himself in front of students to talk about literature, he cannot confine himself to the dead, and let them make their own impact unimpeded. Most academic critics would prefer to do so, but the assumption involved is that students can be left to read contemporary literature on their own, and students are so little inclined to do that that they often regard their teachers as under a moral obligation to devote themselves as much as possible to the living. The university administrator may sometimes feel gratitude to the humanists because their financial demands are less than those of science and technology, but high price and high regard go together, and he more often echoes the attitude of a public who queries the "relevance" of the humanities. The critic has no relevance except what he creates himself, though I suspect that that is equally true of the rest of the human race.

Let us start with the tradition that begins with Aristotle, as a way of introducing the real subject of the critic, the subject that Aristotle calls poetics. I speak of an Aristotelian tradition rather than of Aristotle, because the *Poetics* is a very elliptical treatise, and the notetaker to whom we owe it seems to have been seized with writer's cramp at the most inappropriate times. Whenever we read anything, we have two things to do with the words: fit them together, and relate them separately to what they mean in the world outside the book. As though this were not complicated enough, we also have two aspects of words to struggle with, the unity and the units. The unity is expressed by the narrative, the sequential ordering of the words from the first page to the last. The units consist mainly of the images, the words with their conventional meanings, of which the most prominent are the nouns and the verbs, the names of things and of actions. We may call these two aspects of narrative and imagery the structure and the texture.

At a certain point we may come to feel that what the words mean, outside the book, is taking precedence over their relations to each other. That is, we have a verbal structure which is meant to be set up against something else, to which it is related as an imitation to an original. There are two large and important classes of such verbal structures: those that imitate *praxis*, or human action, and those that imitate *theoria*, or human vision and thought. These can be called the historical and the discursive verbal structures. Here the narrative reflects a corresponding area of action or thought, and is subject to the criterion of "truth." Truth here means truth of correspondence: a verbal structure is compared with a body of phenomena outside it, and is called true if it is a satisfactory verbal counterpart of it. The correspondence may be only occasional and fitful, or may come to be increasingly so in the course of time. This causes us to say that there is "some truth in" what the writer says. The images correspond to the things they conventionally mean: words have to be used in accustomed and consistent senses, and the smaller units are subject to a related but different criterion, the criterion of the factual.

On the other hand, we may come to feel that in what we are reading the interrelations of the words come first, that we have a verbal structure set up for its own sake. In that case it is a secondary verbal imitation of action and thought, and belongs to the group that we call poetic or literary. In the literary work the unifying narrative is simply that, a narrative, *mythos* in Greek, not subject to the criterion of truth of correspondence, or detailed agreement with anything outside it. As an imitation of action, the narrative is not a history but a story, something read for its own sake. Aristotle suggested that in the process the narrative moves from representing the particular to representing the universal. When we go from the early history of Scotland to *Macbeth* we go from what happened to what happens, to a vision of something recurrent and never finished with in human life. The word "vision" implies that *theoria* is involved as well as *praxis*, which is why Aristotle says that poetry is more philosophical than history [*Poetics*, chap. 9].

The *Poetics* says next to nothing about the relations of literature to representations of thought, and in English criticism it is not until the time of Coleridge that this question begins to be dealt with. But the same general principles hold. Primary imitations of thought are made up of predications, particular statements which again are judged by the truth of correspondence. Poetry may use philosophical material, just as it may use historical material, but when it does the context is different from philosophy. On the simplest level, the poet has a peculiar concern for felicity of statement, for saying, in Pope's words, what oft was thought but ne'er so well expressed.[2] The poet has always been admired, and still is much more than we often realize, for a sententious quality in his work, his ability to produce the quotable or easily recognized phrase. If we look more closely, we see that this results from a greater concreteness in his medium. On a more continuous level, a philosophical poet, as compared with a philosopher, is less interested in a system or the relating of ideas, and more in elaborating the metaphorical pictures or diagrams out of which the system comes. Thus Poe's *Eureka*, which talks a good deal about electricity and gravitation, develops these concepts into a positive and negative alternation of movement in the universe, and ends with a vision like that of the days and nights of Brahma in Hinduism. A perhaps more obvious example is [Carlyle's] *Sartor Resartus*, which elaborates the clothes-and-body metaphor implicit in Kant and Fichte. In long and complex literary works, like the epics of Dante and Milton, such world pictures expand into cosmologies, cosmology being, as Valéry says, one of the literary arts.[3]

In literature, then, the narrative is a pure *mythos*, or, in English, a myth, and there are two general types of literary myths, story myths and conceptual myths. As for the units or images, in literary works these are related primarily to each other rather than separately to things in the world outside. When two images are related primarily to each other we have some form of metaphor: thus a work of literature has a structure of myth and a texture of metaphor.

The Aristotelian view of verbal structures, which modulated into the

Coleridgean one around 1800, served us very well down to the beginning of this century, and seems to me still solid and useful. Its main deficiency, apart from the lack of historical perspective, was less in itself than in the fact that it left criticism open to some very dubious social and cultural assumptions. In spite of Aristotle's use of the term "universal," it seemed to imply that the really serious business of words was to tell us the truth about what was going on in time and conceptual space. Hence literary structures were not very serious, unless they had been written in dead languages, where the effort to decipher them, and the obscurity surrounding the effort, helped to make them more so. The real function of literature, it was assumed, was to supply a kind of emotional resonance to the truths that history and philosophy could convey. It is these cultural inferences, not the Aristotelian theory itself, which have fallen to pieces in our day.

We no longer have the same naive confidence in the unlimited ability of words to express all possible phenomena of experience, or show us every kind of reality in a flawless mirror. We realize more clearly how easy it is to talk about things which are not there, or cannot be shown to be there, to discuss the nine orders of angels as concretely as the stratification of rocks. More important, we realize the extent to which words keep twisting away from reality back to their own grammatical fictions, and so entice us to believe that subjects and predicates and objects are built into the nature of things. As a result philosophy in our time has shifted a good deal of its attention from what words tell us, or seem to tell us, to the linguistic structure itself, and the powers and limitations of that structure as a communicating instrument.

Thus we have Heidegger, in *Was Heisst Denken*? [*What Is Called Thinking?*] and in his essays on Hölderlin, minimizing the difference between the poetic and the philosophical thinker. Both, for him, elaborate self-contained verbal structures, and his most typical philosophers are Nietzsche and Parmenides, both of whom could equally well be described as poets. Wittgenstein, a very different philosopher, is more concerned with the negative aspects of verbal structures, and in defining the limits of their capacities, but similar interests are reflected in him. When a verbal structure is called true because it is thought to correspond to a body of phenomena, it becomes univocal: that is, language is being used as pure communication. The *Philosophical Investigations,* in particular, explore the immense difficulties involved in oversimplifying this situation. More positive questions are also involved. As long as literature continues to use words in their accustomed senses, it can never be as abstract or nonrepresentational as music is, or as painting and sculpture can be. On the other hand, there must be another aspect of the kind of truth that can be conveyed by words, a truth of implication, a truth emerging from inner coherence rather than external reference.

There is thus a growing realization, among critics, philosophers, even social scientists, that what words do best, do most accurately, and do most powerfully, is hang together. The ability of words to inform the external world makes them extremely useful, but it seems to be limited as compared with mathematics, and to be to some extent derivative. It would be easy to exaggerate this tendency out of reaction, but it has gone so far that we seem to be nearing a critical situation in which verbal structures can be thought of as literary or as subliterary. This year, 1976, we celebrate the bicentennials of Adam Smith's *Wealth of Nations* and the first volume of Gibbon's *Decline and Fall*. These books were originally historical and discursive accounts of economics and the history of Rome. As such, they "date": accepting them as that would drag us back to outmoded conceptions of their subjects. But as self-contained verbal structures they are more important now than they were in their own day, because they have been graduated to the higher, or literary, category.

Two corollaries follow. One is that when a work survives through such a literary quality, it also acquires a historical dimension. This is what the word "classic" primarily expresses. The fact that the books of Adam Smith and Gibbon are still readable makes them valuable also as eighteenth-century documents, perspectives of another age. We have to look at things sometimes from the point of view of other ages, precisely because they are not our own. Why else does this university celebrate a centennial, and the country it is in a bicentennial? The other is, that every writer, to the extent that he succeeds in producing a coherent verbal structure, is not only a "creative" writer, but, if we are using the word in a proper critical sense, a poet. A third corollary ought to follow, but does not. This is, that literary criticism occupies a central place in everything that has to do with words. Why it does not follow is something we cannot deal with until we have looked at the historical or genetic dimension of the subject. This will take us from the Aristotelian tradition into the eighteenth-century Italian philosopher Vico, with his great vision of the development of social institutions out of what he calls "poetic wisdom," or an original mythology.[4]

The importance of Vico to our present argument is that he grasped so firmly two points: first, that a mythological structure is a poetic structure, whatever nonliterary uses may also be made of myth, and second, that this poetic mythology precedes the development of historical and discursive writing. This is the historical side of the principle that verbal structures are primarily made to hold together rather than reflect: the holding-together aspect is not only primary but primitive, the one that came first. One assumption involved here is that the poetic always precedes the prosaic in the history of literature, which is obviously true, but at once destroys what I have often attacked as the Jourdain fallacy, the notion that prose is the language of ordinary speech.[5] Such a fallacy is particularly foolish at a time when so many students in university can not write or speak prose, and when we are near the point of seeing the smear word "elitist" applied to anyone who habitually does.

Vico sees poetic mythology as something used in society to control human action on the one hand, and human thought on the other. The control of human action is achieved through law, though law in this context includes custom and ritual. Society begins in an age of gods, where laws are assumed to be of divine origin, and are interpreted by oracles and divination; it then moves into an age of heroes, where laws are drawn up in the interests of an ascendant class, then to an age of the people, where man is assumed to be responsible for his own laws, and finally to the various stages of a *ricorso* which starts the sequence over again. The great example of the *ricorso*, for Vico, was the return of the age of gods and heroes after the fall of the Roman republic.

This growth of law is a nonliterary development of mythology, and it involves a new allegorical recreation of the mythology at each social phase. When we pass from an age of gods to an age of heroes, the actions of the gods become an allegory of the actions of an aristocracy or privileged class. When we pass to the age of the people, the actions of the aristocracy become an allegory of what we should now call a class struggle. Each reinterpretation is an effort to say what the original myth "really means." By doing so, it destroys the myth as a structure, and replaces it with the new meaning. The evolution of the inner mythology of law into a parable of exploitation is what Vico himself is mainly interested in, and he begins the tradition followed later by Michelet,

Marx, and Sorel.[6] Vico's normal habit of mind is allegorical, and he insists that the true allegories of the original myths are univocal and historical.

But the original mythology was a product of poetic, or what we should call imaginative thinking, and hence, along with the movement in which mythology mirrors the course of social action, there goes a reshaping of the mythology itself in its own imaginative patterns, a reshaping which is structural and not allegorical, which works by recreation rather than by destroying one meaning and setting up another. This structural reshaping of myth is what we call literature. As the age of gods becomes the age of heroes, the myths of the gods modulate into romances about human champions; as the age of heroes becomes the age of the people, romance becomes more plausible and realistic. But the same mythical structures, the same devices for beginning and developing and ending the story, persist throughout.

The literary development of myth is also different from another development in which myth forms the embryo of philosophy and science. Mythology is not really a form of conceptual thinking, and the development of science, like the development of law, involves destroying and replacing rather than restructuring the myth. Thus seventeenth-century astronomy replaced mythological with scientific space, and nineteenth-century biology and geology replaced mythological with scientific time. We still use the words "sunrise" and "sunset," but we now think of them as allegories of a very different situation. We need, therefore, a third social development of mythology, one which, unlike the other two, preserves its inner imaginative structure, to account for the continuation of the poetic and mythological habit of mind in literature.

A cyclical view of history is in itself a rather pessimistic one, and the ideal course that nations run, under the benevolent eye of a divine providence, is summarized by Vico thus: "Men first feel necessity, then look for utility, next attend to comfort, still later amuse themselves with pleasure, thence grow dissolute in luxury, and finally go mad and waste their substance" [*The New Science*, 78 (par. 241)]. It seems to follow that if there is any sense or moral to history, or even to the study of it, that moral must be connected with the question of how we can arrest the cycle at what seems to us the most desirable point. For most of us this point would be the age of the people, and that appears also to be Vico's attitude. He even seems to suggest that the effort of analysis represented by his book might do something to work against the fatality of another *ricorso*. Perhaps, to borrow a celebrated maxim, it is only those who will not learn history who are condemned to repeat it. The ouroboros might straighten out if it began to feel actual pain while chewing its tail.

In Vico the cycle of history begins with a thunderclap, the noise from the sky that the primeval giants after the flood took to be the voice of God, interrupting their intercourse with their women with what was assumed to be disapproval. The frightened giants got up off their women and dragged them to the caves instead, thus beginning private property. This was the feature of Vico that attracted James Joyce, who was also terrified by thunderstorms.[7] In *Finnegans Wake* Joyce seems to be associating Vico's myth with that of another great eighteenth-century masterpiece, Sterne's *Tristram Shandy*, where the hero ascribes his misfortunes in life to his mother's having interrupted his father, in the act of coition, by asking him if he had wound the clock. Sterne, along with St. Augustine, is clearer than Vico is that the anxieties of sex and of time go together.

Vico's thunderclap, however, also symbolizes a historical and social problem that we do not yet have the conceptual tools to deal with: the problem of whether, and if so to what extent, cultural developments are founded on some forgotten, suppressed, or misinterpreted trauma. Myths of the fall of man or, still more obviously, myths of a major deluge, like the story of Atlantis, seem to indicate something like this. Freud suggests a rite of killing a primal father as the source of a traumatic myth of a similar kind.[8] But for the most part we leave these questions to such speculators as von Däniken and Velikovsky,[9] who follow Vico's suggestive but somewhat freewheeling mythopoeic style. It may seem inherently likely that the real answer, if there is an answer, would be something less picturesque than visits from outer space or the birth of the planet Venus. But the reason for the popularity of such writers in our day opens up another aspect of the problem, and explains why I am putting so much emphasis here on Vico.

Every age, of course, thinks it is the fulfilment of everything up to itself, and tries to interpret history not as cyclical but as evolving towards its *telos* in the present moment. Vico himself, living in the eighteenth century, lays a good deal of emphasis on the improvement of life since giants wandered the world in a state of promiscuous anarchy. Similarly, the popular progressive myths of fifty years ago feature a "cave man" who was much closer to nursery tales of giants and ogres, and closer also to Vico, than to anything that the caves of Lascaux and Altamira actually suggest. But there is so strong a sense today that we are in the last stages of the cycle Vico traces, when luxury gives way to a mad squandering of resources, that our progressive and evolutionary myths have become overlaid by something much more apprehensive.

Of course anyone over thirty may feel that the existence of so many people under thirty constitutes in itself a threat of return to the Dark Ages. But a great intensifying of an otherwise normal feeling seems to pervade our time, and to affect the younger generation even more than the older one. The feeling that another trauma or "thunderclap" is directly in front of us, as something that will come within a generation, extends from depressive fears of a nuclear holocaust to manic forecasts of an age of Aquarius. It is related to the sense of being near the end of a cycle, close to what Blake's *Mental Traveller* calls the birth of the babe.[10] Naturally language and literature are affected by the same feeling. Vico's *ricorso* period was accompanied by the breakdown of language, as Latin turned into the Romance vernaculars. The elaborate communication machinery of our time holds together a traditional normalized form of English which without that machinery would fly off in all directions into every variety of dialect and idiom. I often find in young people a sense of diffidence, almost of something like shame, in speaking this traditional language, as though it implied an attitude to participating in society that they do not share.

Vico tells us that history is made by men, which means that all the gods born of the fear of the thunderclap are human creations too. This is the main reason why he is compelled to bracket the whole Biblical tradition as outside the history he surveys. We can hardly follow him in this, nor am I sure that he wants us to. In the first place, Jehovah, who drowned the whole human race, is quite as much of a thunder-god as Zeus, and the story of the Exodus has cultural trauma written all over it. The real relation of Hebrew to Egyptian culture can only be guessed at: we may note some shrewd guesses in Freud's *Moses and Monotheism*, and a comment in Melville's journal after a visit to the pyramids: "I shudder at idea of [*sic*] ancient Egyptians. It was in these pyramids that was conceived the idea of Jehovah. Terrible mixture of the cunning and awful."[11] Second, and more important, the culture born in so mysterious a way had a revolutionary character that makes it unique in the ancient world, as well as the direct ancestor of a line of revolutionary religions,

Judaism, Christianity, Islam, and Marxism. It begins with God telling Moses that he is giving himself a name and entering on a specific and highly partisan historical role [Exodus 3]. The belief in a revelation starting at a definite time and place, the acceptance of a canon of sacred books, the dialectical habit of mind which polarizes every issue and excludes revisionist or compromising or liberal elements: these are characteristics of a revolutionary religious movement, and they recur in all the progeny of the burning bush. The revolutionary monotheism of the Hebrews is quite different in social reference from the imperial monotheism that appeared early in Egypt, and later in Persia and Rome. Biblical monotheism is that of a small and beleaguered nation: its god is invisible, and in contrast to Egypt, where the Pharaoh was always the high priest and an incarnation of Horus, the Hebrew tendency was toward a separation of spiritual and temporal authority. The main reason for this separation was that the Hebrews possessed, in the institution of prophecy, a third form of authority which, though it often served the kings or priests, was distinguishable from both. The function of prophecy was to remind the people of their contractual relation to their god, in other words to keep restating the original myth.

Out of the teachings of the prophets came the development of the law and the later wisdom literature. But although the Deuteronomic code assumes great differences of wealth and station in society, including slavery, the prophetic insistence on preserving the form of the original direct relation to the god seems to exert an equalizing force. The explicit teachings of the prophets, of Amos, for instance, are full of denunciations of the "great houses" and of the rich grinding the faces of the poor. It is as though the age of the gods and the age of the people were linked in something of a common cause against the tyranny of heroes. Similarly, the tyranny of heroes is what revives with the failure of nerve which starts off the *ricorso*, when the power of the people is surrendered to dictators or Vico's "kings."

The Biblical tradition, then, if I am right, has the three elements of mythology that I have tried to extract from Vico, or see implicit in him: the two centrifugal developments of law and wisdom, and an inner imaginative restructuring of the original myth in prophecy. The structures of law and wisdom are, so to speak, horizontally related to society: they are sustained by what I think of as the anxiety of continuity. Hence the emphasis, for example, on hereditary succession in monarchies, and on the next election and the new leader in democracies. Similarly in religion, where the constant repetition of the same rite is the motive force. Prophecy, on the other hand, breaks vertically and discontinuously into society: it presents a transcending vision of the social order out of which it has come. Its Biblical symbol is the prophet in the desert, the voice crying in the wilderness.[12]

But once a prophetic revelation is accepted and established in society, there can be no more prophets, in the sense of transcendental visionaries, within that establishment. The structures of law and wisdom take over entirely, and social change takes place within an evolutionary and continuous development. Medieval Christendom had its High King and its High Priest, in the Emperor and Pope of Rome, but no recognized prophetic tradition. The liberty of prophesying was one of the things that the Protestant Reformation was all about, but Protestantism can hardly be said to have achieved that liberty: its prophets were preachers, who continued within the priestly orbit, or, as Milton said, new presbyter was old priest writ large.[13] Within any social order, however established, there may be improvement and development, new strategies for new occasions, social criticism, individual or mystical recreations of the original vision. But by definition and hypothesis, nothing can transcend the revelation of the Torah or the Gospel or the Koran or the writings of Marx: whatever appears to do so is only a heresy, an old fallacy in a new disguise.

Such a feeling is intolerable to the mood of many people today, at least in the democracies, and one of the features of our age is an anxious search for some kind of prophetic or transcending vision of the social order. Here again is an intensifying of something that has been with us for a long time. Protestantism, I said, did not succeed in liberating prophecy, but it did produce some remarkable prophetic figures, including Milton. Milton's *Areopagitica* seems to me to represent a turning point in the history of Western culture so far as our present subject is concerned. It is an attack on censorship and a defence of the liberty of the press which is important perhaps less as that than as the first suggestion that the power of prophecy is starting to come from the printing press rather than the pulpit, from secular rather than sacerdotal contexts. This may be expanded into the general principle that the prophet is most likely to emerge from an unrecognized quarter of society, from a place that society has overlooked, or forgotten to enclose and protect.

Ever since the Romantic period, at least, we have tended to recognize a prophetic authority in literature, and in the arts generally. Some writers, notably in the T.S. Eliot and T.E. Hulme generation, have made a good deal of renouncing this attitude, but they usually turned out to be only prophetic plainclothesmen. The original prophets were ecstatics who went into trances and spoke with different voices, and their prestige had much to do with the primitive reverence for such abnormal states of mind. Thus Samuel says to Saul: "It shall come to pass, when thou art come thither to the city, that thou shalt meet a company of prophets coming down from the high place . . . and they shall prophesy: And the Spirit of the Lord will come upon thee, and thou shalt prophesy with them, and shalt be turned into another man" [1 Samuel 10:5–6]. The fact that creative powers come from an area of the mind that seems to be independent of the conscious will, and often emerge with a good deal of emotional disturbance in their wake, provides the chief analogy between prophecy and the arts. The creative people that we most instinctively call or think of as prophetic—Nietzsche, Rimbaud, Blake, Van Gogh, Dostoevsky, Strindberg—show the analogy very clearly. Some people pursue wholeness and integration; others get smashed up, and fragments are rescued from the smash of an intensity that the wholeness and integration people do not reach.

Then too, the prophetic aspect of the arts is reflected in the great difficulty that society has in absorbing its creative people. The fierce persecution of so many of the best Russian writers by the Soviet bureaucracy comes readily to mind, and there are many parallels in the democracies. At the same time, if the prophetic voice so frequently comes from the outsider, it follows that society's most effective defence against prophecy is toleration. The realization of this, in our society, has helped to create an almost obsessive preoccupation with the subcultures or countercultures of various minorities—blacks, chicanos, homosexuals, terrorists, drug addicts, occultists, yogis, criminals like the holy and blessed Genet[14]—wherever it may still be possible to make out a case for social hostility or discrimination. Similarly with the revival of dada and other movements in the arts that spill over into anarchistic activism. We read in the Old Testament of prophets who used various emblematic devices to make their oracular points: "And Zedekiah the son of Chenaanah made him horns of iron: and he said, Thus saith the Lord, With these shalt thou push the Syrians, until thou have consumed them"

[1 Kings 22:11]. There seems some analogy here to the brief vogue of the "happening," when, for instance, large blocks of ice were set up in various street corners in Los Angeles and left to melt, presumably as an emblem of California civilization.

Again, many great writers have been not simply neurotic but called mad, like Blake, or confined in asylums, like Ezra Pound. The assumption in the word "mad," which is a social judgment, is that society as a whole is always sane, a difficult assumption to accept in the twentieth century. We are now told, by R.D. Laing and others,[15] not only that schizophrenia, for example, may be a quite normal reaction to a mad society, but that the primitive sense of the prophetic authority of madness, the ancient linking of the manic and the mantic, may have been more nearly right than some of our notions about mental illness. But however useful the self-criticism involved in exploring every corner of society in search of yet unheard oracles, it may be well, before we settle permanently into a second-coming syndrome, to remember that there is another and more traditional side to prophecy.

Milton's *Areopagitica* has another importance for us in this connection. It was written while Milton was pondering the subject of his epic, and was slowly shifting over from the story of Arthur to the story of Adam. *Paradise Lost* retells one of the original myths of Milton's culture in such a way as to make it a parable of the failure of the revolutionary movement of Milton's time and, by implication, of the failure of all efforts of an age of the people to maintain its own freedom without help from the kind of power that the Son of God symbolizes in the poem. Significantly, that failure went around in a circle, from revolt against Charles I to acceptance of Charles II. However right or wrong his views, Milton's poem illustrates the curious link, which we found implicit in Vico's argument, between the age of the gods and the age of the people. For the story of Adam is the story of Everyman, excluded from Paradise and wandering in the circles of lost direction all through history, yet never quite losing the hope of an eventual return to something that is not the beginning of another cycle. The hero of *Paradise Lost* is a human trinity made up of Christ, Adam, and Milton himself. Adam is man in the cycle of history; Milton is the prophet who restructures the myth and makes Christ and Adam his own and our contemporaries; Christ represents the fact that although man does not much want freedom, there is a power, identical with his own creative power, which is determined to force it on him.

The story of Arthur, on the other hand, is a theme belonging to the Homeric convention, in which the poet's chief function is to glorify a hero. The hero, to revert again to Vico, is one of the ascendant class of rulers who appear as feudal overlords at one end of the cycle of history and as divine Caesars or charismatic dictators at the other end. The glorifying of the hero thus implies acceptance of the cycle with its *ricorso* as the ultimate horizon of human existence. No comparative value judgments are involved here, but Milton's final choice of subject was an act of criticism, and helps us to understand the place of criticism in the literary process. The critical principle involved is the identifying of something in the literary tradition with the activity that we have been calling prophetic.

The work of most middle-class people today consists mainly in the polluting of paper, or what is known as filling out forms. I struggle hard to keep up with the avalanche of poetry and fiction produced in Canada, and the bulk of this, however interesting in itself, consists of filling out conventional forms, no less than filing an income tax return. Similarly with the routine of the critic's work, editing texts, commenting, and researching into historical background. But there is something in the whole enterprise that is different. A work of art is an effort at imaginative communication: if it succeeds in being that, it becomes the focus of a community. The critic is there, not so much to explain the poet, as to translate literature into a continuous dialogue with society.

The word "critic" is connected with the word "crisis," and all the critic's scholarly routines revolve around a critical moment and a critical act, which is always the same moment and act however often it recurs. This act, I have so often urged, is not an act of judgment but of recognition. If the critic is the judge, the community he represents is supreme in authority over the poet; all human creation must conform to the anxieties of human institutions. But if the critic abandons judgment for recognition, the act of recognition liberates something in human creative energy, and thereby helps to give the community the power to judge itself. If the critic is to recognize the prophetic, of course, he needs to be prophetic too: his model is John the Baptist, the greatest prophet of his age, whose critical moment came with recognizing a still greater power than his own. I do not mean by this that the critic's function is to wait for a great poet to come along and then recognize him: practically everything the critic will ever recognize accurately is already here. Still less do I mean that the significant critical act is to recognize the supremacy of poets over critics. That points to an utterly muddled and misconceived notion of the critic's role.

The cultural trauma that Vico symbolizes by the thunderclap is projection, the accepting of a mysterious power outside man which is first called the will of the gods, then incarnated in a ruling class. As the sense of power transfers itself to the people, guilt feelings left over from earlier phases may continue unresolved: every scandal and crime may contribute to a growing sense of failure and muddle and self-contempt, until before we know where we are the charismatic leader is there again. That is why the inner self-transforming of the original myth is so important. In the age of the gods we learn that God made the Garden of Eden for man, that man fell out of it through his own fault and is now shut out of it for ever. In the age of heroes we learn that there are huge parks or enclosures set aside for our great men, where they may hunt and enjoy themselves, but which the rest of us must keep out of. In the age of the people we begin to learn, at last, something of what is meant by the metaphor of "creation."

The world around us is not necessarily a creation: there is no reason why the actual world should have a beginning or an end. But everything human is created: man has created his gods, his rulers, his institutions, his machines, and it is only when he enters the created world, through a door that someone's imagination has opened, that he can participate in this and feel that the word "subject," in all its contexts, no longer applies to him. The sense of freedom and release that we can get from entering the created world is so great that we can also understand why religious and political organizations are so anxious about the creative process, and use every pretext to regulate or control or get rid of it. But the critic is constantly trying to find his and our way back to the original lightning flash which the trauma of the thunderclap has caused us to forget. The door to our Eden is still locked, but he has a key, and the key is the act of recognition.

I began by separating the use of words to illustrate something in action or thought from the self-contained body of words which exists for its own sake. These, I said, are not two kinds of structures: every verbal structure has both aspects. We might distinguish them as what the words mean and what the words say. The psychologist Eric Berne, in a popular handbook called *What Do You Say After You Say Hello?* remarks that when a child is picking up patterns of behaviour from his parents, he listens not to what is said to him but to the imperatives implied in what is said to him. The principle is very similar to that of Frege, referred to by Wittgenstein, that every assertion contains an assumption, the assumption being what is really asserted.[16] Society does the same thing with a revelation: it asks, not, What does it say? but, What does this tell us to do? The prophet, on the contrary, is first of all a sayer and an asserter, even when he does not think of himself as the primary source of what he says.

As a structure of meaning, every body of words is an ideological document, the product of a specific social and historical condition in the cycle of human life. In this context there is nothing really prophetic in any human utterance, outside the group that accepts it as a revelation. Isaiah has a tremendous vision of God treading the winepress of wrath [Isaiah 63:3], but that, historically, is only a squalid jingoism gloating over the future discomfiture of a hated enemy. Elijah hears a still small voice after the earthquake and fire [1 Kings 19:12], but, historically, all that the voice tells him to do is to liquidate the opposition, exterminate the priests of Baal. Similarly, the great prophetic figures of modern literature, Rousseau or Swift or Kierkegaard or Dostoevsky, may often not have been much more than wrongheaded neurotics in their historical and biographical context. What the critic tries to do is to lead us from what poets and prophets meant, or thought they meant, to the inner structure of what they said. At that point the verbal structure turns inside out, and a vortex opens out of the present moment, from the world of the Viconian cycle into the created world.

Literature, including all structures in words which come to be literary in the course of time, shows an extraordinary conservatism and sense of tradition and convention, along with an equally extraordinary power of renewing itself. It thereby suggests that the real course of human life may be neither a closed circle nor a straight line going off into unknown directions and hazards, but an expanding and open-ended cycle, the stages of which may be simultaneous as well as temporal. The ages of gods and of people are opposite poles of the cycle. At one end is a sense of infinite and eternal mystery, at the other a sense of unlimited possibilities. All through literature the tone I have been calling prophetic keeps echoing the sense of the infinite and eternal, not as what is meant, but as what is said in spite of what is meant. In the Bible there are references to a prophecy which has to be sealed up and hidden away until its time has come. That time comes when in the age of the people the gods become names for human powers that belong to us, and that we can in part recover. Ultimately, all criticism is social criticism, and while it is the part of the creative imagination to say, with Eliot, "Do not think of the fruit of action" [*The Dry Salvages*, pt. 3, l. 38], it is the part of the critical intelligence, by recognizing and responding to it, to ensure that something at least of the essential act of creation does bear fruit.

5

Comment on Peter Hughes's Essay

1977

From Yale Italian Studies, *1 (Winter 1977): 91–2, published under the title "Comment by Northrop Frye to Peter Hughes's Essay." Hughes's essay, "Vico and Literary History," appears on pp. 83–90 of the same issue.*

It seems to me that implicit in Vico's conception of poetic myth is a double movement, one centrifugal and one centripetal, that follows the course of history until the *ricorso* brings it around again. Mythology, in his as in the modern sense, is the source of both a literary and a nonliterary development. In the nonliterary context, the primary use of myth is to rationalize law, law including the whole context of custom, ritual, and class structure. Law is first thought to be revealed by the gods; in the heroic age laws are drawn up in the interests of an ascendant class, and after this age there comes a growing sense that the people themselves are the source of the law, and responsible for both changing and administering it. Democratic and Marxist movements today are both, from the Viconian point of view, movements designed to perpetuate the demotic law, and stop the *ricorso* from coming round again. Vico was less sanguine about the possibility of transcending his cycle, but he wasn't hung up on the cycle, and this centrifugal or legal context of myth is what he's chiefly concerned with. His heavy allegorical emphasis in interpreting myth is quite consistent with his social emphasis, and this emphasis is, as you say, the one followed by Michelet, Marx, and Sorel (also by Innis in Canada in his historical theory of communications).[1]

In the literary context, myths stick together to form a mythology, which in turn builds up a mythological or imaginative universe. Within this, literature grows up, literature being a displaced form of mythology,

recreating itself in the various divine, heroic, and demotic contexts of the cycle. Here the recreation takes the form of what you call an "implosion," the self-renewal of the central powerhouse, so to speak, where myth forms a body of imaginative language that changes to make itself intelligible to the different stages of social development. The demotic stage of this language is what is usually meant by realism in literary criticism. Study of the literary aspect of mythology has to be mainly structural in emphasis, not allegorical.

The return to myth and romance in contemporary literature may indicate, from one point of view, a tendency to go round the bend with the *ricorso*. But this return is not necessarily a reactionary or counter-revolutionary movement: it could also form part of a counter-*ricorso*, where mythical and heroic language are recovered within a total demotic context. That would transform the cyclical return into something more like a spiral expansion, which I think is hinted at in Joyce's recreation of Vico's "the same anew."[2]

6

Literature, History, and Language

29 March 1979

Originally presented at a conference on "Theories of Literary History" organized by the Centre for Comparative Literature at the University of Toronto, 28–31 March 1979. From Bulletin of the Midwest Modern Language Association, *12 (Fall 1979): 1–7. Reprinted with minor changes as "Literary History" in* New Literary History, *12 (Winter 1981): 219–25, and in* The Horizon of Literature, *ed. Paul Hernadi (Lincoln: University of Nebraska Press, 1982), 43–51. The typescript is in the NFF, 1988, box 47, file 1.*

When I first became interested in problems of literary history, I became very impatient with the kind of literary history that told me nothing about the history of literature, but was simply ordinary history specializing in the names and dates of authors. Genuinely literary history, I thought, was largely concerned with conventions and genres, and as I looked further into it, it began to take on two aspects, one diachronic, the other synchronic. Diachronically, it showed a kind of Darwinian pattern, throwing mutations out more or less at random and descending through whatever had the greatest survival value. The survival value was derived largely from the ideologies of the ascendant classes, and in each age there was a popular literature which had the special function, for the historian, of indicating what the ascendant conventions would be in the next age. Thus in Elizabethan times the ascendant conventions of prose fiction were exhibited by Lyly's *Euphues* and Sidney's *Arcadia*, while Deloney's more popular stories[1] showed what fiction would be like when the class addressed by Deloney came to power, which it did around Defoe's time. Yet every modulation in convention seemed to throw up much the same patterns as before, so that the genres of comedy and romance, for example, maintained an extraordinary similarity through all the centuries of social change.

I have lately begun to turn my attention to the Bible, not so much as a work of literature but as what Blake calls the "Great Code of Art,"[2] a kind of model for the reading and study of literature. Dante used scripture as a model for literature, including his own poetry, in a similar way. But with the Bible a different kind of historical question arose, which I had not thought much about previously. This question arose out of one of the first problems confronting me: in what language has the Bible been written? The factual answers, Hebrew and Greek, hardly do justice to a book which has exerted most of its cultural influence in translation, whether Latin or vernacular. But this, to use a convenient French distinction, applies only to the *langue* of the Bible, not to its *langage*.[3] It seemed to me that there was a history of *langage* to be considered as well, and this naturally took me to Vico, the first person to think seriously about such matters.

Vico suggested that language followed the three main phases of his cultural cycle—the age of the gods, the age of the heroes, and the age of the people—after which a *ricorso* occurred and started the cycle over again. He called these three phases of language hieroglyphic, hieratic, and demotic. These terms refer to different kinds of writing, because Vico believed that men communicated by signs before they could talk. I think some kind of adaptation of Vico's principle would make a good deal of sense of the history of language, though the adaptation has to be a very free one. I think there have been, since Old Testament times, three phases of language, but these three phases cut across the *ricorso* that Vico postulates for the Middle Ages. Also they seem to me not primarily different kinds of writing, but kinds of communication both oral and written. Again, all three phases overlap and coexist. A Sumerian or Egyptian of 3000 B.C., if he were ordering stone for a building, or dickering with his in-laws about the finances of his marriage, or assessing the amount of tax owed by a farmer, would use much the same linguistic categories of true and false, reasonable and fanciful, that we should use now. I am speaking of the culturally ascendant aspect of the language, the aspect we find in religious or literary documents.

The first phase of language is "hieroglyphic," not necessarily in the sense of sign-writing, but in the sense of using words as signs. In this phase the word evokes the image: it is an active force, a word of power, and there is a magic latent in it which can affect, even control, some of the operations of nature. At the New Year's Day ritual in Babylon the poem of creation, *Enuma Elish,* was read: the reading presumably helped to sustain and encourage the order of nature whose origin it described.[4] Puns and popular etymologies involved in the naming of people and places affect the character of what is given the name. Spirits can be controlled by verbal formulas; warriors begin battles with the boasts that may be words of power for them. Boasting is for the same reason most objectionable to the gods. All words in this phase are concrete: there are no true verbal abstractions. Onians's monumental study of Homer's vocabulary shows how intensely physical such conceptions as soul, mind, time, courage, emotion, thought, and the like are in his poems.[5] Homer's conceptions were evidently not metaphorical to him, but they are to us: we see metaphor, the word that expresses an identity of person and thing, as the controlling figure of this phase of language. The typical expression of metaphor is the god, the being who, as sun-god or war-god or whatever, represents this metaphorical unity of consciousness and objectivity most clearly.

The operations of the human mind are also controlled by words of power, formulas of the type called mantras in Indian religion. Prose in this phase is discontinuous, a series of gnarled epigrammatic statements which are not to be argued about but must be accepted and pondered, transformed into words of power. We can see how the prose of the Bible, for example, breaks down into prose kernels of this discontinuous kind: law and commandment in the opening books, proverb and aphorism in the wisdom literature, oracle in the prophecies, pericope in the Gospels. Presocratic philosophy, so called, is mainly communicated in discontinuous aphorisms of a similar type.

The second phase of language is more individualized, and regards words as primarily the expression of thoughts. It comes into Greek culture with the dialectic of Plato, and is associated by Eric Havelock with the development of writing itself,[6] though I should prefer to think of it as primarily a development of continuous prose. This is the period of the vast metaphysical and theological systems that dominate thought from Plato to Hegel. Such language is "hieratic" in the sense of being produced by an intellectual elite. In this phase the word expresses the idea, and the typical verbal structure is an ordering of ideas, in a long sequacious march from premises to conclusions. The compelling magic of the previous phase is sublimated here into a magic of sequence or linear ordering. "I think, therefore I am," says Descartes:[7] the operative word is "therefore," an antecedent belief in the connectability of words. Similarly with the ontological proof of God, which reduces itself to "I think, therefore God exists."[8] Many notions much more bizarre than these, such as extreme Calvinist views of predestination, may be clung to in spite of what seems to be common sense because of the strength of the feeling: if you accept this, then you must, etc. It is a highly intellectualized form of language, but its tendency is not so much to reasoning as to rationalizing, expanding agreed-on premises into verbal armies marching sequentially across reality. Its central conception is not the god but God, the infinite reality of the person, and its controlling figure is metonymy, which expresses the analogy of the finite verbal world to an infinite God. The second phase comes closest to the first phase in the genre of oratory, which continues to use a highly figured language, and oratory is also "hieratic" in the sense of drawing an audience into a closer unit of agreement. From Cicero's time to the Renaissance, at least, the orator was regarded as the user of words *par excellence*.

The third phase of language begins theoretically with Bacon in English literature, and effectively with Locke. Here words are regarded as the servomechanisms of sense experience and the mental operations which attend sense experience. It is a conception of language as primarily descriptive of nature, and is at the opposite extreme from the first phase: instead of the word's evoking the image, the image evokes the word. This use of language corresponds to Vico's "demotic" phase, and is an approach to language that avoids figuration, whether metaphorical or metonymic. Such devices are regarded as "merely verbal," and the ideal in style is framed on the model of truth by correspondence: a verbal structure is set up beside what it describes and is called true if it seems to provide a satisfactory correspondence to it. As compared with the second phase, it still employs continuous prose, but all deductive procedures are subordinated to a primary fact-gathering process. The predominance of this approach to language, along with the principle of public access to its documents, is the technical invention that makes democracy a practical possibility. The demotic writer, ideally at least, by avoiding all figures of speech appeals only to the consensus of experience and reason. The oratorical figures continue in advertising and propaganda, but these are normally distinguishable genres.

In our day we seem to have reached the end of a gigantic linguistic cycle, but a cycle is a failed spiral, and instead of entering a Viconian *ricorso* and going around the cycle again, we should surely start another one on a higher level. It is one of the few genuinely reassuring features of contemporary culture that there should be so heavy an emphasis on the resources and capabilities of language itself, apart from whatever it embodies itself in. It seems to be, and certainly should be, an essential aspect of this study of language that it recognize the equal validity of all three phases without trying to make any one culturally dominant, as they have successively been in the past.

The Bible belongs primarily to the first phase of language: its chief second-phase features are its metonymic or monotheistic God and its constant use of oratorical devices. There are no true rational arguments even in the New Testament, which for all its late date is still astonishingly close to the first phase. What look like rational arguments, such as the Epistle to the Hebrews, turn out on closer analysis to be disguised forms of exhortation; in other words, oratory. In the Old Testament, metaphors, puns, and popular etymologies occur so frequently that they clearly represent the dominant mode of verbal thinking: in the Gospels Jesus defines his nature and function primarily in terms of metaphor ("I am the door" [John 10:7, 9], and so forth), and many even of the central doctrines of post-Biblical Christianity, such as the Trinity or the Real Presence, can be grammatically formulated only in metaphor.

Literature adapts itself to the dominant phase of language, mainly through allegory in the second phase and through what is called realism in the third. But it is the primary function of poetry, at least, to keep recreating the first phase of language and insisting on it as a valid form of linguistic activity during the domination of the other phases. In, say, the Middle Ages, it was subordinate in cultural authority to the great conceptual systems like those of St. Thomas, and so, in practice if not in theory, was the Bible itself.

Second-phase hieratic writing and thinking tends to deconstruct such metaphorical structures as the Bible and assimilate them to its own deductive and systematic arrangements. This is usually done through allegory, which is a technique of continuously paralleling metaphorical with conceptual language. Allegory in its turn is a special form of analogy. The tendency of allegory is to smooth out and reconcile an originally metaphorical structure by making it conform to a consistent conceptual norm. In this it is greatly aided by its distinctive rhetorical tool of continuous prose, and by the quality inherent in continuous prose of being able to reconcile anything with anything else. The Bible, in this phase, is wrapped up in thicker and thicker coverings of commentary, until finally it loses most of its effective authority apart from the commentary. That is, its essential truth is regarded as being better expressed in the form of the commentary.

In the third phase, where the conception of language is descriptive, allegorical commentary tends to disappear in favour of a direct confrontation with the work itself, either as an object of knowledge or as an object of experience. As an object of knowledge, it is studied in relation to its own time and historical context; as an object of experience, it is studied in relation to its relevance for us. A tendency began with the Protestant Reformation to scrap the accretions of tradition and try to confront the Bible directly, although of course in practice this meant mainly a reabsorbing of it into the rationalizing constructs of the Reformers. A historical criticism gradually developed as a by-product of this tendency, which is now the dominant form of Biblical scholarship. After that, archaeology opened the door from the Biblical to the pre-Biblical, and since then the Bible has been increasingly studied as a mass of traces of pre-Biblical activity, Mesopotamian or Canaanite or Ugaritic or what not, becoming in itself a zero degree of writing[9] in a fairly literal sense. When criticism gets so far back in time that there is no longer any documentary evidence to support it, it has to turn psychological, as the scholar's own subconscious is all that is left which is sufficiently primitive to work on.

The criticism of secular literature, dealing as it does with what are essentially metaphorical documents, shows a similar double movement of commentary and description, one a wrapping-up, forward movement increasing a tradition of commentary, and the other an unwrapping, backward movement to the naked text. The graduate student of literature is asked both to write a thesis incorporating a scholarly tradition and to teach the texts of literature to undergraduates. There is a core of truth in both procedures.

Verbal structures are organized in narrative sequences, or *mythoi*. In the first, metaphorical phase of literature, these *mythoi* are mainly stories; in the second, metonymic phase they are mainly conceptual myths or arguments, which again can be related by analogy to the story myths preceding them. In the third phase the narrative sequence is conventionally assumed to be provided by whatever in the external world is being described. This involves a good deal of rhetorical ingenuity, much of it unconscious, to conceal the fact that it is not, but is being generated by the linguistic movement itself, like the narratives of the earlier phases. In fact narrative structures show very little essential change throughout the three phases, though the characteristics of each phase are still largely unexplored. There is no narrative structure that began in historical times, any more than there is any human being whose ancestry began in historical times. Hence every myth can be traced back until it disappears from view in the Tertiary Age, and traced forward to our own time.

This basis supplies us with a number of critical axioms. First, all argumentative or descriptive verbal structures can be studied diagrammatically, as analogous to story myths. Thus in the title of Gibbon's history the phrase "decline and fall" indicates the mythical shape, the principle on which he selected his material and arranged his sequential narrative.[10] Similarly, the shape of Hegel's *Phenomenology of Spirit* is the same Eros mountain-climb that we have in Dante's *Purgatorio*. Second, a myth "means" everything that it has been effectively made to mean (I say "effectively" because there may be some extreme treatments that dropped out of the tradition or belong to another myth). Thus what St. John of the Cross did to the Song of Songs in *The Dark Night of the Soul* cannot be dismissed as a strained allegorical wrenching of the theme, but is an integral part of its historical development. Third, the profoundest "meanings" of a myth are not necessarily in its very early manifestations. The profoundest treatment of a winter–summer contest is more likely to be in Shakespeare's *Winter's Tale* than in a St. George folk play, though the latter may display the skeleton of the myth more clearly. Fourth, we need not worry about doing violence to the "uniqueness" of a work of literature by studying its mythical ancestry and descent. What is called content, for example, is the structure of the individual work, as distinct from the structure of the convention or genre it belongs to.

It seems to me that the central conception involved in the historical sequence of literary works is the conception of recreation. A reader recreates everything he reads, more or less in his own image; a poet recreates something in previous literature; perhaps a text does not exist at all except as somebody's recreation of it. In all recreation there is a son–father relationship which has a double aspect: an Oedipus relation where the son kills the father, and a Christian relation where the son identifies with the father. This is similarly the relation of gospel to law at the centre of the Bible, and in fact we cannot trace the Bible back to a time when it was not recreating itself. Similarly, when we study works of literature, there is an effort to annihilate tradition by isolating them, and simultaneously an effort to identify with tradition by studying them in their context, historical or contemporary. Out of this paradox criticism is born, where we stumble all night over bones of the dead, in Blake's phrase [*The Voice of the Ancient Bard*, l. 9], and find in the morning that a living organism has rearticulated itself.

7

On Translation

May 1979

Unpublished introduction to W.A.C.H. Dobson's translation of Li Po's poems. From the typescript, in the NFF, 1988, box 47, file 1.

What in poetry is translatable? It is easier to begin with the other side of the question, What is not translatable? What is not translatable are the accidents of language: the features that make words rhyme in one language and not in another, the differences in rhythm that make, for example, the hexameter useful in French but awkward in English, the kind of humour that depends on verbal wit, the associative clusters of meaning around words that are different for every language. With English and Chinese, there is the further difficulty of rendering a sequence of characters into an alphabetical system. Such differences are so perasive, and go so deeply into the process of poetic thought, that we could understand it if a translator gave up altogether. Language is the most fragmented of all human activities, and poetic language is the most fragmented aspect of it.

What can be translated is what is usually called the "sense." Here we see the other side of language: that it is a form of communication, and that there is something intelligible to be communicated. But in poetry the "sense" exists on two levels. There is, as Gerard Manley Hopkins says, an "overthought," the so-called prose sense, and an "underthought," the progression of imagery and metaphor.[1] It is not difficult to convey the overthought: anyone who can read a second language at all can give some account of its prose or manifest sense. It is the underthought which is the translator's real battleground. With poetry he cannot take the easy path of conveying the prose sense and cutting his inevitable linguistic losses. He has to try to show that his poet is thinking poetically in another language, and that nevertheless that process of thought can be adapted to another.

It is through wrestling with this problem that the translator shows us how poetry is a universal language as well as a collection of all the confusions of Babel. We find in this book how Chinese poetry, like our own, keeps recreating itself from its own resources, as one poet adapts the work-song of "hearse-pullers," and then a later poet adapts the adaptation. We learn from Li Po how the "vanities of generals" can transform a huge populous empire into a beleaguered fortress, just as it can do on the other side of the world twelve centuries later. Chinese poets, like European poets, show us how the poet's mind constantly teeters between the discriminations of waking life and the acceptances of dreams, and hence how drunkenness can symbolize that mind. We learn how gorgeous luxuries represent an insane perversion of social values, as they do with us, how a bird incarnates the freedom a prisoner longs for, how in China, as in the Song of Songs, love is as strong as death and jealousy cruel as the grave [Song of Solomon 8:6]. We find out many other things too, but it is high time for the reader to turn the page.

8

Extracts from *The Practical Imagination: Stories, Poems, Plays*

1980

"Preface," "On Fiction," "On Poetry," "On Drama," from the first edition of The Practical Imagination: Stories, Poems, Plays, *ed. Northrop Frye, Sheridan Baker, and George Perkins (New York: Harper & Row, 1980). In 1987, a revised compact edition appeared, with Barbara Perkins as an additional editor. In the revised edition, the preface to which is included below, introductions have been slightly altered and abridged, and the language has been made inclusive; substantial changes are indicated here in endnotes. The typescripts are in the NFF, 1988, box 47, file 3.*

While the works included in the sections on fiction and drama are listed in notes 1 and 8 respectively, the sheer number of poems precludes a similar endnote for the poetry section. The latter was reissued in 1983 as The Practical Imagination: An Introduction to Poetry.

Preface

The Practical Imagination introduces students to the view that literature is both enjoyable and practically useful as it awakens our consciousness of how and where we live: in our imaginations, really—in our perceptions of ourselves as we face the world. Indeed, literature is perhaps our most immediately practical educator, from fairy tale and nursery rhyme onward, engaging our responses as it widens our vision and clarifies our perspectives.

This book is an anthology. It covers the forms and varieties of fiction, poetry, and drama, moving from the simple elements to the more subtle and complex, with introductory principles and questions to guide the student's progress. Each section begins with an introduction to the genre and concludes with a chapter on how to write about it. Some works are given full discussion, with questions; others not. We have been liberal with footnotes to help the student. We have closed few doors. The aim is to acquaint students with good literature in its various modes, to familiarize them with the questions to ask and the principles to support their judgments, and to show them how discussion and writing can deepen their appreciation and understanding, not only of the literary work, but of themselves.

Our generic survey introducing fiction emphasizes the relationship between oral and written traditions. In chapter 1, "The Narrative Impulse," we begin with the oral tale—*Rumpelstiltskin* and *Stone Soup*—and examine the ways the ancient theme of wish-fulfilment has been shaped by three sophisticated modern storytellers, ending with the narrative complexities of Kipling's *The Man Who Would Be King*. In the next four chapters, we explore narrative point of view, stressing at first the "I" narrator in stories as varied as Poe's *The Tell-Tale Heart* and Lessing's *The Old Chief Mshlanga*, before moving on to omniscient narration in Fitzgerald, Lawrence, and Chopin. Chapters 5 and 6 shift the emphasis back from point of view to content, as we illustrate realism and then show metaphor, symbol, and allegory at work: writers range from Dreiser and Langston Hughes through Joyce and Dylan Thomas. Chapter 7 invites students to put their knowledge together in a consideration of meaning, not only in established and realistic writers such as Porter, London, and Dostoevsky, but in newer, experimental, and "absurd" authors such as Le Guin, Lem, Borges, and Pynchon. Chapter 8 presents for extended study two outstanding longer fictions, *The Death of Ivan Ilych* and *The Secret Sharer*. Throughout, we attempt to increase the joy of reading by the pleasure of improved understanding, so that discussion and writing can be attractive challenges, successfully met.

Poetry follows fiction because beginning students generally do best when armed with a confidence, a vocabulary, and a strategy of criticism won through successful study of short stories. Nevertheless, because poetry still strikes some as an alien form, we begin slowly, with additional assistance in definition, discussion, and footnotes. After the introductory overview, we divide the field into "lyric" and "narrative," before considering the elements of dramatic situation and character fundamental to poetry. Then comes a chapter on language, followed by a chapter to show the beginner how poets often turn anew to timeless human themes. Next come images and metaphors; then sound and metre, after which we turn to traditional forms, free forms, consideration of poems in specific times and places, and a small gathering of popular poems. "Poems for Study" presents, chronologically, some valuable poems not otherwise represented. All told, we have printed almost 350 poems, a sampling rich enough for all approaches.

Our plays represent the Western tradition, from the Greeks to the present. We begin with tragedy and comedy, with Sophocles, Shakespeare, Aristophanes, and Molière as examples against which students may measure the plays from later times. A chapter on "Social Drama" directs attention to theme; we pursue the question into "Farce, Fantasy, and the Absurd," with Pirandello, Ionesco, and Albee. In "Writing About Drama," we print and discuss Beckett's *Not I* as a paradigm of how difficulties in interpretation may be met and surmounted. Because many of the plays have been translated, we have taken particular pains to ensure authoritative texts that are also accessible to students, beginning with the Dudley Fitts and Robert Fitzgerald *Oedipus Rex* and the Donald Sutherland *Lysistrata*. Shakespeare's *Macbeth* is presented as edited by Alfred Harbage, with his notes, and *The Tempest* as edited, with notes, by Northrop Frye.

Northrop Frye has written the three generic introductions. Sheridan Baker has written the three "Writing Abouts" and the framework for the fiction section. George Perkins has written the framework for poetry and drama and supplied most of the questions, headnotes, and footnotes. The three of us have put our heads together to pool our concepts and to organize and select the best stories, poems, and plays to illustrate them. We have shared our literary and editorial perceptions as we have revised and aligned our individual contributions into what we feel is a unified and effective whole to bring students the joys and practical understanding of literature.

Of our many debts to innumerable teachers, students, and colleagues, we would like to express particular gratitude to Jane Widdicombe, Robert Elias, and Louis Budd, who gave valuable assistance in the final stages.

Northrop Frye
Sheridan Baker
George Perkins

On Fiction[1]

The Oral Tradition

Stories were told orally long before they came to depend on reading and writing. Many such stories have survived as folk tales preserved in a community's memory, and a few examples of such tales are given here. As a rule folk tales have simple characterization, seldom going beyond, say, a contrast between a clever and a stupid person. The story line is what is important, and it usually drives straight to the end, with few if any surprises. As there is little dependence on local or specific allusion, folk tales can travel through the world past all barriers of language and culture. In *The Pardoner's Tale* Chaucer tells a story that had probably reached him from a French source, but the story itself can be traced to India, where, five centuries later, Rudyard Kipling heard it and put it into his *Second Jungle Book*.[2] Kipling's story is recognizably the "same" story as Chaucer's, even though all the details are different.

Similarly, the motif of the impossible task that is somehow accomplished, in *Rumpelstiltskin*, can be found in a famous Classical myth, the story of Cupid and Psyche, and the story of the soup made of stones forms the subject of a play by W.B. Yeats [*The Pot of Broth*]. In W.W. Jacobs's *The Monkey's Paw*, the three wishes remind us of folk tale again, as does the sardonic treatment of the love potion in John Collier's *The Chaser*. Even Kipling's *The Man Who Would Be King*, for all the realism of detail, turns on the theme of the hero betrayed through a woman that we find in the stories of Samson and Hercules.[3]

The oral story with its linear drive can be, like many simple structures, a very powerful one, and we can see its influence in, for example, Jack London's *To Build a Fire*. Here there is only one character (except for the dog), and the only suspense is that of inevitability. We know what will happen: the story seems to exist in only one dimension, that of time, and we are anxious to reach the end, not because we are bored, but because the end gives us the sense of resolution, of a pattern completing itself. The man in the story is not a sympathetic character, and the workings of his imagination are kept to a minimum. No identification with him is wanted: our attention is wholly absorbed in the sequence of movements he makes to keep alive. The smallest details become gigantic: the spark of life in his body depends on the tiny flame of his match, and as some snow slides off a branch it carries his death sentence with it. Such urgency of narrative movement, even in a story written to be read, still derives from the sense of listening to a speaking voice. Even a story as long and complex as Tolstoy's *The Death of Ivan Ilych* preserves the same feeling of inexorable advance. The emphasis on narrative pacing reaches an extreme in Poe's *The Tell-Tale Heart*, where the movement of time, represented by the ticking of a watch and the heartbeat associated with it, enters the story as, in a way, its chief character.

The Written Tradition

Most stories now, however, are written to be read, and a printed page gives a second dimension, a sense of space as well as time. When the whole story is visually before us, a number of things can go on simultaneously, and the plot may twist unexpectedly. If we read Ambrose Bierce's *The Boarded Window* or Faulkner's *A Rose for Emily* quickly, concentrating on the narrative movement, the last sentence may come as a puzzling surprise, but we can always look back to see what clues the author gave us that we missed. The nightmarish experiences of the young man in Hawthorne's *My Kinsman, Major Molineux* may also impel us to see whether the opening paragraph, about political upsets in prerevolutionary America, was really as irrelevant as it may have seemed on first reading. In a written story a sense of the difference between appearance and reality makes itself felt, so that we feel that we are discovering something behind the narrative movement.

Narrative Techniques

Naturally, most writers will look for some way of preserving both the driving energy of the oral tale and the sense of discovery in the written one. The most common way of doing this is to tell the story through one of the main characters, in contrast to the so-called "omniscient" narrator who is not tied to a single point of view. The urgency of a speaking voice still dominates our attention, but the speaking character is not the whole story, and the interactions with the other characters provide the second or spatial dimension. The narrator is often not aware of all the implications in the story he or she is telling. When the narrator of Ring Lardner's *Haircut* says at the end, "it probably served Jim right, what he got," the reader agrees verbally, but the agreement is on different levels of comprehension. In John Updike's *A&P* the narrator tells us his side of a confrontation of two attitudes that are both quixotic, though for different reasons. The narrator, however, has enough self-knowledge to say, "it seems to me that once you begin a gesture it's fatal not to go through with it," so he also understands that he is only part of the story.

There are two limitations, not necessarily hampering ones, in telling a story through a major character. One is that the author is restricted to that character's speech, and in modern times standard literary English and colloquial speech are often almost different languages. In Faulkner's *A Rose for Emily* the story is told by a minor character whom we never really see, hence a full vocabulary can be used, with such phrases as "stubborn and coquettish decay" in describing Emily's house. But in Sherwood Anderson's *I'm a Fool* the inarticulateness of the boy narrator is part of the point of the story: he knows what has happened to him, but cannot break out of his immature framework of language with its recurrent "gee whiz." The reader has to supply an understanding that makes up for this. On the other hand inarticulateness has its own eloquence, as a failure of expression increases pathos. A more precise vocabulary would not give the concentrated desolation of the last sentence of Hemingway's *My Old Man*: "Seems like when they get started they don't leave a guy nothing." Elsewhere we can see reasons for not using a narrator. Fitzgerald's *Babylon Revisited*, though focused on Charles Wales, is not told by him, and the different technique makes it easier for the author to present the two points of view about the custody of Honoria as equally strong, and, for those who hold them, equally justifiable.

The other limitation is one of positive sympathy: we do not need to "identify" with, or even like, the teller of a story, but we have to accept the narrator sufficiently to be willing to see the story through his eyes. The narrator in Charlotte Perkins Gilman's *The Yellow Wall-Paper* is mad, but madness is not alienating: we have reservations about the reality of what she sees, but a mad world can have both a logic of its own and a logical reason for deviating from the "normal," besides being related to our own phobias. But in Flannery O'Connor's *Good Country People*, where the Bible salesman first appears to us as naive and innocent, we realize, as he gradually turns nastier with every paragraph, how difficult, perhaps impossible, it would be to make him a narrator. We prefer to look at such people objectively: there is something about real evil that has to remain inscrutable.[4]

There is a corresponding limitation in the "omniscient" technique. In

D.H. Lawrence's *Mother and Daughter* the author tells us a good deal about the motivation of his characters, and he has opinions about many other subjects as well, such as the difference between male and female attitudes to holding jobs. We may feel that we are free to disagree with Lawrence, if we like: he gives the impression of "omniscience" only to the extent that he is telling his story. Once he starts commenting on it, he has no more authority than we have. A good story, apparently, has a life of its own, and its author does not so much make it up as release it. Lawrence himself remarked, in fact, that we are not to trust an author, only the story he tells.[5]

Meaning

If these observations have any validity, we seem to be led to some such principle as this: story writers do not moralize, or if they do they are apt to weaken their creative authority, but they keep us in touch with moral realities. What we get from the story, therefore, is not a "message" or any concept to be inferred from the story, but the vision presented by the story itself. In modern stories this vision is normally ironic, in a special sense of seeing more of the whole situation than the characters in the story do. Irony does not, in this context, mean any lack of sympathy, but it excludes the sentimental sympathy that refuses to see the whole picture. Thus in Katherine Anne Porter's *He* we can understand Mrs. Whipple's love for her retarded son, but we can also see an obsessive element in it that is bound to lead to trouble. In James Joyce's *A Little Cloud* we can understand Little Chandler's provincial wistfulness and his envy for the glamorous life of Gallaher, but we can also see that Gallaher's real life is not likely to be glamorous at all.

Even here, however, we are still in a moral and human area, and irony is not confined to that. In Katherine Mansfield's *Bliss* the long dammed-up sexual feelings of the heroine are suddenly released in an enveloping sense of euphoria. The euphoria enables her, while feeling complacent about the rather foolish babble of her guests, to find her real affinity with a blossoming pear tree. This latter is what T.S. Eliot calls an "objective correlative,"[6] a natural image symbolizing, and corresponding to, a human emotion. But it appears that while pear trees usually blossom on schedule, human emotions often do not. There is no moral factor directly involved here: only the irony of a humanity imprisoned in a world that it so often feels it does not belong to. There is a similar irony in Dreiser's

The Lost Phoebe, where the pastoral opening, with its leisurely evocation of the routines of life on a farm, is followed by the account of the shattered life of Reifsneider, which fits no cycle of seasons.

Such a perspective, in which we struggle to see the whole story, as the characters in it ordinarily cannot, brings us closer to the universality of what is presented. The story expands from being that particular story to being a story about human life as a whole. The characters at the opening of *The Death of Ivan Ilych* are very unsure of their most trivial actions and gestures, because they are trying to pretend that they are not thinking only of their own lives and of the fact that at least they are not dead. As the story goes on, we see how utterly unique every person's death is for him, and thus how even the unique can be the universal. When the pilot in Ralph Ellison's *Flying Home* remarks that "jimcrows" is an appropriate name for buzzards, hardly knowing at that moment what he is saying, we begin to see that Ellison's story is not simply a story about an injured pilot, but about the outlook of black people in a society dominated by hostile whites. Literature, then, may be among other things a technique for training us to look at life with an enlarged vision.

But we can hardly stop here, enlarging our vision at the expense of the illusions and frustrations of imaginary characters. In Eudora Welty's *A Memory* a vision from waking life moves across the dream world of a young woman, threatening her emotional security with a reality that she struggles to keep within her picture frame of reverie. But we suspect that she has really grown beyond that point, and is now ready to deal with reality on its own terms. Similarly, at any moment our ironic perspective may go into reverse, and show us that we have illusions too that protect us from reality, and that the story we are reading may be part of that reality. Thus as we read Doris Lessing's account of how a shy white child fails to make any human contact with Africans, the appalling callousness of the white attitude to the blacks looms out of the background of the story and confronts us directly.

But it is not only social and outward realities that literature presents; the conflict of reality and illusion goes on inside our minds too. In John Barth's *Lost in the Funhouse* we eavesdrop on the inner debate in an author's mind about how he is to write his story. The uncertainty in the "funhouse" itself about what is real is a projection of that inner debate. In Conrad's *The Secret Sharer* the story of how an inexperienced sea captain tries to get rid of a stowaway is given a new dimension by the unexplained mystery of the stowaway's resemblance to the captain, "my double," as the captain calls him. The story is told with a psychological resonance that gives to it the universal theme of separating from a self that we do not want and yet is a part of ourselves.

This twofold focus of reality, inside and outside the mind at once, is particularly important when we are reading what is called fantasy. Stanislaw Lem's story of a kingdom created from robots, *The Seventh Sally,* raises questions that have tormented us for centuries, about the relation of God or the gods to man, about the distinction between an organism and a mechanism, about the difference between what is created and what has come into existence by itself. And in Ursula Le Guin's story, *The Ones Who Walk Away from Omelas,* the science fiction setting does not make the central situation less relevant to our own lives; we have all asked ourselves how far it is possible to be happy in a society based on making other people miserable. It is these fantastic stories in particular that lead us to another critical principle. A story presents us with what is technically an illusion, something that did not happen or could not happen. But whatever reality may be, one of the most direct and intense ways that we can grasp it is through the deliberate illusions of literature.

We began with the folk tales that can travel through the world past all social and linguistic barriers, and we end with the suggestion that when a story presents a form of universal experience, there are no limits to its communicating power. In Borges's little story, *The Gospel according to Mark,* we are in a remote part of South America, as far as we can get from all our normal cultural habits and references. Yet the story which is familiar to us in the Gospels makes its way there, too, in a most disconcerting form. The narrator in Dostoevsky's *Dream of a Ridiculous Man* is also remote from us in culture and attitude, and keeps excluding himself from our understanding, so far as he can, by dwelling on his own "ridiculous" qualities. Yet he has a dream of a kind that was described by an English Romantic essayist, Thomas De Quincey, writing many years before Dostoevsky's time. De Quincey says, "Perhaps not one of us escapes that dream . . . every one of us . . . has a bait offered to the infirm places of his own individual will; once again a snare is presented for tempting him into captivity to a luxury of ruin; once again, as in aboriginal Paradise, the man falls by his own choice."[7] In other words, the vision described in the Biblical story of the fall of man has a permanent place in our own minds. This is not a religious doctrine: it is a statement about the intelligibility of great stories, which may come to us from immense distances of time and space, and yet are stories that we recognize because we have lived through them.

On Poetry

Sound

A poet has to accept the language given to him at birth, so we have first to ask what the peculiar strengths and difficulties of the English language are, as a medium of poetry. First, it is a heavily accented language (French critics speak of "the British thump"); second, it has a high proportion of consonants to vowels; third, most of the words in common use, including most of the words of native English origin, are monosyllables or near monosyllables; and fourth, it has very few inflections. There are other characteristics that will emerge in the more specific commentaries, but these will do to go on with. All four, of course, are closely interconnected.

Every monosyllable has a separate accent, however slight, and because the English language is so heavily accented, and so full of consonants as well, the effect is like that of riding a bucking and plunging horse that is capable of great speed and power if brought under control or of merely running away with its rider if not. Partly because of the lack of inflections, English is very full of such phrases as "the house," "by him," "when I," "of love," "to be," and the like. These phrases are iambic (short-long) in rhythm, and help to make iambic the normal metre for English poetry:

> When I consider how my light is spent (Milton, *On His Blindness*).

> And I with thee will choose to live (Milton, *Il Penseroso*).

The first line quoted is iambic pentameter, or five iambic feet; the second iambic tetrameter, or four feet. The iambic pentameter has been the backbone of English poetry from Chaucer to our own day, but tetrameters or octosyllabics are used a good deal too, especially when high speed is wanted. Longer lines than the pentameter are seldom used for long poems, because in English the rhythm is apt to get clattery and turn into doggerel when there are too many beats in a line, especially if rhyme is added. In fact, anything unusual that a poet does to his rhythm or rhyme, in English, is likely to sound obtrusive, to call more attention to itself than would normally be wanted. So such unusual features, when we find them in competent poets, are being used for special effects.

At the beginning of *Paradise Lost*, Milton describes the expelling of Satan from heaven thus:

> Hurled headlong flaming from the ethereal sky.

The rhythm of "headlong flaming" is trochaic (long-short), because the trochaic is a "falling" rhythm and is also a more energetic rhythm in English than the more usual iambic. We notice too that the use of a long word ("ethereal") makes the rhythm lighter because, with the heavy accent in English, a long word brings in a ripple of unaccented syllables. This principle, that the longer words in English (mostly borrowed from Greek or Latin) lighten the rhythm because of their lightly stressed syllables, meets us everywhere: in Cummings's "O sweet spontaneous earth," in Wordsworth's "From low to high doth dissolution climb," in Whitman's "A reminiscence sing," and so on.

Special effect poems in unusual rhythms include Tennyson's *Charge of the Light Brigade*, where the prevailing rhythm is dactylic (long-short-short), because the theme is a cavalry charge. In this passage from Swinburne's *Atalanta in Calydon* an anapestic rhythm (short-short-long) mingles with the iambic one, and goes with the sense of bursting energy that the poem celebrates:

> When the hounds of spring are on winter's traces,
> The mother of months in meadow or plain
> Fills the shadows and windy places
> With lisp of leaves and ripple of rain.

In the second and fourth lines there is also a heavy alliteration (beginning with the same letter) in the texture; this again is there to mark the driving power of emerging life in the spring.

The same principles apply to rhyme. Most rhymes are very resonant in English, and even the simplest double rhymes, like the "traces-places" rhyme above, are generally used rather sparingly. Triple rhymes usually belong to light verse, as in Byron's

But O! ye lords of ladies intellectual,
Inform us truly: have they not henpecked you all?

where the poet is writing deliberate or intentional doggerel. In Hopkins's sonnet *That Nature is a Heraclitean Fire,* we find such rhymes as "resurrection–dejection–deck shone." Here again what would be in other contexts doggerel rhymes are being used for a special reason: they go with the complex and syncopated rhythm of the poem.

Poetry is language used with the greatest possible intensity, and one obvious way in which it can express intensity is in its movement and sound. Poetry is never very far from dancing and singing or from other energetic actions like marching and horseback riding, and, as already suggested, English is an excellent vehicle for high speeds. Thus Edith Sitwell:

Nobody comes to give him his rum but the
Rim of the sky hippopotamus-glum
Enhances the chances to bless with a benison
Alfred Lord Tennyson crossing the bar laid . . . [*Sir Beelzebub*]

Here the movement is so fast that it drags the meaning along after it: there is a meaning, and the words will eventually make some sense, but the meaning can wait. Here we are in the world of the nursery rhyme, where the bouncing rhythm is what carries the poem. We may notice two things in particular. First, a very emphatic rhyme scheme cuts across the arrangement of the lines, which gives a syncopated rhythm suggesting the jazz rhythms popular in the 1920s, which the poem is in part imitating. Second, while there is a rolling dactylic metre, there are also four main beats or accents to the line.

This four-beat line is the most primitive measure in English; it is the rhythm of Old English poetry, where as a rule the first three beats alliterate to increase the emphasis, as in the adaptation of the Old English poem *The Seafarer* by Ezra Pound:

Chill its chains are; chafing sighs
Hew my heart round and hunger begot
Mere-weary mood. Lest man know not . . .

It is also the rhythm of most nursery rhymes, and of most ballads. The ballad is often in a four-lined stanza with four and three accents alternating (or, counting by syllables, eight-six-eight-six, the "common metre" of hymnbooks). This is really a continuous four-beat line with a rest at the end of every other line. Thus in *Sir Patrick Spens*:

> The kíng síts in Dumfeŕling tówn,
> Drińking the bloód-red wíne: (rest)
> "O whére will Í get góod sailór
> To sáil this shíp of mińe?" (rest).

Originally the ballad (from the Latin *ballare*, to dance; cf. "ball") had a background of dancing as well as singing, and for dancing one needs a continuous rhythm.

After English poetry adopted metres in the Middle Ages, the old four-beat rhythm could still be heard as a secondary rhythm syncopating against it. If we look at Hamlet's famous "to be or not to be" soliloquy on the page, we see iambic pentameter lines; but if we listen to an actor speaking the lines on a stage, we also hear something like this:

> To BE or NOT to be, THAT is the QUEStion:
> WHEther 'tis NOBler in the MIND to SUFfer
> The SLINGS and ARrows of outRAGEous FORtune,
> Or to TAKE ARMS against a SEA of TROUBles . . .

The conflict of the two rhythms against each other, in Shakespeare as elsewhere, is largely what provides the subtlety and complexity of what we hear. In a high-speed poem like Browning's *How They Brought the Good News from Ghent to Aix*, the speed comes from both the anapestic metre and the heavy accent of the four main beats:

> I sprang to the stirrup, and Joris, and he;
> I galloped, Dirck galloped, we galloped all three;
> "Good speed!" cried the watch, as the gatebolts undrew;
> "Speed!" echoed the wall to us galloping through . . .

But of course poetry has to have its andante and adagio movements as well. In the stopped couplets of Dryden or Pope, the iambic pentameter takes charge, and the four beats we heard in Hamlet's soliloquy fade into the background:

Tim'rous by nature, of the Rich in awe,
I come to Counsel learned in the Law:
You'll give me, like a friend both sage and free,
Advice; and (as you use) without a Fee.

We can still hear the four main stresses, but a strict metre and rhyme scheme controls them. If such verse as this (from Pope's *Imitation of the First Satire of the Second Book of Horace*) is read aloud to us, we have a sense of constantly fulfilled expectation. If we hear the line "You'll give me, like a friend both sage and free," we don't know what the next line will be, but we do know that it will be an impeccable iambic pentameter, with the last word a perfect rhyme to "free." Such strict metre and rhyme give the effect of *wit*, of high intelligence in full control of its material. Similarly with E.A. Robinson's *Richard Cory*:

So on we worked, and waited for the light,
　And went without the meat, and cursed the bread;
And Richard Cory, one calm summer night,
　Went home and put a bullet through his head.

The punch line is surprising, but, once we have had the surprise, inevitable. Such a combination of relaxed easy movement and deadly accuracy would be impossible without the firmly established metre and rhyme.

The capacity of English for high speed also has something to do with the fact that, because it has so few inflections, it is dependent on a fixed word order. If we hear someone say at a station, "When does go this train?" there is no disturbance of logical order, but we know that the speaker's native language is not English. The skeleton of word order is the sequence subject-predicate-object, as in "John loves Mary," where "John" is the subject, "loves" the predicate, and "Mary" the object. "Mary loves John" is clearly a different statement, and "John Mary loves" means nothing because it could mean both. In Latin we would normally say "Johannes Mariam amat," but we could rearrange the words in any order, because the *m* on the word "Mariam" shows that that is the object whatever the order. Latin verse often seems, to the student who is accustomed to the unvarying linear drive of English from subject through predicate to object, like a very tangled ball of yarn. In Gray's *Elegy Written in a Country Churchyard* we read:

The boast of heraldry, the pomp of power,
  And all that beauty, all that wealth e'er gave,
Awaits alike th' inevitable hour . . .

Here the *s* on "awaits" shows that "hour" is the subject and the first two lines the object. It is very unusual to alter the word order in this way, but in such a slow and meditative movement it is perhaps appropriate sometimes to pause and rearrange our impressions of the words.

In still slower movements we become more aware of such features of English as its clusters of consonants. In the passage given in this book from Pope's *Essay on Criticism,* Pope gives examples of how to vary the speed and rhythm to fit the subject being talked about, and says:

When Ajax strives some rock's vast weight to throw,
The line too labours, and the words move slow. [ll. 370–1]

What makes the first line laborious is the number of consonants we have to stop and spit out before we can go on to the next word. If we are to read poetry with an ear as sharp as Pope's, we have to be conscious of every sound. If we try to introduce "ghost story," "wasp's nest," or "priest's stole" into ordinary conversation, we soon realize how much eliding, or cutting out of consonants, we do, but we cannot read poetry in this way. Thus in Ben Jonson's little song [from *Cynthia's Revels*] beginning:

Slow, slow, fresh fount, keep time with my salt tears

there are two *t*'s in "salt tears," not one, and getting them both out will bring us down to the speed Jonson wants.

The same song goes on:

Droop, herbs and flowers
Fall grief in showers

Here we come back to something noted earlier: that monosyllables have separate accents and thus slow down the rhythm. In a passage just before the one quoted from Pope's *Essay on Criticism,* Pope gives horrible examples of bad ways to write and cautions against an overuse of monosyllables with this one:

And ten low words oft creep in one dull line. [l. 347]

The trouble with this line is not the ten monosyllables but the ten heavy stressed accents: such a line has no rhythm at all. So when Milton is describing the scenery of hell, he says:

Rocks, caves, lakes, fens, bogs, dens, and shades of death
(*Paradise Lost*, bk. 2, l. 621)

Both the rhythm and the harsh discordant inner rhyme "fens-dens" tell our ears that the scenery of hell is not attractive.

Monosyllables, however, are very useful to a skilful poet. Even in an unobtrusive line like Shakespeare's "When icicles hang by the wall," we should notice how the lively anapestic metre can still "hang" the icicle for a suspended instant. Or, again, placing two heavy accents, usually monosyllables, together in the middle of a line (called a spondee), can often give the effect of something ominous or foreboding, as in a wonderful little poem [*My Lute, Awake!*] written by Sir Thomas Wyatt at the beginning of the sixteenth century:

Perchaunce thee lie withered and old
These winter nights that are so cold,
Plaining in vain unto the moon:
Thy wishes then dare not be told.

On the other hand, the absence of inflectional endings means that English can seldom manage the gentle caressing rhythm that we find so often in, say, German lyrics. In the Middle English that Chaucer used there were still a large number of such endings, and modern English can seldom match the lightness of such lines in Chaucer as

But trewėly to tellen attė lastė.

or

And wel we weren esėd attė bestė.
[*Canterbury Tales*, "General Prologue," ll. 707, 29]

Writing lyrics in English is like carving in oak: it can be done all right, but we need to allow for the toughness of the medium. In Housman's *A Shropshire Lad* we have:

With rue my heart is laden
  For golden friends I had,
For many a rose-lipt maiden
  And many a lightfoot lad.

The delicate charm needed is skilfully brought out, but the curiously old-fashioned words used show that the poet is not finding it easy.

So far we have dealt with poetry that is also verse, that is, has certain features like a regularly recurring rhythm that can be identified. But we can have verse that is not acceptable as poetry, or what we usually call doggerel, and we can have poetry in "free verse," with none of these specific features. If we look at, say, Whitman's *Dalliance of the Eagles*, we can see that the furious gyrating and twisting movement is just as effective without a metrical framework. In other free verse, such as we have in William Carlos Williams, we can see what makes it "poetry" if we look at what the arrangement of lines on the page does to our reading of it. There is no continuous linear movement through the syntax of one sentence after another, as in prose; the rhythm keeps returning on itself, driving towards its own centre, forcing us to grasp the total meaning of the words.

Meaning

We said a moment ago that poetry is language used with the greatest possible intensity, and this means, first of all, that in reading poetry we have to step up the intensity of our reading, beginning with the movements and sounds. In prose, or more specifically nonliterary prose, there is a low-keyed intensity, because the words are being used to describe something else. In poetry the words exist for their own sake, and the primary relation of each word, including nouns and verbs, is to the other words, not to the things or actions they describe. In this world, surrounded as we are with such masses of verbiage, mostly passing for prose, we get feelings of panic about the amount of material we have to "cover." We have to start reading poetry by dismissing this panic. Reading poetry is a technique of meditation; we must keep reading and rereading the same poem for quite a while before its real intensity will emerge.

When it does, we can begin to see that poetry is *figured* speech, made up of patterns of words that bring things together in ways that would be quite impossible if the writer were trying to describe something in experience. The most frequent figures are metaphor (this is that), simile (this is like that), and metonymy (this is put for that). We have metaphor in Shakespeare's:

> Thou that art now the world's fresh ornament,
> And only herald of the gaudy spring. [Sonnet 1]

We have simile in T.S. Eliot's:

> When the evening is spread out against the sky
> Like a patient etherized upon a table. [*The Love Song of J. Alfred Prufrock*]

We have metonymy in Dylan Thomas's:

> The force that through the green fuse drives the flower.
> [*The Force That Through . . .*]

These figures are not decorative or ornamental; they are modes of thinking. A great poet is a great thinker too, but he does not think conceptually or in ideas like a philosopher: he thinks in images, and sets these images beside one another or on top of each other, leaving it to us to make the connections. We said that the metaphor usually takes the form "this is that," but Ezra Pound says that real metaphor just puts things together, as in his little two-line poem *In a Station of the Metro*:

> The apparition of these faces in the crowd,
> Petals on a wet, black bough.

We may feel that this is not good grammar, and that we need some predicate in between, such as "is," "is like," "reminds me of," "suggests to me," "is linked in my mind with," or whatever; but it is clear that as soon as we have put one down we have ruined the poem. Similarly:

> O Western wind, when wilt thou blow,
> The small rain down can rain?
> Christ, if my love were in my arms,
> And I in my bed again! [Anonymous, 15th century]

Here the juxtaposing of uncomfortable weather and comfortable bed is easier to follow; it is not a logical connection, but an emotional connection of a kind we have all had in some form or other. The important thing is that the poem simply presents the two images: it does not talk about them, still less about the relation between them.

Thinking in metaphor, simile, and metonymy is in some ways a primitive way of thinking; it has no relation to telling the "truth" as we usually understand truth, where we put a body of words up against something it's supposed to describe and say it's "true" if it's an adequate counterpart of that something. It's because of the primitive nature of poetic thinking that all literatures, in all human societies, begin with poetry; prose develops only much later. But while it's primitive it's also extremely concentrated. Suppose I were writing an essay about eighteenth-century England and were trying to explain how the commonsense philosophy of John Locke helped to establish the cultural climate out of which the Industrial Revolution emerged. This revolution brought in new inventions, like the spinning jenny, but also other things like mass migrations, exploitation, and imperialism, which had very little to do with common sense. As I keep writing, it may occur to me that there is a grotesque analogy here with the Biblical story of the fall of man, with Adam so well adjusted to this world until, with the creation of Eve from his body, another person, and consequently a human community, a wholly unexpected complication, emerged in which he lost that world. But the more I labour at this analogy, the more strained and unconvincing it would get; my readers couldn't follow it, and I would finally have to cut it; one can't do this kind of thing in prose. Yeats, in poetry, can say it all in twenty syllables or so:

> Locke sank into a swoon,
> The Garden died:
> God took the spinning-jenny
> Out of his side. [*Fragments*]

Or, again, Hopkins writes of the instability of all things, and of how, for him, the resurrection of Christ establishes something permanent and solid in the middle of it. He ends:

> This Jack, joke, poor potsherd, patch, matchwood, immortal diamond . . .
> [*That Nature is a Heraclitean Fire*]

Heraclitus said that everything was in a state of flux, a constant flowing or burning, so that one very central image of his pessimistic philosophy (he was called the weeping philosopher) would be a burnt match. If we held the opposite view, that there was something in reality that did not disintegrate, about the best image we could use would be a diamond, the hardest known substance and as precious as the match is the opposite. Yet both match and diamond are made of the same substance, namely carbon, just as the physical body of man ("potsherd" because it's compared in the Bible to a potter's vessel) is of the same substance as the spiritual body that enters the resurrection. Hopkins wrote the poem out of a profound belief in the Resurrection. We don't have to share the belief to respond to the poem, but we do have to see that the belief is imaginatively possible.

The greater intensity of poetry as compared with prose, we said, is partly a greater intensity of sound: that is why rhyme, alliteration, pun, and assonance (similarity of sound) belong to it. Such resemblances of sound are accidents in a language until a poet uses them; then they become elements of design. Here we have "jack-joke," "patch-match," diamond as gem and diamond as suit in a pack of cards. The "jack" in cards, also called knave or valet (servant), suggests man in his ordinary state, of no use except as a servant of God and usually unreliable as that. When Pope describes a card game in his long mock-epic *The Rape of the Lock*, he says

> The Knave of Diamonds tries his wily arts,

indicating that this particular card has a shifty reputation in card lore. The sound link between jack and joke turns up another card, the joker or fool (the fool was often called "patch" in Shakespeare's day). In the background, not in the poem, but within its range of allusions, is the contrast between ordinary humanity, weak and suggestible, and Christ the invincible: Paul calls them the first and second Adam. The Greek word *adamas*, unconquerable, is the origin of our word "diamond."

Poetry, we see, can be endlessly allusive. If you try to write poetry, you will soon find that the kind of poetry you produce will depend entirely on what kind of poetry you have read and will be full of echoes of it. You may be expressing your ideas or emotions, but you can never express them directly; they must go inside some poetic structure, or what is called a convention. Young poets usually gather in groups and write like each other, but as they get older they strike their individual roots into literature and learn more and more from the poets of the past. But the notion that they can write outside the framework of the literary tradition itself is pure illusion, and all great poets gave it up long before they became great poets. When Yeats tells, for the thousandth time in poetry, the Classical myth of Leda and the swan, and says

> A shudder in the loins engenders there
> The broken wall, the burning roof and tower
> And Agamemnon dead

he is indirectly telling us that, because Homer wrote about the Trojan War at the beginning of our literary tradition, that is the most important war for readers of poetry to know about, and the word "Agamemnon" can fall on our ears with a resonant crash that no less familiar name can match. True, Whitman urged his Muse to "migrate from Greece and Ionia" on the ground that we had heard enough about the Trojan War, and come to "a better, fresher, busier sphere" in the United States [*Song of the Exposition*]. But fortunately, Whitman's real Muse made him write like a poet and ignored his advertising copy. The *content* of poetry constantly changes, but its inner structure does not, just as a new baby is always a different individual but never constitutes a different species.

The allusiveness of poetry is a by-product of the fact that the study of literature is as coherent and systematic as the study of any other subject. Just as every genuine discovery in science is true because it is consistent with other genuine discoveries, so every great work of the imagination is imaginatively consistent with other works in the same medium. Even so, this allusiveness in poetry may put some of us off. Why, we may say, should we have to look up so many references? Okay, they may be part of our cultural heritage, and it may be very interesting to see how Classical and Biblical stories and echoes from earlier poets are used in poetry, but, with so complicated a world facing us in this century, is it really worth so much time and effort to learn a special elitist language?

Some poets are explicitly allusive, like Milton, or like Eliot or Yeats in our day. They make us look things up and consult footnotes, and we find ourselves rapidly getting an education in comparative mythology, religion, and literature. Others, like Wordsworth or Robert Frost, keep their language as free of special reference as they can, and they are the ones who may give us a clue to the question we're looking at. We notice that some poems—we might call them emblematic poems—set up a single central image and stare hard at it, as, to take random examples, Blake does with his tiger and worm-eaten rose, William Carlos Williams with his red wheelbarrow, or Whitman with his live-oaks in Louisiana. Sometimes the poet tells us that the image is the distilled essence of an intense experience, as Rossetti does in *The Woodspurge*. The poet doesn't use these images as a pretext for talking about something else, as is done in certain kinds of allegory, where the "real" meaning is something different. If we look at Robert Frost's poem, *Stopping by Woods on a Snowy Evening*, long enough and hard enough, we begin to see that it is collecting a great variety of experiences into that single, solemn, hushed moment. But we can't say, for instance, "the poem is really about death," because it is, just as really, about stopping by woods on a snowy evening. It's as though the central image of the poem had been placed in a reverberating sound chamber and were expressing some kind of infinite resonance in its very concrete and specific theme.

Explicitly allusive poems, then, like Milton's *Lycidas* or Eliot's *Prufrock*, create a resonance by their allusions against everything else we've read in literature, as well as an infinite amount that we haven't. (This goes for the poet too, who hasn't read the poems written after his death that echo him, and that he echoes by anticipation.) Such poems tell us that the whole world of literature is one gigantic imaginative body, and that studying literature is entering into that body of human imaginative experience, not just reading one thing after another. But implicit allusion, like that of Frost's poem, raises an even bigger question.

Wallace Stevens has a poem called *Description without Place*, a long and very difficult poem, which says that man does not live directly in the world of nature, like animals and plants—he lives within his own constructs of the world. These constructs, in their totality, are what we call cultures or civilizations. They are what, as Stevens says, make everything that we see in Spain look Spanish.[8] A great deal of these constructs consists of words, and at the centre of it all is the body of words we call poetry. Because the metaphors and images and analogies of poetry are what tell us most clearly that we cannot see or understand or act or feel except from within the human construct that we entered at birth. Nature knows nothing of up or down, of inside or outside, of beginning or ending, of before and not yet. All these are notions we impose on nature. It is the poets who keep reducing our experience to these simple and essential things, and they who lead us to the engine room of creation, the energy and intensity of the constructing process itself.

On Drama[9]

Spectacle

The word "theatre" is derived from a Greek word meaning "to see," and this indicates that the basis of what goes on in a theatre is spectacle, something to look at. The words in themselves often have a secondary function. Many, if not most, major developments of drama have been closely associated with music, where singing frequently takes over from speaking, and sometimes music and spectacle converge in the dance so that words get squeezed out altogether. In any case it is spectacle that has been the most popular feature of drama in all ages and cultures. If we start to read Shakespeare's plays, for instance, in what scholars regard as their chronological order, we find, very early on, three plays on the Wars of the Roses in the reign of Henry VI, and a tragedy called *Titus Andronicus*. If our only contact with these plays is through reading, we may find the Henry VI plays rather dull, and *Titus Andronicus* in particular almost childishly grotesque and horrible. Yet whenever any dramatic company works up enough nerve to give these plays a proper production, we discover that they can be made into superb pieces of spectacular theatre. We have to realize, then, that Shakespeare was not educating himself through written texts, as we do for the most part, but through experience with audiences who wanted, and were ready to respond to, spectacle.

Later on, Shakespeare began his *Henry V* with a prologue apologizing for not giving his audience more spectacle, and what may be his last play, *Henry VIII*, again seems rather a dull play to read, because it is really a costume piece, a historical panorama with long processions of noblemen in full parade dress. So while an excellent film can be made of Shakespeare's *Henry V* (and of most of his other plays too), still, if Shakespeare's theatre had possessed the resources of the modern cinema, it is clear that we should never have had Shakespeare. The more spectacular the play, the less important the words are, and an audience, unless it is a specially educated audience, will not listen long if there is not enough to see. It's sometimes said that this emphasis on the visual is peculiar to Western culture; it's been suggested that when we say we listen "to" music, the word "to" indicates that we're putting even music into a visual and spatial context. But the emphasis on spectacle is quite as marked in Oriental drama too.

Through most of its history the verbal drama has been squeezed between musical forms on the one hand (opera, ballet, revue) and spectacular ones on the other (pantomime, circus, masque), which, as already noted, often combine to reduce the verbal content still further. One comedy by the best of the Roman dramatists, Terence, was not played through on its first performance, because the audience went out during the intermission to watch a rope-dancing act, and failed to return. In later Roman times, when such circus entertainment had expanded into gladiatorial battles and chariot races, serious drama seems to have disappeared from stage almost altogether. If stage drama is not crowded out today by the competition of movies, television, and ball games, that is partly because of the efforts made by books like this one to stress the importance of verbal education and partly out of a need for greater variety. The most popular dramatic forms, because they are mass produced, tend to be highly conventionalized; this is true of sitcoms and similar stereotyped dramatic forms in television, as it was of their predecessors in radio and cinema a generation or so ago, when they were the most popular forms. It is not much wonder if we find a tendency on the part of playwrights to nag and scold their audiences for wanting something more lowbrow; this tendency has run through the history of drama from Aristophanes to Bernard Shaw and beyond. We may assume that a parallel tendency to say "nothing ever happens in these new-fangled plays; they're all just a lot of talk" has recurred in audiences for the same length of time.

Dramatic Roles

But there are some very profound and central human experiences that only verbal drama can express. We might begin by looking at two types of these experiences in particular. In the first place, we act out dramatic roles constantly in our own lives. Someone we know comes into our room, and we instantly adopt a role that is based on our knowledge of his character and the way he talks. He leaves, and we start dramatizing ourselves to ourselves, like Hamlet; if we aren't consciously talking to ourselves, as he did, we are unconsciously throwing our minds into some sort of inner dialogue. Cutting out all the babble and chatter that goes on inside us takes a high degree of concentration and mental discipline, and all this chatter is dramatic in one way or another. Some people speak of a "persona" as the part of ourselves that expresses the social aspect of our life; the word means mask, and refers to the fact that in the plays of ancient Greece the actors wore masks. The phrase *dramatis personae,* before the list of characters at the beginning of a play, originally meant "the masks to be used for the performance." But we don't have just one mask; we have any number of them, and it's highly significant that our words "person" and "personality" come from the same dramatic metaphor. They suggest that we can never take a mask off and show the "real self" underneath. There's nothing under a "persona" except another persona; there's no core to that onion. The Greek equivalent of persona is *hypocrites,* from which our word "hypocrite" comes. This sounds bad, and suggests that if we are better people we can remove all deceitful disguises and speak with utter sincerity and truthfulness. Perhaps we can, but when we do we are entering into a dramatic role of sincerity and are wearing *that* mask.[10]

So one of the things drama does is to reflect back to us the dramas we carry on with each other and with ourselves. When we first come upon the dialogue in Albee's *American Dream,* we might assume, if we were unaccustomed to this kind of drama, that all the characters were simply insane. But if we listen closely to the interaction of the things we say with the things that are also in our minds that we don't say, along with an occasional echo of things we don't dare say to ourselves or even consciously think, we might hear something not so very different. And we have all gone through conversations that seemed to us so pointless and meaningless, with so many empty clichés mechanically spoken whether they related to anything else said or not, as to make the onstage dialogue in Ionesco's *Bald Soprano* sound like the soberest realism.

Our second type of dramatic experience is an extension of the same principle to the characters in a play, who are so often locked inside subdramas of their own, so that the play we are watching often becomes a bundle of subsidiary dramas. Take the conclusion of Strindberg's *Miss Julie,* a dialogue between two people, Miss Julie herself and Jean, the valet who has seduced her. Miss Julie goes out and kills herself at the end of the play because she feels that fate or God or circumstances or the class structure of nineteenth-century Sweden, or whatever, has woven an ironic drama around her in which she has the role of a sacrificial victim, and she kills herself in obedience to the role she assumes she's cast in.

The valet then hears his master's bell ring, and says that behind his master's hand there's something else moving the hand. That something else is presumably his subdramatist, setting a role for him to go on living, at least through the mess of Julie's death. However we interpret the words of his final speech, they make it clear that there's no simple situation involved where Strindberg merely writes a play and an audience merely listens to it. There's a group of intermediate dramas, some of them within the characters and some of them within our own previous experiences, and it's the interactions of all these that make up the whole drama. Admittedly, the dramatist who is shaping Miss Julie's life into a suicide is a pretty corny dramatist and is really not God or fate or Sweden but Miss Julie herself. In other words both she and Jean are projecting their inner dramas on something outside them. That doesn't, however, reflect on Strindberg, who had the ability to create Miss Julie and Jean both as characters and as the subdramatists of their own lives.[11]

Illusion and Irony

It's also important that when we assume a dramatic role in relation to someone else we become partly a dramatic construct of that someone else. Anyone who has thrown himself into a set role, like Willy Loman in *Death of a Salesman*, is in danger of suddenly realizing that he's not sure whether he's himself or merely a kind of ventriloquist's dummy, an echo of what other people or other people's values have made out of him. Something similar is the reason for the neurotic snoopiness of the people in Pirandello's *It* Is *So! (If You Think So).* It drives them up the wall to think that there may be something about the Ponza family that they can't get to the bottom of once and for all and establish the truth about by documentary or other "certain" forms of evidence. Because, of course, if there is no tangible reality in those lives to be clutched and grasped, there is no such reality in their own lives either. One character, Laudisi, understands that we don't see or touch reality directly: we gradually learn something about it by bouncing illusions off each other.[12]

Similarly, in Shakespeare's *The Tempest*, at the beginning of the second act, we find Antonio and Sebastian in a state of giggling hysteria that gradually turns venomous as they plot to murder Alonso when he's asleep. They plot this because they're realists, because this is the kind of thing you do in the real world to get on and get ahead. Earlier, when Gonzalo says that the island is fresh and green, they see it realistically as totally barren. Later the hero, Ferdinand, sees the masque put on by Ariel and the other spirits working for Prospero, which is of course an illusion, like all dramatic performances. By the end of the play we realize that these notions of reality and illusion are exactly the opposite of those being presented by the play itself. The masque symbolizes a far profounder reality than actual existence ever affords; the squalid plot of Antonio and Sebastian shows that they are the ones who are plunged in illusion. And on top of that we have Prospero's speech after the masque, pointing out that the difference between reality and illusion is itself an illusion, what we call reality being simply an illusion that lasts a little longer.

One form of drama that has been popular at various times is the puppet play, where we can see that the movements and sounds of the characters are being produced by somebody else offstage. But of course human actors are to some degree puppets also, considering how much authors and directors have to do with their acting. Audiences, again, are always in a state of greater freedom than the characters on the stage, simply because they are able to walk out of the theatre; and in the great majority of plays they know more about what is going on in the whole action of the play than the characters on the stage are supposed to know. All this makes for the situation that we call irony, where the spectator knows more than the participator.

Irony is an obvious source of the comic; in many comedies we find a type of character that Shakespeare's friend and contemporary Ben Jonson called a "humour,"[13] a character like a miser or hypochondriac or snob or jealous husband or father or glutton or pedant, who is identified with a single leading characteristic and can't do anything not connected with exhibiting it. Such characters are funny because they have made themselves into puppets, mechanically responding to every stimulus in the same way. Most of Molière's plays are constructed on this principle, where a father forbids a son or daughter to marry the person he or she wants to marry because the father is obsessed with his "humour": in *The Physician in Spite of Himself* this principle is played down, and the father is simply being obstinate about getting his daughter married to a rich man, but the action of the play follows the usual setup. The characters in *The Cherry Orchard* are also humours, wandering around in a daze created by their own dreams and snobberies. Lyubov, who compulsively gives too much money to beggars because she resents the fact that she's not wealthy any more and can't afford to, is the central humour of the play.

But irony is a feature of tragedy also. In *Oedipus Rex* the audience already knows the outlines of the story and so keeps anticipating all the horrific discoveries that Oedipus makes about himself. In *Macbeth,* there's a prophecy that no man born of woman can kill Macbeth, but then Macduff was the result of a Caesarian operation, and so wasn't really born of a woman at all. It sounds like a poor joke, and gives us a glimpse into the sheer idiocy of the world that Macbeth has committed himself to.[14] In *Death of a Salesman,* again, the audience, while it may not know the end of that particular story, still does know that Willy Loman's version of the American dream is a lot of nonsense, and that no good can come of pursuing it.

In general, there's a broad division between tragedy and comedy, which is mainly a difference in endings: a tragedy traditionally ends in the death or disaster of the central character and a comedy with some kind of party, such as a wedding. The pervading mood of tragedy is likely to be sombre and that of comedy festive, but we can have tragedies full of wit and humour, like *Romeo and Juliet,* or "black" comedies that seem very gloomy or bitter. The original idea was that tragedy showed us death and comedy showed us a passage through, if not actual death, at least something quite ominous, to renewed life.

In Aristophanes' *Lysistrata* the women barricade the Acropolis, and the chorus of old men scrambles up with wood to set the place on fire, so as either to roast the women alive or to smoke them out. They are too old to be drafted for military service or to be affected by the sexual strike, but the intensity of their hatred for the women who want to intervene in public affairs long enough to stop the war with Sparta is not just good fun. This is "Old" Comedy, and was succeeded on the stage by "New" Comedy, where, usually, a young man wants a young woman, is opposed by his or her father, but finally gets her. He is often helped, in Roman comedies, by a clever slave, who may be threatened with anything from flogging to crucifixion by the father. We notice how, even in the very lighthearted farce of Molière, when the hero gets the heroine from under the nose of her father through the aid of Sganarelle, Sganarelle is led away to be hanged.

Tragedy usually focuses on a heroic figure, of greater authority or articulateness than we have. Tragedy is an event: it does not depend on the moral quality of the hero. The hero may be the mature and responsible Oedipus, utterly unconscious of anything he could have done to provoke the wrath of the gods, or he may be loaded down with the foulest crimes, like Macbeth. The one thing he must be is a hero, somebody worth writing a tragedy about. Willy Loman may not be what we ordinarily think of as a hero, but, as his wife says, small men can get just as exhausted as big ones, and however absurd his values may be he has fought hard for them. And, in the sight of watching angels or someone equally removed from the human scene, his values might be much less absurd than Macbeth's ambition.

Is the final meaning of drama, then, simply that everything is illusion and that nothing is real? Not quite. We notice that Oedipus keeps driving himself through the most agonizing self-discoveries because, as he says, he is determined to find out who he is. In *Death of a Salesman*, Biff says of his father, "He never knew who he was," but he's reached a profounder level of insight himself when he says of himself simply, "I'm nothing, Pop." Macbeth, after his last hope has failed him, is threatened with the negative dramatic role of being made "the show and gaze o' th' time," [5.8.24] and he realizes that whatever he has done his identity is still that of a warrior.[15] At the end of *The Tempest*, Gonzalo says that "all of us [found] ourselves, / When no man was his own" [5.1.212–13]. At the end of a play, then, there is often left behind some sense of identity that has been attained by somebody, in however perverse a way, and this sense of identity, a reality that can only be pointed to by illusion, seems to be what is really underneath all the masks and stage paint and lighting. Sometimes a character in the play attains it; sometimes, as in *The Cherry Orchard*, nobody does. In that case the gaining of a sense of identity is a job for the people in the audience, as Prospero indicates when he says, in the epilogue to *The Tempest*, the play's over; I've done what I can; now it's all yours.

Preface to the Revised Edition (1987)

In revising *The Practical Imagination* for this new and compact edition, we have kept most of the original features and added others. The new anthology is lighter, more attractive, and easier to handle—and at the same time more effective as a tool for teaching, both because of our own second thoughts and the helpful suggestions of users.

As we observe recent trends toward "practical" education in our colleges and universities—which means, more often than not, narrowly vocational education—it seems to us more important than ever to introduce students to the idea that the imagination is practical, and that literature is uniquely valuable in its capacity to widen vision and clarify perspectives. To support this point, we have made this book both an anthology and an introduction to literature. As an anthology, it includes many forms and varieties of fiction, poetry, and drama. As an introduction to literary study, it moves from simple to more subtle and complex elements. At each step of the way, explanations, discussions, and questions inform students of the principles under consideration and help them to engage in imaginative and intellectual dialogue with the literary texts. Each section begins with an introduction to the genre, broadly surveying the ground to be covered. At the end of the first chapter of the fiction section, we provide students with a few brief suggestions to help them frame their thoughts into essays. At the end of the book, we provide a glossary as a ready reference to terminology.

Our generic survey introducing fiction emphasizes the relationship between oral and written traditions. In chapter 1, "The Narrative Impulse," we begin with the oral tale—*Rumpelstiltskin* and *Stone Soup*—and examine the ways the ancient theme of wish-fulfilment has been shaped by three sophisticated modern storytellers, ending with the narrative complexities of Lawrence's *The Rocking-Horse Winner*. In the next three chapters, we explore narrative perspective, discussing concepts much more fully in this edition than in the earlier one, and enriching the discussion with four newly selected stories: Alice Munro's *An Ounce of Cure*, George Garrett's *King of the Mountain*, Gail Godwin's *A Sorrowful Woman*, and Ernest Hemingway's *Hills Like White Elephants*. Chapters 5 and 6, divisions new to this edition, treat "Character" and "Setting," with Cynthia Ozick's *The Shawl*, E.L. Doctorow's *The Hunter*, and John Cheever's *The Swimmer* newly selected as examples for discussion. Chapter 7 discusses "Metaphor, Symbol, Allegory," and includes for the first time Ann Beattie's *Janus*. In chapter 8, "Theme," we now begin with Margaret Atwood's *When It Happens* and end with Thomas Pynchon's *Entropy*. As before, the last chapter, "Longer Fiction," includes Tolstoy's *The Death of Ivan Ilych* and Conrad's *The Secret Sharer*, but with questions newly added to each and diagrams supplied to assist students toward understanding the Conrad story.

Poetry follows fiction because beginning students generally do best when armed with a confidence, a vocabulary, and a strategy of criticism won through successful study of short stories. Nevertheless, because poetry still strikes some as an alien form, we begin slowly, with assistance in definition, discussion, and footnotes. After the introductory overview, we divide the field into "lyric" and "narrative," before considering the elements of dramatic situation and character fundamental to poetry. Then comes a chapter on language, followed by one on images, metaphors, and symbols. In chapter 5, we explore sound patterns including rhyme and metre, and in chapter 6 the traditional forms of ballad, sonnet, villanelle, and sestina. Chapter 7, much expanded from the earlier edition, introduces the forms of free verse, with examples newly added from Walt Whitman, Lawrence Ferlinghetti, Margaret Atwood, and A.R. Ammons. In chapter 8, our discussion of time and place includes two new poems, Walt Whitman's *Crossing Brooklyn Ferry* and Emma Lazarus's *The New Colossus*. In chapter 9, poems are grouped according to timeless human themes. The last chapter, "Poems for Study," presents chronologically some valuable poems not otherwise represented.

Our plays represent the Western tradition, from the Greeks to the present. We begin with tragedy and comedy, with Sophocles, Shakespeare, Aristophanes, and Congreve as examples against which students may measure the plays from later times. A chapter on "Social Drama" directs attention to theme. In "Plays for Study," we print and discuss Beckett's *Not I* as a paradigm of how difficulties in interpretation may be met and surmounted. We conclude our consideration of drama with two modern masterpieces, Tennessee Williams's *The Glass Menagerie* and Arthur Miller's *Death of a Salesman*. Of the eleven plays that now constitute our introduction to drama, four are new to this edition: *Hamlet*, *The Way of the World*, *Suppressed Desires*, and *The Glass Menagerie*.

Finally, at the request of users of the earlier edition, we have added to this one a complete glossary, drawn from *The Harper Handbook to Literature* and cross-referenced to the pages in the text where the terms are most fully treated.

9

Vision and Cosmos

17 May 1982

Originally presented under the title "The Elizabethan Mythological Universe and Its Biblical Origin," at the First Annual Conference of the Institute for Literary Research, held at Bar Ilan University, Ramat-Gan, Israel, 17–20 May 1982. From Biblical Patterns in Modern Literature, *ed. David H. Hirsch and Nehama Aschkenasy (Chico, Calif.: Scholars Press, 1984), 5–17. The book is a collection of the conference papers, which discuss the influence of the Bible on specific literary works from a variety of cultures, historical periods, and linguistic traditions; Frye's essay appears first as a general introduction. The typescripts are in the NFF, 1988, box 47, file 5, and NFF, 1991, box 36, file 4.*

Every human society, it seems, looks at its environment through a transparent cultural envelope of its own construction. There are no natural societies, in the sense of human groups living directly in and according to nature, able to dispense with such an envelope. There are no "noble savages," or completely natural men, for the same reason. A society's cultural structure normally consists of two concentric circles: an inner one which is peculiarly the "sacred," and an outer one which, though related to the sacred, has the less vigilantly guarded circumference that we describe as secular or profane. Writers on comparative cultural symbolism, such as Mircea Eliade, lay stress on the *temenos,* the drawn boundary that marks off the sacred area, and on the way that this *temenos* is reflected in, for example, the architecture of ancient cities.[1] My own chief interest is in the verbal counterpart of the *temenos,* or what I call a myth of concern, the body of written documents that express what is of crucial importance to a given society. In the Christian culture of Western Europe, from the time of the New Testament down to around the eighteenth century, this central verbally sacred area contained the Christian Bible, assumed to be the definitive revelation to man of the essential knowledge concerning his historical past, his moral present, and his spiritual future or destiny.

Until the power of abstract verbal expression develops, the verbally sacred consists primarily of stories (*mythoi*), and after abstract thought has appeared, a good deal of it is expended on commentary, explanation, and systematization of the sacred narratives. Before this takes place, however, most of the myths have consolidated into the kind of roughly unified, and certainly interconnected, construct that we call a mythology. The constructive principle of a mythology is the metaphor, the statement of identity, A is B, where two different things are said to be the same thing. Examples are in Genesis 49: "Joseph is a fruitful bough," "Issachar is a strong ass," "Naphtali is a hind let loose," and the like. If we ask what is the point of asserting that A is B when A is so obviously not B, we begin to get a clue to its importance in cultural development. A metaphor is not really a connecting of two things by forced and overstrained analogies. It is a way of setting up a current of verbal energy between subjective and objective worlds. It is not referential, in the sense of attempting to describe or set up a verbal replica of the objective world, but a way of absorbing the external world into cultural categories. The unit of metaphor, in most societies, is the god, the sea-god or sky-god or war-god who unites an aspect of nature with an aspect of personality.

A myth of concern is primarily a society's expression of what seems of immediate importance to itself: it deals with that society's views of its origin, its present obligations, and its destiny. It is not really a protoscience, or a primitive attempt to study the natural environment. But its impetus is normally imperialistic: after bringing secular culture into at least verbal consistency with itself, it goes on to deduce, from its sacrosanct writings, certain conceptions of the external world. At this stage the mythology has expanded to include a cosmology, the sense of a framework including the divine, the human, and the natural. But statements about the external world deduced from mythology are of course very apt to collide with what the actual observation of that world suggests. Hence what is often called, inaccurately, the conflict of religion and science, is really a conflict between mythological and empirical views of the natural order.

There have been two major conflicts of this kind: the heliocentric view of the solar system upheld by Galileo and Bruno in opposition to the social concern that demanded a geocentric view, and the evolutionary view of the origin of nature upheld by Darwin and contemporary geologists in the nineteenth century, which seemed to conflict with the doctrine of divine creation.[2] These collisions have established a most important cultural principle. As one aspect of culture develops, science in our present context, the scientist becomes aware of a tension or polarization between the concerns or anxieties of society and the authority of his own discipline. Obviously he has to respect the concerns of society, otherwise he would have no social function at all; but increasingly, as time goes on, he finds he has loyalties and commitments to this science that he may have to defend even in the face of social threats.

This situation is generally admitted in regard to science, even though such things as the energy crisis, the deteriorating of the environment, and the lethal possibilities of atomic warfare indicate that social concern does have its own case. It is much more difficult for society to understand and recognize the fact that literature and the other arts also have an authority within themselves, and that the serious writer or painter must adhere to that authority no matter how much he may be condemned or ridiculed for doing so. Official Marxism (often called "vulgar Marxism" by Marxist intellectuals in the democracies) denies this authority in literature and the arts as a matter of dogma, and there have been startling outbreaks of hysteria nearer home. The reason for this state of affairs, apart from original sin, is that the origin and nature of authority in literature and the arts has not, to my knowledge at least, been investigated. Science's ability to appeal to verification and similar criteria make the question of its authority a relatively simple one; literature and the other arts are in a far more ambiguous and complex position. What follows is a tentative survey of some of the prolegomena needed for such a study.

Western civilization inherited a body of sacred stories, mainly from the Bible, and from the earliest days of Christianity this body of stories had already taken the form of what I have called a myth of concern. In a very short time, too, it had expanded into a cosmology, or view of the natural order. The Bible, as I see it, does not itself provide such a cosmology, but it does provide any number of hints and suggestions for one. It was inevitable, given the social conditions, that what Western Christianity derived from its sacred sources should have been a mythology and cosmology justifying a structure of authority. The metaphorical universe that persisted through the Middle Ages into and even beyond the

Renaissance, in spite of all the cultural changes within society, was a structure on four levels. On the top level, of course, was God: the presence of God, or the real "heaven," was only metaphorically at the top, but the metaphor was usually taken as descriptive also. Below this came God's creation, the geocentric universe with the sky, the "firmament" of Genesis, forming the visible "heaven."

The Biblical myth of creation is an artificial one in which God "makes" the world, instead of bringing it into being like an earth-mother. God being what he is, he could only have created a perfect world, with no sin or death or misery in it: this original creation was what God saw to be "good" in the Genesis account. The alienation myth of the "fall" was therefore necessary to account for the contrast between the model world that a good God must have created in the beginning and the world we live in now. The fall produced a third world, the world into which we are now born, where we are largely alienated from nature, including our own original nature. Before this fall, however, there must have been a fall among the angels, to account for the origin of sin and disobedience in the human mind, and the fallen angelic, or demonic, world constitutes a fourth level. Of these four levels, God is above nature, the demonic world below it, and the two levels of nature itself, or God's creation, come in between.

I have explained all this many times, but each context demands some repetition. World constructs of this type have certain recurrent characteristics. One is that they rationalize the structure of authority in the society. The graduated four levels of the construct we are now discussing has the general model of the feudal conception of protection from above, obedience from below. Everything that is good in this construct comes from above in its origin, and everything good in our own lives comes from responding properly to such inspired impulses. The sacramental system of the Church, again, reconstructs our chaotic lives into a model imitating the form of what God originally intended man to be. In the Renaissance, with the rise of the secular prince, the analogy shifted to the king as the earthly representative of the One Person who was supreme in the universe.

A less interested function of the construct is to put man into a perspective in which his confused activity as a semiconscious being striving for fuller consciousness can be made more intelligible. Our own view of things is blinkered by a schizophrenic subject–object split in which we are constantly stumbling over either/or dilemmas of our own making:

we distrust the "subjective" as unreal (usually with excellent reason) and try to pretend that we can comprehend an independent objective world which is real, with very indifferent success. The conception of God is among other things an attempt to define a kind of existence which is free of all the limitations of the human intelligence. Thus Sir John Davies, in *Nosce Teipsum*, a wonderful grab bag of epigrams setting forth common Elizabethan assumptions about the world:

> But we that measure times by first and last
> The sight of things successively do take,
> When God on all at once His view doth cast,
> And of all times doth but one instant make . . .
> He looks on Adam as a root or well,
> And on his heirs as branches and as streams;
> He sees all men as one Man, though they dwell
> In sundry cities and in sundry realms. [ll. 757–60, 765–8]

Our perception of time as a succession of three unrealities, a vanished past, an elusive present, and an unknown future, is reversed in God's mind into a single eternal present which includes past and future as well. Our ceaseless efforts to unite many things into a single form symbolic of our own unity as an "individual" does not exist for God, for whom the one and the many are merely aspects of the same thing.

One of the most important consequences of this mythological construct, for the understanding of the literature of the period at least, is its conception of two levels of nature. The original "good" creation included the Garden of Eden, but with the fall of Adam this creation largely disappeared, and only the heavenly bodies, made of quintessence and revolving in perfect circles, are left to remind us of its original glory. The planetary spheres are the abode of the blessed spirits in Dante who have passed beyond the Garden of Eden (which is at the top of the mountain of Purgatory in Dante), though Dante distinguishes between their manifestation in the spheres and their abiding place in God beyond the spheres. The use of the planetary spheres as the setting of the *Paradiso* is a spatial metaphor, but by no means an arbitrary or capricious metaphor. With the sin of Adam, man fell into a lower level of nature, the world of experience we now inhabit. This world is ultimately alien to him: animals and plants seem reasonably adjusted to it, but a conscious being cannot be. Man's essential quest, then, is to move from the world of physical nature in which he is born, and which he is in but not of, up to the second level which he was originally created to inhabit. The Garden of Eden has disappeared as a place, but it is recoverable to some extent as a state of mind. Thus Chapman, in his long didactic poem *The Tears of Peace*:

> So when the Soul is to the body given
> (Being substance of God's Image, sent from heaven)
> It is not his true Image, till it take
> Into the Substance, those fit forms that make
> His perfect Image; which are then impressed
> By Learning and impulsion; that invest
> Man with God's form in living Holiness,
> But cutting from his Body the excess
> Of Honors, perturbations and Affects;
> Which Nature (without Art) no more ejects,
> Than without tools, a naked Artisan
> Can in rude stone, cut th'Image of a man. [ll. 373–84]

The way upward from the ordinary to the genuinely human world is the way of morality, law, religion, and education. This means that on the upper level of nature, the level that is specifically the level of human nature, art and nature are the same thing. Many things are "natural" to man, such as wearing clothes, obeying laws, and being in a state of social discipline and intellectual order, that are not natural to anything else in the order of nature. Chapman places this conception of two levels of nature within the framework of the chain of being, which is polarized by the conceptions of form and matter. The chain of being stretches from God to chaos, God being pure form and the "principles" of chaos (hot, cold, moist, and dry) being as close as we can get to matter without form. The essential progress of man upward to his own original home is thus a purgatorial progress, whether an actual doctrine of purgatory is involved or not. Man was created in God's image, but that is not the image he is now born with, and recovering his own original form involves doing a good many things that our hazy post-Romantic superstitions would call "unnatural," such as quieting the mind.

The conception of two levels of nature, the upper one identical with art and the genuine home of man, is still going strong in, for example, Burke's *Appeal from the New to the Old Whigs*, written at the time of the

French Revolution. It underlies Milton's *Comus*, where Comus attempts to seduce the Lady with arguments borrowed from what he calls the state of nature, where sexual intercourse is engaged in without self-consciousness. The Lady informs him that it is her chastity that is really natural, on her proper human plane [ll. 706–99]. It underlies the critical views of Sir Philip Sidney, when he speaks of the poets expressing a golden age in opposition to nature's brazen one (meaning the lower level of nature).[3] It underlies the complications surrounding the word "natural" in *King Lear*, where lower nature becomes Edmund's goddess, and thereby impels Gloucester's "natural" son into some very unnatural forms of behaviour, such as betraying his father and brother. It underlies the last book of *Gulliver's Travels*, where we are informed that the "natural society" so much discussed in the eighteenth century might be possible for a gifted animal, like Swift's talking horses, but is certainly not possible for a "Yahoo" (i.e., man considered purely as an animal).

In God's mind, we saw, time is a pure present, and space would be similarly a pure presence: the "now" and the "here" that never quite come into existence in our own lives are realities for him. Man is the only being in creation who is out of his natural place ("kindly stead," as Chaucer calls it),[4] and when he is in that natural place his experience of space and time become very different. Space in this higher world is a category that suggests a feeling of belonging rather than alienation: our word "home," suggesting as it does a space essentially related to ourselves, preserves something of the feeling. In fact the word "space," during the period we are examining, is usually expressed by "place," space *there*, emphasizing the importance of taking one's rightful position in the hierarchy of the created order. Time, again, on the second or genuinely human level, is more an expression of inward exuberance and energy than the compulsory succession of events symbolized by a ticking clock. The traditional symbol for this sense of time as inner energy is the dance, and more generally music, including the "music of the spheres" which symbolizes the harmony of the genuine creation.[5] Thus Davies again, in the long poem *Orchestra*, an extraordinary vision of the world as seen as an interwoven cosmic dance:

> Since when all ceremonious mysteries,
> All sacred orgies and religious rites,
> All pomps and triumphs and solemnities,
> All funerals, nuptials, and like public sights,

All parliaments of peace, and warlike fights,
All learned arts, and every great affair,
A lively shape of dancing seems to bear. [st. 77]

What Davies means by dance includes the element of ritual in human life, the sense of the sacred occasion or moment of time related to a spiritual reality. It also includes the vision of man as *homo ludens*,[6] engaged in the play which is energy expended for its own sake and not for a further external end as work is.

We have emphasized the fact that this purgatorial upward quest of the soul, however central and significant, cannot be made on its own volition. In a universe of authority all initiation of essential action must come from the source of authority: grace must descend before merit can ascend. Even the revolutionary Milton does not think of liberty as anything that man wants or has a "natural" right to. Liberty for him is good for man because it is something that God wants him to have: man left to himself could not desire liberty, much less achieve it. John Donne, in an *Eclogue* [*at the mariage Of the Earle of Somerset*], applies this downward-moving initiative to the temporal as well as the spiritual life:

The earth doth in her inward bowels hold
  Stuff well dispos'd, and which would fain be gold,
But never shall, except it chance to lie
  So upward, that heaven gild it with his eye;
As, for divine things, faith comes from above,
  So, for best civil use, all tinctures move
From higher powers; From God religion springs,
  Wisdom and honour from the use of Kings. [ll. 61–8]

The figure employed here is one of the corollaries of the chain-of-being aspect of this mythological universe. Metals have been employed since Plato's day as metaphors for an aristocracy in the inanimate world with analogies (hence the word "mettle") in human life. They were enabled to "grow" out of the ground by the influence of the planets: the nearer or larger planets, the sun and the moon, brought out the "noble" metals gold and silver, and the smaller and more distant ones, Jupiter and Saturn, produced the "base" metals tin and lead. This gives Donne the illustration for his theme of all good coming from above, and for the social authority of a monarchy as representing by analogy the authority of God in the secular world. Monarchy is thus, for most people at the time in England (1613), the "natural" form of government for man, because it manifests the same kind of descent of order and law and harmony into a chaotic world that religion does. Such a view of monarchy is often dramatized in masques, especially those of Ben Jonson, where we move from a vision of disorder (the antimasque) upwards through society until we reach the person, often the king or queen, who is in the audience and in whose honour the masque has been held.

The initiative from above can generate a response from below, because, while everything in nature has an inborn tendency to death, it also has a tendency to return to its creator, which can be set free under the right conditions. In human beings, the soul is a substance different from the four elements that make up the body, and it struggles to liberate itself from the "mortal coil" surrounding it. Thus Marvell employs the figure of the drop of dew descending to an alien world and longing to return from it:

> Because so long divided from the Sphere,
> Restless it rolls and unsecure,
> Trembling lest it grow impure:
> Till the warm Sun pity its Pain,
> And to the Skies exhale it back again,
> So the Soul, that Drop, that Ray . . .
> Does, in its pure and circling thoughts, express
> The greater heaven in an Heaven less. [*On a Drop of Dew*, ll. 14–19, 25–6]

Marvell goes on to compare the dew drop with the manna of the Exodus, the food descending from heaven which was reabsorbed into its origin if not gathered. As in the apocryphal Book of Wisdom, manna is described as though it were snow [16:20–3].

In the period I am chiefly dealing with here (English literature from ca. 1580 to ca. 1660), perhaps the most illuminating portrayal of the four-level universe I am dealing with is to be found in the pendant to Spenser's *Faerie Queene* known as the *Mutabilitie Cantos*. In this poem Mutability, a demonic goddess of the lower world of change and decay, the third and fourth levels we have been describing, claims jurisdiction over the world of the planetary spheres as well, on the ground that they revolve, and therefore change. Nobody questions Mutability's claim to be the supreme sovereign of the sublunary world, but Jove is the ruler of the upper part of Nature, and he resists her intrusion strongly. Mutability ignores him, or at any rate addresses him as "Saturn's son" [canto 6, st. 34, l. 7], stressing the degree of change that operates even in divine lives, and appeals to "the God of Nature" [canto 6, st. 35, l. 6], the Christian God, over the head of this minor functionary.

The *Mutabilitie Cantos* are secular and not religious poetry: there are one or two Christian references, as we shall see, but the discussion itself keeps to secular terms. So it is simply the goddess Nature, who is supreme over both Jove and Mutability, to whom the appeal is brought. The evidence Mutability brings forward is evidence of change in the world below—her kingdom—which is caused or aligned with similar changes in the upper world, and so indicates that change, or mutability, goes on there as well. The evidence is chiefly that of the cyclical movements in nature: the months, days, hours, the cycles of life and death, and the like. Nature's decision is:

> I well consider all that ye have said,
> And find that all things steadfastness do hate
> And changed be: yet being rightly weighed
> They are not changed from their first estate;
> But by their change their being do dilate:
> And turning to themselves at length again,
> Do work their own perfection so by fate:
> Then over them Change doth not rule and reign;
> But they reign over Change, and do their states maintain. [canto 7, st. 58]

The effect of Nature's decision is to confine Mutability to the sublunary world, and to confirm the authority of Jove in "his imperial see" [canto 7, st. 59, l. 7]. But that is not the real point of Nature's decision, which speaks of "all things," including evidently the things of this world as well. The cycles of nature are geared to two final movements, one downward into death and annihilation, the other upward into "perfection." The former is the direction of Mutability herself: "For thy decay thou seekst by thy desire" [canto 7, st. 59, l. 3], Nature says to her. The latter is what we have called the purgatorial progression, where cyclical movement becomes the basis for a perfecting of form. In ordinary life repetition may be dull and mechanical, leading to nothing but more repetition, or it may be the basis of a growth in freedom, like practising to play the piano. Hence there is a direction in change which is not simply into death, but is an upward movement into the oneness of being in which "all things" find their rest. Spenser concludes the poem with a pun on Sabbath, the final day of rest, and Sabaoth, multitudes or hosts.[7] It is not a very good pun in Hebrew, where the two words do not even begin with the same letter, but in the Vulgate and English versions of the Bible that Spenser is using it is more convincing. Its significance for Spenser's society is indicated by the second part of the passage from [Sir John Davies'] *Nosce Teipsum* quoted above [p. 217].

The *Mutabilitie Cantos* are high metaphysical comedy, worked out in a secular context. We get an indication of the tone of the poem, and the mood in which it ought to be read, very early, in the description of Mutability's invasion of the sphere of the moon, the lowest point of the higher world over which she claims jurisdiction:

> Thence to the circle of the Moon she clambe,
> Where Cynthia reigns in everlasting glory,
> To whose bright shining palace straight she came,
> All fairly deck'd with heaven's goodly story:
> Whose silver gates (by which there sat an hoary
> Old aged sire, with hour-glass in hand,
> Hight Time) she entered, were he lief or sorry:
> Ne stay'd till she the highest stage had scann'd,
> Where Cynthia did sit, that never still did stand. [canto 6, st. 8]

This is deliberate doggerel: the run-on fifth line in particular is a device Spenser does not employ in a serious context, and the bits of metrical putty in the seventh and ninth lines bring it closer, by Spenser's standard, to *Sir Thopas* than to, say, the descriptions of the Bower of Bliss or the Gardens of Adonis. It is consistent with such a tone that Spenser should incorporate into his poem a story of how Faunus the satyr bribed a nymph to allow him to see Diana naked. When he is discovered, he is hunted by his own hounds like Actaeon and finally both he and his nymph are turned into rivers. A stanza comparing Diana's rage with that of a farmer's wife who catches a "wicked beast" in her dairy house tells us, by all the rules of Renaissance decorum, that we are still within the area of light verse.

The story of Diana and Faunus is obviously parallel to the main theme: the violation of Cynthia's sphere by Mutability is in counterpoint to Faunus's glimpse of the genitals of Diana. Diana and Cynthia are in Classical mythology both aspects of the threefold goddess whose infernal name is Hecate, and Mutability, though not identified with Hecate, is associated with her and comes from the same world. The theme of metamorphosis is one of the most popular in Classical mythology, and in the Christian centuries it became roughly a secular version of the fall of Adam. In terms closer to our present subject, a metamorphosis is a story of the dissolving of a metaphor into its original elements. That is, a being with personal qualities turns into a silent or at least unconscious object, a tree or bird or star or what not, the underlying theme being the reassertion of the gap between subject and object that all creative activity attempts to overcome. Metamorphosis stories are not common in the Bible: according to Sir Thomas Browne, the story of Lot's wife is the only one it offers.[8]

We have said that the decorum of this poem is secular, avoiding explicitly reference to the Christian framework which Spenser's readers would assume to contain both levels of nature. Mutability, brushing Jove out of the way, says that she appeals to the God of Nature over his head, and while contemporary readers would identify this deity with the Christian God, the latter does not appear, and Nature herself conducts the inquiry. There is however one exception, a stanza indicating that even Nature is subject to a greater power:

> That well may seemen true: for well I ween
> That this same day, when she on Arlo sat,
> Her garment was so bright and wondrous sheen,
> That my frail wit cannot devise to what
> It to compare, nor find like stuff to that:
> As those three sacred saints, though else most wise,
> Yet on Mount Tabor quite their wits forgat,
> When they their glorious Lord in strange disguise
> Transfigur'd saw: his garments so did daze their eyes. [canto 7, st. 7]

The fact that it is the Transfiguration episode that Spenser uses for almost his only Christian reference is doubtless connected with the fact that the word rendered "transfiguration" in English New Testaments is metamorphosis. This supplies the key to Nature's decision: metamorphosis moves simultaneously downward to the inevitable death of everything under the moon, and upward to the changeless being of the divine presence.

This use of a metamorphosis story, derived, in its general outline, from

Ovid, is an example of the way in which Classical mythology had been adapted to a Christian framework by the poets of the Christian centuries. Strictly speaking, the Classical fables were to be regarded as demonic parodies of divinely revealed truths, especially when their similarity to those revelations was unmistakable. But in practice this view had been modified in a way indicated by Milton. In the *Nativity Ode* (a poem which is not about the Nativity but about the Incarnation), Milton describes the flight of pagan gods before the coming of the true God. Our feelings about these deities are mixed: nobody wants Moloch back, but the "parting Genius" [l. 186], the "yellow-skirted fays" [l. 235], even the Lars and Lemures of the Roman household, leave a good deal of genuine nostalgia behind them. In *Paradise Regained* this situation is doctrinally clarified: there Jesus is offered the imaginative and philosophical riches of the Greek world, and refuses to have anything to do with them [bk. 4, ll. 285–364]. This looks at first like an irritable obscurantism on Milton's part, but it is nothing of the kind. Because Jesus rejects the whole Classical tradition at that moment, before he enters on his ministry, he is safe from being taken over by it, from deserting the prophetic tradition for a speculative one rooted in the theology of hell as described in the second book of *Paradise Lost*. But at the same time his rejection of it in the context makes it possible for his followers, including Milton, to accept so much of it: the "Genius," we note, has a very positive role to play in *Comus*, *Lycidas*, and *Arcades*.[9] In short, Christ's rejection of Classical imagery redeems it, and creates two categories within it: the category of demonic parody, represented in Milton by Comus and his followers, and the category of positive analogy. Thus Giles Fletcher, in *Christ's Victory and Triumph*:

> Who doth not see drown'd in Deucalion's name,
> (When earth his men, and sea had lost his shore)
> Old Noah; and in Nisus' lock, the fame
> Of Samson yet alive; and long before
> In Phaethon's, mine own fall I deplore;
>   But he that conquer'd hell, to fetch again
>   His virgin widow, by a serpent slain,
> Another Orpheus was than dreaming poets feign.
>
> [pt. 3, "Christ's Triumph over Death," st. 7]

Here the story of Deucalion in Ovid is a positive analogy of the story of Noah in Genesis, the fall of Phaethon similarly an analogy of the fall of

Adam, and even the descent of Christ to the lower world to conquer death and hell and redeem his bride the Church is adumbrated by the failure of Orpheus to redeem his bride from the lower world. The last phrase in Fletcher's stanza indicates that Christian poets, for doctrinal reasons, had to express a conventional ingratitude to the Classical poets from whom they took their allusions; but the difference between the doctrinal demonic parody and the poetic positive analogy is clear enough.

The central conception of this analogy is that of Eros, the love that springs from the sexual nature of humanity. The word *eros* does not occur in the New Testament, where love means either *agape*, God's love for man reflected in man's love for God and for his neighbour, or *philia*, the kind of social cement that may be comprehensively called gregariousness. And although the conception of Eros did enter Christian thought later, it is a fact of primary importance for the history of literature that Christian poets simply appropriated it as something that Christian doctrine had omitted and was of vital importance to them. The theme of metamorphosis itself is actually a by-product of Eros, a story of either the frustration or the fulfilment of erotic love. In the *Mutabilitie Cantos* there is no question of the love of Faunus for Diana, his ambitions regarding her being pure voyeurism and nothing more, but presumably he does love the nymph he bribes, and the mingling of his streams with hers when he is changed into a brook is in the central tradition of such things, the best-known example being the story of Alpheus and Arethusa.[10]

It is well known that medieval poetry developed an elaborate parallel to Christian imagery in which the God of Love was not Jesus but Eros or Cupid. The parallel was extraordinarily detailed: the God of Love was both an infant in the arms of Venus and the power that created the world and held all the gods in subjection; he possessed the equivalent of grace; he had his saints and martyrs, his devotees and his heretics. We can see the parallel worked out as late as, say, *Romeo and Juliet*, where hero and heroine are obedient children going for confession to Friar Laurence, but who die as martyrs to another god whom Romeo describes as "my bosom's lord" [5.1.3]. Its imagery was by no means purely pagan: a lurking sexual element in the descriptions of Paradise, where Adam is the conscious presence in the garden and Eve's body is associated with the garden itself, is frequently employed, and this Edenic imagery modulates to "a garden inclosed . . . a fountain sealed," which is the body of the bride in the Song of Songs [4:12]. Thus in a familiar poem by Thomas Campion:

There is a garden in her face,
Where roses and white lilies grow;
A heav'nly paradise is that place,
Wherein all pleasant fruits do flow.
There cherries grow which none may buy
Till cherry-ripe themselves do cry . . .

Her eyes like angels watch them still;
Her brows like bended bows do stand,
Threat'ning with piercing frowns to kill
All that attempt with eye or hand
Those sacred cherries to come nigh,
Till cherry-ripe themselves do cry.

[*There Is a Garden in Her Face*, sts. 1 and 3]

Echoes of the Garden of Eden, including the forbidding angels at the end of the story, and of the Song of Songs, mingle with echoes of the garden of the Hesperides and of the theme of forbidden fruit which underlies both the Biblical and the pagan myths.

The deeper significance of the poetic emphasis on Eros does not become really obvious, however, until towards the end of the eighteenth century, when the authoritarian four-level structure was beginning to cease to carry an imaginative conviction and was dissolving as a context for poetry. Actually it had only lasted so long because it was a structure of authority and had the resources of spiritual and temporal authority to back it. The older structure, with its two levels of nature, obviously was one that put its main emphasis on the aspect of nature known as *natura naturata*, nature as a structure, order, or system. An emphasis on Eros, then, would go much further than simply the inclusion of sexual love as a poetic theme: it would also bring into the foreground the *natura naturans*, nature as a process of growth, which in turn suggested that man was as much a child of nature as he was a child of God, and that many of his impulses had the moral ambiguity of nature when considered apart from humanity.

So from Rousseau through the Romantics, the framework of imagery behind poetry began to turn into something very different. Human civilization, with its laws, its reason, its social discipline, its clothes, and its figures of authority, still sits on top of what in previous ages was the "fallen" or alienated world of physical nature. But the latter world is now thought of increasingly as something containing a nonhuman Other which is needed to complete human nature itself, and yet is not God. The relation of this *natura naturans* to ordinary human civilization may vary according to the poet's temperament: in Wordsworth it is profoundly benevolent for the most part; in others it may be sinister and terrible, even the kind of thing it is in the Marquis de Sade. Meanwhile, the stars in their courses can no longer symbolize the original divine creation with any real convincingness. In a post-Newtonian world the sky looks more like a mechanism than a product of divine wisdom. If it is a mechanism, of course, that leaves the organism as the highest form of creation we know of, and the world of "outer space" becomes increasingly a place of alienation, inhabited either by emptiness or, at most, by the idiot "immanent will" in Thomas Hardy[11] which man has projected on it. But if nature contains an otherness that man needs to complete his own nature, the descent into it may be, as it was in pre-Christian times, thought of as a perilous but rewarding descent for the greatest of all buried treasures, the treasure of identity.

In the older model, themes of descent had survived mainly because of the prestige of Virgil, where a Classical Hades was substituted for the Christian hell. From Romantic times on, however, themes of descent take on an increasingly oracular quality, and are often associated with the world of dreams. In De Quincey's great mail-coach essay, for example, the dream world is the place where the fall of man is reenacted each night—a suggestion anticipatory of [Joyce's] *Finnegans Wake*. In short, under Romanticism the old four-level cosmos is turned on its head, with a dead mechanical space above, a world of experience below it, a world of rapprochement between man and his natural origin metaphorically below that, and a world of final identity, sometimes, as in [Shelley's] *Prometheus Unbound*, associated with Atlantis, below that again. In the first poet of English literature who gives us this upside-down view of the old cosmos of authority, William Blake, it is interesting that once again all the imagery comes from the Bible, except of course that different proof-texts are supplied.

No human imagination can remain satisfied with an antithesis, and there have been many attempts to set up some outline of a cosmos that will escape from the overriding constraints both of authority and of revolution. Poe's *Eureka* was an early one, and it suggested to the poet and critic Valéry that cosmology, as distinct from the areas explored by science and philosophy, was a literary product.[12] Since then there have been many others, ranging from Yeats's *Vision* to Graves's *The White Goddess*, not of course new constructs, but new ways of rearranging traditional elements in the older ones. The subject has yet to be explored, though the immense contribution the Bible has already made to the subject suggests that it will remain central to all explorations. In any case one hopes for a vision of the imaginative cosmos that will show us our own imaginative creations against a background of equality and freedom rather than the limiting order provided both by a hierarchical vision and by the resistances made to it.

10

Literature as a Critique of Pure Reason

29 September 1982

Originally presented as the second of the 1982–83 Wiegand Lectures at the University of Toronto. This was the inaugural year of the Wiegand Foundation Lecture Series, devoted to a dialogue between science and faith in the modern world. The five speakers in this first lecture series, "Irrationality in Western Society," were Sir Kenneth Dover and Professors Northrop Frye, Jacob Arlow, Allan Bloom, and George Steiner. From Descant, *14 (Spring 1983): 7–21. Reprinted in* Literary Half-Yearly, *24 (July 1983): 134–49, and in* MM, *168–82. The typescripts are in the NFF, 1988, box 48, file 4, and 1991, box 39, file 3 (annotated).*

The word "irrational" is derived from "reason," and the word "reason" summons up the ghost of the old faculty psychology, in which "reason" is a thing man has, and frequently regards as uniquely his, to be distinguished from other things called "will" or "feeling" or "desire." These latter seem to be found among animals, or at least analogies to them are, and so "reason" has been traditionally considered the crown that man wears as the king of nature. It is the faculty that shows off man as the only organism in nature whose horizon is not wholly bounded by the needs of survival and adaptation. However, looking at the mind as an assemblage of parts or different capacities no longer seems very productive, and is generally thought of now as metaphorical, like the theory of four humours in medicine.

But calling such terms "metaphorical" hardly gets rid of them. Some time ago, in reading through Bertrand Russell's *History of Western Philosophy,* I noted a comment he makes in introducing Aristotle's conception of physics: "To understand the views of Aristotle, as of most Greeks, on physics, it is necessary to apprehend their imaginative background. Every philosopher, in addition to the formal system which he offers to the world, has another, much simpler, of which he may be quite unaware. If he is aware of it, he probably realizes that it won't quite do; he therefore conceals it, and sets forth something more sophisticated, which he believes because it is like his crude system, but which he asks others to accept because he thinks he has made it such as cannot be disproved."[1] A passage in Whitehead's *Science and the Modern World*, also about the Greeks, makes much the same point: "Every philosophy is tinged with the colouring of some secret imaginative background, which never emerges explicitly into its trains of reasoning."[2] Whitehead connects this background, in the Greek period, with the Greek sense of the dramatic.

We get, then, from two highly reputable philosophers, a conception of philosophy as a verbal clothing worn over the indecent nakedness of something called its "imaginative background," so as to allow it to appear in public. It is this retreating nude that I have been trying to study all my life. I call it a metaphorical or mythological structure, and it seems to me that while a good deal of philosophy, as Russell and Whitehead say, consists in disguising it in various ways, literature approaches it more directly and recreates it, age after age. One major function of literary criticism, as I see it, is to help us to become more aware of this "secret imaginative background," as it has operated in the past and continues to operate in the present. I do not think that Russell and Whitehead are talking simply about the prejudices of one's upbringing: if they were they would not use the term "imaginative."

Our primary thinking, then, is not rational but metaphorical, an identifying of subjective and objective worlds in huge mental pictures. Metaphors are statements of identity: they tell us, for instance, that the poet and the lady he loves are shadow and sun. Here two quite different things are said to be one thing. To say that A is B when A is so obviously not B is absurd and illogical, and, as Russell says, it won't quite do, at least for argumentative purposes. But it is also a primary structural effort of consciousness. Metaphor does not evoke a world of things linked together by overstated analogies: it evokes a world of swirling currents of energy that run back and forth between subject and object. Such metaphor may be followed by, or even translated into, more continuous or rational thinking, but when it is, it is not superseded by rational thinking: it remains in the background as its constant source of inspiration. About two generations ago there was a vogue among philosophers, including Russell himself, for saying that no statement had meaning unless it was either empirical or analytic, and that if it had no meaning it was obviously not rational. The trouble with this position was that it was a dead end: it cut philosophy off from the metaphorical basis of its own creativity, and there was nothing to do but to scrap it and go on with something more fruitful. The present age seems fascinated by Nietzsche and Heidegger, and so we are unlikely to lose sight of the connection between the philosophical and the metaphorical as long as the present attention span lasts.

Let us ask ourselves, first of all, What are the customary metaphors applied to reason? One of them, clearly, is light: we instinctively think of an age of reason as an age of "enlightenment," and whatever we can add to the world's structure of rational knowledge we call throwing more light on it. Another is dryness, often associated with coolness. The dispassionate thinker rises above the tumultuous storms and tempests of the passions into the clear air, etc.— one can easily paint such metaphorical pictures by numbers. The same metaphors operate negatively for anti-intellectuals. Long ago I spoke of a popular prejudice about poets, of the type often called romantic, as based on a hazy metaphorical contrast between warm mammalians who tenderly suckle their living creations and the cold reptilian intellectuals who lay abstract eggs [*FS*, 20; *FS2*, 28].

This metaphorical ambience of sunrise and mountain air surrounding the reason suggests that we highly approve of ourselves when we feel that we are rational beings. The metaphors were not born yesterday: they are all in Heraclitus, who associated his conception of Logos with "dry light," a contrast to the soggy moist sensuality in which most people are soaked for most of their lives.[3] More important for historical influence, the same metaphors enter into the first two acts of creation in Genesis, which begins with a primordial light, followed by the separation of the dry land from the sea. The account of creation in the Bible does not describe the origin of nature, and was probably never intended to: if it were, it would have been a little cleverer, and not had the trees created the day before the sun was [Genesis 1:11–19]. Creation is rather the presenting to human consciousness of what Heidegger says is the first riddle of existence, Why are there things rather than nothing?[4] The creation resulted also from a divine commandment: light and dryness appeared because they were told to do so. Metaphors of reason, then, are connected with an activity, one that we often distinguish as will.

This connection of reason and will, a connection implying both an identity and a distinction, is complex and confusing. The distinction is often linked to the difference between Hellenic and Hebraic influences on our culture. Many Classical scholars, and some philosophers, including Whitehead, think of reason as something uniquely developed by the Greeks, as though what we call philosophy in Chinese or Indian traditions rested only on some kind of analogy to the techniques of logic and dialectic introduced by Plato and Aristotle. Others, following Nietzsche's lead, have claimed that the conception of "will" is a Christian one, unknown before the New Testament and developed mainly by St. Augustine. But whatever historical constructs we adopt, surely reason has always been active and the will conscious, so that they are really aspects of the same thing, even if at times they seem to be separated. In traditional Christianity creation was not the product of the simple will of God but of the Logos of God, a reasoning and conscious as well as an active will. And it is clear in, for example, Plato's *Republic* that reason should be, and in the wise man is, the commander of the soul, not simply exploring or speculating about the environment but giving orders to the subordinate appetites. Plato expects reason to be what some psychologists call "top dog"[5] in the wise man's mind, and a top-dog reason is clearly an executive. At the same time Plato was well aware that self-conflict would arise in the best-regulated minds, and Christianity can hardly have introduced a new conception in this regard, though it did place much greater emphasis on the psychology of self-conflict. But Paul's statement "what I hate, that I do" [Romans 7:15] is not really so different from Ovid's "deteriora sequor."[6]

Another kind of example also shows how inseparable "reason" is from a controlling activity, whether called "will" or not. Will is frequently associated with motion, and man's impulse to move has developed a sequence of vehicles of transport, starting with domesticated animals and continuing to machines that can go faster and farther than sound. We have also started to build computers that can calculate infinitely faster than the human brain by itself can do. This second development has created in many people a sense of the eerie and uncanny: surely, they protest, a machine may calculate but it can't *really* think: that would endanger man's status as king of nature. Here again "will," as another aspect of "reason," seems to provide us with at least a verbal solution, which is perhaps all we need here. Whatever a machine may do, *qua* machine it has no will to do it. Leave an automobile in a garage unused, and it will rust away to nothing without the slightest sign of impatience.

And so far no computer has exhibited a will to compute until it's plugged in by a human being, and I do not see how it can acquire such a will unless computers in the future come equipped with DNA molecules and genetic codes impelling them to fight every moment for their own survival and reproduction. We may notice in passing that when science fiction stories depict computers beginning to use their own powers for their own ends, like the computer HAL in *2001*,[7] the effect is frightening, as it is intended to be, but the computer has nonetheless turned into a fellow creature. However sinister when in power, there is a genuine pathos in his destruction.

This example suggests that machines are both fascinating and frightening to us because they work without self-conflict. The behaviour of many social insects, such as ants and bees, affects us in a similar way. When we think of the "irrational" in the modern world, we first of all think of such tyrannies as the Nazi movement in Germany, and then smaller but equally mad phenomena like the Jones debacle in Guyana or the Manson group in California.[8] These impress us not simply as erratic behaviour, but as mechanical behaviour in which the mechanism has gone out of control, like an automobile with a blacked-out driver. Certainly there can be no doubt about the self-destructive element involved: when a mass suicide occurs in such groups, one feels that the essential suicide has already taken place, and the essential life already given up.

We may recall the impression given to Hannah Arendt by her experience of attending the Eichmann trial, as recorded in her book *Eichmann in Jerusalem*. What disconcerted her about Eichmann was not a sense of great wickedness or even of great stupidity, for either of which she would have been prepared. She felt rather that, so to speak, he wasn't there: something impossible to define, but nonetheless at the core of real humanity, was simply missing. She developed from this a conception of "the banality of evil," which, I take it, was a philosopher's way of putting clothes over the naked metaphor of "lost soul." Let us look more closely at the metaphor.

In Plato, we said, an active reason has to be top dog in the wise man's mind. As few of us are wise, our top dogs are usually capricious tyrants continually changing their moods, but even people who are wise may have underdogs who hate their wisdom and are ready to look anywhere except in themselves for a new master. An external master has a strong appeal because he puts an end to the sense of self-division in the soul. He makes the sense of responsibility unnecessary, if we have such a sense, or he releases us from self-hatred and self-contempt if we do not. Michael explains to Adam in the last book of *Paradise Lost* that there will always be tyranny in society because the great majority are tyrants to themselves, but prefer to project their tyrannical impulses on something or somebody outside. The affinity of such irrational movements as those we have mentioned with hypnotism, which depends partly on a willingness to be hypnotized, and with hysteria, which is an attempt to cover up something suppressed, has often been noted.

Plato's remedy for self-conflict was a dictatorial one. The active reason employs, as a part of itself, a thought police, hunting down and exterminating every lawless impulse, or else a brainwashing indoctrinator makes sure that no such impulses are formed in early life. The political side of Plato's *Republic,* at least, is not, in my view, its primary one: I think the just state envisaged there is really an allegory of the wise man's mind. But of course the political analogy is present, and there must be something wrong with a psychology that makes for such frightful tyranny when translated into political terms. Christian remedies, though they had a different context, were also dictatorial: whatever rebels against the active controlling reason is evil and must simply be stamped out. Here again the political analogies have tended to be authoritarian: it has been urged that man is so desperately wicked that the strongest possible restraints, secular and spiritual, are needed. In a Christian context such an attitude is arbitrary: the obvious political inference from original sin is democratic. There is no point in giving unlimited authority to others who by definition cannot be any better than we are.

It seems clear that the active consciousness we have spoken of is really human life itself, and choice and responsibility are aspects of biological survival. The presence of an inner commander is a sign of autonomy or freedom, and the hundreds of books demonstrating that we cannot be free willers and ought not to be free thinkers may safely be ignored as containing, in Hume's phrase, nothing but sophistry and illusion.[9] And yet a dictatorial maintaining of this inner authority is a panic-stricken attitude that soon ends in the very hysteria it is trying to fight. In society, irrational impulses may have at least a comprehensible cause, such as the vacuum left in the soul by the departure of political loyalty, religious faith, family affection, or social vision. In the individual, it would be more practical to regard the mind as more like a parliamentary democracy. The active reason should be not a dictator but a government in power which has, like the Liberal party in Canada, a divine right of re-election. The irrational or self-destructive impulse is the view of the honourable member from Redneck Gulch, representing a constituency from a more primitive area of the brain. What he says is not to be acted on, but it is better to know that he is there and holds the views he does. And gradually, as we listen to the parliamentary debate that goes on inside ourselves, and which we hear the instant we stop to listen, we begin to understand that while there are elements in the mind that are perhaps grammatically "irrational," they may not be self-destructive at all, and hence can coexist with reason, or even form a part of it.

In speaking of reason, we have come to characterize it as primarily something that maintains an inner freedom, rather than something that tries to arrive at an objective truth, which is the more conventional view of it. For most of us today, the word "truth" has a rather empty and rhetorical sound: what is true today will be either disproved tomorrow or carried on to another stage, and in any case may be only a choice among many truths, as we imply when we use phrases like "the real truth." To revert to *Paradise Lost*: when the yet unfallen Adam asks the angel Raphael whether or not other planets are inhabited besides the earth, Raphael discourages the question as a distraction. The primary knowledge for Adam is the knowledge Raphael gives him, the story of the fall of Satan which will help him to preserve and maintain his freedom in Paradise. Knowledge of nature for itself, to satisfy the mere desire of knowing, has to take second place. For St. Augustine, much earlier, intellectual curiosity verged on a sin of presumption.

This attitude, so hard for us to sympathize with now, arose partly because Christianity had come to think of all natural knowledge as a set of deductions in a vast synthesis of reasoning, with the primary revelations of faith acting as the major premises. The essential truths, those that tell us what we must do to be saved, have already been given us. Such a conception of knowledge, we may observe, is one that annihilates the distinction between reasoning and rationalizing, or carrying a reasoning operation to a predetermined goal. Rationalizing, apart from private and subjective contexts, has, as its primary aim, the bolstering of some ideology held in one's society, and is still with us in both sacred and secular contexts. The general attitude is, If you want to philosophize, don't just stand there. Do something socially functional, that is, work out proofs that your society is right in believing what it wants to believe. The principle formulated by St. Anselm, *credo ut intelligam*, "I believe in order to know" [*Proslogium*, chap. 1], is the axiom of this kind of rationalizing.

Most of us, nonetheless, feel that there is a difference between reasoning and rationalizing, however easy it may be to show that every point of view is culturally conditioned and subject to preceding social assumptions. We are now fairly sure that no deductive approach to knowledge founded on unquestionable premises is going to work. Any individual's line of reasoning, then, may achieve a break with the structure and tradition of the reasoning he started with: it may become a genuine mutation with a survival value for a quite new society. One sees this most clearly in scientific method. Science is an activity like anything else, and it has to begin in the same chaos of I-wonder-if and let's-see-whether that any activity would do. But here the activity is directed toward the external world, which acts as the answering authority. Hence the activity is reinforced by an observant, sometimes almost a passive, receptivity in regard to the evidence coming from nature. If a cattle tick will wait for years to hitch a ride on a passing cow, the science that records this fact has to be equally patient.

The poet Browning, in his early poem on Paracelsus, the sixteenth-century doctor and occult philosopher who was a contemporary of Luther, Rabelais, and Erasmus, makes Paracelsus say, at the outset of his career:

> There is an inmost centre in us all,
> Where truth abides in fullness . . .
> . . . and, to KNOW
> Rather consists in opening out a way
> Whence the imprisoned splendour may escape,
> Than in effecting entry for a light
> Supposed to be without. [*Paracelsus*, pt. 1, ll. 728–9, 733–7]

Browning may have thought of Paracelsus, as he did of Fra Lippo Lippi, as a spokesman of the new attitudes coming in with Renaissance humanism, the period he was particularly interested in. But Paracelsus, as we have seen, is speaking for the whole traditional attitude to knowledge before him in thinking of knowledge as primarily an activity directed by the subject towards the object. Browning himself, however, seems to assume that this attitude would be something of a paradox to Paracelsus's contemporaries. Here, I think, he is reflecting the growing ascendancy of a more receptive attitude to nature that had grown up since Descartes and had been codified by Locke's theory of knowledge. According to this, man is first of all equipped with five senses and is surrounded by a world which those senses must take account of. Hence there comes a strong emphasis on the inductive side of reasoning, on the receptivity of the scientific attitude, its impartial taking in of sense impressions, its uninvolved observation of phenomena, the patience with which it checks its data and repeats its experiments to make sure the observations are correct.

We have now a conception of two aspects of reason, one active and aggressive, the other receptive and suspending judgment. Scientific method on this basis has come to symbolize, for us, the typically rational procedure of our time. This method is founded on the Cartesian paradigm, where consciousness resides only in the perceiving subject, so that the object has to be treated as mechanical, and, by extension, as quantitative and measurable. In recent times there has been a growing chorus of objections to the Cartesian paradigm, asserting that what was a brilliant and innovative idea in the seventeenth century has become a positive danger in the twentieth, especially in the social sciences. It is argued that the active and passive aspects of reason are wrongly related: what is observed is affected by the observation, and when it is man himself that is being observed, a detached attitude is only a disguise for reactionary prejudice. Perhaps, then, there is not only an active and a passive side to reason, but different levels of it, the two aspects being closer together on higher levels.

In Hindu philosophy, as we have it in the *Bhagavadgita* and elsewhere, there is a conception of three *gunas* or moods of the soul.[10] Perhaps "modes" would be a better rendering than "moods." There is an active and aggressive *rajas* mood, a passive and receptive *tamas* mood, and a balancing or neutralizing *sattva* mood which is superior to them both, because it includes them both, and which is the foundation of all genuine wisdom. All three, being modes of consciousness, are modes of reason as well, even though they include other factors. The *rajas* or aggressive mood is typically what we have been calling the actively rational. The *sattva* or balancing mood is closer to what we generally call the reasonable. For, as Samuel Butler pointed out over a century ago, the reasonable is often the opposite of the rational.[11] The reasonable pursues the middle course that keeps life unified and integrated. Emotional and other factors are balanced and compromised with, but not ignored. The rational attitude, in contrast, pursues extremes rather than the middle way. It is fascinated by reason as a machine, and by the compulsions in it that seem to do away with self-conflict. If you accept A, then B necessarily follows and you must do that, however out of proportion to human life as a whole it may be.

Reason pursued in this exclusive way eventually becomes a mental cancer, fostering its own growth at the expense of the whole organism. A few steps further along, the excessively rational turns into the irrational, which, as we saw, is the rational gone out of control. As a modern French poet has said, the madman is the victim of the rebellion of words.[12] Orwell's nightmare world of *1984* is a mad world, but a triumph of pseudo-logic also. Some years earlier, E.J. Pratt had used Orwell's imagery in describing the Nazi invasion of France as reason in the service of the irrational:

> Seven millions on the roads in France,
> Set to a pattern of chaos
> Fashioned through years for this hour.
> Inside the brain of the planner
> Not tolerance befogged the reason—
> The *reason* with its clear-swept halls,
> Its brilliant corridors,
> Where no recesses with their healing dusk
> Offered asylum for a fugitive. [*Dunkirk*, ll. 30–8]

There is a Western analogue to the Hindu conception of two levels of reason in the psychology of Jung, where there are said to be four types of consciousness: thinking, feeling, intuition, and sensation.[13] Jung suggests that people can be classified according to the proportion of these elements within them. The "thinking" type, if he is primarily that, is often a hard-driving aggressive person, impatient with the untidiness of people who never seem to understand that the shortest distance between two points is a straight line. He is the direct opposite of the "feeling" type, and it takes all the opaqueness of Jung's prose style to conceal the fact that by a feeling type he means a receptive thinker. Such a person would make a good chairman, collecting the sense of a meeting, or a good teacher, presenting the thoughts or events of the past, but his record of accomplishment in the world might be less impressive. For Jung there is an ideal of "individuation" beyond them both, and when we reach it one typical activity is an outbreak of symmetrical doodling, or drawing that Jung calls mandalas or geometrical designs.[14]

To see the point of this we have to turn to Kant, for whom there are also two levels of reason, which he distinguishes as *Verstand* and *Vernunft*. If I have grasped the distinction correctly, *Verstand* is what we have called the Cartesian paradigm, a surmounting of clearly delimited problems by an alternation of active search and passive consideration of evidence. *Vernunft* is a freer activity of reason, concerned not so much with things as with consciousness itself, asking Montaigne's question "What do I know?"[15] and limited only by the categories within which the mind operates. There is a distinction between "pure" and "practical" forms of *Vernunft*, corresponding to the distinction between the theoretical and active aspects of a commanding and executive reason, and consequently two critiques.[16] For pure reason the world is objective and phenomenal; hence pure reason cannot make contact with the ultimate realities, including God. The practical reason, however, can feel its attachment to a divine or creative Logos that knows nothing of any distinction between pure and practical aspects of itself, and nothing of any limitations on either.

We are now back to the metaphor of creation in Genesis. We notice that the climax of the creation was a day of rest, which God presumably spent in contemplating the "good" world he had made [Genesis 1:31, 2:2–3], which once finished had become objective to himself. On the previous day he had taken the precaution of making man among the other animals, so that there would be at least one member of an appreciative conscious audience. Man's imitation of the sabbatical aspect of creation is the subject of Kant's third critique, the *Critique of Judgment* (*Urteilskraft*). Here the mind is neither reflecting on itself nor motivated by desire, but is studying that curious assimilation of nature and art that seems to underlie so much of what we call beauty, design for its own sake, purposiveness without purpose, as Kant says.[17] There is no reason why we should feel that a snowflake has an exquisite and subtle design: we just do, and there is a feeling of wonder and mystery about this that mathematical explanations of the forming of crystals do not affect: they are made in a different area. The words "speculation" and "reflection" remind us of how deeply our view of nature is bound up with metaphors of mirrors, of seeing in nature, traditionally the second Word of God, the same free play of design that we find in our own consciousness. Hence, as Matthew Arnold insists, many things are not really seen at all until they are seen as beautiful,[18] and this kind of perception is really the fulfilment of consciousness itself. Sir Thomas Browne goes much further, with an explicit reference to the Sabbath of creation: "I hold there is a general beauty in the works of God, and therefore no deformity in any kind or species of creature whatsoever. . . . Nature is not at variance with Art, nor Art with Nature, they being both servants of His Providence. Art is the perfection of Nature. Were the World now as it was the sixth day, there were yet a Chaos."[19]

But as soon as we enter the world of design, beauty, play, and the assimilating of nature and art, we begin to wonder whether creation itself, rather than the exercising of consciousness within it, is not the primary human activity. The Romantics who followed Kant developed a conception of "imagination," designed to express this. Imagination is a constructive, unifying, and fully conscious faculty that excludes no aspect of consciousness, whether rational or emotional. As such, it is for many Romantics the primary activity of human consciousness. In Blake, for example, the word "reason" usually has an unfavourable sense, because for him it means the Cartesian split between subject and object that all creation begins by trying to overcome. But the words "mental" and "intellectual" in Blake are consistently synonyms for imaginative. For Shelley, the language of imagination is the key to human freedom and equality, because it is purely constructive, in contrast to the language of assertions that carry their own negations along with them, and are consequently aggressive and hostile. For Coleridge, there is a "primary" imagination, an existential consciousness very close, it seems to me, to Kant's practical reason, and a "secondary" one which embodies itself in its artefacts.

This takes us back full circle to the metaphorical world with which we began, the world of the poets which is older than the world of the philosophers, and is still the verbal matrix of civilization. The Romantics tell us that to get to the furthest distance from the irrational we have to move from the balance and prudence of the reasonable to the creative energy of culture, more particularly as embodied in, or symbolized by, the great works of art, music, and literature. The creative person or "genius," in the Romantic view, does not simply avoid the irrational but grapples with it and transforms it, dealing with the fantastic as well as the real, and often in the grip of neurosis himself. In creation the alternating of activity and receptiveness recurs: there is no question about the mental energy that creating works of art requires, but poets constantly tell us that much of that energy has to take the reverse form of allowing what is being created to assume its own independent existence without interference from the poet's conscious will. Many of Keats's most dazzling letters are concerned with the principle that "that which is creative must create itself."[20]

Of course, especially in the theologically-minded Coleridge, there is an analogy between man as creator of art and the Logos of God as the creator of nature. This analogy is not new with the Romantics: we find it in the Elizabethan critic Puttenham, writing in the 1580s:

> A Poet is as much to say as a maker. And our English name well conforms with the Greek word, for of *poiein*, to make, they call a maker *Poeta*. Such as (by way of resemblance and reverently) we may say of God; who without any travail to his divine imagination made all the world of naught, nor also by any pattern or mould, as the Platonics with their Ideas do fantastically suppose.[21]

Well, the Platonics may be fantastic, but it was they who supplied Puttenham with his metaphor. The word rendered "created" in the first verse of Genesis is never used in the Bible to describe anything that man can also do. But in, say, Plato's *Timaeus*, where the creator is a demiurge working by a model like a human craftsman, the way is wide open for such a parallel.

There are two obstacles here. In the first place, nothing that man makes is genuinely alive: Pygmalion's statue, in ordinary experience, never really becomes Galatea. Milton says that books are not absolutely dead things,[22] but the very defensiveness of the phrase indicates that they are relatively dead things, mechanisms that repeat what they say. This is the point at which the Bible inserts its warnings against idolatry: an idol is a human artefact, therefore dead, or animated only by some spirit that has forgotten or ignored its real creator. Thus man invented the wheel thousands of years ago, and promptly turned it into an idol of external fate or fortune. An attempt to idolize human culture would be equally futile: the Romantics reach a conception of the elitism of genius, and many of them, even Blake, often speak as though they were content to leave it at that, but we cannot.

In the second place, metaphors of the dead or the mechanical seem to get attached even to God's creation in the Bible. God's making of Adam is very like the animating of a corpse, and man's occasional grumbles that he never asked to get thrown into so stupid and meaningless a world are supposed to be refuted by the statement that pots do not raise this sort of question with their potters. We find however that that remarkable

Victorian novelist, clergyman, and writer of fantasy George Macdonald ends a short allegorical fable with a very unusual prayer dealing with precisely this point: "We thank thee that we have a father, and not a maker; that thou hast begotten us, and not moulded us as images of clay; that we have come forth of thy heart, and have not been fashioned by thy hands."[23] To adopt the male-centred Biblical terminology that Macdonald uses, can man beget as well as create? Or, more accurately, what do human beings bring forth that is alive?

Their children, of course, and by extension a new society. But if we bring something to life, we have to respect its freedom; otherwise it is not really alive. I am not speaking here of what is often called "permissiveness": that is not a genuine respect for freedom, but a deliberate prolonging of the frustrations of dependence. The "adolescent" or "teenager" is a twentieth-century invention, and a most ill-advised one. I am saying rather that there can be no progress in human life except progress in the formula "live and let live," releasing more and more members of society from exploitation, from the inherited conditioning of conventions that keep us from dealing with change, from the panic that perverts all experience into a form of possession. Our word "manufacture" shows how deeply we are involved in the clutching, grasping, possessive activity of the hand, and we also speak of seizing or grasping ideas. The genuinely human reason for technology was the abolition of slavery, but slavery is partly a state of mind and can coexist with the most highly developed technology. I do not mean only human society: the domination and exploiting of nature is part of a slave economy too. I have occasionally wondered, in looking at the approaches to our cities, whether nature possesses the capacity to make a convulsive lunge of self-preservation that would rid her of this horrible strangling parasite of humanity once and for all.

The arts, whatever their limitations, have an essential role to play in the liberating of the human mind. They do not work by magic, and are not mind-altering drugs: they cannot make people "better" unless there is already a reasoning will to be made better. But the work of literature (the art we are at present concerned with) forms a focus for a community. It reflects the concerns of that community but is detached from immediate action, so that the community remains a community and does not turn into a mob. Literature cannot by itself prevent the total destruction that is one of the many possible fates in store for the human race, but I think that that fate would be inevitable without it. No one has really studied the function of literature in society, but it must be one of major importance. In Canada today, for example, with its demoralized government and chaotic economy, it seems to me only its lively and articulate culture that holds the country together. Everything else seems to me irrational, in the sense I have given the word of machinery out of control. But if we place the works of the human imagination in the centre of the community and make sure they stay there, we shall be able eventually to see that community itself as the total form of what human beings can bring forth, their own larger life that continues to live and move and possess its inward being.

11

Approaching the Lyric

14 October 1982

Originally presented as the opening address at a conference on "Lyric Poetry and the New New Criticism," Victoria University, University of Toronto, 14–17 October 1982. From Lyric Poetry: Beyond New Criticism, *ed. Chaviva Hošek and Patricia Parker (Ithaca, N.Y.: Cornell University Press, 1985), 31–7. Reprinted in* EAC, *130–6. Typescripts of both the written paper and the oral version (in which, as Chancellor of Victoria University, Frye first welcomes conference participants and at the end introduces the second speaker of the evening, Jonathan Culler) are in the NFF, 1988, box 48, file 4.*

Some people believe that literary terms can be defined: there was a purist in the *Greek Anthology* who maintained that an epigram is a poem two lines long, and that if you venture on a third line you're already into epic.[1] But that seems a trifle inflexible. At the other extreme, there is a popular tendency to call anything in verse a lyric that is not actually divided into twelve books. Perhaps a more practicable approach would be to say that a lyric is anything you can reasonably get uncut into an anthology. Or perhaps we can at least limit the subject by saying what the lyric is not.

The kind of formulaic, half-improvised poetry that, we are told, lies close behind the Homeric poems is poetry of pure continuity. Like motion in Newton, there is nothing to stop it except some external factor, such as the end of the story it tells or the beginning of the occasion it was composed for. If the poet does not read or write, the poem exists only in the one dimension of pure continuity in time, because such a poet is not thinking of lines on a page. If the poem is written, it appears in two spatial dimensions, across and down a page, as well as in time, and the crucial term "verse," with its associations of turning around or turning back, becomes functional. The poem may still be continuous, but in "verse," where we keep coming to the end of a line and then starting another, there is a germ of discontinuity. The more this sense of the discontinuous increases, the more closely we approach the lyrical area.

In the lyric, then, we turn away from our ordinary continuous experience in space or time, or rather from a verbal mimesis of it. But we cannot simply identify the lyrical with the subjective. Continuous poetry may also be subjective, like [Wordsworth's] *Prelude* or [Byron's] *Childe Harold*, and lyrical poetry may be a communal enterprise, like the Old Testament Psalms or the odes of Pindar. As these examples show, the discontinuous element in poetry is often linked to a specific, usually ritual, occasion, and the element of occasion means that the poem revolves around that occasion, instead of continuing indefinitely. If there is no public occasion, what corresponds to it may be a private occasion like drinking or love-making, to cite two standard themes. But even in this kind of "occasional" verse there is still an identity of subject and object. Many years ago, when logical positivism was in vogue among philosophers, I picked up one of their books and read the following: "Many linguistic utterances are analogous to laughing in that they have only an expressive function, no representative function. Examples of this are cries like 'Oh, Oh,' or, on a higher level, lyrical verses." This remark put me off reading philosophy for some years, at least until philosophers stopped chasing these red herrings of expressive and representative functions.

The private poem often takes off from something that blocks normal activity, something a poet has to write poetry about instead of carrying on with ordinary experience. This block has traditionally been frustrated love, as in the Petrarchan poetry of Elizabethan England, where the frustration is normally symbolized by the cruelty and disdain of a mistress. Such a block has much to do with creating the sense of an individualized speaker. Something similar occurred in ancient Greece: in fact, Bruno Snell, in his book on the evolution of what he considers a unique type of individual consciousness in the period between Homer and the age of Socrates, associates the decisive turning point with the early lyrical poets, Archilochus, Sappho, Anacreon, and their contemporaries.[2]

Here the blocking point makes the lyrical poem part of what biologists call a displaced activity, as when a chimpanzee crossed in love starts digging holes in the ground instead. In another lyrical genre the block relates to the reader rather than the poet: this is what we find in the epitaph convention that we have had from Greek times on. Here the reader is assumed to be a traveller, pursuing his normal course through time and space, who is suddenly confronted with something he should stop and read. What he reads is the verbal essence of a life which has once had its own context in space and time but is now enclosed in a framework of words. He is often told, at the end, that he has been looking in a mirror: his own context is still in ordinary space and time, but it will eventually disappear, and the verbal essence of *his* life may make an equally short poem.

We notice in, for example, Mallarmé, a good many occasional pieces as well as poems called *Toast funèbre* or thought of as inscribed on tombs. So we are not surprised that it is Mallarmé who gives us the best-known parable of the displacing operations of lyric in *L'Après-midi d'un faune,* where a faun tries to pick up a nymph and finds that he has two nymphs stuck together, interested in each other but not in him. There is nothing for it but to retreat into the dream world where verbal creation begins, and where, as he says, he will see instead the shadows that they will turn into.

When the block ceases to be opaque and becomes transparent, the lyric of frustration expands into the lyric of mental focus. Gerard Manley Hopkins speaks of two kinds of poetic process: a transitional kind, which operates in narrative and storytelling, following the rhythm of the continuity of life in time, and a more meditative kind, which turns away from sequential experience and superimposes a different kind of experience on it. The superimposing provides an intense concentration of emotion and imagery, usually on some concrete image. It is on this level that we have Keats's contemplation of the Grecian urn, Hopkins's recognition of the presence of God in the windhover, Rossetti's remembering from a moment of anguish that "the woodspurge has a cup of three." In this kind of meditative intensity the mind is identified with what it contemplates.

In Oriental poetry the tradition of meditation is so well established that a poem can often simply give a few verbal clues and leave it to the reader to recreate the process. The meditative power of Japanese or Chinese lyric may have something to do with the nature of the written language, which seems to provide a visual supplement to the verbal intensity, so that the seventeen syllables of the haiku, for instance, can become a kind of exploding verbal atom. However much may be lost through ignorance of Japanese, no one can miss this exploding power that comes through a haiku of the poet Rippo, which must surely be one of the world's greatest death songs.

> Three lovely things . . .
> Moonlight . . . cherry blossoms. . .
> And now . . .
> The untrodden snow.

This hieroglyphic quality is mentioned by Hart Crane in one of his rare critical essays: "It is as though a poem gave the reader as he left it a single, new *word*, never before spoken and impossible to actually enunciate, but self-evident as an active principle in the reader's consciousness henceforward."[3]

So far I have touched mainly on the visual side of the lyric, but of course traditionally the lyric is primarily addressed to the ear. A good deal has been said about the deferring of written language to the spoken word: much less has been said about the deferring of written poetry to music, especially in lyrical poetry, where the very word "lyric" implies a musical instrument. For centuries poets refused to admit that their expression was verbal: they insisted that it was song, or even instrumental music. In pastoral poetry the instrument was often a flute or reed, like the "oat" of [Milton's] *Lycidas* or the pipe of Blake's *Songs of Innocence,* regardless of the fact that it is impossible to sing and play a wind instrument at the same time. The sixteenth century, more realistically, featured the lute: poets who do not think musically give us some curious musical images, such as Coleridge's damsel lugging a dulcimer across Abyssinia [*Kubla Khan,* ll. 37–41].

This association with music has two elements of importance. One is that the lyric turns away, not merely from ordinary space and time, but from the kind of language we use in coping with ordinary experience. Didactic or even descriptive language will hardly work in the lyric, which so often retreats from sense into sound, from reason into rhyme, from syntax into echo, assonance, refrain, even nonsense syllables. The strict forms of traditional lyric—villanelles, ballades, sonnets, and the like—form part of the same tendency. Many lyrics are written in stanzas, and the metaphor of "room" inherent in "stanza" suggests a small area complete in itself even though related to a larger context. So a stanza unit may impart a lyrical quality even to a long continuous poem: *The Faerie Queene* seems "lyrical" in a way that *Paradise Lost* does not. "We'll build in sonnets pretty rooms," as Donne says [*The Canonization*, l. 32]. If we start to read this poem of Wyatt—

> Process of time worketh such wonder,
>   That water which is of kind so soft
> Doth pierce the marble stone asunder,
>   By little drops falling from aloft
>
> [*Process of Time Worketh Such Wonder*, ll. 1–4]

—we can hear the imitative harmony in the rhythm that suggests a self-contained world where reality is verbal reality. Imitative harmony is sometimes called a trick of rhetoric, but in Wyatt, who is better at it than anyone else I know in English literature, it is certainly no trick. More important, we are circling around a defined theme instead of having our attention thrown forward to see what comes next. We hear, so to speak, the end in the beginning: we have stepped out of experience into something else, a world like the rose-garden in [Eliot's] *Burnt Norton* from which we must soon return.

The second factor connecting lyric with music is that, for the most part, musical sounds are in a special area, different from the sounds we hear in ordinary life. The poet, however, has to use much the same words that everyone else uses. In lyric the turning away from ordinary experience means that the words do not resonate against the things they describe, but against other words and sounds.

Sometimes this verbal resonance comes from allusiveness, from deliberate echoes of Classical and other myths, as in Swinburne:

> And the brown bright nightingale amorous
> Is half assuaged for Itylus,
> For the Thracian ships and the foreign faces,
> The tongueless vigil, and all the pain. (*Atalanta in Calydon*, ll. 69–72)

Here we are psychologically close to magic, an invoking of names of specific and trusted power. At other times the resonance is not allusive but, more vaguely, or at least more indefinably, an evoking of some kind of mysterious world that seems to be concealed within ordinary time and space. Verbal magic of this kind has a curious power of summoning, like the proverbial Sirens' song. When Keats says that the nightingale's song has "Charmed magic casements, opening on the foam / Of perilous seas, in faery lands forlorn" [*Ode to a Nightingale,* ll. 69–70], half our brain closes down and says it doesn't know what Keats is talking about. The other half wakes up and recognizes a strange environment that still has something familiar in it. The poet, in the ancient phrase, unlocks the word hoard, but the word hoard is not a cupboard: it is something more like a world that our senses have filtered out, and that only poets can bring to awareness.

It is very common for a single line to possess this quality of resonant and summoning magic. There is the line from Thomas Nashe's elegy, "Brightness falls from the air,"[4] which many people know who know nothing else of Nashe. One critic has suggested that the line may be too good for Nashe, who perhaps wrote the more commonplace "Brightness falls from the hair," the present version being a printing accident. I dislike the suggestion, but it is true that accident can play some part in verbal magic. There is a Newfoundland folk song with the original refrain, "I love my love but she'll love no more." Through a lucky short circuit in oral transmission, this turned into "I love my love and love is no more," a line that teases us out of thought like the Grecian urn.

So the frustrating or blocking point, the cruel mistress or whatever, becomes a focus for meditation rather than brooding, and thereby seems to be the entrance to another world of experience, "the fitful tracing of a portal," as Wallace Stevens calls it [*Peter Quince at the Clavier,* l. 52]. This world is one of magic and mystery, one that we must soon leave if we are to retain our reputations as sober citizens of the ordinary one. But there is still a residual sense that something inexhaustible lies behind it, that it is good not merely to be there, but, as Ferdinand says at the masque in *The Tempest,* to remain there [4.1.22–4]. Two highly cerebral poets, Mallarmé and Rilke, have said that the end and aim of lyrical poetry is praise.[5] They did not say this in any sort of conventional religious context: they were not talking about a prefabricated heaven, but an earthly paradise we stumble on accidentally, like the castle of the Grail, a paradise we can bring to life for ourselves if we ask the right question, which is, according to Chrétien de Troyes, "Who is served by all this?"[6]

For many centuries the lyric was content to be a relatively minor aspect of poetic experience, but Poe's essay "The Poetic Principle" reacted against this and identified the lyrical with the authentically poetic, dismissing all continuous poems as fragments of genuine lyric stuck together with versified prose.[7] This essay had, as is well known, a tremendous influence on the French school that runs from Baudelaire to

Valéry, and that influence made its way into English poetry in the generation of Eliot and Pound. I imagine that one reason for its influence was the belief that the standard metres of continuous verse had exhausted their possibilities, so that narrative shifted to prose, while long poems, even the poems of that master of the interminable, Victor Hugo, tended to become increasingly fragmented.

One of the by-products of this movement was the critical approach that developed two generations ago, which I suppose this volume would call "the old new criticism." This was a technique of explication that approached all literature, whatever the genre, in terms of its lyrical quality, and tended to place the great continuous poets—Milton, Goethe, Victor Hugo—below the poets of the greatest fragmented intensity—Hopkins, Hölderlin, Rimbaud. This movement in criticism seems to me essentially a practical one, excellent for classroom discussion but not well grounded in critical theory. Theoretical developments since then have tended to focus on continuous qualities and on narrative. I take it that the present book owes its existence to a feeling that it is high time for critical theory to come to firmer grips with the lyrical element in literature. I share this feeling, and I have therefore an additional reason for being interested in it.

12

The Survival of Eros in Poetry

16 February 1983

Originally presented as a lecture under the title "Romance as the Survival of Eros" at the University of New Mexico. From Romanticism and Contemporary Criticism, *ed. Morris Eaves and Michael Fischer (Ithaca, N.Y.: Cornell University Press, 1986), 15–45. The lecture is reprinted in* MM, *44–59; the questions and answers are reprinted under the title "Freedom and Concern" in* WGS, *281–302. The typescript is in the NFF, 1988, box 47, file 5.*

In the preface to their volume, Eaves and Fischer explain that the "sets of questions and answers that follow each essay began as three-hour classroom sessions focusing on the work of each contributor, including the essays published here. Credit for the demanding lines of questioning pursued in and out of class belongs entirely to the undergraduate and graduate students of 'The Romantic Self,' 1982–1983." They note that "the final versions, based on tapes of those sessions, have been extensively edited by us and reworked by the contributors" (10–11).

Every society is characterized by concern, a term so broad that it is practically equivalent to conscious awareness itself, or at least to the awareness that life is serious, on both its individual and its social sides. The verbal expression of such concern is, in modern times, mainly conceptual and theoretical, taking the form of political, religious, psychological doctrines. Before the rise of conceptual language, however, such verbal expression most naturally took the form of stories, stories tending to explain or identify the gods, the structure of authority in the society, the legendary history, and the like. It is obvious that a great many societies had two categories of stories, one "sacred" or particularly serious and important, telling the society what it essentially needed to know, and one more relaxed and secular, stories told for entertainment or mere sociability.

Our own culture, by which I mean essentially the culture of Western Europe from the beginning of the Christian era to the present day, along with its descendants in the New World and elsewhere, was characterized, for many centuries, by a group of sacrosanct stories derived from the Bible. These stories had consolidated into a mythology, a reasonably coherent account of the relations of God to man from creation to, in the future, the end of the world; and the metaphors within the mythology had taken the form of a cosmology. Like most mythologies of concern, its primary function was to illuminate and rationalize the structure of authority, both spiritual and temporal, within its society. Although its cosmology, in some respects, was admitted to be metaphorical, still most of it enjoyed the prestige of a science for a long time. But the cosmology remained essentially related to the sense of concern about human duties and destiny that had inspired it, and it was not really a proto-science.

This cosmos of authority envisaged a universe on four main levels. At the top was heaven in the sense of the place of the presence of God. The word "top" is a metaphor, but it was so pervasive a metaphor that it got into practically every type of reference to God, who was invariably thought of as "up there." This God was a Creator, the creation myth of the Bible being an artificial creation myth in which the universe is made by a divine sky-father, in contrast to others where it is brought into being by an earth-mother. Such a God could have created only a perfect world, with no sin or death in it: this perfect world is described in the Book of Genesis in its first chapter, and in the story of Adam and Eve in the Garden of Eden. An alienation myth or fall is necessary to account for the difference between this originally perfect world and the one we are now in. The latter forms a third level, also part of the order of nature, and below it is the demonic world or hell—again a metaphorical "down," but an inescapable metaphor. There are, then, a divine presence above nature, a demonic world below nature, and two levels of the order of nature itself, or the created world.

The third or "fallen" world is the one we are born into, and animals and plants seem to be relatively well adjusted to it, but man is not. His natural home is the perfect world God originally created for him and intended him to live in. Nothing remains of this world physically except the stars in their courses, along with the legends concerning the stars, that they are made of quintessence, that they move in perfect circles about the earth, that they give out an inaudible music. Otherwise, the original home of man is no longer a place, but may to some degree be achieved as a state of mind. Man's primary duty, in fact, is to move upward on the scale of being, coming as close to his original state as possible. Many things are "natural" to man that are not natural to any other organism: the wearing of clothes, the being in a state of social discipline, the practice of religion and law, the possession of consciousness. Everything good for man in religion, law, and education has for its end his promotion from the lower to the higher level of nature. Man's pilgrimage is a purgatorial one, whether an actual doctrine of purgatory is involved or not.

If we take such a period as the Elizabethan age in English literature, we can soon see how impossible it is to understand, in many crucial aspects, without realizing that for Spenser, Sidney, Shakespeare, and their contemporaries there are two levels of nature, an upper level of human nature, where nature and art are much the same thing, and a lower level of physical nature, from which man's essential humanity feels alienated. Thus Sidney says that nature's (i.e., lower nature's) world is brazen, in contrast to the poet's golden world, and that (on the higher level) art is a "second nature."[1] In *King Lear* the nature whom Edmund accepts as his goddess [1.2.1–2] is lower nature; what Lear's own references to nature are concerned with is an order of nature that Edmund has shut out of his mind. Such a conception of nature, it is obvious, is one that throws a very heavy emphasis on the aspect of nature called *natura naturata*, nature as a structure or system.

This emphasis derives from the Biblical horror of nature worship, that is, of finding anything numinous in nature to adore. This is primarily what the Bible means by idolatry, and the corollary of its condemning of idolatry is the principle that man is to turn away from nature and seek his God through human institutions. Nature was of course created along with man, and the traces of its original perfection may still be seen in it, but whatever we find to admire in it must be instantly referred back to its Creator. Everything God has created possesses two impulses: an impulse to die or decay, which is inevitable in a fallen world, and an impulse to return to its Creator, something that only man can do consciously.

Not that man can set out to do such a thing of his own volition. In this cosmos all the initiative comes from above, the initiative that in human life is known as grace. Even a revolutionary thinker in this period, such as Milton, could not think of liberty as anything that man can achieve for himself or even wishes to achieve. Liberty is good for man because God wants him to have it, but without grace no man wants it. There is a current of love flowing from God to man, and it is man's duty to accept that love and communicate it to his neighbour. That is Christian love in its pure form of *agape* or charity. Whatever springs from the sexual instinct is mainly something that belongs to the behaviour of a gregarious animal.

All of this represents a very considerable divergence from the tradition of Classical literature, starting with Plato and continuing through Virgil and Ovid, which assigns a powerful impetus in human life to Eros, the energy of a love rooted in the sexual instinct, which can be a destructive passion or an ennobling power. It is profoundly significant for the central question in literary criticism of the social function of the arts, that poets from the medieval period on simply inserted Eros into their cosmos, as something the religious and philosophical authorities had left out, and ought not to have left out.

There is no need to rehearse in detail the familiar story of courtly love in medieval poetry. Influenced largely by Virgil and Ovid, the poets worked out an elaborate correspondence between sexual love and Christian *agape*. One might be living one's life carelessly, in complete freedom from the perturbations of love; then the God of Love, Eros or Cupid, would suddenly strike, and from then on one was Love's abject slave, supplicating the favour (usually) of a mistress. Sometimes, as in Dante, the cult of Eros is sublimated, in other words assimilated to the Christian one. It is Eros who inspires Dante with his *vita nuova* that started from his first sight of Beatrice, but Beatrice in the *Paradiso* is an agent of divine grace. In another great medieval epic, however, *The Romaunt of the Rose*, the climax of the poem is a clearly sexual allegory, and in Petrarch, who did far more than Dante to popularize the theme, at least in English literature, love for Laura is rooted in Eros throughout, even though again it is sublimated, involving no sexual contact and easily surviving her death.

In these sublimated forms the love of a mistress becomes a parallel quest to the purgatorial one: it is what inspires a hero to great deeds and a poet to great words. A poet who attempts poetry without experiencing the power of Eros is conventionally assumed to be a rather poor creature. Sublimation usually means that the mistress is an inspiring object but not a sexual one; love poetry, however, covers the whole spectrum from idealism to bawdiness. What is essential, normally, is a long period of frustration during which the mistress is proud, disdainful, cruel, and the like. Lovers who die or go mad through such frustration are the saints and martyrs of the God of Love: in Chaucer's *Legend of Good Women*, meaning women good by Eros's standards, we find Helen of Troy, Cleopatra, and Dido. The question has been raised of whether Romeo's suicide would, in the minds of Shakespeare's audience, involve him in damnation. Most of the audience would recognize that Romeo has his own religion, which does not conflict with Christianity but nevertheless goes its own way: when Romeo speaks of "my bosom's lord" [5.1.3] he means the God of Love, and he dies a martyr in the odour of erotic sanctity.

Although the main sources of such love poetry are Classical, there are certain Biblical allusions that reinforce it and help to assimilate it to other types of poetry. The Song of Songs, whatever the commentators had done to it, still remained a great monument of poetry inspired by sexual love, and there the bride is described as "a garden inclosed . . . a fountain sealed" [4:12]. The imagery of trees and water reminds us of the Garden of Eden, and there too the love of Adam and Eve before the fall remains a pattern of sexual union, even though not everyone shared Milton's view that sexual intercourse as we know it took place before the fall. Let us glance at a familiar lyric of Campion:

> There is a garden in her face,
> Where roses and white lilies grow;
> A heav'nly paradise is that place,
> Wherein all pleasant fruits do flow.
> There cherries grow which none may buy
> Till cherry-ripe themselves do cry . . .
>
> Her eyes like angels watch them still;
> Her brows like bended bows do stand,
> Threat'ning with piercing frowns to kill
> All that attempt with eye or hand
> Those sacred cherries to come nigh,
> Till cherry-ripe themselves do cry.

[*There Is a Garden in Her Face*, sts. 1 and 3]

The theme of forbidden fruit is associated with sex; the Biblical image of the angels forbidding entrance to Eden after the fall is assimilated to the lady's disdain; echoes of the garden of the Hesperides mingle with the memories of Eden suggested by such words as "paradise" and "sacred." Similarly with Fulke Greville:

> Caelica, I overnight was finely used,
> Lodged in the midst of paradise, your heart;
> Kind thoughts had charge I might not be refused,
> Of every fruit and flower I had part.
>
> But curious knowledge, blown with busy flame,
> The sweetest fruits had in down shadows hidden,
> And for it found mine eyes had seen the same,
> I from my paradise was straight forbidden. [*Caelica*, no. 38]

The "heart" is invariably a respectable suburban address: if the lover moves into the downtown business section other complications arise. More accurately, the theme of forbidden knowledge is given an even more explicitly sexual connotation than it has in Genesis.

Another association involved here is that between the mistress's body and the garden itself. If we look carefully at the imagery of *Paradise Lost*, we can see how subtly but constantly Milton associates the Garden of Eden with the body of Eve. Marvell's well-known poem *The Garden* describes a union first of the body and then of the soul of the narrator with the garden, and then goes on to make the paradoxical point that the garden itself was the only mistress that Adam needed, the creation of Eve being the beginning of the loss of paradise.[2] A different aspect of the same kind of identification appears in Bartholomew Griffin's *Fidessa* sequence:

> Fair is my love that feeds among the lilies,
> The lilies growing in that pleasant garden
> Where Cupid's mount, that well belovèd hill is,
> And where that little god himself is warden. [Sonnet 37]

The first line contains an echo of the Song of Songs, but "Cupid's mount" can hardly be anything but the *mons veneris*. The same imagery, according to most Spenserian scholars, appears in the Gardens of Adonis episode of *The Faerie Queene*, where the gardens are also referred to as a paradise.[3] In a very long poem called *Loves Martyr* by Robert Chester, best known now because a group of rather better poets, including Shakespeare, wrote pendants to it (Shakespeare's contribution was the poem called *The Phoenix and Turtle*), a conventional feature of such poems, the detailed description of the heroine's body, is provided. In case our attention relaxes, the author places in the margin the feature of the lady's anatomy he is talking about: we begin with "Hair," "Brow," "Eyes," and the like, and finally work our way down to "Bellie." Just as we are beginning to get a flicker of interest in this dreary poem, the next stanza has in the margin merely "Nota," and the stanza itself talks about the four rivers of Eden. If the author had been a distinguished poet, we might assign this to a quirky originality, but when he is Robert Chester we can be sure that nothing but straight convention is involved.

Shakespeare's *Phoenix and the Turtle* is a different matter: there the Biblical metaphor of two people becoming "one flesh" in marriage [Genesis 2:24; Ephesians 5:31] is applied, in an erotic context, to the union in "death," which can mean sexual union, of a red bird and a white bird on St. Valentine's Day. Some of the paradoxes resulting from two things becoming the same thing almost read like parodies of the Nicene creed on the persons and substance of the Trinity.[4] Donne uses the same kind of imagery, especially in *The Canonization* (the title means that the narrator and his mistress have become saints in Eros's calendar):

> The phoenix riddle hath more wit
> By us; we two being one, are it.
> So to one neutral thing both sexes fit,
> We die and rise the same, and prove
> Mysterious by this love. [ll. 23–7]

And, of course, the same Biblical paradisal imagery, the same identification of God-created garden and the body of his bride (or virgin-mother) could occur in a straightforward Christian poem with no courtly love overtones at all. Thus in Henry Vaughan's *Regeneration*:

> With that, some cried, Away; straight I
> Obey'd, and led
> Full East, a fair, fresh field could spy
> Some call'd it, Jacob's Bed;
>
> A Virgin-soil, which no
> Rude feet ere trod,

> Where (since he stepped there) only go
> Prophets, and friends of God. [ll. 25–32]

The epigraph to this poem is again the passage in the Song of Songs that includes the reference to the enclosed garden and the sealed fountain [Song of Solomon 4:12].

The points I have been making up to now are not particularly novel; my purpose in making them is to bring out certain aspects of historical criticism that are less frequently discussed. One is the status of allusions to Classical mythology. From the very strict orthodox point of view, all the resemblances between Classical and Biblical stories and images result from the activity of the devils, who seized control of the Classical oracles (Cowley, for example, speaks of "the fiend Apollo" [*On the Death of Mr. Crashaw*, l. 22]) and instilled demonic parodies of the sacred myths into the minds of the heathen. Such demonic parodies may be called negative analogies. But there are other Classical myths that can be regarded as positive analogies, as moving, from the poet's point of view, in counterpoint to the sacred texts. It was a commonplace in the Renaissance period that many of the Classical myths, especially those in Ovid's *Metamorphoses*, could be used contrapuntally in this way. Thus Giles Fletcher [*Christ's Victory and Triumph*]:

> Who doth not see drown'd in Deucalion's name
> (When earth his men, and sea had lost his shore)
> Old Noah; and in Nisus' lock, the fame
> Of Samson yet alive; and long before
> In Phaethon's, mine own fall I deplore:
> But he that conquer'd hell, to fetch again
> His virgin widow, by a serpent slain,
> Another Orpheus was than dreaming poets feign.
> [pt. 3, "Christ's Triumph after Death," st. 7]

The story of the worldwide deluge in Ovid, which Deucalion and Pyrrha alone survived, is a positive analogy of the story of Noah in Genesis; the story of "Nisus' injur'd hair," as Pope calls it [*The Rape of the Lock*, canto 3, l. 124], has resemblances to the Samson saga; the story of the fall of Phaethon is an analogy of the fall of man; the descent of Orpheus to hell to reclaim his bride Eurydice is an analogy of the harrowing of hell by Jesus and his rescue of his bride the Church. The final phrase about "dreaming poets" is an example of the traditional ingratitude of Christian poets who levy such tribute on the Classical writers while officially denouncing the truth of their stories. Similarly, in the first canto of the *Paradiso*, Dante uses the Classical images of Marsyas, who was flayed alive for challenging Apollo to a contest in flute-playing (the Olympians were notoriously poor losers, but Apollo had not even the excuse of losing), and of Glaucus, who ate some miraculous grass that turned him into a sea-god. The images are exquisitely precise: Marsyas stands for the divesting of the garment of flesh in Paradise and Glaucus for the plunge into a new and unknown element. But the touch of grotesquerie in the same images still keeps a hint of negative analogy or demonic parody.

To understand this more clearly we may turn to the passage in *Paradise Regained* in which Satan suggests that Jesus, if he does not want earthly power of any kind, might become one of the great Athenian philosophers. Here Jesus, in a passage which has troubled many of Milton's commentators [bk. 4, ll. 285–364], rejects the whole of the Classical tradition as worthless. Its taproot is the theology and culture of hell described in book 2 of *Paradise Lost*, and Jesus must reject every atom of it if he is to proceed with his ministry. But having rightly rejected it in the right context, he thereby redeems it, at any rate for his followers. In the *Nativity Ode* all the heathen gods are put to flight by the rising sun of the Incarnation. Our own sympathies are divided: nobody wants Moloch back, and he will always be a demonic parody, but we have more sympathy with the "parting Genius" who is "with sighing sent" from his habitation [l. 186]. Milton can use Moloch only as a devil, but the "Genius" is a positive analogy of a Christian guardian angel, and appears as such in *Lycidas*, *Arcades*, *Comus*, and *Il Penseroso*.[5]

The cult of Eros in medieval and later poetry, then, is a special case of imaginative conquest by Classical poetic mythology, sometimes in the teeth of religious opposition, but steadily increasing the range and power of poetry in the Western world. As society became more complex and sophisticated, other types of analogies grew up: in Protestant England, for example, Jewish or Catholic imagery could be used either as types or as aesthetic analogies of what would be acceptable to authority. In Milton's *Il Penseroso* the narrator, choosing to live in the melancholy tonality, so to speak, for the rest of his life, speaks of dwelling among cloisters, stained glass, Gothic architecture, organ music, and finally a hermitage. All these were deprecated in strictly Puritan circles, but in a mood poem, where aesthetic feelings are so important, they are acceptable as aesthetic analogies. It is probable, but not absolutely necessary, that the nun who is the muse of this poem is more of a Classical vestal virgin than a Christian nun. The poem closes with a phrase that delicately indicates the analogical nature of its imagery, specifically in the passage about becoming a hermit: "Till old experience do attain / To something like prophetic strain" [ll. 173–4].

To anticipate a little, a poet with strong Christian commitments might use Classical imagery as analogical to Christian themes, but he would do so, presumably, with the assumption that the Christian theme was primary and the Classical one peripheral. Thus Francis Thompson, in *Assumpta Maria*:

> I am the four Rivers' Fountain
> Watering Paradise of old;
> Cloud down-raining the Just One am,
> Danaë of the Shower of Gold. [ll. 31–4]

The same imaginative link between the Virgin Mary and the story of Danaë is made by Ezra Pound, in the fourth *Canto*, but this time there is no sense of the greater reality of one story than of the other: they are simply two themes in poetic counterpoint:

> . . . upon the gilded tower in Ecbatan
> Lay the god's bride, lay ever, waiting the golden rain.
> . . .
> Across the Adige, by Stefano, Madonna in hortulo,
> As Cavalcanti had seen her. [ll. 117–18, 124–5]

Cavalcanti has a poem which tells us that the miraculous cures ascribed to a picture of the Virgin were the result of the fact that the model for the Virgin was his mistress:[6] a further secularizing piece of counterpoint.

The general principle this argument is leading to may be expressed as follows. In the earlier stages of a culture, there is usually a dominating myth of concern which controls the arts. In the Middle Ages, for example, the ecclesiastical authorities who were the main patrons of painting prescribed the subjects to be painted and the way they were to be treated, stated which saints were bearded and which clean-shaven, which ones barefooted and which shod, and insisted on certain conventions, such as clothing the Madonna in blue. As painting grew more complex and its patronage widened, the artist became increasingly aware of technical discoveries to be made in the art of painting itself, which might command his loyalties no matter what his patrons wanted. By the time we reach the Salon des Refusés of the French Impressionists,[7] we have gone a long way in this direction. The principle is more easily illustrated by science. Galileo and Bruno felt a commitment to the scientific conception of a heliocentric solar system even when the anxieties of the time demanded a geocentric one. Darwin and Huxley, opposing Bishop Wilberforce on the question of evolution and creation, were committed in the same sense.[8] Today the authority of science is generally recognized, even though the lethal dangers of our time indicate that the conflict of science and social concern is a two-way street, that concern still has its own case, and that there can be such a thing as socially irresponsible science.

But society is much less willing to grant literature or the other arts any degree of inner authority of this kind. Certain Marxist regimes, such as Stalinist Russia with its "socialist realism" and the so-called Gang of Four group in China,[9] deny such authority as a matter of dogma and insist that the arts, including literature, must be hitched to the bandwagon of ideology. In theory, of course, there is no ideology, merely the natural creativity of workers released from the constraints of other ideologies, but it would take a fairly gullible observer to accept that. There have been some startling outbreaks of hysteria in the democracies, too, that indicate similar feelings there, even when not expressed in government action. In the period that we have been looking at, there were certainly tensions between the anxieties of the prevailing social concern and the poet's loyalty to his own craft, though their expression was necessarily very oblique. In the thirteenth-century French romance *Aucassin and Nicolette*, for example, Aucassin is warned that his uncompromising pursuit of his lady may place him in danger of hell fire. He replies that hell is clearly the only place to go, because everything that makes life worth living seems headed for it, whereas nobody cares about heaven except for a few old crocks who are fit for nothing else.[10] For all the gossamer-light humour, there were contemporaries of the *Aucassin* poet who would have said the same thing in grim earnest. An even more familiar example is the *Retraction* at the end of Chaucer's *Canterbury Tales*, where the poet repudiates those of his tales "that sownen into synne," a phrase that takes his Friar and Summoner at their own valuation. There is a strong aroma of "sign here" about the *Retraction*, but if it is a voluntary composition of Chaucer's it merely demonstrates the conflict of concern and craftsmanship within the same mind, a conflict that has raged in many great poetic minds before and later. Tasso and Tolstoy are obvious examples.[11]

It seems to me that the question of the authority of poetry within a culture, which is much the same thing as the question of the social function of poetry, is a central problem of critical theory. It is obvious that such authority has no direct or simple connection with content. Most literary critics would recognize a core of authority in the essential visions of Pound or D.H. Lawrence, while admitting freely that they talked a good deal of nonsense as well. As W.H. Auden apostrophizes Yeats: "You were silly like us: your gift survived it all" [*In Memory of W.B. Yeats*, pt. 2, l. 1]. But what constitutes a "gift"? If we accept the poet's own answer, the ability to write well, we are simply going around in circles.

Around the latter part of the eighteenth century, or about the time of Rousseau, the older cosmos of authority began to break down. What was at issue, as far as literature was concerned, was not the objectively true but the rhetorically convincing: within literature, the word "truth" is a term in rhetoric and means what carries one along in emotional agreement. The cosmos of authority could not outlive the authority that supported it; and the American Revolution, the French Revolution, and the later Industrial Revolution were cracking up the authority on all sides. Let us look first at the metaphorical association of the presence of God with the upper heavens. After Newton's time, it was no longer believed that the stars were made of an imperishable substance, that they moved in perfect circles, or that they symbolized the underlying harmony of the universe. A universe held together with gravitation suggests a mechanism, not a design, and within literature there is a sharp difference between the two. In Romantic thought the superiority of the organism to the mechanism is a central principle: there being no visible organism in the skies, the upper world becomes increasingly a symbol of alienation, as it still is, for the most part, in science fiction.

More central to our present argument is the poetic treatment of Eros, which from this period on begins to acquire a larger reference. Human sexuality comes to be seen increasingly as an aspect of the neglected *natura naturans*, nature as a vast reservoir of life and reproductive power. Such nature is indissolubly linked to man: man is, therefore, as much a child of nature as he is of God. And so another cosmos began to grow up in poetry, with much the same set of levels as before, but, in effect, the older world stood on its head. At the top was empty space, filled by an emotionally meaningless world of stars. This world suggested nothing to the human imagination except the involuntary and mechanical: hence the sky-god in Romantic and much later poetry—Blake's Urizen, Shelley's Jupiter, Hardy's Immanent Will—becomes a source of tyranny.[12] Below this is the world we live in; below that again is a nature, huge, mysterious, morally ambivalent, an otherness that is still an essential part of our own identity. In more optimistic writers, this "nature" is what man needs to complete his own being, a wise and benevolent teacher, as normally in Wordsworth. Elsewhere it is a sinister image, predatory, ruthless, and totally indifferent to human values, but man is inescapably attached to it nonetheless.

In the older construct, the two levels of nature were arranged so as to put the ordinary world we are all born into—or thrown into, according to some—metaphorically below an ideal or paradisal world where man was, at one time, fully integrated with his natural surroundings. In the newer Romantic construct the world of ordinary experience sits on top of a world in which man rediscovers his integration with nature but does not necessarily find this discovery beneficial. Some writers in the Rousseau orbit associated the natural with the rational, and assumed that a natural society would also be a rational one: it is this attitude that changed the word "artificial" from a term of approval to a deprecatory one. In Shelley a relation of sexual love normally includes the reintegration of nature with humanity: thus in *Epipsychidion*: "Let us become the over-hanging day, / The living soul of this Elysian isle, / Conscious, inseparable, one" [ll. 538–40]. Such an integration with nature as environment would have been impossible for, say, Donne, with his conviction that there is nothing paradisal outside the regenerate human mind. Elsewhere the sense of otherness in nature is associated with its size and strength: the feeling of awe that produced the "sublime" in Romantic and pre-Romantic aesthetics. I have elsewhere spoken of the curious "drunken boat" construct in nineteenth-century thought, where the world of experience seems to float precariously on something immensely powerful that both supports it and threatens it.[13] Examples are the world as will in Schopenhauer, the world of unconscious impulse in Freud, the world of the excluded proletariat in Marx, the world of evolutionary development in Darwin, and the social applications of Darwinism. In some of these constructs the lower world contains only monsters of the deep; in others there is a submarine Atlantis to be reached.

It is particularly the latter group who revive the ancient theme of the quest of descent, which had been kept alive because of the prestige of Virgil's *Aeneid* and the extraordinary vision of its sixth book, but which in Christian constructs was usually demonized. With the Romantic period there begins that inner quest to something oracular in the depths of the mind which has developed, among other things, the technique of fantasy. In De Quincey, for example, particularly in the great mail-coach essay, there is, first, a long, diffuse, and digressive piece of reminiscent writing, as though the author were scanning the ground for clues; this suddenly tightens up into a moment of intense action, except that the action is not performed but observed by him, and after that it funnels into the dream world in a descending spiral. The dream world is, like all the levels of the Romantic cosmos, morally ambivalent: the *Confessions* ends with two sections, one on the pleasures and the other on the pains of opium, the good and the bad trips, after which there is a succession of visions representing the fact that the greatest intensity of the imagination is to be found at the bottom rather than the top of experience, as in the Classical oracles, which were also assisted by drugs or narcotics. In the mail-coach essay the experience described dramatizes to the writer the essential weakness of human consciousness as based on observation, and hence on the lack of a crucial spontaneity where action is needed. Perhaps, De Quincey concludes, the central thing that dreams are trying to tell us is that man's rational and observing consciousness is his original sin: "Upon the secret mirror of our dreams such a trial is darkly projected, perhaps, to every one of us. That dream, so familiar to childhood, of meeting a lion, and, through languishing prostration in hope and the energies of hope, that constant sequel of lying down before the lion, publishes the secret frailty of human nature—reveals its deep-seated falsehood to itself—records its abysmal treachery. Perhaps not one of us escapes that dream; perhaps, as by some sorrowful doom of man, that dream repeats for every one of us, through every generation, the original temptation in Eden."[14]

We are reminded of the fact that the *Confessions* ends with a line from the end of *Paradise Lost* about the angels expelling man from Eden,[15] and, by anticipation, of the dream of Finnegan, or rather of HCE, in Joyce, with its feelings of primordial guilt as the unreached source of the dream pilgrimage itself. For modern literature the essential link between man and nature seems to be the sexual one, and the great battle between sexuality and self-consciousness, or what Lawrence called sex in the head,[16] is so prevalent a theme in literature now as to suggest that the integration of Eros is close to the centre of whatever new cosmos will replace the Romantic one.

I spoke at the beginning of concern as one of the essential elements of all civilization. It seems to me that there is primary concern and secondary concern. Primary concern is based on what can be expressed only in the baldest and biggest of platitudes: the sense that life is better than death, happiness better than misery, freedom better than slavery. Secondary concern has to do with the structure and source of authority in society, with religious belief and political loyalties, with the desire of the privileged to keep their privileges and of the nonprivileged to get along as well as they can in that situation. I think the present age, with its threats of nuclear warfare and environmental pollution, is an age in which secondary concerns are rapidly dissolving. Down to the Romantic period, and for many poets later than that, the cosmos within which most writers worked was either the cosmos of authority already described, or the cosmos of revolt, which we said was essentially the same kind of structure upside down. As the sixteenth-century Anabaptist theologian Hans Denck remarked, after publishing a list of antithetical statements culled from scripture, "Whoever leaves an antithesis without resolving it lacks the ground of truth."[17]

Occasionally one discovers a writer who is not satisfied to inhabit his world unconsciously, or by instinct, or whatever the right term is. Thus Poe's *Eureka* is an essay on speculative cosmology which sounds as though it were using scientific or philosophical language, but which Poe himself says at the beginning he wishes to be considered as a poetic product. Paul Valéry's note on *Eureka* remarks that cosmology is primarily a *literary* art: it is based, not on the scientific or philosophical ideas of its time, but on metaphorical analogies to them that appeal to poets.[18] The purpose of such cosmologies is to give us some notion of the kind of context within which literature is operating, the imaginative counterpart of the worlds explored by intellect and sensation. Since then a good many such speculative cosmologies have emerged, some disguised as historical or scientific treatises, and eventually, one hopes, we shall have a clearer notion of what kind of world our creative writers are living in.

Such a world is dominated by forces that were originally gods—Eros, Prometheus, Cybele (perhaps the closest approach to Graves's white goddess), and others. In consequence some modern writers have accepted a polytheistic outlook: Hölderlin did, and Ezra Pound often talked as though he did. But it is only a nervous habit that keeps us calling such forces gods: they are states of the human mind with metaphorical identities in nature. More important, they are the shaping powers of poetry, the authentic muses. In Greek myth the muses bore the names of literary genres and were in the aggregate daughters of memory, that is, of literary convention. In our day they bear names like Anxiety, Absurdity, and Alienation, and they are the daughters of Frustration; but their power is as great as ever, and their cultural achievements could be as impressive as ever.

Questions and Answers

QUESTION: "The Survival of Eros in Poetry" is typical of your work in its focus on Christian metaphors and beliefs. I want to ask a question that might help me understand the relation between metaphors in art and beliefs in religion. In the conclusion to his review of your book *The Great Code* and Robert Alter's *The Art of Biblical Narrative* for *The Georgia Review*, Herbert Levine remarked that "the Christian notion of original sin, claiming that man cannot fulfill his destiny without divine help, simply expresses (in Frye's liberated view) man's fear of his own freedom. The ex-Christian Frye, who has apparently passed beyond good and evil, imagines us as self-delighting, self-enlightening beings capable of our own redemption. The liberal Jew [Robert Alter] imagines no redemption whatsoever, only the difficult task of living in history."[19] Did you write *The Great Code* as an ex-Christian, and do you agree with Levine's judgment?

ANSWER: Well, I don't know this audience very well, so I can't express my opinion of those sentences in a language that I think is appropriate to them. The United Church of Canada, of which I am an ordained clergyman, would be surprised to hear that I am an ex-Christian. I think that the answer to the reviewer's puzzlement is simply that all my life I have learned my views of Christianity more or less from Blake, who would never split the efforts of man from the efforts of God. He would say that God works only through man, and that only when the divine and the human become identified is man himself created and genuinely alive. And certainly mere man, or natural man, can do nothing about it by himself—and to that extent the conception of original sin is quite valid. The reviewer has accepted it and so have I. It doesn't mean, however, that you are going to call an objective God down out of the sky to help man in his state of original sin. The God that will help not only works through the man but is the man.

QUESTION: That way of explaining original sin seems similar to your explanation of the passage about the fall of man being reenacted in dreams from De Quincey's mail-coach essay, which you use to show a change in metaphorical constructs brought about by Romanticism. That passage comes at the end of the description of the running down of the two trapped people by the mail coach. The scene has the quality of a nightmare, but I can't see a connection between that kind of dream and the fall of man. Could you put that together for me, please?

ANSWER: De Quincey is one of the great pioneers of a principle which we largely take for granted today. He was one of the first people to understand the spiritual world in metaphorical terms. Dante uses categories of time and space: the Inferno is underneath the surface of the world, and the people there know the future, not the present. Purgatory is a mountain on the opposite side of the spiritual world, and paradise is in the stars. These are all to some degree metaphorical constructs that suggest that the real drama of the spiritual life of man is going on elsewhere: real eternal life is after death, and souls are saved across the world in Purgatory.

Ever since the Romantic period, we've become increasingly aware that all the drama and spectacle of heaven and hell is enacted inside the human mind. I remember some years ago a manic depressive who was caught by the BBC—this is the kind of thing that could only happen on the BBC—and asked on the radio what it was like to be a manic depressive. His answer contained one thing which struck me; he said, "It's no good arguing with me about heaven and hell. I've been there." One of the earliest statements of that realization is in the passage where De Quincey proposes that in every dream, every night, the original sin that brings about the fall of man is reenacted. The drama is within our consciousness the whole time and never leaves us.

Original sin is not being born with the capacity to murder and rape. Original sin is essentially inertia, the feeling of helplessness—that beyond a certain point we can't go. It is that nightmare feeling of being stuck with our feet in concrete which De Quincey seizes on as the psychological essence of the doctrine.

QUESTION: The key to the explanations of your own Christianity and of the passage from De Quincey's essay seems to be metaphor. How do you define it?

ANSWER: The grammatical form of metaphor is A is B—Joseph is a fruitful bough and Issachar is a strong ass—although it is extremely obvious to any sane person that A is not B at all. So what is the point of saying that A is B and making it the cornerstone of poetic expression when A is not B? I suggest that the function of metaphor is the opening of a channel of verbal energy between the subjective world and the objective world, which is easiest and most natural at a period of society when the subjective and objective worlds are not clearly distinguished.

QUESTION: Do you agree then with Paul Tillich that symbols, which in clusters become myth, are the highest possible articulation of experience and belief, and that using words metaphorically is superior to using them literally?[20]

ANSWER: I certainly do agree with Tillich on that point, but I would make a slight alteration in your phrasing. People who say the Bible is literally true, for example, usually mean that here in a book is a stack of words which is related by correspondence to certain events in the spiritual and historical world outside. Now it seems to me that one should read the Bible literally, but one should remember that the literal meaning is in fact the metaphorical meaning, that it is the symbolic meaning, because the structure of words cannot be literally anything but a structure of words. So the things that bind the structure of words together—the metaphors, the images, the symbols, and the like—are the bedrock of the reading of anything.

QUESTION: In *The Great Code* you describe three phases of language—metaphoric, metonymic, and descriptive—and allude to a fourth phase that you seem to believe we might be entering.[21] Can you describe the fourth phase?

ANSWER: In *The Great Code* [6–7] I spoke of the origin of thought in metaphor, the sense of an undifferentiated energy flowing between personality and nature. The essential unit of this phase is the god. That phase is displaced by more abstract language, in particular the dialectical language of Plato, which I connect with metonymy: A is *put for* B. Then, the distinctively modern form of expression is close, accurate description, in which the verbal structure A is *like* B, the body of phenomena that is being described. These phases perhaps give you the keys to the immanent language that the Romantic poet wants in connecting man with nature, the transcendental language that the theologian and metaphysician want in connecting man with the world of ideas, and the descriptive language that the scientist wants in getting a clear account of things in words. A fourth stage, which I mention as a future possibility, would unite these three and perhaps do other things by uniting them. But one of the functions of poetry, as I see it, is to keep alive the metaphorical habit of mind and to make sure that its significance remains obvious to all receptive people.

QUESTION: The marvellous capacity of your system for categorizing suggests the possibility of a metacriticism that would categorize other critical theories. Can you categorize your own system?

ANSWER: I rather gave up categorizing forms of criticism after I published the *Anatomy*. Increasingly since then I've felt that bringing critical theories in is really a job for somebody else, preferably somebody younger. I can only pursue my own course at this point. I can't see myself in perspective.

QUESTION: Would it make sense to describe your critical theory as Romantic?

ANSWER: Oh, it's entirely Romantic, yes. I see the Romantic movement as the first great step in clarifying the role of criticism and bringing in a conception of creativity that could unify the mental elements in the creative process. While Samuel Johnson's criticism is an unmatchable instance of its type, it is also the kind of criticism that follows literature at a certain distance, commenting on it and thereby mediating between works of literature and the reading public. For all his limitations, Johnson was an extraordinary critic who is right nine times out of ten, but his kind of criticism does not go on to study what literature is doing in the world. But Coleridge's criticism—for all the blither—does give me some sense of that, and some sense of the autonomy of the creative person. A critic like Addison will say that the artist has to meet the standards of taste established in his day, whereas the Romantics are more apt to say that if the standards of taste in my day don't like what I'm doing, so much the worse for the standards of taste. That's rather a difficult axiom to live by, but Blake survived for seventy years.

QUESTION: You compared your Christianity to Blake's. Is your theory of literature different in any way from Blake's?

ANSWER: It probably doesn't differ very much, because I've learned everything I know from Blake. At the same time, I do live in a later age among different social phenomena, and I'm an academic, which means I'm much fuzzier around the edges, much less certain of my certainties, than he was.

QUESTION: Does your identity as a Romantic critic affect your teaching?

ANSWER: Teaching is a very difficult art. One of the first things to remember is that you are not the source of the student's knowledge. That is, teaching is not a matter of conveying information from somebody who has got it to somebody who has not got it. The teacher has to try to transform himself into a kind of transparent medium for whatever he is teaching. If he's lucky, there may come a point at which the entire classroom is pervaded by the spirit of the subject—of Blake, or Shakespeare, or romance. And then the relationship between teacher and student, which in itself is a somewhat embarrassing relationship, disappears, and you are all united in the same vision.

QUESTION: You said that you can't see yourself in perspective. But you do go so far as to characterize your theory as Romantic, and your description of Romantic criticism seems to suggest, at least implicitly, that Romanticism made it possible for critical theory to progress. Has critical theory progressed?

ANSWER: The most I could say is that it can and should progress.

QUESTION: Doesn't your comparison of Johnson to Coleridge imply that criticism progressed from neo-Classicism to Romanticism?

ANSWER: I think that Romanticism brought in some essential things that we need for a coherent criticism, and one can trace certain new ideas about criticism—including some twentieth-century ideas—back to Romanticism. At present, the fact that there are various schools of critical theory indicates that it's still a relatively immature discipline. I believe, however, that the materials are being collected which will permit criticism to improve and expand, and that there's a fair chance that it will.

QUESTION: If conflicting schools of thought are a sign of immaturity in a discipline, then do you conclude that metaphysics, philosophy, and theology are immature disciplines?

ANSWER: You are quite right in picking me up on that. I was expressing myself rather carelessly. I think there are different criteria in the different disciplines, and that there is a sense in which science tries to escape from controversy. I don't mean that a subject like genetics can ever be noncontroversial, but that the authority that science appeals to, the authority of established facts and repeatable experiments and certain methods of proof of validity, is a way of trying to get away from controversy to a body of evidence beyond controversy. At the same time, philosophical and theological and undoubtedly humanistic studies as well are existential. They are too deeply rooted in immediate human concerns ever to avoid the collision of different schools and modes of agreement.

When I spoke of the immaturity of criticism, I was thinking specifically of the number of false antitheses that flood the critical journals. Most of the major critics of our time are, I think, in fairly solid agreement about the value of literature. Their differences are differences in methodology and techniques of approach, but those will always be there.

QUESTION: When you say that criticism is in a sort of prescientific state, are you suggesting that it's in roughly the same prescientific state that it was in when you wrote the *Anatomy*? Has the *Anatomy* helped to make criticism more scientific? With the proper historical perspective, might we see the roots of systematic criticism in the work that you have done in these decades?

ANSWER: When I said in the *Anatomy* that criticism is a branch of social science [*AC*, 16], that attracted a great deal of adverse comment because of the strength of the rather provincial prejudice of humanists against social scientists as "those fellows over there who can't write." But if you read through the program of an MLA meeting, you'll find it in many respects almost indistinguishable from a meeting of social scientists. To that extent certain changes have taken place which would probably have taken place if the *Anatomy* had not been written. I have some hopes, however, that in a few minds changes have taken place with a bit more clarity because it was written.

While, as I say, I believe that criticism can and should improve and become more comprehensible as a whole as it goes on, it happens that I have no worries about my own place in it. If posterity doesn't like me, the hell with posterity—I won't be living in it anyway. And while I'm a little disappointed that there is still so much clutter and confusion in critical theory, at the same time I am interested and even exhilarated by the variety of things that do appear, and by the number of approaches to the study of literary documents that would have been inconceivable half a century ago.

QUESTION: You've said that literature may recur and expand but may not progress, while criticism may progress [*AC*, 344]. What accounts for the difference?

ANSWER: The title of Hazlitt's essay "Why the Arts Are Not Progressive" lays down one of the central conditions with which the literary critic has to work. There is nothing in literature corresponding to the accumulation of knowledge within a science. The literary tendency is to produce the masterpiece, and that remains *sui generis*—something that can be seen in a context but cannot be compared in value with anything else. So, as long as the human mind remains what it is, it is not really possible to have literature in the future which will be on the whole better than the literature that we already have. On the other hand, I think criticism is close enough to a social science to have different conditions underneath it—conditions that make progress possible. Of course, saying that criticism can progress and ought to progress is like saying that we can be wise and good and ought to be. Saying it isn't going to make us wiser or better—and criticism will probably be floundering as wildly in 2083 as it is in 1983—but still one has the hope. The work of criticism as I see it is to understand the place of the creative imagination in society—to see what it's doing and why society can't get along without it.

QUESTION: Concerning the potentially scientific nature of criticism, it seems that in the physical sciences there is a self-motivating impetus toward system. You don't have to urge the physical sciences to be systematic or to develop broad hypotheses. That just happens. But in criticism, judging from what you called the clutter and confusion in literary theory, the natural tendency seems to be a resistance to system. Might that resistance have something to do with the nature of criticism or of literature?

ANSWER: The difference does have to do with the nature of the disciplines. But we need to distinguish the sciences, which are one thing, from arts and skills, which are another. The practice of medicine—of meeting a patient, diagnosing what is wrong, and prescribing accordingly—has to have a considerable amount of art or skill in it, however scientific its basis. That is also true of a great many forms of critical contact with literature, and many of those critical contacts are attempts to formulate the experience that one has had in making the contact. They are really forms of psychological criticism, and that's all right, except that there are no words for the direct experience of literature. I once had a student who, after a performance of *King Lear*, walked the streets until the sun came up and it was time to go to breakfast. It seems to me that that is a perfectly valid response to *King Lear*, but there's no sense trying to put it into words.

We have criticism simply because the direct experience of literature is never adequate. We build up the analogical structure of criticism as a means of compensating us for the fact that we do not enter directly into the work of literature, for the same reason that we cannot eat our food until it has to some extent been cooked and processed. I think it's that sensitivity to the central importance of experience that makes people distrust any form of systematization. You build up what you hope will be a critical palace like the Alhambra, and people stand back to look at it and say "Look at that jail." All the psychological overtones of a *system* as a spider web that might catch and hold you if you're not careful seem to me superstitions.[22]

QUESTION: If literary criticism is a systematic, even scientific, discipline, how narrow are its boundaries? Is the language of linguistics, for example, an encroachment on a language of criticism that comes—as you say it should—from literature itself? Is textual linguistics, which attempts to study scientifically all discourse, part of criticism or criticism part of textual linguistics?

ANSWER: I'd have to look at instances. Of course there are no rigid boundaries. Back in my younger days, a literary critic could carry on quite happily with the subject of literature without even being aware that there was such a subject as linguistics. Those days are gone. You can no longer study literary criticism without immediately realizing that linguistics is another area of what you're doing. With the gradual breaking down of barriers—which, after all, were never established as matters of theory, only of practice and of the limitations of the human mind—we can begin to enter a period in which literary criticism becomes an aspect of the whole study of words, the function of words in human society and its relation to the conscious mind.

But when a discipline is trying to find its boundaries it does tend to break up into a variety of technical approaches. In the dissolving of boundaries, if there are occasional acts of looting and raiding—if Chomsky's linguistics takes over certain techniques of criticism or Derrida's deconstruction takes over certain others—that again is not a thing that harrows me particularly, because it's the machinery of a very complicated discipline trying to function as best it can. But I would certainly like to see a more coherent theory of poetics built up in the centre of literary criticism. I dislike the notion of shifting the centre of the study of literature from literature to something else.

QUESTION: Then what is your view of Marxist and Freudian literary criticism?

ANSWER: I want the study of literature to arise from the actual conditions and modes of expression that are within literature itself. That is why I am opposed to any construct—Marxist, Freudian, Thomist, or whatever—that is going to annex literature and simply explain literature in its own terminology. What happens in that case may be illuminating for Marxists, Freudians, and Thomists, but it does nothing for the subject of literary criticism.

QUESTION: You are saying then that the critic's responsibility is to criticize an art in its own context rather than to force upon it social concerns which may not belong to it?

ANSWER: The last part of your question is practically a definition of bad criticism. The first part of your question is connected with another:

what makes some literature endure? And if literature endures because it is good, what makes it good? I have never been able to answer that question, although it is the most natural kind of question to ask. The fallacy in most ways of putting such questions is that the standard is the audience's response: what the critic has rather than what the work he is studying has. I have been saying all through my critical career that the old metaphor of the critic as judge is totally wrong. The critic does not judge literature, he studies it and tries to understand it and thereby understand its social functions, but if he is up against something the size of Shakespeare, the critic is the one getting judged. The best he can offer is none too good. In some lectures on Shakespeare earlier this year,[23] I said that for the nineteenth century the central play of Shakespeare was *Hamlet*, because it dramatized the conflict between experience and structures of thought about experience, which was the nineteenth century's preoccupation. The twentieth century, with its existential absurdity and anguish contemplating nothingness and the like, found that *King Lear* was the central play of Shakespeare, and the twenty-first century will almost certainly find the central play of Shakespeare to be *Antony and Cleopatra*, because it deals with the grotesque dislocation between the fate and fortunes of world history and the private lives of two or three highly spotlighted people in the middle. But these are not reflections that make the plays of Shakespeare good. The plays of Shakespeare are the standard: they illuminate the preoccupations and diseases of *our* time. It is in that direction that one has to direct questions about the greatness of literature.

A critic conditioned by a certain time and place will make value judgments against certain works. But these value judgments don't prove to be immortal, and the next age may discover that what he said was bad wasn't bad at all. A critic is to be judged as a critic primarily by the authors he has understood. That is, T.S. Eliot is to be judged by what he has said about Dante and about Marvell and about Dryden, but on Blake and Thomas Gray and D.H. Lawrence, Eliot is just in the position of somebody saying "I pass."[24] If you open F.R. Leavis anywhere, you will find appreciative references to D.H. Lawrence and sneers at Joyce. Well, what Leavis says about Lawrence is genuine criticism, because he understands Lawrence. What he says about Joyce is rubbish, and we have to wait for somebody else to deal with him.

QUESTION: But doesn't the act of theorizing about literature entail implicit value judgments?

ANSWER: I would certainly express a lot of value judgments about my own theory and fewer about other people's theories, but I do not say that value judgments have no place in literary criticism. What I say is that they are an expression of certain social attitudes, that social attitudes are subject to change, and consequently, that the study of literature always has the power of veto over any value judgment.

You may develop a passion for a poet at the age of ten, and at the age of twenty you may outgrow him, or you may stay with him for the rest of your life. But value judgments are like happiness in life. The American Constitution talks about the pursuit of happiness, but that's bad grammar. You can't pursue happiness: you pursue the course of your life and if you're lucky it may produce happiness from time to time. Similarly, you pursue the study of literature and from time to time these value judgments keep popping up as a kind of emotional response to what you are studying. So I'm not calling for the abolition of value judgments but merely for their rigid subordination to the study of criticism generally. I'm constantly being told that when I select one writer to talk about rather than another I'm implying a value judgment.

Of course I am. And that is where value judgments belong, in the preliminary area of original hunch. They may remain at the original level or they may be qualified, but they must always be regarded as subject to change.

QUESTION: Concerning factional disputes in literary theory, do you see poststructuralist criticism as a direct attack on Romantic critical theory?

ANSWER: It may look like that, but these are eddies in the general swirl. Around the time of T.E. Hulme an anti-Romantic movement caught the early Eliot and the early Pound, but that movement turned out to be actually a development of Romanticism itself. Similarly, it seems to me, Derrida's analysis of Rousseau[25] is an eddy in a current which eventually brings one of the world's first and greatest Romantics into focus with regard to his social function as a writer. The action and counteraction, thesis and antithesis, in criticism are probably a necessary part of the process—something that ought to be seen wherever possible in the light of an expanding totality.

QUESTION: Would you disagree with Dame Helen Gardner that some contemporary schools of criticism threaten to destroy the imagination?[26]

ANSWER: Nothing like that is going to destroy the imagination. Anything that could destroy the human imagination would have to be infinitely more powerful and infinitely more evil than any of the critics with whom I am personally acquainted.

QUESTION: Are you suggesting that deconstruction differs from other criticism in matters of technique or methodology but isn't really different in its view of literature?

ANSWER: I don't think that in the long run deconstruction will seem different in its view of literature. It may seem to be different for a while, but wherever you have deconstruction, you also have construction. Wherever you have somebody analysing the metaphorical structure of Rousseau, you will have somebody else wondering what the metaphorical construct in itself means by being there. The two methods of approach, it seems to me, are complementary rather than antithetical.

QUESTION: A deconstructionist is like a microbiologist, then, while the constructionist is like an ecologist—both part of the same field of study?

ANSWER: That's more or less what I would feel, yes.

QUESTION: When faced with gloomy local possibilities, you often seem to look for a broad optimistic view that will outshine the gloom. I wonder if you have an optimistic view of language to outshine the gloomy view of language being highly advertised by poststructuralists.

ANSWER: I have often been told that I'm optimistic and I usually reply by saying that there are two kinds of people: those who in the face of a new social phenomenon point out its dangers and those who point out its opportunities. Once when somebody took me for a ride in British Columbia, I saw on the highway a sign saying "Watch for falling rocks," and then we turned the corner and saw another sign saying "Prepare to meet thy God." I realized then that the impulse to warn is very deeply imbedded in human nature. I don't need to worry about it: there's always somebody there to tell you what the results of an all-out nuclear war will be. Our own age is an extremely apocalyptic one, and there are always two aspects to an apocalypse: the vision we finally get when it clears away, and the sun and moon turning to blood before that happens.

QUESTION: You've been accused of optimism by Harold Bloom in particular:[27] he says that you exaggerate the cheerfulness with which poets share archetypes, and that the actual process of displacing archetypes is much more anxious and dark than you've made it out to be. Do you care to comment?

ANSWER: Oh, sure. The creation of literature is a process of human nature, and nothing that involves human nature is going to be devoid of anxiety and darkness. It is the job of the critic, when he reaches a point of anxiety and darkness, to fish out his flashlight and see what is happening in that dark corner.

QUESTION: As far as those "dark corners" of human nature are concerned, haven't you been accused of allowing criticism to avoid human nature and society by drawing a line around literature? To put it another way, do works of literature have meaning beyond the myth that unifies them, or does criticism stop at identifying the myth?

ANSWER: Yes, the meaning goes beyond that identification simply because identifying the mythical construct is a matter of putting it into a literary context. The literary context extends from the individual work into a study of all the aspects of literature that are in the least like that particular work. That study of context takes you out, in its turn, to the frontiers of literature as a means of working within society. So there is really no end to the directions in which you can go from that identification. If you identify the myth behind *King Lear*, the next step, or at least one next step, is to see it as being tragedy, and that leads you to thinking about the role of tragedy in literature. Consequently, the study doesn't tend to detach what you're reading from its social context; it's quite the opposite. The function of criticism is to try to find out enough about literature to determine the nature of its social autonomy and its social authority. And that in a way is parallel to the clarifying of the limits of the authority and autonomy of the sciences.

QUESTION: What kinds of connections do you see between literature and society in this century?

ANSWER: It seems to me that literature has been increasingly over the last century or so a fact of social, moral, and political significance, although to my knowledge there is very little critical theory that explains very coherently just what that social, moral, and political significance is. But if we look at, say, literature in Russia over the last fifty or sixty years, what we most cherish is the work of people who are banned by the Soviet government. And over here we have cases like Ezra Pound and the people who were hounded by the McCarthy hearings in the 1950s, so that there is obviously a very great tension between the sense of social concern and the feeling of loyalty to one's own art which is characteristic of genuine writers.

Of course the sense of social concern, by the time it gets expressed, has filtered down into some pretty crude categories. The McCarthy hearings in the United States and the flat-bottomed bureaucracy of Russia do not represent the actual concerns of those societies by a long, long way. Nevertheless, the tension does remain, and in consequence it puts a rather sharper light on the social function of literature. Compare the Galileo and Giordano Bruno crises in science: you can't judge the Christian church by its attitude toward Bruno, which involved a specific aspect of the church in a remarkably jittery time. But the tension itself highlighted the conflicting claims of social concern and loyalty to a discipline of increasing coherence.

QUESTION: Galileo, Bruno, and the McCarthy hearings are negative examples of the connection between social and vocational responsibilities. What positive social obligations does a writer have?

ANSWER: The positive obligations are the ones that arise from his loyalty to his own art. As I've said, the old doctrine of the muse means that the writer has a very limited choice in what he writes. He writes out what takes shape in his mind. That's his muse. And if he is not faithful to that, he is not faithful to what makes him a writer. His positive obligation is to remain loyal to his muse, however horrified society may pretend to be as a result.

QUESTION: Milton believed that in order to write great poems, you have to make yourself as pure a vessel as possible—and pure for Milton clearly meant morally pure. Do you believe that great art can ever come from the mind of a racist or anti-Semite?

ANSWER: Yes. I think great art can arise in any kind of mind. An example is the French novelist Céline, who was a fascist and an anti-Semite and generally a most reprehensible person, but whose novels nevertheless have a kind of intensity that interests people in that field. I can't get through him myself, but I know there are other people who can and do. The whole history of literature is strewn with neurotics and people with wrecked lives who nevertheless saw with the most tremendous power. There are the Goethes who see life steadily, see it whole, and bring a great sanity to bear on whatever they see, and there are the Rimbauds, the Hölderlins, and the Nietzsches who smash their lives up but rescue fragments of the smash that have an even greater intensity. Just as God is no respecter of persons, so literature is no respecter of persons either. Any kind of person may come through as a person of unforgettable insight.

QUESTION: In *The Critical Path* you say that no writer's work is inherently revolutionary or reactionary and that any writer's work "may be potentially useful to anybody, in any way" [*CP*, 126]. Are you sure that Hitler's *Mein Kampf* would become something besides programmatic anti-Semitism in a different social context?

ANSWER: I'm not saying that any critical power can turn *Mein Kampf* into a good book. I was really repeating what Milton says in *Areopagitica*: that a wise man will make better use of an idle pamphlet than a fool will make of holy scripture.[28] Consequently, the reactionary or revolutionary tendencies within an age, after that age has passed, become things for the critic to observe in any way he can. A better example than *Mein Kampf* is, again, the fiction of Céline. People regard his power of imagination as something worth investigating. It is the critical use made of him that is really decisive. The actual tendency in the author's own life fades out when its social context has gone by.

QUESTION: While you're discussing the social context of literature, would you explain the balance between what you call concern and freedom [*CP*, 55]?

ANSWER: Man being a social being, there is an interplay between his social concern and his individual freedom. The freedom of a society depends entirely on the degree of genuine individuality that it permits, because there are many essential aspects of freedom that only the individual can really experience. I would even say there is no such thing as social freedom as such. However important it is to get legislation properly worked out, social freedom still remains an approximate and potential thing, and the actual experience of freedom is that of the individual. Either the sense of concern which binds society together or the sense of freedom which makes individuals individual can of course break its connection with the other. When that happens social concern freezes into intolerance and bigotry and unreflective dogmatism, while freedom freezes into nihilistic scepticism. Obviously both of those extremes are undesirable.

QUESTION: What is the position of education with respect to concern and freedom?

ANSWER: One very important role of education is to determine the relationship between them. Social concern comes from a desire to integrate society, and by itself that desire would go in a totalitarian direction. It would proscribe the expression of disciplined belief and would compel the whole of society to believe the same things—or to say it believed them, which in that kind of atmosphere would be much the same thing. On the other hand, the myth of freedom, if it works without any awareness of its social function, ends in a kind of directionless anarchy in which people have no standards beyond the ones that have been suggested by their own subconscious. That is why I think that education has a crucial function in society. A scientist has a loyalty to the conditions of his science and a loyalty to the particular research that he is doing, but, at the same time, in an age like ours he can hardly work without the awareness that science has a social function and is an expression of social will to that extent. It's not so hard to see that in science, though it's perhaps a little harder in literature where, for instance, a poet has a loyalty to his own means of expression within literature and at the same time has a social function.

QUESTION: Why do you say that the myth of concern precedes the myth of freedom? [*CP*, chap. 2].

ANSWER: Because all of us belong to something before we are anything: I was conditioned to be a twentieth-century Canadian middle-class intellectual nine months before I appeared on earth. In the process of acting out the social conditioning we have acquired, we come to understand something of the strength and the unity of the social concerns around us, and we take part in those. But then gradually an individuation process—the growth of the genuine individual, not the ego—takes place in us as well. The genuine individual takes his concerns from society and reabsorbs them in his own individual way. The question often raised in criticism about whether analysing a work of art will kill it is connected with this process. Every work of literature has to die and to be reborn in the individual studying it. It doesn't just stay out there; it becomes part of him or her. Without that death and resurrection, there is no genuine possession of literature. When it is possessed, then what I call the myth of freedom is being formed.

QUESTION: Why do you call the myth of freedom a myth? Is that meant to suggest that the criteria of detachment, objectivity, and the like are illusions?

ANSWER: I would certainly want to keep well away from the vulgar use of myth to mean that which is not really true. Myth to me always means primarily *mythos*, that is, story or narrative. In early societies these stories are stories in a fairly restricted sense. As time goes on they become more flexible narratives, so that you can get a type of mythos which is essentially a description of a lifestyle. You could, I think, define the mythos of the Middle Ages or Marxist Russia or democratic America in certain recognizable verbal terms. It wouldn't be a story in the restricted sense, but it would be a narrative in the sense that it would see society as going in a certain direction and moving toward a certain vision, as in the quest themes of romance.

QUESTION: When you define the myth of freedom in isolation from the myth of concern, you say that it would be totally incoherent, valuing detachment in and of itself. But can't we imagine science as an isolated myth of freedom without any myth of concern to attach it to a culture? In fact, don't we imagine science that way all the time in the nightmares of science fiction?

ANSWER: The myth of freedom by itself would minimize the sense of social concern and therefore ultimately would minimize the sense of social function. A poet or a novelist working hard to express what he sees in the world in his own terms would still resent very much being told that what he was doing had no relevance to society. In science that problem hardly exists psychologically. Certainly in fields like nuclear physics or in genetics the immediate relevance of the science to the concerns of society is pretty obvious. In societies that have pushed the myth of concern as far as it will go—the European Middle Ages in certain respects, China during the Cultural Revolution, and the Soviet Union—the arts have been made to serve as instruments of the social and political program. In the past there were efforts in this country to say that certain things are American and certain things un-American, but those voices of concern were never representative voices. The representative voice of concern spoke for democracy and certain rights of the individual.

It's difficult to define the conception of freedom by itself because it really can't exist by itself. It always has a social context of some kind, and it exists to diversify and make more flexible that context. It's misleading in some respects even to use the word "freedom," because the ability to set yourself free to play the piano or tennis or to paint pictures or anything of that kind is made possible by a repetition of habit and practice, so that genuine freedom and genuine necessity become the same thing. If you're still exercising your free will as to whether to play the right notes on the piano, you still don't know how to play the piano. For a painter like Cézanne, who is said to have cleaned his brushes after every stroke, it is clear that what he wanted to do and what he had to do were the same thing. On that level there isn't very much argument about relevance to the needs of society.

QUESTION: Freedom of will is usually opposed to necessity, and yet you say that what artists want to do and what they have to do ultimately become the same thing. Could you clarify that?

ANSWER: If a person says "I want to do what I like, that is what freedom means to me," he will very soon discover that what he likes to do involves certain impulses in him that are pushing him around. So we start with the conception of freedom in the child's mind as what he wants to do, which is up against its antithesis, what society will allow him to do, and we generally work out a kind of uneasy compromise: the feeling of freedom is what we want to do minus whatever society will let us do. But the word "want" in that case refers to something which is pushing the mind around, usually undeveloped impulses within the mind that are demanding expression but are not understood.

There are two kinds of repetition, habit and practice. One kind of repetition is inorganic: you keep on doing the same thing over and over because you are too dumb to think of doing anything else. Naturally, that goes nowhere. The other kind is the accumulating repetition that builds up some kind of skill. If you play the piano or tennis or chess, there is a great deal of repetition in the practice that makes you skilful. But if you want to play the piano, what you are really saying is that you wish to be set free to play the piano. If you have arrived at that pitch of freedom, then, as I said, you'll find that the notes that you want to play and the notes that you have to play are exactly the same notes. If you are playing so that in a sense you cannot play the wrong notes, then you are really free to play. What a painter wants to do is paint his picture. What he has to do to paint the picture that he wants to paint is to put this stroke there and that stroke there and so on. The freedom and the necessity are simply aspects of the same activity.

QUESTION: Are you dissociating free will from choice?

ANSWER: I don't see anything wrong with associating free will with choice. The issue of freedom, of course, is bound up not simply with the act of choosing but with a perception of the possible consequences of choosing, and that is where the question of awareness comes in. To my mind, the free person is primarily in a state like that of the freedom called academic freedom. I sometimes think there is no genuine freedom except academic freedom, where the resources of human knowledge are open for people to assimilate as they best can. Then they are faced with the tactical difficulties of working in a society made up of people who hate the very idea of freedom and can't stand having it anywhere near them. In situations like that the question of choice may come up, but choice in relation to freedom seems to me to have a great deal to do with the tactical manoeuvring of the free individual in a hostile world.

QUESTION: There appears to be an astounding amount of reading behind everything you write. What kind of preparation do you actually do?

ANSWER: Someone asked me how I find time to read everything I read. I said it's simple—I don't. It's very seldom that I do any program of reading before embarking on a piece of writing except when I'm writing about something specific; when you write about Blake you read Blake. Otherwise my reading is rather random and is largely confined to primary sources. That is not arrogance on my part, just self-preservation.

I do find that I often am attracted to subjects that would kill a younger unestablished writer with stage fright. The thought of leaping into a field like the Bible and trying to write a general popular introduction which would still make sense as literary criticism is rather petrifying when one thinks about it. And therefore I think about it as little as possible. When you write such a book you know that the actual scholars in that field will react much as the sons of Jacob reacted to the rape of Dinah [Genesis 34]. It means simply that you have to draw on everything you have read, because it is a corollary of my own view of literature that any verbal document may be potentially useful, and that what counts is not so much the amount and variety of what you've read as the intensity with which you have read it. As Henry James said in giving advice to a young novelist, "Don't worry about getting enough experience to write novels, just try to be the kind of person on whom nothing is lost."[29] I'm an omnivorous reader in the sense that I can read almost anything in words—as Charles Lamb said, "I can read anything that I call a book"[30]—and one never knows when that is going to come in handy.

13

The Ouroboros

Summer 1983

From Ethos, *1 (Summer 1983): 12–13. The typescripts are in the NFF, 1988, box 48, file 4.*

The ouroboros ("tail-eater") is one of the images that grew up in the tangled complex of symbols that accompanied the Gnostic, hermetic, and, more particularly, alchemical speculations of the early centuries of the Christian era. Its origins are Egyptian and may go back to very ancient times. It is not a Biblical symbol, though it could be adapted to a Jewish or Christian framework by alchemists or Kabbalists, and its first literary appearance is in a poem [*On Stilicho's Consulship*, bk. 2, ll. 427–30] by Claudian, one of the last of the pagan Latin poets.

The image of the serpent with its tail in its mouth is primarily an image of the natural cycle, continually devouring and continually renewing itself. Sometimes, in early illustrations, half the serpent is black and the other half white, symbolizing the cycle of light and darkness. Sometimes the serpent is a winged dragon, like the Mexican "plumed serpent," and in this form it unites the qualities of heaven and earth. Sometimes it represents the sexual aspect of the cycle, the tail being the male and the mouth the female principles.

Like most images in the occult tradition it can be identified or associated with practically anything else. The oriental figure of yang and yin, the two aspects of the natural cycle interlocked like two big commas, has the same general reference. Perhaps the serpent became the vehicle of the symbol because its ability to shed its skin makes it a natural image of death and renewal. Death and renewed life are the two balancing forces that hold together the energy of the earth itself and the same idea is portrayed in the double or balancing serpents on the wand or caduceus of Mercury. What is inside the circle formed by the ouroboros is the earth itself: the conception of the earth as held in a serpent's coils meets us everywhere in mythology, the world serpent Midgard in Scandinavia being an example.

In alchemy the ouroboros stands for both the *prima materia* and the *lapis*, that is, for both the beginning and the end of whatever process it was that the alchemists were trying to accomplish. Like all images of its type, it is binary; it has two contexts, and one is the opposite of the other. Similarly, the serpent itself may be an image either of insinuating deception or of genuine wisdom, of man's primordial sickness, as in the Book of Genesis, or of genuine health, as in the Indian symbolism of Kundalini yoga. Purely as an image of the cycle of nature, it can represent an inexorable fate that we never escape from but are simply dragged around with forever. The acceptance of this turning cycle of fate is often regarded (by Nietzsche, Robert Graves, and perhaps Yeats) as characteristic of the genuine hero. In E.R. Eddison's fantastic romance, *The Worm Ouroboros*, the ouroboros is a sinister image employed by the magician-villain, but when the heroes have conquered him they find that a world of peace after victory is too boring for words, and invoke the same image to start the same action all over again. This may strike some readers as a somewhat feeble-minded conclusion but then they might find Nietzsche's doctrine of identical recurrence, from which it may have been derived, a rather feeble-minded notion too.

Writers with a strong sense of apocalyptic vision, like Blake and Shelley, who feel that man's destiny is to smash all his squirrel cages, because he originally built them himself for the pleasure of getting caught in them, speak of ouroboros and similar imagery mainly with contempt. Blake, adopting the common belief of his day that the megalith monument at Avebury, near Stonehenge, had been built by the "Druids" and consecrated to serpent worship, speaks of the "serpent temple" as an "image of infinite shut up in finite revolutions."[1] Similarly, Shelley speaks at the end of *Prometheus Unbound* of "spells" to ward off the threats of the serpent that tries to clasp eternity and so bring tyranny and fatalism back to mankind. In Thomas Pynchon's *Gravity's Rainbow* there is a continual opposition of human creativity and human self-destructiveness. The former is founded largely on dreams; the latter is symbolized by the discovery of the atomic structure of benzene by the nineteenth-century German chemist Kekulé, a discovery that made so much of modern warfare possible. Kekulé's discovery was the result of his having a dream of—guess what—a serpent with its tail in its mouth.

However, it would also be possible to reverse Blake's phrase and say that an image of finite revolutions could also be an image of the infinite, just as Augustine defines God as a circle whose centre is everywhere and circumference nowhere.[2] In Joyce's *Finnegans Wake* we have a book that goes round in a circle, a book of "Doublends Jined," as Joyce calls it,[3] so that the sentence that ends the book is completed by the opening sentence. Yet the circularity is not purely fatalistic: the circle is perhaps the only figure for conceiving an infinity that is beyond the circle. When a contemporary poet (James Merrill, in *The Book of Ephraim*) speaks of Joyce as forging a snake that swallows its own tail, he puts him in a context of dragon-slayers, as one of those creators who destroy the anticreative by defining it.

14

Literary and Linguistic Scholarship in a Postliterate World

29 December 1983

Originally presented at the MLA Centennial Convention in New York. From PMLA, *99 (October 1984): 990–5. Reprinted in* MM, *18–27. The typescripts are in the NFF, 1988, box 47, file 5, and 1991, box 39, file 3. For Frye's response to criticism of this article, see no. 21.*

The title of this paper is not mine: I do not know what the word "postliterate" means, and I have finally decided to take it as a synonym for education itself. Society supports compulsory education because it needs docile and obedient citizens. We must learn to read to respond to traffic signs and advertising, learn to cipher to make out our income tax. These passive acquirements make us literate, and society as such has no great interest in education beyond that stage. Teachers take over from there: their task is to transform a passive literacy into an active postliteracy, with the responsibility and freedom of choice that are part of any world we want to live in.

A hundred years is not a long time, geologically speaking: I have been teaching for nearly half that time myself, and for well over a third of it I have belonged to the MLA and watched its letters come increasingly to stand for Miscellaneous Linguistic Activities. In 1883 the picture of a scholar reading a book was a fairly adequate icon for the humanities. It was a Cartesian icon, a thinking subject confronting a mechanically produced object. However, as the MLA has grown it has become clear that texts, like dragons or beautiful princesses in romance, attract a great variety of visitors. Some want to devour the text; some want to surrender to it; some want to read it; some want to misread it; some want to extract its essence; some want to proclaim its existence; some critical engineers want to build bridges connecting the images; some critical developers want to build new structures in the empty spaces.

It is apparently the policy of the MLA, as of most such gatherings, to allow all of these a share of time on the program, in the hope that the procession will eventually shake down into some sort of community, or group of communities. The fact that a relatively stable text becomes the focus of a community is so patent now that the old individualized reader, shut away from the community to read in quiet, begins to look like a self-dramatizing abstraction. In the process it has also become generally accepted that criticism is not a parasitic growth on literature but a special form of literary language.

It would be unreasonable for me to object to this development, when I have been advocating so much of it for so many years. But still only postliterate communities are involved, and they still operate within a society that neither sees nor much wants to see the importance of what they are doing. The critics in turn seem to have equally little interest in trying to demonstrate that importance. It is curious, considering the brilliance of the leading scholars in the field, how much critical theory today has relapsed into a confused and claustrophobic battle of methodologies, where, as in Fortinbras's campaign in *Hamlet* [4.4.56–65], the ground fought over is hardly big enough to hold the contending armies. One central critical question, it seems to me, is that of the writer's social authority, but we seem unable to deal with this. Yet it is a very old question: when Dante expounds the meaning of a verse in the Psalms, and then says that his own *Paradiso* is written on the same principle [*Letter to Can Grande*], he is not simply describing a critical method but trying to find a place for his authority as a poet by attaching his work to another text that already has such authority.

It is easy to see in science, say, in Galileo or Darwin, how the integrity of the science itself commands a loyalty and a commitment from the scientist even when it conflicts with social concerns and demands. It seems much more difficult and complex to locate the source of the writer's social authority. We know that there is often a core of authentic vision at the heart even of writers who admittedly also wrote a good deal of blithering nonsense. We know how hideously powerful perverted rhetoric can be, and how a deliberate debasing of language can wipe out all genuine freedom and culture in a society. We also know—and this is the centre of the issue for me—how many writers of recent years have faced ridicule, persecution, even martyrdom, in order to remain loyal to a vision that they felt had been entrusted to them. Many writers have been suppressed or exiled or murdered for ideological reasons, and many have committed suicide because of social and political as well as psychological stress.

What I am speaking of is not a question of the last century only. Writers have always been torn by the conflicting demands of their own craft and those of a society that usually finds something quite different more acceptable. One thinks of Petrarch, spreading throughout Europe the gospel of the frustrations and sublimations of love, yet writing in his *Secretum* a rueful dialogue between himself and Augustine, a mother-fixated saint whose view of the workings of Eros in human life was seldom genial, and yet who stood much closer to the centre of spiritual authority in Petrarch's day. One thinks of Chaucer and his *Retraction* [at the end of the *Canterbury Tales*], disowning his allegedly sinful tales, as though his Friar and Summoner were after all to be taken at their own valuations. One thinks of any number of self-conflicts, ranging from Tasso to Gogol, from Rimbaud to Yukio Mishima, that have nearly or quite destroyed the creative powers of those in whom they raged.[1] Around us today we see a great variety of social groups—Christian, Marxist, Moslem, anarchist, liberal, conservative—all of them full of hardliners who simply deny, in the interests of their own dogmas, that poets have any authority except what they might derive from whatever ideology the dogmatists themselves want to advance. Their confident and self-hypnotized assurance has influenced many of the more timid critics to believe or assume that if there is any value in the study of literature, it cannot inhere in literature itself. And if we speak vaguely, as Auden does about Yeats, of a "gift" for "writing well" [*In Memory of W.B. Yeats*, pt. 2, l. 1, pt. 3, l. 16], we are only going around in circles.

It should go without saying—but it doesn't, so I have to say it—that the social authority of the critic and the literary scholar is an inseparable part of the same question, because text and reader can no longer be thought of as standing in a simple object–subject relation. I know too that the word "authority" will sound disquieting to many. I use it because it is impossible to raise the issue of the social function of writing without a complete redefinition of authority, and such a redefinition would have to extend to every aspect of social life. In a world where authority now resides in power structures that are confronted by one another and by most of their own citizens with equal apprehensiveness, this reconsidering of authority would take us a long way. It might conceivably give the MLA itself a new kind of social relevance.

Literature develops out of mythology, a body of stories with a specific social function, and mythology in its turn is an outgrowth of concern, a term that I hope is self-explanatory. There is primary concern, and there is secondary concern. Primary concern is based on the most primitive of platitudes: the conviction that life is better than death, happiness better than misery, freedom better than bondage. Secondary concern includes loyalty to one's own society, to one's religious or political beliefs, to one's place in the class structure, and in short to everything that comes under the general heading of ideology. All through history secondary concerns have had the greater prestige and power. We prefer to live, but we go to war; we prefer to be free, but we keep many people in a second-class status, and so on. In the twentieth century the dangers of persisting in the bad habits of war, and of exploitation of both human beings and nature, have brought humanity to a choice between survival and extinction. If we choose survival, the twentieth century will be the first period in history when primary concerns have some real chance of becoming primary.

Poets are the children of concern: they normally reflect the ideologies of their own times, and certainly they are always conditioned by their historical and cultural surroundings. Yet there has always been a sense of something else that eludes this kind of communication. Gerard Manley Hopkins speaks of an overthought of syntax and an underthought of metaphor and imagery, a distinction between what is said and what is shown forth.[2] What is said may sometimes be only a perfunctory disguise, a concession to the censor in the reader, burglar's meat for a watchdog, in Eliot's phrase.[3] But even what is shown forth by the figurative structure, if more disinterested, may be a choice among alternatives, which are repressed but still in some sense there.

As we pursue this question, one landmark after another begins to disappear. The writer disappears as an individual, and the question of authority shifts from him or her to the authority of literature as a whole. Then we see that there are no clear boundaries between literary and other verbal structures, so that the question becomes one of the authority of language. Similarly the reader merges into the community of criticism and scholarship, which again cannot be separated from what it acts on. Every effort of criticism is a recreation. So we are left only with language and users of language. But on further reflection we can no longer be sure whether it is humanity that uses language or language that uses humanity.

It might be prudent to stop here, with the retrospective view appropriate to a centennial, surveying our progress from the scholar and book of a century ago to the reduction of all solid elements into a heaving sea of melted-down categories. But if any members of the larger social public I mentioned earlier are waiting to have the significance of all this explained to them, they are still waiting. And even if they have gone home, we, if we survive, need something to keep us going for another hundred years. So I have to venture on one more step.

Primary concern is clearly not confined to life and the pursuit of happiness; it is not confined even to the leisure, privacy, and freedom of movement that for most of us indicate the higher levels of culture. It includes also the concern of a conscious being to enlarge that consciousness, to get at least a glimpse of what it would be like to know more than we are compelled to know. In short, conscious primary concern is postliterate, in the sense I have given to that word.

Just as there is primary and secondary concern, so there is primary and secondary mythology. Primary mythology sees the environment in terms of the human impulse to expand into it. The chief instrument of this expansion is metaphorical identification. If we look at the drawings of bisons and stags in Palaeolithic caves, and consider the conditions of positioning and lighting under which they were done, we can see that the titanic strength and urgency of the motivation involved is something we can no longer find words for.[4] Such words as "aesthetic," "magical," "religious," or words relating to social solidarity or survival, are merely thrown at it: they express nothing of the intensity of identification involved. Later we find the metaphorical imagination expanding into the worlds of dream, belief, vision, fantasy, ideas, as well as human society and nature, and annexing them all to the enlarging consciousness.

But every society is structured, and there is always another or secondary tendency to attach what is imagined to the ideals of some ascendant group or class. Thus medieval and Renaissance romances were attached to the aristocratic or monastic ideals of their time, nineteenth-century fiction to contemporary bourgeois ideals—every age shows the same pattern. We never get a work of imagination that is wholly primary or secondary; it is invariably both at once. Yet the two aspects are still two: primary mythology is anthropocentric; secondary mythology is ethnocentric. Much of the critical process revolves around the effort of distinguishing them.

For instance, when Shakespeare presents the career of Henry V, he supplies his audience with their own prefabricated prejudices. He traces his hero through his madcap disguise as prince, his emergence as responsible king, his invasion of France, and his victory, leaving him as he is about to marry the French princess. He throws in Falstaff as comic relief to diversify the same ideology and removes him when he has served his purpose. But if we listen carefully to the progression of images and to other things said that are subordinated but still audible, we can see and hear how much else is happening. We become aware of the misery of France, the fact that Falstaff is a powerful presence whatever his moral status, the shaky morale of many of the English soldiers. Above all, we become aware that Henry's victory is shot through with the illusions of fortune, and that he died almost at once and left a legacy of sixty years of disaster for England. This does not mean that the play is a palimpsest with a perfunctory patriotic message on top and an ironic one underneath to be discovered by cleverer students. It means that as we progress in understanding, the play's expression of primary concern, as a metaphorical vision of life, begins to become distinguishable from an ideology of patriotism that is also present.

In our day, this distinction is so clear that we now instinctively think of a mythology as a structure of phoney ideas that embodies the entrenched interests of some ascendant or pressure group, whether its vehicle is advertising or propaganda. It is obvious too that if there is a strong tension between two political powers, the greatest long-term danger, so far, comes less from what either power directly does than from the mythology that each projects on the other. Hence there would clearly be some point in trying to develop a technique of making ourselves more aware of our mythological conditioning, of removing the ideological cataracts from our social vision. Using the criticism of literature as a remedy for the abuses of ideology is unreliable and hazardous, and in practice it has hardly ever worked. But that is true of criticism as it is, not as it could be, and I see nothing else that has any chance of working at all.

Henry V is a history play, and it builds up a sense of an irresistible historical destiny and of cause-and-effect logic. These things are realities, or seem so until the total annihilation of everything they bring before us shows that they are also illusions. What we notice increasingly are, first, the immense power of counter-logic in the metaphorical structure, and, second, the equally powerful counterhistorical movement in the myth, the total story being told. We begin by thinking that the myth of the play follows history except for some poetic licence. But it does not "follow" history: it absorbs the historical movement and then confronts it.

We are reminded of Nature's judgment at the end of Spenser's *Mutabilitie Cantos*, where she decides against Mutability's claim to be the supreme power in the universe. If, says Nature, we are ruled by change, there is only mechanical repetition leading to death, the normal drift of time and space into entropy. But we can reverse the movement and rule over change, making repetition a progress toward freedom, as repeated practice sets us free to play the piano or tennis. This latter repetition, she says, is a working of our own perfection, a dilation of our own being [canto 7, st. 58, ll. 4–7]. "Dilate," incidentally, is also a rhetorical term referring to the writer's copiousness or creative energy.

It seems to me that all creative impulses, including the literary one, begin in the sense of the unreality of time and space in ordinary experience, where the central points that we call here and now never quite come into existence. The counterlogical and counterhistorical movements of metaphor and myth have to do with trying to establish or reconstitute a sense of a present moment and a spatial presence as the basis of whatever significance the verbal imagination can find in life. I conclude with an example or two of what I mean.

In Plato's dialogue *Phaedrus* we first meet Phaedrus himself, deeply impressed by a speech about love given by the rhetorician Lysias. As Socrates begins to ask him about the speech, it becomes obvious that it is the personal impact rather than the content of Lysias's address that has impressed Phaedrus. So he pulls a written copy of the address out of his pocket to refresh his memory of it. At the end of the dialogue we are told that the god Thoth, having invented writing and proclaimed its virtues as an aid to the memory, was informed by his critics that his invention had far more to do with forgetting than with remembering, and that it would only encourage mental laziness. Beginning and end fit together exactly. For Phaedrus at the beginning and for Thoth's critics at the end, writing is a vestige of a presence that has vanished, and in fact was continuously vanishing even while it was appearing. The same principle would apply to the oral discourse of Socrates, in that context.

But in addition to the Socratic irony that pervades the dialogue, there is a Platonic irony inherent in the arrangement of the dialogue itself. In the middle of it we hear Socrates taking off into the blue in one of his wonderful mythical journeys, telling us of the power of Eros, how it pushes us upward in a staggering chariot drawn by two unequal horses, how it crashes again to the earth as we are reborn once more in a cycle of thousands of years. He also says that Lysias's speech has no shape: his points simply follow one another as minute follows minute, whereas a *logos* or discourse ought to be also a *zoon*, a living being from which nothing can be taken without injury. Socrates is speaking to that unified and organic awareness which is one of the things he means by equating knowledge with recollection; our response to him should be, in part at least, that of the narrator in Eliot's *Marina*: "I made this, I have forgotten / And remember" [ll. 23–4]. The implication is that Socrates' speech does not merely follow Lysias: it does not even merely confute him. It reverses his movement; it is a tide coming in again after low ebb.

In the New Testament the Gospels record the words uttered by Jesus. Few if any scholars believe that the authors of the Gospels were eye-witnesses, or rather earwitnesses, of the original utterances; they are recording after a lapse of time. The orthodox doctrine says that they were inspired to give a definitive transcription of what Jesus said. The critical principle involved is that the text is not the absence of a former presence but the place of the resurrection of the presence.[5] Or rather, it is not a place but what Wallace Stevens calls a description without place, a description he identifies with revelation or apocalypse.[6] In this risen presence text and reader are equally involved. The reader is a whole of which the text is a part; the text is a whole of which the reader is a part—these contradictory movements keep passing into one another and back again. The Logos at the centre, which is inside the reader and not hidden behind the text, continually changes place with the Logos at the circumference that encloses both.

In Donne's poem *The Extasie* two bodies joined in sexual union produce two souls that merge into a single entity. The barrier between subject and object disappears, and the single entity is thereby enabled to enter an experience that is not wholly in time. But of course the clock still goes on ticking in the ordinary world, the united soul dissolves and returns to the two bodies, and ordinary experience is reestablished. It is obvious that Donne is not talking exclusively about sexual union: in such concluding phrases of the poem as "the body is [love's] book" [l. 72] and "dialogue of one" [l. 74], he seems to be glancing at some of our own concerns. Similarly, another poem, *The Canonization*, describes a sexual union in which "we die and rise the same" [l. 26] but moves from there into metaphors of text and reader. In the sexual union two separate egos form a soul that is still not quite a body; in the reading process the object as book and the subject as reader merge into an identity equally fragile and temporary. But the reader belongs to a community of readers, the text to a family of texts, so that both text and reader have the support of an extending world of a kind that sexual experience, confined as it is to two individuals, cannot provide.

In each of these examples certain beliefs are suggested: reincarnation in Plato, plenary inspiration in the New Testament, a dichotomy of soul and body in Donne. But in the full critical operation there must always be a catharsis of belief which belongs to secondary concern and secondary mythology. What they all open up to us is a world of recovered identity, both as ourselves and with something not ourselves. That does not mean that we ever escape from paradox into certainty: paradox and self-contradiction are if anything greater than they were before. But these new paradoxes come from the counter-movements of myth and metaphor against the annihilations of time and the alienations of space, and one can not only live with such paradoxes, but live more intensely with them.

Our fondness for words beginning with "post-" and "meta-," whether we are speaking of the postliterate or poststructural, of the metaphysical or the metaphorical, indicates the importance we place on the renewing aspect of tradition. We look for the child who comes after the parent, bringing a youthful vision of revived hope in place of stability and fixed order. The real reference in "post-" and "meta-," however, is less to the future than to another dimension of the present, where time flows back on itself and space collapses in upon itself, and where a sense of reality replaces, for however brief an instant, our normal fear of the unknown.

15

The End of History

10 May 1984

Transcript from the Canadian Broadcasting Corporation. Broadcast on the CBC program "Ideas" as the first in a four-part series, "History and the New Age," which in introducer Lister Sinclair's words "explores the changed relationship of history to nature in the nuclear age." This first program, "The End of History," was written and presented by David Cayley. Cayley began by suggesting the bankruptcy of the Western notion of history as progress, and used Frye's words to introduce "the aboriginal human conception of time in myth."

In the first place, the myth is a *mythos*, a story, a narrative. And if you're attending a play of Shakespeare's, the story of that play is its *mythos*, it's its myth. And if Shakespeare is writing a history play, for example, you'll find that he alters some details. He makes Hotspur and Prince Henry the same age, where historically, according to his sources, they were twenty years apart. Well, then we say that the story, the play, follows history except for some poetic licence, but that's got the whole thing backwards. The myth of Shakespeare's play incorporates historical material, but it twists the events around so that they confront the audience. You cannot listen to a myth without moving into a higher dimension of time than the purely sequential one. If you take, say, the Crucifixion of Christ, that was a historical event, because even if Jesus was not crucified, a lot of other people were. And as a historical event, it is simply part of the continuous psychosis that we know as human history; but as a myth, this particular Crucifixion confronts us—confronts us with our own moral bankruptcy. Time is arrested at that point. You've got to stop and think of what you do with this.

16

Myth as the Matrix of Literature

Fall 1984

From Georgia Review, *38 (Fall 1984): 465–76. The typescripts are in the NFF, 1991, box 35, file 2 (annotated), and 1988, box 48, file 5.*

At the beginning of the *Anatomy of Criticism*, there is a statement to the effect that that book is "pure critical theory" [vii]. I now somewhat regret that phrase, not simply because one tends to lose faith in purity with advancing years, but because of the discovery, which I made soon afterward, that I was much less interested in "pure critical theory" than I thought I was. My central interest is really in practical criticism, which I had originally hoped the *Anatomy* would be; and my two central conceptions have always been myth and metaphor. The *Anatomy* speaks of the modes of literature as fictional and thematic, which are conceptions developed from Aristotle's *mythos* ("plot," "narrative") and *dianoia* (often translated as "thought") [*Poetics*, chap. 6]. Every work of literature has both a narrative movement, which carries us from a beginning to an end in a temporal sequence, and an underlying "structure" (a term derived from the motionless art of architecture), which we try to study as a simultaneous and spatialized arrangement of metaphors.

I have arrived at an age where a good deal of my energy has to go into writing *Festschriften* for my contemporaries, and recently, faced with such an assignment, I found myself getting interested in William Morris again.[1] I say again because I was fascinated by him when I was still a junior instructor. One reason for the fascination was his remarkable temperamental affinity with Blake; another was that, like Blake, he was unfashionable, and unfashionable writers have always interested me. To be unfashionable implies a negative collective value judgment, and while value judgments tell us nothing reliable concerning the poet about whom they are made, they tell us a great deal concerning the cultural conditioning of the person who makes the judgment. For a writer to be unfashionable may, and often does, indicate that his writing exemplifies a different set of standards from the ones in the ascendant during his lifetime. William Morris was obviously one of the most remarkable, productive, and creative personalities of his century; yet except for *News from Nowhere*, which was tolerated as a kind of curiosity, and a few of his poems that kept getting into anthologies, nearly his entire literary output seemed to critics for a long time to be almost stillborn.

We can perhaps see why if we turn to another Victorian poet who is about as far apart from Morris as one could get, Gerard Manley Hopkins. In Hopkins's letters and sketches for critical essays there are certain suggestions thrown out that seem to be different aspects of one central conception. He distinguishes, for example, between two levels of meaning in poetry: a level of "overthought," the explicit meaning conveyed by the syntax, and a level of "underthought," the deeper meaning conveyed by the imagery and metaphors.[2] (If, for example, we study carefully the images used in the opening scene of Shakespeare's *Henry V*, attending particularly to their emotional resonances, we shall hear something very different from the rather simple-minded patriotism of the explicit meaning.) There is also in Hopkins the much better-known distinction between running rhythm and sprung rhythm, the running rhythm being dependent on the constant coincidence of accent and metre, and sprung rhythm being syncopated and more closely related to the rhythms of music. Finally, most significant of all, Hopkins distinguishes between what he calls a sequential or transmissional form of thinking and another type which he calls meditative, which stops at one point and groups its ideas around itself.

In all three conceptions there is an obvious preference for the underthought, the sprung rhythm, the meditative circling around a theme. To this discontinuous and centripetal view of poetry Morris forms a complete antithesis. Morris is interested primarily in telling stories, in moving from point A to point B in a narrative; and to make his stories readable he preserves a clarity and lucidity of texture designed for sequential reading. He sticks to the standard "running" metres that English literature imported from French and Italian; he avoids the kind of discontinuous meditative quality that would obstruct continuous reading; his overthought and underthought are nearly always the same thing.

In this Morris was continuing the tradition of the great Romantics, all of whom cultivated the long verse narrative, usually leaving their greatest achievement in such narrative unfinished at their deaths. The Romantics wrote for a market that responded to stories in verse: Byron even remarks that he is writing *Don Juan* in verse rather than prose because verse is "more in fashion."[3] But the vogue for continuous narrative poetry vanished with the twentieth century: Eliot's remarks about "dissociation of sensibility"[4] were a polemic against it; Hopkins, many decades after his death, entered English literature as a typical *twentieth*-century poet; and critics trained in the standards of the modern period tended, like my late friend and colleague Marshall McLuhan, to develop out of those standards a preference for simultaneous apprehension in contrast to linear modes of understanding.

Yet if one reconsiders Morris, one finds an oddly prophetic quality about him which is disconcerting in someone who has been so confidently assigned to the lumber room of minor poets. His interest in Marxist socialism, for example, was regarded by most of his contemporaries, including even his very sympathetic biographer Mackail, as the kind of regrettable perversion that genius is often attracted to. But while Marxism was a minority movement in the England of the 1880s, one would hardly say now that Morris's interest in it was freakish or peripheral. He was certainly a bourgeois sympathizer with socialism rather than a proletarian, but then socialism has since become—at least in the Soviet Union—a bourgeois adversary of capitalism rather than a new development of society. Then again, Morris produced at the end of his life a series of prose romances, which all have much the same title—*The Wood beyond the World, The Well at the World's End, The Water of the Wondrous Isles*—and seem to be very full of trees and water. Nobody paid much attention to these books at the time, and they seemed to represent an almost schizophrenically different interest from his political views. The few who were interested in the romances, like Yeats, had little interest in his socialism; the few who sympathized with his socialism, like Shaw, had even less interest in the romances.

If one looks at the various long romances which have followed upon the sensational success of Tolkien, however, one finds a tradition developing which was quite obviously initiated by the prose romances of Morris (who was among other things a major influence on Tolkien himself). In such works as Frank Herbert's "Dune" books, Roger Zelazny's "Amber" books, and Ursula LeGuin's "Earthsea" books, both history and geography have been invented, as in Morris; and while such stories are often classified as "science fiction," there is relatively little interest in technological hardware. What emerges is a rather primitive type of romance, sometimes in the form of adventurous intrigue, sometimes reminding us of folk tales. So here again Morris committed himself to something almost totally ignored in his own time, and ignored with even greater enthusiasm later on, which has had an odd resurrection in our own day. Similarly, Morris's cultural enthusiasm for the Middle Ages is often regarded as imaginatively inconsistent with his revolutionary attitude to his own time, but this also is nonsense, and the contemporary romances we have just spoken of often drift back into a kind of medieval ambience, even when they are close enough to conventional "science fiction" to avoid Morris's anti-technological attitudes. Along with the flourishing of such romance we have a lively development of retold mythological themes: Arthurian, ancient Egyptian, Scandinavian, and others. So Morris's curious compulsion, not merely to write stories but to retell all the famous stories of the past, seems to have some contemporary relevance as well.

Value judgments, as I said above, express the cultural conditioning of the period that makes them. The cycle of fashion that ignored Morris for so long, and then brought him (or the cultural interests he followed) again into the centre, seems to me to be an aspect of a larger cycle, one that keeps moving from structural interests to an interest in texture, from a constructive interest in what literature is building up to a more analytical interest in the material that literature is made of. Perhaps the structural and poststructural schools of criticism today represent another phase in that cycle, repeating to some degree the complementary interests of the historical criticism and the rhetorical or "new" criticism of the 1930s and 1940s, and even going back to the interest of Elizabethan critics in, on one hand, mythological commentary explaining something of the shape and structure of the great mythical stories, and on the other, textbooks of rhetoric analysing the various devices of verbal figuration. I imagine that this pendulum of fashion will keep swinging back and forth between one interest and the other until critics finally get it through their heads that they have to have both going on at once.

This brings me back to the point that the two elements of literature are the myth, the narrative that moves, and the metaphor, the link that connects. Myth is a word I prefer to anchor in its literary context, where for me it is essentially and always Aristotle's *mythos*, narrative or plot, which in turn refers to the movement of literature. The paradox of using the spatialized metaphor of "structure" for something that moves has its confusing aspect, but it does express the fact that all the arts, whether mobile like music or static like painting, have both temporal and spatial aspects. A Chinese jar, as Eliot says, moves in its stillness;[5] music is played from a score that can be studied as a simultaneous unit. A simultaneous comprehension of a play or novel or poem as a motionless structure seems to me quite feasible and desirable, except that as soon as attained it has to be abandoned and a new cycle of understanding begun.

Mythos or narrative exists in both literary and extraliterary types of verbal entities, in anything which we read in sequence. It does not necessarily have to be a story, although in early verbal cultures almost all narratives are likely to be stories. In more complex cultures there are conceptual narratives in works of philosophy and books where we call the narrative an "argument." In fact, narrative exists in everything that has a sequence even if we do not read it sequentially, like a telephone book. The words "history" and "story," again, have come to mean different things, and we adopt a rough practical distinction between a history which is paralleled against certain events going on outside the book being read, and a story which exists for its own sake without any continuous paralleling of this sort. But *mythos* or narrative will be present whether the work is history or story: the phrase "decline and fall" in the title of Gibbon's history indicates the underlying narrative, along with the principle on which he selected and ordered his material.[6]

We may raise the question in passing whether it is really possible to write history diachronically, except in special forms like that of Pepys's *Diary*. It seems more probable that every historian has to stand outside the history he is recording and take a synchronic view of it. The implication is that a history is at once "true" and "untrue"—"true" because it deals with verifiable statements, "untrue" because these statements are being selected and arranged in a form that is no longer purely sequential. "Myth" is often vulgarly used to mean a false statement, or mirage of ideology: this is because every narrative conveys to a reader both the assertion that this event happened and that it could not have happened in precisely that way and in that identical context.

Literature seems to begin in a corpus of stories, and some of these stories, which are classified as folk tales, show an extraordinary versatility in surmounting all barriers of culture and language and making an appearance in one society after another. In another development, however, a group of stories does take root in a specific society, and when that happens they seem to draw a kind of *temenos* or magic circle around themselves, and begin to exist in time. Eventually, this produces a distinction between the popular and the canonical, the folk tale and the myth, which are not really two distinct kinds of literature but two social adaptations of the same original corpus of stories. Mythical stories will show structural analogies to other stories all over the world, but despite this structural similarity, they will contain traditional names and specific affinities to religion and legendary history that establish them within a single society. If we examine certain features of culture even today, we can see both of these tendencies operating. Just as we find creation and flood and fall myths with similar structural features all over the world, so, in any given period of history, we find techniques in fiction and poetry that spread rapidly from one language or culture to another. But this goes along with a curiously decentralizing rhythm that has been very consistent in the history of literature.

Great empires, as such, seldom produce great literature, with the most obvious exceptions, such as Virgil, illustrating the rule. There seems to be something vegetable about the creative imagination, something that seems to want a relatively limited environment, so that in proportion as a literature becomes more mature it tends to settle into relatively smaller units. The population of England was small enough for English literature to be essentially a London literature down to the end of the eighteenth century, but after Wordsworth the situation changed rapidly. In another century or so we find that "English literature" produces a Dylan Thomas growing out of south Wales, a Hardy out of Dorset, a D.H. Lawrence out of the Nottingham area, a Yeats out of Sligo, and so on. As early as the preface to Shelley's *Prometheus Unbound* we find the statement that for England's literary production to be broadened, the country should be broken down into a number of self-contained units, states like those of Renaissance Italy. The statement also illustrates the confusion between the decentralizing rhythms of culture and those of political and economic developments, which tend rather to centralize.

Similarly, if we look at American literature, we find an aggregate of Southern literatures, New England literatures, expatriate literature, and so on over all the country. If we want to know what the creative imagination tells us about American life, we learn it by adding together what Faulkner tells us about Mississippi, Robert Frost about New Hampshire, and so on. The same development has occurred very dramatically in

Canada within the last twenty years. This odd paradox of techniques common to the whole world but developed within a local, even a provincial, area, seems to be the way in which a great deal of literature operates. After a brief visit to Guyana, I got interested in Wilson Harris,[7] and immediately after reading one of his novels I read a Canadian novel set in Alberta. The two novels were not at all like each other, but they used certain techniques, such as telling the story on two levels of time at once, that marked them both as mid-twentieth-century novels.

I suggested above that such cultural developments are quite different from political or economic ones, which not only centralize but become more uniform as they grow. One cannot take off in a jet plane and expect to find a radically different way of life in the place where the plane lands. If we try to unite a political or economic movement with a cultural one, certain pathological developments, such as fascism or terroristic anarchism, are likely to result. If we try to annex culture to a centralizing political or economic movement, we get a pompous and officialized imperialism in the arts. It is simplistic to make too sharp a distinction between two aspects of human life that must always both be present—for example, the production of a literature may be local, but its marketing follows economic rhythms—but still the lurking antagonism between cultural and political phenomena is important. It means that one social function of literature in our time is to help create a kind of counter-environment.

So far I have been speaking mainly of spatial patterns, of the way in which literature seems to break down into smaller geographical units and, even in this very unified world, still continues to exploit differences in language—language being, especially in its literary aspect, one of the most profoundly fragmented of human activities. The question then arises, How does this phenomenon act in time? I have always, from the very beginning of my critical interests in literature, been impressed by the stability of literary genres and conventions, by the uniformity of, say, comic characterization from Greek times to our own, by the way in which traditional myths and folk tales keep on being adapted by poets and novelists century after century. This recreation of traditional patterns, in particular, makes mythology a real and continuing presence.

Mythology, in its origin, is a structure of what I think of as human concern. That is, it is an expression of the fact that man not only lives in nature, but builds a human world out of nature. That human world, so far as it is verbal, is made out of human beliefs and anxieties and hopes and ambitions, and consequently it faces inward towards human society and its concerns, not outward towards nature. That is, mythology is not a proto-science. But it is bound to make certain assumptions about nature that may be contradicted by further examination of nature; these assumptions are likely to be defended by entrenched social interests, and so collisions of mythology and science result, as in the kind of opposition provoked by Galileo and Darwin. But genuine mythology tends to become a literary structure, and is recreated by the poets: collisions between literary and scientific views of the world are both rare and insignificant. For one thing, poets may be quite content with a world of four elements, phases of the moon, alchemic or astrological imagery, and other constructs no longer used in science; for another, when concern becomes really important and no longer merely an anxiety of superstition, as in the concern about atom bombs and pollution, scientists are as much involved in the concern as poets are.

To return briefly to William Morris: I referred earlier to what seemed almost a compulsion on his part not merely to write stories but to retell all the great stories of the past, to translate the *Aeneid, Beowulf,* the *Odyssey,* old French romances, and Icelandic Sagas. This suggests something double-edged about the relationship of cultural developments to the temporal sequence of history. As the historical examination by scholars of the motifs of mythology and folk tales gets carried back further into the past, it comes up against the sense of a very remote time in which the complete story with all its implications was intact, of which only broken and garbled fragments have survived. One sees this occasionally spoken of as a possibility—for instance at the beginning of Jessie Weston's *From Ritual to Romance*—but it is almost certainly an illusion. To understand what a myth fully means one has to look forward in time to the various ways in which the poets have treated it. Certain very primitive stories about the triumph of summer over winter might be more clearly understood from a complex and late work like Shakespeare's *Winter's Tale* than from the St. George folk dramas of the English countryside. In fact, anyone who studies the folk drama is sure to have the later literary developments affecting his understanding of it, however unconsciously.

My reference to Jessie Weston's book has another aspect: whatever the view that Arthurian scholars take of it, it was a major influence on *The Waste Land,* one of the seminal poems of our time. I suspect that it proved so suggestive to Eliot because its author got many of her ideas out of Wagner: in other words, her treatment of the Arthurian legend was unconsciously based on a feeling of the legend's being recreated and moving forward in time. For when Wagner started working on *Parsifal*, his obvious source was Wolfram von Eschenbach, who had already made an appearance as a character in an earlier Wagner opera [*Tannhäuser*] and had suggested the subject matter of another.[8] But Wagner found that there were certain elements in the Grail legend which seemed very central and very primitive, or at least far more suggestive metaphorically, that Wolfram did not know about. In Wolfram the Grail is not a chalice or cup, nor is the spear carried in the Grail procession the spear of Longinus. Hence the word "primitive," just used, need not necessarily mean earliest in time.

There is another sense in which the temporal movement of culture tends to be reactionary, in a specialized way. Every country in the world today is committed by the nature of twentieth-century technology to some kind of social revolution, and the social consequences of revolution are normally in the direction of greater uniformity. Intellectuals have a great desire to help pitch in and turn the wheel of history, and thereby show that ideas of the kind they have amount to something in the historical process after all. This is the activity that has been described as the *trahison des clercs*, the betrayal by intellectuals of their real social function.[9]

To understand this better, we may turn to Plato, where the central figure is Socrates, and where the martyrdom of Socrates is the crucial event around which most of Plato's work revolves. The imagination of posterity has naturally focused on the unforgettable dignity and serenity of Socrates in the *Apology* and the *Phaedo*. But Plato himself was a revolutionary thinker and devoted many of his late years to the construction of the *Laws*, a blueprint for a revolutionary society where Socrates does not appear, and where no such figure as Socrates ever could appear, because one of its main principles is that teachers are to be rigidly censored in everything that they say and teach. Something similar happened, perhaps, with the growth of Christianity into a social institution. Culture is often, and I hope rightly, thought of as a progressively liberalizing force in society. But it seems to be also a force that continually moves backward to what is symbolically, at least, a prerevolutionary time, a time when Jesus or Socrates is still alive, and when the vital ideas of vital people are still of profound social significance.

In the tendency to recreate an earlier time as a cultural model for the present or future, the significance of the use of mythology by poets and novelists comes into focus. Myth, we saw, differs from history in that it is not bound to a sequence of events, but is a presentation of human history in a participating form, so that in a myth one can feel that one's own life and fortunes are involved in the story being told. The black spiritual "Go down, Moses: let my people go" indicates what power a myth can have long after its connection with history has disappeared. The medievalism of William Morris had nothing to do with any desire to return to the political or economic or religious structures of the Middle Ages: the medieval period for him was a cultural model only, and its standards of art and craftsmanship were the only elements that he wished to apply to his own time.

The mythology that has been decisive for the cultural tradition which we ourselves inherited is the Biblical one. Biblical mythology is revolutionary, formulated by a people who were tribal and never imperial, who thought in terms of an eventual overturn of the historical process in which the power of the kingdoms of Egypt and Babylon would be destroyed. The Biblical myth is intensely patriarchal and male-centred: its own deity was male, and it consistently opposed the mother-goddess cults that were so prominent in the east Mediterranean world at the time.

The reason for this is that the mother-centred mythology tends to be associated with the natural cycle, which may lead to the implication that man is essentially an unborn being, that he remains all his life imprisoned within the cycle of nature, emerging from its womb but returning to its tomb. This is the mythological kernel, perhaps, of the story of Oedipus, the ruler who comes to grief through an unconscious clinging to the mother. In Genesis the first woman is formed out of the body of the first man; Adam is related only to a father, and in renouncing that relationship he returns to his only mother, the mother earth who for him is only a principle of death. The Genesis story is not simply a rationalizing of patriarchal values: it is also a revolutionary break from the cyclical view of human destiny: we have to be cut off from the mother to get born. As Yeats pointed out [in *A Vision*], Classical civilization developed both a cyclical view of history and a tragic version of the Oedipus myth, whereas Christianity gives us a revolutionary view of history and a comic Oedipus myth—comic of course only in the sense of an action leading to reconciliation.

The Bible sets up an ideal of love which is primarily God's love for man, *agape* or *caritas*, a disinterested love which acts as a model for the love that man must develop towards God and his neighbour. Love rooted in the sexual instinct is described by the New Testament as (or rather is included in the conception of) *philia*, which makes it really a form of gregariousness. The word *eros* does not occur in the New Testament, nor does what it describes. But of course Eros, which suggests an essential kinship with nature (particularly nature as *natura naturans*, the proliferating and bursting forth of life in an organic process), was central to Classical mythology. In the Middle Ages the poets developed, mainly out of Virgil and Ovid, a cult of Eros which was in effect reminding the religious, political, and other authoritarian establishments that they had left something out that was essential to the human imagination, something that had to be reckoned with as a powerful cultural force.

The structure of authority that derives from the Bible was founded on spatial metaphors in which God is associated with the sky—with a world "up there"—and a demonic world located somewhere "down below." Because of the immense prestige of Virgil and the sixth book of the *Aeneid*, the downward journey still survived in poetry, and the notion of a titanic figure who was imprisoned underground, yet retains a forbidden knowledge of a mysterious future, also remains latent in Western consciousness. This is the figure of Prometheus, and Eros and Prometheus represent an aspect of reality that was minimized in the Biblical and Christian mythological tradition, but was potentially present all along and has reemerged most powerfully in our own time.

In a sense, poetry is always polytheistic, because the central form of metaphor is the god: the identification of some kind of personal spirit with some aspect of the order of nature. Gods are ready-made metaphors and fall into poetry with a minimum of adaptation. A rigid monotheism like that of Judaism or Christianity or Islam would have considerably narrowed the variety of culture if it were not that in the Western world, at any rate, the poets insisted on clinging to the great gods that were still immanent in the form of gigantic human powers. The old structure of authority was an ordered hierarchy with God on top, the perfect world he had made (and to which it is our primary duty to return) directly underneath, the "fallen" world into which we are born below that, and the demonic world at the bottom. This cosmology had many analogies to the human body, from the upper regions corresponding to the human brain to the lower regions corresponding to that mixture of the sexual and the excretory which has always bothered poets. We now live at a time when that inherited structure of authority in the Western world is undergoing a process of revolutionary change and imaginative recreation. There is a profound awareness of this process among our serious writers, though not always a conscious awareness.

The metaphor, like the myth, opens up a channel or current of energy between subjective and objective worlds. Its typical formulation, "A is B," both asserts an identity and conveys the sense that this identity makes no sense in everyday experience. Hence it is a microcosm of an order of reality that is neither subjective nor objective, but bridges the gap between them. (We note in passing that it is impossible to characterize metaphors except by other metaphors.) Because the metaphor asserts an identity that we cannot, in an ordinary context, take seriously, literature becomes a form of play, keeping an ironic distance from the use of words in which their conventional meanings (and their consequent differences from one another) are primary.

The development of a literature which is aware of its mythical and metaphorical basis seems to be a central factor in helping us to get through a profoundly revolutionary period without a loss of freedom. The criticism of literature can make us conscious of our mythical and metaphorical conditioning, as well as of its opposite, our activity as subjects in an objective world where words do not form models of experience, but are only servomechanisms for acquainting us with things and events. Writers today, in particular, have developed a growing interest in fantasy, where our conventional notions of time and space are shaken up and mixed together. A process of recreation and metamorphosis, which enables new mythical forms to emerge in all kinds of unpredictable ways, is what I look forward to in the literature of the present and immediate future: an imaginative exploration that is not confined either to the mythical or the nonmythical, but moves with creative freedom between both.

17

The *Koiné* of Myth: Myth as a Universally Intelligible Language

4 October 1984

Originally presented to the Society for Mediterranean Studies at Victoria University, Toronto. First published in MM, *3–17. The text below is from the typescript in the NFF, 1988, box 48, file 5.*

The word "myth" is used in such a bewildering variety of contexts that anyone talking about it has to say first of all what his chosen context is. Mine is the context of literary criticism, and to me myth always means, first and primarily, *mythos*, story, plot, narrative. The words "story" and "history" were originally identical, but they are now distinguished, and the word "story" seems to lie along an axis extending from history to fantasy. In theory, we have at one extreme the "pure" history which is all "true," in the sense of being a verbal structure that corresponds closely, or satisfactorily, with events that actually occurred. At the other extreme we have stories that are not intended to possess "truth," but are "just stories," which may be fantastic enough to be improbable or so far as we know impossible.

Obviously, such extremes do not really exist. The most pedestrian history must not only select its material, but also have some principle of selection. So a form–content type of distinction arises between the historian's sources and whatever it is that enables him to arrange what he finds there into a sequential narrative. This sequential narrative, which is not present in the nonverbal events themselves, is his *mythos*. My stock example for this has always been Gibbon's *Decline and Fall of the Roman Empire*, where the phrase "decline and fall" indicates the mythical principle that controls the selection of material and various other factors, such as the tone used in presenting it. A myth, in nearly all its senses, is a narrative that suggests two inconsistent responses: first, "this is what is said to have happened," and second, "this almost certainly is not what happened, at least in precisely the way described." It is this latter aspect of myth that has given it the vulgar sense of something simply untrue, something that did not occur. Even Gibbon's *mythos* contains an element of something imposed from outside on the material: very few of the people he discusses had much notion that they were declining and falling.[1]

There is a more positive side to this "untrue" aspect, however. The phrase "decline and fall" is a fairly literal translation of the word "catastrophe," which is a technical term in literary criticism, and suggests that Gibbon's *mythos* is in part an imaginative construct, something the historian has in common with the poets. We notice that as the purely historical element in Gibbon's scholarship dates, as historians discover more and more about the period, his book tends insensibly to shift from the historical to the literary category. It now becomes something of a poetic meditation on the theme of decline and fall as illustrated by the Roman Empire, and its "truth" has, on Aristotelian principles, shifted from the particular to the universal.

As we follow the spectrum leading away from the historical, we find ourselves in literature properly speaking, and at the end of the spectrum is fantastic romance, like the works of "science fiction" where the history and the geography have both been invented. There is no reachable extreme here either. A fantasy completely discontinuous with its social context would be impossible to write: nobody's mind is capable of getting so detached from its social milieu. Even the writings of psychotic or similarly disturbed people are still bound to their surroundings, however off-course their interpretations.

Now that we have located the centre of gravity of myth as the narrative of literature, we can see that such narratives descend directly from myth in its more customary sense of a story about a god which is frequently employed in connection with ritual. Being a story, it is always potentially literary, and very soon becomes actually so, or has close relatives that do. Two categories of stories crystallize in most societies. At the centre is a body of "serious" stories: they may be asserted to have really happened, but what is important about them is not that, but that they are stories which it is particularly urgent for the community to know. They tell us about the recognized gods, the legendary history, the origins of law, class structure, kinship formations, and natural features.

These stories do not as a rule differ in structure from other stories that are told simply for entertainment, but they have a different social function. The less serious stories become folk tales, travelling over the world through all barriers of language and culture interchanging their motifs and themes with other stories. Their literary life is at first nomadic, and only later, often not until the rise of writing, do they become absorbed into the general body of literature. The more serious stories, on the other hand, become the cultural possession of a specific society: they form the verbal nucleus of a shared tradition. The stories of the Bible had this distinctively mythical status for Christian Europe down to the eighteenth century at least; the stories of Homer had it for Greek and much Roman culture.

One should not exaggerate this, of course: myths can also migrate, just as two of the world's greatest mythological systems, the Christian and the Buddhist, have moved outside their places of origin. In the *Odyssey*, we meet Odysseus on Calypso's island, resisting her importunities to marry her, which include the promise of immortality if he does. Later we learn that Odysseus has spent a year with Circe, after he was enabled to overcome the enchantments by which she had turned his companions into animals. In the Gilgamesh epic, many centuries earlier, the hero resists a similar proposal from the goddess Ishtar, telling her that she had not only abandoned her earlier lovers but turned them into animals and birds by enchantment. The older story brings us much closer to what Robert Graves calls the white goddess cycle, where the Earth Mother takes a new lover each year and then abandons or sacrifices him, renewing her virginity and destroying her memory before the next year begins.[2] The similarity of theme points to a good deal of mythological diffusion in the intervening centuries. It does not follow, incidentally, that we can always reach the most authentic form of a myth by tracing it backwards in time. The poets who recreate the myths may also deepen and expand them. Shakespeare's *Winter's Tale* brings a complex richness out of the Demeter and Proserpine myth that is unique in its history, and the same is true of Wagner's treatment of the Parzival story.

The response to a narrative, of whatever kind, has two stages to it, the first being most frequently described in metaphors of hearing, the second in metaphors of seeing. Someone who is about to tell a joke may say, regrettably, "Stop me if you've heard this one," indicating that what follows is addressed primarily to the ear. But if we "see" the joke, the joke is all over, and we are considering the afterimage of its total structure. The metaphors should not prevent us from realizing that we can have a narrative presented in visual terms, such as a ballet, or a response presented verbally. But nonetheless there does seem to be a movement in time, which is the *mythos* properly speaking, up to and followed by an act of understanding where the *mythos* is "seen," or apprehended as a unit. It is this final act of understanding the whole, which for a complex work is more ideally than actually present, that has made the word "structure" so pervasive a metaphor in literary criticism, although the traditional term *anagnorisis* ["recognition"] seems to me less misleading. The apprehension of a total structure may exist on any level from the simplest to the most profound. We hear a joke, but as soon as we "see" the joke we do not want to hear it again. We read a detective story to reach the identification of the murderer, but as soon as we reach it we do not normally want to continue studying the story, at least not until we have forgotten how, as we say so significantly, it "turned out." But in something like a play of Shakespeare there is an indefinite sequence of these final apprehensions: as soon as we have reached one, we become dissatisfied with it and try to regroup our forces for a new and, we hope, better understanding. The kind of literary work we describe as a "classic" could perhaps be defined as one in which the process goes on through the whole of one's life, assuming that one keeps reading.

This conception of two phases of apprehension, one metaphorically aural and the other metaphorically visual, helps to explain the connection of religious myth with ritual. Many types of ritual begin with the reciting of a myth, as the creation myth was read at the festival of Marduk in Babylon, telling again the story of how Marduk created the present world out of the body of the dragon (or whatever she was) Tiamat and then imposed laws on mankind, or the only part of mankind that mattered, the Babylonians.[3] Here the reciting of the myth is part of a ritual which, so to speak, epiphanizes or makes present the myth, that is, repeats the original assumed event in the present. Sometimes the ritual centres on the exhibiting of a visual symbol. In a Christian mass the reciting of the Creed, the summary of mythical events recounted in the Gospels, leads up to the elevation of the Host, and the initiations at Eleusis are said to have reached their climax with the exhibiting of a reaped ear of corn.[4] Zen Buddhism has a legend that after the Buddha had preached a sermon, he held up a golden flower, which caught the eye of the only auditor who got the point, that auditor being, of course, the founder of Zen.[5]

At this stage it becomes clear that myth is inseparable from another verbal phenomenon, the metaphor. A typical metaphor takes the form of the statement "A is B," examples being found in Jacob's prophecy of the twelve tribes of Israel in Genesis 49: "Joseph is a fruitful bough," "Issachar is a strong ass," "Naphtali is a hind let loose." Here again, as with the myth, we have two contradictory messages presented. There is, or seems to be, an assertion that A is B, along with an undercurrent of significance that tells us that A is obviously not B, and nobody but a fool could imagine that it was. Joseph is clearly not a fruitful bough, and the metaphorical attributes seem purely arbitrary and interchangeable. Here again, as with the myth, there is a more positive side to the obvious unreality of what is being said. "Joseph" is an element of personality, and "fruitful bough" a natural object. Metaphor, then, suggests a state of things in which there is no sharp or consistent distinction between subject and object. That is, a metaphorical statement is not so much an assertion that A is B as an annihilation of the space separating A and B. I shall return to this in a moment: just now we must note that the myth does to time what the metaphor does to space. It does not say so much "this happened long ago" as "what you are about to see, or have just seen, *is* what happened long ago." The present becomes a moment in which, in Eliot's phrase, the past and future are gathered [*Burnt Norton*, pt. 2, l. 19].

In watching, say, a historical play of Shakespeare, we discover that Shakespeare has, as we say, taken some liberties with the historical facts, such as making Prince Hal and Hotspur the same age when they were in fact twenty years apart. So we say that the *mythos*, the total story being told in Shakespeare's play, "follows" history except for some poetic licence, which we allow to poets for much the same reason that liberty of speech used to be allowed to court fools. But if we stop to think, we can see that the *mythos* is not "following" history at all: it includes a historical theme, but it twists it around so that it confronts us in the present. It shows us the glorious English victory over the French; it also shows us the misery of France and the low morale of many of the English soldiers. It shows us a triumphant young king about to marry a foreign princess; it also indicates that this king died almost immediately and left a legacy of sixty years of unbroken disaster for England. It is neither patriotic nor ironic: it simply presents all imaginative aspects of a historical situation. The departures from historical fact are in the direction of giving greater symmetry to the story, that is, of throwing emphasis on the unique form of *this* story, rather than on the content of a historical episode which is like so many other episodes. Similarly, the story of the Crucifixion of Christ is presented mythically in the Gospels, although there is no reason to doubt that a historical event forms the kernel of it. But as a historical event, the Crucifixion of Christ is like any other execution, one more manifestation of the continuous psychosis of brutality and stupidity that is human behaviour. It is only as a myth that it has the power to confront us in the present tense, and tell us that what was done then is what we are doing now.

The metaphor, by saying "A is B," is not being logical, the identity of two different things being an impossibility, but neither is it antilogical. It is counterlogical; it introduces us to a world where the inevitable movement from cause to effect, the inevitable separation of one thing from another thing, no longer exist in the same way. A creation or deluge myth, by saying at once "this happened" and "this didn't happen quite like that," is not being historical, nor antihistorical. It is counterhistorical, which I take it is what Biblical scholars mean by the term *Heilsgeschichte*:[6] it opens up a world whose laws are quite other than those of this world of differing and deferring.[7] The Elizabethan critics used the Horatian tag *ut pictura poesis* [*Ars Poetica*, l. 361], poetry as a speaking picture, to emphasize this quality of representing and recreating something otherwise out of reach.

A *mythos*, a story being told in time, is what Jacques Derrida would call logocentric: it suggests the presence of a teller of the story, even if it is presented as a drama. But when we reach the end, it turns into something for which some visual metaphor, like Derrida's own term *écriture*, expanded, as he expands it, from writing to any visualizable system of meaning, is what seems appropriate.[8] This something, this simultaneous pattern to be apprehended all at once, is itself a cluster of metaphors, images and events linked together in identity by the previous movement of the story. Sometimes this metaphor cluster is expressible by a diagram, a pictorial design, or a single image. For example, as Gibbon's *Decline and Fall* moves increasingly from the historical to the literary category, we begin to see it more and more clearly as an eighteenth-century book. That is, there is an act of simultaneous apprehension of the whole theme which Gibbon could have attained only in the eighteenth century, when he could look at the story of late Rome as a growing descent from the Antonines into the triumph of barbarism and religion, after which history struggled out on the other side to a plateau of enlightenment from which Gibbon could survey the whole process and pass his vision on to us. What we see is a U-shaped curve declining and falling until it reaches its nadir with the fall of Byzantium, after which a Renaissance begins to bring history up again to something like the original level.

After absorbing Gibbon's vision of history, we may turn to Ruskin's *Stones of Venice* in the next century, and learn that in fact the shape of that period was precisely the opposite, an inverted U beginning in the "servile" art of the late Romans, rising to a pinnacle of disciplined spontaneity with decorated Gothic, and declining through what Ruskin calls the "fall" of the Renaissance. Both visions are true, just as both the comic and the tragic visions are true: they merely select different data. It is in this metahistorical form that history reaches the general public. Not everyone has read Spengler's *Decline of the West*, but everyone has unconsciously absorbed a good deal of his application of the "decline and fall" *mythos* to our own culture. Similarly with the cyclical myth of Vico, the progressive myth advanced in the democracies from Condorcet[9] on, the revolutionary myth of Marxism, and so on. Here again the ambivalence of myth, in saying "this happened" and "this isn't the whole truth about what happened" at the same time, continues to operate. All these myths are oversimplified diagrammatic formulas, and the advance of scholarship has a great deal to do with qualifying their symmetry by pointing to more complicating factors. And yet the advance of scholarship itself seems also to move toward the reconstruction of some such vision, however more flexible.

What I have said about historical narrative applies in general to dialectic, or philosophical narrative. Philosophers themselves point out that their philosophy is a kind of garment woven over a more primitive and naked vision. Philosophical narrative, like historical or fictional narrative, does more than narrate: it reaches an end and stops, and where it stops it points to a simultaneous structure of how, say, the world looked to Spinoza in the seventeenth century or Kant in the eighteenth. This simultaneous structure is a kind of cosmology, and a cosmology is *écriture* in the sense of being a structure of meaning written over the heavens. As usual, we can see this more clearly in religious or imaginative literature. Most religions, including the Biblical ones, begin with a creation myth. But creation, at any rate in the Book of Genesis, is not a story of how the order of nature came into being, but a vision of nature as *écriture*, as an interlocking system of signs. "Let them be for signs" [Genesis 1:14], is what God says when he creates the sun and moon. Every cosmology is a renewed effort to see the creation as an end rather than a beginning.

As a book to be read consecutively, the Christian Bible is logocentric, a continuous discourse, traditionally ascribed to God speaking through his prophets and scribes, and reaching a climax in the Incarnation, which though visible was invisible to practically everyone. But what it all points to is an apocalypse, or ultimate vision of creation, the world book with its seals taken off. Within the Old Testament, the climax of the narrative is the return of Israel to its Promised Land, after its bondage in Egypt and its forty years in the desert. Here the leader, Moses, climbs a mountain and sees, without entering, the Promised Land [Deuteronomy 3:27–8, 34:1–5]. The inference is that nobody actually saw the Promised Land except Moses, because as soon as it is entered it turns into Canaan, and another cycle of history begins. At the end of the Book of Job, God makes a long speech ending with hymns on the animals Behemoth and Leviathan, which are presented, again, in visual metaphors: "Behold now behemoth" [40:15], etc. Job responds: "I have heard of thee by the hearing of the ear, but now mine eye seeth thee" [42:5]. In Dante we reach the corresponding point when Beatrice finally resigns her oral schoolmistress role and points to the Virgin Mary. In Milton, whose theme is tragic, we go in the opposite direction and end with a logocentric summary of human history, as recorded in the Bible, after which human experience as we know it begins.

Let me give one fairly extended example of how narratives lead up to some sort of visualizable emblem, myth or narrative frozen into a complex metaphor. Mythology from primitive times to Tolkien and beyond has always thought of the world we live in as a "middle earth," with two other theatres of reality above and below it. "Above" and "below" are once again spatial metaphors, but they are no less pervasive for that. So we get the image of climbing to a higher sphere of existence, represented usually by a ladder, sometimes by a mountain or tree.

In the Bible we have the ladder, or rather staircase, seen by Jacob in his dream at Bethel [Genesis 28:12]. Angels go up and down the ladder, but the ladder is clearly not of human construction. It has a demonic parody in the story of the Tower of Babel, built by arrogant man himself to reach the heavens. The Tower of Babel in its turn is related to the Mesopotamian ziggurat, the temple in the midst of the city that provided the means of ascent to the gods, a kind of artificial mountain transplanted to a flat country. Here we have a recessed building with a stairway going up, usually in a spiral form. The image of the spiral, suggesting among other things the organic process of birth from nothing and death into a second nothingness, gets associated with ladders and mountains very early. Brueghel's painting of the Tower of Babel, and Blake's of Jacob's ladder, show them as spirals. There were spiral staircases in Solomon's temple, even though it was only three storeys high. According to Herodotus, Babylon and Ecbatana had more elaborate temples, seven storeys high, with each stairway coloured differently to represent the seven planets.[10] On top was the chamber of the bride, who was placed there to receive the embrace of the descending god: the myth of Danaë, courted by Zeus in a shower of gold, seems connected with this.[11] In Egypt the step pyramids may have had a similar reference, and one of the names for Osiris was "the god at the top of the staircase."[12]

The Tower of Babel illustrates a problem in mythology that troubled both Judaism and Christianity. How was one to explain the close resemblance between Biblical and non-Biblical myth and imagery, if the adherents of the Biblical religion claimed a unique revelation? The simplest answer was the hardline one: all non-Biblical myths had been invented by the devils to deceive mankind by a close simulacrum of the truth. But gradually a more liberal view prevailed that nothing need necessarily be demonic unless it is attached to false belief or cult, and that Classical myths and images, purely as that, could be taken as metaphorical analogies of the myths and images that revealed God's actual purpose in history.

Even so, the central emphasis on the ladder image in Mithraism, where the soul's ascent through the seven planets was so much insisted on, provided a good deal of imaginative rivalry with early Christianity. But by Dante's time it was clear that the ladder had been fully absorbed into the victorious religion. Dante's Purgatory is a vast ziggurat, a mountain on the other side of the earth, up which the souls of the redeemed ascend spirally to the top. There are the traditional seven complete turns around the mountain, and progressing through each turn removes one of the seven deadly sins. The laborious climb reminds us that man's ability to raise himself in the scale of creation is limited, as he cannot fly to heaven. John Donne remarks in a sermon how the angels, who traditionally can fly, still are demurely plodding up and down a ladder in Jacob's vision.[13] At the top of Dante's Purgatory is the Garden of Eden, the home originally destined for man. The female figures that appear here, first Matilda and then Beatrice, indicate the descent of the theme from the ancient bridal chamber. The Virgin Mary does not appear until later in the poem, but in contemporary iconography she was, at the time of the

Incarnation, the "garden inclosed . . . fountain sealed" of the Song of Songs [4:12], or Eden in an individual form. Her mythological connection with Danaë is frequently noted by poets: Francis Thompson [*Assumpta Maria*] and Ezra Pound [*Canto* 4] both provide examples. With the *Paradiso* comes the climb through the planetary spheres, and in the sphere of the last of the planets, Saturn, we see Jacob's ladder again, symbolizing the final ascent to the presence of God [canto 22, ll. 68–74]. As the Greek word for ladder, *klimax*, reminds us, it is the last step on the ladder that is the crucial one. Perhaps it is worth noting that the word "climax" entered the English language originally as a term in rhetoric, a name for a certain way of arranging words.

Dante's poem also reflects the two great cosmological ladders that dominated the thought of his time, the chain of being, polarized by form and matter, that extended from God to chaos, and the Ptolemaic universe, extending in a parallel fashion from the *primum mobile* through the heavenly bodies and the four elements to the earth we stand on. The conception of a ladder of elements goes back to Presocratic times. Heraclitus appears to think in terms of a soul struggling upwards from soggy wet mud at the bottom to the dry light of the *logos* or shared consciousness at the top, and of this again as part of an incessant process of ascent and descent, one in which we live each other's deaths and die each other's lives.[14] With the Renaissance, the ladder of Eros in Plato's *Symposium* began to re-enter the European world picture, on a more heterosexual basis than Plato provides, but still one where the driving force is a love rooted in the human body in a way that Christian love (*agape*) is not. Sometimes the two aspects of love are united: in Dante's *Commedia* Beatrice is purely an agent of *agape*, but her original appearance in Dante's soul, as described in the *Vita Nuova*, was the work of Eros.

We noted that the Bible contains both an ideal and an ironic version of the mounting image. The Classical counterpart of the ironic version is the story of the revolt of the Titans, the sons of earth who piled mountains on top of each other to reach their enemy in the sky. There are also widespread folk tales that associate the attempt to build a ladder to heaven with futility. One such tale is current among British Columbia Indian tribes, where there is an original war between the Sky People and the Earth People, the latter being apparently animals. One animal or bird, generally the wren, shoots an arrow into the moon; another shoots a second arrow that hits the notch of its predecessor, and so on until there is a complete ladder of arrows from earth to sky. Then the animals climb up, until the grizzly bear breaks the ladder by his weight. One is reminded of Blake's sequence of drawings called *The Gates of Paradise*. One of these drawings has the caption "I want! I want!" and shows a young man starting to climb a ladder leaned against the moon. There is a young couple making a gesture toward him, but he ignores them, no doubt in the spirit of Longfellow's mountain-climbing youth, shouting "Excelsior!" when invited to sleep with an Alpine maiden [*Excelsior*, st. 5]. There is an ominous bend in the ladder, however, and we are not much surprised to find that the next engraving, with the caption "Help! Help!" shows him fallen into water, like his prototype Icarus.[15]

In the Bible the difference between Bethel and Babel is the difference between a stairway created by God between heaven and earth and an attempt to build one up from the earth by man. In Milton, where naturally the emphasis on divine initiative is always primary, we encounter, in the third book of *Paradise Lost*, the "paradise of fools" on the smooth surface of the *primum mobile*, or circumference of the universe, where those arrive who have tried to take the Kingdom of Heaven by force or fraud. A reference to the Tower of Babel precedes this description, and indicates its archetype. There follows a vision of stairs descending from heaven to earth, which, Milton tells us, were "such as whereon Jacob saw" the angels of his vision. These stairs are let down from heaven and drawn up again at God's pleasure: Satan, on his journey to Eden, arrives at a "lower" stair, from which he descends to earth by way of the planets.

The ladder cosmology of the chain of being and the geocentric universe began to fall apart in the eighteenth century. By then the centred perspective had vanished, and it became increasingly obvious that the conception had held sway so long because it was a structure of authority, and rationalized the religious and secular structures that claimed to embody it in society. The chain of being was still in place for Pope, early in the eighteenth century, but Voltaire was very doubtful about the *échelle de l'infini*,[16] which he realized to be a weapon in the armoury of the social establishment. However, the ladder remained in the centre of thought, though it took other forms. Hegel's *Phenomenology* is called a ladder by its author,[17] but it is really a tower or mountain stood on its head, its apex the concept that can hardly be found between subject and object, but steadily broadens until it becomes absolute knowledge. Such a structure could not exist in nature, only in thought, and perhaps only in

Hegelian thought at that. But with the coming of evolution, pop science broke out in another rash of ladders, all designed to show that Nature had been patiently climbing one until she reached her supreme and once-for-all masterpiece, namely ourselves. In the meantime, the ladder had settled into place in the two great workshops of models, science and the arts. The Latin word for ladder, *scala*, has given us "scale," the techniques of measurement on which all the sciences depend, and which inform the arts as well, notably music.

If we had asked in 1930 who were apparently the most significant writers in English at the time, most critics would have included T.S. Eliot, W.B. Yeats, Ezra Pound, and James Joyce in their list. In Eliot the staircase is an almost obsessive image in the earlier poetry, and *Ash-Wednesday* (1930) recounts an ascent up a spiral stair to the enclosed garden of the Virgin at the top. The choice of image is not surprising, given the poem's open and avowed debt to Dante's *Purgatorio*, but around the same time Yeats, from a very different point of view, was collecting his poetry in books entitled *The Tower* (1928) and *The Winding Stair* (1933), and finding spirals not only in staircases but in human history and the afterlife. Yeats even went to the point of buying one of the round towers, with a spiral staircase, that still exist in Ireland, although he did not spend much time living in it. After completing *Ulysses* (1922), Joyce went on to construct his epic on the story of Finnegan, the drunken hod carrier who fell off a ladder, an event identified on the first page of the book with both the fall of Adam and the flood of Noah. Falling off ladders reminds us of the story of Elpenor in the *Odyssey*, which enters Pound's first *Canto*, and even the terrible experience of being confined in a cage at Pisa did not destroy Pound's ambition for his poem, which was, he says in the opening lines of the *Pisan Cantos*, "To build the city of Dioce whose terraces are the colour of stars" [*Canto* 74, l. 11], a reference to the ziggurats mentioned in Herodotus.

One could go on for a long time with these images, and others closely related, such as the tree that stretches into the heavens, whose fruit is the planets, or descending staircases and whirlpools leading to worlds below. Nearly all of these are images of what is called the *axis mundi*, the vertical dimension that connects our world with the others above and below it. About the *axis mundi*, we can say two things, first, that it is not there, and second, that it won't go away. The difficulties in such a metaphor begin with projecting it, thinking of it as something with an independent being, and nothing could be more obvious, in this context, than Yeats's remark that all ladders are planted in the foul rag-and-bone shop of the human heart [*The Circus Animals' Desertion*, ll. 39–40]. But to psychologize or subjectivize such an image is equally misleading, as it simply emphasizes the other half of the subject–object split. Such images are not subjective or objective: they are units of creative activity with words, the roots of a language spoken from China to Peru that never affirms and can never be refuted, but always makes its own kind of sense. They belong to the world man builds out of nature, not to the order of nature itself.

Our next and final step takes us back to metaphor. I said a moment ago that such a metaphor as "Joseph is a fruitful bough" asserts an identity between something personal and something natural. There is no question of belief or reader's involvement here, except that originally the reader was assumed to be an Israelite who would be, however distantly, a relative of Joseph or his tribe. But this kind of literary metaphor is a later development of a type of metaphor that links together a divine personality and an aspect of nature in which he has a particular interest or function. To say, for example, "Neptune is the sea" would be a genuine identity for those who accept the cult: the statement would in fact be almost a tautology, like saying that Elizabeth II is Queen of England. The identity of Neptune and the sea is the base of a triangle with its apex pointing to the social group that addresses prayers or sacrifices to Neptune when starting on a sea voyage.

Such a god is, so to speak, a prefabricated metaphor: it unites a personality and a natural object, and is the entering wedge of that union between subjective and objective worlds that all creative activity depends on. It is part of the function of literature, more especially poetry, to keep alive in society the metaphorical habit of mind, and gods are invaluable to poets because they are traditional and recognized metaphors. Gods are supposed to be immortal in contrast to the mortality of man, but in practice the situation is reversed. After all the temples to Jupiter and Venus had been closed down and their cults abandoned, Jupiter and Venus continued to live a far more intense imaginative life than ever before within literature.

More psychologically primitive than such literary or imaginative metaphors, if not necessarily earlier in time, is what we could call ecstatic metaphor, the sense of being actually linked with a divine power, as in the worship of Dionysus in Greece or in states of direct inspiration or possession by a god. Theseus in Shakespeare's *Midsummer Night's Dream* speaks of "the lunatic, the lover and the poet" [5.1.7] as the people who take metaphor seriously. The inclusion of the lover is a throwback to ecstatic metaphor, as lovers traditionally attempt to create a single soul out of two bodies. In Shakespeare's day it was conventionally assumed that a poet began by fixing his whole mental and emotional life on a lady, whose disdainful repelling of his advances forced him into poetry as an outlet for his frustration.

Behind the lover the rather limited horizon of Theseus contains only lunatics. Today we think also of, say, members of totemic societies who feel an identity with the totemic animal, primitives who engage in ritual dances and initiation ceremonies, shamans who make journeys to upper and lower worlds. All these have their present-day counterparts, as the popularity of yoga and Zen meditation and of such books as those of Carlos Castaneda shows.[18] Mystics, too, though they also show a great affinity for climbing ladders and mountains, like the Mount Carmel of St. John of the Cross, arrive at an ecstatic union with the divine, the precise degree of union being determined by the dogmas of whatever religion commands their allegiance.

These ecstatic or directly experienced metaphors are not crude forms of the literary metaphors we encounter in literature and in religions no longer believed in, but the extension into life of their meaning.[19] A genuine progress in the study of literary or religious mythology would not "outgrow" or impoverish the ecstatic stage but reabsorb it. Moments of ecstatic union, or "peak experiences,"[20] as they are often called, may come and go like flashes of lightning, but such moments are, we said, the frozen or simultaneously grasped aspects of a *mythos* or continuous narrative. Within the limitations of human life, the most highly developed human types are those whose lives have become, as we say, a legend, that is, lives no longer contemplating a vision of objective revelation or imprisoned within a subjective dream. The New Testament presents the ultimate human life as a divine and human Logos, but the Logos has transcended its relation to logic and has expanded into *mythos*, a life which is, so to speak, a kind of self-narration, where action and awareness of action are no longer clashing with each other. I conclude with this reference because the New Testament was written in a *koiné* in the ordinary sense,[21] a simplified Greek understood over most of the Mediterranean world. What it had to say with this language was a *mythos*, a story of immense scope and suggestiveness which was the spearhead of its advance through the Western world. Anything that proposes to become a significant part of human consciousness today will have to use the same kind of mythical *koiné*, narratives with a verbal shape that can inform other arts and sciences as well, and draw them together in a unity of thought and action.

18

The Symbol as a Medium of Exchange

26 October 1984

Originally presented at a symposium in memory of George Whalley, organized by the Royal Society of Canada, at Queen's University, Kingston, 26–28 October 1984. From Symbols in Life and Art, *ed. James A. Leith (Montreal: McGill-Queen's University Press for the Royal Society of Canada, 1987), 3–16. Reprinted in* MM, *28–43. The typescripts are in the NFF, 1988, box 48, file 5, and 1991, box 39, file 5.*

The word "symbol" is a term of such Protean elusiveness that my instinct, as a practical literary critic, has always been to avoid it as much as possible. However, the title of this conference, "Symbols in Life and Art," indicates, quite correctly, that it is a word of major importance in an aspect of criticism which has also been central to my interests, the linking of the arts, including literature, to other social phenomena, and the study of the place and function of the arts in social life. "Symbol" comes, we are told, from the Greek *symballein*, which means to put together, or, in many contexts, to throw together. A *symbolon* was a token or counter, something that could be broken in two and recognized again by the identity of the break. By an easy derivation it acquired the meaning of a ticket, say to a theatrical performance. Emily Dickinson writes:

I never spoke with God,
Nor visited in Heaven—
Yet certain am I of the spot
As if the Checks were given—[1]

"Checks" means railway checks, which validate the ticket and guarantee that one is going to the right place. The word is a symbol that takes us back to one of the most ancient and primitive senses of the term.

There is also a closely related masculine noun *symbolos*, which means an omen or augury, such as predictions made from entrails of birds or the positions of the stars. This brings us a little closer to the "throwing" meaning in *ballein*, the sense of something random or accidental which partly reveals something not fully understood. When Mallarmé tells us that a dice throw does not abolish chance, and ends his poem on the subject by saying "Toute Pensée émet un Coup de Dés,"[2] he is using a symbol that takes us back to its other primitive sense. In these two Greek words we can see the beginning of a distinction in our conception of symbolism that has run all through its history. A *symbolon* is something that is not complete in itself, but needs something else, or another half of itself, to make it complete. A *symbolos*, in contrast, links us to something too complex or mysterious to grasp all at once.

In the chapter on "Symbol and Myth" in his book *Poetic Process*, George Whalley remarks that "a symbol, like a metaphor, does not stand for a 'thing,' or for an idea; it is a focus of relationships."[3] This is true of the literary context of the word "symbol" with which Whalley is concerned: it is not true of all its contexts. It is very common to use a symbol to stand for a thing or an idea: every noun in language represents a thing or idea in one of its aspects, and every verb an action or event. The relation between a word and the thing or event it represents is arbitrary, or more accurately fixed only by convention. But if we are going to use words in this way we must employ the words that convention has decreed to be the suitable ones. In medical diagnosis, for example, the doctor studies a set of symptoms and tries to find the verbal *symbolon* that unmistakably fits them. Such *symbola* of course need not always be verbal: in driving in traffic, red and green lights are symbolically related to actions that the driver must complete by performing.

But if we turn to other symbols, such as national flags, we find ourselves moving closer to the *symbolos*, the omen or portent. A Greek flag on a ship may be a simple sign telling us that the ship is Greek in origin. But a nation is a very complex entity, and its flag can be used in any number of contexts with any number of possible responses. Here we are definitely in the area that Whalley describes as "a focus of relationships." Flags belong to a group of what may be called metonymic symbols: the symbol is *put for* a cluster of phenomena indicating what kind of social contract a certain body of people has been born into. If Joe Snitch the cat burglar is on trial for stealing, his case is called Regina versus Snitch. Everyone knows that the Queen has never heard of Snitch and has not the least awareness that she is going to law with him: the metonymy is there to show (among other things) that the Canadian social contract has a central British and monarchical strain in its cultural traditions. Similarly with religious symbols, like the cross in Christianity or the symbols that appear on the flags of Israel and South Korea.

When such symbols are simple visible or audible stimuli, like a flag or a slogan, they possess a tremendous condensing power. Their focusing of relationships can act as a burning glass, kindling a flame of response from the heat of myriad social concerns that they draw together into a single impact. At the same time they are displacements of those concerns: they are not the concerns themselves, with all our conflicting and critical feelings about them. The words "condense" and "displace" remind us of Freud's conception of the dream symbol.[4] And certainly there is something dreamlike about a social symbol of this kind. Like the dream image, it is a mirror of our own identity: it looms up out of a mass of vanished or submerged impressions, and speaks to us from a context of silence. Like the dream image, again, it bypasses all mental conflict. Once seen, it is to be accepted (or rejected, if it is a symbol of something hostile to our concerns), and accepted on a deep emotional and uncritical level. Such symbols may be essential to social unity, especially in a crisis, where their function is to stop debate and initiate action. But because of the uncritical element in the response to them, there are lurking dangers in their use. Such words as "flag-waving" express our awareness of these dangers.

Secular loyalties, however, have the built-in safeguard that they cannot be believed to have an ideal form. A sufficiently ferocious tyranny may prevent its citizens from expressing all criticism of it, but that merely makes it more obvious that such criticisms are possible. It is different with religious symbols. Take the symbol of the Christian church in a well-known hymn:

> We are not divided,
> All one body we:
> One in hope and doctrine,
> One in charity.[5]

Anyone who had been, let us say, on an ecumenical action committee might well wonder how even a hymn writer could bring himself to write this appalling blither. But such a perfectly unified church of pure love and compassion not only could conceivably exist in a spiritual world, but according to its own doctrine it does. Hence it is possible to define the church in a way that would have, to a visitor from Mars, not the slightest discernible connection with that building on the corner advertising a rummage sale. This fact has in the past given a peculiarly venomous quality to disputes over religious symbols, and it is all the more essential to keep in mind that a spiritual church, so far as ordinary experience is concerned, is the same thing as a dream church in a dream world.

One of the best-known discussions of symbolism occurs in Carlyle's chapter on symbols in *Sartor Resartus*. The chapter begins with a praise of silence and secrecy as the atmosphere in which all creative work takes shape, and goes on to say, "in a Symbol there is concealment and yet revelation: here therefore, by Silence and by Speech acting together, comes a double significance."[6] I have tried to show that this is true of the metonymic symbols I have been discussing, and why it is true. Carlyle then goes on to distinguish extrinsic from intrinsic symbols: symbols without value in themselves, like the flags mentioned above, and symbols that have inherent value. These latter include, first, works of art, and, secondly, charismatic personalities, heroes, leaders, prophets, and finally Jesus of Nazareth. The implication is fairly clear that the intrinsic symbol is the reality to which the extrinsic symbol points.

It seems to me that in this conception of an intrinsic symbol Carlyle made the fatal misstep that sent him on the way to becoming a prophet of fascism. A human personality, whether of Jesus of Nazareth or of our local member of Parliament, is not a symbol but a presence. Certainly some persons, like the Queen or the Pope, incorporate many symbolic attributes, but the symbolism is still extrinsic to them so far as they are persons. In the title of Kantorowicz's great book,[7] the king has two bodies: if they are not separable, we have a human leader who claims a more than human authority, which I think is one of the things that the New Testament means by Antichrist.

In his inclusion of works of art among intrinsic symbols, again, it seems clear that Carlyle thinks of the work of art as essentially its creator's personal rhetoric, a by-product of the artist's life. It is true that in poetry, at least, there is a constant association of the poem with the poet speaking. But this is a literary convention based on the fact that the poem is being referred back to an original performance. If we ask a poet what his poem means (or, in still clumsier language, what he meant by it), the only truthful answer he could give would be to recite the poem. The poets themselves, from the authors of the Homeric Hymns invoking the deity they were celebrating to T.S. Eliot invoking a catalyser in a chemical laboratory,[8] have insisted that their poetry was not their personal rhetoric but something that seemed to emerge with an origin of its own. The poet, then, like the king, has two bodies, one a maternal body where the poems are gestated and born, the other the person who is, in Yeats's phrase, the bundle of contradictions that sits down to breakfast.[9]

We have now to turn to the question of symbols in works of art, and the obvious art to begin with is literature. Every word is a verbal symbol with two contexts. First, it is half of a *symbolon* which must be matched up to its other half, its conventional meaning, in memory or in a dictionary. Second, it is a *symbolos*, with a meaning related to its context which will give us one more clue to the sense of the whole verbal design of which it forms part. What makes a word a word is its difference from all other words, but what makes verbal arrangement, or syntax, possible is the opposite: a prehensile quality that words have of linking up with one another. To speak in the romantic idiom of early theories of social contract: no sooner has a noun discovered its identity as a word apart from all other words than it also discovers that it is in fact a subject, and must go off looking for a predicate. The predicate meanwhile has been searching for an object; adjectives and adverbs leap in to extend the world of things and actions into a world of qualities and universals and values, and so on until finally an articulated verbal society takes shape. But in, say, a poetic structure, where the bonding of words is so concentrated, there is a second level of linking up which may cooperate with the syntactic links or may override them. This is the level of metaphors and other figures of speech.

The double nature of the symbol, as something completed both by its context and by its relation to something outside the world of words, still remains: as long as it continues to use words, literature can hardly become as abstract, as removed from all direct representation of what is external to itself, as painting or music can. We see this in a late development of the theory of symbols, Eliot's conception of an "objective correlative": "The only way of expressing emotion in the form of art is by finding an 'objective correlative'; in other words, a set of objects, a situation, a chain of events which shall be the formula of that *particular* emotion; such that when the external facts, which must terminate in sensory experience, are given, the emotion is immediately evoked."[10] There are many things wrong with Eliot's conception: it contains an unnecessary mechanical metaphor (the word "automatically" occurs in a sentence following the quotation), and it is a theoretical principle invoked to rationalize a bad value judgment. It occurs in an essay on *Hamlet* in which Eliot asserts that *Hamlet* is an artistic failure because Hamlet's personal disgust and nausea are in excess of the "correlative" they are projected on, namely his mother. But the excess of Hamlet's feeling is precisely what the play is about, and the hinge on which the tragedy turns. Nonetheless the conception is a useful one, and is closely related to such metonymic images as the flag and the dream symbols that we have just been looking at.

We most frequently find such correlatives in the titles of works of fiction, where a central symbol conveys what the author feels his book is "about," what its main theme is. The Canadian novel *White Narcissus*,[11] for example, tells the story of a young man whose love for a young woman is frustrated by the latter's parents, who are emotional vampires: for some reason they have quarrelled and have retreated into a mutual sulk in which they communicate only through their daughter, while the mother spends her energies raising white narcissi. Clearly the flower, with its sickly-sweet smell, funereal colour, and mythical affinities conveys the sense of psychological deadlock more clearly than any description would do.

We may take the metaphor, the statement or pseudo-statement that A is B, as the basic form of verbal figure, perhaps the essential figure of which all the others are variants. Let us look at the following verse from Isaiah (55:12): "For ye shall go out with joy, and be led forth with peace: the mountains and the hills shall break forth before you into singing, and all the trees of the field shall clap their hands." Passing over for the moment the rhythm of parallelism which makes the whole verse poetic, we can accept the first part of it as a more or less conscious syntactic statement. The concluding part seems to come from a less conscious part of the mind which is nonetheless linguistically structured. Our normal response to such a statement as "the trees of the field shall clap their hands" is something like "Of course we can't take this literally, but—." What follows the "but" is usually some qualification that turns the response into "This doesn't make sense, or appear to make sense, and yet it does make its own kind of sense." What we have to do with such a metaphor is look into the empty space between what it appears to be saying and what is obviously untrue about what it is saying. What we find in that empty space is, first, a *symbolon*, the counter or other half of the first or more conscious part of the total statement. Second, it is a *symbolos*, a portent or augury of a state of existence in which nature is totally humanized and responsive to human life.

Syntactic and metaphorical meanings, the meaning conveyed by statements or quasi-statements and the meaning conveyed by the sequence of imagery, have long been distinguished. Gerard Manley Hopkins speaks of them as "overthought" and "underthought."[12] In very ironic structures the stated meaning can even be a disguise for the figurative one, or, in Eliot's phrase, a piece of meat thrown by a burglar to keep a watchdog quiet.[13] The watchdog in this case is the anxiety of a reading or listening public. If we listen to the opening scenes of Shakespeare's *Henry V*, for instance, we hear, superficially, what the original audience wanted to hear, the patriotic nobles of England urging a heroic king to invade France and clean up on a lot of foreigners. If we listen more closely to the metaphorical imagery, we hear something much more ominous and foreboding. England, says the Archbishop of Canterbury, a century earlier sent the King of Scotland a prisoner to Edward III, then fighting in France:

> To fill King Edward's fame with prisoner kings,
> And make her [England's] chronicle as rich with praise
> As is the ooze and bottom of the sea
> With sunken wrack and sumless treasuries. [1.2.162–5]

It is also generally recognized that the metaphorical texture is less under the control of the conscious will than the syntactic one. Ever since Aristotle's *Poetics* it has been said that the ability to think metaphorically is the distinguishing mark of the poet, what he must be born with, and is the one thing that he cannot learn from others.[14]

If we examine these two levels of meaning in a major poet, we usually find that the syntactic meaning is infinitely varied and flexible, but that the metaphors used are much less so. They tend to cluster around certain repeating images, as though they were building up a kind of structure based on recurring units. Let us look at a sonnet by Sir Thomas Wyatt, written in the reign of Henry VIII:

> My galley chargéd with forgetfulness
> Thorough sharp seas, in winter nights doth pass

'Tween rock and rock, and eke mine enemy, alas,
That is my lord, steereth with cruelness;
And every oar a thought in readiness,
As though that death were light in such a case.
And endless wind doth tear the sail apace
Of forcéd sighs and trusty fearfulness;
A rain of tears, a cloud of dark disdain,
Hath done the wearied cords great hinderance;
Wreathéd with error and eke with ignorance.
The stars be hid that led me to this pain;
Drownéd is Reason, that should me comfort;
And I remain, despairing of the port.

This poem is based on a sonnet of Petrarch, and is sometimes said to be a translation, though "paraphrase" is more accurate. I think it a tighter and more completely realized poem than Petrarch's. It was first published, not in Wyatt's lifetime, but fifteen years after his death in an anthology known as *Tottel's Miscellany*. The Tottel editor provides the poem with a fancy title: *The Lover Compareth his State to a Ship in Perilous Storm Tossed on the Sea*. This suggests that the poem is an allegory, a narrative illustrating a concept. Perhaps it is: it certainly uses allegorical techniques, such as personification ("Wreathéd with error and eke with ignorance"). But I should prefer to think of the controlling design as analogical metaphor. Two vivid pictures, of a despairing lover and a foundering ship, are set up facing each other, each reflected in the other, with occasional points of coincidence such as the "lord," who is both the master of the ship and the god of love, and the hidden "stars," which are both the concealed stars of a stormy sky and the averted eyes of an indifferent or absent lady.

The narrative of the sonnet proceeds straight ahead, glancing at a great variety of entities on its way. But its metaphorical meaning, its under-thought, is totally absorbed into this single structure of two reflecting pictures. We note that the specifically poetic features in the sounds of the poem reinforce the metaphorical rather than the syntactic organization. Rhyme emphasizes recurring and echoing sounds; metre recurring and echoic movement. There is also an unobtrusive imitative harmony, as "'Tween rock and rock, and eke mine enemy, alas," where the *k*'s stick up like rocks, or "Thorough sharp seas," where the sibilants hiss like wind in sails. The relation between words and the things they describe is arbitrary: the effect of these devices is to minimize the arbitrariness, to suggest an incantation with some hidden link between what is said and the objective world it is, so to speak, said *at*. Modern free verse may dispense with formal devices like rhyme or metre, but its discontinuous rhythm breaks up the syntactic structure into meditative fragments. Instead of a suggestion of a magical connection between words and the world, it suggests, not exactly that reality is verbal, but that our only possible contact with reality must be verbal or something closely related to the verbal, such as the pictorial or the musical. In modern poetry, reality is absorbed into what Wallace Stevens calls "a world of words to the end of it" [*Description without Place*, pt. 7, l. 5].

One inference from all this is familiar to students of literature. Poetry speaks the totality of language, the language of the subconscious as well as the language of consciousness; the language of emotion as well as the language of intelligence. The units of this language, whether words or images or even letters, are symbolic in relation both to their own verbal context and to the external entities they represent. The Romantic poets, beginning with Blake, adapted the word "imagination," which had previously had the general meaning of hallucinatory vision, to express this linguistic union of conscious and unconscious, the language of reason united to the language of feeling. One principle that emerges here is that every conscious verbal construct, such as a metaphysical system, is founded on less conscious metaphorical ones, usually diagrams of some kind. The other is that criticism cannot deal with literature unless it recognizes the creativity of metaphor in poetic language, and recognizes also that metaphor cannot be described except by another metaphor.

Sometimes such a metaphorical understructure of thought changes without notice. The Romantic critics put metaphorical above syntactic language, a "higher" against a "lower" reason. In this post-Freudian era, aware of the connection of creative power with repression and dream states, we tend to put it below. In between came the *symboliste* movement, which put them side by side, with their backs turned to each other. It is common knowledge that *symbolisme* was a development mainly in French literature, influenced by Wagner and Baudelaire, and, through Baudelaire, Edgar Allan Poe. *Symbolisme* emphasized how words made their own kind of reality, and were not merely servomechanisms calling up nonverbal elements of experience. It reacted against rhetorical poetry, and often seemed hermetic and puzzling, because it insisted that the reader should think metaphorically, instead of regarding metaphor as "poetic licence," a concession to immature intelligence.

Earlier critics, such as Edmund Wilson, had an easy way of writing off this movement: they described it as a movement of almost total subjectivity, where reality consists of one's own moods and perceptions, which have to be indirectly suggested or evoked rather than described.[15] Certainly the subjectivity is there, to a degree that is occasionally funny or grotesque. For example, Des Esseintes, the hero of Huysmans's *À Rebours*, who admires Dickens, decides to take a trip to England.[16] He packs his bags, takes a train to Paris, and a taxi to Galignani's, buys a guide to England, and visits a restaurant that caters to English tourists, where he eats an English meal surrounded by people he identifies with characters from Dickens. Then he goes home. He does not have to get sick on a channel crossing, endure any more English weather (it is pouring rain in Paris), or eat any more English food. He has had all the pleasure and none of the trouble of a trip to England, and to follow this symbolic journey with a real one would be most pedestrian and literal-minded.

In Villiers de l'Isle-Adam's dramatic romance, *Axël*, there is a somewhat grislier version of the same principle. The hero is sitting on top of a vast treasure: he goes down to it and finds the heroine about to plunder it—how she got there would take too long to explain. She tries to kill him, but they fall in love instead. The hero decides that, again, they have had the one moment worth living for in their lives, and to go on to consummate their union, or, worse still, go on the extended honeymoon that the heroine proposes, would be simply anticlimax. So the hero proposes mutual suicide: "as for living," he says, "our servants will do that for us."[17] It is not said what the surviving servants are to live on.

The conception of "peak experiences,"[18] as they have come to be called, is found in other writers too, notably Pater.[19] Such experiences are symbolic, and reflect our two traditional meanings of "symbol": they are portents or auguries of what life could be, and it is worth any amount of commonplace life to purchase one of them. But *symbolisme*, the movement that produced Mallarmé and Laforgue and Valéry and Rilke, is very much more than merely a paradoxical cult of introversion, and it gives the conception of "symbol" a new dimension.

The earlier poetry of Rilke, for example, the poetry of the *Neue Gedichte* of 1907–8, is a poetry full of "things," of emotions let loose in a world of Eliot's "correlatives" ready to respond to and complete them. The main influences on him at that time, Rodin's sculpture and Picasso's blue-period painting, are representational, even to some degree realistic. Rilke then fell into a long period of silence, and at the end of it came two works, the *Duino Elegies* and the *Orpheus* sonnets, almost simultaneously. According to a long letter he wrote at the time, the world of things had to be interiorized, the visible world transmuted into the invisible, before the later poetry could take shape.[20] Man's spiritual evolution has to proceed in the direction of moving from a physical into a symbolic world. In the *Elegies* the symbol of the "angel" appears, representing the kind of being for whom this transcendence has been accomplished, and of course Orpheus is preeminently the artist who can transform his physical environment at will. Rilke emphasizes that his conception is not Christian, but it is clearly religious in most senses of the term, an almost Neoplatonic or Gnostic effort to find through words, and through the symbolic relationships of words, a more intense mode of life and experience.

In Mallarmé it is clearer that what Rilke calls an invisible world is a verbal world created in a certain way. In one place Mallarmé speaks of "transposition" and "structure" as characteristic of the poetic process.[21] The poet has to use the same words that everyone else uses, but as they do not belong in ordinary syntactic structures, words in poetry become as distinct from their everyday use as the tones of a violin are from noises in the street. The verbal world is the form for which external reality supplies the material. But there is a single verbal or symbolic world, not just a pile of poems, and this symbolic world, or "supreme fiction" as Wallace Stevens calls it,[22] is forged in defiance of external reality. The world of reality dies into nothing; the symbolic world is born from nothing, for a symbol to begin with is nothing apart from the context that forms around it and completes it.

So although Mallarmé speaks of God as an old scarecrow whom he has at last overcome,[23] he also speaks in his letters of a symbolic death and resurrection that he has attained through his search for a pure poetry, and speaks also of the poet who creates in the teeth of *the* creation, so to speak, as though he were the vehicle of a holy spirit. "Man's duty," he says, "is to observe with the eyes of the divinity; for if his connection with that divinity is to be made clear, it can be expressed only by the pages of the open book in front of him."[24] He also describes himself, in a letter to Cazalis, as "one of the ways the Spiritual Universe has found to see Itself, unfold Itself through what used to be me."[25]

Mallarmé's monologue drama, or whatever it is, called *Igitur*, depicts a man (though he is said to be a young child) descending to the tombs of his ancestors, where he blows out his candle, throws dice, and lies down on the ashes of his ancestors. A throw of dice does not abolish chance,

Mallarmé says, but it is a gesture of defiance against the totality of chance: it defines a world where chance and choice are one, in Yeats's phrase.[26] So the ashes may be phoenix ashes after all. Igitur does not commit suicide (if he does) merely because, like the lovers in *Axël*, he is afraid that the rest of his life will be an anticlimax. He has entered the world of nothingness because it is there that everything has to renew itself.

Mallarmé's symbolic world, then, is not a Platonic world above the physical one, nor a world of buried treasure below it, nor a private world inside it. It is the world where human creation comes to be, where meaning is, where chance is not abolished but where a world that within itself is not chance has taken shape. It is not a subjective world, because, as Rilke says, all poets are manifestations of the same Orpheus.[27] Symbols intercommunicate: they are not, like dream symbols, parts of a code to be interpreted by unknown or repressed desires within a dreamer. So although we have become increasingly aware, in the last century, of the close connection between dreaming and the poetic process, it seems to me that Keats's principle that "The poet and the dreamer are distinct" [*The Fall of Hyperion*, canto 1, l. 199] still holds up.

It should be becoming clearer that a symbol is a unit of meaning, that is, an image *plus*. If someone knowing nothing of physics examines the traces left in an atom-smashing cloud chamber along with a physicist, or if someone knowing nothing of geology goes for a walk with a geologist and sees a mountainside exposing a series of rock strata, the two see the same images, but only the trained eye sees them symbolically, as units meaning something in a context of knowledge. Freud became one of the great pioneers of contemporary thought as soon as he realized that dream images were dream symbols, in the subjective context I just mentioned. On the other hand, there is probably no human society that has not attached some kind of symbolic value to dream images. So perhaps the ability to see the image as a symbol, as a unit to be completed by an understander or by a context, may be, as Cassirer among others suggests, the distinctively human element in consciousness.[28]

The word "symbol" enters the English language in the fifteenth century in the sense of a dogma, or articulated doctrine of religion. We find "the credo and symbol of our faith" in Caxton.[29] This meaning of the word is a late derivation of *symbolon* through Latin. Since then, the meanings of symbolism and faith have widely diverged: symbolism now means to us something that may or may not suggest a belief, but bypasses belief, and does not commit us to acceptance of any specific body of values. It is in their doctrines or conceptual languages that religions disagree: symbols form part of a universal language. And yet a historical religion does establish a framework of understanding that confers symbolic meanings on images, and such a framework may persist unconsciously, however strongly repudiated by the consciousness. In studying poets who have talked about symbolism, I find those who, like Mallarmé and Rilke, explicitly repudiate the association with doctrinal Christianity most useful, because it is in them that the historical Christian shape of the framework organizing their conceptions emerges most clearly, more clearly than it does in, say, Claudel or Auden. It is not surprising in any case to find that the whole program of nineteenth-century *symbolisme* was anticipated in the seventeenth century by Andrew Marvell, the Puritan member of Parliament for Hull, in the familiar lines of *The Garden*:

> Meanwhile the mind, from pleasure less,
> Withdraws into its happiness;
> The mind, that ocean where each kind
> Does straight its own resemblance find.
> Yet it creates, transcending these,
> Far other worlds, and other seas,
> Annihilating all that's made
> To a green thought in a green shade. [ll. 41–8]

I have now come within sight of my title, "The Symbol as a Medium of Exchange." The basis for the title is an aphorism of Heraclitus: "There is exchange of all things for fire and of fire for all things, as there is of wares for gold and of gold for wares."[30] Heraclitus is concerned with the perennial theme of the one and the many, the world of "all things" and the sense of unity that the mind constantly struggles for,[31] which emerges in some form in practically every effort to make sense of a pluralistic world. Heraclitus's teaching appears to include some metaphorical conception of a ladder of elements. Earth, wet mud, and water are at the bottom of this ladder: people with undisciplined emotions and undeveloped intelligence are soggy and moist. As they rise in the scale of being they become drier and warmer, and capable of sharing in the common light of experience that Heraclitus calls the *logos*. On the top level of fire, where there is dryness and light, we begin to experience the unity of things instead of simply their plurality. But unity, the oneness of things, cannot be expressed except by such a symbol as the word "fire" provides. Heraclitus apparently does not think that we go up to an "other" world where, in Yeats's phrase again, we stand indefinitely in God's holy fire [*Sailing to Byzantium*, l. 17]. Sooner or later the descent back to the world of things takes place, and we begin to sink from the dry light of fire to the mud-vision of the dreaming ego. Perhaps everything consists of these two movements: of death passing into nothingness, of new life coming to birth from the same nothingness. We live each other's deaths and die each other's lives,[32] he says: we move from "all things" to the unity they symbolize, and find that the symbol of unity, the fire, is also the symbol of all things. If so, then the illustration of buying wares with gold is to be taken seriously: we may have one or the other, but not both.

And yet it is possible that he is speaking of an interchange rather than simply an exchange. "All things" are wholes, yet surely every one of them must have something of what Heraclitus symbolizes by fire in it. What he calls fire, on the other hand, is a whole which may illuminate "all things" rather than causing them to disappear. Let us go back to the early English meaning of symbol as dogma. One of the central dogmas in Christianity is that of the Eucharist, which develops from Paul's conceptions both of being in Christ and of having Christ in himself. Christ is a whole of which we are parts, and at the same time we as individuals are wholes of which Christ is a part. The rite of the Eucharist expresses this paradoxical interchanging of part and whole, the world of fire and the world of all things. The Reformation did not change this doctrine, so far as its symbolism is concerned, but it put more emphasis on another aspect of it. We exist in Christ as the Word of God; as individuals reading the Word of God in the Bible, we are wholes of which the Word is part, so part and whole interchange again.

These are statements of belief, because they are attached to the centre of a specific religion. They could be loosely or vaguely attached, as in Edgar Allan Poe's cosmological essay *Eureka*, which ends in the contemplation of "this Divine Being, who thus passes his Eternity in perpetual variation of Concentrated Self and almost Infinite Self-Diffusion."[33] Poe puts in the word "almost" because he will not concede the infinity of the universe. But they could be stated with no such attachments at all, and then they would cease to be statements of belief, or gestures toward it like Poe's, and become simply statements of experience. The teachings of Zen Buddhism have been summarized in the formula: "First there is a tree and a mountain; then there is no tree and no mountain; then there is a tree and a mountain."[34] First, simple images, then a state of enlightenment in which particulars vanish, and finally a return to the world of images, now not the less images for having been transformed into symbols of enlightenment. Whatever the English word "enlightenment" may translate from Sanscrit or Japanese, the word itself is clearly not far away from Heraclitus's "fire." Every creative achievement is an invention, and to invent something is, subjectively, to construct it, and, objectively, to find it. A scientist discovers something new in his science, alone, or, more likely nowadays, with the help of forty or fifty colleagues, collects his Nobel Prize, and adds something to the total structure of the science in his time. Before long the entire world picture of which that scientific structure forms part begins to change, in the manner set out in Thomas Kuhn's now classical study, *The Structure of Scientific Revolutions*. I have only to add that no scientific revolution is confined to science: there are invariably parallel and closely related revolutions going on in all other areas of culture, even though they may come at slightly different times. Whenever they come, that curious union of thing and meaning that we call a symbol shows once more that it is neither static nor arbitrary, but part of the continuing presence of our own becoming and being.

19

The Expanding World of Metaphor

8 December 1984

Originally presented as a plenary lecture at the 75th anniversary meeting of the American Academy of Religion in Chicago. From the Journal of the American Academy of Religion, *53 (December 1985): 585–98. Reprinted in* MM, *108–23.*

Frye presented two slightly different versions of this paper in April of the same year; substantial variants are indicated here in endnotes. The first, "Expanding the Boundaries of Literature," was given as an address to the Victoria University Alumni, Toronto, 10 April 1984. The second, "The Social Authority of the Writer," was presented at the Library of Congress, Washington, D.C., 24 April 1984. The typescript of the former talk is in the NFF, 1988, box 48, file 6; typescripts of the latter are in the NFF, 1988, box 48, files 5–6. "The Social Authority of the Writer" is also available on audiotape and videotape at the Library of Congress.

I

Let us start with literature, and with the fact that literature is an art of words. That means, in the first place, a difference of emphasis between the art and the words. If we choose the emphasis on words, we soon begin to relate the verbal structures we call literary to other verbal structures. We find that there are no clearly marked boundaries, only centres of interest. There are many writers, ranging from Plato to Sartre, whom it is difficult, or more accurately unnecessary, to classify as literary or philosophical. Gradually more and more boundaries dissolve, including the boundary between creators and critics, as every criticism is also a recreation. Sooner or later, in pursuing this direction of study, literary criticism, philosophy, and most of the social sciences come to converge on the study of language itself. The characteristics of language are clearly the essential clue to the nature of everything built out of language.

The developments in linguistics and semiotics in the last quarter-century have shown us how language both expresses and structures our consciousness in time and space. I speak of these developments only in passing, because there are many scholars who can speak about them with more authority than I can. In this area of study a word is primarily a signifier, related arbitrarily, or more precisely by convention, to what it signifies. What makes a word a word is its difference from other words, and what gives words a public meaning for a community is the disentangling of them from the associations of those who use them, including the author. Jacques Derrida in particular has emphasized that this attitude to language is one in which writing or printing is logically prior to the spoken word.[1] In oral discourse the words are still, in a manner of speaking, unborn, still attached to an enclosing presence or speaking personality.

We can also, however, turn to the other emphasis on the *art* of words, where we begin with a practical commonsense distinction in which, say, Keats and Shelley are poets and not philosophers, and Kant and Hegel philosophers and not poets. Again there are no definable boundaries, and no one asserts that there are, but we do have, in practice, a distinctive area in which literature has the same kind of integrity that music has when distinguished from songs of birds or noises in the street. The painter René Magritte painted a highly representational picture of a pipe and gave it the title *This Is Not a Pipe*, and one can see very well what he means. The centre of the art of words is poetry, and from here on I shall be speaking of poetry.

In poetry, accidental resemblances among words create sound patterns of rhyme, alliteration, assonance, and metre, and these have a function in poetry that they rarely have outside it. The function of these sound patterns is to minimize the sense of arbitrariness in the relation of word and meaning, to suggest a quasi-magical connection between the verbal arrangement and the things it evokes. Puns and different or ambiguous associations bound up in a single word seem to be structural principles rather than obstacles to meaning. Above all, in poetry we are in the area of figurative language, where the status of the word as a word is called to our attention, and the relation of that word to its context has to be given special treatment. Of course we use figurative language everywhere, but in poetry what seems to be dominant in importance is not so much the relation of signifiers to signifieds as the *resonance* among the signifiers.

The poet may be very remote in time, place, language, and cultural context from his reader. Hence there are two directions in the study of poetry. One is an attempt to determine, so far as is humanly possible, what a poem meant in its own original context; the other tries to see what the qualities in it are that make it still communicable to us. The critical reader of a poem is one of a large number of people who have read it, hence he cannot dream of any definitive criticism of it, for the simple reason that he is not all those other people. He is a spokesman for a community of readers, and fails if he replaces the poem with himself. But his reading is only his, and it may range in motivation from devoted discipleship to a kind of ritual murder of his poet. We might say that the reader invents his text, the word "invention" having its double meaning of something subjective that we make up ourselves and something objective that we find outside us. An invention comes out of an inventor's mind, but an invention that works must have some roots in the external world. It is normally best to begin reading our poem in a mood of Leibnizian optimism that the words chosen for that poem are the best of all possible words.[2]

So far, there is not much difference between the role of the reader of poetry and that of any other reader. But the poem (one might have to modify the statement in regard to prose fiction) seems to be radically an *oral* production, an utterance. This utterance is not a direct address to the reader; it is broadcast, like a radio program, and is separate from both reader and poet. Poets have always said that they did not feel that they were making their poems; they felt more like mothers bringing an independent life to birth. The written poem comes into being partly because of this independence. If there is anything to be said for Marshall McLuhan's axiom that the content of any given medium is the form of a previous medium,[3] then the content of written poetry is the form of oral poetry, which seems invariably to precede it historically. The subordinate and secondary status assigned to writing, of which so many poststructural critics complain,[4] is derived from a literary convention, but within literature the convention is rooted in the facts of literary experience.

The source of the convention is the fact that the poem, like a musical score, but unlike other types of verbal structure, is being referred back to an actual performance. If we want to know what a poem "really means," we have to read the poem itself aloud. The poet may be replaced by a reciter, as Homer is by Ion in Plato, or the oral reader may not be present at all, except as a minor element in a silent reader's response. But, except in poetry where literature is encroaching on the visual arts (as in concrete poetry, shape poems, and typographical designs like those of E.E. Cummings), there is always a priority of utterance to writing. This convention is closely related to another convention within poetry itself that the spoken words are actually being sung or played as a musical composition. Thus Milton says halfway through *Lycidas*, "But now my oat proceeds" [l. 88], "oat" meaning a reed, or a kind of rustic oboe, and at the end, "Thus sang the uncouth swain to th' oaks and rills" [l. 186]. The impossibility of singing and playing a wind instrument at the same time does not bother Milton. The written text of a poem is a kind of charm or spell: a spell that, so to speak, knows and repeats the *names* of the poem, and has the power to summon an absent present into reappearance.

II

Of all figures or rhetorical devices that emphasize the relation of signifiers to one another, the simplest and most direct is the metaphor, the figure that tells us that one signifier *is* another signifier, even if each term keeps its own conventional relation to a signified. That is, the metaphor is usually presented in some variant of the grammatical model "A is B." Stock examples of such metaphors may be found in Jacob's prophecy (Genesis 49) concerning the tribes of Israel: "Joseph is a fruitful bough," "Naphtali is a hind let loose," "Issachar is a strong ass," and the like.

Such metaphors are curiously self-contradictory. First, they assert, or appear to assert, that A is B. But they also imply that A is quite obviously not B, and nobody could be fool enough to imagine that it was. The metaphor is totally illogical, for logic preserves the commonsense principle that A is always A, never B, and the only metaphors that make logical sense are tautologies with one term, such as "Elizabeth II is Queen of England." Accepting the assertion "A is B" as a statement of fact we call "taking a metaphor literally." I have often enough attacked this addled use of the word "literal," but as soon as we raise the question of "literal meaning," as that phrase is generally used, each term is related to a separate signified meaning and the metaphorical link between them vanishes. So our first problem is, What is the point of saying that A is B when anyone can see that A is not B?

Let us first try to put the question into some form of historical perspective. We notice that a typical metaphor, such as "Joseph is a fruitful bough," identifies some aspect of human personality or consciousness ("Joseph") with some aspect of the natural environment ("fruitful bough"). If we were to think of a permanent relationship of this sort which we might in some contexts have to "take seriously," we should come to the conception of a god, or, at least, a nature-spirit. The god is an early form of socially postulated metaphor, but the god has many mutations and derivations, such as the totemic animal in totemic societies. The Bible does not accept gods or nature-spirits, but still "Joseph is a fruitful bough" is a development of the same mode of thinking that elsewhere identifies Neptune with the sea or Baal with the fertility of the land.

Metaphor, then, arises in a state of society in which a split between a perceiving subject and a perceived object is not yet habitual, and what it does in that context is to open up a channel or current of energy between human and natural worlds. The gods are not simply projections of the human mind on nature: they are evocations of powers of nature as well. The starting point of metaphor, then, seems to be what I propose to call, taking a term from Heidegger,[5] ecstatic metaphor, the sense of identity of an individual's consciousness with something in the natural world. I say an individual, but of course a social or group consciousness is what is almost always primarily involved. If we look at the cave drawings of animals in Altamira or Lascaux, and think of the fantastically difficult conditions of lighting and positioning in which they were done, we can get some sense of the titanic will to identify that they represent.[6] We can distinguish certain aspects that seem more reasonable to us, such as the magical wish to evoke by art a supply of animal food, but the will to identify is what is in the centre. Similarly, the chief "primitive" use of music seems to have been ecstatic, designed to merge the consciousness with another kind of being, like the Dionysus cult in Greece that has given us the word "enthusiasm," and the school of prophets in the Old Testament whom King Saul briefly joined (1 Samuel 10:5–6).

Such forms of ecstatic identification survive in modern religion, and have left many traces in literature. In drama, for example, we require the actor to be ecstatically identified with his role. But gods suggest a more stabilized social relationship of a sort that produces cults, statues, temples, myths, prayers, and sacrifices. Any such metaphor as "Neptune is the sea" is the base line of a triangle with its apex pointing to the group of worshippers who acknowledge the identity. The sense of a subjective consciousness separated from the physical world seems to become continuous around the time of the earliest civilizations, although some would put it much later. In proportion as it does so, the ecstatic response becomes individualized: the social conditioning is of course still there, but its workings in the individual mind become harder to trace. Along with this goes the specifically "literary" response to metaphor: the sense of it as assumed, as putting something in a way that does not assert or deny anything about the "real" world. Poetry thus becomes a form of play, to use Francis Bacon's term,[7] or, as we should now say, there is an ironic distancing between literature and experience. I am not sure that the modern phrase is an improvement on Bacon.

Literature thus becomes detached from the kind of commitment that we call "belief." In the poetry of the Christian centuries Jupiter and Venus are readily absorbed, the more readily because they are not believed in. Of all works of Classical literature, the one that had the most pervasive influence over the next thousand years was probably Ovid's *Metamorphoses*. The metamorphosis, in Ovid, is typically a story of the disintegrating of metaphor, the breaking down of some conscious personality into a natural object, as when Daphne becomes a laurel tree [bk. 1, ll. 452–567] or Philomela a nightingale [bk. 6, ll. 424–674]. When Jupiter assumes the form of a bull or a swan for one of his amours, the original story may have actually identified the god and the animal, but in the age of poetry he is merely putting on a disguise to fool Juno, usually without success.

A literary age tends to think of ecstatic forms of identification as primitive and something to be outgrown, as modes of behaviour that would seem hysterical in our society. Such terms as Lévy-Bruhl's *participation mystique*[8] suggest an attitude of keeping them at arm's length. We are afraid of losing our sense of the distinction between fiction and fact, like Don Quixote at the puppet show,[9] and the tendency of younger readers to identify with (or, in the fashionable euphemism, "relate to") some figure in a book or movie or rock band they admire we think of as immature. Yet it seems clear that one of the social functions of literature is to keep alive the metaphorical way of thinking and of using words. So our next problem is, why should it be kept alive?

I have often reverted to the lines from *A Midsummer Night's Dream* in which Duke Theseus summarizes the three types of people who, from his point of view, take metaphor, as we say, literally or seriously: "The lunatic, the lover and the poet / Are of imagination all compact" [5.1.7–8]. We see that the word "imagination" already contains the twofold emphasis it still has in the contrast between "imaginary" and "imaginative." Theseus's emphasis is on the whole on the pathological side: lunatics, lovers, and poets for him are people disturbed emotionally who see things which are not there. He goes on to say that lunatics see more devils than hell can hold, and that the poet's eye moves from heaven to earth and from earth to heaven, suggesting that the poet is essentially a lunatic on a good trip. The inclusion of the lover is particularly interesting, because sexual love is a throwback to ecstatic metaphor. The sexual drive is symbolically toward a union of two people in one, or, as Sir Thomas Browne says, "United souls are not satisfied with embraces, but desire to be truly each other." He goes on to say, however, "which being impossible, their desires are infinite, and must proceed without a possibility of satisfaction."[10] It seems to Browne, as perhaps to most of us, safer to stay with embraces.

The association of lover and poet is what enables John Donne to write such poems as *The Extasie* and *The Canonization*, which begin with a celebration of sexual union and end with images of books and sonnets. It also accounts for the hundreds, if not thousands, of poems bewailing the cruelty and indifference of a poet's mistress. Few poets in medieval or Renaissance times would set up as poets without declaring themselves head over heels in love: a poet not a lover is conventionally a rather poor creature. The same convention assumes that poetry is the normal result of frustration in love: Eros is the presiding genius of the awakening of the imagination, and poetry is written as what biologists now call a displaced activity, the baffling of love by a lady's cruelty. But Eros is still the driving force of the poetry, and Eros does not care how casual or inappropriate any given metaphor may be: he only wants to get as many images copulating as possible.

Behind the lover, the practical and rather commonplace mind of Theseus sees nothing but lunatics. But even in this paper we have already seen that many of the most intense forms of human experience take some form of ecstatic metaphor. The hypothetical nature of literature, its ironic separation from all statements of assertion, was as far as I got in my *Anatomy of Criticism*, published nearly thirty years ago. The literary imagination seemed to me then, as in large part it does now, to be primarily a kind of model-thinking, an infinite set of possibilities of experience to expand and intensify our actual experience. But the *Anatomy* had led me to the scripture or sacred book as the furthest boundary to be explored in the imaginative direction, and I then became increasingly fascinated with the Bible, as a book dominated by metaphor throughout, and yet quite obviously not content with an ironic removal from experience or assertion. Clearly one had to look at other aspects of the question, and reconsider the cultural context of metaphor, as something that not only once had but may still have its roots in ecstatic experience.

I had noticed, for example, that many of the central Christian doctrines (e.g., Christ is God and man) were grammatically expressible only in metaphor. At that time, however, existential questions of "commitment" and the like were still in the ascendant,[11] and in that cultural frame of mind, committing one's beliefs and values to metaphor seemed like crossing a deep gorge on a rope bridge: we may put all our trust in its ability to get us across, but there will be moments when we wish we hadn't. At the same time I was not happy with the merely "let's pretend" or "let's assume" attitude to literature. Nobody wants to eliminate the element of play from literature, but most poets clearly felt that what they were doing was more complex.

The complexities begin when we realize that metaphor, as a bridge between consciousness and nature, is in fact a microcosm of language itself. It is precisely the function of language to overcome what Blake calls the "cloven fiction" [*The Keys of the Gates*, l. 13] of a subject contemplating an object. In the nineteenth century the German philosopher [Wilhelm] von Humboldt had arrived at the principle that language was a third order of reality, coming between subject and object. Saussure, the founder of modern linguistics, also spoke of a world of "signification" in between the signifier and the signified. Language from this point of view becomes a single gigantic metaphor, the uniting of consciousness with what it is conscious of. This union is Ovid's metamorphosis in reverse, the transfiguring of consciousness as it merges with articulated meaning. In a more specifically religious area this third order would become Martin Buber's world of "Thou,"[12] which comes between the consciousness that is merely an "I" and a nature that is merely an "it."[13]

III

To turn now to a slightly different aspect of the subject. We started with the conception of the god as a socially stabilized metaphor. The metaphor "Neptune is the sea" becomes a social datum if we build a temple to Neptune or address prayers to him when starting a voyage. The next step in this social stabilizing of a god is the story or narrative (*mythos* in Greek, whence "myth" in English) that is associated with a god and gives him a specific character and activities. We find such myths in the Homeric Hymns in an unusually concentrated form. Such myths, or stories about gods, are a normal part of every society's verbal culture: in structure they hardly differ from folk tales, but the social use made of them is different. Folk tales may be told for amusement, and tend to lead a nomadic existence, wandering over a wide area through all barriers of language. But myths, though they also travel widely, form in addition a central body of stories that it is particularly important for a specific society to hear, because they set out what are regarded as the essential facts about its gods, its history, and its social structure. Hence myths, in contrast to folk tales, have a higher proportion of stories about recognized deities in them, and they also unify into a mythology and form the core of a body of shared imaginative allusion and shared experience for a society. They add the dimension of history and tradition to a society's verbal culture.

The myth, like the metaphor, conveys two contradictory messages. One is "this happened." The other is "this almost certainly did not happen, at least not in precisely the way described." The latter aspect has given us the common but vulgar sense of myth as simply a false statement. In Western culture the Biblical myths formed an inner core of sacrosanct legend, where, in contrast to Classical or other non-Biblical stories, the assertion "this happened precisely as described" was maintained for centuries by brute force. Thus at the end of the seventeenth century Bishop Burnet's *Sacred Theory of the Earth* explains how the world was originally smooth and uniform, without mountains or sea, until human sin provoked the Deity into causing the deluge, after which Nature appeared in its present preposterous and asymmetrical shape. The Last Judgment by fire will start with volcanic explosions in which Great Britain will burn faster than most of the world, because it has so much coal. However, in expounding these matters his orthodoxy was suspected and he lost an official job under William III, an example of the way in which people of that time, especially if they were clergymen, were effectively disqualified from trying to think seriously about such subjects as ancient history or the earth sciences. But as, later, people became freer to speak of creation, deluge, and even gospel myths, the positive as well as the negative side of myth became clearer.

A myth is a story, a word now distinguished from history, and of course many stories are "just" stories, making no claim to be anything else. But consider what happens when a great poet treats a historical subject. In studying Shakespeare's plays on Henry IV and V, for example, we can see that Shakespeare used the historical sources available to him, but made some deliberate changes, such as giving Hotspur and Prince Hal the same age when they were in fact twenty years apart. So we say that the myth, the story, of Shakespeare's plays follows history except for some deviations which are permitted only to poets, and are called "poetic licence," poets being assumed to be too weak-minded to handle documents accurately.

But let us look again at, say, *Henry V*. We see the victorious king winning Agincourt and becoming king of France; we also see something of the ghastly misery of France, the greatness of personality which still remains in the abandoned Falstaff, the fact that Henry is being merely pulled upward on an automatic wheel of fortune, that he died almost at once and that sixty years of unbroken disaster in England resulted. This growing "alienation," as Brecht would call it,[14] means that the myth or story of the play is not "following" history at all. It incorporates a good deal of historical material, but it twists the events around so that they *confront* the audience. The audience is compelled to respond to a dimension of time that is no longer purely sequential. That is why the changes that poets make in their sources are so often in the direction of providing a greater symmetry in the narrative.

Similarly, the Crucifixion of Christ was a historical event, or at least there is no discernible reason for its not being one. It is presented mythically in the Gospels, and that implies a certain amount of arrangement and contrivance, such as the way in which the sensibilities of Roman authorities are clearly being soothed down. But to concern ourselves only with the negative aspect of myth, its departure from history, would be to miss the whole point. As a historical event, the Crucifixion of Christ is merely one more manifestation of that continuous psychosis which is the substance of human history, the activity of what Cummings calls "this busy monster, manunkind."[15] It is only as myth that *this* crucifixion has the power to confront us with the vision of our own moral bankruptcy.

Poets, on the whole, prefer to work within their own history. That history tells us that the central event in the past was a ten-year siege of Troy by the Greeks, that Rome was founded as an aftermath of that siege, that Britain was settled as a later aftermath, and that out of the British settlement there arose the titanic figure of King Arthur, with whom no other British sovereign can compare for an instant in majesty and power. Tennyson closes his account of that king's passing with the somber lines: "The darkness of that battle in the West, / Where all of high and holy dies away."[16] It would be difficult to write with this kind of resonance about an actual event, where the chaotic untidiness and continuous anticlimaxes in human behaviour would be bound to get in the poet's way.

The value and importance of getting actual history as accurate as possible is not, of course, in question here. But our ordinary experience in time has to struggle with three unrealities: a past which is no longer, a future which is not yet, a present which is never quite. The myth is presented to us now, a present moment where, as Eliot would say, the past and future are gathered [*Burnt Norton*, pt. 5, l. 19]. Similarly, in metaphors of the type "A is B," the "is" is not really a predicate at all. The real function of the "is" in "Joseph is a fruitful bough" is to annihilate the space between the "Joseph" who is there, on our left as it were, and the "bough" which is there, on our right, and place them in a world where everything is "here." And as it becomes increasingly clear that the words "infinite" and "eternal" do not, except in certain aspects of mathematics, simply mean space and time going on without stopping, but the reality of the "here" and "now" that are at the centre of experience, we come to understand why all language directly concerned with the larger dimensions of infinite and eternal must be mythical and metaphorical language.

IV

My next step begins with what may sound like a digression. Several bestselling books lately have been telling us how the most advanced societies of our time, that is to say our own, are moving from an industry-based to an information-based form of social organization. This thesis doubtless appeals strongly to a middle management who would rather issue memoranda than produce goods at competitive prices. But what is really curious about such books is the conception of information involved. Surely everyone knows that information is not a placid river of self-explanatory facts: it comes to us prepackaged in ideological containers, and many of these containers have been constructed by professional liars. There is such a thing, of course, as a genuine information explosion, but in even the most benevolent forms of acquiring information, such as research in the arts and sciences, most of the work involved consists in extricating oneself from a web of misinformation, after which the researcher hands over to posterity what he has put together, with *its* quota of mistakes and prejudices. The issue here has a direct bearing on the social function of writing.

A mythology is not a proto-science: it does not, except incidentally, make statements about the natural environment. It is a structure of human concern, and is built out of human hopes and fears and rumours and anxieties. When a mythology is looked at spatially, as a unified construct of metaphors, it turns into a cosmology, and in that form it may include or imply pseudoscientific fallacies. The cosmologies of Dante and Milton are full of what is now pseudoscience, but that does not affect their worth in the literary structures they inform, because, as Paul Valéry remarks, cosmology is an aspect of literature.[17] It still often does not matter to a contemporary poet whether his cosmology is in accord with the science of his day or not. Twentieth-century poets continue to talk about four elements and phases of the moon and other such features long excluded from the scientist's universe. In fact, as Valéry also says, the word "universe" itself, with its suggestion that all the millions of galaxies out there turn around one point, is mainly a word to be consumed on the licensed premises of poetry.[18]

There is primary concern and there is secondary concern, and correspondingly there is primary mythology and secondary mythology. Primary concern is based on the simplest and baldest platitudes it is possible to formulate: that life is better than death, freedom better than slavery, happiness better than misery. Secondary concern is what we call ideology, the desire of a particular social group, or a class or priesthood or bureaucracy or other special interest within that group, to preserve its ascendancy, increase its prestige, or proclaim its beliefs. Every work of literature, as something produced for its own time, is in part an ideological document. The relation of a poet to the ideology he expounds or reflects is the genuine form of the "anxiety of influence," and it affects all writers without exception. The psychological and Freudian aspect of it celebrated by Harold Bloom seems to me mainly a by-product of the law of copyright.[19]

What we call classics are works of literature that show an ability to communicate with other ages over the widest barriers of time, space, and language. This ability depends on the inclusion of some element of insight into the human situation that escapes from the limits of ideology. Thus Shakespeare's *Henry V*, just referred to, contains the kind of ideology that his audience would want, and shows a heroic English king victorious over a swarm of foreigners. It was still exploiting that ideology in the Laurence Olivier film version in the Second World War, where the invasion of France became an allegory for a second front against Nazi Germany.[20] At the same time the immense variety of events and moods in the play, which show us the context of such a war in the total human situation, constitutes a vision of life in terms of its primary concern with the struggle against death.

All through human history secondary concerns have kept an ascendancy over primary ones. We prefer to live, but we go to war; we prefer to be free, but we may accept authority to the point of losing our freedom; we prefer happiness, but may allow our lives to self-destruct. The century that has produced atom bombs and a pollution which threatens to cut off the supply of breathable air and drinkable water is the first period in history we know of when humanity has been compelled to face the conclusion: primary concerns must become primary, or else. Surely this suggests that it is becoming a central task of criticism, in literature or outside it, to try to distinguish the disinterested vision from the interested ideology. As the critic has his own ideology to become aware of, this is very difficult to do, and it is very natural for him to regard his own ideology as the Aaron's rod turned serpent that will eventually devour all its rivals. But as it becomes clearer that all the ideologies presented by political, economic, and religious bodies fall short of a genuine mythology of primary concern, it becomes more and more urgent for critics to increase the awareness of their own and of others' mythological conditioning, and thus take up some of their real social functions.

And what good would it do if they did? I wish I had a glad confident answer to this. Previous decades in this century assumed that revolutionary action, self-determination on the part of third-world colonies, and the like, could revitalize our social consciousness, but that has led to one disillusionment after another. Today it is hard to dodge the fact that any form of intensified ideology is pernicious if it leads to another excuse for war or for exploiting either other men or nature. In the late 1960s a state of mind developed that we might characterize as a feeling that the old subject–object consciousness, in which the individual is merely one of a social aggregate, had to give way to a new and heightened form of consciousness. Hence many forms of ecstatic metaphor reappeared. Certain drugs seemed to bring about something close to a sense of identity with one's surroundings; teachers of yoga and Zen forms of concentration became immensely popular; folk singers and rock music festivals seemed to symbolize a new conception of comradeship. It was a period of neoprimitivism, of renewed identity through ecstatic music or contemplation of a visual focus. McLuhan suggested that the physiological impact of television and other electronic media would create a new sensibility, forming bodies of social awareness in which nations and states as we know them would wither away and be replaced by a revitalized tribal culture. In the 1970s he became less sanguine about this, but something of his earlier view survives as a vague hope that some technological gimmick will automatically take charge of the human situation.[21]

At the same time it seems clear that metaphorical and mythical habits of mind are much more taken for granted today than they were thirty years or so ago. There seems little interest in reviving gods or nature-spirits: in contemporary academic journals, references to Nietzsche and Heidegger are all over the place, but nobody seems to want to buy Nietzsche's Antichrist Dionysus or Heidegger's murky and maudlin polytheism. The feeling is rather a new awareness of a common identity of human consciousness engaged with a total nature. This conception of a total human consciousness is central to all the more serious religions: in Christianity it takes the form of the vision of Christ as total man, as the Word or total intelligibility, and consequently as the key to all metaphor as well as all myth, the identity of existing things.[22] But it extends so far beyond Christianity as to strain our best "ecumenical" efforts. The notion of an antithesis between the religious and the secular-humanistic does not work any more, if it ever did. Everyone knows that all religious social phenomena have a secular aspect to them, and the same principle holds in reverse. The specific entity pointed to by the word "religious" seems to me to be closely connected with the principle of ecstatic metaphor that I have been expounding. What a man's religion is may be gathered from what he wants to identify himself with, and except perhaps for those who are devoted one hundred per cent to pursuing their own interests, all activities have a religious aspect as well as a secular one.

In reading contemporary criticism, I have been interested to notice how the religious origin of many critical questions still peeps out of odd corners: in the tendency to capitalize "Word"; in the theological subtleties of distinctions among *verbe, parole, langue,* and *langage;* in the pervasive uncertainty about whether human consciousness is using language or is being used by it. Similarly with poets: Wallace Stevens speaks of a "central mind" or "major man," which or who includes all other minds without destroying their individuality.[23] He also has a poem in which a fisherman with his river and his fish and the doves cooing around him consolidate into one form, though, again, the individual forms remain. One thing that is interesting about this poem is its title, *Thinking of a Relation between the Images of Metaphors*. Scientists too: the physicist Erwin Schrödinger, the founder of quantum mechanics, informed an audience at Cambridge about thirty years ago that "consciousness is a singular of which the plural is unknown."[24]

Well, of course, there are those who emphasize, quite rightly, the social and cultural conditioning that underlies every thought or experience we have, and they could just as readily say that consciousness is a plural of which the singular is unknown.[25] But the real significance of such statements is in a different category from assertions that anyone can instantly refute.[26] What is involved is rather the interchange of reality and illusion that language brings about. We start with the notion that the perceiving subject and the perceived object are the essential realities, brought together by the fictions of language. But in proportion as subject and object become illusory, the world of intelligibility connecting them becomes reality, though always the sort of reality that Wallace Stevens, again, calls a supreme fiction.[27] To the extent that the subject–object relation is the sole reality and the metaphors and myths connecting them illusory, the poet will be a relatively unpopular leisure-class entertainer with a limited function and no authority. To the extent that the subject–object relation grows illusory and the fictions connecting them real, the poet begins to recover something of the social authority which, according to tradition, he originally had.[28] But we can never understand the poet's authority without Vico's principle of *verum factum*,[29] that reality is in the world we make and not in the world we stare at.

I mentioned Bishop Burnet and his discussion of the deluge myth, the story of how human sin and folly caused the entire world to be destroyed. His treatment of the myth may seem to us naive, but the myth itself seems far less so now than it might have done not so long since. If the human race were to destroy both itself and the planet it lives on, that would be the final triumph of illusion. But we have other myths, myths telling us that time and space and life may have an end, but that the sense of identity with something other than these things will not, that there is a word which, whether flesh or not, is still dwelling with us [John 1:14]. Also that our ability to respond to what it says is the only sensible reason yet proposed for our being here.

20

Extracts from *The Harper Handbook to Literature*

1985

From the handbook coauthored with Sheridan Baker and George Perkins (New York: Harper and Row, 1985). The entries reproduced are those written by Frye. In view of the fact that life dates appear in the index of the present volume, life dates supplied occasionally by Frye have been omitted.

Preface

The Harper Handbook to Literature, arranged in alphabetical order, aims to satisfy curiosity about terms like *syzygy* or *zeugma*, concepts like *structuralism* or *phenomenology* or *unity*, and literary genres and movements like *Afro-American literature* or *Goliardic verse*. It is a supplementary text for college students beginning their literary study, a handy guide for casual readers, and a ready reference for advanced students and instructors. Entries range from a few words to summary essays with bibliographies for further study. Cross-references lead from short definitions to larger concepts. A *Chronology of Literature and World Events*, at the end of the text, ranges from the first pictographs to contemporary names and titles. The aim is comprehension, in coverage and in understanding.

We focus on literature in English but include those influences and terms that have flowed in from the great matrix of world literature. *Drama*, for instance, begins with the Greeks; *Romanticism*, with the French Jean-Jacques Rousseau. Students may follow the history of *printing* all the way from China, or the more recent story of the *Beat Generation* in the United States or the *Angry Young Men* in England. SMALL CAPITAL LETTERS indicate terms treated elsewhere in the *Handbook*. The entry on **Irony**, for instance, mentions ROMANCE, TRAGEDY, and COMEDY. Terms introduced and discussed under a larger heading are printed in *italics*. *Individualized characters*, for example, appears this way under **Characters**. We have tried to include all useful terms, but not all terms ever used. Readers will find clarified most terms that might puzzle them when encountered elsewhere, or they may browse through the corridors of literary history and critical thought, discovering innumerable surprises and satisfactions within the rich literary heritage of English-speaking people.

Northrop Frye
Sheridan Baker
George Perkins

Allegory. A story that suggests another story. The first part of this word comes from the Greek *allos*, "other," and an allegory is present in literature whenever it is clear that the author is saying, "By this I also mean that." In practice allegory appears when a progression of events or images suggests a translation of them into conceptual language. Thus when Sir Guyon, the knight of Temperance, enters the house of Medina, in book 2 of Spenser's *Faerie Queene*, and finds himself attracted to her but not to her two sisters, the prudish Elissa and the wanton Perissa, the episode is clearly to be taken as an allegory of Aristotle's doctrine of the ethical mean, as a way intermediate between opposed extremes. Allegory is normally a continuous technique, like counterpoint in music, and a work of literature that seems to have a continuous parallel between its narrative and conceptual or moral ideas, or historical events looked at as illustrations of moral precepts, may be called an allegory. Examples in English literature would include Spenser's *Faerie Queene* and Bunyan's *Pilgrim's Progress*; in American literature, some of Hawthorne's stories, such as *The Birthmark*.

The simplest form of allegory is usually conveyed by personification: thus in the *Pilgrim's Progress* the hero, Christian, with his companion Hopeful, is imprisoned in the castle of Giant Despair, but they escape by means of a key to the prison door called Promise. This technique is very old in literature: the two characters who bind down Prometheus, in Aeschylus's *Prometheus Bound*, are called Power and Force. More complex techniques occur when literary criticism examines, say, a sacrosanct myth which does not seem to conform to approved moral standards. Thus the episode in the *Odyssey* of the fornicating Aphrodite and Ares caught in the net of Hephaistos, Aphrodite's husband [bk. 8, ll. 266–366], was subjected to allegorizing on Plutarch's principle that gods of whom indecent stories can be told are no gods [*Moralia*, 417e–f]. This tendency was far enough advanced by Plato's time for Plato to ridicule it, and it became, despite the ridicule, an important critical trend in later Alexandrian times. Similarly, when in Exodus 33:23 God turns his "back parts" to Moses, because a direct view of him would be destructive, the back parts of God are explained in later commentary to mean the material world.

Allegory is thus a technique of aligning imaginative constructs, mythological or poetic, with conceptual or moral models. In the Middle Ages Dante's *Commedia* was written in continuous allegory because at that time imaginative structures were regarded as rhetorical analogues to the revealed truth, which was communicated more directly in conceptual (and mainly theological) language. As a method of reading Scripture, it was permitted as long as it did not conflict with the "literal" or historical meaning, but there was still a suspicion that it was too flexible to be trustworthy. If A can mean B, the way is open for making it mean C or D as well. In book 1 of *The Faerie Queene*, Spenser introduces the character Duessa to represent falsehood and duplicity: her main associations are with the Great Whore of the Apocalypse in the New Testament, identified by Protestant polemic with the Roman Catholic church. When she reappears in book 5 she is clearly identified with Mary Queen of Scots. Thus Sir Thomas Browne, in his *Religio Medici*, grants that for some Biblical obscurities "allegorical interpretations are also probable,"[1] but it is clear that he finds that allegorical interpretations in general as a way of reading Scripture do not apply to allegory in a professedly literary work.

The assumption that it was a primary social function of literature to provide rhetorical analogues to the truths of morality and revelation maintained the prestige of allegorical techniques until, roughly, the seventeenth century. The medieval habit of thinking of nature as a second Word of God produced among other things the bestiaries, catalogues of the habits of animals, mostly fabulous, which illustrated some moral or scriptural truth. Thus the unicorn, which can be hunted only by using a virgin as a decoy, is a type of the Christ who was born of a virgin. The dramatic rise of science from the seventeenth century onward greatly weakened this attitude of mind. With Romanticism came the revolt of the poets themselves, who could no longer accept the view that it was their duty to be an answering chorus to morality.

If we say that a work of literature "is" an allegory, we mean that allegorical techniques are continuous throughout; but there are many such works which make only an episodic and sporadic use of allegory. Examples may be found in Tasso's *Gerusalemme Liberata*, in the second part of Goethe's *Faust*, and in several plays of Ibsen. The garden scene in *Richard II* [act 3, scene 4] seems to be one of Shakespeare's very rare ventures into allegory. But in Melville's *Moby-Dick* it is to be noted, first, that the author, like the majority of post-Romantic writers, deprecates having the book called an allegory,[2] and, second, that while Moby Dick himself clearly represents many things besides an albino whale, the imaginative effect of the book depends on the sense of a great variety of suggested meanings, and would be spoiled by the pinning down of such meanings to explicit alignments with specific conceptions. It would be insensitive to say that Moby Dick represents the noumenal world or the demonic elements in nature or a projection of Captain Ahab's mind.

Hence it is not surprising that in Romantic times a distinction should grow between allegory and SYMBOL, the latter being preferred because of its greater suggestiveness and because it does not suggest that a poem can be fully "explained" in other terms than its own. The effect of the new reliance on symbol is to break down the continuities of allegory, as when Stéphane Mallarmé speaks of avoiding the naming of objects and concentrating instead on the effect produced on the observer by the object.[3] Similarly, such a conception as Eliot's "objective correlative,"[4] where an image represents an emotion, tends to turn the allegorical technique inside out, so that instead of images being aligned with concepts, they are aligned with the poet's feelings. In the present day allegory survives chiefly in parody: thus Kafka's *The Castle* is a kind of parody of the quest of the soul in *The Pilgrim's Progress;* and science fiction romances allude, usually in the tone of parody also, to social and political trends on this earth.

Reference

Angus Fletcher, *Allegory: The Theory of a Symbolic Mode* (1964).

Archetype. A term that has come down from Neoplatonic times, and has usually meant a standard, pattern, or model. It has been sporadically employed in this sense in literary criticism down to at least the eighteenth century. An archetype differs from a prototype (even though the two words have often been used interchangeably) in that *prototype* refers primarily to a genetic and temporal pattern of relationship. In modern literary criticism *archetype* means a recurring or repeating unit, normally an image, which indicates that a poet is following a certain convention or working in a certain GENRE. For example, the PASTORAL ELEGY is a convention, descending from ritual laments over dying gods, and hence when Milton contributes *Lycidas* to a volume of memorial poems to an acquaintance who was drowned in the Irish Sea, the poem is written as a pastoral elegy, and consequently employs a number of conventional images that had been used earlier by Theocritus, Virgil, and many RENAISSANCE poets. The conventions include imagery of the solar and seasonal cycles, in which autumn frost, the image of premature death, and sunset in the western ocean are prominent; the idea that the subject of the elegy was a shepherd with a recognized pastoral name and an intimate friend of the poet; a satirical passage on the state of the church, with implied puns on *pastor* and *flock* (naturally a post-Virgilian feature); and death and rebirth imagery attached to the cycle of water, symbolized by the legend of Alpheus, the river and river god that went underground in Greece and surfaced again in Sicily in order to join the fountain and fountain nymph Arethusa.[5]

One of the conventional images employed in the pastoral elegy is that of the red or purple flower that is said to have obtained its colour from the shed blood of the dying god. *Lycidas* contains a reference to "that sanguine flower inscrib'd with woe" [l. 106], the hyacinth, thought to have obtained red markings resembling the Greek word *ai* ("alas"), when Hyacinthus was accidentally killed by Apollo. Milton could of course just as easily have left out this line: the fact that he included it emphasizes the conventionalizing element in the poem, but criticism that takes account of archetypes is not mere "spotting" of such an image. The critical question concerns the context: what does such an image mean by being where it is? The convention of pastoral elegy continues past Milton to Shelley [*Adonais*], Arnold [*Thyrsis*], and Whitman's *When Lilacs Last in Dooryard Bloom'd*. Here again are many of the conventional pastoral images, including the purple lilacs: this fact is all the more interesting in that Whitman regarded himself as an anti-archetypal poet, interested in new themes as more appropriate to a new world. In any case the gathering or clustering of pastoral archetypes in his poem indicates to the critic the context within literature that the poem belongs to.

The archetype, as a critical term, has no Platonic associations with a form or idea that embodies itself imperfectly in actual poems: it owes its importance to the fact that in literature everything is new and unique from one point of view, and to the reappearance of what has always been there, from another. The former aspect compels the reader to focus on the distinctive context of each particular poem; the latter indicates that it is recognizable as literature. In other genres there are other types of archetypes: a certain type of character, for example, may run through all drama, like the braggart soldier, who with variations has been a comic figure since Aristophanes' *Acharnians*, the first extant comedy. The appearance of a braggart soldier in a comedy by Shakespeare or Molière or O'Casey is quite different each time, but the archetypal basis of the character is as essential as a skeleton is to the performing actor. Thus the archetype is a manifestation of the extraordinary allusiveness of literature: the fact, for example, that all wars in literature gain poetic resonance by being associated with the Trojan War.

In JUNGIAN CRITICISM the term *archetype* is used mainly to describe certain characters and images that appear in the dreams of patients but have their counterparts in literature, in the symbolism of alchemy, in various religious myths. The difference between psychological and literary treatments of archetypes is that in psychology their central context is a private dream. Hence they tell us nothing except that they appear, once we leave the psychological field of dream interpretation. The dream is not primarily a structure of communication: its meaning is normally unknown to the dreamer. The literary archetype, on the other hand, is first of all a unit of communication: primitive literature, for example, is highly conventionalized, featuring formulaic units and other indications of an effort to communicate with the least possible obstruction. In more complex literature the archetype tells the critic primarily that this kind of thing has often been done before, if never quite in this way.

Bible as Literature. The Bible considered for its narrative and imaginative qualities, as distinct from its religious content. Studies of the Bible as literature often treat the Bible as a kind of anthology, concentrating on parts of it, such as the Book of Job, that seem analogous to the reader's other literary experiences. But this does violence both to the Bible and to the traditional way of reading it. The Bible has always been regarded as a self-consistent unit and not as a miscellaneous pile of small books, and its cultural influence, including its literary influence, has derived from that view of it.

While it is not possible to say that the Bible simply "is" a work of literature, no book could have exerted its immense literary influence without having literary qualities. Its narrative is submerged for the most part, but still the Christian Bible begins with the beginning of time at the Creation, ends with the end of time at the Last Judgment, and surveys the history of humankind—under the symbolic names of Adam and Israel—in between. Its climax is reached near the end with the revelation in the Gospels of the hero of the story. Again, the language of the Bible is metaphorical and figurative throughout, and proceeds by a repetition of concrete images (sheep, mountains, rivers, bread, wine, bride and bridegroom, trees, serpents, monsters, cities, gardens, etc.) which recur so often that they clearly point to some kind of overall structure of imagery.

The fact that the Bible includes a kind of total narrative, with a beginning at Creation and an end at the Last Judgment, has enabled it to form an imaginative framework for later Christian centuries. For example, Shakespeare's *Richard II* begins with a scene in which Bolingbroke accuses his enemy Mowbray of a murder he compares to Cain's murder of Abel [1.1.104]. It ends with Henry IV (the same Bolingbroke) dissociating himself from the murder of Richard II that he had ordered himself, and sentencing the actual murderer to banishment "with Cain" [5.6.43]. In between comes a scene with a gardener who discourses allegorically on the proper way to govern a country and who is addressed by the queen as "old Adam's likeness" [3.4.73]—that is, Adam after the fall, tilling resisting ground. There are also several references to the trial of Christ during Richard's abdication [act 4, scene 1]. None of this makes *Richard II* a Christian allegory, but it puts the story into a frame of reference that the original audience might be assumed to have brought into the theatre with them. The same is true of the opening description of the London fog in Dickens's *Bleak House*, recalling the flood, and the references to the judgments of the law courts as a kind of parody of the trial and judgment metaphor in the Bible.

All through the history of literature, there have been two major modes of organization of imagery. The model for one mode is the cycle of nature: images are arranged in cyclical patterns corresponding to the daily cycle of the sun, the yearly cycle of seasons, the lunar cycle, and the larger historical cycles in which empires decline and fall and others arise. This arrangement suggests an environment of death and rebirth, with despondency accompanying every decline and hope attached to every return. Cyclical imagery, though present in the Bible, is not the dominating pattern there: the Bible seems to insist on an absolute beginning and end. The second organizing mode is that of polarity, in which images of an ideal world are separated from and opposed to demonic images of a hideous or repulsive world. The latter, after separation, seem to be parodies of their ideal counterparts. This polarized imagery is the mode on which the Bible is primarily based: the trees and water of Eden are contrasted with the wasteland and dead seas of heathen kingdoms, Jerusalem is contrasted with Babylon, lambs and sheep are contrasted with beasts of prey or dragons, and the like. This polarized imagery, where instead of death followed by rebirth we have eternal death and permanent resurrection—or what later Christianity identified as heaven and hell—is the major contribution of the Bible to literary craft, as Classical literature's major contribution was cyclical imagery.

Actual literature is purely hypothetical: the poet makes certain assumptions that readers must accept if they are to read at all. The assumptions themselves are not questioned, and it is only what the poet does with them that is relevant to criticism. The Bible can hardly be confined to the hypothetical literary world in this way. But there is an intermediate form between the imaginative or literary and the discursive or direct-address use of words: this is the form traditionally known as rhetoric, where there is an element of persuasion bound up with the figurative use of language. Rhetoric is often (and often rightly) distrusted, but the style of the Bible can hardly be separated from rhetorical address. The term *kerygma*, "proclamation," applied by Biblical scholars in particular to the New Testament, seems to apply to the whole of the Bible so far as its figuration of language is concerned.

Bible, Translations of. Renditions of the Bible in languages other than those of its first composition. The Christian Bible consists of an Old Testament, a New Testament, and a body of writings known as the Old Testament APOCRYPHA. The Old Testament was written in Hebrew (except for a few passages in Aramaic, the language which succeeded Hebrew in Biblical countries), and its text was established in the New Testament period. It is known as the Masoretic, or traditional text. The greatest difficulty in achieving it lay in the fact that the twenty-two letters of the Hebrew alphabet are all consonants, and hence practically all the vowels are editorial. Some centuries earlier, the Old Testament had been translated into Greek for the benefit of Jews living in various parts of the Greek-speaking world. This translation is known as the Septuagint (abbreviated LXX), from the traditional number of translators. Because it is earlier than the final Masoretic text, it sometimes preserves earlier and more primitive readings. The recent discovery of DEAD SEA SCROLLS, which include versions of most books of the Old Testament, indicates that the textual tradition was far more conservative than many scholars had previously considered it to be.

The New Testament was written in the colloquial and conversational Greek, known as *koiné*, which was the general linguistic medium of the Near East at the time. Its writers were doubtless familiar to varying degrees with the Hebrew text, but when they quoted from the Old Testament they tended to use the Septuagint. Throughout its history Christianity has been more dependent on translation than either Judaism or Islam. As the centre of Christianity shifted to Rome, the need for a Latin Bible became urgent, and this was supplied by St. Jerome in the fifth century A.D., in the version known as the Vulgate, or version in common use. In Western Europe, Jerome's Latin or Vulgate Bible *was* the Bible for the next thousand years.

The Apocrypha consists of fourteen books excluded by Hebrew scholars from the canon because, although most if not all of them were almost certainly originally written in Hebrew, the Hebrew original had disappeared, and they could be read only in Greek or Latin. Jerome translated the Apocrypha, but placed it in a separate section. The Catholic church overruled him on this point, but Protestant Bibles also put it in a separate section, when they bother to include it at all. Hence the Old Testament ends with Malachi in Protestant Bibles, and with 2 Maccabees in Catholic ones, both versions deriving their order from the Septuagint. The Jewish arrangement of the books is much more schematic: five books of the Law, as in Christian Bibles; four "Former Prophets" (Joshua, Judges, Samuel, Kings); four "Latter Prophets" (Isaiah, Jeremiah, Ezekiel, and the twelve minor prophets); and a miscellaneous group called the "Writings," including the Psalter and ending with Chronicles.

In England, the followers of the reformer John Wyclif, in the fourteenth century, translated the Vulgate into English. The fact that the move to translate the Bible into the vernacular was associated with reforming or heretical sects led to great resistance to such translation among church authorities, and caused great bitterness on both sides. A translation of the Bible from Greek and Hebrew originals was made under the direction of Martin Luther in Germany, as one of the first efforts of the Reformation, and this German version is a cornerstone of German literature as well. In the reign of Henry VIII, William Tyndale, a refugee working on the Continent, made the first attempt to translate the Bible into English from Greek and Hebrew, but he was kidnapped by Henry's secret police and taken to England, where he was burnt along with many copies of his translation. However, Henry changed his mind and his policy, and by the time of his death a complete English Bible, edited mainly by Miles Coverdale, was available for use in English churches.

Under Elizabeth I there were two English Bibles: one the "Bishop's Bible," a product of conservative scholarship and approved by the Church of England; the other the "Geneva Bible," produced by Puritan scholars working on the Continent as refugees, like Tyndale earlier, during the reign of Mary I. It was also called the "Breeches Bible," because of its rendering of Genesis 3:7.[6] Its scholarship was not in question, but its strongly polemical marginal notes brought it under official disapproval. Shakespeare is thought to have used a Bishop's Bible for his earlier plays and a Geneva Bible for the later ones, almost certainly by pure chance. When James I succeeded Elizabeth in 1603, one of his first acts was to call a conference at Hampton Court in an effort to reconcile Episcopalian and Puritan wings of the Church of England. The conference accomplished little beyond a resolution to provide an "authorized" translation of the complete Bible, including the Apocrypha, which would be a joint effort of the two bodies of scholars. This translation appeared in 1611, and has been known ever since as the Authorized Version or King James's Bible.

This version was an astonishing literary success. It was conceived as a traditional rather than a scholarly translation, and it keeps very close to the Vulgate tradition. The translators thought of it as primarily a version to be read aloud in churches, and their sensitivity to the rhythms and sounds of spoken language was very keen. Among Christian groups only the Roman Catholics attempted to rival it for many centuries. Once again working as refugees on the Continent, they produced an English New Testament at Rheims in 1582, and a complete English Bible at Douai in France in 1609. These were translations of the Vulgate, following the directive of the Council of Trent, which had declared that version to be the authentic one. Because of this the Douai Bible is further removed from ordinary speech, and contains a greater number of learned and abstract words.

It was not until the nineteenth century that a need for new translations made itself felt: by that time there had been many discoveries of new manuscripts and of historical and archaeological material, along with greatly increased scholarly knowledge of such matters as the nature of

Hebrew poetry. The earlier revised versions (English in 1881–85, American in 1900) were not very successful; considering what was available, the improvements in scholarship were not enough, and the prestige of the Authorized Version was more of a hindrance than a help. Twentieth-century translations are too numerous to be considered here: of Protestant Bibles, the Revised Standard Version of 1952 and the New English Bible of 1970 may be mentioned; among Catholic translations, the Jerusalem Bible, and the Anchor Bible, employing Jewish, Protestant, and Catholic scholars, is an ambitious though still incomplete project.

Comedy. One of the typical literary structures, originating as a form of drama and later extending into prose fiction and other genres as well. The word is usually derived from *komos*, "a revel," suggesting that comedy sprang from the kind of festival which, like the Roman Saturnalia, inverted normal social customs in memory of a lost Golden Age. Comedy has preserved throughout its history the sense of two levels of existence, one an absurd reversal of the normal order, the other pragmatically more sensible. The first comedies extant are those of Aristophanes; they belong mainly to what is called *Old Comedy*, a highly conventionalized form that included personal attacks, Socrates and Euripides being among the targets. Later came *New Comedy*, of which the best-known Greek practitioner was Menander, whose work is known only by fragments except for one complete play recently discovered.[7] The Greek New Comedy dramatists were imitated and adapted by Plautus and Terence in Rome, and about two dozen plays from them survive. When drama revived in the Renaissance period, these plays served as the main Classical models for comedy.

What frequently happens in a New Comedy is that a young man wants to marry or become sexually allied to a young woman; that other characters with more money, influence, pretences, or social position are opposed to this; and that toward the end of the story some device in the plot reverses the current of the action and allows hero and heroine to be united. A tricky or resourceful servant is often the hero's ally; the hero's father or a rival supported by his father is often in the opposition. Thus in New Comedy an absurd or obviously unjust situation forms most of the comic action, and a more sensible order of things is reached at the end of a teleological plot. In comic drama there is, as a rule, a final scene in which everyone is assembled on the stage, forming a new society that crystallizes around the united pair.

The characterization of New Comedy fits the plot. The hero and heroine are usually likable but not very interesting people, because their real lives are assumed to begin just after the play stops. The chief character interest thus falls on the blocking characters. In Molière, for example, the central blocking character—a miser, a hypochondriac, a snob, or a hypocrite—usually has the play named after him. Earlier than Molière, Ben Jonson's theory of "humours" had described the character appropriate to a New Comedy plot. A humour, Jonson said, is a person dominated by a single obsession, and is thus confined to a simple repetitive and mechanical behaviour, which is the source of the amusement caused by the character.[8]

The New Comedy formulas held the stage until the nineteenth century, and were disseminated also by the half-improvised type of drama known as the COMMEDIA DELL'ARTE, which was a major influence on Shakespeare, Molière, and Carlo Goldoni. In the eighteenth century the comic formulas expanded into the genre of prose fiction, and can be found in Henry Fielding, Jane Austen, and Dickens. With Oscar Wilde and the Gilbert and Sullivan operas, the formulas are presented in the form of parody, indicating that the conventions were wearing out. Flanking New Comedy are variants which take it in either a romantic or an ironic direction. A mystery of birth, affecting either hero or heroine, is often the means of bringing about the comic resolution. This theme is central in [Fielding's] *Tom Jones* and is frequent in Dickens. In Shakespeare's comedies a symbolic representation of the freer world reached at the end is often hidden within the action, where it takes the form of a forest or enchanted island or a world connected with mystery, magic, fairies, identical twins, dreams, or wish fulfilment. This romantic development of a "green world"[9] comedy was taken over by Shakespeare from his predecessors—Peele, Greene, Lyly, Nashe—but tends to the spectacular and operatic rather than the purely verbal.

The other direction is the ironic or realistic direction, in which the blocking activities of stupid or obsessed characters are triumphant and the hero's efforts are crushed in frustration and despair. In the twentieth century, when writers became weary of the rigidities of New Comedy plots with their compulsory happy endings, this ironic structure has predominated. The darker comedies that begin with Ibsen, Strindberg, and Chekhov present anything from farce to brutality or terror, but remain within the general comic area because the dominant impression they leave is one of absurdity—in fact, many such black comedies belong explicitly to the THEATRE OF THE ABSURD.

Characterization in comic drama is somewhat limited in scope, because comedy deals with people in groups rather than concentrating on isolated figures of heroic size. The most fully realized comic figure in Shakespeare is Falstaff, because he appears in history plays. Prose fiction has more scope to develop full-scale comic characters: the most notable example is Don Quixote, whose dream of a chivalric society, however ridiculous, is still not discreditable, and suggests again another order of things behind the absurdity. See TRAGEDY.

Epic. A long narrative poem, typically a recounting of history or legend or of the deeds of a national hero. In the earliest poetry of Greece, long poems were delivered on specific occasions, usually religious ritual, which were normally not written down but delivered orally, and were improvised or partly improvised, perhaps by poets who did not read or write. They were known as *epos* or, in the plural, *ta epe*. Improvised poetry of this sort demands a strict metre and a number of fixed epithets, known as formulaic units, which fitted into an established metre. Even as late as Homer one can see the importance of these formulaic epithets in giving to the long dactylic hexameter line an impression of masterly ease. Formulaic poetry still survives, mainly in Slavic countries, and the study of it is illuminating in understanding the background of Homer (see Albert B. Lord, *The Singer of Tales*, 1960). The so-called Homeric Hymns illustrate a related type of *epos*, poems celebrating the birth and accomplishments of a god. The most familiar type of epic now is a presentation of a heroic event in the past, where the material is partly historical and partly legendary. The two great poems ascribed to Homer, the *Iliad* and the *Odyssey*, are the only early epics to survive intact, although we are told of many "cyclical" poets who filled out the total body of traditional history and legend with other poems.

Epic poetry ever since has reflected the overwhelming influence of Homer. In Greek literature the best-known surviving example of post-Homeric epic is the *Argonautica* of Apollonius Rhodius. Roman literature produced a similar dominating influence in Virgil, whose *Aeneid* owes much to Homer, particularly the *Odyssey*. Virgil was followed, in the Silver Age of Latin, by Lucan, whose *Pharsalia* deals with the wars of Caesar, and Statius, whose *Thebaid* goes back to the Greek legends about Thebes. The latter gained a considerable reputation in the Middle Ages through the legend that he had been converted to Christianity. Such epics, whatever their diversity, tend to be organized on a basis of straightforward narrative: what makes the *Iliad*, *Odyssey*, and *Aeneid* attain a distinctive rank in epic is the careful shaping of the foreground action of the poem in relation to a total action that covers the whole story of Troy. The *Odyssey* and the *Aeneid* begin in the middle of the total action, with the hero far from his home and the end of the quest, and then work forward and backward to the end and the beginning of the total action. Alexandrian editors divided the *Iliad* and the *Odyssey* into twenty-four books each; the *Aeneid* has twelve books, and it seems clear that these divisions correspond to a genuine symmetry in the poems as a whole.

Another great semi-legendary figure in early Greek poetry is Hesiod (eighth century B.C.), often paired with Homer. Hesiod's *Theogony* is concerned with myths of the gods; *Works and Days*, despite its personal tone, indicates one of the primitive social functions of the poet, who in times before writing was the walking encyclopedia of society, the one who knew the myths, legends, maxims, proverbs, magic, and practical science of the community. The poet held this function because verse provides the simplest framework for memorization. Hesiod is more closely related than Homer to the tradition of the DIDACTIC poem, the poem on a philosophical or scientific subject, of which Lucretius's *De Rerum Natura* (*On the Nature of Things*) is the supreme Classical example. The combination of the long didactic poem and the long heroic narrative produced what became in Renaissance critical theory the supreme GENRE that only the greatest poets could hope to succeed with: the encyclopedic epic poem, the poem that summarizes the learning of its time as well as telling one of the central stories in its society's mythology.

This encyclopedic quality is already present in Virgil, where the story of Aeneas is embedded in a profound Stoic philosophy of history (see STOICISM) and of the role of the Roman Empire in that history. In the Middle Ages the encyclopedic survey of all knowledge, whether in verse or in prose, was a fairly frequent form, partly because of the interlocking shape of the different disciplines of the time, dependent as they all were on the axioms of the Christian faith. The encyclopedic shape of the Bible, which runs from the beginning of time, at the creation, to the end of time, at the apocalypse, and surveys the history of mankind in between under the symbolic names of Adam and Israel, became the model for such surveys as the *Cursor Mundi* in fourteenth-century England. The supreme medieval example, however, is of course the *Divine Comedy* of Dante, which covers the entire "comedy" or mythology of Christianity in the three great journeys through hell, purgatory, and paradise.

In the RENAISSANCE, critical theory emphasized two assumptions glanced at above: (1) the encyclopedic knowledge needed for major poetry, an ideal fostered by the belief that the oldest poets were the most learned people of their time and by such models of scholarly virtuosity as those of Cicero's *De Oratore*, and (2) an aristocracy of genres, according to which epic and TRAGEDY, because they deal with heroes and ruling-class figures, were reserved for major poets. The influence of these views is clear in Milton, for whom the encyclopedic epic, achieved in *Paradise Lost*, was the supreme effort of his life, "long choosing and beginning late" [bk. 9, l. 26], as he says, and one that could be made only once. In the next age came a change of taste, epitomized in the antimythological attitude of Boileau and in Pope's axiom that "the proper study of mankind is man" [*An Essay on Man*, Epistle 2, l. 2], which meant that long poems in the age of Dryden and Pope tended to be satires.

ROMANTICISM revived both the long mythological poem and the verse romance, but the prestige of the encyclopedic epic still lingered, and when Byron speaks of "an epic from Bob Southey every spring" [*Don Juan*, 3.97.4], the implication is that Southey's romances are too facile to be called genuine epics. Victor Hugo's *Légende des Siècles* (1859–83) is perhaps the most impressive epic achievement in nineteenth-century poetry, though it is not a unified work but a procession of episodes on a loosely chronological basis. The influence of such critical views as that of Poe in his "Poetic Principle," that poetry is essentially discontinuous, and that long poems are poetic passages connected by versified prose,[10] led to a technique of fragmentation, in which separate poems or episodes imply an unwritten epic framework holding them together. T.S. Eliot's *Waste Land* is a familiar example. Contemporary with Eliot were James Joyce and Ezra Pound, both of them writers of great erudition interested in history and in comparative mythology. The *Finnegans Wake* of the former and the *Cantos* of the latter are once again encyclopedic epics, and *Finnegans Wake* in particular, written in a synthetic associative language based on English but incorporating echoes from many other languages, seems to have reached a kind of limit in the genre.

Freudian Criticism. The analysis of literature based on Freudian principles. Freud changed directions often during his life, but each change seems to have had important effects on the criticism of literature. His great pioneering work on *The Interpretation of Dreams* (1900) was accompanied by various other conceptions that explained a good many mysterious literary phenomena. The dream was treated in that book as a construct of wish fulfilment made by the repressed unconscious: the repression, and the fact that the wishes are often forbidden in ordinary experience, made it an oblique symbolic construct, subject to certain mechanisms called "condensation" and "displacement," which enabled it to get past the socially disapproving attitude in the mind called the "censor." Along with this view of the dream came the view of wit as an escape of something normally repressed or subordinated from the unconscious, and the conception of the Oedipus complex as an infantile impulse to get rid of the father and possess the mother. Sophocles' *Oedipus Rex* was seen as owing its power to its dramatization of a forbidden or buried impulse, and one of Freud's followers, Ernest Jones, interpreted *Hamlet* as a play in which Hamlet is unable to kill Claudius because Claudius has done precisely what something in Hamlet wanted to do—kill his father and go to bed with his mother.[11] Such critical works as D.H. Lawrence's *Studies in Classic American Literature* and Leslie Fiedler's *Love and Death in the American Novel*, as well as many works by Kenneth Burke and Norman Holland, show how Freud's view of the crucial importance of repressed sexuality in social life can be made a valuable instrument for literary criticism. There is also what might be called vulgar Freudianism, the attempt to explain literary works by a hypothetical psychoanalysis of their authors, but this is out of fashion and has seldom produced anything of permanent value.

Freud's later work, represented by such books as *The Future of an Illusion* and *Civilization and its Discontents*, took a somewhat stoic and pessimistic view of society, partly because Freud came to think of the sexual driving force as closely related to a death instinct. However, this attitude was transformed into a revolutionary doctrine by Norman O. Brown in *Life against Death* and *Love's Body*, and by Herbert Marcuse in *Eros and Civilization*. In other writers, such as Lionel Trilling, the influence of Freud operates in a more conservative direction, stressing the Freudian connection between sanity and the sense of self-limitation. Freud's later view of narcissism as the means by which the ego maintains its autonomy has been combined with the Oedipus theme in some of Harold Bloom's criticism, notably *The Anxiety of Influence*. Narcissism again bulks large in some of the Freudian conceptions brought to literary criticism by Jacques Lacan, notably his view of the *stade du miroir* and his conception of the myth of the lost phallus.[12] Lacan has also suggested that the unconscious is itself linguistically structured, which is the factor that enables dialogue to form part of psychoanalytical treatment, and naturally such a view of the unconscious, if established, would have far-reaching implications for criticism.

Genre. A term often applied loosely to the larger forms of literary convention, a kind of analogy to "species" in biology. The root of the conception of genre, however, seems to be the relation of the literary work to its audience. The Greeks spoke of three main genres of poetry—lyric, epic, and drama—each of which indicates a specific and distinct form of presentation. The EPIC developed out of *epos*, poetry which takes the form of an oral recitation by the poet, or rhapsode, directly confronting the listening audience. DRAMA is marked by the concealment of the author from the audience behind an external MIMESIS of plot and characters. LYRIC is marked by the concealment of the audience from the poet, who internalizes the mimesis of sound and imagery, presenting it in relation to self only. Since the Greeks, literature has developed a fourth relationship, the presentation by means of a written text that we have in prose fiction.

Clearly these forms of presentation readily merge into one another: for example, anything written down can be read aloud. The epic is a development of the genre of oral presentation by a reciter. In Homer, the written text is closely related to conventions of oral presentation, whereas Milton's *Paradise Lost* is, in practice, a poem to be read in a book. But because Milton preserves certain *epos* conventions—such as the invocation to a Muse at the opening, the assumption that the poem is "dictated" to him by her, and references to himself as singing—he is indicating what tradition he associates with his poem. Hence to clarify the notion of genre it is necessary to speak of a *radical* of presentation, which relates to the origin of the tradition within which the poet is operating rather than to what in practice would be the poet's mode of communication. The dramas of Shakespeare are practical plays for the stage; Milton's *Samson Agonistes* is not intended for the stage, according to Milton himself, although it could be acted; Shelley's *Prometheus Unbound* would probably be impossible to stage, yet in its form it is clearly being associated with the dramatic genre. Again, a novel of Dickens is generically fiction, though readings from it to an audience would turn it, or some of it, into *epos*, and of course, stage or movie adaptations of it would assimilate it to drama.

Because of this relationship to the form of presentation, genre must be an aspect of RHETORIC. In *epos* there is normally a uniform metre throughout: dactylic hexameter in Homer, the four-beat alliterative line in *Beowulf*, blank verse in Milton. In the lyric there is an associative rhythm distinct from the material, the lyric being a discontinuous form which, so to speak, revolves around itself and does not propel the reader into a narrative movement. In written fiction the semantic rhythms of prose tend to dominate, and drama possesses what may be called a rhythm of decorum, where the rhythmical movement is continually adapted to changing characters or moods, as Shakespeare in *Henry IV* switches from blank verse to prose for the Falstaff scenes.

Within each major genre there are, naturally, subgenres. In written forms dominated by prose, for example, there is a broad distinction between works of FICTION (e.g., the novel) and thematic works (e.g., the essay). Within the fictional category we note, first, a distinction between NOVEL and ROMANCE, the latter featuring greater emphasis on plot, more flexibility about including fantastic or supernatural elements, greater emphasis on pacing, which often means using a narrator, and the like. Then there are forms that seem to be literary but emphasize intellectual rather than social conditioning, such as the MENIPPEAN SATIRE, which comes down through Lucian in Greek, Petronius in Latin, Erasmus in Renaissance times, Voltaire and Swift in the eighteenth century, Thomas Love Peacock in the Romantic period. The CONFESSION form used by St. Augustine and Rousseau also seems to have literary affinities. In drama, besides the TRAGEDY and COMEDY inherited from the Greeks, there are ironic plays, black comedies, and the like, where the boundary between comedy and tragedy seems to disappear; we have the subgenre of MIRACLE PLAY in the Middle Ages, which continues in Calderón in seventeenth-century Spain, and a group of spectacular dramatic forms, the MASQUE, the OPERA, many movies, the puppet play, among others. The object of making these distinctions in literary tradition is not simply to classify, but to judge authors in terms of the conventions they themselves chose. Readers accept Jane Austen because they are familiar with the novel form, but Peacock is often regarded as dull or fantastic or amateurish because the convention he worked in is not recognized.

Jungian Criticism. Literary examination based on the writings of Carl Jung. Jung, beginning as an associate of Freud, broke with Freud over the conception of the unconscious, which Jung thought of not as the individual's repressed unconscious but as a COLLECTIVE UNCONSCIOUS which all individuals possessed in common. The process of what Freud called psychoanalysis and Jung analytical psychology thus moved, for Jung, in the direction of reaching certain archetypes common to all experience and recorded in literature and in various occult studies, notably alchemy. Jung regarded this as a crucial step in achieving what he called "individuation," a process in which individuals shift their centre of gravity from the reasoning and sensational ego to that of a fully integrated human being. Jungian psychology, while it cannot compare in extent of influence with FREUDIAN CRITICISM or MARXIST CRITICISM, has nonetheless had a considerable influence, if perhaps more in the area of comparative religion than in literary criticism. It is, however, notably represented in literary criticism by Maud Bodkin's *Archetypal Patterns in Poetry* (1934) and Joseph Campbell's *Hero with a Thousand Faces* (1949). See ARCHETYPE.

Lyric. A poem, brief and discontinuous, emphasizing sound and pictorial imagery rather than narrative or dramatic movement. Lyrical poetry began in ancient Greece in connection with music, as poetry sung, for the most part, to the accompaniment of a lyre. The earliest Greek poets were markedly individualized writers (Anacreon, Sappho, Archilocus), but the lyrical cannot be identified with the subjective. Many long continuous poems are subjective (Wordsworth's *Prelude*, Byron's *Childe Harold*), and many lyrics are connected with public occasions, such as the Pindaric ODE and the Old Testament Psalms. The lyric is, rather, a discontinuous poem, in contrast to the continuous epic and dramatic forms. In the lyric we can, so to speak, hear the end in the beginning; the rhythm revolves around a centre instead of thrusting forward in a narrative linear motion. In contrast to *epos*, in which the poet, or rhapsode, faces an audience directly, or drama, in which the poet is concealed behind the production, the lyric is a GENRE in which the audience is concealed from the poet. That is, lyric poets normally pretend to be talking to themselves, to a Muse, to a god, to another person not the reader; or else, as in the Psalms, they represent the collective "I" of the group.

The study of literature makes us aware of its position between music, the art of the ear alone, and the pictorial arts, which address the eye alone. The lyric emphasizes the musical and pictorial contexts of words most clearly. Apart from the great number of lyrics that can be or have been set to music, lyric continually relapses from sense into sound: refrains full of "fa la" or "hey nonny nonny," and elaborate schematic arrangements of sound in the VILLANELLE, TRIOLET, BALLADE, and RONDEAU. On the other side are lyrics focused on a particular image, as with Keats's Grecian urn or Hopkins's windhover. In early Greece much lyrical poetry was "melic," or sung to music; much of it, too, was in the epitaph convention frequent in the *Greek Anthology*, where we are suddenly confronted by a poem thought of as inscribed on a visible object. As late as Mallarmé we have lyrics thought of as a *Toast funèbre*, or an epitaph on a tomb, and Rimbaud's *Illuminations* represent not a psychological but a strictly pictorial metaphor.

This suggests that lyric is the genre of arrested movement, in contrast to the narrative genres of linear progress. If this is true, it would account for the characteristic brevity of the lyric and for its frequent sense of the inadequacy of purely verbal elements of communication. Even when brief, a lyric is usually divided up still further into stanzas, and the word "stanza" suggests "room," a part of something else that is nonetheless complete in itself. The rhetorical device known as imitative harmony, or making the sound, in Pope's phrase, an echo to the sense,[13] is most common in lyric, where it helps to suggest a self-contained world withdrawn from that of the ordinary external environment.

Lyric was for long generally regarded as a relatively minor form of poetry, better adapted to lesser poets than epic or drama. As a historical fact, many lyrical poets have reached the height of their powers in early life, whereas drama, for example, has never been a genre for infant prodigies. But in the nineteenth century Poe's essay "The Poetic Principle" reacted against this and set forth the thesis that continuous poems were, strictly speaking, fakes, being moments of genuine lyrical emotion strung together with versified prose.[14] This essay had a profound influence on the school of French poetry that runs from Baudelaire to Valéry, and to such English adherents of it as Eliot and Pound. Many of these developed techniques of "fragmentation," or presenting only vivid flashes of poetic experience, leaving it up to the reader to make the connections. Among the critical axioms that sprang from this movement are Eliot's conception of "unified sensibility,"[15] Mallarmé's dictum that poets should not name or describe objects but deal only with their effect on the poet;[16] Joyce's conception of "epiphany," or vivid flash from actual experience that illuminates the work of imagination as well;[17] and Hopkins's conception of "inscape" and "instress," which are intuitions of the inwardness or "this-ness" of something, and hence separate it from its surroundings.[18] See DRAMA; EPIC.

Mimesis. A term meaning "imitation." It has been central to literary criticism since Aristotle's *Poetics*, which included, or at least implied, a critique of the conception of mimesis in Plato, more particularly in the last book of the *Republic*, that made Socrates exclude poets from his ideal state. The ordinary meaning of *imitation* as creating a resemblance to something else is clearly involved in Aristotle's definition of dramatic plot as *mimesis praxeos*, the imitation of an action [*Poetics*, chap. 6]. But there are many things that a work of literature may imitate, and hence many contexts of imitation.

Socrates remarks in Plato's *Phaedrus* that a *logos*, or discourse, should resemble a *zoon*, or organism, a unity from which nothing can be taken away without injury. This organic conception of verbal structure recurs in Romantic criticism: in Coleridge, for instance, a literary work resembles or imitates nature in being an organic unity.[19] At the same time there is a pervasive resemblance in the literary work as a whole to something in the external environment; otherwise, it would be impossible to understand. Similarly in the art of photography, the resemblance in the picture to its original "subject" is the first aspect of it to strike us, though this is reinforced by a corresponding sense of the differences between a photograph and an ordinary sense impression. Literature too may appear as "realistic," or like what the reader knows, though the differences created by its literary structure are at least equally important.

In Aristotle himself *imitation* appears to mean, not an external relation of a copy to its original, but an internal relation of form to content: a tragedy, for example, is a form that has some aspect of "nature," or actual experience, for its content. From this point of view literature surrounds an aspect of experience and transforms it into its own shape. We are aware of the resemblance of the tragic action to human behaviour, but we are also aware of the containing conventions of tragic drama that differentiate that action from all other forms of action.

Works of literature may imitate other works of literature: this is the aspect of literature that comes into such conceptions as CONVENTION and GENRE. Thus when Milton is asked for a memorial poem to an acquaintance drowned in the Irish Sea and produces *Lycidas*, he is imitating the convention of the PASTORAL ELEGY established by Theocritus and Virgil, and makes this point very explicitly in the course of the poem. Sometimes the title of, say, a novel, such as Tolstoy's *Resurrection* or Faulkner's *Sound and the Fury*, will indicate a relationship to something within literature that the author is calling attention to. Here again the difference between what is produced and what is being imitated or recalled is as important as the point made by the resemblance or connection.

In a larger sense every work of literature imitates, or finds its identity in, the entire "world of words," in Wallace Stevens's phrase [*Description without Place*, pt. 7, l. 5], the sense of the whole of reality as potentially literary, as finding its end in a book, as Mallarmé says.[20] Such a world is in one sense bigger than the "reality" it started by reflecting, because the limits of the verbal imagination are not the real but the conceivable, and may include fantasy or nonsense as readily as analogies to previous experience. See FICTION.

Myth. From Greek *mythos*, "plot" or "narrative." The verbal culture of most if not all human societies began with stories, and certain stories have achieved a distinctive importance as being connected with what the society feels it most needs to know: stories illustrating the society's religion, history, class structure, or the origin of peculiar features of the natural environment. A distinction arises between "serious" stories and stories told for amusement, and this distinction develops into the literary distinction between myth and FOLK TALE. The difference between myth and folk tale is thus one of social function rather than structure: in structure there are many analogues to myths in folk tales, and vice versa. But the specific social function of myth gives it two characteristics of its own. First, it defines a cultural area and gives it a shared legacy of ALLUSION, as the Homeric epics did for Greek culture and the writings that eventually became the Old Testament did for Hebrew culture. Second, they link with one another to form a *mythology*, an interconnected body of stories that verbalizes a society's major concerns in religion and history particularly. Folk tales, by contrast, lead a nomadic life, passing from one culture to another through all barriers of language. A literature develops mainly out of mythology, but as it develops it tends to absorb the secular or folk tale aspect of verbal culture as well, an expansion made easy by the structural similarity of folk tales to myths. In the Western world, Dante and Milton devoted their main efforts to recreating the Christian mythology; Chaucer and Shakespeare drew rather from folk tale and legend.

A third factor in this development is the taking over by poets of a mythology which is no longer "believed in," as the Greek and Roman mythologies were taken over by Western European poets after Jupiter or Venus had ceased to be connected with temples or cults. This process indicates the close association of the literary and the mythological: mythology goes on being recreated by poets whatever the degree of its social acceptance. The myths of Christianity possessed a distinctive status in Western Europe until about the eighteenth century; for the last two centuries such mythological material has been used or referred to by poets who may or may not be writing from a commitment of belief.

For many reasons the great bulk of myths are stories about gods or other beings beyond the orbit of ordinary experience (dragons, human heroes of supernormal powers, etc.). As literature develops, there comes a greater demand for stories that conform to plausibility or likelihood; but these often use the same themes as myth, adapted to a greater demand for "realism." Thus the theme of the mysterious or portentous birth of a divine infant, like Zeus or Dionysus in Greek mythology or Jesus in the Gospels, is carried on in ROMANCE, and eventually into the fictions of novelists. Fielding's Tom Jones, like many of Dickens's heroes, is a foundling of mysterious parentage, and the mystery is cleared up only at the very end. One important implication from this is that myths have much the relation to realistic stories that abstract or stylized pictures have to representational painting. As the characters are usually gods, who by definition can do anything, myth normally conveys the kind of events that happen only in stories, just as highly stylized paintings present the visual formal relationships that occur only in pictures. Hence, a movement toward abstraction in twentieth-century painting and a deliberately self-conscious use of mythical patterns (for instance, the *Odyssey* in James Joyce's *Ulysses*) in twentieth-century fiction are part of the same cultural development.

The social function of myth divides into two aspects. First, it is a structure of concern, telling a particular society what that society most wants to know: the names and relationships of its gods, its laws, and the origins of its class structure, its legends and historical reminiscences, and the like. Second, it is a means of symbolizing the ideals and aims of an established spiritual or temporal hierarchy. Thus MEDIEVAL ROMANCE embodies the ideals of a chivalric aristocracy, or, in the Grail stories, of a religious intellectual elite, along with being distantly related to universal mythical themes. If the ideals of an ascendant class are distrusted by a large proportion of the society, mythology acquires the sense of something not true, stories told merely to advance an ideology or rationalize the existing social structure. In contemporary society there is an acute awareness of the false or interested type of mythology that is communicated through advertising and propaganda (see Roland Barthes's *Mythologies*, 1957).

Plot. The events of a story. The word that Aristotle used for plot in the *Poetics* is *mythos*, which is the origin also of the word MYTH. In its broadest sense *mythos* means narrative or sequential movement, such as any form of verbal structure designed to be read sequentially would possess. But in practice there is a rough distinction between fictions, or narratives that are stories, and thematic narratives, or arguments, as in essays. Aristotle appears to identify the *mythos*, or plot, with his central conception of drama as a *mimesis praxeos*, or imitation of action. The plot is thus the central form, or metaphorically the soul, of the drama [*Poetics*, chap. 6].

Such a plot has, Aristotle said, a beginning, middle, and end [*Poetics*, chap. 7]. This distinguishes the plot from the type of narrative which is merely sequential, starting and stopping arbitrarily, as in a diary or in some of the more naive forms of ROMANCE. If a plot begins and ends, the beginning must somehow suggest an end, and the end return to the beginning. Thus *Oedipus Rex* begins with the king determined to discover why his land is suffering from a drought: the reader or audience assumes that his discovery of the reason will end the play. He eventually discovers that *he* is the reason; he has killed his father and lives in incest with his mother. Two things are involved here: one is "reversal" (*peripeteia*), or sudden change in fortune; the other is "discovery" (*anagnorisis*) [*Poetics*, chaps. 10–11]. The word *anagnorisis* could also be translated as "recognition," depending on how much of a surprise it is. In some plots, such as those of detective stories, the *anagnorisis* is a discovery, because it is a surprise to the reader; in others, such as those of most tragedies, it is a recognition by members of the audience of something they have come to realize long before, though it may still be a surprise to the chief character.

The plot, then, is not simply an arrangement of events in a straight line. There is always something of a parabola shape about a story that ends in some kind of "recognition" that aligns the end with the beginning. Again, a plot has a shape that, to use a word appropriate to Aristotle's mode of thought, is teleological: it has a purpose in moving as it does, and its purpose is to illuminate the beginning by the end, and vice versa. Plot in this sense is not wholly disconnected from plot in the sense of a planned conspiracy; in fact, most comic and tragic plots include actual conspiracies of one kind or another.

Thus a plot does not simply move with time, but spreads out conceptually in metaphorical space, just as a musical composition has a score that can be studied as a simultaneous unit. This static way of looking at a plot suggests the metaphor of STRUCTURE. Aristotle speaks of *dianoia* [*Poetics*, chap. 6], which means "thought" or "meaning," and it seems clear that *mythos* and *dianoia* are really aspects of the same thing, as poetic meaning can never be separated from poetic structure.

Romance. In its broadest possible meaning, a continuous narrative in which the emphasis is on what happens in the plot, rather than on what is reflected from ordinary life or experience. Thus a central element in romance is adventure; at its most primitive, romance is an endless sequence of adventures—endless in the sense that the story simply stops, with no structural ending built into it. However, a life capable of continuous adventure is clearly a life for young people, and is in fact a sublimated form of eroticism. Hence today there are two popular forms of romance, one an ADVENTURE STORY, such as the spy thriller or the DETECTIVE STORY, the other a highly conventionalized love story (see POPULAR ROMANCE).

Romance began historically in the Western tradition with late Greek fictions, the most elaborate being Heliodorus's *Ethiopica,* in which the themes of continuous adventure and the postponement of the sexual union of hero and heroine until the end of the story are obvious enough. More sentimental stories with more continuous erotic interest, such as Longus's *Daphnis and Chloe,* remind us that a PASTORAL, idealized setting is very common in quieter forms of romance, and in fact varieties of pastoral may appear in other romance forms: the WESTERN story, for instance, is a modern form of pastoral. In the Middle Ages romance became absorbed into the chivalric and courtly-love codes of a feudal society: the hero is often a knight-errant who destroys giants, robbers, and other disturbers of the peace as tributes to his inspiring lady. Here and there, as notably in the Grail romances, we can see that romance is closely related to MYTH. The chief characters are human beings, if sometimes magicians or disguised animals, but the setting is a world in which the laws of nature do not consistently operate. Again, the central Christian myth includes a romance pattern in which Christ destroys the dragon of death and hell and redeems his bride the Church, just as in the romance of St. George, the hero kills a dragon, releases a lady threatened by it, dies himself and revives, and succeeds to the kingdom. Such proximity to myth, even to sacred myth, gives a dimension of dream and wish fulfilment.

Thus in Spenser's *Faerie Queene,* which is related not directly to MEDIEVAL ROMANCE but to RENAISSANCE developments of it, especially Ariosto's *Orlando Furioso,* the first book shows St. George setting off to kill his dragon as an imitator of Christ. In the first canto he and his lady disappear into a dreamy magical forest so dense that no light from the sky can penetrate it. In this first canto, too, St. George kills a dragon called Error, as a kind of rehearsal for his supreme achievement. Bunyan's *Pilgrim's Progress* is a simpler example of a romance which is a continuous allegory of the Christian life.

In later centuries a greater demand for some similarity to ordinary experience caused various modifications in romance patterns. Some romances became simply love stories, often of great length. In 1764 Horace Walpole's *Castle of Otranto* started a vogue for fantastic or GOTHIC elements in storytelling: the setting is pushed back to an earlier age, where the intrusion of ghosts, magicians, and similar apparatus seems more appropriate (see GOTHIC NOVEL). In Scott, the historical setting, because of its greater distancing, helps the romancer to emphasize the adventurous plot, with its intrigues and mysteries and exciting episodes. Scott was not an allegorical writer, but the possibilities for ALLEGORY in the romance form interested later nineteenth-century writers, including Nathaniel Hawthorne and Bulwer-Lytton, the latter having strong occult interests. The ghost story, which is mainly a nineteenth-century phenomenon, was a by-product of this fashion.

The later Victorian William Morris marks a further development of romance. Morris collected a great number of traditional romances, which he versified or translated or adapted, most of them in the book called *The Earthly Paradise.* Later in his life he turned to a form of prose romance in which the setting, though vaguely medieval, was in fact purely imaginary, both the history and the geography being invented, as the titles suggest (*The Wood beyond the World; The Well at the World's End,* and so on). These stories were out of fashion at the time, but after a remarkable mid-twentieth-century success in somewhat the same idiom—Tolkien's *Lord of the Rings*—a good deal of what is sometimes known as SCIENCE FICTION began to take on romance themes. A strange, magical, even miraculous setting seems appropriate enough when the setting is another planet, and what relation the story still has to our own experience contributes the allegorical dimension. See NOVEL.

Satire. Literature that ridicules vices and follies. The term comes from *satura*, a mixed dish or, metaphorically, a medley, although a derivation from *satyra*, and the belief that satire had developed from the Greek SATYR PLAY, has influenced its history. Satire arose as a specific verse form in Latin literature, practiced by Horace, Juvenal, and Persius. It has no real counterpart in Greek literature, but another form of satire, in prose with verse interludes, or simply in prose, was allegedly invented by the Greek cynic Menippus, whose works are lost, and was the form (without the verse) used by Lucian. It is called the MENIPPEAN SATIRE, or sometimes the *Varronian satire* (from the Latin writer Varro, whose works are also lost except for fragments).

Verse satire, as the specific form of that name, was revived in English literature by Joseph Hall in *Virgidemiarum* (1597). Hall claimed to be the first English satirist, though he had been preceded by Gascoigne's *Steel Glass* (1576). His followers John Marston and John Donne emphasized the harsh, rugged, obscure style of Persius, and wrote in a deliberately irregular metre. This tendency survived in satire with the intentional doggerel and comic rhymes of Samuel Butler's *Hudibras*, Byron's *Don Juan*, and W.S. Gilbert in Victorian times. With the RESTORATION, and partly under the influence of Boileau in France, satire acquired the more Horatian characteristics of strict metre and a prevailing tone of urbanity and good temper, sometimes deepening to harsh and ferocious condemnation of social evils in imitation of Juvenal. This type of satire is the form most frequently employed by Dryden and Pope. Pope even rewrote two of Donne's satires in a more regular metre, to make them more acceptable to the taste of his time.

Menippean satire in prose also revived with Erasmus and others in the humanist period, and continues through Swift and Voltaire to Thomas Love Peacock (who revived the use of verse interludes), thence to Aldous Huxley and others in our day. But before long, satire changed its meaning. It now means, not two specific genres or subgenres of narrative, but a tone of antagonism between the writer and the material which may be found in any genre. Thus we speak of satire in Chaucer or Ibsen or Evelyn Waugh without regard to the genre in which it occurs. Satire in this sense is a type of IRONY which is normally in a comic context, in contrast to tragic irony, and is more militant in tone than the irony which depends on the suppression of all attitudes of commitment or engagement on the part of the writer. Direct satire—that is, personal or individualized attack—is certainly found in literature, as in Byron's early satire, *English Bards and Scotch Reviewers.* But most personal satire belongs to the pamphlet wars in religion and politics that fall outside the normal orbit of literature.

Indirect or more purely literary satire seems to be a combination of the ironic with the fantastic: Swift's fantasy settings in *Gulliver's Travels* and the romantic adventures of Voltaire's characters and of Byron's *Don Juan* are typical. Pure fantasy without the tone of antagonism is at one extreme: the Alice books appear to be straightforward fantasy, but the fact that their interspersed poems are often parodies of well-known writers dips them lightly into satire. Pure irony, where the attitude is too detached for the characteristic antagonistic tone of satire to appear, is at the other extreme. Of the two words derived from the metaphor of the masked actor, *hypocrite* and *person,* the former carries a moral charge, and what the satirist sees is normally a society in which all forms of personality are more or less hypocritical. Satire is usually what is called obscene—that is, outspokenly scatological—because under the hypocrisy of dressing up there is a democracy of the body usually concealed in public. It also includes parodies of literary form itself, which again is a way of allowing one's creative efforts to appear in a conventional dress. Many satires are anonymous, fragmentary, or deliberately disorganized and chaotic in structure. It is also characteristic of satire, especially in the Menippean tradition, to present people as representatives of certain intellectual attitudes, the social consequences of which are ridiculed by their sponsorship of them.

Perhaps the most concentrated form of fantasy is the presentation of the imaginary ideal state known as the UTOPIA, where all activity is ritualized and where every individual fits perfectly into the social mould. And perhaps the most concentrated form of satire is what is now called the DYSTOPIA, the Utopian parody of a world turned by malice or cunning into a nightmarish hell, as in Orwell's *Nineteen Eighty-Four,* Yevgeny Zamyatin's *We,* or Aldous Huxley's *Brave New World* and *Ape and Essence.* A good deal of SCIENCE FICTION is based on dystopian allegories (for example Ray Bradbury's *Fahrenheit 451* and Walter M. Miller's *A Canticle for Leibowitz*), where the relation to the social pitfalls in contemporary technology is close enough for frightening plausibility in the fantasy. See HORATIAN SATIRE; JUVENALIAN SATIRE; SATIRIC POETRY.

Structure. The construction or organization of a literary work. This word is a METAPHOR from architecture, and hence can hardly be applied to an art that moves in time, as literature does, without making allowance for its origin. Aristotle spoke of the importance of PLOT in tragedy [*Poetics*, chap. 6]: if we examine a tragedy or any other literary construction in terms of its plot, we soon see that we can look at the entire work simultaneously, "frozen," as it were, just as we can examine the score of a musical composition. At the same time the effect of its movement must be kept in mind, and so a structure cannot be static even if the metaphor is. According to Jean Piaget, the conception of structure includes three aspects: wholeness, transformation, and self-regulation.[21] All these aspects are characteristic of literature: the necessity for wholeness or UNITY in a literary work has been recognized since Plato [*Phaedrus*]; transformations are seen in the endless retellings of familiar stories and in the persistence of certain genres, or types, along with the typical characters (comedy and such comic types as the braggart, parasite, etc.); self-regulation is evident in the fact that literature is not dependent on factors external to itself. As this reference to Piaget shows, structure became the basis of the critical movement known as STRUCTURALISM, which derived largely from the work of the anthropologist Lévi-Strauss, who suggested that kinship in tribal communities corresponded to certain elements in their language.[22] His work was influential in leading to the conception of the "linguistic model," of finding in language the key to other social structures that were also forms of communication.

The emphasis on structure in literary CRITICISM first arose in the twentieth century (although of course the conception itself had been there from the beginning) as a reaction against the emphasis on "texture" among the so-called new critics (John Crowe Ransom, Cleanth Brooks, and others—see NEW CRITICISM). For them, a text was also a *textus*, or fabric of verbal interrelationships; but such elements as the genre the literary work belonged to, the conventions it employed, the totality of the impression its ambiguities and overlapping meanings led up to, were less clearly brought out. Study of structure thus increased the critic's awareness of the importance of historical setting and social conditioning in literature.

Symbol. Any unit of any verbal structure that may be isolated for critical attention. The word has been used in such a bewildering variety of contexts in literary CRITICISM that it seems most helpful to give it the broadest possible meaning for itself and then look into the different relationships implied by that variety. The smallest units, in an alphabetical language, are the letters; next come words, to which we shall confine ourselves here.

A symbol is a SIGNIFIER: it has a potential relation to something being SIGNIFIED. In that relation there are three aspects of particular importance. First, it conveys to the mind the sense of something specific which is signified; second, its relation to the signified is an arbitrary and conventionally assumed relation; third, it is intelligible only because it is different from every other signifier. Thus in reading we are, first, trying to unite the human consciousness with some aspect of experience which the verbal structure brings into signification. Second, we are continually searching in our memories for the conventional and socially agreed-upon significance of the verbal units. If we are reading something in a language we know imperfectly and have to keep looking words up in a dictionary, we soon see how urgent this aspect of reading is. Third, we are trying to make sense out of what we read—that is, we are building bridges between the differences that each unit has from the others.

In some tendencies in literature, such as the French movement known as *symbolisme,* stress is placed on relating the verbal units to one another, turning away from description or any aspect of words that seems to be fixed by convention in the interests of greater fluidity. On the other hand, there are other tendencies that lay stress on the descriptive aspect of symbols, their generally understood meanings that convey to the reader some experience through words with the least possible difficulty. This is the tendency often spoken of as REALISM using words in a context of externalized MIMESIS. Or a symbol may recall similar symbols previously used in similar contexts within literature; this use of a symbol may be called an ARCHETYPE, or recurring unit of literary convention. Or certain words may appear to us as keys to a whole complex of verbal meaning, as a philosopher's total meaning may be suggested by some such word as *form, time, substance,* or *being.* This last usually means that the word has a great variety of significations, and in literature more particularly double or multiple meanings of words play a major role in unifying the work. Thus in Horatio's first words to the ghost in *Hamlet,* "What art thou that usurp'st this time of night?" [1.1.46], the word "usurp" introduces the ambiguity on which so much of the play as a whole turns: the question of the reality of the relationship between the ghost and Hamlet's father. Such variety in approaching the term *symbol* is evidence of the fact that literary structures in particular have

POLYSEMOUS MEANING—that is, have many aspects of meaning, and can be approached from many points of view. See SYMBOLISM.

Tragedy. Fundamentally a serious FICTION involving the downfall of a HERO OF HEROINE. In ancient Greece the ritual of the dying god Dionysus included the singing of a choral ode, known as the *dithyramb*, in his honour. The dithyramb contained among other things the tone of passionate lamentation appropriate to the story of a dying god. The semilegendary Thespis is said to have amplified this ode into a potentially dramatic form by including a narrative from the leader of the chorus. Aeschylus, by adding a second actor (a third, apparently introduced by Sophocles, appears also in Aeschylus's later plays) brought in dialogue, and with it a fully matured dramatic form. Tragedies were acted mainly during the spring festival of Dionysus, and the priest of Dionysus was present. Three dramatists competed each year for a prize, and presented, at least at first, a group of three tragedies (trilogy) on related themes, followed by a SATYR PLAY which was lighter in tone, the four plays together making a tetralogy.

Greek tragedy was strongly influenced by the conception of a contract of order and stability in which gods, human society, and nature all participated. An act of aggression (Greek *hybris*, often spelled *hubris*) throws this cosmic machinery out of gear, and hence it must make a counter-movement to right itself. This counter-movement is usually called *nemesis*, and a number of words often translated "fate" (*heimarmene, moira, ananke*) also refer to this recovery of order, which makes the tragic action seem inevitable. The conception of a contract is a moral conception, but the particular action called tragic that happens to the hero does not depend on moral status. Aristotle spoke of a tragic *hamartia*, usually translated "flaw," as essential to the hero, but this flaw, despite the fact that *hamartia* is the ordinary New Testament word for sin, is not necessarily a moral defect, but rather a matter of being in a certain place exposed to a tragic action [*Poetics*, chap. 13]. According to Aristotle, a tragic action should, by raising pity and terror, effect a *catharsis*, or purification of these emotions [*Poetics*, chap. 6]. Whatever Aristotle meant by this, in dramatic experience this catharsis appears to be essentially a detachment of the spectator from feelings of attraction or repulsion toward the characters, particularly the hero.

Thus in Sophocles' *Oedipus Rex* the king of Thebes, an able and responsible ruler, attempts to discover the reason for the drought that has been causing famine in his land, and learns that he has unknowingly killed his father and is living in incest with his mother. In his horror at this discovery he tears out his eyes. A second Oedipus play, *Oedipus at Colonus,* shows Oedipus's reconciliation to and acceptance by the gods at his death: that does not make the play a comedy, but manifests the order and stability that caused the earlier tragedy. Similarly, in Aeschylus's trilogy the *Oresteia,* we first see the murder of Agamemnon by his wife and her lover, then the revenge of Agamemnon's son Orestes on the murderers, then the pursuit of Orestes by the Furies, who in that form are agents of a mechanical or automatic form of nemesis. In the third play of the series, *The Eumenides,* the Furies are incorporated into the more flexible and humane contract announced by Athene, so that that play, again, manifests the basis of order for tragedy and is not a comedy, even though it ends in great serenity. In Euripides, on the other hand, some of the actions, notably those of *Alcestis* and *Ion,* seem to move in the direction of COMEDY.

In these examples three main themes of tragedy are evident. One is the theme of isolation, in which a hero, a character of greater than ordinary human size, becomes isolated from the community. Mortal heroes of divine ancestry, like many Greek heroes, must discover the limitations of their humanity; if they are gods, like Aeschylus's Prometheus, they are isolated by the power of the much stronger god Zeus. Then there is the theme of the violation and reestablishment of order, in which the neutralizing of the violent act may take the form of a revenge. Finally, a character may embody a passion too great for the cosmic order to tolerate, such as the passion of sexual love. This theme is more conspicuous in Euripides (e.g., *Hippolytus*).

In Roman literature tragedy was cultivated by Seneca, whose plays may not have been intended for the theatre of his time. When drama revived in the Renaissance, Seneca was the only Classical model directly available to Shakespeare and to most of his contemporaries. Renaissance tragedy seems to be essentially a mixture of the heroic and the ironic. It tends to centre on heroes who, though they cannot be of divine parentage in Christianized Western Europe, are still of titanic size, with an articulateness and social authority beyond anything in our normal experience. In Shakespeare the theme of the social isolation of the hero appears at its most powerful and concentrated in *King Lear,* where the king's abdication of royal power leaves him exposed to the malignancy of the two of his three daughters who supplant him. REVENGE TRAGEDY, a common Elizabethan and Jacobean form, appears in *Hamlet*, with revenge being imposed on the hero as a moral obligation. The tragedy of passion, in its most common form of sexual love, is the mode of *Romeo and Juliet*, and a different form of it appears in Racine's *Phèdre*.

After the Renaissance, the most notable development of tragic drama was in Germany, with the works of Schiller and the younger Goethe, especially the first part of *Faust*. Many other tragic dramas were literary imitations of the great Classical and Renaissance models, and have not worn well on the stage. Prose fiction (*Crime and Punishment, Anna Karenina, Moby-Dick, Madame Bovary*) has been the genre of most of the really powerful modern tragedies. Even here the ironic component of tragedy predominates over the heroic one, because of the difficulty of assuming the convention of a tragic hero who is larger than life size. Such a figure as Willy Loman in Arthur Miller's *Death of a Salesman*, for example, gains his heroic aura only through being a representative of a specific social development, the emphasis on hustling and hard-selling capitalism which at one time, at least, formed a prominent part of what is called the American dream. Loman's isolation in itself is simply ironic: it is the collapse of the dream he embodies that is tragic. See DOMESTIC TRAGEDY; MELODRAMA; TRAGIC FLAW; TRAGIC IRONY; TRAGICOMEDY.

21

Letter to the Editor of *PMLA*

March 1985

From PMLA, *100 (March 1985): 238. A response to a letter from Lawrence W. Hyman (Brooklyn College, City University of New York), which questions the sociopolitical potential in the literary experience posited by Frye in his article "Literary and Linguistic Scholarship in a Postliterate World" (no. 14).*

I think of literature not as ironic but as hypothetical, its central axiom being not so much "nothing is certainly true" as "everything is to be tentatively accepted." Such an axiom certainly has its ironic aspect, but the primary concerns I speak of are not, for me, "immutable values" but limits to the irony. Thus the irony of Swift's *Modest Proposal* has a limit in the reader's continuing conviction that, as the saying goes, eating people is wrong. Here Swift is on our side, but when Yeats, in his *On the Boiler* essays, advocates a "just war" and a new "science" based on spiritualism and racist breeding,[1] he does not know whether he is being ironic or not, so that the critic's task is more complex. This is the kind of thing Auden had in mind when he said of (or to) Yeats, "You were silly like us: your gift survived it all" [*In Memory of W.B. Yeats*, pt. 2, l. 1]. Auden is expressing what I imagine most of us feel, that literature as a whole has a moral solidity to it that can absorb any amount of a poet's silliness or a critic's triviality. But I want to know more about the "gift," where it gets its survival value and authority, and why so many of those who have it will fight to preserve it against social pressure instead of adapting to that pressure.

I should agree that we cannot counter an ideology except with another ideology, that literature cannot, except incidentally, be "harnessed" to a social vision, and that we cannot use literary experience directly to improve society. But we can use it to improve experience itself, where it can put in proportion the actions that arise from practical concerns. Primary concerns are not practical, but they do spring from the imagination and are linked to what literature addresses. In the days before concern moved into the foreground, when most people did not read seriously and no one questioned the indefinite survival of humanity, literature had little social function beyond a working alliance with (rarely against) the religious and political ideologies of its time. Things are different now, even for the present criticism of past literature. At the time of writing (mid-November 1984), most MLA members have recently voted for either Reagan or Mondale, and I doubt that their primary concern for human life and freedom was much alleviated by doing so. That suggests a social imagination of a different order from what any conceivable political action can attain to by itself. What I am urging is a sharper look at the connection between our primary concern with human life and our professional concern with language.

Whatever the adequacy of this reply, I am greatly obliged to Lawrence Hyman for his courteous and thoughtful letter.

22

Lacan and the Full Word

April–June 1985

Originally published in French as "Lacan et la parole dans sa plénitude," Ornicar, *33 (April–June 1985): 11–14, translated by Jacqueline Carnaud. The English version appeared as "Lacan and the Full Word" in* Criticism and Lacan: Essays and Dialogue on Language, Structure and the Unconscious, *ed. Patrick Colm Hogan and Lalita Pandit (Athens, Ga.: University of Georgia Press, 1990), 187–9, from which the text below is taken. Correspondence (in the NFF, 1988, box 59, file 5) reveals that Frye had written his piece at the request of Patrick Hogan for inclusion in a projected* Annual of Lacanian Studies, *edited by Hogan and Lacan's literary executor, Jacques-Alain Miller. The annual never appeared, but Miller subsequently published the unauthorized French translation without the knowledge of either Frye or Patrick Hogan. The typescripts are in the NFF, 1988, box 48, file 5, and 1991, box 39, file 3.*

My own chief interest at the moment is in the place of the Bible in the imagination of Western culture, a subject which does not directly concern Lacan. Yet I find Lacan a most rewarding writer to "misread"—this word is taken from Harold Bloom, but Lacan's own dictum that every *méconnaissance* implies a *connaissance* behind it amounts to much the same conception.[1] Lacan's aphoristic and discontinuous style, his unique fusing of the oracular and the witty, affords his reader at least two kinds of stimulus. On the one hand, even if one is not a special student of Lacan, one feels the impulse to arrange his oracles into an interlocking system, even though it is clear from the start that Lacan is the sort of writer who keeps suggesting the systematic in order to be free to break out of system. On the other hand, readers like myself, concerned with matters remote from his psychoanalytical techniques, may find his epigrams profoundly illuminating for some very unlikely areas.

In my book *The Great Code* I attempted a preliminary study of the narrative and imagery of the Bible. The rationale of the procedure was the hypothesis that the narrative of the Bible, specifically the Christian Bible that stretches from creation to apocalypse, describes a vast spiritual development which the reader grasps sequentially as he reads. When the Bible is taken on its own terms as being what it obviously is intended to be, a revelation, that revelation develops progressively within the narrative—that is, there is no "progressive revelation" except within the process of reading itself. The first major "revelation" in the Bible is the account of creation. This is not a history of how the order of nature came into existence, but, in Lacanian terms, a transformation of an "imaginary" world into a "symbolic" one, a transformation which of course brought the "real" world into the picture as well. Creation is the presenting to the consciousness of an objective world as a mass of *écriture*: it forms, traditionally, an idea of Nature as a second "Word" of God, a book to be read on the assumption that we do not see Nature so much as our own constructs of Nature.

The response to Creation and its attendant phenomena (the myths of the fall, the flood, the Tower of Babel are all visions of the circumscribing of the subject into a roughly predictable response role) becomes eventually the calling of Israel out of, first, Mesopotamia, with Abraham, then Egypt, with Moses. Why the chosen community should be tribal rather than imperial raises social and political issues that I have found no counterpart to in Lacan. But in any case the chosen community is given the Law, the codifying of Lacan's *nom du père* into a social contract. The God who gives the Law is presented as very alive, but in the Christian perspective, where a revised revelation makes the Law a "type" of something greater than itself, a something that culminates, as far as human history is concerned, in the Crucifixion of Christ, the *nom du père* stands first in the place of absence and then in the place of death. The response to Law is Wisdom, which begins in the sense of the permeation of individual life by the Law, and which attempts to unify and systematize the apparently arbitrary miscellany of commandments. The life before and the life after the growth of wisdom in the mind marks a transition perhaps roughly comparable to Lacan's distinction between *connaissance* and *savoir*.

With Prophecy we begin to hear the voice of the Other, the *Autre* with a capital A, in a quite new area: what we now call the unconscious. Prophets appear first as thaumaturgists and "inspired" people who go into trance and speak with a different voice; later they enter into a dialectical struggle with secular policy. Consequently their normal role is frequently one of exclusion or martyrdom, and the tradition culminates, for Christian readers, with the New Testament martyrs John the Baptist and Jesus. The response to Prophecy, as finally formulated in the teachings and career of Jesus, is that of the Gospel or spiritual community, and the word "Spirit" is pushed into the forefront of the Biblical narrative.

Paul distinguishes the *soma pneumatikos* or spiritual body from the *soma psychikos*, the body-soul unit. The latter, Paul says, cannot understand the Word of revelation, because Word and Spirit are both aspects of God, and the "all too human" soul-body cannot hear its dialogue. I take Lacan's *stade du miroir* to mean that one cannot become a genuine "subject" in our subject–object world of ordinary experience until one has become an object to oneself. There must be a split within the subject, and the sense of the subject as bound up with something alien is thereby formed. This conception threw a good deal of light, first, on my reading of Shakespeare. Richard II, for example, bedevilled by what has been called the king's two bodies,[2] and finding his royal self not only alienated but lost, tries to add himself together in the abdication scene by calling for a mirror and gazing into it. Hamlet, too, seems to me a gigantic force of personality imprisoned within an alienated self, thrashing around within it in his soliloquies and gazing hard at all the other characters, including Ophelia and Yorick's skull, in an effort to de-objectify himself, so to speak, or return to the pre-mirror stage. The same conception underlies many literary treatments of the double, who is so fundamental a structural principle of romance.

Paul's conception of the spiritual body seems to include a conflict within the psyche in which self and other exchange roles. The Spirit becomes the genuine self, and the self an alienated ego, Lacan's *moi*. In proportion as the Spirit grows, the "natural man" or ego, man in the prison of what he is, becomes consolidated as the residue of physical, social, and parental identifications (compare Jesus' remark that a disciple of his must "hate" his father and mother [Luke 14:26]). The conflict is resolved, in the New Testament, by a "second coming" of the Word, or Apocalypse, in which both the imaginary and the real disappear and only the symbolic world is left. The last page of the Bible, ending with an invitation to the reader to drink of the water of life, seems to be saying to him that he has now had the complete vision of the "full Word," and what he does in response to the vision is up to him. As Lacan says, every Word demands a reply.

I am not trying to kidnap Lacan for a religious program: I am merely trying to indicate the places where, in my study of the Bible, epigrams and observations I had read in Lacan began to reverberate. Both the Bible and Lacan present visions of the human situation, with occasional points of contact. But to see these points clearly we have to separate Lacan's vision from his practice as a psychoanalyst, and the Biblical vision from questions of faith, with their many emotional imponderables. Any contemporary journal devoted to religious topics will confirm that thinkers who have withdrawn from most or all religious belief—Freud, Marx, Nietzsche, Heidegger—are quite as useful in defining those topics as those who have aligned themselves with such beliefs. The reason for this must be sought for within the nature of language, and the study of language, as I imagine few will deny, has not yet progressed so far into its real depths.

23

Literature and the Visual Arts

6 May 1985

Originally presented at a conference of the Associazione Internazionale per gli Studi di Lingua e Letteratura Italiana in Toronto. First published in Italian as "La letteratura e le arti figurative," trans. Francesco Guardiani, Lettere Italiane, *37 (August–September 1985): 285–98. Subsequently published in English in* MM, *183–95. The text below is from the typescript, in the NFF, 1988, box 49, file 3.*

I

I should like to approach the relation of literature to the visual arts through some of the general principles involved, and hence I am not confining myself to Italian examples. Also, if I am to keep the discussion contained within the limits of a short introductory paper, I shall be able to discuss only one of the visual arts: the one I choose is painting.

The verbal and musical arts that address the ear are presented as temporal experiences, where we move along with the presentation from beginning to end. Those that address the eye, including painting, sculpture, and architecture, are presented spatially. But before long we realize that there is something accidental about the presentation, that every art has both a temporal and a spatial aspect. We may, by studying the score, perceive a musical composition as simultaneous, spread out all at once in front of us, as it were. We may also see a painting or other spatial work of art as an instant of arrested movement. T.S. Eliot speaks of how "a Chinese jar still / Moves perpetually in its stillness" [*Burnt Norton*, pt. 5, ll. 6–7]. Literature seems to be closer to the visual arts than music, as it depends on imagery as well as rhythm. We may think of it as midway between the musical and the visual. We experience this double context most obviously in drama, where we not only hear a narrative but often a background of music as well, along with seeing a spectacle on the stage. But even if we are silently reading a work of literature, there is still a metaphorical hearing and seeing that is never wholly out of our consciousness.

The metaphorical "hearing" of literature, more particularly poetry, is often expressed in metaphors of music. Thus Milton's *Lycidas* has in its invocation the line "Begin, and somewhat loudly sweep the string" [l. 17], implying that the poem has a *mezzoforte* musical accompaniment on a lute or lyre. At the end we read

> Thus sang the uncouth swain to th' oaks and rills
> When the still morn went out with sandals gray:
> He touch'd the tender stops of various quills
> With eager thought warbling his Doric lay. [ll. 186–9]

The word "quills" implies the use of a reed or a kind of rustic oboe, called an "oat" earlier in the poem. Milton had a good deal of musical taste and knowledge, but the impossibility of singing and playing a wind instrument at the same time does not seem to bother him. *Paradise Lost*, again, invariably uses the metaphor of singing whenever the poet appears in his own person.

But when the process of reading or listening to a body of words in time is ended, we make an effort to understand what the body of words conveys, in a simultaneous or comprehensive act that we metaphorically call "seeing." Someone about to tell a joke may begin with some such formula as, "Have you heard this?" Once we hear it, we "see" the joke; we "grasp" (turning to another group of tactile metaphors) the essential point or meaning of the joke, or what Aristotle would call its *dianoia* [*Poetics*, chap. 6]. But once we "see" the joke we do not want to hear it again. Similarly, we may read a detective story in order to identify the murderer at the end, but once we "see" who the murderer is, we normally do not want to read the book again until we have forgotten his identity.

If, on the other hand, we are presented with something as complex as *King Lear*, we hear or read the play, and make a tentative effort to understand what it all means. This effort soon falls to pieces; its inadequacy becomes oppressive; we read or listen to the play again, and attempt a more satisfactory understanding. Such a process, if one is professionally concerned with studying literature or drama, may go on for the whole of one's life. Any feeling that we have "seen" the meaning of a work of literature in a final and completely adequate way implies a rather low estimate of it. This conception of "seeing" a body of words is so deeply involved in our response to literature that the metaphor of "structure," literature studied as a simultaneous pattern, has become a central critical term.[1]

The metaphor of "seeing," however, has two frames of reference. It may refer us to a conceptual meaning, an understanding which is a *Gestalt* of apprehension, but in itself, when expressed, is primarily another kind of verbal structure. Thus the fable is a story we listen to like other stories, but understanding it is a matter of understanding a "moral," the reconstruction of the story in conceptual or didactic verbal terms. Most allegories call for a response of this kind also. Here the "seeing" is the response of simultaneity that appears to take place in some kind of conceptual space. Sometimes a poet will indicate what kind of response he expects by providing a suggested "moral" of his own to his fable, as with Gray's *On a Distant Prospect of Eton College*: "No more: where Ignorance is Bliss, / 'Tis Folly to be wise" [ll. 99–100]. Another example would be the "truth is beauty" proposition at the end of Keats's *Ode on a Grecian Urn*, where the urn itself suddenly comes to life and speaks, in the figure of speech technically known as *prosopopeoia*. This is the same figure of speech that is employed in Anglo-Saxon riddles, where a visual object describes itself verbally and challenges the reader to guess its identity. The Grecian urn in itself, apart from the poem, belongs to the visual arts, and suggests that a verbal moral can be attached to a pictorial image as well as to a story. This is what is done in the emblem, where an allegorical picture is the occasion for verbal commentary.

Poetry depends heavily on concrete sense experience, and has a limited tolerance for the language of argument, thesis, or proposition. Within the last century we have had a series of manifestos directed against the moral and didactic type of writing where the act of understanding, being itself verbal, keeps the literary work "logocentric," in the current phraseology. Thus Verlaine adjures the poet to "wring the neck" of rhetoric,[2] meaning by "rhetoric" the alliance of poetry and oratory that seems to evoke only a verbal response. In English literature the early years of this century produced the movement known as "imagism," which demanded that the response to the total meaning, or what we may call the theme, of a poem should be at least metaphorically pictorial.[3] Imagism was a minor movement in itself, but similar tendencies led Eliot, for example, to praise the "clear visual images" of Dante, contrasting him in this respect with the blind Milton to the latter's disadvantage.[4] William Carlos Williams, though working in a very different idiom from imagism, formulated the principle[5] that forms the title of the last poem in Wallace Stevens's *Collected Poems*: "Not ideas about the thing but the thing itself." In prose fiction it is a very common device to have some visual emblem represent the simultaneous meaning or theme of the novel. Examples include Henry James's *The Golden Bowl*, D.H. Lawrence's *The White Peacock*, and Virginia Woolf's *To the Lighthouse*.

The geometrical shapes of the letters of Western alphabets make it difficult to assimilate the literary and pictorial arts as completely as can be done in the Orient, where calligraphy often seems to bridge the gap between writing and drawing. However, there are enough experiments with shape poems and concrete poetry to indicate a considerable interest in this area. There is much less to note on the musical side: poets are no longer as liberal with metaphors of harps or lyres or lutes, or even singing, as they used to be. We occasionally run across the term "voice" as a metaphor for hearing, as in Herbert Read's *The True Voice of Feeling* or Malraux's *Les Voix du silence*, but these are critical works.

But the combination of verbal and visual appeal, with each art functioning by itself, has had a long history in our tradition. Its more modern forms begin with Hogarth's sequential pictures on a verbal program, such as *Marriage à la Mode* and *The Rake's Progress*,[6] and reach their highest development in the illuminated books of William Blake, where we have again a sequence of plates that may show any proportion of verbal and visual material, from a plate that is all text to one that is all design, and anything in between. These are not illustrated poems, for illustration punctuates a verbal text and brings it to periodic halts: in Blake there is a continuous counterpoint of the two arts from beginning to end. On a popular level an easygoing intermixture of drawing and text forms the staple of younger readers today, the comic book, where one art continually feeds on the other, so that the deficiencies in each art by itself are less noticeable.

II

We next notice that in our cultural traditions the specifically Biblical and Hebrew influences, the ones that underlie the religions of Judaism, Christianity, and Islam, have in common a reverence for the spoken word of God and a corresponding distrust in any association of deity with the eyesight. Moses turns aside to see why the burning bush does not burn up: the visual stimulus is merely to awaken his curiosity, and it is the voice that speaks from the bush that is important [Exodus 3:2–4]. God constantly speaks in the Bible, and there seems to be no theological difficulty about hearing his voice. But the editorial and redacting processes in the Old Testament seem to get very agitated where any suggestion of a vision of God is concerned. We are solemnly adjured to make no image either of the true God or any of the gods concocted from nature,[7] and this commandment has led to the practical extinction of representational painting in all three religions at various times, more particularly in Islam. In Christianity, any swing back to the primitive revolutionary fervour of the first Christian age has been normally accompanied by iconoclasm, in both Western and Eastern churches. In the *Clementine Recognitions* St. Peter enters a building decorated with frescoes, and it is noted with emphatic approval that he is totally indifferent to the impressions of pictorial art.[8] Of course the Bible is full of imagery, as full as any work of literature would be. But apparently this imagery is intended to be internalized, and assimilated to the silent hearing which is the approved response to the Word of God.

The attitude of Plato toward the arts of *techne*, painting and sculpture particularly, was not greatly different: he began the critical tendency to regard the painter as simply a master of representational illusion that lasted until after the Renaissance. But in a polytheistic religion we must have statues or pictures to distinguish one god from another, and in Greek culture we see two powerful emphases on the visual: the nude in sculpture and the theatre in literature. For, whatever the importance of the music and poetry heard in a theatre, the theatre remains primarily a visual presentation of literature, as its derivation from the Greek word for seeing (*theaomai*) shows. In contrast, the iconoclastic tendencies in Christianity are often accompanied by a strong dislike of the theatre, and complaints about the moral indecency of portraying naked bodies need no elaboration of reference. Again, in Homer a god or goddess will appear to a hero in the guise of someone he knows well: the Christian notion of a uniquely portentous incarnation of a deity in a human form is very remote from the Homeric world.

At the same time the transition from hearing to seeing metaphors that we noted in the encounter with literature also seems to operate in religious texts and rituals. In the Christian mass the collect or scripture readings are followed by the elevation of the Host; the Eleusinian mysteries culminated, we are told, in exhibiting a reaped ear of corn to the initiates; Zen Buddhism has a legend that the Buddha, after ending a sermon, held up a golden flower, the only member of his audience who got the point being, naturally, the founder of Zen.[9] The Christian Bible ends with the book of "Revelation," a tremendous vision of the whole order of nature being destroyed and succeeded by a new heaven and earth. Though a very imperfectly visualized book, it is said to be a "vision," and clearly follows the religious tradition in which the crucial transition from physical to spiritual life is described in the visual metaphor of "enlightenment." Similarly Job remarks, at the end of his long ordeal, "I have heard of thee by the hearing of the ear, but now mine eye seeth thee" [Job 42:5].

When the relation of the art of words and the art of drawing and colouring becomes less metaphorical and more concrete, the tension between them greatly increases. The elaborate descriptions of paintings that are occasionally found in literary works belong to a specific rhetorical device, usually called *ecphrasis*, which is often considered a sign of "decadence," or whatever term we use to indicate that the writer has embarked on what we consider a misleading path. Many such descriptions belong to late Classical fiction: the romance of *Leucippe and Clitophon*, by Achilles Tatius, is triggered by a picture, elaborately described, of the rape of Europa, which leads a bystander to tell his story to another bystander. However, when he ends the story eight books later, the author has forgotten his opening and does not return to it. It is usually a woman's nudity that a writer counts on to hold his reader's attention in such a device, but even so his resources are limited. Two heroines are exposed naked to a sea monster in *Orlando Furioso*, but despite the fullness of Ariosto's description, the reader is apt to conclude that, in a verbal setting at any rate, one luscious nude is very like another. In still more elaborate examples, such as the shield of Achilles in Homer [*The Iliad*, bk. 18], we quickly forget about the connection with the visual arts—that is, we stop asking ourselves if it is really possible to get all that on a painted or carved surface, and simply accept the shield for what it is: a description of a calm world at peace that forms a beautiful contrast to the weary hacking of bodies that is the foreground action. It has been a generally accepted principle, since Lessing's *Laokoon* at least, that one art cannot really do what another art is especially equipped to do.[10] The principle involved here is quite distinct from the one implicit in Blake's illuminated poems: there we have two arts running side by side, each doing its own work, and not one art attempting to reproduce the effect of another in its own medium.

The same principle would apply to the attempt in painting to imitate verbal effects, but there the issue is more complex. In the Middle Ages, when the church was the chief patron of the visual arts, an elaborate code of iconography prescribed at least the content of the picture. There were verbal reasons for presenting one saint as bald and another with hair, and for supplying martyred saints with the instruments of their martyrdom—Catherine's wheel, Laurence's gridiron, and the like. When in the Renaissance the market for secular painting began to expand, the situation was not very different: painting the birth of Venus or the apotheosis of Louis XIV is equally a commitment to a verbal program. Still later come the anecdotal pictures of the eighteenth and nineteenth centuries, which are part of the development of the visual arts known as illustration.

We have said that verbal media internalize the imagery they use, so that the reader is compelled to build up his own structure of visualization. The illustration relieves the strain of this by supplying a ready-made equivalent for the reader's mental picture: hence its proverbial vividness, as expressed in the journalistic cliché that "one picture is worth a thousand words." In the nineteenth century books were illustrated to an extent hardly conceivable today, when the development of film and television has obviated the need for most of it. What's the use of a book, inquires Lewis Carroll's Alice, without pictures or conversations?[11] The same close association with words is present in paintings themselves: the pre-Raphaelite movement in Britain, for example, was primarily a development of painting as illustration—to medieval romance, to Shakespeare, to contemporary life, to the Bible.

A contradiction seems implied in what we have said thus far. We have spoken of the iconic art of the Middle Ages, and also of the prejudice against representational art of any kind that pervades the Biblical religions, and accounts for the recurring movements of iconoclasm. The explanation is that the Word of God, or doctrine of the church, being verbal, is, we said, supposed to be internalized, and the status of the painting or sculpture related to it depends on the previous existence of that internalization. If there is none, the picture or whatever could be an idol, something that brings us to a reverent full stop in front of something presented as both objective and numinous. But in the Biblical tradition nothing objective can be numinous: art is a creation of man and nature a creation of God, and no deities lurk in either. If the internalized verbal structure is already there, however, the picture becomes an icon, intended to elicit meditation instead of closing it off. The same principle, working inside the Christian tradition, makes for a progressive domestication of the major religious figures. We go from the great Torcello Madonna, who seems a million years old with no sign of aging, through the highly stylized Byzantine figures like the Rucellai Madonna of Duccio, to the comparatively humanized Madonna of Giotto, and from there to the still more familiar Quattrocento Madonnas,[12] who look so much more like simply attractive young women with their babies.

In later periods of painting we become increasingly aware of the principle stated by William Carlos Williams in relation to literature: "The classic is the local fully realized, words marked by a place."[13] Substituting "pictures" for "words," we see the principle operating in Dutch realism, including the realism of landscape in Hobbema and Ruysdael, in the first generation of French impressionism, in the earlier Barbizon school, in the southern English landscape tradition headed by Constable. Such movements in painting are opposite in tendency to what is called the "picturesque," the search for a particular spot (often called "unspoiled") that lends itself to certain pictorial conventions, again usually verbal in origin. In our day the picturesque has been mainly taken over by photography, but a contrast remains between two approaches to visual art: that of the tourist looking in from the outside and that of the native looking out from the inside. Such contrasts are more familiar in culturally new countries, including Canada, but picturesque bandits and gypsies have been celebrated by European painters too. The picturesque is typically a conservative, idealized vision, and hence rather distanced: if it comes much closer it turns into the genuinely realistic. John Ruskin, who in this respect was more of a lay preacher using pictures as moral documents than a critic making objective analyses of works of art, is full of denunciations of the picturesque that gets too close to its subject. Thus in *Stones of Venice* he contrasts Holman Hunt, who "loves peasant boys, because he finds them more roughly and picturesquely dressed, and more healthily coloured, than others" with Murillo's drawing of a beggar's dirty foot, which "is mere delight in foulness."[14]

The issue involved here takes us a long way. Traditionally, the painter has been judged by his representational skill: there are Greek legends about painters painting grapes that birds would peck at,[15] and the Elizabethan critic Puttenham says that the artist of painting or carving is "only a bare imitator of nature . . . as the marmoset doth many countenances and gestures of a man."[16] It is somewhat chastening to realize how triumphant the tradition of painting has been, in the face of such infantile critical theories. The justification for the theories was that, as Sir Thomas Browne said in the seventeenth century, "Nature is the art of God,"[17] hence in theory all the original part of the painter's work had already been done. And yet the painter often agrees with such critics, maintaining that he paints only what he sees, and just as he sees, without realizing how impossible this is. What he sees he sees from within the conventions of painting in his day, which in turn are determined by a cultural and social framework. Any frequenter of art galleries can determine, with a little practice, what century any picture he is looking at was painted in, and this clearly could not be done if it were true that any painter in any age could simply reproduce nature at second hand. The development of photography has complicated this situation, but has not essentially changed it: photography has its conventions and fashions also.

In any case the assumption that painting is essentially representation has persisted up to a century or so ago, and it is part of the assumption that the painter is permitted only selection, not recreation. The selective process is supposed to operate on a quasi-moral principle: what the painter selects to record should, traditionally, be the "beautiful." The trouble is not only that beauty, at least the beauty that is connected with the erotic feeling, is proverbially fleeting, but that conventions of beauty are fleeting also. Whatever is considered beautiful in any given period of culture tends to imprison itself within an increasingly narrowing convention. A beautiful body should be only a body in good physical condition between the ages of eighteen and thirty, and in a white society it must be obviously white. Even in the nineteenth century it was widely assumed that the Greeks had invented beauty, and that Asian and African artists had deliberately made a cult of the grotesque and hideous out of sheer perversity.

This constant closing off of the "beautiful" in academic dead ends and blind alleys is accompanied by a corresponding exhaustion of resources in the techniques of producing it. We recall Browning's melancholy monologue of "the faultless painter" Andrea del Sarto, obsessed with a sense of futility and disillusionment not merely in his personal life but in his painting as well.[18] It has been remarked that probably nobody in Andrea's own time would have understood that faultlessness could itself be a fault: the point is, however, that technical "perfection" implies a convention narrowing so rapidly that there is soon nothing left to explore within it. When such perfection is reached it becomes mechanical, and there is nothing to do but abandon the convention and try something else. Nobody would call Magnasco, or for that matter even Caravaggio, a faultless painter, but they were exploring pictorial conventions that Andrea del Sarto could not have dreamed of.

III

We should not be surprised to find a fairly consistent tradition of revolt in the painting of the last two centuries or so, first against the tyranny of verbal conventions, then against the assumption that the painter's primary function is to represent nature, which makes the content of the picture and the "accuracy" of its representation functional elements in criticism. The landscape painters in England, Turner, Constable, Bonington, and their impressionist successors in France, were in the forefront of the struggle against too exclusive a demand for emblems, illustrations, and other forms of subservience to the verbal. By the end of the nineteenth century this resistance had spread to the dominance of representation itself. One of the most common stories about twentieth-century painters, ascribed to both Picasso and Matisse and doubtless many others, is the response to the complaint that a picture, let us say of a fish, was not a fish: "Quite right: it is not a fish, it is a picture." The issue at stake here is, of course, the autonomy of painting, the right of the painter to deal only with the pictorial shapes and colours that belong to his art.

The development of the verbal arts has followed parallel directions, though the sequence is harder to trace because as long as literature uses ordinary words, it can never be as abstract or autonomous as painting or music can be. Some representational aura will still cling to the words, however strong the embrace of their metaphorical context in poem or story. Also, the external forces trying to dominate literature mostly take the form of other verbal structures. But the same resistance to conventionalizing standards of beauty, to an idealizing representationalism that stays well away from its subject (unfortunately there is no exact literary equivalent of "picturesque"), to the tyranny of religious or political anxieties, has operated in literature as well as in the visual arts.

One result of this is that instead of making a sterile and canonized ideal beauty the model for the artist, the entire spectrum of cultural traditions, from the most primitive to the most sophisticated, from the most immediate to the most exotic, is spread before him as a source of possible influences. A contemporary artist without a strong sense of inner direction would be more likely to suffer from agoraphobia than claustrophobia. A by-product of the same expansion has been the breaking down of the barrier between the work of art and the ordinary visual object. The *objet trouvé* may be not only the subject for a picture but the art object itself; in collage the picture is not painted but assembled from pictorial data; "pop" art and similar developments are based on the principle that anything may become a work of art when a consciousness is focused on it. In the Renaissance it was assumed, not only that nature was the art of God, but that the order of nature was a metaphorical book, a secondary Word of God, and that the properly instructed man could read its riddles for almost any purpose, magical, medical, scientific, or religious. A rather similar assumption, that nothing exists merely as itself, seems to inform the visual arts today, however different the context. A well-known picture by Boccioni, *The Street Enters the House*,[19] may serve as an allegory for an age in which the separation of works of art inside buildings from miscellaneous objects outside on the street is breaking down.

The oldest paintings we possess, and the oldest works of any art by many thousands of years still extant, are the Palaeolithic paintings and drawings in the caves of southern France and northern Spain.[20] The firmness and assurance of the drawings would be impressive anywhere, but in such surroundings, with such formidable difficulties of positioning and lighting, they are little short of miraculous. There were doubtless representational motives for drawing the animals of the hunt on which the food supply depended, but this can hardly have been the entire motivation, as some of the figures are human beings, probably sorcerers, clothed in animal skins. Wherever we turn in studying this art, we are constantly brought up against the cave itself, as a shrouding maternal womb containing the embryos both of human society and of the beings of the natural environment to which that society was most closely related. The persistence of the cave setting for fresco painting in Anatolia, India, Etruscan Italy, and many other places makes us wonder whether painting may not have a special relationship to the sense of something embryonic, present within the human imagination but suggesting the outlines of a human civilization not yet born.

Whatever may be thought of this, the sense of something unborn and embryonic turns up recurrently in the history of painting. We see it in the grotesque fantasies of Hieronymous Bosch and Brueghel, in the naive staring faces of primitive painters, in the melting or deliberately incongruous shapes of the surrealists, in the spidery childlike scrawls of Miro and Klee. It is as though, in Klee's words, the painter "places more value on the powers which do the forming than on the final forms themselves."[21] We are very far away here from the notion of the painter as a supermonkey reproducing the art of God in nature. In the cultural history of Canada, painting was the first of the arts to come to maturity, and it formed a very important aspect of the exploring and settling of the country. Perhaps a worldwide metamorphosis of the visual arts indicates the coming of a new age in man's attitude to the globe he inhabits.

A corresponding metamorphosis of the verbal arts would probably come later, though some elements of it can already be glimpsed. In the Western tradition literature seems to have run through a cycle beginning with myth and romance and ending with an ironic realism which disintegrates into various forms of paradox, such as the theatre of the absurd. In our day we see many signs of the cycle being repeated: the retelling of the great myths, the reshaping of romance formulas in a science fiction setting, the revival of a primitive relation to a listening audience in rock and ballad singing. But nothing repeats exactly in history, and in any case the end of a cycle does not compel us to repeat the same cycle, but gives us a chance to transfer to another level.

It is obvious that most of the movements in the arts mentioned above are political statements. Many of them are regarded as bourgeois erosions of socialist values in Marxist societies, even though they often assert those very values in a democratic setting. It seems to me that behind the political statement lies a fundamentally antipolitical attitude, an anarchism tending to break down all social mythologies devoted to promoting special social interests. Such an attitude may be unrecognized by the individual artist himself, or may even be the exact opposite of what he thinks he is trying to do. The movement known as Dada, which arose after the First World War, was explicitly anarchist in this sense as a total movement, whatever the variety of social opinion within it. At present we are confronted by a movement in all the arts which, for all its tremendous creative variety, has incorporated the spirit of Dada within it. Such a movement is to be welcomed, as long as we see it not as a kind of extreme unction for the bourgeois soul or as a morbid preoccupation with chaos for its own sake, but as the opportunity for renewed imaginative energy and a new freedom in seeing the world.

24

The Journey as Metaphor

8 October 1985

Originally presented as a lecture at the Applewood Centre in Toronto, a Jungian study centre devoted to spiritual understanding. First published in MM, *212–26. The text below is from the typescript in the NFF, 1988, box 49, file 1. There is an additional typescript in the NFF, 1991, box 39, file 3.*

A journey is a directed movement in time through space, and in the idea of a journey there are always two elements involved. One is the person making the journey; the other is the road, path, or direction taken, the simplest word for this being "way." In all metaphorical uses of the journey these two elements appear. In pure metaphor the emphasis normally falls on the person; in proportion as we approach religious and other existential aspects of metaphorical journeys the emphasis shifts to "way." I should like to begin with some common examples of the metaphor of journey, and see how they are intertwined with the still larger metaphors of the directions taken.

"Journey" is a word connected with *jour* and *journée*, and metaphorical journeys, deriving as they mostly do from slower methods of getting around, usually have at their core the conception of the day's journey, the amount of space we can cover under the cycle of the sun. By a very easy extension we get the day's journey as a further, perhaps more concentrated, metaphor for the whole of life, life being thought of as a cyclical process of birth, death, and renewed life. Thus in A.E. Housman's poem *Reveille*:

> Clay lies still, but blood's a rover;
> Breath's a ware that will not keep:

> Up, lad: when the journey's over
> There'll be time enough to sleep. [ll. 21–4]

Here the awakening in the morning is a metaphor for continuing the journey of life, a journey clearly ending in death. The prototype for the image is the Book of Ecclesiastes, which urges us to work while it is day, before the night comes when no man can work, and which is also dominated by the vision of life as a cyclical movement under the sun. The Biblical vision includes a plug for the work ethic: in the much less realistic Housman, the ethic seems to relate to war or adventure rather than simply the effort of life itself.

In the Housman poem there is also, in the background, the figure of the forking road, where one route leads to death and the other to a resuming of life. Such a figure may appear in any situation of extreme danger or despair, but it is also common in more ordinary ones: there is a famous and beautifully muted example in Frost's poem *Stopping by Woods on a Snowy Evening*. Here a night traveller pauses to contemplate the stillness of the snow in the woods, which seems to express not only serenity but welcome, but he soon returns to his journey, because he still has "miles to go before I sleep." In Blake's poem *Ah! Sun-flower*, the flower that turns its face to the sun through its passage across the sky is the emblem of all those who have repressed or frustrated their desires to the point at which they all consolidate into a desire for the sunset of death: "Seeking after that sweet golden clime / Where the traveller's journey is done."

A journey is a movement from here to there, from point A to point B, and as a metaphor for life the two points are obviously birth and death. But this is true only of the individual: the containing way or direction is cyclical. When the cyclical movement enters the individual life, we have the form of journey we call the quest, where a hero goes out to accomplish something, kill a dragon, deliver a heroine from a giant, help destroy a hostile city, or what not. The hero of a quest first of all goes "away": that is, there must be some direction for his movement. Home, as Eliot says, is where one starts from [*East Coker*, pt. 5. l. 19]. If the quest is successful, he normally returns home, like a baseball player, the great model for this returning journey being of course the *Odyssey*. The cyclical framework for the journey may have different emotional overtones. In a pure cycle the hero is trapped in a squirrel cage: there is nothing for him to do except to do it all over again. A rather silly example of this is in one of the romances that had some vogue in the wake of the success of Tolkien, Eddison's *The Worm Ouroboros*. The serpent with its tail in its mouth is a common emblem of an unending cycle, and when the heroes accomplish their quest in this book they invoke this emblem to repeat the whole performance, on the ground that it is so boring with nothing now to do. Other cycles are connected with evil: Psalm 12:8 tells us that the wicked travel in circles. At least, that is what the Septuagint and Vulgate say: the Hebrew and Protestant versions seem to me to make no sense.[1]

The genuine quest cycle is of the type in which the conclusion is the starting point renewed and transformed by the quest itself. In a way Virgil's *Aeneid* is a quest of this type: Aeneas moves from old to new Troy, setting up a new cycle of history with the same race of people. The cyclical movement is emphasized by the fact that the Trojans or Dardanians came from Italy to Asia Minor in the first place. Similarly with the Biblical Exodus, the movement from Egypt to the Promised Land which is also a return to the Promised Land, and the quest of the Messiah as developed by Christian liturgy, where the Word of God begins as a person of the Trinity in the presence of God, then departs for the earth to redeem mankind, and returns to the same presence.

Let us turn to the word "way," which is one of the most common words in English, and is an excellent example of the extent to which language is built up on a series of metaphorical analogies. We are constantly using metaphors based on "way" without realizing it. The most common meaning of "way" in English is a method or manner of procedure, but method and manner imply some sequential repetition, and the repetition brings us to the metaphorical kernel of road or path. One "way" may be straight and another winding: such a phrase as "that's a funny way to go about it" indicates a winding one. If the situation is one where we get to the same destination whichever course we pursue, we use the word "anyway." If we are speaking of a time when all possible journeys have been completed, we use the word "always."

In the Bible, "way" normally translates the Hebrew *derek* and the Greek *hodos*, and throughout the Bible, though very emphatically in the New Testament, there is a strong emphasis on the contrast between a straight way that takes us to our destination and a divergent way that misleads or confuses. This metaphorical contrast haunts the whole of Christian literature: we start reading Dante's *Commedia*, for example, and the third line speaks of a lost or erased way: "che la diritta via era smarrita."[2] Other religions are based on the same metaphor: Buddhism speaks of an eightfold path.[3] In Chinese Taoism the word *Tao* is usually rendered "way" in English, by Arthur Waley and others, though I understand that the character representing the word is formed of radicals meaning something like "head-going." The sacred book of Taoism, the *Tao te Ching*, begins by saying that the Tao that can be talked about is not the real Tao: in other words we are being warned to beware of the traps in metaphorical language, or, in a common Oriental phrase, of confusing the moon with the finger pointing to it. But as we read on we find that the Tao can, after all, be to some extent characterized: the way is specifically the "way of the valley," the direction taken by humility, self-effacement, and the kind of relaxation, or nonaction, that makes all action effective. Tao is said also to mean art, and every art or skill is founded on sequential repetition or practice. The Middle Ages used the word *habitus* to describe the "way" in which one acquired skills: one who could read Latin was said to have the "habit" of Latin. The metaphor of road or track here seems to have a counterpart with something in the objective world, or so we gather from modern studies of the way the nervous system operates in cultivating such "habits."

The figure in the Sermon on the Mount, contrasting the straight and narrow way to salvation with the broad highway to destruction [Matthew 7:13–14], has been the basis of a number of sustained allegories, the best known being Bunyan's *Pilgrim's Progress*. To keep the figure of a "way" going for a whole book, the course pursued has to be a very laborious one: this is theologically defensible for Bunyan, even though we can see that the difficulty of the journey is a technical as well as a religious requirement. Towards the end of the second book Bunyan says: "Some also have wished, that the next way to their Father's house were here, that they might be troubled no more with either hills or mountains to go over; but the way is the way, and there is an end."[4] One wonders if there is not a suppressed voice also in Bunyan's mind asking: why do we have to be stuck with a malicious and spiteful God who puts so incredibly difficult an obstacle course between ourselves and himself? In the great *danse macabre* with which the second book concludes, where the dying Valiant-for-Truth says, "though with great difficulty I am got hither, yet now I do not repent me of all the trouble I have been at to arrive where I am,"[5] the suppressed voice is almost audible.

Whatever the dissenting voices, the spatial aspect of the journey metaphor, the movement from here to there, is obviously essential to Bunyan. The City of Destruction and the City of God must be thought of as different places: there must be an explicit repudiation of the attitude that regards "the next way to their Father's house" as "here," though many equally religious poets, such as Blake, would adopt that attitude. We are here in a curious limbo of language where the metaphor seems to be something "more" than a metaphor. My own view is that every form of speech can be reduced to metaphor, but metaphor is primary language, and metaphor cannot be reduced to another kind of language: as long as we use words at all we can never escape metaphors, but only change them. I want to return to this point later.

Less dogmatic writers than Bunyan adopt more flexible forms of journeys. Even Bunyan's figure is Y-shaped, that is, there is a choice to be made between the right way and the wrong way. A similar figure turns up in Greek mythology in the story of the choice of Hercules, who chooses between pleasure and virtue in the form of a forking road. But, of course, the doctrine of original sin, and parallel doctrines in other religions, indicate that every man is on the wrong path to begin with. Hence the frequency of such themes as that of Robert Frost's *The Road Not Taken*, which is based on the fact that every choice excludes every other choice, and that every life is full of roads not taken that continue to haunt us with a sense of possible missed opportunities. Eliot's *Quartets* begin by saying that some rigorously fatalistic cause–effect philosophies may tell us that the phrase "it might have been" is entirely futile, but, as soon as it has told us that, we instantly begin again with "it might have been" fantasies.[6] The reason is ultimately that mankind took the wrong way at the fall, and all such fantasies are connected with nostalgia for the unfallen state. Here again, of course, the same theme can be treated ironically: Borges's story *The Garden of Forking Paths* encloses a number of paths within a cycle of unvarying identity.

So far we have been speaking of journeys over the surface of the earth. But in mythology our world has always been a middle earth, with different forms of experience above and below it. Once again the "above" and "below" are spatial metaphors, but metaphors that are very difficult to confine to the purely hypothetical area of the literary metaphor. Mircea Eliade tells us of the shamanism centred in Siberia, where a major part of the shaman's arduous spiritual training consists of journeys to heights and depths.[7] The symbol of ascent may be a tree, a mountain, or a ladder. The ladder, or staircase, appears in the Book of Genesis [28:12] with Jacob's vision, and the same figure of a ladder recurs in Plato's *Symposium* as the image of the progress in love from fascination with a physically beautiful object to union with the ideal form of beauty. The Greek word for ladder, *klimax*, and the Latin word, *scala*, will give us some notion of the immense proliferation of this image. Scale, or marks of degree, represents the indispensable instrument of all physical science, and nature seems to lend itself to such measurement, as in the electromagnetic ladder that runs up through the colours to gamma rays. The dependence of the art of music on the scale needs no elaboration, and it was a common view not many centuries ago that scale and degree were essential to the form of human society as well.

Very frequently the image of ascent takes the form of a spiral path going around a mountain or tower. Such towers or ziggurats were common in the ancient Near East, and the story of the Tower of Babel [Genesis 11:1–9], which was designed to reach heaven from earth, is the demonic parody of the vision of Jacob in Genesis. According to Herodotus some of these towers had seven turnings, each coloured differently to represent the seven planets.[8] The greatest literary development of this image is of course the *Purgatorio* of Dante, where purgatory is represented as a vast mountain on the other side of the world, with seven turnings, at each of which one of the seven deadly sins is removed. At the top is the Garden of Eden, where Dante recovers his freedom of will and the original innocence that he possessed as a child of Adam before the fall. The garden at the top of the mountain descends symbolically from the chamber at the top of the ziggurat, where, according to Herodotus, the body of the god's bride was laid to await the descent of the god.[9] The connecting symbolic link in the Bible is the identity of the Garden of Eden with the body of the bride described in the Song of Songs [4:12] as "a garden inclosed . . . a fountain sealed." Dante passes over this identification, but two female figures, first Matilda and then Beatrice, appear at the top of the mountain, and the latter conducts Dante through another journey past the seven planets into the presence of God.

The assumption underlying such journeys is the same as the assumption underlying the chain of being, namely the assumption that every created thing has its "natural place" in the chain of being. Medieval physics even held that anything in its natural place had no weight. And yet the whole conception of a natural place ("kindly stead" is Chaucer's phrase for it)[10] is disturbed by the fact that every creature has impelled within it a desire to return to its creator, and so until everything is in God and God is all in all, in Paul's phrase [1 Corinthians 15:28], there will still be a motive for a journey of some kind. God being above nature, there is strictly speaking no such thing as a natural place at all, at least in this eschatological context.

The immense suggestiveness of the spiral climb up the mountain may be connected with the fact that each revolution on the spiral is circumferential: that is, one acquires a complete vision or understanding of what one is doing at each stage. It has been suggested that some actual mountains may have been equipped with spiral paths for ritual purposes. One writer claims to have found such an ancient spiral climb on the Glastonbury Tor, and it is possible that some of the Psalms in the Bible, especially those marked "a song of degrees," were connected not merely with ritual pilgrimages to Jerusalem but more specifically with a climb up one of its hills, whether spirally or not. The figure itself retains its power in literature until our own time. In the seventeenth century John Donne says of Truth:

> on a huge hill
> Cragg'd, and steep, Truth stands, and he that will
> Reach her, about must, and about must go;
> And what the hill's suddenness resists, win so. [Satire 3, ll. 79–82]

The disciples of the Renaissance grammarian in Browning's poem are not necessarily going up a spiral, but the symbolic appropriateness of ascent is as strong as ever:

> Leave we the unlettered plain its herd and crop;
> Seek we sepulture
> On a tall mountain, citied to the top,
> Crowded with culture! [*A Grammarian's Funeral*, ll. 13–16]

In our century T.S. Eliot, in *Ash-Wednesday*, builds his poem around the figure of a staircase, modelling his metaphor explicitly on Dante's *Purgatorio*, although his earlier poetry also shows a constant fascination with the image. Contemporary with *Ash-Wednesday*, Yeats was producing books of poems with such titles as *The Tower* and *The Winding Stair*, even buying himself a round tower, of a type frequent in Ireland, to live in. James Joyce was also writing at the same time the epic of *Finnegans Wake*, founded on the story of the Irish hod carrier who fell off a ladder, an event he associates on the first page of his book with the fall of man. Ezra Pound in the *Cantos* was, according to his own statement, erecting a verbal tower corresponding to those in Herodotus, whose terraces were the colour of the stars [*Canto* 74, l. 11].

There are, naturally enough, variant patterns of this metaphorical journey: there is the journey to the sea or the bank of a sacred river like the Ganges or Jordan, where sins are metaphorically washed off: the pilgrimage of the initiates at Eleusis, where the greatest of the Greek mysteries was held, was to the sea, and perhaps the great resonance of the cry of "the sea!" in Xenophon's *Anabasis* is connected with it.[11] Again, Jacob saw the angels going up and down on his "ladder," and, as Donne remarks, it is interesting that the angels, who presumably can fly, are portrayed as going up and down the ladder one step at a time.[12] In fact that dreary and totally unauthenticated story that one of the subjects discussed in the Middle Ages was the number of angels that could stand on the point of a pin probably owes what basis it has to the question of whether angels occupied space or not when they moved or simply manifested themselves in different places. The answer to the question would therefore be either none or an infinite number, depending on whether the metaphor of a journey was appropriate to angels.

In any case, angels are often invoked to account for one recurring feature of mystical experience, the involuntary journey, where a seer or visionary suddenly finds himself in a quite different place. Ezekiel in the Old Testament represents himself as being physically in Babylon with other Jewish captives, but transported to Jerusalem to see visions of its present desolation and future glory [Ezekiel 8:3]. Mohammed also had an experience, alluded to in the Koran, of a journey from Mecca to Jerusalem at night: accounts of this introduce a magic flying horse and add a further journey through the seven heavens like that of Dante. In the seventeenth century the poet Henry Vaughan, describing his conversion in his poem *Regeneration*, tells us that he first climbed the mountain of morality to no purpose, and was then suddenly transported to the earthly paradise alluded to earlier:

With that, some cried "Away!"; straight I
Obey'd, and led
Full East, a fair, fresh field could spy
Some call'd it, Jacob's Bed . . . [ll. 25–8]

Such involuntary journeys are, of course, usually associated with a dream state, and were a common feature of shamanism, referred to earlier. We remember that in *King Lear* Edgar assumes the role of Tom o' Bedlam, and Tom o' Bedlam is associated in a ballad, first collected in the eighteenth century but quite possibly going back to something very similar in Shakespeare's day, with a shamanic vision of this kind:

> With an host of furious fancies
> Whereof I am commander,
> With a burning spear, and a horse of air,
> To the wilderness I wander.
> By a knight of ghosts and shadows
> I summoned am to tourney
> Ten leagues beyond the wide world's end,
> Methinks it is no journey.

But of course the central involuntary journey is death, where the metaphor of travelling seems inescapable. We can find an example without leaving *King Lear*, in Kent's dying speech: "I have a journey, sir, shortly to go: / My master calls me, I must not say no" [5.3.322–3]. Many initiate and mystery cults were founded on a practice of giving instruction to their members about what they would meet after death and how to deal with it. This aspect of journeying forms the theme of the various sacred books written for the guidance of the dying, of which the Egyptian and Tibetan Books of the Dead are the best known.[13] The Egyptian journey was to a world very like this one, where anything dangerous or sinister could be warded off by spells or by a proclamation of one's virtue during life. This conception of a postdeath "better land" is ignored in the Old Testament, though it seems to have been well known in Greece, judging from Plato's attacks on it, and even in popular Jewish belief. But it was in Christianity that it made its most energetic revival, and a quasi-material heaven very like the ancient Egyptian one was central to most forms of Christianity as late as the nineteenth century—still is, of course, in some quarters. *The Tibetan Book of the Dead*, on the other hand, is set in the framework of the Buddhist belief in reincarnation. Here the recently dead soul is informed, by the reading of the book to him, that he will see a series, first of benevolent, then of wrathful, deities, and that as all these are hallucinations projected from his own mind, he should not commit himself to any belief in their substantial existence. In practically all cases the discarnate soul is assumed to wander in an intermediate world between death and birth known as "Bardo," until he is finally attracted to a female womb and enters it. Here again there is a continuing cycle within which all journeys take place.

In the majority of these journey metaphors, the journey is seldom regarded as a good thing in itself. It is undertaken because it must be: if the journey is a metaphor for life, life has to be followed to the end, but the end is the point of the journey, or at least the quality of the end is. It is conceivable, however, that a journey might have a value in itself. If so, obviously there would have to be something inside the traveller to resonate against the experience, so the theme of journeying for the sake of the experience of journeying would often be at the same time a journey into oneself. Such a journey implies not a progress along a straight path leading to a destination, as in Bunyan, but a meandering journey. Instead of going from point A to point B. the journey might have a moving series of point B's, a further B appearing in the distance as soon as one reaches the nearest one. Thus Tennyson's *Ulysses*:

> I am a part of all that I have met;
> Yet all experience is an arch wherethro'
> Gleams that untravell'd world, whose margin fades
> For ever and for ever when I move. [ll. 18–21]

We may contrast this with Homer's Odysseus, with his consuming passion to return home, turning down the offer of immortality itself from Calypso in order to be with his Penelope [*Odyssey*, bk. 5], and with Dante's Ulysses, whose restless curiosity is regarded as a kind of blasphemy, and leads him eventually to hell [*Inferno*, canto 26]. Tennyson's type of journey, which is frequent in the Romantic period, is a continuous discovery, and any final destination can be only stagnation. We find such meandering journeys in the knight-errant romances of the Middle Ages, where the journey takes the form of a continuous series of adventures in a world that is never likely to run out of a sufficient supply of giants and dragons and suppliant heroines in a fix. The wrong kind of meandering journey is the labyrinth or maze. In the meander the route may be indirect or unexpected, but there is no danger of getting lost because the traveller is always where he is. In the labyrinth there are many false turnings, so that the journey may end nowhere, in a state of total confusion and loss of direction, unless a guide appears, as Ariadne with her clue appeared to Theseus.

Archaeologists have discovered many designs, going back to very ancient and primitive times, for both meander and labyrinth patterns. The meander, which seems to form part of the Avebury construction near Stonehenge,[14] was associated by eighteenth-century antiquarians with serpent worship. Troy also seems to have been linked with similar ritual journeys, and even the word "Troy" has been derived by some scholars from Western European Celtic or Teutonic origins.[15] In the *Aeneid* we are told of a "game of Troy," the concluding act in the war games of the fifth book, which sounds like a military tattoo or series of cavalry manoeuvres, and which had a tradition passing through ancient Troy to contemporary Rome (contemporary with Virgil, that is).[16] In the sixth book we have Aeneas's journey to the lower world, through the cave of the Sibyl, the structure of which is associated by Virgil with Daedalus, the builder of the Cretan labyrinth. Even in Romantic times, where the journey with value in itself is so frequent, we may get a labyrinthine parody, as in Shelley's *Alastor*, where the journey is a pursuit of a mocking illusion.

Throughout the Christian centuries journeys downward tended to be demonized: in the metaphorical cosmos of the Middle Ages hell was what was "down," and only the prestige of Virgil kept the convention of the downward journey going at all. It is Virgil, of course, who guides Dante through hell, hell being a descending spiral, a parody of the upward-tending spirals of purgatory and paradise. The symbolic ambiguity of the spiral meets us all through the history of symbolism: on one side there is the cornucopia, on the other the whirlpool of death. Again, journeys into the interior of the self were not common in earlier ages, because according to Christian doctrine the self was in possession of demonic forces, and one should search rather for the source of grace, such as the "cloud of unknowing" of a fourteenth-century mystical treatise.[17]

But with the Romantic movement in particular, the sense of levels of the self below consciousness, which might be evil but might also be connected with the creative powers, or with more neutral and ambiguous phenomena, notably dreams, began to complicate the journey metaphor. Such a poem as Browning's *Childe Roland to the Dark Tower Came* describes what is clearly a journey into the self, a perilous and sinister journey towards what may very well be evil, but a journey that must be undertaken nonetheless. Perhaps the definitive modern form of this type of journey is Conrad's *Heart of Darkness*, where there is a quite credible journey into the interior of Africa, almost traceable on a map, which is at the same time a journey into the darkness of the human heart as represented by the figure of Kurtz. What is remarkable about this story is that there is really nothing strictly allegorical in it: that is, the journey to the interior of the human self and the journey to the interior of Africa are simultaneous, independent, and equally significant.

The contrast we drew earlier between the meandering and the labyrinthine journey, the journey where one keeps finding things and the journey where one gets lost, often meets us in contemporary poetry. The American poet Theodore Roethke has a poem called *Journey to the Interior*, which begins, "In the long journey out of the self / There are many detours,"[18] but the journey is into the self as well, as the title suggests. We begin with the figure of a speeding car, and this suddenly stops as the self becomes motionless but the world around it continues speeding. The poem ends with an extraordinary mystical vision where all the powers of death come to life in the soul and burst into song. It is interesting to contrast the poem with another of the same title by Margaret Atwood, which tells us rather of the dangers of interior journeys, the absence of signposts and the ease of getting permanently lost.[19] It seems to me that a significant number of contemporary Canadian poets seem to be following up the nineteenth-century theme of fascination with a huge, threatening, largely unexplored environment with a theme of exploring this environment and the poet's self at the same time. In an article on the subject I gave examples from A.M. Klein, Gwendolyn MacEwen, Jay Macpherson, and others.[20] The moral ambiguity of meeting both good and evil in the depths of the self comes out vividly in a little poem by Alden Nowlan, who ascribes the same journey to St. Francis of Assisi and to Bluebeard.[21]

T.S. Eliot tells us, on the authority of Heraclitus, that "the way up and the way down are one and the same,"[22] but Heraclitus seems to have had some conception of the journey of life as travelling in opposite directions at once, so that we are continually dying one another's lives and living one another's deaths.[23] The meandering journey recurs in Yeats's "winding path," called in his occult cosmos the *Hodos Chameliontos*, the way that continually changes colour.[24] But there seems to be in him also a continuous unwinding of the winding path, which he speaks of in his poem *Byzantium* [l. 12]. He often associates this unwinding process with a purgatorial afterlife, but clearly this way of expressing it is not a doctrine for him, only one of several possible metaphors. The ancestry of this image goes back to the ancient theme of the cosmic dance, where movement and counter-movement are of equal importance. In the great

Elizabethan poem of Sir John Davies on the cosmic dance, *Orchestra*, the contradictory movements are associated also with the story of Penelope, winding and unwinding her web.

In another poem of Robert Frost, *West-Running Brook*, there is a dialogue between a male and female speaker taking place on a mountain watershed where all the brooks are flowing toward the east except one that has decided to go in the opposite direction. As they continue to examine this contrary motion, the man notices an eddying movement in its current that punctuates the sequential movement toward the west with a stasis where the water seems to be standing still. He says:

> It is this backward motion toward the source,
> Against the stream, that most we see ourselves in,
> The tribute of the current to the source.
> It is from this in nature we are from.
> It is most us. [ll. 68–72]

One thinks also of the journey to the source of the river at the end of Yeats's *The Tower*. A modulation of this arrested movement in the journey is the interrupted journey, of which perhaps the greatest example in literature is Shakespeare's *Tempest*, the arresting of the Court Party returning from Africa to Italy and the rearranging of their lives in consequence. *The Tempest* owes a good deal to the *Aeneid*, where the midway interruption of Aeneas's journey in the visit to the lower world is also what enables him to see the point of his quest. The corresponding theme in the Bible, I should think, is the interruption of the Exodus by the death of Moses, who climbs a mountain to see the Promised Land in the distance [Deuteronomy 3.27–8, 34.1–5], leaving younger successors to complete the quest. It has not been sufficiently remarked, I think, that Moses was the only man in history ever to see the Promised Land. Those who went further merely entered Canaan, and started another cycle of history.

We have seen that many of these journey metaphors come from the teaching of Jesus in the Gospels. They occur mainly in the more exoteric part of his doctrine, the Sermon on the Mount [Matthew 5–7] and other addresses to a public still immersed in a time-world, where it seems appropriate to suggest extensions of time, in such conceptions as "the next world" or "the afterlife," to unknown forms of existence, and to keep the metaphor of the completed journey for this life. But in the dialogues between Jesus and his disciples in the Gospel of John we seem to be in a more esoteric area. The discussion in John 14 is so familiar that it tends to slide in and out of the mind without leaving much impression, and the paralysing paradox of what is being said misses us entirely. Jesus tells his disciples that he is going to prepare a place for them, that they know where he is going, and consequently they know the way. They protest that they don't at all know where he is going, and therefore they can't possibly know the way. Jesus' answer, "I am the way" [John 14:6], explodes, or, as some would now say, deconstructs, the whole metaphor of journey, of the effort to go there in order to arrive here. Philip asks to be shown the Father, and gets the same type of answer: there is nothing there; everything you need is here. In the synoptics Jesus makes the same point in telling his disciples that the kingdom of heaven, the core of his teaching, is among them or within them. Nothing in Jesus' teaching seems to have been more difficult for his followers to grasp than his principle of the hereness of here.

Gertrude Stein remarked of the United States, "There is no there there,"[25] meaning, I suppose, that the beckoning call to the horizon, which had expanded the country from one ocean to the other in the nineteenth century, had now settled into a cultural uniformity in which every place was like every other place, and so equally "here." This is a kind of parody of Jesus' conception of his kingdom as here [Luke 17:21], but nevertheless it forms a useful starting point. Several religions, notably Zen Buddhism, emphasize first of all the fact that "there is nowhere to go," attempting to drive us into an intolerable claustrophobia from which there is no escape except by a kind of explosion of the ego-self into the spiritual body that is the real form of itself. Similarly with Jesus' "I am the way." Once we form part of the body of the Word which is both ourselves and infinitely larger than ourselves, the distinction between movement and rest vanishes: there is no need for a "way," because the conception "away" is no longer functional.

Metaphor, I said earlier, is primary language: every type of language can be reduced to metaphor, but when we are speaking in metaphorical language itself there can be no further reduction: we can only exchange one metaphor for another. But metaphor is normally a statement of identity, of the type "A is B." In literature metaphor is asserted only: we say that A is B, but we know quite well that A is not B and that no one is confused enough in his mental processes to think that it is. The essential point here is that literary metaphor, which is purely hypothetical, grows out of an existential type of metaphor, as we might call it, where a subject does identify himself with something not himself, in an experience that has no further need for language, although it has also fulfilled the entire function of language. As long as we say, for example, "I believe that," we are caught in a verbal trap, because we don't know who "I" is or what "that" is: all we know is that the barrier between subject and object is still there, so that we can't distinguish between what we believe and what we believe we believe, or might believe if we knew more, like Philip [John 14:8–10]. But when we pass from the language of metaphor into the identities that metaphor asserts, we have reached the kind of faith the New Testament is talking about: the *hypostasis* of the hoped-for, the *elenchos* of the unseen.[26]

25

Framework and Assumption

24 October 1985

Originally presented at a conference on "Convention and Knowledge: Anatomy of Agreement in Contemporary Intellectual Culture," at Smith College, Massachusetts. First published in the Northrop Frye Newsletter, *1, no. 1 (Fall 1988): 2–10. Reprinted in* MM, *79–92. The text below is from the typescript in the NFF, 1988, box 49, file 1. There is an additional typescript in the NFF, 1991, box 39, file 3.*

As this conference is concerned with convention and knowledge, I should like to begin by talking about the role of convention in literature. A convention is an aspect of the identity of a work of literature: it is what makes it recognizable for what it is, and it is also the aspect that welcomes and invites the reader. Conventions may appear in minor roles within other conventions. In *Romeo and Juliet,* for instance, the great courtly love convention that dominated so much of the Middle Ages extends only to the Romeo–Rosaline affair that precedes the action of the play. Convention can even be merely a traditional custom, like the *topoi* used so much in medieval literature or the fourteen lines of the sonnet. When the convention is big enough to include the entire work, we call it a genre, and this is the aspect of convention I shall be mainly concerned with. A genre establishes the identity of a work of literature in two ways: it indicates what the work is, and it suggests the context of the work, by placing it within a number of other works like it. Any large bookshop will illustrate the role of genre in reading by dividing its stock into sections labelled science fiction, detective fiction, romance, Westerns, and the like. Such divisions continue the role of convention in inviting the reader: if you want this kind of book, the label says, here is where you find it.

In ordinary speech convention implies that a thing is just like a lot of other things. This may be a reason for feeling indifferent to certain conventions: it is also a reason for feeling interested in certain others. I know of no reason, beyond the whims of personal taste, why members of one convention should impel us to say "they're all much the same," and why members of another should rouse our interest in distinguishing all the variety we can. The only criterion I can think of is the number of normal conventions that have to be sacrificed to keep a central one intact.

For example, I was once in the shop of an old and cranky bookseller who had put up his labels according to his own reactions, which were precritical. One such label read, simply, "Filth." There were some books approaching pornography in this section, and they started me thinking about pornography as a genre. Most pornography plays down the traditional conventions of story line, characterization, description, and comment, and confines itself to a prodding of certain reflexes or an evoking of certain fantasies. Such things are always formulaic, and the formulaic represents convention at its most primitive, a level at which the work may emerge, like the popular songs in Orwell's *1984*, untouched by human intelligence. I notice too that in bookstores and publishing houses the categories of genre have been uninfluenced by critical theory. I glanced at a row of books by Carlos Castaneda recently, and saw that the earlier books were labelled "nonfiction" by the publisher and the later ones "fiction."[1] I dare say an interesting story lies behind that, but as the earlier and the later books appeared to be generically identical, the distinction was of little critical use.

There is a certain amount of snobbery among some readers tending to assume that a book is of minor importance if its genre is easily recognizable, like the science fiction and detective stories just mentioned. The detective story, in particular, is written in a convention that follows certain prescribed rules, and so resembles a game, like chess. That is nothing new in literature, though earlier rules-of-a-game conventions were usually smaller in range and mostly confined to verse. At present there is a widespread impression that flexible conventions are a mark of serious writing. The days are gone when Jane Austen could protest against the snob phrase "only a novel," and point out that a "novel" could be on the same level of seriousness as any book of sermons.[2] But of course she had her conventions: there are no writers who are unconventional or beyond convention. Sometimes a writer may seem unconventional because his readers are accustomed to different conventions and do not realize it, or else assume that what they are used to is the normal way of writing. Such reactions to convention may vary from Samuel Johnson's dictum, "Nothing odd will do long: *Tristram Shandy* did not last," to the claim of a twentieth-century formalist critic that *Tristram Shandy* was the most typical novel ever written.[3]

Browning's poem on Andrea del Sarto, called "the faultless painter," makes the point, among others, that faultlessness can be itself a fault.[4] The reason is that if a painter can be called faultless it means only that the particular convention he followed has come to a dead end. When this happens, all the critics who decided that other painters were "faulty" because their grasp of the convention was less complete are swept into the dust bin of the history of taste. Today we try to be more liberal and eclectic in our responses, but government and other boards entrusted with the duty of giving grants to promising artists still often respond only to certain fashionable conventions, so that artists who are interested in different conventions have to go without grants until the fashion changes. The word "beauty" has become suspect as a critical category, because it has meant, so often and for so long, conforming to an established convention. In the nineteenth century there were still critics who assumed that the Greeks had invented beauty in their statues and architecture, and that everything pre-Greek or outside the Greek tradition was deliberately and perversely ugly.

Thirty years ago, when I wrote the *Anatomy of Criticism*, I paid some attention to the question of genres, because I felt that lack of careful reflection in that area made for many confusions and illiterate critical judgments. The wheel of fashion that moves the history of taste has turned since then, though that does not mean that the issues involved have turned with it. I now frequently encounter objections to my alleged passion for ticketing and labelling things, where reference to an excessive toilet training in my infancy is clearly being suppressed with some reluctance. But when I turn to other areas of critical theory, and am informed, for example, that the privileging of interdiscursivity problematizes the differentializing of contextuality, I do not feel that I am being released from an obsession. I feel only that I am facing different conventions about what it is important to find names for.

I think of literature as a specific field of imaginative activity, but the metaphor of "field" I have in mind is something like a magnetic field, a focus of energy, not a farmer's field with a fence around it. I also think of genres as fields in the same way. A literary genre being a part of literature, that means, as long as we hang on to the farmer's field metaphor, a smaller field with a smaller fence. Hence we instinctively think of Shakespeare, for instance, as a poet who wrote mainly plays, rather than as a dramatist who used mainly verse. That will sound like a quibble only to those who do not understand the issues involved. A modern reader of Shakespeare may be put off by the dullness he finds in the Henry VI plays, the brutality of *Titus Andronicus*, the anti-Semitism of *The Merchant of Venice*, the sexism of *The Taming of the Shrew*, and so on through a large part of the canon. The point is that all these plays, whatever our present ideological values, are superb theatre, and with Shakespeare the actable and the theatrical always come first. If we had been Shakespeare, we feel, we would have used the theatre for higher and nobler purposes. Shakespeare never used the theatre for anything except putting on plays, which is one reason why he is Shakespeare. The surrender to the genre, the entering into its conventions as they were at his time, is the mark of the professional craftsman, who outlasts most of the well-meaning amateurs.

In Shakespeare's day schoolboys were trained in the three parts of the trivium: grammar, meaning Latin grammar, rhetoric, and formal logic. Deductive logic became increasingly arid with the rise of science and its more inductive attitude, along with the growing suspicion that the syllogism yielded no new knowledge. The decline of rhetoric continued through the eighteenth century and was fairly complete by the Romantic period. Grammar, even English grammar, declined in the twentieth century, partly through the influence of linguists who maintained that the English grammar taught in schools was still Latin grammar, English analysed in a way that had no relevance to the real structure of English.

I have thought about this a good deal, and my present view is that the linguists were pedagogically wrong: I think that English grammar should be taught from the point of view of a more highly inflected language, Latin being the obvious one. Such a training gives an insight into the structure of English that cannot be obtained from English alone, and it also provides an elementary introduction to philosophical categories, the concrete and abstract, the universal and particular, and the like, which the student will be encountering all his life. But this is by the way: the essential point is that in the twentieth century writers learn to write mainly by instinct and practice, supplemented by the study of older writers who had, or took, greater educational advantages, such as Joyce and Pound. As a result the conventions of writing are acquired but not learned, and while this may be an advantage for some kinds of writers, it makes the general bulk of contemporary writing more conventional than ever. A writer who has studied and practised certain conventions may develop more distinctive and individual ways of handling them; a writer who does not know that he is being conventional becomes a mass voice in a mass market.

As a result of the collapse of the trivium there grew up an attitude to the arts represented by the title of a book by Herbert Read, *The True Voice of Feeling*. This was a refinement of the Carlyle view that all writing was the personal rhetoric of the author. Jacques Derrida would quickly recognize it as one more way of using writing in order to denigrate writing. I spent ten years reviewing poetry in Canada,[5] where the doctrine of the true voice of feeling was the established one, and had ample experience of the monotony that resulted. I noted with interest the other day that one or two Canadian poets were talking of basing more of their poetic themes on the routine work of their society, on the jobs people held and the way their social functions affected their imagination. They had finally realized, after a steady downpour had been going on for half a century, how many Canadian poets were still as obsessed by certain sexual themes as the most pedantic Elizabethan sonneteer.

This is a far cry from the days when a poet would begin his work by making an appeal to the Muses. The great advantage of the Muses was that they were confined to specific generic territories: if you wanted to write a love lyric there was a Muse for that (Erato), but you wouldn't call on Calliope or Clio, otherwise it might take you twelve books to get to your first orgasm.[6] The poet who is his own Muse, regarding his own imagination as an unconditioned will like Calvin's God, gains a facile victory over nothing: he has no angel to fight with, like Jacob [Genesis 32:24–30]. Walter Benjamin connects this autonomous aesthetic with fascism:[7] I would not go as far as that, though I can see some of the affinities. And I would certainly not want to leave the impression that all Muses are soft cuddly nudes: some of them are ravening harpies who swoop and snatch and carry off, who destroy a poet's peace of mind, his position in society, even his sanity.

I think I understand what Derrida means by the use of writing to denigrate writing, though I hesitate to draw the portentous inferences from it that some of his disciples do. What I find much more difficult to understand is the continuous use of criticism to denigrate criticism, the continued assumption that literary criticism has no skeleton, and cannot stand up unless some philosophical or psychological construct provides one. If we start by regarding criticism as parasitic on literature, we invariably end by regarding literature as parasitic on the other verbal structures that convey actual information. Again, language is certainly one of the contexts of every verbal discipline, but to obliterate all distinctions between reader and poet, between criticism and creation, between literature and other verbal structures, because they are all forms of language, seems to me to fall under the law in the Book of Deuteronomy that says "Cursed be he that removeth his neighbour's landmark" [27:17]. There are many distinctions that may be difficult, even impossible, to establish in theory that are nonetheless essential to employ in practice. Ignoring them transforms all the products of language into a vast alphabet soup in which those two essential letters, Alpha and Omega, the beginning and the end, are nowhere to be found. There is no reason in the mind of God or the design of nature why I should now be in an area called Massachusetts, but life would get very confusing without such arbitrarily designated areas.

I notice that an increasing number of literary critics are moving outside the literary field and developing interests in other verbal disciplines. Some of them, including myself, are following the lead of Kenneth Burke's pioneering study, *The Rhetoric of Religion*.[8] Of the many reasons for my growing preoccupation with the Bible, two are particularly relevant here. One is that a literary critic, in studying metaphor, is confined to the hypothetical metaphor of literature, the statement of identity that remains purely verbal and simultaneously denies what it asserts. The Bible expands metaphor into what might be called existential metaphor, the actual identifying of a conscious subject with something objective to itself. As Shakespeare's Theseus ought to have said, every human being is of imagination all compact.[9] The other reason is the double perspective the Bible presents: from one point of view it is a completely unified whole of metaphor and imagery, and from another it is totally decentralized. It continually, in other words, constructs and deconstructs itself.

II

I see a writer or a work of literature as at the centre of a cross like a plus sign. The horizontal bar represents his historical and cultural situation, the assumptions he was bound to make as a man of his time, the ideology he was bound to reflect when he wrote. The vertical bar represents the literary tradition from which he descended and the continuing of that line of descent to ourselves. Let us look at the horizontal line first. It runs in theory from complete acceptance of the social and ideological environment the poet is in to its complete rejection. In practice nobody could live continuously at such extremes, and there is always some conflict within the mind of the writer himself. This, rather than the influence of a predecessor, seems to me to constitute the primary anxiety besetting a poet. Certainly an influence can also be an anxiety, but I should call this a special factor in a writer's struggle with his contemporary culture, rather than putting it on the socially isolated Freudian basis that Harold Bloom does.[10] Gerard Manley Hopkins, for example, found himself in conflict with the prevailing ethos of Victorian England, and adopted a dogmatic Catholic position partly in opposition to it, partly for the positive values it supplied in place of the negative reaction. But the religious position he adopted was a terrifying anxiety in itself, however much we as readers may profit from the tensions it created. Other poets—Tasso, Gogol, Rimbaud—have had their lives shattered or drastically altered by similar tensions.[11]

Of course it is obvious that we cannot keep horizontal and vertical dimensions separate: Hopkins's Catholicism had also a great deal to do with the literary traditions he attached himself to. But again there are practical distinctions. To take the next step I must return to a point made in the *Anatomy of Criticism* [95–104]. Young writers huddle together in schools and issue manifestos, announcing their conventions as something new, or as about to produce something new. As they grow older and acquire more authority, they do not become less conventional, but their notions of convention become more deeply rooted in the history of the art and are less a reflection of a contemporary fashion in ideology. It is at this point that the really crucial form of originality comes into view. Painters of the Barbizon school in nineteenth-century France followed certain easily recognizable conventions, though they achieved a great deal of individual variety within them. When we come to Manet, we feel that we have got past those conventions and are on something new. But after a while we realize that the new, though certainly new, is also deeply traditional. There is a deeper link with certain painters of the past—Goya, Velasquez, Rembrandt—being established. This aspect of tradition forms the vertical bar of my diagram: it refers to the traditions of the art rather than to contemporary situations. But, unlike the more obvious conventions linking the Barbizon painters with one another, there is a discontinuous quality in the larger historical tradition. Something that has disappeared for years or centuries may suddenly reappear; conventions long ignored or forgotten suddenly materialize again, like the angels who traditionally do not move in time or space but simply become visible somewhere else.

It seems to me that this historical relationship is an integral part of an artist's or writer's relation to us. What might otherwise be an insoluble mystery, the way in which a writer incredibly remote from us in time, space, social conditioning, and cultural assumptions, can still make imaginative contact with us, becomes intelligible when we remember that we are still living within the history of literature and the other arts, and can recognize the current of that history flowing into us. It should go without saying that this current is not only that of the Western tradition, but includes Oriental and other cultures as well. If we are interested in our ancestry, it is natural to trace our direct ancestry first, but we all know that we eventually come to a point at which everyone alive was an ancestral relative.

If we keep this cross diagram in mind, it may give us some understanding of the artist's situation vis-à-vis his own time. In studying, let us say, Shakespeare, we confront a dramatist working around 1600 in a society with very different assumptions and organization from ours. We cannot study him intelligently without noting the nuances that the differences in social rank among his characters bring into the dialogue, nor without allowing for the prejudices and cultural preferences his audience brought into the theatre with them. Without this context of Shakespearean scholarship, we simply kidnap Shakespeare into our own age, and judge him by all the prejudices and assumptions that *we* bring into the theatre with us. At the same time, there is still the mystery of how such a writer does communicate with us, and for that we need a different dimension from the one provided by a knowledge of Elizabethan ideology. That communicating ability, it seems to me, is the other half of the historical relation to the dramatists and other writers of earlier ages, starting with his immediate precursors of the Greene and Lyly period, and going back to the great Greek writers. This is a genuinely historical relationship, but it cannot all be reached by historical methods, as Shakespeare did not know the Greek tragic writers directly and knew the formulas of Menandrine comedy mainly in prose romance distortions. Here only a comparative generic analysis will establish the relation.

I can understand the fascination of what Roland Barthes calls the zero degree of writing, the impulse to rid oneself of all conventions and confront one's subject directly.[12] I can understand Picasso's remark that it was easy to learn to paint like Raphael and very difficult to learn to paint like a child.[13] In a related field, I can understand the nostalgia of Husserl for an abandoning of preconceived mental categories and an unimpeded view of the things themselves.[14] In painting, again, we prize the work of the so-called primitives because of their freshness of insight, their freedom from secondhand formulas, from stock pictorial quotations and allusions. But if we look at a collection of primitives, we see the same doll-like figure drawing, the same psychedelic colouring, the same crowding of detail in the composition, over and over again. Directness of vision is not for us: everything objective is also in part a mirror, and human creation is an ontogenetic development that must recall its phylogenetic ancestry before it can bring it to life once more. Adam may have had a direct vision of reality on the sixth day of creation, but after the seventh day the world became conventionalized to God himself. I think the cult of unmediated vision really relates to something quite different.

I have often enough insisted that every human society exists within a cultural envelope that separates it from its natural environment: that there are no noble savages, and no men sufficiently natural to live in a society without such an envelope. Most people call this envelope an ideology, which is accurate enough for fairly advanced societies. The word "ideology" suggests argument as well as ideas, because of the Hegelian principle that every proposition contains its opposite. That is why a writer living in his own ideology is subjected to stress and anxiety: thesis and antithesis are bound to be in his mind at once. I suggest that an ideology is a secondary and derivative structure, and that what human societies do first is make up stories. I think, in other words, that an ideology always derives from a mythology, as a myth to me means a *mythos*, a story or narrative. I am speaking of course of story types, not of specific stories.

It is mythology that we find in primitive societies, and mythology that we find at the historical beginnings of our own, and it is again mythology that underlies our present ideologies, when we examine them closely enough. In Shakespeare's day the Christian ideology his contemporaries accepted was a derivation from Christian mythology, the story Christianity had to tell from its sacred books. In our day we are surrounded by various historical ideologies, progressive and revolutionary, Jeffersonian and Marxist, but these go back, in their inception, to various forms of comic plot superimposed on history. I think also that the poet, in particular, has an instinct for the mythological core of his culture and goes directly to it to try to recreate it so far as he can. The quest for unmediated vision, then, is really a quest for the recovery of myth, the word hoard guarded by the dragons of ideology.

The growth of an ideology in society is a product of concern, a word that I find very difficult to define or even describe, but which I hope is to some degree self-explanatory. It is our concern for living in social units that builds up societies into nations to be defended in war, into religious confessions to be maintained by enforced agreement and the persecution of dissidents, into class structures where the different strata of society have different rights and privileges. These are, it seems clear, secondary and derivative concerns, and the ideologies that maintain them are based on rationalization. The primary concerns underlying them are simpler: they are the concerns for food, for shelter, for sexual relations, for survival; for freedom and escape from slavery; for happiness and escape from misery. Paul Tillich distinguishes the religious concern as "ultimate": it may be that, but it can hardly be primary. One cannot live a day without being concerned about food, but one may live all one's life without being concerned about God. At the same time one hesitates to rule out the conscious and creative concerns from the primary ones. When a society comes close to the level of bare subsistence, and has no leisure or technology for the so-called "frills," the arts, including the literary arts, do not disappear: they leap into the foreground among the essentials of survival. Examples range from Palaeolithic cave drawings to Inuit life today. Again, the opening sentence of Aristotle's *Metaphysics*, "all men by nature desire to know," seems to me to put the expanding of consciousness, too, on its proper primary footing.

All through history secondary concerns have taken priority over primary ones. The primary concern for survival has to give way periodically to going to war; the concern for a sexual partner gives way to the demands of celibacy enforced by a religion or by certain other types of social calling. I say "all through history," and in fact history itself is created by the continuity of such secondary concerns. Literature obviously reflects these ideologies in every period, but they enter literature as elements of content, not as forms or shaping principles. The conventions and genres of literature are essentially untouched by them: these seem to look back to the earlier mythological time, some of them, like the pastoral, looking very longingly and nostalgically to them. Certain mutations of genres take place as the social structure alters and the reading public changes: it is clear, for instance, that the classical novel as we know it rose along with a certain kind of bourgeois reading public in the eighteenth century, and will disappear with the disappearance of that class. But the middle-class novel was not a new entity in literature: it was a new format for storytelling, and the shape and pattern of the stories told remained much the same.

What we said earlier, that ideology is primarily an anxiety to a writer and not a guide to the form of what he should write, makes it not surprising that so many of the best and most influential writers—Balzac, Dostoevsky, Ezra Pound, D.H. Lawrence—should have adopted such bizarre, even perverse, forms of ideology. It is clear that their mythological interests, the kinds of imaginative themes that preoccupied them, fitted very awkwardly and uneasily into the ideological structures confronting them.

The historical nature of ideology makes it quite feasible to study the history of ideas, but, as explained earlier, the history of mythology is more discontinuous. The best we can do with mythology is to try to sketch out the large interlinking patterns in it, and when we do this we find a curious affinity between mythology and primary concerns. Because of the unorthodox methods that are essential, those who deal with the informing role of mythology in literature often seem close to being cranks. Frazer's *Golden Bough*, for instance, while it is by no means as fundamentally wrong and full of holes as some anthropologists and classicists say, is still a very vulnerable book. Nonetheless it retains its fascination as a book that brings an astonishing number of mythological patterns into alignment with one of the primary concerns: the food supply, more particularly the agricultural supply. Frazer's dying god cycle has an intimate connection with a female figure who usually represents the earth as the dying god does the vegetation. Frazer leaves out most of her mythological role: Graves's *White Goddess*, another vulnerable book, attempts to fill this in. However, the primary sexual concerns of humanity are reflected more directly by modern psychologists when they touch on mythology, as they so often do. The work of Freud and his followers, orthodox and heretic, is of course indispensable here. Jung moved further away from the sexual concern than most of the others, even though his biggest, most complex, and most totally unintelligible book is called *Mysterium Coniuctionis*. Some works in archaeology, such as G.R. Levy's *Gate of Horn*, deal with the primary concerns of providing shelter for the living, the dead, and the gods.

Because the history of mythology rides on top of, or gets submerged under, actual history, it suggests a state of innocence or Golden Age that we do not look for in actual history. Every age had cruelties and horrors parallel to our own, but we can still read their literature and look at their visual arts with pleasure. This is partly because the creative imagination suggests an intimacy with the natural environment which emerges in the metaphorical structures of poetry, metaphor being the language of identity. In its more pastoral and romantic genres it creates a nature that responds to human desire; in its more tragic and ironic ones it surveys the human situation from a point of detachment. The language of ideology is metonymic: it urges that this particular structure of authority is the closest we can get to the ideal one, and so is being "put for" the ideal.

The twentieth century saw in its earlier years a very explicit and conscious revival of mythological themes in its literature, especially in the group of writers who peaked around 1922, the year of [Joyce's] *Ulysses* and [Eliot's] *The Waste Land*. What happens in the arts indicates what is going to happen in the world a generation or so later, and from mid-century on we have come to realize, from the nuclear bomb and from the polluting of the supply of drinkable water and breathable air, that our age is the first in history to exhibit clearly the principle: primary concerns must become primary, or else. Some people in various parts of the world, including this one, may still think it highly desirable to go to war to smash somebody else's ideology, but the primary concern with human survival tells us that we cannot afford such gestures any more. And for the first time the primary concern is beginning to speak with authority.

It seems, then, if this argument has any cogency, that criticism, the theory of the language of myth and metaphor in which primary concern expresses itself most directly, is very far from being the game of trivial pursuit that it so often appears to be. In the title of my paper, "Framework and Assumption," the "framework" is the ideological structure, or the great variety of them, surrounding us in the contemporary world. Such frameworks, whether religious or secular, are reasonably well known in their general outlines. Studying the assumptions on which they are based brings us to the mythological structures from which they are derived, and which literature recreates directly. We have no coherent surveyed maps of the mythological area yet: we have only exploratory and tentative maps of the "here be dragons" type. It has been recognized at least since Sir Philip Sidney's time that because literature, the mythological imagination at work in the world, makes no assertions, it escapes from argument and refutation. In criticism, of course, as in any theoretical field, disagreement is as essential and as creative as agreement is. Subordinating it to primary concerns means only that it should be kept impersonal. Nonetheless the vision of a created order where, in Blake's phrase,"no dispute can come,"[15] is essential to the total picture.

If we are working solely on the basis of ideology, and regard it as the basis from which literature and the other arts emerge, we shall eventually come to a vision of humanity as a crazy Oedipus obsessed by two overmastering desires: to kill his father God and to rape his mother Nature. By "his father" I mean the source of his life, whether we call it God or not. For such a rabid animal, as Gulliver's Houyhnhnm master told him, reason is simply a faculty that intensifies his viciousness.[16] With the mythological perspective, we can see ourselves capable of creation as well as destruction, with reason a means to an end of ultimate consensus, however distant. In that perspective, what this conference is studying, the role of convention in knowledge, becomes more intelligible. The two meanings of the word "convention" coincide: the convention is the agreed-on place of meeting for a community, where variety and difference are always needed, where individual distinctiveness is as prized as it is anywhere, but where the total disruption caused by wholesale commitment to secondary issues cannot break in.

26

Maps and Territories

25 May 1987

Originally presented at a conference devoted to the work of Northrop Frye in Rome. From Ritratto di Northrop Frye, *ed. Agostino Lombardo (Rome: Bulzoni Editore, 1990), 11–16. The typescripts are in the NFF, 1991, box 38, file 6 (annotated), and 1991, box 39, file 3.*

Many things must be said that should go without saying. It should go without saying that I regard this occasion as an extraordinary honour to me, so I am saying it with all the emphasis I can. The honour is independent of whatever may be said about me, because what is in the centre of discussion is not me but literary criticism. Fifty years ago there was a widespread feeling that criticism was a series of reactions to works of literature, but did not form a coherent subject in itself. There was a reluctance to examine the theoretical assumptions of criticism: it was felt that that would be only "the criticism of criticism," which it was assumed would be a most trivial and pedantic pursuit. The maturing of our sense of the importance of critical theory is, I hope, part of a new seriousness about the social function of literature.

I think that, with the exception of my early book on Blake, everything I have written has grown in some way out of my interests as a classroom teacher. In my younger days I was often on committees with university and secondary school colleagues discussing curriculum. I noticed that the primary question was nearly always, What books should a student have read by the time he or she is ready for university? Any other subject would have raised the question in the form, How much should a student know of this subject by that time? It is of course true that nothing can replace the reading of one book after another. But an educational process accompanies it, and I felt that this process should be plainly visible and not some kind of occult osmosis.

The *Anatomy of Criticism* was based, first, on the principle that it is not literature itself but the criticism of literature that is directly taught and learned, and, second, that meaning derives from context, hence most of the meaning of a literary work depends on its context within literature. This last implies paying a good deal of attention to the conventions and genres that link literary works together. No one would buy a detective story without a clear idea of the conventional and generic features of such a story, and I could not see why the student of what is usually called literature in school should be less well informed. Then again, a student has a great many literary experiences, in films and television as well as books, outside his literary curriculum. Where these represent serious interests, surely a conscientious teacher would want to show, by the structural features of such works, how the student's literary experience was forming the same kind of unity that would appear in, say, his experience of mathematics.

Such an outlook on literature aroused at first some opposition from what I think of as the read-and-feel squad. They often talked about "pigeonholing," which seems to me a silly metaphor: the relevant metaphor is that of a map. A map is not the territory being explored but is normally the best guide to it, and maps improve in refinement and accuracy with further study. But for some time there were many who followed the tactics of the "Bellman" in Lewis Carroll's *The Hunting of the Snark* as he set out on his sea voyage:

> He had bought a large map representing the sea,
> Without the least vestige of land:
> And the crew were much pleased when they found it to be
> A map they could all understand.
>
> "What's the good of Mercator's North Poles and Equators,
> Tropics, Zones, and Meridian lines?"
> So the Bellman would cry: and the crew would reply
> "They are merely conventional signs!"[1]

If criticism is not a structure of knowledge it is nothing very interesting, and if it is a structure of knowledge it is objective to the knower, distinct from the experience of reading or the like that led up to it. I often used to hear about the "uniqueness" of the literary work, but while every experience is unique, the unique is never known as such: knowledge is based on likeness within difference. We know this creature to be a cat, disregarding the fact that there are millions of cats, all of them perceptibly different in appearance and temperament from this one. Again, it is true that the understanding of literature includes the recapturing of one's experience with it, but the structure of knowledge must mediate, otherwise the criticism ends where it began and has no content.

When I was a student, literature was set within a mainly historical framework, which was roughly satisfactory for most purposes but did not include the real history of literature. This was understandable: the history of literature is full of gaps that actual sources and influences do not always fill. The tragedies of Shakespeare are generically related to the tragedies of fifth-century Athens, but there is no direct influence involved; Dante knew that Homer was at the headwaters of his own literary tradition, but he did not know Homer at first hand. In our day, a writer may deliberately avoid a predecessor whom he knows critics will connect him with, as Joyce claimed that he had never read Rabelais. The real literary tradition has to be established in large part from a comparative generic study, which may often sound speculative or even eccentric. True, every writer is surrounded by a cultural conditioning which for many critics constitutes the whole critical area. But a past writer's historicity is always, so to speak, a great deal deader than he is. It is only the central line of literary descent, with all its gaps, that enables us to understand poets utterly remote from us in time and culture, and to admire them for reasons that they themselves, to say nothing of their contemporaries, would have found unintelligible.

I see the producer of literature as the spokesman for what I have come to call primary concern, the human preoccupation with such things as food, sex, happiness, and freedom. Human life being what it is, literature is concerned mainly with the anxieties and frustrations about not getting such things. Romance for example, is concerned largely with sexual frustration, whatever the last page may tell us, and all the literature going back to dying god myths is linked to anxiety about the food supply. Secondary concerns, the ones arising from the social contract, are the concerns connected with patriotism, religious belief, class solidarity, and the like, and are expressed in some form of ideology. All through history secondary concerns have had an ascendancy over primary ones: we want to live, but we go to war; we want freedom, but put up with exploitation. But the century of nuclear bombs and a pollution that threatens the supply of air to breathe and water to drink may be the first century in history when it has become obvious that primary concerns must become primary, or else. This fact ought to give a new social importance to the writer.

The writer knows instinctively that he has a social function that cannot be annexed to anything else. I suppose there is an "anxiety of influence" within the literary tradition itself,[2] but I think a writer's really obsessive anxieties come from his ambivalent feelings about the ideologies that surround him in society. Writers who adopt freakish and perverse ideologies, like Yeats, Ezra Pound, or D.H. Lawrence, illustrate this principle negatively. There are many writers in this century who have been silenced, exiled, imprisoned, murdered, or driven to suicide by ideology-obsessed governments. Every writer today is surrounded by ideologues who not only urge him to write according to their formulas, but have suborned a large proportion of critics to explain his work in their own terms. Surely it is a central part of a critic's function to try to determine the sources and context of a writer's distinctive authority, and help him both to understand what it is and to resist external invasions and assaults.

Lewis Carroll had more to say about maps. In *Sylvie and Bruno Concluded* there is a professor who speaks of mapmakers in his country who actually succeeded in creating a map on a scale of an inch to an inch.

> "Have you used it much?" I enquired.
> "It has never been spread out, yet," said Mein Herr: "the farmers objected: they said it would cover the whole country, and shut out the sunlight! So we now use the country itself, as its own map, and I assure you it does nearly as well."[3]

The word "nearly," which turns the passage from fantasy into satire, often comes into my mind when I pick up some of the journals of critical theory which have blossomed since the innocent 1950s when I entered the field. Surely there must be a middle ground between a map that tells us nothing about the territory and a map that attempts to replace it.

Going back to the classroom, the teacher, especially the elementary teacher, is in contact with a student's entire verbal experience, of which everything that we normally call literature forms about one per cent. The student ought to know something about the rhetorical devices employed by advertising; he ought to be able to tell when his political leaders are lying, especially when they are technically telling the truth; he ought to know what is really being said when something else is being explicitly said; he should understand the meaning of the public statements that are made to conceal meaning. Most people are left to pick up these verbal skills for themselves, which, considering the quality of most elementary school literary training, is just as well. Outside literature the texture of what one reads and hears as a concerned citizen is, or is a disguise for, some kind of either historical or conceptual framework.

So there are at least three aspects of our social training in words. First is the study of literature, which is based essentially on myth or story, and on metaphor or juxtaposed imagery. Myth says two things to us at once: "this happened" and "this cannot have happened in precisely this way." Similarly, metaphor says to us "A is B," two things are the same thing, and at the same time conveys the meaning "A is clearly not B, and no one could be fool enough to think it was." Literature releases us from the obligation of trying to relate everything we read to external standards of verification. Second, we learn from words information, as coded in historical and other descriptive forms of writing, where such categories as truth and established fact are constantly appealed to, and from which we derive most of our serious and fundamental convictions. Third, this area shades off into ideology, which pretends to be true, and which we know contains a great deal that is not. Much of it in fact is simply sick myth and sick metaphor. This area and literature form the two aspects of what has always been called rhetoric, the use of words to concentrate the mind and the use of words to persuade us out of our minds.

My survey of literary genres in *Anatomy of Criticism* led me to the sacred book as the most comprehensive of all genres. The sacred book is not really literature, but it is written mainly in the mythical and metaphorical language of literature. The literature that deals with primary concern and the book that deals with what Tillich calls ultimate concern, the origin, nature, and destiny of mankind, apparently have a common language. I then thought, What would happen if I turned this thesis inside out, starting with the Bible, and then seeing how the Bible has affected Western literature? After all, no one would attempt a study of Islamic culture without starting with the Koran, or of Hindu culture without starting with the *Vedas* and *Upanishads*. I hesitated much too long, I think now, before attempting a book on this subject, although in the meantime the number of critics interested in the Bible, and of Biblical scholars interested in literature, had greatly increased. *The Great Code*, when it finally appeared, was a very vulnerable book, and I regret its deficiencies. However, I am not through with the subject yet, and still have hopes that I may be among those who will be studying over the next few years the interrelations of education in words. Out of this study, I hope, would come something of a consensus on the social function and responsibilities of both poets and literary critics.

27

Epilogo

May 1987

Originally offered as the concluding remarks at the Rome conference on the work of Frye, where the paper "Maps and Territories" (no. 26) was also presented. First published as "Epilogo" in Ritratto di Northrop Frye, *ed. Agostino Lombardo (Rome: Bulzoni Editore, 1990), 419–20, from which the text below is taken.*

I can only repeat what I said at the beginning: what an enormous honour this is to me. And add that the conference was organized with extraordinary efficiency. The uniform excellence of the papers rendered me almost—you will be glad to know—almost speechless.

I have often been asked how I feel about being discussed in the third person, and I usually say that I meet it with a kind of controlled schizophrenia. That is, one splits off one's private preoccupations from one's public work, because if you get the two attached and begin to yield to temptations to correct misunderstandings or to counterattack hostility, then you are heading for a very dangerous quarrel.

Sometimes it becomes unnecessary anyway. During the Gang of Four Maoist regime in China,[1] a pamphlet came out describing me as a high priest of obscurantism, and the cover was decorated with a number of black, cold figures suggesting both monks and the Klu-Klux-Klan.[2] However I discovered two things about this attack. Well I didn't discover the fact that the Gang of Four regime was in the ash can of history in a very few years. But what I did discover was that the whole series of attacks on me at that time were struck by a CIA infiltrator who happened to be there. So one never knows.

But what I have to stress here is the positive side of the same thing.

Ever since I read Schiller's essay on the aesthetical education,[3] I have been stressing in my writing the difference between work and play. Work as energy for a further end and view and play as energy for its own sake. And play, according to Schiller and people who follow him, is the core of civilized human existence. And it is not just an accident of language that makes us speak of dramas as plays and of people as playing *Hamlet* or Bach and Beethoven.

So, while work is required for playing well, it looks very different when the goal of play is visible. Work by itself can accommodate things like slavery and exploitation and evil things of all kinds. Work directed towards play in this sense cannot. So that is what they spoke of as the civilized way of God and man in Paradise.

The difference, therefore, is that the fact of play is always associated with freedom. And all the arts and all the things that teaching is dedicated and directed to are also forms of freedom. And there is a poem of Irving Layton, who is a friend of mine but by no means a disciple, in which we read that "Whatever else poetry is freedom."[4] So I am always delighted to hear any evidence that I have encouraged, and therefore assisted, other people to do what they want to do in their way. I regard words like "disciple" and "follower" as somewhat disreputable. They are rather extensions of the Ego.

I regard also the fact that my dedication to these things has been fairly constant, and during fifty years of teaching experience I have become more and more impressed with a similar dedication in my colleagues.

In short I believe very deeply in the values of liberal education, which seems to me to have something to do with liberating people, with genuineness of freedom, and while sincerity of intention is not in itself a virtue necessarily—I imagine that even the phoniest or greediest of television evangelists shares it to some degree—still it does mean that I am very heavily dependent on the good will of those whom I try to communicate with as a scholar and as a critic.

It is that good will of which I have had such an overwhelming, overflowing abundance within the last three days. And it is that good will that I will cherish all the rest of my life. Thank you very much.

28

Auguries of Experience

28 December 1987

Originally presented at the special session on Northrop Frye at the Modern Language Association convention in San Francisco. From Visionary Poetics: Essays on Northrop Frye's Criticism, *ed. Robert D. Denham and Thomas Willard (New York: Peter Lang, 1991), 1–7. Reprinted in* EAC, *3–8. The typescripts are in the NFF, 1991, box 38, file 7.*

In days so remote that I can barely remember them now, I was reading books on Blake in preparation for writing one myself. In those early times it was an unquestioned axiom that one should read everything available on a subject before trying to write about it, and for Blake in the 1930s that was still humanly possible. So I immersed myself in the two or three good books and the hundred and fifty or so bad ones that had been devoted to Blake up to that time. One of the bad ones quoted a couplet from *Auguries of Innocence*, "He who the Ox to wrath has mov'd / Shall never be by Woman lov'd" [ll. 31–2], and objected that a poet less mentally confused would know that it was quite possible to be both brutal to animals and attractive to women. The critic forgot to look at the word "shall," and also forgot to take the title of the poem into account. I was still so green that it took me a while to work this out, but when I did I had a new insight into Blake and had acquired the first of my own auguries of experience, that is, the scaled-down expectations acquired from one's own life. Good books may instruct, but bad ones are more likely to inspire. Since then, as the author of criticism which some have found useful and others objectionable, I trust I have done something to inspire as well as instruct.

After finishing my Blake book, I went on to the *Anatomy of Criticism*, which in the innocent 1950s, when it was published, was regarded, even by me, as an essay on critical theory. So in a way it was, although my conception of theory has always been different from those generally held. In this age of structural, poststructural, feminist, phenomenological, Marxist, metahistorical, dialogist, and any number of other schools, the word "theory" is essentially pluralistic: a theory is one of many dialectical formulations that proceed from specific assumptions and conclude with special emphases. My own conception of theory, though in many respects it may look much the same, is closer to the Greek *theoria*, a vision or conspectus of the area of literature, an area distinguishable from, though with a context relating it to, the other arts and the other forms of verbal discourse.

From this point of view there is a very broad consensus among all critical schools, a consensus which the variety of dialectical approaches more or less deliberately conceals. In the *Anatomy of Criticism* I pointed out the existence of this consensus, and even made suggestions for promoting it. Such suggestions look very naive now, and I have no longer any interest in making them. The procedure is rather like proposing the union of the various Christian churches on the ground that they accept most of the same major doctrines, or say they do. It is of course the differentiating dialectics and the special interests of conflicting groups that fill the foreground, and fill it so completely that the area of agreement remains largely unexamined, as no one is interested in it except the charitable.

This is my fortieth year as an MLA member, and so I have just acquired what is called, somewhat ironically, a life membership. Forty years ago literary criticism was dominated by a rather narrow historical approach to criticism which was neither genuinely historical nor genuinely critical. The first MLA meetings I attended resounded with the triumphs of this approach in the seminar rooms and with complaints about it in the corridors. A superstition grew up in graduate schools that only the obscurest aspects of the obscurest poets were still available for thesis material, and that the whole industry was approaching stagnation and exhaustion. When any discipline gets to this point, it blows up and a new conception of it takes its place, as happened in physics around 1900, when Planck and Einstein blew up its nineteenth-century mechanical synthesis. Similarly, it is now taken for granted that not only is the variety of individual works of literature inexhaustible, but the variety of critical treatments of them is equally so.

My own scholarly deficiencies in contemporary critical theory do not imply indifference, much less hostility, to what in itself is a most lively and exhilarating cultural growth. Even if it were not, its development was inevitable if we are to maintain the ideal that everyone on a university staff should be a productive scholar. Whether this ideal is either possible or desirable is not the point; it exists, and it cannot continue to exist without a large number of school badges, so to speak, ensuring one of a seat in front of a cue screen that will suggest some specific critical approach in advance. I have been assigned a badge of sorts myself, usually reading "mythical" or "archetypal," but my view of a latent consensus keeps me in a middle-of-the-road position, cherishing the belief of my age group that in all polarized situations there is much to be said on both sides. The only disadvantage of this position is that so much is *said* on both sides. My Canadian criticism, for example, has led to my being called a formalist critic who ignores or is unaware of the relation between literature and society, and to my being called a thematic critic who exaggerates that relation. I can only feel that as long as the two groups of objectors are approximately equal in numbers, I am still more or less on course, or at least on my course.

No one questions, or is ever likely to question, the right of literary scholars to discuss critical issues indefinitely. What could be questioned is whether the present critical activity exists for its own sake, a type of glass bead game, or whether it is going somewhere in the direction of increased and progressive understanding of both literature and criticism. Despite Enobarbus, nothing is staled by custom more quickly than infinite variety.[1] This would be true even if all the infinite variety were new, but I keep finding also that venerable critical fallacies, whose funerals I thought I had attended many years ago, were not, as I had assumed, buried, but merely stuffed into cryonic refrigerators to await revival in future journals of theory.

Such issues may not matter in themselves, but a crisis may arise when the question of critical debate is confronted by the question of curriculum, of what should be taught to students, or at least undergraduates, over a limited period of time. There is always public concern over what the public is paying for, and the explosive success of some recent books that seem to be largely repeating what many teachers have been saying for half a century indicates one more revival of that concern. I have been listening to such expressions of concern most of my life, and have spent a fair proportion of my own critical energies on trying to do something about them. Another augury of experience I acquired in this process was that all such movements tend to focus on something we shall assuredly never get: a Messianic super-Archimedes who can say: "Give me a place to stand, and I will move the educational bureaucracy." But this time the dissatisfaction does seem to reflect back, however indirectly, on the critical situation I have been discussing. It is as though a psychiatric patient, already hundreds of dollars in arrears, had suddenly realized that his treatment was by definition interminable.

I happen to be one of those who believe that contemporary criticism is going somewhere, although my notion of where it is going antedates most of the activity itself, and has changed very little since. I have spoken of a vision of literature, because I think that there is a literary universe, which, like every other universe, is unbounded and finite. The variety of individual literary works may be infinite; the total body of what can be produced as literature is not. Any given period of criticism, no doubt every period, may have too narrow a view of this total body. The permanent value of, for example, women's studies or black studies is in reminding criticism of the narrowness of its scope of recognition. But there is a totality to what the mythical and imaginative forms of verbal discourse can do: they may be unlimited in depth and complexity, but they are finite in range.

It was this conviction that led me, in the *Anatomy of Criticism*, to consider what I called encyclopedic forms, works of a scope that seemed to suggest a circumference within which the verbal creative imagination operates. Such forms include some epics, some novels, and, above all, sacred books. They also include mythologies, cosmologies, like those incorporated into Dante and Milton, cosmological principles like the chain of being, and ideologies in their primary, or mythical, shape. Such frameworks are always imaginative, and hence literary, in origin, however much science or political theory may be called in to rationalize them. Of the sacred books, the central one for a Western critic was the Bible. The Bible is the only place in our tradition I know where one can get a view of literature that goes beyond literature, and so establishes its relative finiteness, and yet includes all the elements of literature. In this age of posts and metas, I can find nothing in our cultural tradition except the Bible that really illustrates the metaliterary.

It then occurred to me, after finishing the *Anatomy*: suppose one were to reverse the process, starting with the structure of the Bible, and working outwards to literature? No one would attempt a study of Islamic culture without starting with the Koran, or of Hindu culture without starting with the *Vedas* and *Upanishads*. I hesitated for many years before attempting to say anything about this, but another augury of experience, this time directly derived from Blake, pushed me toward writing: the axiom not to trust prudence, and to persist in folly.[2] The preliminary study that I produced in 1982, *The Great Code*, bore the subtitle *The Bible and Literature*. The operative word was "and": all studies of the Bible *as* literature that I had read treated the literary aspect of the Bible as incidental, even as ornamental.

It seemed obvious to me that while the Bible can hardly be called a work of literature, every word of it is written in the literary language of myth and metaphor. By myth I mean story or narrative (*mythos*), and by metaphor a verbal formula of identity. These are the central elements of literature, but in literature itself they are hypothetical: in the Bible they are existential, incorporating the reader with a completeness that literature cannot attempt. So in the Bible a literary texture forms the content of something else. For this something else I retained the term *kerygma*, "proclamation" or "revelation," even though that meant opposing the formidable authority of Rudolf Bultmann, for whom *kerygma* and myth are mutually exclusive.[3] I am now engaged in disentangling myself from the final chapter of a sequel to this book [*WP*].

I can hardly hope to summarize a complex argument in the minute or two I have left, but a few suggestions about it may interest you. Literature seems to me to revolve around what I call the primary concerns of humanity, those that have to do with freedom, love, and staying alive, along with the ironies of their frustration, as distinct from the secondary or ideological concerns of politics and religion, for which the direct verbal expression is expository rather than literary. Because the content of literature is hypothetical, assumed rather than asserted, it has always been regarded as a form of verbal play, and it is only recently that we have come to understand that play may well be more important than the serious activities promoted by ideology, such as going to war or exploiting other people or the other lives in nature. As long as the *kerygma* or proclamation of the Bible is opposed to myth, it will be identical with ordinary ideological rhetoric; when it is made to include myth, it gives us a new perspective on the social function of literature. By squeezing a mythical and metaphorical proclamation into one book, however long and inexhaustible a book, the Bible provides a kind of experimental model for what I have called the finiteness of literature. Once again, what

I mean by finiteness is not something that limits or imposes barriers, but something that allows for a progressive increase of understanding.

Naturally the Bible, being a historical product even though it transcends history, cannot avoid suggesting specific Jewish and Christian ideologies, and one has to try to set out its mythical and metaphorical structure as something distinct from them. It should go without saying that this applies even more obviously to all the authoritarian, patriarchal, sexist, racist, and sectarian ideologies that profess to derive from the Bible, as well as from doctrinal and other aspects of what is usually meant by "religion," which is still an ideology expressed in rhetorical or hortatory language.

I was asked recently why I could never write anything without mentioning Shakespeare's *Tempest*. The reason is that I know of no other work of literature that illustrates more clearly the interchange of illusion and reality which is what literature is all about. In drama the illusion on the stage *is* the reality, and *The Tempest* is a play about the creation of a play through Prospero's magic, where illusion becomes the raw material for a new creation, while the old objective reality turns into illusion in its turn and disappears, leaving not a rack behind.[4] The Bible similarly begins with the creation, the presenting of objective order to a conscious mind, and ends with a new creation. It is written throughout in the language of myth and metaphor because that is the language of illusion. Freud was quite right, however unconsciously, in talking about "the future of an illusion," because nothing can possibly have a future except an illusion. "Reality" can only be what does not change or changes entirely on its own terms: as far as we are concerned, its future has already occurred. But when we wake up from a dream in our bedroom, we are confronted, not with "reality," but with a collection of human artefacts. The essential "reality principle," then, consists of what human beings have made, and what human beings have made they can remake. Whether they will or not will depend on the strength of the illusory desires expressed in their dreams.

All this can be taught by literature alone, but literature alone gives us only a relative perspective; every way of turning illusion into reality is equally valid within its orbit. One needs also to try to get outside literature without simply returning to ideology. I am certainly no Moses proposing to lead criticism out of Egypt and a plague of darkness, though I may resemble Moses in not having any very clear notion of where the Promised Land really is. On the contrary—and this is my last augury of experience—for many years now I have been addressing myself primarily not to other critics, but to students and a nonspecialist public, realizing that whatever new directions can come to my discipline will come from their needs and their intense if unfocused vision.

29

Literary and Mechanical Models

6 June 1989

Originally presented at a conference on "Computing in the Humanities" at the University of Toronto. First published in EAC, *9–20. The text below is from the typescript, in the NFF, 1991, box 38, file 9. An abbreviated version, the typescript of which is in the NFF, 1991, box 38, file 10, was given as "Technology and Literature" at the Marconi conference in Bologna, 27 April 1989.*

I

My qualifications for addressing a conference of this kind are as close to absolute zero as it is possible to get, except for one thing. Nobody can have lived through three quarters of this century without being aware of the immense number of major revolutions, political, economic, religious, and above all technological, that one has lived through during that time. So nowadays I almost invariably begin an address with personal reminiscence: this is not (yet) simple senility, but a means of providing some historical perspective on the contemporary world.

When I was an undergraduate student at Victoria College, I had as a teacher the scholar Pelham Edgar, who in the early years of the century had gone to Johns Hopkins and done a doctoral thesis on Shelley's imagery. The bulk of the thesis was a catalogue of various images Shelley used with their contexts. Clearly it was of immense benefit for the author of the thesis to steep himself so thoroughly in Shelley's poetic vocabulary, but still most of the thesis could have been done by an appropriately programmed computer in a matter of seconds. From Toronto I went to Oxford, where, at that time, the greatest prestige and highest status in literary scholarship belonged to editors "establishing" the texts of standard authors. I remember hearing one senior scholar meeting another on Broad Street, and on asking him what he was doing these days, getting the answer, "Oh, collating, collating." I remember a preface to another established text in which the editor, in the tone of a triumphant St. George with a very dead dragon, thanked his wife for holding his hand while he fought out his titanic battle with a room full of bulky folios.

However, these achievements, useful as they were then, are not so highly regarded now. Such editions were routinely described as "monumental," but monuments, from Ozymandias onward, tend to crumble with the years, and the two editions I have referred to are already out of date. It was not the fault of such scholars that there were no computers then, nor am I belittling them in any degree. I am simply calling attention to the amount of difference the computer has made, even in its most elementary activities, to literary scholarship.

A Canadian scholar whose field was early Tudor literature told me that after the first edition of the *OED* appeared, he found earlier uses of many words in his reading than any that the editors had recorded, and sent them along to the continuing committee. His contributions were received, he told me, not with expressions of gratitude but with snarls of resentment, presumably because it meant filing more handwritten slips into more pigeonholes. Concordances, again, were partly the work of what Samuel Johnson would call harmless drudges, but were also acts of piety founded on private value judgments. One might devote a large part of one's life to making a concordance to Chaucer or Shakespeare or the 1611 Bible or a favourite Romantic poet, but hardly to a "minor" writer.

One principle stands out here: the direct mental control of a mechanical operation never guarantees accuracy. One may see that as early as Chaucer's pungent epigram on the Adam Scriveyn who transcribed his manuscripts by hand [*Chaucers Wordes unto Adam, His Owne Scriveyn*]. The moral seems to be: in some areas of scholarship human intelligence is a crude and primitive form of mechanical intelligence, and anything that can be done better and faster by machinery obviously should be.

Just as societies have to go through a food-gathering stage before they enter a food-cultivating one, so there had to be a stage of gathering information about literature that might be relevant to it, even when there was still no clear idea of what literature was or how to arrive at any structural principle that would direct research from the heart of literature itself. This period of literary scholarship, which was dominant until about 1935, is sometimes called the *Wissenschaft* period, and its great scholars amassed an awesome amount of information. Its imaginative model was the assembly line, to which each scholar "contributed" something, except that the aim was not to produce a finite object like a motor car, but an indefinitely expanding body of knowledge. However, there was still a principle of finiteness involved in the methodology. Before the subject of a doctoral thesis would be accepted by a graduate department, there would be a check to see whether the subject "had already been done," and this is still a necessary precaution to take with some types of thesis. But the assumption behind it was "done on a *Wissenschaft* level."

In those days what general principles of scholarship existed were philological, and I remember a graduate classmate, interested in pre-Chaucerian literature, being told by his supervisor: "Go into Middle English. Don't bother about Old English: the work there has been done." But while it was true that the philological conquest of Old English had been very impressive, it seemed to me that, apart from R.W. Chambers's book on *Beowulf*,[1] hardly a word of anything that I should call genuine literary criticism had yet appeared in that field. As for Middle English, I remember saying to a medieval scholar, a very decent human being but one of the dullest pedants I ever knew, how as a student I had been led to Chaucer through John Livingston Lowes's book on him.[2] My friend said: "Well, I don't know: it's a—a—an inspirational sort of thing, isn't it?"

Whenever there is this conception of doing work, there arises the spectre of exhaustion: sooner or later everything essential will be done, and the humanists of the future will have nothing new to do. To revert to Lowes, I remarked once to Kathleen Coburn how impressed I had been by the sheer narrative excitement of his account in *The Road to Xanadu*[3] of reading through a thousand pages of (I think) Priestley's *Optics*, and finding what he wanted on practically the last page. The great Coleridge scholar said, "Yes. Of course he had the wrong edition." There are still many scholars who would be frightened by the thought of a computer scanning all the editions on machine time, perhaps leaving them less able to answer the stock idiot's question, How do you manage to get through so long a summer with nothing to do? But the fear of exhaustion is totally illusory. Around the year 1900 there was a widespread feeling that physics was in this near-exhaustion state. Physicists had constructed a mechanical model of the universe that in its overall design seemed immutable, and only a few details remained to be worked out. A year or so later along came the first work of Planck and Einstein, and there was no more talk of physics being exhausted. The same principle applies to the humanities. As soon as we seem to approach the horizon of what can be done with *Wissenschaft* philological criticism, or any other kind, the horizon vanishes and a new world spreads out.

I have to turn personal for a short time now, because I am coming to the period when, with the *Anatomy of Criticism*, I began to enter the critical scene myself. At that time the limitations of *Wissenschaft* philological criticism were apparent on all sides, and the first efforts to squirm out from under it were beginning. One of these was the judicial criticism of the *Scrutiny* group headed by Leavis; another was the "ambiguity" or close reading movement fostered by Empson and others.[4] But, as I saw it around 1950, there was still no critical structure that could prevent criticism from being regarded as parasitic on literary practice, or from being sucked into some ideological vortex like Marxism or Freudianism or (then) Thomism.

There was, however, one form of *Wissenschaft* scholarship that seemed to me to open a wider horizon. This was the scholarship applied to ballads and folk tales, where themes and motifs could be identified and indexed. I felt that the difference between this kind of popular literature and the whole of what we ordinarily call literature was a difference in degree of complexity but not a difference in kind. In other words, the conventions, genres, and what I called archetypes or recurring units of literature could form the basis for a new and comprehensive perspective on literature. It would give a shape to the history of literature, which was then only a history of everything in general plus a catalogue of biographical and publication dates; it would expand the arbitrary division of literature into the different languages to a real interdisciplinary study; it would establish context as the basis of literary meaning.

I also, in my introduction, used the word "scientific," by which I meant essentially progressive. My structural vision of criticism was very generously received, but there was also a revival of the old fears about exhaustion. One critic even asked me if I proposed to lock up all critics in that goddamned jail, where they would do nothing but clean out its cells. Most of this misunderstanding, I now see, came from the word "scientific," which I used because my view was the opposite of the one assumed by the hostile question. I wanted criticism set free to do something with a direction to it, instead of fighting civil wars on judgmental grounds, or disintegrating a text into ambiguous units, or following the course of a history which had nothing to do with the actual history of literature. Not that I wanted to abolish these activities, merely to prevent them from becoming dead ends and abolishing themselves.

I have never been impressed by the "hard" and "soft" metaphors applied to science, nor did I care two pins that the conception of science I invoked was as soft as a marshmallow. But such conceptions as "software programming" and "computer modelling" were as yet unknown, and if I were writing such an introduction today I should probably pay a good deal of attention to them and talk less about science. Ballads and folk tales are an obvious area for computer assistance, and an approach to literature through its recurring conventional units might be equally so. Again, I had always suspected that the basis for the prestige of judicial and evaluative criticism was social snobbery: for it, criticism was a gentlemanly, and therefore an unsystematic, occupation. But this was only an intuitive hunch, which the coming of computers has done much to clarify.

Apart from the analogies of ballad and folklore scholarship, I was also influenced by the twentieth-century fluidity of media, in which a story might begin as a magazine serial, then become a book, and then a film. I remember the shock of picking up a copy of [Dostoevsky's] *The Brothers Karamazov* and seeing it described as "the book of the film," but I also realized that certain verbal cores, of the kind I usually called archetypes, were constants throughout the metamorphoses. The variety of media, in fact, was what made the conventions and genres I was interested in stand out in such bold relief.

It was this that made it impossible for me to go along with McLuhan's "the medium is the message" axiom, despite my general sympathy for what McLuhan was trying to do. McLuhan's formula was essentially an application of the Aristotelian form–content unity. He says, for example, that the form of one medium is the content of a later medium. I could see the identity of form and content: the content of a picture, for example, is the form of that picture, as long as we are talking about it as a picture and not as a representation of something else. I could also see the essential identity of content and "message." But the McLuhan aphorism also implied an identity of form and medium, and that I could not buy. A medium is precisely that, a vehicle or means of transmission, and what is transmitted are the real forms. The form of a Mozart quartet is not affected by whether it is heard in a concert hall or over the radio or read in a score, though there would be psychological variants in reacting to it, of the kind that McLuhan made so much of. The real forms are not media but verbal or pictorial structural units that have been there since the Stone Age.

There is now, of course, a large number of critical "schools" concerned with the humanities. What I have called the *Wissenschaft* or philological school grew up in precomputer days: it would be absurd to regard it as obsolete merely because it has been around for some time, but the necessity of supplementing it with other approaches is fairly obvious. Most of the schools that have appeared since the *Anatomy of Criticism* have their centre of gravity in linguistics or semiotics, or else represent some ideological interest, religious or psychological or politically radical or feminist or whatever. I think that as long as all these critical perspectives are thought of as competing schools, the whole critical enterprise becomes a Tower of Babel, a vast structure largely abandoned, so far as it is a cooperative effort, because its builders have become unintelligible not only to the general public but increasingly to one another. It is on the whole fortunate that they have, because most such schools contain a hard core of imperialists anxious to dominate all the others.

I think here of a friend of mine who, about fifty years ago, started an academic career in philosophy. At his first job the department chairman called all the new recruits together and wrote on a blackboard a list of nineteen "isms," which they were required to teach their students. My friend felt that while philosophy might be a genuine subject these "isms" were not, so he did the philosophical thing: resigned and joined an advertising firm. Critical schools, like philosophical ones, are better thought of as programming models. The importance of the computer is in bringing them down to manageable scope, so that their essential assumptions can be worked through in a reasonable time before they modulate into or merge with something else.

The *Anatomy of Criticism* was written just as the Babel clamour was beginning, hence it has come to be regarded as a document of a "mythological school," and its schematic overview taken to be a "system," which is a schematism petrified into dogma. There is a sentence in the introduction about the schematism being a scaffolding to be knocked away when the building is in better shape [*AC*, 29]. Those who disregard this sentence have totally misunderstood both the book and the spirit in which it was written. The personal reference is not important, but the critical principle is highly relevant to my subject.

II

Humanists are often said to be "Luddites" or machine-breakers, resisting new technology as much as possible. C.P. Snow even cites Orwell's *1984* as an example of the humanist wish that the future should not exist,[5] though I should think any sane man would wish that *that* future should not exist. But resistance to mechanical developments is a matter of personal habits combined with age: it has nothing to do with whether one is a humanist or not. Humanists can come to terms with technology when it seems feasible. At Oxford I picked up a rumour that Sir James Frazer, author of *The Golden Bough* (twelve volumes), *Totemism and Exogamy* (six volumes), *Folklore in the Old Testament* (three volumes), an edition of Pausanias (two volumes), and a whole shelf of other books, had recently, in his last years, switched to a fountain pen.

I myself have been a touch typist since the age of sixteen, am also a very laborious and endlessly revising writer, and hence I tend to resent the word processor with its itch to jump around and perform miracles, and stay with my typewriter. But younger people, naturally, have a different attitude. Of course in so experimental a field some developments are certain to be a bust: one thinks of how badly boards of education got stung on the teaching machines of the 1950s, with their inept Pavlovian programming as transmitted by B.F. Skinner and others. The translating machines of the same period, again, have developed their own folklore, of which the most famous story is the rendering of "out of sight, out of mind" as "invisible lunatic."

The Luddite thesis overlooks the fact that three of the most seminal mechanical inventions ever devised—the alphabet, the printing press, and the book—have been in humanist hands for centuries. The prestige of humanists in the past came largely from the fact that they lived in a far more efficient technological world than most of their contemporaries. It is true that today they are sometimes confused about the new possibilities opening up in front of them, though hardly more so than the rest of the human race, and some of them may also be put off by overenthusiastic forecasting. I often find that, when I read books about the technology available in the near future, the author's eyes are starry while mine are still glazed. One such book, written around 1970, predicted quite astonishing technical developments for the 1980s, almost none of which occurred. Everything the author predicted may eventually come true, but he did not allow for the normal rate of social metabolism.

At present, in the humanities, computers are doing an immense amount of word-crunching, and could easily do much more. Concordances have multiplied; dictionaries are no longer assembled from handwritten slips; in the study of literature the prospect opens up of having the entire verbal corpus of any given literature placed within easy reach. Those who remember the precomputer age are reminded at every turn of the changes new technologies have made. A few days ago a good deal of material landed on my desk from a spelling reform enthusiast. My mind went back forty years to the time when supporters of "Anglic" and similar schemes predicted that English would become a world language overnight if its spelling were made as phonetic as Italian. I also thought how quaint this interest looked now, when not only has English become a world language anyway, in spite of its spelling anomalies, but we have computers with entire dictionaries built into them.

When the historian Michel Foucault wrote his book *Les Mots et les choses*, he gave it the prophetic subtitle *An Essay on the Archaeology of Knowledge*. The word "archaeology" seems to me deeply significant here. Archaeology emerged as an essential basis of historical research, especially for the ancient period, about two centuries ago, and its first efforts were in the general area of treasure hunts, or at least the recovery of startling artefacts. It has now become a patient soil-sifting and strata-separating enterprise, with the aim of reconstructing the continuity of the past: that is, of filling in the gaps in society's record of its own earlier life. Society, like the individual, becomes senile in proportion as it loses its continuous memory. The humanist's preoccupation with the past is concerned with reconstructing that past, not, as in the "two cultures" thesis,[6] with nostalgia for it. The computer can add a fantastic amount of detail to that reconstruction.

My own technological fantasies are very limited. I should hope that within a few years the most mind-numbing of humanist activities, the marking of undergraduate essays, would disappear as the essays were fed into a machine that would not guess at the mark, would not be affected by prejudice or exasperation, and would not respond to the protests of failed students. It would also, of course, have a complete file of the essays written in the fraud factories, and when it received one would start bellowing the name of the student who had bought it over a public address system. I should also hope to see the end of the conception of "productive scholar," with its nineteenth-century industrial overtones, and "creative scholar" put in its place. In the future, perhaps, someone proposing a doctoral thesis, let us say on the Adonis myth in Milton or metaphors of nature in Wordsworth or colour imagery in Tennyson, would look to see whether it had already been done, and discover that there were in existence 9,842 theses on precisely that topic, of which 7,235 were in Japanese. The department would nod its collective head and remark that any thesis that had been written as often as that must be an excellent one. The thesis would add nothing to knowledge, but nobody would read it anyway, and if there were something in it that could conceivably be used it could be made available by other means. So the crazy chain of thesis, thesis rewritten as book, book published, book bought by libraries, book added to an already groaning bibliography, would be broken. The computer would play only a minor role in reducing this academic counterpart of the national deficit, but its role would be crucial.

Such a reverie need not be taken with desperate seriousness, but it contains a genuine point, and the analogy of learning a language may help to explain what that point is. Despite the teaching machines, computers could help a great deal in the learning of language. But no machine will learn the language for us: we have to digest all those idioms and irregular verbs ourselves. In this learning process we are not contributing to any body of knowledge except our own; yet there is normally an advance in fluency and competence. I think of language partly because it is so prolific a source of guilt feelings among humanists: we never know enough languages, and the languages we do know we never know well enough.

Literature itself, especially poetry, is also written in a language of its own, the language of myth and metaphor, which graduate students pick up piecemeal by luck and instinct but are never systematically taught. The kind of thesis I have spoken of would be a pure academic exercise and not, in the *Wissenschaft* formula, "a contribution to knowledge worthy of publication." But it would also be an immersion in the thought and vocabulary of a great poet, which would teach the author the language of poetry in a way analogous to the learning of composition through the study of models. I began this talk with a reference to Edgar's Shelley thesis, which I said could be done now by a computer very quickly, but which undoubtedly represented an experience of great value to Edgar himself. I should like to see most doctoral theses, also, take the form of documents that have educated the author without driving the rest of the scholarly world out of its mind.

III

It is a cliché to say that computers can do only what they have been programmed to do. But a few decades ago biology came up with the DNA molecule and the genetic code, which showed that much the same principle applies to the human organism. For example, there have been experiments in ESP and telepathy which may have established the fact that some human beings possess such powers. They certainly established the fact that the majority of people either do not possess them at all or possess them in an erratic, unreliable, and very largely useless form. Perhaps our remote ancestors possessed them when they had more survival value and they have merely atrophied since; perhaps strenuous efforts of meditation training in yoga or Zen schools could awaken these and other dormant mental abilities.

But the simplest way of looking at this question is to say that human evolutionary history has produced a unique but still limited and finite being, and that there are many theoretically conceivable powers for which our nervous wiring, so to speak, is not well adapted. What we do have is the capacity to construct machinery that can compensate for what is impossible for the human organism, such as the ability to explore the electromagnetic spectrum far beyond the colour range or report on what is going on on the planet Neptune. Telepathy and the like, again, may exist in human minds, but it seems to be a poor thing there compared to what the technology of telephones and wireless has been providing for a century.

The question of whether computers are or can become conscious or thinking beings is of course a pseudo-issue. There is a pernicious tendency in the human mind to externalize its own inventions, and pervert them into symbols of objective mastery over us by alien forces. The wheel, for example, was perverted into a symbolic wheel of fate or fortune, a remorseless cycle carrying us helplessly around with it. Again, as soon as human beings learned to write books and keep records, there arose the nightmare of being confronted after death by a book containing the record of our misdeeds written by a recording angel. The same dreary superstition turns up with computers.

In Samuel Butler's *Erewhon*, written in 1870, the imaginary society he calls Erewhon once had a flourishing technological civilization, but on the urging of a prophet who might fairly be called a Luddite, they destroyed it and refused to allow any more mechanical progress. The argument was that machines were developing so quickly that the human being was certain to become very shortly "an affectionate machine-tickling aphid,"[7] a parasite useful only for feeding and grooming machinery. Some writers talk about the computers of the future in very similar terms, predicting the imminent arrival of superintelligent mechanisms that will—well, I'm not sure what: you write the book. After fifty years of teaching I feel that I know something about the strength of the human impulse to say "enough is enough." And when a silicon microchip begins to take on the proportions of a world-conquering Messiah, it is perhaps time to say "enough."

What makes human beings unique in the scheme of things is not simple consciousness, but consciousness directed by an autonomous will. Machines extend human capacities in all directions including mental ones, but no machine has yet appeared that has any will of its own to exert its power, that is independent of being plugged in or turned on. In short, there are no perpetual-motion machines. Computers look mysterious and spooky to some people because of the Cartesian fallacy, which survives as an unconscious assumption, that the human being is made up of two separate components, a mind (or soul or whatever) and a physical body which the mind inhabits, and which by itself is a mechanism. So a machine that runs faster than our legs, like an automobile, arouses no emotional disturbance, as it belongs to the mechanical body-world, but a machine that can do what only the mind is traditionally supposed to be able to do may seem to threaten our supremacy as lords of the earth. As soon as we put such an assumption into words we can see how absurd it is.

Destruction is the mother of invention, and tyranny its stepfather. Technological development has been largely prompted, in every age, by military conflict, and further advance is often frozen by the determination of an ascendant class to preserve its ascendancy. Consciousness is the critic of the directing will, and when the will does not pay attention to its criticisms human ingenuity is put to very wrong uses. With the coming of the Industrial Revolution a different but related social element entered the scene. Alluding for the last time to the "two cultures" polemic, it is true that many nineteenth-century literary figures—Blake, Dickens, Carlyle, Ruskin, Morris—attacked and ridiculed the material civilization of their time on the ground of its ugliness and filth.[8] But they were not making a mere shudder of refined distaste: they saw in the physical ugliness of their time the sign of a far more sinister spiritual ugliness. Ruskin and Morris in particular denounced the drudgery and misery caused by the division of labour in factories into intolerably monotonous tasks, and emphasized that bad or mindless design in mass-produced goods was invariably connected with exploitation.

Marx of course had a far more comprehensive vision of all this, but the aesthetic criteria were the distinctively humanist ones. And while much of the squalor of working-class nineteenth-century life may have been inevitable, given its coal-based economy, the humanist's opposition to it was in some respects even more deeply prophetic than the Marxist one. Some of it has developed into the "green" political parties of today, which are growing rapidly at a time when Marxism seems to be entering a decline. The main principle of the humanist case was: humanity can be genuinely civilized only when it loves and cherishes nature. The exploiting of nature is, in the long run, just as wrong and evil as the exploiting of one's fellow men. This is not really a Marxist doctrine, as Marxism paid as little attention to environmental factors as *laissez-faire* capitalism did, so far as the exploiting of nature was concerned. At present, with the apparent weakening of the adversary situation between the two systems, a more centrally conscious attitude is emerging. At least we now know that graphite fires and oil spills are major disasters, not minor incidents to be hushed up by whatever authority gets there first.

In the development of computer technology there are two possibly reassuring features. It is a relatively clean technology, and it seems to have a curious kind of democratic dynamic built into it. Each advance, so far, seems to have made the mechanism involved simpler, cheaper, and more available to more people. Obviously this can hardly be the whole story, and there could well be "Big Brother" features in it that would make Orwell's "telescreen" look very rudimentary as a means of paralysing all moves toward freedom. But I am concerned here with scholarship in the humanities, which in itself cannot enslave anyone. Besides, whenever a new instrument of production emerges in society, there are both opportunities to be taken advantage of and dangers of reinforcing existing or future power structures. Everybody likes to warn of the dangers; some, including myself, tend to be more attracted to the opportunities. As for how these opportunities may be extended and applied in our own field, I come up against the blank wall of my own technical ignorance once again, and must turn the next chapter over to you.

30

Literature as Therapy

23 November 1989

Originally presented in the Samya Moranis Chris Special Lecture Series on Science and Culture at Mount Sinai Hospital in Toronto. Frye spoke from notes, rather than from a manuscript, and the lecture was taped by Dr. John Roder. A transcription was made by Robert D. Denham (in the NFF, 1991, box 39, file 5) and published in the Northrop Frye Newsletter, *3, no. 2 (Spring 1991): 23–32, from which the text below is taken. Reprinted in* EAC, *21–34.*

When I was looking over the connections that came to my mind between literature, more particularly English literature, and the medical profession, I remembered that in the Middle Ages the doctors had a popular reputation for scepticism and that there was a medieval proverb that said that wherever there are three doctors there are at least two atheists. When Chaucer introduces a physician on his Canterbury pilgrimage, he remarks that "His studie was but litel on the Bible,"[1] and that was a sort of in-joke, picking up the general assumption. That notion lasted even as late as the seventeenth century, when Sir Thomas Browne, who was a doctor himself, wrote a book called *Religio Medici*, the doctor's religion, which, even at that time, was a catchy title because a doctor's religion would sound like something of a paradox. In fact, Browne speaks in his opening sentence of the general scandal of his profession. Nevertheless, he writes a book on his religion, because it relieves him of the tedium of what he elsewhere calls "the fruitlesse importunity of Uroscopy."[2]

Well, considering how much hysteria there was at that time about the smallest deviation in doctrine, to say nothing of atheism, one wonders why this remained on the level of a relatively harmless joke. One or two things occur to me on that point. There's a very shrewd comment in

George Eliot's *Middlemarch* about a doctor who had a reputation for being a sceptic, but, instead of that ruining his reputation in a small Victorian town, his scepticism actually raised his stock very considerably because his patients greatly preferred to deal with somebody who thought entirely in terms of natural causes and natural cures.[3] Then again, the doctors' study of medicine, which at that time was derived very largely from Galen, was intensely materialistic, in the sense of dealing with the body and the mind as a single and indivisible unit. Of course, the practice of medicine then was full of magic, but it was based on the conception of natural sympathies and natural antipathies, a notion which we'll come to later in the context of literature.

A key idea in Chaucer's day was the conception of what we call complexion or temperament. Both words mean mixture, and they referred to the balancing of the four humours or liquids of the body, together with the balancing of the seven planetary influences under which the patient was born. The doctor of Chaucer's time would look first of all to see what complexion or temperament his patient had. His pharmacopia was a much more elaborate one than we would use now. He would use lapidaries, that is, treatises on precious stones, all of which had some use, and herbals, because there was no herb growing in the ground that was not of some use. That is typical of the medieval mind: there is nothing in the world that does not refer directly to human values.

A good deal of what we think of as Chaucer's freshness and insight, his concrete view of people, is actually made up of these observations about humours and planetary temperaments. He says of his Franklin, for example, "of his complexion he was sanguin."[4] That is, of the four humours the blood was the one that dominated in his complexion. That would immediately for Chaucer's readers have summoned up a picture of a ruddy-faced English country squire. The medical principle that came from this was that you were liable to certain diseases because of the temperament or complexion you were born with. If you were tall and dark and sallow, you were probably of a melancholy temperament, probably born under Saturn or the moon, and you would be liable especially to emotional mental disorders or to such diseases as jaundice. If you were short and thickset and quick-tempered and red-headed, you were choleric and probably born under Mercury. That meant that you would be liable to whatever Chaucer's contemporaries recognized as high blood pressure.

The interesting thing about this knowledge was that it was available to the layman, as well as to the doctor—a fact that sometimes rather disturbed the medical profession. The Wife of Bath, for example, in telling the story of her life, explains her numerous love affairs by the fact that she was born under a conjunction of Mars and Venus, who, as we remember from Greek mythology, carried on in a rather uninhibited way. In *The Nun's Priest's Tale,* which is a story about a cock and a hen, the hen feels that there is something the matter with her husband and, with the greatest confidence, prescribes remedies for him out of the best authorities, having clearly read the fourteenth-century equivalent of *The Reader's Digest.*

In Shakespeare's day this theory of humours and, to a large degree, planetary temperaments was still there, except that of the four humours—the sanguine, the phlegmatic, the choleric, and the melancholic—the melancholic one had assumed the leadership and was the supreme example of the mental/physical disease. You are probably familiar with the wonderful passage in *Macbeth,* where Macbeth, in discussing his wife's illness with a doctor, says in a remarkably prophetic passage:

> Canst thou not minister to a mind diseas'd,
> Pluck from a memory a rooted sorrow,
> Raze out the written troubles of the brain,
> And with some sweet oblivious antidote
> Cleanse the stuff'd bosom of that perilous stuff
> Which weighs upon the heart? [5.3.40–5]

All the doctor says is, "Therein the patient / Must minister to himself," and so Macbeth says, "Throw physic to the dogs, I'll none of it." Well, the reason why the doctor makes this extremely helpless and unenterprising answer is that he sees quite clearly that there's a lot going on in Lady Macbeth's mind that he can't afford to get mixed up with. Consequently, he simply backs out, and that is what earns him the contemptuous remark of Macbeth.

In the second scene of *Hamlet,* we have the court of Denmark all dressed up in their best court finery and Hamlet, just a little withdrawn, dressed in black clothes, allegedly in mourning for the death of his father. The audience of Shakespeare's day would see at once that Hamlet was of a melancholy disposition. They would not be at all surprised at the fact that the scene ends with Hamlet reciting a soliloquy expressing a nauseated vision of the world. But although the physical side of melancholy was left out of *Hamlet*, it was in Shakespeare's day a physical disease, and at the end of the seventeenth century there was a song book published under the title of *Pills to Purge Melancholy*. The conception of the humour lingered on in various forms. Ben Jonson, Shakespeare's younger contemporary, invented a type of comedy in which the humour becomes a kind of obsession, such as miserliness or hypochondria, of which the chief character is either cured or not cured by the end of the action of play.[5]

A little later than Shakespeare we have Burton's *Anatomy of Melancholy*, a great encyclopedic treatise on this mental and physical disease. The physical reason for it was the excess of what was called "black bile," but it extended over the entire psychiatric area as well. Burton's *Anatomy of Melancholy*—I'm expressing my own opinion here—is one of the supreme masterpieces of English literature. It ranks with Chaucer and the novels of Dickens as a survey of the life contemporary with him, except that it uses books instead of characters. Sir William Osler of McGill paid it the rather chilly and left-handed compliment of saying that it was the greatest book on medicine ever written by a nonmedical person.[6] Burton was an Oxford don and a clergyman. Samuel Johnson paid it a much higher and much more concrete compliment when he said it was the only book that ever got him out of bed to read two hours earlier than he wanted to.[7]

As Burton deals with the disease, melancholy tends to spread over the entire area of human feelings and inadequacies of both body and mind. In the three long volumes of the *Anatomy* there are some amazing digressions. There is, first of all, a "Digression of Spirits," where he talks about devils, demons, fairies, elves, and so forth, and about what hundreds and hundreds of authorities have all said about them and what role they actually play in disease. Here, for example, he is speaking of various books on melancholy of which he doesn't take a very high view because he doesn't believe what they say:

> Many such stories I find amongst pontifical writers, to prove their assertions; let them free their own credits; some few I will recite in this kind out of most approved physicians. Cornelius Gemma related of a young maid, called Katherine Gualter, a cooper's daughter, *anno* 1571, that had such strange passions and convulsions, three men could not sometimes hold her; she purged a live eel, which he saw, a foot and a half long, and touched himself, but the eel afterwards vanished; she vomited some twenty-four

> pounds of fulsome stuff of all colours twice a day for fourteen days; and after that she voided great balls of hair, pieces of wood, pigeons' dung, parchment, goose dung, coals; and after them two pounds of pure blood, and then again coals and stones, of which some had inscriptions, bigger than a walnut, some of them pieces of glass, brass, etc., besides paroxysms of laughing, weeping and ecstasies, etc. "And this I saw with horror." They could do no good on her by physic, but left her to the clergy. Marcellus Donatus hath such another story of a country fellow, that had four knives in his belly, indented like a saw, every one a spân long, and a wreath of hair like a globe, with much baggage of like sort, wonderful to behold: how it should come into his guts, he concludes, could assuredly only have been through the artifice of the devil.[8]

Well, it's clear that Burton knows that he is describing a case of hysteria, but what he doesn't know is whether it was the doctor or the patient who had it. We read about sixty pages of this digression about demons and their power and their shape (because some people say that they're all completely spherical), and we realize that there is probably not an atom of genuine information in the entire passage. It doesn't follow, of course, that we've wasted our time reading it. On the contrary, what it does is recreate for us the incredible seventeenth century. But all of this had started in the sixteenth century, with the heavy dose of magic which Paracelsus reintroduced into medicine and the development of the magus figure. The medical man was very frequently a magician whose cures were magical and, consequently, miraculous. In the seventeenth century the magus figure was giving way to what we would think of more as science, but it gave way very slowly, and in Burton's time almost anything could be true. Magical and scientific explanations could both be given for the same phenomena. Even as late as Sir Isaac Newton, for example, you have a scientist who was just as interested in alchemy and in Biblical numerology as he was in the laws of gravitation and motion.

Burton does not say that literature is a therapy for melancholy, except in a wider context of recreation generally. On the other hand, he begins his book by saying that he wrote the book because he was melancholy himself. In other words, it was a form of autotherapy that inspired him to write it. The other reason for writing it is that *we* are: everybody suffers from melancholy. Consequently, the book itself may have a therapeutic value. It's perhaps worth noting that the longest and most popular section of the book by far is the section on love melancholy, which, of course, coincided with one of the central conventions of the literature at that time. If you wanted to write poetry in Shakespeare's day, it was practically obligatory to fall in love and to complain about the cruelty and disdain and neglect with which your mistress treated you. The effect of this was to drive you into a state of melancholy, which, again, was partly physical and partly emotional and self-induced.

In later literature, it seems to me that doctors are rather less of a target than lawyers or the clergy, the chief exception being Molière. In Molière's last play, *La Malade imaginaire*, the central figure is a hypochondriac. He is waited on by two doctors whose names are Purgon and Diafoirus (*diaforus* is the French word for diarrhoea). Their techniques consist almost exclusively of purging and bleeding. Diafoirus has heard of Harvey's theories of the circulation of the blood, but thinks that that's just a new fad that will very soon wear out and he'll then be able to return to his purging and bleeding. The play ends with a magnificent ballet in which a student is admitted to the medical college and is examined by being asked such questions as "Why does opium put people to sleep?" To which he answers, "Opium puts people to sleep because it has a dormant effect." Then there is a dance at the end about the routines of purging and clystering and repurging and reclystering and so forth. A little later, in the eighteenth-century novel [Lesage's] *Gil Blas*, the hero is apprenticed to a doctor for a time, who carried out these routines of bleeding and purging so thoroughly that his patients invariably died. For this he took the greatest credit to himself, as a compliment to the thoroughness of his methods.

Another aspect of medical theory was that the digesting of food distilled in the stomach what were called "the vegetative spirits," which were still further distilled and refined into "cordial spirits," located in the heart. By a still further distillation, they became "the animal spirits"—a phrase we still use in a different sense—in the brain or consciousness. This conception or metaphor was of great aid and comfort to Swift in the eighteenth century. It enabled him to explain most of the phenomena of his time of which he disapproved. That is, if the vegetative spirits went up into the brain too suddenly or prematurely, the result was fantasy and illusion. Consequently, you had things like the Nonconformist enthusiasts, of which Swift, who was the dean of St. Patrick's Cathedral, took an extremely dim view. The same view of the spirits led Swift to some extraordinarily penetrating psychological observations on the erotic origin of idealism and ambition and various other things. He says, for example, "The very same principle that influences the bully to break the windows of the whore who has jilted him, naturally stirs up a great prince to raise mighty armies, and dream of nothing but sieges, battles, and victories."[9]

With later writers, like Bernard Shaw in *The Doctor's Dilemma*, the interest tends to shift to the doctor as the product of a certain kind of society, as a member of a social establishment and under certain kinds of social pressures. But my central point in trying to trace out this intertwining of literary and medical references is that there was a medical tradition unifying body and mind long before modern psychology. The doctors of the nineteenth century, for example, while they may have lacked a good deal of what we would consider scientific training, may have made up for it partly by their close personal relations with their patients and their familiarity with both the physical and the mental constitution of their patients.

This inseparability of body and mind naturally leads to the question of whether such imaginative constructs as literature and the other arts would have a direct role to play in physical health. The art with the longest record in therapy is, of course, music. Even the most inflexible and uptight Puritan could not deny the possible therapeutic power of music because of the story in the Bible of David's playing a harp in an effort to cure the melancholy of King Saul [1 Samuel 16.14–23]. Musical theory down to the end of the sixteenth century included a great deal of speculative cosmology, which turned on terms like "harmony" and "rhythm" and assumed a certain correspondence between the balance which made for good health in the body and the balance which kept the world in a state of harmony. Some time ago a book came out called *The Romeo Error*, referring to Romeo's mistake in thinking that Juliet was dead when she was actually suffering from a drug-induced coma.[10] The point of the book, so far as I gathered, was that a person may be clinically dead for a long time without being actually dead. This is a standard device in many of the romances of the time, especially the late plays of Shakespeare. In *Pericles*, for example, the hero, Pericles, goes to sea with his wife, Thaisa. His wife dies. The sailors insist on putting her in a coffin and throwing the coffin overboard, on the grounds that it's bad luck to a ship to have a corpse in it. So her coffin is thrown overboard, but, being made of wood, it drifts to shore. It's picked up there, and her body is brought to the doctor, who says,

'Tis known, I ever
Have studied physic, through which secret art,
By turning o'er authorities, I have,
Together with my practice, made familiar
To me and to my aid the blest infusions
That dwells in vegetives, in metals, stones. [3.2.31–6]

And one of his attendants says, "Your honour has through Ephesus pour'd forth / Your charity, and hundreds call themselves / Your creatures, who by you have been restored" [3.2.43–5]. That is, he can bring people back to life again. We're still, of course, within the orbit of the magus, who works in terms of the mysterious virtues of herbs and so on. But my reason for referring to this passage is that what the doctor is most anxious about is getting the music started. He has a kind of private orchestra as a part of his practice. He starts the music going, which is obviously the initiating power in bringing Thaisa back to life. One occasionally sees, even in contemporary newspapers, the suggestion that in thinking of the turmoils of Eastern Europe today one should not overlook the direct influence of American jazz and rock. In any case, there's always a certain amount of mystery about music. We never know quite what's going on in it. Perhaps it's partly to that that it owes its therapeutic reputation.

Literature has never had the prestige of music in that context, partly because, I think, literature is not really defined clearly as a category until about the Romantic period—though, of course, people spoke of the poets. Literary criticism goes back to Aristotle's *Poetics,* which is apparently a set of incomplete lecture notes. At least, what has come down to us is incomplete. Aristotle deals mainly with tragedy. He begins with a definition of tragedy in which he says that it is a form that is complete and of a certain magnitude, varied by different poetic devices, and raising the emotions of pity and fear in order to affect a *catharsis* of those emotions.[11] Now that is undoubtedly the most celebrated sentence that has ever been written in the history of literary criticism. One wonders why it turns on the word *catharsis,* which is a medical metaphor. The question naturally arises, Would it apply to other genres besides tragedy, such as comedy?

There must be at least fifty theories on the market about the meaning of *catharsis.* I can perhaps save time by giving you the correct one, which by coincidence happens to be mine. I think that by "pity and fear" is meant the moral feelings that draw you either toward or away from certain characters. In such a play as *Othello*, for example, we feel pity for Desdemona, because she is so utterly innocent, and we feel terror for Iago, because he is so unrelieved a villain. But the central figure of the play is Othello, and our feelings about him are very much mixed. If we are watching something in which these emotions of pity and terror predominate, if they are the leading features that we react to, we have something that is usually today called melodrama, rather than tragedy. Melodrama impels us, of course, to hiss villains and applaud heroes. But if these emotions of sympathy and repulsion, "pity and terror," are purged through catharsis, as they are in tragedy, then the response to tragedy is a response of emotional balance, a kind of self-integrating process. That is, what we feel when we respond to a tragic action is, well, yes, this kind of thing does happen: it inevitably happens given these circumstances. With Othello, who's the central figure, it doesn't really matter whether he is a good man or a bad man. He is obviously a mixture of both, or at least a mixture of strength and weakness. In any case, the particular thing called tragedy that happens to a tragic hero does not depend on his moral status. The hero of tragedy may be a very good person or a very bad one. But tragedy itself is the working out of an inevitability which the audience recognizes to be such. There is, according to Aristotle, a kind of excessive action on the part of the tragic hero, which Aristotle calls *hybris*. That is bound to lead to the restoring of balance in the natural order—what he calls *nemesis*. So the action of tragedy is almost physically intelligible, almost as intelligible in terms of a cosmos and the workings of nature as it is in moral or human terms.

Irony is an important genre for us because so much contemporary literature is ironic in its tone. What irony appeals to is a sense of normality on the part of the audience. That is, we recognize a certain action to be grotesque or absurd or evil or futile or whatever, and it is that sense of normality in the audience that enables irony to make its point as irony. Without that sense of the normal, irony would cease to be ironic and become simply a description. That is the trouble that so many writers complain of—that the world itself is so much more ironic a place than any kind of ironic construction they themselves could dream up. In a way, their work has all been done for them.

The appeals to and responses of audiences in the tragic and ironic modes have a great deal to do with confrontation. The sense of confrontation is something which writers themselves use within their own fictions, partly to demonstrate how very effective it is. There is a story [*Signor Formica*] by the German Romantic writer E.T.A. Hoffmann, for example, about the painter Salvator Rosa, who walks into a situation of a very familiar comic type. There is a young heroine languishing under an old and miserly uncle, who is determined to marry her, and there is a perfectly acceptable hero who wants her instead. The painter gets the old miser out to a theatrical performance in which he acts the part of the miser himself on the stage. This shatters the miser so completely that he loses his miserliness and becomes immediately converted, and the heroine is able to marry the hero. A rather more familiar example would be Shakespeare's *Taming of the Shrew*, where we realize that the story is, to put it mildly, somewhat improbable. Its preposterous sexism, of course, was never taken very seriously even in its own day. Nevertheless, it is tremendously good drama, and it is that partly because it deals with such an admirable dramatic device. Petruchio confronts Katherina with a shrew—with the mirror reflection of her own shrewishness—and so shows her exactly what it looks like when she can see it objectively. It is her recognition of that that casts her shrewishness out of her and converts her. The point is that by putting on a certain dramatic act, Petruchio has also performed an act of therapy.

There is also the question of *catharsis* in comedy. Either Aristotle didn't write a treatise on comedy or we've lost it if he did. In any case, we have to go a little further from Aristotle to discuss comedy. In Greek mythology, there is the earth goddess Demeter who lost her daughter Persephone and went mourning all over the world in search of her. She was in a practically catatonic state. She just sat and stared gloomily in front of her until a servant girl named Iambe made some obscene remarks and an old nurse named Baubo performed an obscene dance, which eventually persuaded her to smile.[12] There is a very similar story, curiously enough, in Japanese mythology.[13] When we look at the earliest of comic writers, Aristophanes, we find that his text is rather startlingly obscene, even for these enlightened days. One wonders how it would have been tolerated in his time, in a culture in which drama, including comic drama, had something of a sacerdotal and ritual side to it. It is obvious that the obscenity is important as a form of psychological release. That kind of release helps to build up the festive atmosphere of comedy, which had at that time a very close connection with certain festival periods of the year.

The Czech writer Milan Kundera has made a very profound remark about comedy. He says that the great comic geniuses are not the ones that keep us laughing, because laughter is simply a reflex: you can laugh for a whole evening and still be bored out of your mind. The great comic geniuses, Kundera says, are those who have discovered or uncovered for their audiences the comic aspects of what those audiences have not previously thought of as comic.[14] If you apply a statement like that to the novels of Dickens, for example, you can see how profoundly true that is. There are many aspects of Victorian civilization which seem so humourless and grim. If you take a look at Engels's *Condition of the Working Class*, you can see how grim the conditions sometimes were. But the comic side of them emerges in Dickens. There is little doubt, I think, in the therapeutic importance of Dickens in his impact on Victorian society. The same thing is true of such figures as Charlie Chaplin or Buster Keaton. Chaplin is an almost unbearably pathetic figure, with his mixture of the dapper and the seedy in his appearance and of the timid and the jaunty in his manner. He seems to dramatize everything that is crushed and neglected and treated with contempt in the world, and yet he uncovers the whole comic side of that, which, again, restores a balance, in those who watch him, of something that has been repressed. So, of course, does the sick joke, which brings us back very close to Aristotle's *catharsis*, because the sick joke expresses forms of pity and fear which achieve something of a purgation of those emotions. It is very familiar how a certain type of sardonic joke arises among oppressed people or people living under totalitarian governments. Such rather subversive humour clearly has a survival value for such people. That is true of the oppressed. It is true also of the other end of the society. One thinks of the role of the fool in *King Lear*, whose function is to tell Lear the exact truth about himself. This makes what he says funny because nothing is funnier than the sudden escape of the exact truth of any situation. That is why Renaissance princes kept fools around them—to remind them of the more human aspects of their own situation and to set out for them a feeling of proportion and balance, which, again, seems to have a great deal to do with both mental and physical health.

I am suggesting that in all this we are really coming back to Galen's principle of magical sympathies and antipathies, except that they are not regarded any longer as forces existing in nature itself. That is, we don't believe in cures by sympathetic magic any more, and we do not, so far as I know, prescribe saffron as a cure for jaundice simply because it is yellow. And so far as I know, Alcoholics Anonymous does not recommend the wearing of amethysts because, being wine-coloured, they will keep you sober. The word "amethyst," in fact, is Greek for "not drunk." The magical sympathies and antipathies that exist now, I think, are rather those that exist between words or pictures and the social environment. That is, literature and painting, particularly, constitute a kind of counter-environment in which the follies and evils of the environment are partly reflected in the arts but within a context which, again, achieves that type of purgation and, ultimately, of balance which Aristotle is talking about. Such a use of words is rather indirect, and there is the strong temptation for many writers to become ideologues, to use the same kind of language that political people do, and, to some extent, to turn their backs on their own specific assignment.

Poetic language is very different from rhetorical or ideological language. Rhetorical language appeals to an audience to integrate as a unit and to do certain things or avoid certain other things. Poetic language tends rather to turn its back on the listener and set up something which requires the reader to detach himself. It is the language of rhetoric and the language of ideology that are the spark plugs of history. I have lived through seventy-seven years of the history of this century myself, and the number of changes which have taken place in that three quarters of a century is, of course, immense. But it has left me with the general feeling that history is a kind of dissolving phantasmagoria, and that all ideologies are sooner or later illusory. To the question of social change there seem to me to be prior questions, such as, Has anything improved in the course of that time? Has anything remained stable? My own view, which my life continually confirms, is that nothing has improved in the twentieth century except science, and that nothing has remained stable except the arts.

In the art of literature, particularly, I've never found any better place to start from than the observation of Duke Theseus in *A Midsummer Night's Dream*, where he says in the last act of the play that "the lunatic, the lover, and the poet / Are of imagination all compact" [5.1.7–8]. By imagination, Theseus means essentially seeing things that are not there. Lunatics and lovers and poets have a family likeness in that regard. The kernel of truth in Theseus's remark is that in the arts reality and realism are rather different things. Realism is a perfectly legitimate form of literature, but it only takes you so far. Ultimate reality, which includes fantasy and romance and a great many other things as well, is something which is verbal. The structural principles of literature are myth and metaphor, and both of these violate the rules of common sense and logic. A myth, by which I mean the Greek word *mythos*—"plot" or "narrative"—is a story which in literature says explicitly, "This is what is happening," and implicitly, "This is what is not happening at all." You have to swallow both statements before you can read a novel. A metaphor says, "This *is* that," or, if you look at Jacob's prophecy in the Book of Genesis, "Joseph is a fruitful bough," "Naphtali is a hind let loose," "Issachar is a strong ass," and so forth [Genesis 49]. The metaphor similarly conveys the explicit statement, "A *is* B," and also implicitly the statement, "Nobody but a fool would really imagine that A was B."

That is partly what I mean by saying that the arts form a kind of counter-environment, setting something up which is really antipathetic to the civilization in which it exists. I said that reality is a much more inclusive term in literature than realism is. It seems to me that at a certain point of intensity what literature conveys is the sense of a controlled hallucination. That is, in literature things are not really seen until they become not actual hallucinations, because that would merely substitute a subjective experience for an objective one, but a controlled hallucination, where things are seen with a kind of intensity with which they are not seen in ordinary experience.

I remember my mother telling me of undergoing a very serious illness after the birth of my sister, and in the course of the illness she became delirious. Her father, who was a Methodist clergyman, came along with the twenty-five volumes of Scott's Waverley novels and dropped them on her. By the time she had read her way through them she was all right again. What impressed me about that was her own conviction that the Scott novels were in fact the curative agent. While I suppose any kind of new and absorbing interest might have been equally beneficial, still I've read most of those novels myself, and would not be at all surprised if the plots of Scott's novels did not form a kind of counter-delirium which had to do with her own recovery.

Certainly one can find in the whole therapeutic area of the arts many ways that the best words in the best order, which is somebody's definition of poetry,[15] can act in a physical way. Many years ago, when I found myself teaching Milton's *Paradise Lost* with considerable intensity, I discovered that his tremendous lines tended to detach themselves from their context and become individual beings chasing themselves around inside my head. On one occasion when I was very tired and still couldn't get to sleep, I examined the contents of my brain, so far as I could, and I found there the line from book 10 describing the building of the bridge over Chaos to Hell: "Disparted Chaos overbuilt exclaimed" [l. 416]. I thought to myself, well, nobody can sleep with a line like that chewing away in the back of his skull, so I concentrated on the line about the planets from book 8, "With inoffensive pace that spinning sleeps" [l. 164], and was asleep in no time.

I am not suggesting, or at least not yet suggesting, that literature ought to be read under medical supervision. What I am suggesting is that we should not overlook the immense recuperative power that literature, along with the other arts, could provide in a world as crazy as ours. Poets themselves often do not realize their own potentiality in this regard. I think filmmakers, of all the producers of art, have perhaps the clearest and most consistent notion of it. But in an age when there is such a vogue for forms of meditation and psychosynthesis and the like, it is just barely possible that literature might be what all the great poets have invariably said that it was, that is, a means of concentrating and intensifying the mind and of bringing it into a state of energy, which is the basis of all health.

31

Response to Papers on "Northrop Frye and Eighteenth-Century Literature"

April 1990

Originally given as a response to papers by Eric Rothstein and J. Paul Hunter at a special session on "Northrop Frye and Eighteenth-Century Literature" at a meeting of the American Society for Eighteenth-Century Studies in Minneapolis. From Eighteenth-Century Studies, *24 (Winter 1990–91): 243–9. Frye's "Varieties of Eighteenth-Century Sensibility," a plenary address at the meeting, was published in the same issue of* Eighteenth-Century Studies, *along with expanded versions of the papers by Hunter and Rothstein.*

I am very grateful for these thorough, well-written, and very sympathetic critiques. I don't feel too happy about being in a position of response. It would be ridiculous to be defensive about a book that I started to write forty years ago. I am interested mainly in seeing what changes of perspective have taken place since that time. At the same time, there are disconcerting aspects of being treated as the author of only one book which was published a full generation earlier, and has been overlaid in my own mind by twenty-odd books since. It reminds me a little of the television programs they used to do in Canada, and perhaps do here, where an interviewer talks to somebody purporting to be Julius Caesar or Cleopatra and says, "What do you think of the world now that you have come back from the dead?" I would be the first to agree that *Anatomy of Criticism* is a book very much of its own period, and I have steadfastly refused to revise it or to try to update it in any way. You don't put your grandmother into Bermuda shorts.

There are other things that look a bit quaint with the passing of years. I talked about the "scientific" nature of criticism in the introduction: by scientific I meant, of course, systematic and progressive, and there was also a touch of wilfulness in the use of the word. I have never had much use for the "hard" and "soft" metaphors applied to science, and thought it might be fun to use the word in a context where it obviously meant something as soft as a marshmallow. One should remember, however, that in those days computers were still in the dinosaur phase, and perhaps if I were rethinking a polemical introduction now, I would talk less about science and more about software programming. Again, one of the problems which seemed to me crucial at the time was the defence of criticism against the charge of being parasitic on literature. That defence is hardly necessary to make today, and in insisting on it I may very well have overseparated the poetic from the rhetorical and the critical from the creative operation.

I think, however, that I have revolved with fair consistency around a single principle with two aspects. One aspect is that meaning is derived from context, and a context, for an individual work of literature, may be internal or external. The New Critics, as they were called then, had done their best, or worst, with the internal context, and I knew that that would always be a central area of critical investigation. Then there was an external context which was also external to literature itself. Critics in this area were often called *Wissenschaft* critics then: they called themselves (as they still do) historically-minded critics. For them, eighteenth-century literature had to be set against a background of what might be called ordinary history: the background of Walpole, Wilkes, the American Revolution, the agricultural movement, Gin Lane, and the rest of it. I had nothing to say against this as long as it avoided the distortions of reductionism, Marxist or Thomist or whatever. But it seemed to me that there was an intermediate order between the internal context of the individual work and an external context outside literature: an order that was external to the individual work but not to literature as a whole. This was the order established by the study of literary conventions and genres. The word "tragedy" forms part of the context of both *Macbeth* and *Oedipus Rex*, whatever the historical relation between them. When Fielding wrote *Tom Jones* he thought in terms of entering an area of a "comic epic in prose";[1] when he wrote *Journey from This World to the Next* he thought in terms of the context, established by Lucian and followed by Swift, of the Menippean satire. I suppose words like "intertextualism" do define to some extent what I meant.

This was really a conception of a specifically literary history that involved a difference in the literary critic's sense of history. The other aspect of my central principle is: all literary criticism has to be grounded in history, but again there are different divisions of history relevant to literature. There is an inner literary history concerned with authors and the editing of their texts. The latter was a major critical enterprise during the 1940s, and many scholars made their reputation by editing texts in whatever way would best represent their original appearance and make them most forbidding for the modern reader. The rest of this inner history consisted of biographies of writers and the dates of their publications—the latter essential if not invariably interesting to students. The outer history I have already mentioned. But again there seemed to me an inner lining, neglected by literary scholars, a history of conventions and genres that came unpredictably into fashion, flourished, went out of fashion, went underground or disappeared for centuries, then suddenly reappeared.

In short, there was a mimetic quality in literary history that ordinary history does not provide, a quality that accounts for the consistency and stability of literary conventions. This stability was one of the first things that attracted me to the study of literature. The lyrical poems of the contemporaries of Chaucer in Richard II's England and the poems written by Sedley and others in the age of Charles II are much closer together, in their literary qualities and conventions, than the immense difference in social history between the two periods would lead one to expect. To go further, the plots and characters of Aristophanic comedy not only are intelligible to us, but are still being recreated on the twentieth-century stage. There is nothing in this that strictly speaking transcends history, but it does give literary history certain peculiar features, enough to distinguish it from other history. These features include the recreation of certain conventions, in the way that Pope and Johnson recreated Horace and Juvenal in their satires; another, closely related, is the use of parody, where a convention reappears in a kind of reversing mirror.

So I find it difficult to buy the panhistorical visions of so many contemporary literary scholars. They seem to me to operate only within history as such: when you're studying history you're inside a historical cosmos where everything is historical. If you're studying philosophy, you're inside a philosophical cosmos where what you do is climb a philosophical mountain, like Hegel, to find yourself on a pinnacle of absolute knowledge where you know everything except where to get the oxygen for the next breath. Similarly there seems to me to be a total cosmos of literature, within which everything is literary. So far as I can see, only three people have been inspired by that last vision. Two of them were Blake and Mallarmé; the third has learned what he knows about it from them. But of course these are not differing universes, and they have no boundaries; they interpenetrate with one another.

When I read Freud on dreams and learned that the major operations of the dream work were condensation and displacement, it struck me that the same operations took place within literature, although, of course, the literary context is totally different from that of a dream. For some mysterious reason, I left out any discussion of condensation in the *Anatomy*. It probably dropped out somewhere around the twelfth revision. By displacement I meant the adapting of story patterns to canons of ordinary experience. To me literature descends historically from mythology, and mythology presents narratives that are almost by definition incredible in terms of ordinary experience, because the characters are gods who can do anything. My special attraction to romance was based on the fact that romance is closely related to myth, and so is particularly useful as a means of showing how certain narrative structures hang together and how certain characters function just on the boundary line between the credible and the incredible. The more realistic forms, I felt, were being handled by other critics in a way which needed no extra comment from me.

By condensation, I mean the opposite process, a concentration on metaphor and the interrelation of words. The most condensed work of literature ever written is [Joyce's] *Finnegans Wake*, but one gets strong tendencies toward condensation in the French *symbolistes*, especially Mallarmé, and in fantasy writing of various types throughout the nineteenth and twentieth centuries. But it enters into all metaphor, in fact into all figuration of language. And if I didn't mention condensation, *Anatomy of Criticism* was still primarily a study of the mythical and metaphorical elements of literature, and so, for tactical reasons, it was better to concentrate on the great mythopoeic periods of English literature which provided the examples that would make it easiest for a reader to follow. Those mythopoeic periods in English literature were the Renaissance period from Spenser to Milton, the Romantic period from Blake to Keats and Shelley, and the great early twentieth-century period of Eliot, Joyce, Yeats, and Pound from 1920 to 1950.

The scope of such a work as *Anatomy of Criticism* made for many difficult technical decisions about how much space one should give to any work of literature or to any tendency within that literature. If I made a mistake in that regard I was in danger of throwing the whole book out of proportion. And if I mentioned too many works, the book would degenerate into a kind of catalogue. So if something got passed over or slighted it doesn't necessarily mean that I was unaware of it or was implying a negative value judgment on it. Actually I thought it was rather a compliment to the eighteenth century that I felt I could let it speak for itself.

I was well aware too that many readers of the *Anatomy* would draw very different inferences from it than those I intended. Many people have spoken of it—these two gentlemen here[2] are two very honourable exceptions in that regard—as presenting a system into which everything must "fit" or else. An irritated colleague of mine at Harvard, where I was visiting when the book first appeared, asked, "Are you seriously proposing to lock up all critics inside that goddamned jail?" My real intention was precisely the reverse of that: I looked forward to an age of criticism that would provide what Professor Rothstein calls a "differential supplement."[3]

I've talked a good deal about holism in criticism, of assuming that what one is examining is a unity and going on from there, but I am not speaking of the end of the critical enterprise but of its beginning. Holism is a preliminary assumption undertaken for heuristic purposes, a tentative exploring axiom one adopts in the hope that something will come out of it. So the normal method of procedure is to go after the unifying factors first. For *Tom Jones* one would first of all look at the shape of the plot, and the generic elements that Fielding himself spoke of in his introductory chapters.[4] I think such a study would reveal a most impressive unity in the book. But in all novels of that size and scope an entire panoramic world is summoned up. That is true of *Tom Jones*; it is true of [Stendhal's] *The Charterhouse of Parma*; it is true of [Tolstoy's] *War and Peace*. Some material in such books may resist any critical treatment which tends to assimilate it into a formal unity. Usually that is only because the critic gets tired and stops halfway. Sometimes it may be that the writer himself has lost his direction or is simply throwing things in, like a French soup, to diversify and give variety to his narrative. If the novel is often a loose or baggy form, that doesn't mean that I consider it inferior because it doesn't follow my critical rules: I have never formulated any such rules. Nor does it mean that my holistic approach to it was necessarily wrong to begin with. It can also mean that the work has passed through the stage of formal unity and come out on the other side.

There it forms a world in itself, like the epics of Homer or the plays of Shakespeare, which one can study to the end of time and still feel that one is inside an epitome of the entire literary cosmos. A deliberately disorderly text, like [Swift's] *A Tale of a Tub*, presents different conventions, but the critic has to take account of them before he starts.

In the opening chapter of the *Anatomy*, I spoke of a sequence of modes ending with the ironic mode, and said that we were still in an ironic mode. I knew that it would last a long time, probably to the end of the century, because many writers tend to pursue conventions automatically even after they have been exhausted. What has happened since that time in criticism was also, I think, predictable at the time of the *Anatomy*, that the spirit of irony has entered into criticism as well as into poetry and fiction. It seems to me, however, that irony cannot really make its point as irony unless it is bounced off an attitude on the part of the reader which contains a standard of normality. That is, irony is not irony unless it is a divergence from something that the ironist is implicitly appealing to in the reader. The individual critic, like the individual word, exists by differentiating himself from others. His song defends his territory. But he discovers that it is perhaps easier to defend that territory if he has the support of others, just as the individual word belongs to one of the parts of speech, of which there are a limited number: nouns, verbs, adjectives, and the rest. Similarly, critics group themselves into a number of competing schools. It seems to me that while the conscious enterprise may be a differentiating one, there is an underlying consensus of which critics are sometimes subliminally aware but would often prefer not to call too much attention to. I think most of them implicitly accept much the same values about the work they are doing, and so a consensus emerges from the subtext, as it were. It is a belief in an underlying consensus that keeps me as hopeful as I am about the critical enterprise as a whole.

The critic has often been seduced into feeling that his job is to judge poets and writers, and that kind of metaphor was used a great deal in eighteenth-century criticism. I think that that rather skews the function of the critic. I don't think the critic judges the writer or his work, except incidentally. I think he judges the common condition of humanity *with* the writer, and of course a writer may let a critic down because there are as many lies in literature as there are truths, and there are some social conditions, such as the socialist-realist program in Stalinist Russia, where a writer has to lie from beginning to end or find himself in a concentration camp. Here what is demanded is not realism but the scruffy pseudo-idealism of a party line. In such a context no critic can trust the writer, and has to supplement what the writer says in other ways. Or the critic may be so blinkered by prejudice that he lets his writer down. And even when they both struggle for truth they are still finite human beings, and in a world of finite beings we need pluralism both in the creative and in the critical enterprise. I am forced to speak of criticism and creation as though they were different things, as to some extent they are, but once again they interpenetrate, and are constantly merging their activities.

I was very interested in what Professor Rothstein said about the metaphor of *sparagmos* or tearing to pieces which runs through my whole writing.[5] The way I begin a book is to write detached aphorisms in a notebook, and ninety-five per cent of the work I do in completing a book is to fit these detached aphorisms together into a continuous narrative line. I think that Coleridge worked in the same way, though he seems to have had unusual difficulty when it came to the narrative stage, and so instead of completing his great treatise on the Logos he kept much of the best of what he had to say hugged to his bosom in the form of fifty-seven notebooks. Holism is not only not the end of the critical enterprise: it is an axiom pursued for its own rewards which at a certain point may turn inside out. I may work hard enough to weld my books into a narrative unity, but it is possible that many of my readers tend to find their way back to the original aphoristic form, finding me more useful for detached insights than for total structures. However, if bits and pieces of me float down to Lesbos with the head still singing,[6] it doesn't matter to me if some of those pieces (I'm mixing metaphors violently here, but the mixing seems to fit the context) get swallowed by someone and grow up again from inside him.

Thank you very much.

Notes

Introduction

1 For critical perspectives on questions of NF's reception and influence, see Joseph Adamson, "The Treason of the Clerks: Frye, Ideology, and the Imaginative Authority of Culture," in *Rereading Frye: The Published and Unpublished Works*, ed. Imre Salusinszky and David Boyd (Toronto: Toronto University Press, 1999), 72–102; and Arnd Bohm, "Northrop Frye: The Consolation of Criticism," *Monatshefte*, 95 (2003): 310–7.

2 As NF himself comments on the aspect of recurrence in his work: "I reflect . . . that a writer has increasingly less that is radically new to say unless he has previously been wrong. One of my less perceptive reviewers remarked recently that I seemed to be rewriting my central myth in every book I produced. I certainly do, and would never read or trust any writer who did not also do so. But one hopes for some growth in lucidity, or at least an increase of the presbyopia that normally comes in later life, as one proceeds" (*CP*, 9).

3 See also the discussion of "displacement" in *AC*, 136–8. NF persistently challenges contemporary ignorance of "poetic and imaginative thought": "mythological thinking cannot be superseded, because it forms the framework and context for all thinking" (*WP*, xvi).

4 See Wallace Stevens, *An Ordinary Evening in New Haven*, in *The Collected Poems of Wallace Stevens* (New York: Knopf, 1954), 468.

5 "The Argument of Comedy," *English Institute Essays, 1948*, ed. D.A. Robertson, Jr. (New York: Columbia University Press, 1949), 58–73.

6 For a discussion of the importance of Vico's work in the evolution of NF's literary theory, see Caterina Nella Cotrupi, *Northrop Frye and the Poetics of Process* (Toronto: University of Toronto Press, 2000).

7 Luke 4:32: "And they were astonished at his doctrine: for his word was with power."

8 Or, as he puts it in *WTC*: "What the critic as a teacher of language tries to teach is not an elegant accomplishment, but the means of conscious life. Literary education should lead not merely to the admiration of great literature, but to some possession of its power of utterance. The ultimate aim is an ethical and participating aim, not an aesthetic or contemplative one, even though the latter may be the means of achieving the former" (47).

9 For a discussion of NF's view of the relation between ideology and literature, see Imre Salusinszky, "Frye and Ideology," in *The Legacy of Northrop Frye*, ed. Alvin A. Lee and Robert D. Denham (Toronto: University of Toronto Press, 1994), 76–83; and Joseph Adamson, "The Treason of the Clerks" (see n. 1, above).

10 NF's concept of "primary concerns" overlaps in significant ways with the progressive and social democratic vision of some contemporary liberal thinkers. Compare, for example, the conception of "primary goods" in John Rawls's *A Theory of Justice* (Cambridge, Mass.: Harvard University Press, 1971), or the idea of "basic capabilities" in Martha Nussbaum's "Women and Cultural Universals," in *Sex and Social Justice* (Oxford: Oxford University Press, 1999), 29–54.

1. The Secular Scripture: A Study of the Structure of Romance

NOTE: References in the notes to published portions of Notes 56 are designated "Notes 56a" and accompanied by their assigned paragraph number and page reference in the *Notebooks on Romance*: for example, "Notes 56a.28 (*NR*, 191)." Passages from the unpublished portions of Notes 56, because these are intermingled with the published sections, have not been assigned paragraph numbers and are simply designated as "Notes 56b." Readers desiring to examine these passages more closely are directed to their location in the Victoria University Library: NFF, 1991, box 28, files 5–6.

1 Friedrich Schiller's *On Naive and Sentimental Poetry* distinguishes "naive" poetry, exemplified in the art of the ancient Greeks and characterized by spontaneity and a natural simplicity, from "sentimental" poetry, the expression of a humanity estranged from nature, self-conscious, and reflective.

2 Heliodorus, the *Ethiopica* or *An Ethiopian Story*; Achilles Tatius, *Leucippe and Clitophon*; Longus, *Daphnis and Chloe*; Xenophon of Ephesus, the *Ephesiaca* or *An Ephesian Tale*. There is considerable attention to these works in both Notes 56a and Notes 56b. For an annotated anthology, in English translation, of the Greek romances discussed by NF, see *Collected Ancient Greek Novels*, ed. B.P. Reardon (Berkeley: University of California Press, 1989). The following editions are in the NFL: Heliodorus, *An Aethiopean History*, trans. Thomas Underdowne (London: Chapman & Dodd, 1924); Heliodorus, *Ethiopian Story*, trans. Walter Lamb (London: Dent, 1961); *Three Greek Ro-*

mances (*Daphnis and Chloe* by Longus, *An Ephesian Tale* by Xenophon, *The Hunters of Euboea* by Dio Chrysostom), trans. and with an introduction by Moses Hadas (Garden City, N.Y.: Doubleday, 1953); all page citations are to the reprint edition (Indianapolis: Bobbs-Merrill, 1964).

3 For the Latin origin of the Apollonius story, see Ben Edwin Perry, *The Ancient Romances* ([Berkeley: University of California Press,] 1967), 300. [NF] Lucius Apuleius, author of *The Golden Ass*, a second-century Latin romance, based on a Greek tale, that recounts the adventures of a young man transformed into an ass. Annotated copies of the English translations by William Adlington and Robert Graves are in the NFL. Adopting the view that the fifth or sixth-century Latin version is very likely an adaptation of an early third-century Greek original, B.P. Reardon includes it in his anthology of Greek romances (see n. 2, above). An English version, "The Tale of Apollonius of Tyre," which appears in John Gower's *Confessio Amantis*, is used by Shakespeare in *The Comedy of Errors* and as the basis for *Pericles*, where Gower appears in the role of Chorus. NF discusses the tale in Notes 56b.

4 For an English translation, see *The Writings of Tatian and Theophilus; and the Clementine Recognitions*, vol. 3 of *Ante-Nicene Christian Library: Translations of the Writings of the Fathers* (Edinburgh: T. & T. Clark, 1868). The *Clementine Recognitions* is a theological romance originally written in Greek, most likely in the early third century, passed down in the Latin translation by Rufinus of Aquileia. Concerned with Clementine's conversion and dedication as a follower of Peter in the latter's struggle against the magician Simon Magus, the tale culminates in a recognition scene in which Clementine is reunited with his family, from whom he had been separated as a child.

5 For an English translation, see *Barlaam and Ioasaph*, Loeb Classical Library. A medieval romance based on the life of the Buddha, it tells the story of Barlaam's conversion of Josaphat, the son of an Indian king, to the Christian faith. The eleventh-century Greek text, whose authorship is uncertain, is an adaptation of a Georgian recension from Arabic and Persian texts, composed about the ninth century; NF's suggestion (later in the chapter) of the eighth century corresponds to the currency of the Arabic source.

6 William Morris (1834–96), an author of particular interest to NF, was also founder of the Socialist League, and a painter, engraver, and decorator. He wrote poems, utopian fiction, and romances such as *The Earthly Paradise*, a retelling of many ancient tales. In Notes 56b, NF discusses in detail a number of Morris's works, including his translation of *The Volsunga Saga*. See also NF, "The Meeting of Past and Future in William Morris," *Studies in Romanticism*, 21 (Fall 1982): 303–18; rpt. in *MM*, 322–39.

7 Richard Blackmur (1904–65), an influential literary critic, whose major works include *The Art of the Novel* (1934) and *Form and Value in Modern*

Poetry (1952). He taught at Princeton, where NF delivered four public lectures in 1954, the substance of which was published three years later as *AC*.

8 In Notes 56b, NF has much to say about Scott's "usual hay-waggon prose style."

9 This exploration in fact led to two books: *GC* and *WP*.

10 See *The Complete Plays of Aristophanes*, ed. and with an introduction by Moses Hadas (New York: Bantam, 1962). *The Birds* shows the gods negotiating their sovereignty when a new city, "Cuckoonebulopolis," is founded in the sky, while *The Frogs* follows Dionysus to Hades, where he seeks a superior tragic poet, "a poet who can *write*!" (371).

11 The Latin writers of New Comedy, Plautus (254–184 B.C.) and Terence (190–159 B.C.), were inspired by the model of Athenian precursors such as Menander (342–292 B.C.), who broke with the tradition of Old Comedy practised by Aristophanes. For a summary of the distinction between Old Comedy and New Comedy, see the opening section of no. 2, "Romance as Masque."

12 From an essay on Shakespeare called "St. George's Day, 1564." [NF] George MacDonald, *A Dish of Orts. Chiefly Papers on the Imagination, and on Shakspere* (London: Sampson Low Marston, 1893), 83: "But, besides *the* Bible, every nation has *a* Bible, or at least *an* Old Testament, in its own history." In Notes 56b, the passage appears verbatim; the somewhat free citation here suggests that NF was working from memory.

13 See A.D. Nock's critique of Karl Kerenyi in *Gnomon* (1928), 485–92. [NF] This refers to Nock's review of Kerenyi's *Die griechisch-orientalische Romanliteratur in religionsgeschichtlicher Beleuchtung. Ein Versuch* (Tubingen: Mohr, 1927). Nock takes issue with the main thesis, "that the typical scheme of the Greek novel . . . is due to the Egyptian sacred story of Isis and Osiris" (485), and concludes that it is "on the whole very much easier to explain the development of the novel from pathetic history, the story as a rhetorical exercise, and the rise of romanticism" (489).

14 See n. 24, below.

15 See [Bede], *Ecclesiastical History [of the English People]*, bk. 4, chap. 24. The quotation is from the translation of Leo Sherley-Price, in the [Harmondsworth:] Penguin Classics (1955), [249–50], quoted by permission of Penguin Books. [NF] The Venerable Bede, an Anglo-Saxon monk, was one of the most learned men of his time.

16 For the story of Christ's descent into Hell, see *The Apocryphal New Testament*, trans. J.K. Elliott (Oxford: Clarendon Press, 1993), 185–204.

17 Compare Hadas's remarks in his introduction to *Three Greek Romances* (see n. 2, above): "If *An Ephesian Tale* is an absorbing tale of love and improbable adventure, it is also a tract to prove that Diana of the Ephesians (who was

equated with Isis) cares for her loyal devotees. . . . The Latin *Golden Ass* of Apuleius is clearly propaganda for the cult of Isis" (ix–x).

18 At the end of Chaucer's *Troilus and Criseyde*, the poet, who has until this point maintained his neutrality, denounces the "payens corsed olde rites" and their gods as "rascaille" or rabble (bk. 5, ll. 1849–55).

19 Jorge Luis Borges, *The Gospel according to Mark*, in *Doctor Brodie's Report*, trans. Norman Thomas di Giovanni in collaboration with the author (New York: E.P. Dutton, 1972), 19.

20 "The Englishman described me as being expelled from heaven by cannons and gunpowders; and to this day every Briton believes that the whole of the silly story is in the Bible." George Bernard Shaw, *Man and Superman: A Comedy and A Philosophy* (Harmondsworth: Penguin, 1946), 143 (act 3).

21 *Henry V*, 4.8.114–16: "And be it death proclaimed through our host / To boast of this, or take that praise from God / Which is his only."

22 See Moses Hadas, *Hellenistic Culture* ([New York: Columbia University Press,] 1959), 121. [NF] Hadas writes: "In the formulation of Asclepiades of Myrlea, echoed in other theorists, narrative prose falls into three categories: true history (*alethes historia*), false history (*pseudes historia*), and history as it may likely have happened (*plasma* or *hos genomena*)."

23 John Henry Newman, *Apologia Pro Vita Sua*, ed. Dwight Culler (Boston: Houghton Mifflin, 1956), 30.

24 [For Alcuin,] see H.M. Chadwick, *The Heroic Age* ([Cambridge: Cambridge University Press,] 1912), 41. [NF] The passage from St. Paul referred to seems likely to be 2 Corinthians 6:15: "And what concord hath Christ with Belial? or what part hath he that believeth with an infidel?" (AV). The question "What has all this to do with Dionysus?" can be found in Plutarch, *Moralia*, trans. Paul A. Clement and Herbert B. Hoffleit, Loeb Classical Library ed. (Cambridge, Mass.: Harvard University Press, 1969), 8:21 ("Table-Talk" [*Questiones Convivales*], 1.1.5, 615a).

25 In *The Life of Pope*, Johnson asserts: "That *The Messiah* excels the *Pollio* [Virgil's *Fourth Eclogue*] is no great praise, if it be considered from what original the improvements are derived" (Bronson, 388).

26 *The Golden Asse of Lucius Apuleius*, trans. William Adlington (London: The Bodley Head, 1923), xxii–xxiii. The quotation is actually from Adlington's dedication to the Earl of Sussex.

27 See his [Arthur Waley's] preface to the translation of the *Chin P'ing Mei* [*The Adventurous History of Hsi Men and His Six Wives*], [trans. Bernard Miall] ([New York:] Capricorn Books, 1960) [ix–xix]. [NF]

28 Stephen Gosson's *The Schoole of Abuse* (1579) was the pamphlet that inspired Sir Philip Sidney to write his *Defence of Poetry*.

29 On 6 December 1933, District Judge John W. Woolsey admitted *Ulysses* into the United States, concluding that, "whilst in many places the effect of

Ulysses on the reader undoubtedly is somewhat emetic, nowhere does it tend to be an aphrodisiac." See *The United States of America v. One Book Entitled "Ulysses" by James Joyce*, ed. Michael Moscato and Leslie LeBlanc (Frederick, Md.: University Publications of America, 1984), 312.

30 For a collection of the popular sixteenth-century author's works, see *The Novels of Thomas Deloney*, ed. Merritt E. Lawlis (Bloomington: Indiana University Press, 1961).

31 See W. Jackson Bate, *The Burden of the Past and the English Poet* ([Cambridge, Mass.: Belknap Press,] 1970). [NF]

32 "A mighty maze! but not without a plan" is line 6 of Pope's *An Essay on Man*. In *The Life of Pope*, Samuel Johnson discusses the revision of the line: "The subsequent editions of the first Epistle exhibited two memorable corrections. At first, the poet and his friend 'Expatiate freely o'er this scene of man, / A mighty maze *of walks without a plan*.' For which he wrote afterwards, 'A mighty maze, *but not without a plan*:' for, if there were no plan, it was in vain to describe or to trace the maze" (Bronson, 350).

33 See particularly the first essay, "The Noble Rider and the Sound of Words," in *The Necessary Angel*[*: Essays on Reality and the Imagination*] ([New York: Vintage,] 1951) [1–36]. [NF]

34 The Sigurd saga is *The Saga of the Volsungs*, an Icelandic prose epic from the thirteenth century. See *Volsunga Saga: The Story of the Volsungs and Niblungs*, ed. and trans. William Morris (New York: Collier, 1962); annotated copy in the NFL. See also vol. 7 of *The Collected Works of William Morris* (New York: Russell & Russell, 1966).

35 [S.T. Coleridge,] *Biographia Literaria*, [vol. 7, pt. 1 of *The Collected Works of Samuel Taylor Coleridge* (Princeton: Princeton University Press, 1983), 305,] chap. 13. [NF]

36 Author of popular works such as *The King Stag*, *The Serpent Woman*, and *Turandot*, Carlo Gozzi quarrelled with the modern theatrical tradition championed by Goldoni, and espoused a style that incorporated strong elements of romance and fantasy. See Notes 56b: "Gozzi was the man quoted by Goethe as having maintained that there were only thirty-six dramatic situations: . . . a dramatist whose work is so undisplaced would be the most likely person to think in such terms."

37 Central characters, respectively, in Flaubert's *Madame Bovary*, Tolstoy's *Anna Karenina*, Conrad's *Lord Jim*, and Henry James's *The Portrait of A Lady*.

38 In a letter to J.B.S. Morritt, 24 July 1814; quoted from [J.G.] Lockhart's [*Memoirs of the*] *Life of Sir Walter Scott*, [(London: Macmillan, 1900), 2:334,] chap. 27. [NF]

39 Marie Corelli (1855–1924) is the pen name of Mary Mackay, author of *Barrabas*, *The Sorrows of Satan*, and other bestselling romances, which featured theosophical themes and extravagant plots. John Buchan (1875–1940)

wrote romantic adventure novels, the most famous of which is *The Thirty-Nine Steps*, annotated copy in the NFL. Elinor Glyn (1864–1943) was another writer of popular fiction, best known for her society novels.

40 Wilkie Collins (1824–89), a friend and collaborator of Dickens, and author of *The Moonstone* and *The Woman in White*, was one of the founders of the English detective novel. Edward Bulwer-Lytton (1803–73) was a politician and the prolific author of occult and historical fiction, such as *The Last Days of Pompeii*, *A Strange Story*, and *Zanoni: A Rosicrucian Tale*. Lewis Carroll (1832–98) is the pseudonym of Charles Lutwidge Dodgson, mathematician and logician, and author of the immensely popular *Alice's Adventures in Wonderland* and *Through the Looking-Glass*, as well as *The Hunting of the Snark*, *Jabberwocky*, and the two-volume fantasy novel *Sylvie and Bruno*. For William Morris, see n. 6, above. Annotated copies of many of the works of these four authors are in the NFL.

41 In Notes 56a.28, NF uses the more pointed term "embalmed": "This allegorical and descriptive approach to literature is embalmed in Leavis's Great Tradition" (*NR*, 191).

42 George MacDonald (1824–1905), a clergyman who eventually left the ministry in order to devote himself to writing. Author of popular and enduring children's stories, *At the Back of the North Wind*, *The Princess and the Goblin*, and *The Princess and Curdie*, as well as essays and the fantasy novels *Phantastes*, *Lilith*, and *The Portent*. Annotated copies of the works are in the NFL, and MacDonald is discussed in detail in Notes 56b. See also n. 12, above. For Carroll, see n. 40, above; for Morris, see n. 6, above.

43 See n. 3, above.

44 See Edmund Wilson, "Why Do People Read Detective Stories?" "Who Cares Who Killed Roger Ackroyd?" and "Mr. Holmes, They Were the Footprints of a Gigantic Hound!" in *Classics and Commercials: A Literary Chronicle of the Forties* (New York: Farrar, Strauss, 1950), 231–7, 257–65, 266–74. The "Roger Ackroyd" article is reprinted in *Detective Fiction: A Collection of Critical Essays*, ed. Robin W. Winks (Englewood Cliffs, N.J.: Prentice-Hall, 1980), 35–40.

45 Oscar Wilde, "The Decay of Lying," in *De Profundis and Other Writings*, ed. Hesketh Pearson (Harmondsworth: Penguin, 1973), 87.

46 The first entry in NB 10 concerns this distinction between the "hence" and the "and then" narratives: "The hence story initiates waking consciousness: the and then story initiates the dream. That's why it holds interest in spite of" (*NR*, 275). Compare Hadas's remarks in his introduction to *Three Greek Romances* (see n. 2, above): "There is no logic nexus between event and event or between event and character. But in a world where the links of causality are broken and Fortune has taken control of the affairs of men it is the very incalculability of events that absorbs interest. Logic is supplanted

by paradox and emotion becomes sentimentality, to be savored for its own sake" (ix). As concerns Coleridge's observation, NF is likely referring to the conversation with John Payne Collier on 17 October 1811: "It was true that in reading them [the *Arabian Nights*] you were obliged to imagine yourself in a kind of dream in order to make some of the relations even possible but the author . . . never required you to be awakened by any touches of fine feeling or sentiment. Your sleep was undisturbed while your fancy was on the wing." *Table Talk*, vol. 14, pt. 2 of *The Collected Works of Samuel Taylor Coleridge* (1990), 328. See also Coleridge's remarks in a lecture of 3 March 1818, in *Lectures, 1808–1819: On Literature*, vol. 5, pt. 2 of *The Collected Works* (1987), 191.

47 See. n. 3, above.

48 Ben Jonson, *Ode to Himself*, in *The Complete Poems*, ed. George Parfitt (Harmondsworth: Penguin, 1975), 283 (ll. 21–2).

49 T.S. Eliot, *Marina*, in *Ariel Poems*. See *The Complete Poems and Plays of T.S. Eliot* (London, Faber & Faber, 1969), 109–10. The reference to the Phoenician sailor suggests "Phlebas the Phoenician" of the fourth section (*Death by Water*) of Eliot's *The Waste Land* (in *The Complete Poems and Plays*, 71).

50 For W.H. Auden's *The Sea and the Mirror: A Commentary on Shakespeare's "The Tempest,"* see *Selected Poems*, ed. Edward Mendelson, new ed. (New York: Vintage, 1979), 127–75.

51 The most probable derivation of the word "religion" is from the Latin *religare*, "to bind," and thus suggests the idea of being bound or tied to a community through one's belief.

52 George Peele, *Old Wives' Tale* (1595); and *A Most Pleasant Comedie of Mucedorus* (1598), a romantic comedy of uncertain authorship. NF discusses the late romances of Shakespeare in *NP* and, in relation to the "problem comedies," in *MD*.

53 The jingle "To Mr Ben Johnson demanding the reason why he called his plays works" was written after the appearance of Johnson's first folio in 1616: "Pray tell me, Ben, where doth the mystery lurk? / What others call a play you call a work." In Herford, 9:13.

54 Johan Huizinga, *Homo Ludens: A Study of the Play-Element in Culture* (1938); annotated copy (Boston: Beacon Press, 1955) in the NFL.

55 Each book of Sidney's *Arcadia* ends with a "tournament" of eclogues sung by the shepherds. The romance is discussed in detail in Notes 56b.

56 As Marcel negotiates the uneven paving stones in the courtyard of the Guermantes mansion, he experiences the same happiness as that which he felt upon tasting the madeleine dipped in tea, described in the opening volume of the work. Inside the mansion, the sound of a spoon knocked against a plate and the feel of a napkin continue to trigger sensations linked

to the striking disappearance of doubts about "the reality of [his] literary gifts, the reality even of literature." Marcel Proust, *Time Regained*, trans. Andreas Mayor and Terence Kilmartin, revised by D.J. Enright, vol. 6 of *In Search of Lost Time* (New York: Modern Library, 1999), 255.

57 Sir Henry Rider Haggard (1856–1925), author of romances of adventure set in the heart of a legendary Africa, such as *King Solomon's Mines, She: A History of Adventure*, and *Ayesha: The Return of She*. Haggard was a friend of Rudyard Kipling (1865–1936), the Nobel laureate whose romances set in India, *The Jungle Book, The Second Jungle Book*, and *Kim*, reflect values and attitudes of the period of British colonial expansion. Annotated copies of both authors' works are in the NFL. For Buchan, see n. 39, above.

58 See Eric Berne, *Transactional Analysis in Psychotherapy: A Systematic Individual and Social Psychiatry* (New York: Grove Press, 1961) and *What Do You Say After You Sa'y Hello? The Psychology of Human Destiny* (New York: Grove Press, 1972).

59 "Poor Tom" alludes to the disguise of a Bedlam beggar put on by Edgar in Shakespeare's *King Lear*. Feigning madness, he complains throughout act 3, scene 4 that he is being tormented by the "foul fiend." The allusion here is to 3.6.17: "The foul fiend bites my back."

60 An allusion to Julien Benda's *La Trahison des clercs* (1927), which criticizes intellectuals who would sacrifice universal principles of truth and justice in the interests of particular political goals. For an English translation, see *The Treason of the Intellectuals*, trans. Richard Aldington (New York: Norton, 1969).

61 As Virgil explains to Dante in *Inferno*, canto 11, ll. 16–66.

62 The fable concludes with a restatement of "the seeming Paradox . . . that Private Vices by the dextrous Management of a skilful Politician may be turn'd into Publick Benefits." Bernard Mandeville, *The Fable of the Bees*, ed. Phillip Harth (Harmondsworth: Penguin, 1970), 371.

63 A prince "should choose from among the beasts the fox and the lion; for the lion cannot defend itself from traps and the fox cannot protect itself from wolves. It is therefore necessary to be a fox in order to recognize the traps and a lion in order to frighten the wolves." Niccolò Machiavelli, *The Prince*, trans. Peter Bondanella and Mark Musa (Oxford: Oxford University Press, 1984), 58 (chap. 18).

64 In *SeS*, though not in all his writings, NF consistently uses the Roman form "Ulysses" rather than the Greek name "Odysseus" to refer to the hero of Homer's *Odyssey*.

65 See Thomas Love Peacock, "The Four Ages of Poetry," in *Memoirs of Shelley and Other Essays and Reviews*, ed. Howard Mills (London: Rupert Hart-Davis, 1970), 117.

66 See *King Harald's Saga*, trans. Magnus Magnusson and Hermann Pálsson ([Harmondsworth:] Penguin Classics, 1966), 129, quoted by permission of Penguin Books. [NF]

67 *The Saga of Grettir the Strong*, a medieval Icelandic romance, in vol. 7 of *The Collected Works of William Morris*. An annotated copy of the translation by George Ainslie Hight (London: Dent, 1972) is in the NFL.

68 See the opening sections of Lucian's *A True Story* and *The Lover of Lies, or The Doubter*.

69 *Odyssey*, bk. 13, ll. 291–9. There are many translations, but I find A.T. Murray's Loeb Library version irresistible for this passage. [NF] This is the unrevised translation by Murray, published in 1919.

70 *To Hermes*, in *Hesiod, Homeric Hymns, Homerica*, Loeb Classical Library; annotated copy in the NFL.

71 Examples of this in the Grimms' *Fairy Tales* include *The Riddle* and *The White Snake*. In Carlo Gozzi's *Turandot*, the eponymous heroine, daughter of the emperor of China, demands that her suitors solve three riddles; the cost of failure is death. For the story of Atalanta, daughter of the King of Arcadia, see Ovid, *Metamorphoses*, bk. 10, ll. 560–680; and Apollodorus, *The Library*, 3.9.2. The swift-footed Atalanta insists on the trial of a foot-race with her suitors, who are beheaded if they fail. The suitor who finally wins the race does so with the aid of a stratagem devised by Aphrodite.

72 See Robert Graves, *The White Goddess: A Historical Grammar of Poetic Myth* (London: Faber & Faber, 1948); annotated copy in the NFL.

73 See [Samuel Butler,] *The Authoress of the Odyssey* (1897) [Chicago: University of Chicago Press, 1967]. [NF]

74 See n. 11, above.

75 The most convenient and reliable translations of *Daphnis and Chloe* and (see below) of the *Ephesiaca* by Xenophon of Ephesus are those by Moses Hadas in *Three Greek Romances* (1953). [NF] See n. 2, above.

76 The quotation from Heliodorus is from Thomas Underdowne's Elizabethan translation (made not directly from the Greek but from a Latin version), [112]. [NF] See n. 2, above.

77 Annotated copies of Terence's plays are in the NFL: *The Comedies of Terence*, ed. Robert Graves (Garden City, N.Y.: Doubleday, 1962); and *The Complete Roman Drama*, ed. George E. Duckworth (New York: Random House, 1942), which includes all the extant comedies of Plautus and Terence.

78 Except that Jane Austen, who never oversimplifies, adds a sentence remarking that Fanny's resistance might have been broken down with some increase of pressure. [NF]

79 Jane Austen, *Mansfield Park*, vol. 3 of *The Novels of Jane Austen*, ed. R.W. Chapman, 3rd ed. (London: Oxford University Press, 1934), 318 (chap. 32).

80 The edition referred to is Henry Fielding, *Tom Jones* (New York: Modern Library, 1950).

81 "The author, though himself a professional talk maker, does not believe that the world can be saved by talk alone. He has given the rascal the last word; but his own favourite is the woman of action, who begins by knocking the wind out of the rascal, and ends with a cheerful conviction that the lost dogs always find their way home. So they will, perhaps, if the women go out and look for them." Bernard Shaw, *Too True To Be Good, Village Wooing, and On the Rocks* (London: Constable, 1934), 108.

82 Bernard Shaw, *Too True To Be Good*, 93 (act 3). Spoken by "The Patient," the heroine of the play.

83 This is the story of Serena, who is captured by a savage people and stripped bare on an altar to be sacrificed and eaten, when she is rescued at the last moment by the good Sir Calepine. See Spenser, *The Faerie Queene*, bk. 6, canto 8, sts. 31–51.

84 The story of the Trojan princess Hesione, rescued by Hercules from sacrifice to a sea monster, is told in Ovid, *Metamorphoses*, bk. 3, ll. 194–220, and Apollodorus, *The Library*, 2.5.9.

85 *Paul et Virginie* (1788), by Jacques Henri Bernardin de Saint-Pierre.

86 Sir Walter Scott, *The Pirate* (Edinburgh: Edinburgh University Press, 2001), 386 (chap. 42).

87 See n. 2, above.

88 John Webster, *The Duchess of Malfi*, 4.2.131.

89 [Sir Philip Sidney, *Arcadia*,] bk. 1, chap. 13 (1590 version). [NF]

90 See *Poems of Heaven and Hell from Ancient Mesopotamia*, ed. N.K. Sandars (Harmondsworth: Penguin, 1971). For a discussion of this myth, see Thorkild Jacobsen, *The Treasures of Darkness: A History of Mesopotamian Religion* (New Haven: Yale University Press, 1976), 55–63. Annotated copies of both works are in the NFL.

91 *Das Ewig-Weibliche* or "Eternal Feminine" is the term that appears at the end of Goethe's *Faust*: "Das Ewig-Weibliche / Zieht uns hinan" ("The Eternal Feminine / Draws us on high").

92 This is an elegant paraphrase of Yeats's conception of historical cycles as outlined in his poetry and in the occult theorizings of *A Vision* (London: Macmillan, 1962). See also NF, "Yeats and the Language of Symbolism," in *FI*, 218–37, and "The Rising of the Moon," in *SM*, 245–74. Yeats's system is based on the primary (objective and solar) and antithetical (subjective and lunar) movements of interlocking gyres or historical cycles of culture, the antithetical motion being the creative impulse. Here NF develops the implications of *A Vision*, in an "antithetical" manner, as he works out his own wide-angle lens approach to literary history. For a more detailed discussion, see Notes 56a.3–19 (*NR*, 183–9).

93 In "On the Affection of Fathers for Their Children" (*Essays*, bk. 2, chap. 8), Montaigne refers to the story of Heliodorus, Bishop of Tricea, who gave up his bishopric rather than burn the *Ethiopica*, "his daughter," as Montaigne refers to it.

94 *Earth's Answer* is the second poem in Blake's *Songs of Experience*, and is presented as a reply to the call of the bard in the first poem (*Introduction*) for the Earth to return (Erdman, 18). The figure of the jealous Covering Cherub, associated with the fall into Selfhood, is based on Genesis 3:24 and Ezekiel 28:16, and appears in Blake's *Milton* and *Jerusalem*. See *FS*, 137–43 (*FS2*, 140–6).

95 NF defines the term in *WP*: "One theme involved in the story of Ruth is the custom of levirate marriage, prescribed in the Mosaic code as a means of protecting widows in a patrarichal society. A dead man's brother or other close relative was obliged to marry a widow in the family to enable her to retain her status as, in the expressive French phrase, a *femme couverte*. The most famous story illustrating this custom is that of Tamar (Genesis 38), the daughter-in-law of Jacob's son Judah, the eponymous ancestor of the tribe of that name" (211).

96 For a diagrammatic form of this scheme, see *WP*, 169.

97 This is Sweeney's refrain in the unfinished poem *Sweeney Agonistes*. See *The Complete Poems and Plays of T.S. Eliot*, 122.

98 For an account of the birth of Zeus, see Hesiod, *Theogony*, ll. 453–91; for that of Dionysus, see Ovid, *Metamorphoses*, bk. 3, ll. 287–315; and Apollodorus, *The Library*, 3.4.3. The relevant Biblical passages are Exodus 1–2 and Matthew 1–2.

99 William Wordsworth, *Ode: Intimations of Immortality from Recollections of Early Childhood*, ll. 66–70: "Heaven lies about us in our infancy! / Shades of the prison-house begin to close / Upon the growing Boy, / But He beholds the light, and whence it flows, / He sees it in his joy."

100 Cf. the reference to "Durante" in chap. 10. [NF] In George MacDonald's *At the Back of the North Wind* (London: Collins, 1958), Durante's account echoes in detail the description of the Earthly Paradise in Dante's *Purgatorio*, canto 28. The final lines of canto 27 are specifically recalled in the characterization of the people back of the north wind as "so free and so just and so healthy, that every one of them has a crown like a king and a mitre like a priest" (87).

101 Longus, *Daphnis and Chloe*, in *Three Greek Romances*, 54. See n. 2 and n. 75, above.

102 Anthony Trollope, *An Autobiography* (London: Oxford University Press, 1950), 126 (chap. 7).

103 William Wordsworth, *Ode: Intimations of Immortality from Recollections of Early Childhood*, l. 58: "Our birth is but a sleep and a forgetting."

104 Lewis Carroll, *Alice's Adventures in Wonderland*, in *The Complete Works of Lewis Carroll* (London: Nonesuch Press, 1939), 100 (chap. 10, "The Lobster-Quadrille").

105 *Sakuntala* is the masterpiece of Kalidasa, author of classical Sanskrit literature. See *Great Sanskrit Plays*, trans. P. Lal (New York: New Directions, 1964); annotated copy in the NFL.

106 Jane Austen, *Henry and Eliza*, in *Minor Works*, vol. 6 of *The Works of Jane Austen*, ed. R.W. Chapman (London: Oxford University Press, 1969), 33–9. Austen wrote the burlesque in her early teens.

107 The story of Actaeon is recounted in Ovid, *Metamorphoses*, bk. 3, ll. 138–252, and Apollodorus, *The Library*, 3.4.4.

108 See the discussion of structures as systems of transformation in Jean Piaget's *Structuralism*, ed. and trans. Chaninah Maschler (New York: Harper & Row, 1970); annotated copy in the NFL.

109 For the story of Daphne and Apollo, see Ovid, *Metamorphoses*, bk. 1, ll. 452–567; for that of Syrinx and Pan, see bk. 1, ll. 682–712.

110 The NFL contains an annotated copy of Carlo Gozzi, *The King Stag*, trans. Carl Wildman, in *Six Italian Plays*, vol. 1 of *The Classic Theatre*, ed. Eric Bentley (Garden City, N.Y.: Doubleday, 1958).

111 *The Magic Flute* (1791), Mozart's final opera, with a libretto by Emmanuel Schikaneder.

112 Samuel Johnson, *Rasselas*, chap. 16 (Bronson, 543). In Notes 56a.52, NF remarks on the "Rasselas archetype" (*NR*, 196).

113 In his dramatic theory and the plays he wrote and staged, Brecht championed the *Verfremdungseffekt* ("alienation effect") as a means of provoking critical reflection on the part of the spectator. See Bertolt Brecht, *Brecht on Theatre*, ed. and trans. John Willett (New York: Hill & Wang, 1964).

114 [William Blake,] *Jerusalem*, pl. 43 in some copies and editions; 29 in others. [NF] In Erdman, 192: "We heard astonishd at the Vision & our heart trembled within us: / We heard the voice of slumberous Albion, and thus he spake. / Idolatrous to his own Shadow words of eternity uttering" (pl. 43, ll. 44–6).

115 In Ovid's version, Narcissus does not in fact drown, as in some other versions of the myth, but simply pines away: "He drooped his weary head on the green grass and death sealed the eyes that marvelled at their master's beauty." *Metamorphoses*, bk. 3, ll. 502–3.

116 See [Cao Xueqin,] *The Story of the Stone*, trans. David Hawkes ([Harmondsworth:] Penguin Classics, 1973), 1:44. [NF] The page reference is to Hawkes's introduction, which discusses the novel's preoccupation with "the interplay between dream and reality" associated with the motif of the mirror.

117 In act 1 of Henrik Ibsen's *Peer Gynt*.

118 Sir Walter Scott, *The Antiquary* (London: Heinemann, 1950), 96, 99 (chap. 10, "The Green Room").

119 J.W. Mackail, *The Life of William Morris* (London: Longmans & Green, 1899), 1:11.

120 The reference is to the three watercolours painted by Jane and shown to Rochester in chap. 13 of the novel. Charlotte Bronte, *Jane Eyre* (Harmondsworth: Penguin, 1966), 156–7.

121 Amos Tutuola, *The Palm-Wine Drinkard* (London: Faber & Faber, 1952); Anthony Burgess, *A Clockwork Orange* (London: Heinemann, 1962).

122 In episode 9 ("Scylla and Charybdis"), Buck Mulligan teases Stephen about his review of Lady Gregory's poetry, the "drivel" of "that old hake Gregory." James Joyce, *Ulysses* (Harmondsworth: Penguin, 1971), 216. Joyce's reading of his work can be heard in *James Joyce reading from Ulysses and Finnegans Wake,* Caedmon TC 1340. The ALP (Anna Livia Plurabelle) chapter of *Finnegans Wake* is bk. 1, chap. 5.

123 On "charm," see *AC*, 278–80, and "Charms and Riddles," in *SM*, 123–47.

124 See n. 3, above.

125 See Allardyce Nicoll, *The World of Harlequin*[*: A Critical Study of the Commedia dell'Arte*] ([Cambridge: Cambridge University Press,] 1963). [NF]

126 See Gertrude Rachel Levy, *The Gate of Horn: A Study of the Religious Conceptions of the Stone Age, and Their Influence upon European Thought* (London: Faber & Faber, 1948); annotated copy in the NFL. Pt. 1 deals with the Palaeolithic stage of human culture and the rock drawings in the caverns of southwestern France and northwestern Spain.

127 Hesiod's *Theogony* tells of Zeus's deposing of his father Cronos and his victory over the insurgent Titans, the first race born of Earth and Heaven, driven far beneath the earth to a bitter imprisonment in Tartarus.

128 In *The Man of Law's Tale*, a work discussed in detail in Notes 56a and Notes 56b, Chaucer refers to the Biblical stories of Daniel in the lions' den, Jonah and the whale, and the crossing of the Red Sea.

129 In her introduction to Rider Haggard's *She* (New York: Modern Library, 2002), xxii, Margaret Atwood cites all but the penultimate sentence of this paragraph from *SeS*.

130 William Blake, *The Four Zoas* (pl. 138, ll. 30–2): "He walks upon the Eternal Mountains raising his heavenly voice / Conversing with the Animal forms of wisdom night & day / That risen from the Sea of fire renewd walk oer the Earth" (Erdman, 406).

131 For a discussion of the "grateful dead man" motif and its relevance to the Book of Tobit, see Stith Thompson, *The Folktale* (New York: Dryden Press, 1946); annotated copy in the NFL. See also *WP*, 233–4. The Book of Tobit is one of the deuterocanonical books of the Bible, treated as apocryphal in the Protestant tradition.

132 See Robert Graves, *The White Goddess*, 48. [NF]
133 *The Saga of Grettir the Strong*, chaps. 21–2 (see n. 67, above).
134 Not the modern noon, but nones, the ninth hour, the time of the death of Christ on the cross. [NF]
135 For a discussion of this creation myth, see chap. 6 of Jacobsen's *The Treasures of Darkness* (n. 90, above).
136 Dr. Diogenes Teufelsdröckh, "devil's dirt" or "devil's dung," is the fictive philosopher of clothing whose life and opinions are the comic subject of Thomas Carlyle's *Sartor Resartus*.
137 Lucian, a second-century Greek author, master of the ancient tradition of Menippean satire, whose dialogues of the dead place the once famous and powerful in a comic "upside-down world," where they find themselves in lowly occupations, humbled and mocked by those they lorded it over during life. See NF's discussion of Menippean satire in *AC*, 309–12.
138 [Jessie L. Weston,] *From Ritual to Romance* ([Cambridge: Cambridge University Press,] 1920), chap. 6. [NF]
139 See *The Book of the Dead*, trans. E.A. Wallis Budge (London: Routledge & Kegan Paul, 1953); annotated copy in the NFL.
140 This is the mouse's tale (tail) in *Alice's Adventures in Wonderland*, in *The Complete Works of Lewis Carroll*, 35 (chap. 3, "A Caucus-Race and a Long Tale").
141 The poet's opening address to the reader in *The Earthly Paradise*, vols. 3–6 of *The Collected Works of William Morris*, 3:1.
142 The prologue of the *Arabian Nights* explains Scheherezade's motivation in telling the thousand and one tales.
143 See Robert Graves, *The Greek Myths* (Harmondsworth: Penguin, 1955), vol. 1 (chap. 24, "Demeter's Nature and Deeds"); annotated copy in the NFL.
144 [Plutarch,] *De Genio Socratis* [*On the Sign of Socrates*], [in *Moralia*, 590a–b] 21: as with Jesus' three days in the lower world, the actual interval is two nights and one day. The statement in the text comes partly from Pausanias [*Description of Greece*], 9.39. [NF]
145 *The Prose Works of Sir Philip Sidney*, ed. Albert Feuillerat (Cambridge: Cambridge University Press, 1963), 2:83.
146 Ibid., 4:247.
147 See n. 71, above.
148 See Ernest Jones, *On the Nightmare* ([New York: Liveright,] 1951). [NF]
149 See n. 4, above.
150 See Margaret Schlauch, *Chaucer's Constance and Accused Queens* ([New York: New York University Press,] 1927). [NF]
151 In chap. 3 of *Culture and Anarchy*, ed. J. Dover Wilson (Cambridge: Cambridge University Press, 1948), Matthew Arnold applies "three distinct terms . . . to denote roughly the three great classes into which [English]

society is divided" (105). The working class is referred to as the "Populace," the middle class as "Philistines," and the aristocratic class as the "Barbarians."

152 Chaps. 59–61 [the verdict is "lunacy"]; the phrase "thief o' the world" [referred to in the preceding paragraph] is from chap. 27. [NF]

153 Jane Austen, *Mansfield Park* (see n. 79, above), 208–9 (chap. 22).

154 See *Of the Wonderful Dispensations of Providence, and of the Rise of Pope Gregory*, tale 81 of *Gesta Romanorum: or, Entertaining Moral Stories*, trans. Charles Swan, rev. Wynnard Hooper (New York: Dover, 1959), 141–54.

155 [Andrew Marvell,] *The Garden*, l. 47. [NF] "Meanwhile the mind, from pleasure less, / Withdraws into its happiness; / . . . / Annihilating all that's made / To a green thought in a green shade" (ll. 41–8).

156 D.H. Lawrence, *The Man Who Died*, in *The Short Novels* (London: Heinemann, 1956), 2:27.

157 *The Wood beyond the World*, in *The Collected Works of William Morris*, 17:128 (chap. 36).

158 A poem by an anonymous author, in which the poet is reconciled to the loss of his young daughter through an allegorical vision of her in paradise. See *The Pearl: A Middle English poem*, ed. Charles G. Osgood (Boston: D.C. Heath, 1906); annotated copy in the NFL.

159 "A garden inclosed is my sister, my spouse; a spring shut up, a fountain sealed" (Song of Solomon 4:12). See NF's discussion of the metaphoric structure of erotic imagery in *WP*, chap. 6.

160 *The Romaunt of the Rose* is an English translation, attributed to Chaucer, of the thirteenth-century allegory *Le Roman de la Rose* by Guillaume de Lorris and Jean de Meun. Seeking the "rosebud" in a garden, the poet-lover gains entry with the help of Fair Welcome, but is then blocked by a series of allegorical figures and finally driven off by Jealousy, who imprisons the rose in a tower.

161 Dylan Thomas, *Fern Hill*, ll. 37–40: "And honoured among foxes and pheasants by the gay house / Under the new made clouds and happy as the heart was long, / In the sun born over and over, / I ran my heedless ways."

162 See *The Romance of the Rose*, trans. Harry W. Robbins ([New York: Dutton,] 1962), 441 ff. [NF]

163 I have used the translation [*Hymn of the Soul*] by M.R. James, in *The Apocryphal New Testament* ([Oxford: Clarendon Press,] 1924), 411 ff. [NF] A revised and newly translated edition, by J.K. Elliott, appeared in 1993 (see n. 16, above).

164 Ibid., 414.

165 This refers to the concluding passage of *Through the Looking-Glass*, in *The Complete Works of Lewis Carroll*, 249.

166 Horatio Alger was the popular American writer of numerous rags-to-riches sagas at the end of the nineteenth century. The titles of the novels—*Struggling Upward; The Errand Boy, or, How Phil Brent Won Success; Bound to Rise, or, Up the Ladder; Joe the Hotel Boy, or, Winning Out by Pluck*—capture the basic direction of the stories.

167 Chaucer, *The House of Fame*, bk. 3, l. 1468, and *Troilus and Criseyde*, bk. 1, l. 394, bk. 5, l. 1653.

168 See [John Middleton Murry,] *Keats and Shakespeare* ([London: Oxford University Press,] 1925), chap. 13. [NF]

169 Ibid., 199.

170 Jorge Luis Borges, *Pierre Menard, Author of the "Quixote,"* in *Labyrinths: Selected Stories and Other Writings*, ed. Donald A. Yates and James E. Irby (New York: New Directions, 1964), 36–44.

171 I am referring, with appropriate inaccuracy, to [Anatole France,] *L'Île des pingouins* [(Paris: Calmann-Lévy, 1921), 152–9] (bk. 3, chap. 6). Except for the first clause in the next sentence, this passage was written before the appearance of Harold Bloom, *A Map of Misreading* [New York: Oxford University Press, 1975]. [NF] France's satire includes the tale of Father Marbodius's descent into hell, where Virgil denounces Dante's account in the *Inferno*: "The thing is monstrous and scarcely credible, but when this man returned to earth he disseminated the most odious lies about me. He affirmed in several passages of his barbarous poems that I had served him as a guide in the modern Tartarus, a place I know nothing of. He insolently proclaimed that I had spoken of the gods of Rome as false and lying gods, and that I held as the true God the present successor of Jupiter. Friend, when thou art restored to the kindly light of day and beholdest again thy native land, contradict these abominable falsehoods." *Penguin Island* (New York: Modern Library, 1960), 110.

172 The anabasis or "rising" of Kore was part of the Eleusinian mysteries in ancient Greece. Demeter and her daughter Kore were the two "Great Goddesses" worshipped in Eleusis, where their sanctuary was located.

173 See [Maxim Gorky,] *Untimely Thoughts*, trans. Herman Ermolaev ([New York: Paul S. Eriksson,] 1968), 32 ff. [NF]

174 In *The Way to Wealth* (1758) and his *Autobiography* (1771), Benjamin Franklin writes about his daily routine and the principles of moral conduct behind his rise to success.

175 Don Quixote interrupts a puppet show representing the pursuit of Sir Gaiferos and his wife Melisendra; thinking he is coming to their aid, he starts attacking the pasteboard figures (Cervantes, *Don Quixote*, pt. 2, chap. 26). In chap. 22 of Mark Twain's *The Adventures of Huckleberry Finn*, Huck goes to the circus and is enchanted by the show; he feels genuine concern

when a performer, obviously only pretending to be drunk, wanders out of the crowd and starts doing tricks on one of the horses.

176 The passage is from the story *A Tempered Wind*, in O. Henry, *The Gentle Grafter* (Garden City, N.Y.: Doubleday, 1917), 163–4.

177 *Purgatorio*, canto 27, ll. 139–42. See n. 100, above.

178 [Wallace Stevens, "Imagination as Value," in] *The Necessary Angel* [n. 33, above], 142. [NF]

179 Jack Kerouac (1922–69), author of *On the Road* (1957), a picaresque novel of the "beat" generation. NF is alluding here to the film *Easy Rider* (1969), directed by Dennis Hopper.

180 See Robert Graves's poem *To Juan at the Winter Solstice*. [NF]

181 Kant's discussion of the "admittedly ideal" kingdom of ends follows his establishment of the categorical imperative ("Act only on the principle of which, then and there, you would be willing to make a general law"): "The conception of the rational being as one who can see his own personal rules as universal legislation, and judge himself and his behavior from this point of view, leads to another and very fruitful conception which is related to it: the idea of the kingdom of ends." Kant, *Metaphysical Foundations of Morals*, in *An Immanuel Kant Reader*, ed. and trans. Raymond B. Blakney (New York: Harper, 1960), 182, 190–1.

182 *Odyssey*, bk. 23, l. 296. [NF] "And they then came in joy to the rite of their old-time bed." This line, as noted in the 1995 Loeb edition, "was regarded by Aristophanes and Aristarchus" as the end of the poem (406).

183 "I leave Sisyphus at the foot of the mountain! One always finds one's burden again. But Sisyphus teaches the higher fidelity that negates the gods and raises rocks. He too concludes that all is well. This universe henceforth without a master seems to him neither sterile nor futile. Each atom of that stone, each mineral flake of that night-filled mountain, in itself forms a world. The struggle itself toward the heights is enough to fill a man's heart. One must imagine Sisyphus happy." Albert Camus, *The Myth of Sisyphus and Other Essays*, trans. Justin O'Brien (New York: Knopf, 1969), 123.

184 [William Blake,] "Annotations to Wordsworth's *Poems*," 1815 [Erdman, 666]. For Hobbes see [J.E.] Spingarn, *Critical Essays of the Seventeenth Century* ([Oxford: Oxford University Press,] 1908), 1:28. [NF] See also Blake's *Milton*, pl. 14, l. 29, pl. 41, l. 4 (Erdman, 108, 142).

185 Blake makes repeated reference to the "Spectres of the Dead"; see his *Milton*, *Jerusalem*, and *The Four Zoas*.

186 In Plato's *Meno*, Socrates argues that the soul already possesses knowledge and that the acquisition of the latter therefore involves an act of recollection.

187 In his suggestion that the title of Mallarmé's *Igitur* is derived from the Vulgate text of Genesis 2:1, NF is following Rolland de Renéville,

L'Expérience poétique (Paris: Gallimard, 1938), 90. In *WP*, NF acknowledges that Renéville's claim "has been discredited for lack of evidence," but that "it is a most penetrating comment nonetheless" (*WP*, 292). Many of the themes in *Igitur* appear in the much later and highly experimental poem *Un Coup de dés* (*A Throw of the Dice*).

188 John Ball was one of the leaders of the Peasants' Revolt of 1381, and is famous for the couplet, "When Adam delved and Eve span / Who was then the gentleman?"

189 Cervantes, *Don Quixote*, pt. 2, chaps. 42–55. Don Quixote gives Sancho advice both immediately before he departs (chaps. 42–3) and in a letter while Sancho is governing (chap. 51).

190 See *AC*, 348: "The corruption out of which human art has been constructed will always remain in the art, but the imaginative quality of the art preserves it in its corruption, like the corpse of a saint." See also *EAC*, 163.

191 For the symbolic and poetic relevance of this in Goethe, see Peter Salm, *The Poem as Plant* ([Cleveland: The Press of Case Western Reserve University,] 1971), 27. [NF]

192 Garcin says this at the end of Jean-Paul Sartre's one-act play *Huis clos* (*No Exit*).

193 [James Joyce,] *Finnegans Wake* [Harmondsworth: Penguin, 1976], 120 ([bk. 1] chap. 5). [NF]

194 Richard Allestree's *The Whole Duty of Man (Laid Down in a Plain and Familiar Way, for the Use of All . . . With Private Devotions for Several Occasions)*, a seventeenth-century work, which takes its title from Ecclesiastes 12:13, "Fear God, and keep his commandments: for this is the whole duty of man."

195 "Immortals become mortals, mortals become immortals; they live in each other's death and die in each other's life." See *Heraclitus*, ed. Philip Wheelwright (Princeton: Princeton University Press, 1959), 68 (Fragment 66).

196 See Murasaki Shikibu, *The Tale of the Genji*; this eleventh-century romance tells the story of Prince Genji and his entanglement in the erotic and political life of court society.

197 Letter to Robert Bridges, 25 September 1888. [NF] "The effect of studying masterpieces is to make me admire and do otherwise. So it must be on every original artist to some degree, on me to a marked degree." *The Letters of Gerard Manley Hopkins to Robert Bridges*, ed. Claude Colleer Abbott (London: Oxford University Press, 1955), 291.

198 *Tractatus Logico-Philosophicus* (1922), 7. [NF] No. 7 is the last proposition of the *Tractatus*: "What we cannot speak about we must pass over in silence." Ludwig Wittgenstein, *Tractatus Logico-Philosophicus*, trans. D.F. Pears and B.F. McGuinness, 2nd impression (London: Routledge & Kegan Paul, 1963), 151. The proposition immediately preceding this one is also of

significance, given NF's theme of ascent and vision: "My propositions serve as elucidations in the following way: anyone who understands me eventually recognizes them as nonsensical, when he has used them—as steps—to climb up beyond them. (He must, so to speak, throw away the ladder after he has climbed up it.) He must transcend these propositions, and then he will see the world aright." Cf. *WP*, 165.

2. Romance as Masque

1 See no. 1, n. 11.
2 See in particular Asper's speech in the introduction to Jonson's *Every Man out of his Humour*, "After the Second Sounding," ll. 87–114 (Herford, 3:431–2).
3 *Fidelio* (1814), Beethoven's only opera, was plagued by a history of difficult composition and repeated failure with an unsympathetic public.
4 See NF, "Dickens and the Comedy of Humours," in *StS*, 218–40.
5 P.G. Wodehouse is the pen name of Sir Pelham Grenville (1881–1975), author of comic novels featuring Bertie Wooster, a young, upper-crust gadabout, and his butler Jeeves, a "tricky servant" type, whose ingenuity rescues his hapless employer from one predicament after another.
6 Socrates appears in *The Clouds*, Euripides in *The Acharnians*, *The Frogs*, and *Thesmophoriazusae*. Cleon, whose demagoguery is satirized in a number of Aristophanes' plays, appears in *The Knights*.
7 George Puttenham, *The Arte of English Poesie*, in *Elizabethan Critical Essays*, ed. Gregory Smith (London: Oxford University Press, 1904), 2:34.
8 The American comedy duo, whose partnership led in 1960 to "An Evening with Mike Nichols and Elaine May" on Broadway.
9 *MacBird* (New York: Grove Press, 1966) is Barbara Garson's political satire of Lyndon Johnson's presidency of the United States during the Vietnam war.
10 *A Most Pleasant Comedie of Mucedorus* (1598) was a popular romantic comedy of uncertain authorship. Sir Thomas More's *Utopia* (1516), a critique of contemporary society and a depiction of an ideal commonwealth, was first translated from Latin into English in 1551.
11 Francis Bacon, "Of Masques and Triumphs," in *A Critical Edition of the Major Works*, ed. Brian Vickers (Oxford: Oxford University Press, 1996), 417.
12 Ben Jonson, *Conversations with Drummond* (Herford, 1:133).
13 Cardinal Nicholas of Cusa (or Nicholas Cusanus), *Vision of God*, trans. Emma Gurney Salter (New York: Ungar, 1960); annotated copy in the NFL.
14 Carl Fabergé, goldsmith and jeweller (1846–1920), whose most celebrated creations were commissioned by the imperial family in Russia.

15 The son of a London cloth-worker, Inigo Jones studied painting and architecture in Italy before returning to London in 1605 as Queen Anne's architect. In charge of the production of court masques, he created innovative stage and costume designs, and collaborated frequently with Ben Jonson until their argument in 1631, after which Jonson was dismissed.

16 [James Shirley,] *The Triumph of Peace*, ed. Clifford Leech, in *A Book of Masques* [*in Honour of Allardyce Nicoll*] ([Cambridge: Cambridge University Press,] 1967). [NF] Many of the masques discussed by NF, including the anonymous *Masque of Flowers*, are collected in this volume. Annotated copy in the NFL.

17 NF is alluding here to the last line of the dedicatory quatrains to Blake's *Milton*. The hymn *And Did Those Feet in Ancient Time* (commonly known as "Jerusalem," after its tune) is no. 157 in *The Hymn Book of the Anglican Church of Canada and the United Church of Canada* (1971), for which NF was a consultant.

18 Ezra Pound, *Canto* 74, l. 11: "To build the city of Dioce whose terraces are the colour of stars." See also the reference to Ecbatana in *Canto* 4: "The camel drivers sit in the turn of the stairs, / Look down on Ecbatan of plotted streets, / 'Danaë! Danaë! / What wind is the king's?' / . . . / It is Cabestan's heart in the dish, / Vidal, or Ecbatan, upon the gilded tower in Ecbatan / Lay the god's bride, lay ever, waiting the golden rain." *The Cantos of Ezra Pound* (New York: New Directions, 1970), 425, 16.

19 For a description of Deioces and the construction of the city of Ecbatana, see Herodotus, *History*, bk. 1, sec. 98; for that of the Babylonian temple of Baal, see bk. 1, secs. 181–2. Annotated copy of Herodotus, *The Histories*, trans. Aubrey de Sélincourt (Harmondsworth: Penguin, 1965) in the NFL.

20 [Enid Welsford,] *The Court Masque* [*A Study in the Relationship between Poetry and the Revels*] ([Cambridge: Cambridge University Press,] 1927), [184 ff.]. [NF]

21 NF's concept of the "green world" was originally presented in "The Argument of Comedy," the essay cited in the introduction to the present volume (see n. 5). See also *AC*, 182–4, and *NP*, 140 ff.

22 The allusion is to Carlos Castaneda's *A Separate Reality: Further Conversations with Don Juan* (New York: Simon & Schuster, 1971).

23 Spoken by Hippolito in act 2, scene 2 of *Love's Cruelty*, in *The Dramatic Works and Poems of James Shirley*, ed. William Gifford and Alexander Dyce (New York: Russell & Russell, 1966), 2:213.

24 Spoken by Calchas in the final scene of James Shirley's *The Contention of Ajax and Ulysses*, ibid., 6:396.

25 G. Wilson Knight, *The Shakespearian Tempest: With a Chart of Shakespeare's Dramatic Universe* (London: Methuen, 1960).

26 Ben Jonson, *Timber: or, Discoveries* (Herford, 8:626).

27 In the *Republic*, Plato associates music with the harmonious order of the planetary spheres. Adapted by Christian mythology in the early centuries, ideas of the "music of the spheres" culminate in the great vision of music and dance presented in Dante's *Paradiso*. See Kathi Meyer-Baer, *Music of the Spheres and the Dance of Death: Studies in Musical Iconology* (Princeton: Princeton University Press, 1970).

28 Ben Jonson, *Bartholomew Fair*, Introduction, l. 131 (Herford, 6:16).

29 George Ivanovitch Gurdjieff, *Meetings with Remarkable Men* (New York: Dutton, 1969), 120.

4. The Responsibilities of the Critic

1 See Edmund Burke, *Reflections on the Revolution in France* (1790), Thomas Carlyle, *The French Revolution* (1837), and Matthew Arnold, *Culture and Anarchy* (1868).

2 Alexander Pope, *An Essay on Criticism*, ll. 297–8: "True Wit is Nature to advantage dress'd, / What oft was thought, but ne'er so well express'd." In *Poetical Works*, ed. Herbert Davis (London: Oxford University Press, 1966), 72.

3 Paul Valéry, "On Poe's *Eureka*," in *Leonardo, Poe, Mallarmé*, trans. Malcolm Cowley and James R. Lawler, vol. 8 of *The Collected Works of Paul Valéry*, ed. Jackson Mathews (Princeton: Princeton University Press, 1972), 170. Valéry speaks of Poe's poem as "one of the rare modern examples of a total explanation of the material and spiritual universe, a *cosmogony*. It belongs to a department of literature remarkable for its persistence and astonishing in its variety; cosmogony is one of the most ancient literary forms."

4 In his *Scienza Nuova*. See *The New Science of Giambattista Vico: Revised Translation of the Third Edition (1744)*, trans. Thomas Goddard Bergin and Max Harold Fisch (Ithaca, N.Y.: Cornell University Press, 1968); annotated copy in the NFL.

5 In Molière's *Le Bourgeois Gentilhomme*, Monsieur Jourdain learns from his philosophy instructor the difference between prose and verse. Upon discovering that it is the former when one says something like "Nicole, bring me my slippers, and give me my nightcap" (2.4.150–1), Monsieur Jourdain expresses his delight at having unwittingly been speaking prose for more than forty years. For an example of NF's attack on the "Jourdain fallacy," see *WTC*, 17–18.

6 Vico's grand conception of history as a human creation and as a progressive advance in the direction of democratic freedom anticipates historical views developed in the nineteenth century, most dramatically in the writings of Karl Marx (1818–83). The *Scienza Nuova* was translated into French by Jules Michelet (1798–1874), best known for his *History of France* and *History of the*

French Revolution. Reflections on Violence, by the socialist thinker Georges Sorel (1847–1922), was published in 1908; annotated copy in the NFL.

7 For biographical information on Joyce and his interest in Vico, see Richard Ellmann, *James Joyce* (New York: Oxford University Press, 1959); annotated copy in the NFL. See also two essays by NF: "Quest and Cycle in *Finnegans Wake,*" in *FI,* 256–64, and "Cycle and Apocalypse in *Finnegans Wake,*" in *Vico and Joyce,* ed. Donald Philip Verene (Albany: State University of New York Press, 1987), 3–19; rpt. in *MM,* 356–74.

8 In *Totem and Taboo,* Freud postulates an originary collective act of patricide by a fraternal horde who act out of resentment at their father's monopolization of women and property. This murder leads to deep guilt and a new "social contract" based on the institution of a system of taboos aimed at precluding a repetition of the original act of violence.

9 Erik von Däniken, *Chariots of the Gods? Unsolved Mysteries of the Past,* trans. Michael Heron (New York: Bantam, 1971), and Immanuel Velikovsky, *Worlds in Collision* (New York: Dell, 1970).

10 For an explanation of "*The Mental Traveller* cycle," see *FS,* 229 (*FS2,* 229).

11 Herman Melville, *Journal of a Visit to Europe and the Levant: October 11, 1856–May 6, 1857,* ed. Howard C. Horsford (Princeton: Princeton University Press, 1955), 118. In *GC,* 239, NF cites the introduction to Walter E. Bezanson's edition of Melville's *Clarel: A Poem and Pilgrimage in the Holy Land* (New York: Hendricks House, 1960); annotated copy in the NFL.

12 See Isaiah 40:3, and the references to John the Baptist in Matthew 3:3, Mark 1:3, Luke 3:4, and John 1:23.

13 Milton's poem *On the New Forcers of Conscience under the Long Parliament* views the new rule by presbytery as tantamount to another episcopacy: "To force our Consciences that Christ set free, / And ride us with a Classic Hierarchy" (ll. 6–7).

14 An allusion to the "canonization" of ex-convict and writer Jean Genet in Jean-Paul Sartre's *Saint Genet: Actor and Martyr,* trans. Bernard Frechtman (New York: New American Library, 1963); annotated copy in the NFL.

15 R.D. Laing, *The Divided Self* (1969) and *The Politics of Experience and the Bird of Paradise* (1967); see also David Graham Cooper, *Psychiatry and Anti-Psychiatry* (1967) and *The Language of Madness* (1978).

16 Ludwig Wittgenstein, *Philosophical Investigations,* trans. G.E.M. Anscombe (Oxford: Blackwell, 1997), 10–11 (pt. 1, no. 22).

5. Comment on Peter Hughes's Essay

1 Harold Innis (1894–1952), Canadian political economist, whose works *Empire and Communications* and *The Bias of Communication* are recognized as landmarks in communication studies. See NF, "Harold Innis: The

Strategy of Culture," in *EAC*, 154–67. For Michelet, Marx, and Sorel, see no. 4, n. 6.

2 James Joyce, *Finnegans Wake*, 215 (bk. 1, chap. 8): "Then all that was was fair. Tys Elvenland! Teems of times and happy returns. The seim anew. Ordovico or viricordo. Anna was, Livia is, Plurabelle's to be." See also no. 4, n. 7.

6. Literature, History, and Language

1 See no. 1, n. 30.

2 William Blake, *Laocoön* (Erdman, 274). Blake's statement "The Old & New Testaments are the Great Code of Art" provided NF with the title for his first book on the Bible.

3 *Langue* is the particular "tongue" shared by a people or nation, as opposed to *langage*, a more general sense of language or "speech." Saussure, in his *Cours de linguistique générale*, further distinguishes *langue* from *parole*. See Ferdinand de Saussure, *Course in General Linguistics*, trans. Wade Baskin (New York: Philosophical Library, 1959), 77: "Language [*la langue*] is speech [*le langage*] less speaking [*la parole*]."

4 See *The Creation Epic*, trans. E.A. Speiser, in *Ancient Near Eastern Texts Relating to the Old Testament*, ed. James B. Pritchard, 3rd ed. (Princeton: Princeton University Press, 1969), 60–72; annotated copy of the 1950 edition in the NFL.

5 Richard Broxton Onians, *The Origins of European Thought* (Cambridge: Cambridge University Press, 1951); annotated copy in the NFL.

6 Eric Havelock, *A Preface to Plato* (Cambridge, Mass.: Belknap Press, 1963); annotated copy in the NFL.

7 René Descartes, *A Discourse on Method*, trans. John Veitch (London: Dent, 1912), 27.

8 See, for example, St. Anselm's ontological proof of God's existence in his *Proslogium*, which is the starting point of St. Thomas Aquinas's proof in the first part of his *Summa Theologiae*.

9 The allusion is to Roland Barthes, *Le Degré zéro de l'écriture* (1953), translated by Annette Lavers and Colin Smith as *Writing Degree Zero* (London: Jonathan Cape, 1967); annotated copy in the NFL.

10 On Gibbon's *Decline and Fall of the Roman Empire*, see *LN*, 219: "Gibbon was, from a naive point of view, chasing a ghost, at best a metaphor inscribed within his sources, there being nothing 'out there' that actually declined and fell."

7. On Translation

1 See his letter to Alexander Baillie, 14 January 1883, in *Further Letters of*

Gerard Manley Hopkins, ed. Claude Colleer Abbott, 2nd ed. (London: Oxford University Press, 1956), 252–3. Hopkins speaks of the overthought as "that which everybody, editors, see," whereas the underthought is "conveyed chiefly in the choice of metaphors etc used and often only half realised by the poet himself." The underthought "is commonly an echo or shadow of the overthought . . . an undercurrent of thought governing the choice of images used."

8. Extracts from *The Practical Imagination*

1 In this introduction, NF refers to works included in the anthology's section on fiction, as follows: chap. 1 ("The Narrative Impulse"), *Rumpelstiltskin; Stone Soup: A Folk Tale*; W.W. Jacobs, *The Monkey's Paw*; John Collier, *The Chaser*; Rudyard Kipling, *The Man Who Would Be King*; chap. 2 ("The Narrator as Participant"), Edgar Allan Poe, *The Tell-Tale Heart*; Charlotte Perkins Gilman, *The Yellow Wall-Paper*; Sherwood Anderson, *I'm a Fool*; Eudora Welty, *A Memory*; John Updike, *A&P*; chap. 3 ("The Narrator as Observer"), Ernest Hemingway, *My Old Man*; Doris Lessing, *The Old Chief Mshlanga*; Ring Lardner, *Haircut*; William Faulkner, *A Rose for Emily*; Ambrose Bierce, *The Boarded Window*; chap. 4 ("The Omniscient Narrator"), F. Scott Fitzgerald, *Babylon Revisited*; D.H. Lawrence, *Mother and Daughter*; Kate Chopin, *The Storm*; chap. 5 ("Realism"), Theodore Dreiser, *The Lost Phoebe*; William Carlos Williams, *The Use of Force*; Langston Hughes, *Feet Live Their Own Life*; Flannery O'Connor, *Good Country People*; Ralph Ellison, *Flying Home*; Vasily Aksenov, *Halfway to the Moon*; chap. 6 ("Metaphor, Symbol, and Allegory"), Joyce Cary, *Evangelist*; Nathaniel Hawthorne, *My Kinsman, Major Molineux*; Katherine Mansfield, *Bliss*; James Joyce, *A Little Cloud*; John Barth, *Lost in the Funhouse*; Dylan Thomas, *After the Fair*; chap. 7 ("Theme"), Ursula K. Le Guin, *The Ones Who Walk Away from Omelas*; Katherine Anne Porter, *He*; Stanislaw Lem, *The Seventh Sally*; Jack London, *To Build a Fire*; Fyodor Dostoevsky, *The Dream of a Ridiculous Man*; Jorge Luis Borges, *The Gospel according to Mark*; Heinrich Böll, *The Thrower-Away*; W.S. Merwin, *The Ford*; Thomas Pynchon, *The Story of Byron the Bulb*; chap. 8 ("Longer Fiction"), Leo Tolstoy, *The Death of Ivan Ilych*; Joseph Conrad, *The Secret Sharer*.

2 *The King's Ankus*, in Rudyard Kipling, *The Second Jungle Book* (London: Macmillan, 1910), 147–75.

3 For the story of Samson, see Judges 14–16. For a portrayal of Deïaneira's unwitting betrayal of Hercules, see Sophocles' *Women of Trachis;* and Ovid, *Metamorphoses*, bk. 9.

4 Compare NF's observation in *WP*, illustrated with reference to Shakespeare's Iago: "We can, up to a point, understand motivated evil, but unmotivated evil has something bafflingly inscrutable about it" (281).

5 See D.H. Lawrence, "The Spirit of Place," in *Studies in Classical American Literature* (New York: Penguin, 1964), 8: "Never trust the artist. Trust the tale. The proper function of a critic is to save the tale from the artist who created it."

6 T.S. Eliot, "Hamlet" (Kermode, 48).

7 Thomas De Quincey, "The English Mail-Coach," in *Confessions of an English Opium-Eater and Other Essays* (Oxford: Oxford University Press, 1985), 212 (sec. 2, "The Vision of Sudden Death").

8 *Description without Place*, in *The Collected Poems of Wallace Stevens*, 345 (pt. 7, ll. 7–12): "As, men make themselves their speech: the hard hidalgo / Lives in the mountainous character of his speech; / And in that mountainous mirror Spain acquires / The knowledge of Spain and of the hidalgo's hat— / A seeming of the Spaniard, a style of life, / The invention of a nation in a phrase."

9 In this introduction, NF refers to works included in the anthology's section on drama, as follows: chap. 1 ("Tragedy"), Sophocles, *Oedipus Rex*; William Shakespeare, *Macbeth*; chap. 2 ("Comedy, Satire, and Romance"), Aristophanes, *Lysistrata*; Molière, *The Physician in Spite of Himself*; William Shakespeare, *The Tempest*; chap. 3 ("Social Drama"), Henrik Ibsen, *An Enemy of the People*; August Strindberg, *Miss Julie*; Anton Chekhov, *The Cherry Orchard*; Arthur Miller, *Death of a Salesman*; Lorraine Hansberry, *A Raisin in the Sun*; chap. 4 ("Farce, Fantasy, and the Absurd"), Luigi Pirandello, *It* Is *So! (If You Think So)* (see n. 12, below); Eugène Ionesco, *The Bald Soprano*; Edward Albee, *The American Dream*; final section ("Writing About Drama"), Samuel Beckett, *Not I*.

10 See NF, "The Stage Is All the World," in *MM*, 196–211.

11 In the revised edition, the discussion of *Miss Julie* is replaced by the following: "Take the conclusion of Miller's *Death of a Salesman*, where we observe the personas that the Loman family have adopted in relation to one another forcefully challenged as fraudulent. Wife and sons must now confront Willy in the light of new knowledge and a new understanding of their own roles—either that or refuse the knowledge and its implications and allow life to go on as it has in the past, with each family member adopting an old mask again. And Willy's final choice when he goes off to die is to continue to play the role he has cast himself in from the beginning, saving the family with an act he persists in viewing as heroic, however hollow others might judge that heroism to be. However we interpret the words at the end of the play, they make it clear that Miller is not simply writing a play and the audience merely listening to it. There's a group of intermediate dramas, some of them within the characters and some of them within our own previous experiences, and it's the interactions of all these that make up the whole drama. Miller's genius as a playwright resulted in part from his ability to create the

Loman family both as characters and as the subdramatists of their own lives."

12 Pirandello's play *Così è (se vi pare)* (1917) has also been translated as *Right You Are (If You Think You Are).* In the revised edition, the discussion of Pirandello is replaced by the following: "Something similar is the reason for the tensions between the people in Williams's *The Glass Menagerie,* as Tom and Laura try desperately to find their own identities apart from the expectations of their mother. Laura, we discover, succeeds at most in establishing a quite fragile identity, easily shattered, and Tom becomes himself only by satisfying his mother that he is a 'selfish dreamer,' although that is certainly not his preferred view of himself, nor is it one we are sure an audience should accept. The play abounds with references to the world as an illusion and to our places in it as illusory."

13 See no. 2, n. 2.

14 In the revised edition, the reference to *Macbeth* is replaced by the following: "In *Hamlet,* the prince, motivated by the desire to set right a monarchy made 'rotten' by regicide, fratricide, and adultery, brings about the total collapse of Denmark's royal family. Order—when it comes—results from the advent of a new dynasty from another country."

15 In the revised edition, the reference to *Macbeth* is replaced by the following: "In *The Glass Menagerie,* Tom finally leaves home, but in his last speech he tells us how his life has been dominated by the persistent reality of his memories."

9. Vision and Cosmos

1 Discussions of boundaries and sacred spaces can be found in a number of Mircea Eliade's works, such as *Patterns in Comparative Religion,* trans. Rosemary Sheed (New York: Sheed & Ward, 1958), *The Sacred and the Profane: The Nature of Religion,* trans. Willard R. Trask (New York: Harcourt, Brace & World, 1959), and *Cosmos and History: The Myth of the Eternal Return,* trans. Willard R. Trask (New York: Harper & Brothers, 1959). See also *The Secret of the Golden Flower: A Chinese Book of Life,* trans. Richard Wilhelm, with commentary by C.G. Jung (London: Routledge & Kegan Paul, 1931), 100–2. Annotated copies of all four books are in the NFL.

2 The Italian philosopher Giordano Bruno (1548–1600) was burned at the stake for heresy, while Galileo Galilei (1564–1642), Italian mathematician and astronomer, was forced to recant his controversial views. Charles Darwin and fellow evolutionists Thomas Huxley and Joseph Hooker were challenged by Bishop Samuel Wilberforce, among others, most famously at a meeting of the British Association for the Advancement of Science, 30 June 1860, at Oxford University.

3 Sir Philip Sidney, *A Defence of Poetry*: "Nature never set foorth the earth in so rich Tapistry as diverse Poets have done . . . her world is brasen, the Poets only deliver a golden." *The Prose Works of Sir Philip Sidney*, 3:8.

4 Chaucer, *The House of Fame*, ll. 730–2 (bk. 2): "That every kyndely thyng that is / Hath a kyndely stede ther he / May best in hyt conserved be."

5 See no. 2, n. 27.

6 See no. 1, n. 54.

7 The last line of Spenser's *Mutabilitie Cantos* is, "O that great Sabbaoth God, graunt me that Sabaoths sight" (canto 8, st. 2, l. 9). See the final paragraph of *SeS* (p. 123).

8 Sir Thomas Browne, *Religio Medici*, pt. 1, sec. 37 (Keynes, 44).

9 The "attendant spirit" appears in Milton's *Comus*, the "Genius of the shore" in *Lycidas*, l. 183, and the "Genius of the Wood" in both *Il Penseroso*, l. 154, and *Arcades*.

10 The story of the river god Alpheus and the nymph Arethusa is told in Ovid, *Metamorphoses*, bk. 5, ll. 572–641.

11 Thomas Hardy's "epic-drama" *The Dynasts* depicts the clashes between peoples in the Napoleonic wars as the working out of "the Immanent Will, "[t]his viewless, voiceless Turner of the Wheel" (Fore Scene). The phrase "all-immanent Will" also appears in various poems by Hardy, such as *God-Forgotten, The Bedridden Peasant to an Unknowing God, By the Earth's Corpse, The Unborn*, and *The Convergence of the Twain*.

12 See no. 4, n. 3.

10. Literature as a Critique of Pure Reason

1 Bertrand Russell, *History of Western Philosophy* (London: George Allen & Unwin, 1961), 213 (chap. 23).

2 Alfred North Whitehead, *Science and the Modern World* (New York: The Free Press, 1967), 7.

3 See *Heraclitus* (no. 1, n. 195), 58 (Fragments 46–51), and 68 (Fragment 65).

4 This is the opening question of Martin Heidegger's *An Introduction to Metaphysics*.

5 See, for example, Fritz Perls, *Gestalt Psychology Verbatim* (New York: Bantam, 1959). Perls uses the terms "top dog" and "underdog" to distinguish different types of manipulators.

6 In Ovid's *Metamorphoses*, Medea speaks of her love for Jason, which is in tragic conflict with her duty to her father: "video meliora, proboque, / deteriora sequor" ("I see the better and approve it, but I follow the worse"), bk. 7, ll. 20–1.

7 *2001: A Space Odyssey*, the well-known science fiction film directed by Stanley Kubrick (Metro-Goldwyn-Mayer, 1968). The screenplay was written

by Kubrick in collaboration with Arthur C. Clarke, author of the novel which appeared in 1967.

8 Cult leader Jim Jones led a band of followers from the People's Temple in San Francisco to a commune in Guyana, where on 18 November 1978 he instigated a mass murder-suicide. In the summer of 1969, Charles Manson orchestrated a series of brutal murders in the vicinity of Beverley Hills, for which he and eight others were convicted.

9 The phrase "nothing but sophistry and illusion" concludes David Hume's *An Inquiry Concerning Human Understanding.*

10 See *Hindu Myths: A Sourcebook Translated from the Sanskrit*, ed. and trans. Wendy Doniger O'Flaherty (Harmondsworth: Penguin, 1975); annotated copy in the NFL: ". . . only a world composed of the full variety of qualities is desirable, let alone possible; the three 'strands' or qualities of matter (*gunas*)—*sattva* (goodness or light), *rajas* (dust, passion, or activity), and *tamas* (darkness or inertia)—must always be balanced; indeed, they are called 'strands' because they are inextricably intertwined everywhere like the strands of a rope" (43–4).

11 Samuel Butler's *Erewhon* suggests that life "would be intolerable if men were to be guided in all they did by reason and reason only. Reason betrays men into the drawing of hard and fast lines, and to the defining by language—language being like the sun, which rears and then scorches. Extremes are alone logical, but they are always absurd; the mean is illogical, but an illogical mean is better than the sheer absurdity of an extreme. There are no follies and no unreasonablenesses so great as those which can apparently be irrefragably defended by reason itself, and there is hardly an error into which men may not easily be led if they base their conduct upon reason only." *The Shrewsbury Edition of the Works of Samuel Butler*, ed. H.F. Jones and A.T. Bartholomew (New York: AMS Press, 1968), 2:163–4 (chap. 21).

12 We have been unable to identify the poet to whom NF is referring here.

13 See *Psychological Types*, vol. 6 of *The Collected Works of C.G. Jung* (Princeton: Princeton University Press, 1971); chap. 10 ("General Description of the Types," pars. 556–671) rpt. in *The Portable Jung*, ed. Joseph Campbell (Harmondsworth: Penguin, 1982), 178–269.

14 See *Psychology and Alchemy*, vol. 12 of *The Collected Works of C.G. Jung* (New York: Pantheon, 1953); pt. 2 ("Individual Dream Symbolism in Relation to Alchemy") rpt. in *The Portable Jung*, 323–455.

15 Montaigne's famous motto *Que sçais-je?* which he had engraved on a medal showing scales in equilibrium, expressed his attitude that certainty is the surest mark of unreason or the irrational.

16 Kant's *Kritik der reinen Vernunft* (*Critique of Pure Reason*) is concerned with reason in the absence of its application to tangible reality; *Kritik der*

praktischen Vernunft (*Critique of Practical Reason*) with the moral law and ethical freedom; and *Kritik der Urteilskraft* (*Critique of Judgment*) with aesthetic and teleological judgments.

17 Immanuel Kant, *Critique of Judgement*, trans. J.H. Bernard, 2nd ed. (London: Macmillan, 1914), 68 (sec. 10), and 241–8 (sec. 58).

18 Matthew Arnold, *Culture and Anarchy*, 155 (chap. 5): "many things are not seen in their true nature and as they really are, unless they are seen as beautiful." In *DV*, NF also mentions in this context Ruskin and Morris, "who insisted that the reality of Victorian civilization was bound up with the sense of how much ugliness was included in it" (*NFR*, 190). The same point is made in *WP*, 226.

19 Sir Thomas Browne, *Religio Medici*, pt. 1, sec. 16 (Keynes, 21–2).

20 In a letter to J.A. Hessey, 9 October 1818, Keats writes: "The Genius of Poetry must work out its own salvation in a man: It cannot be matured by law and precept, but by sensation & watchfulness in itself. That which is creative must create itself." *The Letters of John Keats*, ed. Maurice Buxton Forman, 4th ed. (London: Oxford University Press, 1952), 221; annotated copy in the NFL.

21 George Puttenham, *The Arte of English Poesie*, in *Elizabethan Critical Essays*, 2:3.

22 "For books are not absolutely dead things, but do contain a potency of life in them to be as active as that soul was whose progeny they are; nay, they do preserve as in a vial the purest efficacy and extraction of that living intellect that bred them." John Milton, *Areopagitica*, in *Complete Poems and Major Prose*, ed. Merritt Y. Hughes (Indianapolis: Odyssey, 1957), 720.

23 George Macdonald, *The Castle: A Parable*, in *The Gifts of the Child Christ: Fairytales and Stories for the Childlike*, ed. Glenn Edward Sadler (Grand Rapids, Mich.: William B. Eerdmans, 1973), 1:283–94; rpt. in paperback under the title *The Gifts of the Child Christ: And Other Stories and Fairy Tales* (1996).

11. Approaching the Lyric

1 Cyrillus, no. 728, in *The Greek Anthology and Other Ancient Epigrams: A Selection in Modern Verse Translations*, ed. and with an introduction by Peter Jay (Harmondsworth: Penguin, 1981), 318 (bk. 9, no. 369, in the Palatine Anthology); annotated copy in the NFL.

2 Bruno Snell, *The Discovery of the Mind: The Greek Origins of European Thought*, trans. T.G. Rosenmeyer (Cambridge, Mass.: Harvard University Press, 1953). [NF]

3 Hart Crane. "Appendix I: General Aims and Theories," in Philip Horton, *Hart Crane: The Life of an American Poet* (New York: [Viking,] 1957), 327. [NF]

4 Thomas Nashe, *A Litany in Time of Plague*, l. 17. The song, alternatively called *Adieu, Farewell Earth's Bliss*, a litany mourning the death of summer, is from Nashe's play *Summer's Last Will and Testament* (1600).

5 This is implied in Mallarmé's *Toast funèbre*, *Plusieurs Sonnets*, and *Hommages et tombeaux*; in Rilke, the theme of praise as the function of poetic "song" is explicit throughout the *Sonnets to Orpheus* and in the ninth of the *Duino Elegies*.

6 See the account of Perceval's visit to the castle of the Fisher King, *The Story of the Grail*, in *The Complete Romances of Chrétien de Troyes*, trans. David Staines (Bloomington: Indiana University Press, 1990), 376–85 (ll. 2994–3690).

7 See also Poe's essay "The Philosophy of Composition": "What we term a long poem is, in fact, merely a succession of brief ones—that is to say, of brief poetical effects. It is needless to demonstrate that a poem is such, only inasmuch as it intensely excites, by elevating, the soul; and all intense excitements are, through a psychal necessity, brief. For this reason, at least one half of the 'Paradise Lost' is essentially prose—a succession of poetical excitements interspersed, *inevitably*, with corresponding depressions—the whole being deprived, through the extremeness of its length, of the vastly important artistic element, totality, or unity, of effect." Edgar Allan Poe, *The Fall of the House of Usher and Other Writings*, ed. David Galloway (Harmondsworth: Penguin, 1986), 482.

12. The Survival of Eros in Poetry

1 See no. 9, n. 3.

2 Andrew Marvell, *The Garden*, ll. 57–8: "Such was that happy garden-state, / While man walked there without a mate."

3 Edmund Spenser, *The Faerie Queen*, bk. 3, canto 6, st. 43, ll. 1–3: "Right in the middest of that Paradise, / There stood a stately Mount, on whose round top / A gloomy groue of mirtle trees did rise."

4 The Nicene Creed is a profession of Christian faith established at the fourth-century ecumenical councils, beginning with the Council of Nicaea in 325. It reflects the doctrine of the Trinity and describes the coexistence of divine and human natures in Christ, who is affirmed as "Being of one substance with the Father."

5 See no. 9, n. 9.

6 No. 48a, in *The Poetry of Guido Cavalcanti*, ed. and trans. Lowry Nelson, Jr. (New York: Garland, 1986).

7 Established in 1863, the Salon des Refusés exhibited works such as Manet's *Déjeuner sur l'Herbe*, which had been rejected by the jury of the official Salon.

8 See no. 9, n. 2.

9 Group of four leading members of the Chinese communist party, including Jiang Quing, Mao Tse-tung's companion, who spearheaded the decade-long Cultural Revolution in China in the mid-1960s.

10 *Aucassin and Nicolette*, ed. Anne Elizabeth Cobby, trans. Glyn S. Burgess, in *The Pilgrimage of Charlemagne* and *Aucassin and Nicolette* (New York: Garland, 1988), 126 (sec. 6).

11 After the publication of *Jerusalem Delivered*, Torquato Tasso (1544–95), tormented by religious scruples, feared that his poem had confused the sacred mission of a holy war with the passions and desires of romance. The novelist Leo Tolstoy (1828–1910) underwent a deep spiritual crisis that led to a rejection of the world of the aristocracy, along with the literary form he had used to depict it in *War and Peace* and *Anna Karenina*.

12 For Hardy's "Immanent Will," see no. 9, n. 11. Shelley's Jupiter appears in *Prometheus Unbound*. See *FS* for a discussion of Blake's Urizen, "thunder-god of moral law and tyrannical power" (129; *FS2*, 132), a figure of "Fate or Necessity," who "turns out to be much like our old friend the immanent Will. Perfect obedience to him would be unconscious and automatic, like the circling of the stars" (63; *FS2*, 69).

13 See NF, "The Drunken Boat: The Revolutionary Element in Romanticism," in *Romanticism Reconsidered: Selected Papers from the English Institute*, ed. Northrop Frye (New York: Columbia University Press, 1963), 1–25; rpt. in *StS*, 200–17; revised and expanded in *SR*, 3–49 (*ENC*, 75–91). The "drunken boat" refers to Arthur Rimbaud's poem *Le Bateau ivre*.

14 See no. 8, n. 7.

15 Thomas De Quincey's *Confessions of an English Opium-Eater* ends as follows: "my sleep is still tumultuous; and, like the gates of Paradise to our first parents when looking back from afar, it is still (in the tremendous line of Milton)—'With dreadful faces thronged and fiery arms.'" The line from Milton's *Paradise Lost* is 644 in bk. 12.

16 D.H. Lawrence, *Fantasia of the Unconscious*, in *Psychoanalysis and the Unconscious and Fantasia of the Unconscious* (New York: Viking, 1960), 157–8, 161 (chap. 10, "Parent Love").

17 Qtd. by E.J. Furcha in "The Paradoxon as Hermeneutical Principle: The Case of Sebastian Franck, 1499–1542," in *Spirit within Structure: Essays in Honor of George Johnston*, ed. E.J. Furcha (Allison Park, Pa.: Pickwick, 1983), 112. Denck makes the statement in the preface ("To the Reader") to his *Paradox*, in *The Selected Writings of Hans Denck, 1500–1527*, ed. and trans. E.J. Furcha (Lewiston, N.Y.: Edwin Mellen Press, 1989), 28.

18 See no. 4, n. 3.

19 Herbert Levine, "How Many Bibles?" *Georgia Review*, 36 (Winter 1982): 900–4.

20 See, for example, Paul Tillich, *Dynamics of Faith*: "Man's ultimate concern must be expressed symbolically, because symbolic language alone is able to express the ultimate" (New York: Harper & Brothers, 1957), 41 (chap. 3, "Symbols of Faith").
21 Chap. 1 of *GC* outlines the metaphoric, metonymic, and descriptive phases of language. The fourth phase, the *kerygmatic*, NF introduces at the end of the chapter (*GC*, 29–30), and then develops more fully in *WP*, 100–18.
22 Compare NF's earlier remarks on "the emotional overtones of the word 'system' . . . in this fragmented age": "Jail-building, pigeonholing, providing a glib answering service for undergraduates, overweening ambition on the part of the system-builder, are some of the readiest associations. In the muddled mythology of stock response, the system-builder is the spider who spins nets out of his bowels, as contrasted with the bee who flits empirically from flower to flower and staggers home under his burden of sweetness and light." "Reflections in a Mirror," in *Northrop Frye in Modern Criticism: Selected Papers from the English Institute*, ed. Murray Krieger (New York: Columbia University Press, 1966), 136.
23 These lectures were published as the volume *NFS*.
24 See *TSE*, chap. 2.
25 Jacques Derrida, *Of Grammatology*, trans. Gayatri Chakravorty Spivak (Baltimore: John Hopkins University Press, 1976); annotated copy in the NFL.
26 Helen Gardner, "Present Discontents," in *In Defence of the Imagination*, The Charles Eliot Norton Lectures, 1979–1980 (Oxford: Clarendon Press, 1982), 20.
27 See, for instance, Harold Bloom, *Yeats* (New York: Oxford University Press, 1970), 5; and *The Anxiety of Influence: A Theory of Poetry* (New York: Oxford University Press, 1973), 31.
28 "And again, if it be true that a wise man, like a good refiner, can gather gold out of the drossiest volume, and that a fool will be a fool with the best book, yea or without book, there is no reason that we should deprive a wise man of any advantage to his wisdom, while we seek to restrain from a fool that which being restrained will be no hindrance to his folly." John Milton, *Areopagitica*, in *Complete Poems and Major Prose*, 730.
29 Henry James, "The Art of Fiction," in *The Future of the Novel*, ed. Leon Edel (New York: Vintage Books, 1956), 13.
30 Charles Lamb, "Detached Thoughts on Books and Reading," in *The Essays of Elia* (London: Dent, 1906), 202.

13. The Ouroboros

1 William Blake, *Europe*, pl. 10, ll. 21–13: "Then was the serpent temple form'd,

image of infinite / Shut up in finite revolutions, and man became an Angel; / Heaven a mighty circle turning; God a tyrant crown'd" (Erdman, 63).

2 This Plotinian *topos* was perhaps what Augustine had in mind when he wrote in the *Confessions* that God was "everywhere and nowhere in space" (bk. 6, chap. 3). In his essay "Circles" Emerson writes, "St. Augustine described the nature of God as a circle whose centre was everywhere and its circumference nowhere" (*Selections from Ralph Waldo Emerson*, ed. Stephen E. Whicher [Boston: Houghton, 1957], 169). Pascal says the same thing about "Nature" in his *Pensées* (sec. 72). The version with God as a subject can be found in Empedocles, Hermes Tristmegistmus, Nicholas of Cusa, Bartholomaeus Anglicus, Alain de Lille, Bruno, and Voltaire. The widespread use of the *topos* is doubtless why NF refers to it as a proverb in *WP*, 186.

3 James Joyce, *Finnegans Wake*, 20 (bk. 1, chap. 1).

14. Literary and Linguistic Scholarship in a Postliterate World

1 In the last years of his life, Nikolai Gogol (1809–52) underwent a spiritual crisis that unsettled his emotional and physical health, and made him unable to produce any sustained work. Arthur Rimbaud (1854–91) left behind a fragmentary body of poetry, all of it written before he turned twenty; at the age of twenty-two, he began a life of drifting that took him to North Africa, where he ended his life as a merchant and arms dealer. Yukio Mishimo is the pen name of Kimitake Hiraoka (1925–70), a novelist who adopted extreme right-wing views and committed suicide after a failed *coup d'état* by the political organization he had founded. For Tasso, see no. 12, n. 11.

2 See no. 7, n. 1.

3 T.S. Eliot, "The Use of Poetry and the Use of Criticism" (Kermode, 93).

4 See no. 1, n. 126.

5 NF is alluding to the work of Jacques Derrida, in particular his essay "La pharmacie de Platon," an extensive deconstructive reading of Plato's *Phaedrus* as exemplifying what Derrida calls a "metaphysics of presence." See "Plato's Pharmacy," in *Dissemination*, trans. Barbara Johnson (Chicago: University of Chicago Press, 1981); annotated copy in the NFL.

6 "Description is revelation. It is not / The thing described, nor false facsimile. / . . . / Book of a concept only possible / In description, canon central in itself, / The thesis of the plentifullest John." *Description without Place*, in *The Collected Poems of Wallace Stevens*, 344–5 (pt. 6, ll. 1–2, 10–12).

16. Myth as the Matrix of Literature

1 See no. 1, n. 6.

2 See no. 7, n. 1.
3 This remark appears not in Byron's *Don Juan*, but in *Beppo*, st. 52, l. 8.
4 T.S. Eliot, "The Metaphysical Poets" (Kermode, 64).
5 T.S. Eliot, *Burnt Norton*, pt. 5, ll. 4–7: "Only by the form, the pattern, / Can words or music reach / The stillness, as a Chinese jar still / Moves perpetually in its stillness."
6 See no. 6, n. 10.
7 The Guyanese writer Wilson Harris, author of *Palace of the Peacock* (1960), is noted for his postcolonial themes and experimental style of writing.
8 For further details of this connection, see NF, "The World as Music and Idea in Wagner's *Parsifal*," in *MM*, 340–55.
9 See no. 1, n. 60.

17. The *Koiné* of Myth

1 See no. 6, n. 10.
2 See no. 1, n. 72.
3 For details of the Babylonian creation myth, see Theodor H. Gaster, *Thespis: Ritual, Myth, and Drama in the Ancient Near East* (Garden City, N.Y.: Doubleday, 1961), 89 ff.; annotated copy in the NFL. See also no. 6, n. 4.
4 For details of the Eleusinian initiations, see Gertrude Rachel Levy, *The Gate of Horn* (no. 1, n. 126), 297–8.
5 See *Zen Buddhism: Selected Writings of D.T. Suzuki*, ed. William Barrett (Garden City, N.Y.: Doubleday, 1956), 59 (chap. 3, "The History of Zen"); annotated copy in the NFL.
6 *Heilsgeschichte* or "salvation history": the Biblical narrative as the history of the redemptive activity of God.
7 NF is playing on Derrida's term *différance*, a neologism based on the French words *la différence* ("difference") and *différant* (the present participle of *différer*, "to differ" and "to defer"), and so a play on words that can only be read, not heard, and therefore an effect of writing rather than speech. The term points to the fact that signification depends on both a differential relationship among signifying terms in space (*écriture*) and an unarrestable deferral of "presence" in time. See Jacques Derrida, *Of Grammatology* (no. 12, n. 25), and *Writing and Difference*, ed. and trans. Alan Bass (Chicago: University of Chicago Press, 1978); annotated copies in the NFL.
8 Écriture or writing, according to Derrida, is the fundamental condition of all signification, inasmuch as the intelligibility of any sign, spoken or written, depends on a differential network of signifiers; this means that the possibility of a "presence" of meaning or truth is "always already" disrupted by differentiation in space and deferral in time. See Jacques Derrida, *Of Grammatology* and *Writing and Difference*.

9 In *Outline for an Historical Picture of the Progress of the Human Spirit* (1795), French political philosopher Antoine-Nicolas de Condorcet depicts humankind as progressing in stages, through the force of reason, to a fully enlightened form of society.

10 See no. 2, n. 19.

11 Ezra Pound's *Canto* 4 makes the connection between the bride in the chamber of the ancient temples and the myth of the imprisoned Danaë, whose tower the descending god enters in the form of a golden shower. See no. 2, n. 18.

12 See E.A. Wallace Budge, *The Gods of the Egyptians* (1904; rpt. New York: Dover, 1969), 2:116–17.

13 "And even angels, whose home is heaven, and who are winged too, yet had a ladder to go to heaven by steps." *Devotions on Emergent Occasions*, in *The Complete Poetry and Selected Prose of John Donne*, ed. Charles M. Coffin (New York: Modern Library, 1952), 417 (Meditation 2).

14 See no. 1, n. 195.

15 William Blake, *For the Sexes: The Gates of Paradise*, emblems 9 and 10 (Erdman, 264).

16 Voltaire, "Chaîne des Êtres Crées," in *Philosophical Dictionary*, ed. and trans. Theodore Besterman (Harmondsworth: Penguin, 1972), 107–9.

17 G.W.F. Hegel, *Phenomenology of Spirit*, trans. A. V. Miller (Oxford: Oxford University press, 1977), 14 (Preface).

18 Carlos Castaneda, popular author in the 1960s and 1970s of a series of books on his initiation into the shamanistic practices of Mexican sages, through the use of peyote and meditation. His most famous books are *Teachings of Don Juan: A Yaqui Way of Knowledge* (1968), *A Separate Reality* (1971), and *Journey to Ixtlan: The Lessons of Don Juan* (1972).

19 We might draw attention to Paul Tillich's definition of ecstasy as "not a negation of reason," but "a state of mind in which reason is beyond itself, that is, beyond its subject–object structure. In being beyond itself reason does not deny itself. 'Ecstatic reason' remains reason; it does not receive anything irrational or antirational—which it could not do without self-destruction—but it transcends the basic conditions of finite rationality, the subject–object structure." See his *Systematic Theology* (Chicago: University of Chicago Press, 1956), 1:112; annotated copy in the NFL.

20 See Abraham Maslow, *Toward a Psychology of Being* (New York: D. Van Nostrand, 1968), especially pt. 3, chaps. 6 and 7.

21 See NF's entry on "Bible, Translations of" in no. 20, "Extracts from *The Harper Handbook to Literature*." "*Koiné*," as the subtitle of the present essay suggests, came to refer to a common dialect, after the lingua franca that emerged in post-Classical Greece.

18. The Symbol as a Medium of Exchange

1 *Complete Poems of Emily Dickinson*, ed. Thomas H. Johnson (Boston: Little, Brown, 1960), 480 (Poem 1052).
2 "Toute Pensée émet un Coup de Dés" ("All thought emits a throw of the dice") is the last line of *Un Coup de dés* (*A Throw of the Dice*), in Stéphane Mallarmé, *Oeuvres complètes*, ed. Henri Mondor and G. Jean-Aubry (Paris: Gallimard, 1945), 477.
3 George Whalley, *Poetic Process* (London: Routledge & Kegan Paul, 1953), 166.
4 See *The Interpretation of Dreams*, vols. 4 and 5 of *The Complete Psychological Works of Sigmund Freud*, trans. James Strachey (London: Hogarth Press, 1962); 1965 Avon edition of Strachey's translation in the NFL.
5 In verse 3 of the nineteenth-century hymn *Onward! Christian Soldiers*, lyrics by Sabine Baring-Gould, music by Arthur Seymour Sullivan. The hymn is no. 178 in *The Hymn Book of the Anglican Church of Canada and the United Church of Canada* (1971), for which NF was a consultant.
6 Thomas Carlyle, *Sartor Resartus* (London: Dent, 1984), 165 (bk. 3, chap. 3).
7 Ernst Hartwig Kantorowicz, *The King's Two Bodies: A Study in Medieval Political Theology* (Princeton: Princeton University Press, 1957). Kantorowicz's work is a landmark study of the political theology of the Middle Ages, which he argues was based on the central principle of the splitting of the king's identity between the "body politic" and the "body natural."
8 T.S. Eliot, "Tradition and the Individual Talent" (Kermode, 40–1).
9 W.B. Yeats, "A General Introduction for My Work," in *Essays and Introductions* (London: Macmillan, 1961), 509. Yeats speaks of "the bundle of accident and incoherence that sits down to breakfast."
10 See no. 8, n. 6.
11 *White Narcissus* (Toronto: Macmillan, 1929), by Raymond Knister.
12 See no. 7, n. 1.
13 See no. 14, n. 3.
14 Aristotle, *Poetics*, chap. 22: "It is a great thing to make a proper use of each of the elements mentioned, and of double words and rare words too, but by far the greatest thing is the use of metaphor. This alone cannot be learnt; it is the token of genius. For the right use of metaphor means an eye for resemblances."
15 Edmund Wilson's study of the symbolist movement is *Axel's Castle: A Study in the Imaginative Literature of 1870–1930* (New York: Scribner's, 1931).
16 *À Rebours* (1884), by Joris-Karl Huysmans, pen name of Georges Charles Huysmans. The episode discussed by NF occurs in chap. 11 of the novel, a

translation of which (*Against the Grain*), with an introduction by Havelock Ellis (New York: Modern Library, 1930), is in the NFL.

17 "The quality of our hope forbids us life on earth, henceforth. What is there left for us to ask of this unhappy planet, where our sadness lingers on, save only pale reflections of such moments as these? . . . Live? Our servants will do that for us!" Auguste, Count Villiers de l'Isle-Adam, *Axël*, trans. H.P.R. Finberg, preface by W.B. Yeats (London: Jarrolds, 1925), 284 (4.2.5, "The Supreme Choice").

18 See no. 17, n. 20.

19 The reference is to Pater's statement that "All art constantly aspires towards the condition of music." Walter Pater, "The School of Giorgione," in *The Renaissance: Studies in Art and Poetry*, ed. Donald L. Hill (Berkeley: University of California Press, 1980), 106.

20 An extract from the letter can be found in Rainer Maria Rilke, *Duino Elegies*, ed. and trans. J.B. Leishman and Stephen Spender (New York: Norton, 1939), 128–30; a longer extract is in Rilke, *Sonnets to Orpheus*, trans. M.D. Herter Norton (New York: Norton, 1942), 131–6; annotated copies in the NFL.

21 Stéphane Mallarmé, *Crise de vers* (*Crisis in Verse*), in *Mallarmé*, ed. Anthony Hartley, with plain prose translations (Harmondsworth: Penguin, 1965), 171; annotated copy in the NFL.

22 Wallace Stevens, *Notes toward a Supreme Fiction*, in *The Collected Poems of Wallace Stevens*, 380–408.

23 Stéphane Mallarmé, letter to Henri Cazalis, 14 May 1867 (Caws, 87).

24 Stéphane Mallarmé, "The Book: A Spiritual Instrument" (Caws, 80).

25 See n. 23, above.

26 W.B. Yeats, *Solomon and the Witch*, l. 15. See also *A Vision* (no. 1, n. 92), 136.

27 See Sonnet 5 of pt. 1, and extracts from letters quoted in the notes by Norton in Rilke, *Sonnets to Orpheus*, 141.

28 See in particular vol. 1 of Ernst Cassirer, *The Philosophy of Symbolic Forms*, trans. Ralph Mannheim (New Haven: Yale University Press, 1953); annotated copy in the NFL.

29 The phrase "the credo and symbole of the fayth" appears in William Caxton's *The Art and Craft to Know Well to Die* (*The Art of Dying*), his translation (1490) of an anonymous Latin text.

30 See *Heraclitus* (no. 1, n. 195), 37 (Fragment 38).

31 Ibid., 90 (Fragment 112): "From out of all the many particulars comes oneness, and out of oneness come all the many particulars," and 102 (Fragment 118): "Listening not to me but to the Logos, it is wise to acknowledge that all things are one."

32 See no. 1, n. 195.

33 Poe, *Eureka*, in *The Science Fiction of Edgar Allan Poe*, ed. Harold Beaver (Harmondsworth: Penguin, 1976), 309.

34 "Before a man studies Zen, to him mountains are mountains and waters are

waters; after he gets an insight into the truth of Zen through the instruction of a good master, mountains to him are not mountains and waters are not waters; but after this when he really attains to the abode of rest, mountains are once more mountains and waters are waters." *Zen Buddhism: Selected Writings of D.T. Suzuki* (no. 17, n. 5), 14.

19. The Expanding World of Metaphor

1 Jacques Derrida, *Of Grammatology* (no. 12, n. 25), and "Plato's Pharmacy," in *Dissemination* (no. 14, n. 5); annotated copies in the NFL. See also no. 17, nn. 7 and 8.

2 Leibnizian optimism follows from the notion of "the supreme perfection of God," who, in producing the universe, "has chosen the best possible plan. . . . For as all possible things in the understanding of God claim existence in proportion to their perfections, the result of all these claims must be the most perfect actual world that is possible." Gottfried Wilhelm Leibniz, *Principles of Nature and Grace, Founded on Reason*, no. 10, in *The Monadology and Other Philosophical Writings*, trans. Robert Latta (London: Oxford University Press, 1948), 417.

3 Marshall McLuhan, *Understanding Media: The Extensions of Man* (New York: McGraw Hill, 1964).

4 In particular, Jacques Derrida and other deconstructionists. See n. 1, above.

5 In *Being and Time*, the term "ecstatic," in the sense of *ex-stasis* or "standing outside," is used with reference to temporality, "the primordial 'outside-of-itself' in and for itself." NF applies Heidegger's concept of "the 'ecstases' of temporality" in the primarily spatial context of metaphor. Martin Heidegger, *Being and Time*, trans. John Macquarrie and Edward Robinson (New York: Harper & Row, 1962), 377. See also no. 17, n. 19.

6 See no. 1, n. 126.

7 Francis Bacon, *The Advancement of Learning*: "For as for Poesy, it is rather a pleasure or play of imagination, than a work or duty thereof." In *A Critical Edition of the Major Works* (no. 2, n. 11), 218 (bk. 2).

8 In *Primitive Mentality* (London: George Allen & Unwin, 1923), French philosopher and anthropologist Lucien Lévy-Bruhl argues that "the primitive mind" is characterized by a prelogical, intensely intimate participation in the beings and world of its social and natural environment. In *AC*, 295–6, NF calls one of the "specific thematic forms" of the lyric *participation mystique*.

9 See no. 1, n. 175.

10 Sir Thomas Browne, *Religio Medici*, pt. 2, sec. 6 (Keynes, 75).

11 The reference is to the currency of the existentialists in the 1950s, and in particular to the work of Jean-Paul Sartre, which called for a situational ethics based on "engagement" or commitment.

12 Martin Buber's major work, *Ich und Du* (1923), translated as *I and Thou* (Edinburgh: Clark, 1938), expounds a philosophy of "relation," of authentic dialogue with other beings based on the difference between a person-and-thing relationship ("I" and "it") and a person-and-person relationship ("I" and "Thou"), which includes that between a human being and God.

13 The two earlier versions of the paper contain a further paragraph here (cited from "The Social Authority of the Writer"): "As we saw earlier, the progressive unifying of experience brought about by language is by no means confined to verbal language. In fact, metaphors from painting and music are often used to suggest a heightening of intensity in our verbal experience: that is, an art which is 'beyond words' may suggest a possibility of going beyond words within words as well. The Elizabethans used Horace's tag *ut pictura poesis* [*Ars Poetica*, l. 361], poetry as a speaking picture, to suggest that a poem was a kind of controlled hallucination, a summoning of the past into the present. This century speaks of verbal icons, where a poem becomes a stational focus of meditation. It also uses the word 'structure,' a spatialized metaphor derived from architecture, to suggest that the study of a poem leads up to a complete and simultaneous act of apprehending it. This is both a practicable and a desirable goal, whatever the poststructuralists may say, subject only to the proviso that, if reached, it must be immediately abandoned, which means that we either abandon the poem or start a new cycle of understanding it. If, on the other hand, we prefer to stress the linear experience of reading the poem, we might fall back on the musical imagery that we have seen to be frequent in poetry itself. Thus Walter Pater spoke of all the arts approaching the condition of music, because he was interested in experience, and realized that the arts could provide an intensifying of it" [see no. 18, n. 19].

14 See no. 1, n. 113.

15 E.E. Cummings, no. 14 from *1 x 1 [One Times One]*, in *Complete Poems, 1910–62* (London: Granada, 1981), 2:554.

16 These are the last lines of *To the Queen* in Tennyson's *Idylls of the King*.

17 See no. 4, n. 3.

18 Paul Valéry, "On Poe's *Eureka*" (no. 4, n. 3), 175–6.

19 See Harold Bloom, *The Anxiety of Influence* (no. 12, n. 27).

20 The film *Henry V* (UK, 1944), directed by Sir Laurence Olivier, is dedicated "To the commandoes and airborne troops of Great Britain, the spirit of whose ancestors it has been humbly attempted to recapture in some ensuing scenes." Olivier was released from wartime duties and granted permission to make the film, which was planned as a patriotic work on the eve of the Normandy invasion, when the Allied victory was in sight; references to things such as the British execution of French prisoners are cut from this cinematic version of Shakespeare's play.

21 See, for example, Marshall McLuhan, *The Gutenberg Galaxy: The Making of Typographic Man* (Toronto: University of Toronto Press, 1962), 30–2.

22 The two earlier versions of the paper contain the following example (cited from "The Social Authority of the Writer"): "The specifically Christian view reappears, as we should expect, in poets who are strongly committed to it. Thus Gerard Manley Hopkins: 'I say more: the just man justices; / Keeps grace: that keeps all his goings graces; / Acts in God's eye what in God's eye he is / Christ. For Christ plays in ten thousand places, / Lovely in limbs, and lovely in eyes not his. / To the Father through the features of men's faces'" [*As Kingfishers Catch Fire, Dragonflies Draw Flame*, ll. 9–14].

23 For the "central mind" or "major man" in Wallace Stevens, see his *Chocorua to Its Neighbour*, l. 52, *Final Soliloquy of the Interior Paramour*, l. 16, and *Notes toward a Supreme Fiction* (*It Must Be Abstract*, cantos 8–10), in *The Collected Poems of Wallace Stevens*, 298, 524, 386–9.

24 In *Mind and Matter* (Cambridge: Cambridge University Press, 1958), 55, Erwin Schrödinger speaks of "the empirical fact that consciousness is never experienced in the plural, only in the singular." See also Schrödinger, "Seek for the Road," in *My View of the World*, trans. Cecily Hastings (Cambridge: Cambridge University Press, 1964), 34.

25 The two earlier versions of the paper contain the following sentence: "Also, in the deadlock of scowling superpowers which is contemporary history, it is not very reassuring to be told that my consciousness is identical with President Reagan's."

26 The earliest version of the paper contains the following: "I gave this talk the title 'Expanding the Boundaries of Literature,' and have been trying to show that, in its content and the experience of it at any rate, literature has no boundaries. What it does is remove the boundary built into us by the subject–object world we live in and the categories of time and space within which we struggle to make sense of it. And as these realities dissolve into illusions, the absurd paradoxes of myth and metaphor bring us further illusions that seem to have intimations of a different kind of reality."

27 See no. 18, n. 22.

28 In "The Social Authority of the Writer," NF adds, "the sort of authority expressed in Shelley's phrase 'unacknowledged legislator'" ["Poets are the unacknowledged legislators of the world" is the last line of Percy Bysshe Shelley's *Defence of Poetry*].

29 In sec. 331 of his *Scienza Nuova* (no. 4, n. 4), 96–7.

20. Extracts from *The Harper Handbook to Literature*

1 Sir Thomas Browne, *Religio Medici*, pt. 1, sec. 34 (Keynes, 41).

2 NF may be thinking of the narrator's admonition in chap. 45, "The

Affadavit": "So ignorant are most landsmen of some of the plainest and most palpable wonders of the world, that without some hints touching the plain facts, historical and otherwise, of the fishery, they might scout at Moby Dick as a monstrous fable, or still worse and more detestable, a hideous and intolerable allegory." Herman Melville, *Moby-Dick* (Harmondsworth: Penguin, 1992), 223.

3 Stéphane Mallarmé, *Crise de vers* (*Crisis in Verse*), in *Mallarmé* (no. 18, n. 21), 174–5.

4 See no. 8, n. 6.

5 See no. 9, n. 10.

6 Genesis 3:7 (AV): "And the eyes of them both were opened, and they knew that they were naked; and they sewed fig leaves together, and made themselves aprons." In the Geneva Bible, what is translated here as "aprons" appears as "breeches."

7 NF is referring to Menander's *Dyskolos* (*The Grouch*), which was recovered in 1957.

8 See no. 2, n. 2.

9 See no. 2, n. 21.

10 See no. 11, n. 7.

11 A lengthy footnote in Freud's *The Interpretation of Dreams* suggests that *Hamlet* "has its roots in the same soil as *Oedipus Rex*." See vol. 4 of *The Complete Psychological Works of Sigmund Freud*, 264 (chap. 5, sec. d, "Typical Dreams"). Ernest Jones pursued the idea both in his article "The Oedipus-Complex as an Explanation of Hamlet's Mystery: A Study in Motive," in *The American Journal of Psychology* (1910), and in his book *Hamlet and Oedipus* (London: Victor Gollanz, 1949).

12 For the concept of the "lost phallus," see Jacques Lacan, "The Signification of the Phallus," in *Écrits: A Selection*, trans. Alan Sheridan (New York: Norton, 1977), 281–91. Lacan's concept of the *stade du miroir*, also elaborated in *Écrits*, is a notion to which NF returns in no. 22, "Lacan and the Full Word" (394).

13 Alexander Pope, *An Essay on Criticism*, ll. 364–5: "'Tis not enough no harshness gives offence, / The sound must seem an Echo to the sense." In *Poetical Works* (no. 4, n. 2), 74.

14 See no. 11, n. 7.

15 This conception is developed in Eliot's essay "The Metaphysical Poets" (Kermode, 59–67).

16 See n. 3, above.

17 James Joyce, *Stephen Hero*, ed. John J. Slocum and Herbert Cahoon (New York: New Directions, 1963), 211–13.

18 Hopkins refers to these two concepts throughout his journal and letters. See, for example, *A Hopkins Reader*, ed. John Pick (London: Oxford

University Press, 1953), 46 (extract from his journal, 1875); 91 (letter to Robert Bridges, 15 February 1879); 210 (letter to R.W. Dixon, 30 June 1886).

19 Coleridge, lecture on Shakespeare of 16 December 1811, in *Lectures, 1808–1819: On Literature*, vol. 5, pt. 1 of *The Collected Works of Samuel Taylor Coleridge* (1987), 358; and "Essays on the Principles of Genial Criticism," in *Shorter Works and Fragments*, vol. 11, pt. 1 of *The Collected Works* (1995), 353–86.

20 "All earthly existence must ultimately be contained in a book." Stéphane Mallarmé, "The Book: A Spiritual Instrument" (Caws, 80).

21 Jean Piaget, *Structuralism*, trans. Chaninah Maschler (New York: Harper & Row, 1970), 5.

22 See Claude Lévi-Strauss, *The Elementary Structures of Kinship*, ed. Rodney Needham, trans. James Harle Bell and John Richard von Sturmer (Boston: Beacon Press, 1969).

21. Letter to the Editor of PMLA

1 See W.B. Yeats, *Explorations* (London: Macmillan, 1962), 437, 441.

22. Lacan and the Full Word

1 For this and other Lacanian concepts addressed in NF's essay, see Jacques Lacan, *Écrits: A Selection* (no. 20, n. 12), and *The Language of the Self: The Function of Language in Psychoanalysis*, ed. and trans. Anthony Wilden (New York: Dell, 1975); annotated copies in the NFL. The text by Harold Bloom to which NF refers is *A Map of Misreading* (1975).

2 See no. 18, n. 7.

23. Literature and the Visual Arts

1 See NF's entry on "structure," in the *Harper Handbook to Literature* (no. 20).

2 "Prends l'eloquence et tords-lui son cou!" ("Take eloquence and wring its neck!") Verlaine, *Art poétique*, l. 21. In the typescript, the quotation is ascribed to Valéry, but NF corrects the error in NB 44.534: "Verlaine said take rhetoric & wring its neck *not* Valéry" (*LN*, 215).

3 The movement, associated with poets such as Ezra Pound, Hilda Doolittle, and Amy Lowell, and inspired by T.E. Hulme's anti-Romantic critical prescriptions, was launched around 1912. The imagists advocated the use of nonconventional forms and sharp, objective visual images.

4 See T.S. Eliot, "Dante," and "Milton I" (Kermode, 205–30, 258–64).

5 The principle formulated by William Carlos Williams is "No ideas but in things." See the shorter poem *Paterson*, in *The Collected Earlier Poems* (New York: New Directions, 1951), 233; *A Sort of Song*, in *The Collected Later Poems*,

rev. ed. (New York: New Directions, 1963), 7; *Paterson* (New York: New Directions, 1963), 14, 18 (bk. 1, sec. 1); and *The Autobiography of William Carlos Williams* (New York: Random House, 1951), 390 (chap. 58).

6 William Hogarth (1697–1764), English painter and engraver, famous for his satirical depictions of contemporary life. The eight plates of *The Rake's Progress* narrate the decline of Tom Rakewell, who squanders his inheritance in the pursuit of fashionable life. *Marriage à la Mode* tells, in six plates, the story of a disastrous marriage of convenience between the daughter of a wealthy merchant and the son of a ruined aristocrat.

7 See, for example, Exodus 20:4, 23:24, Leviticus 26:1, Deuteronomy 4:23, 5:8, and Psalm 97:7.

8 See no. 1, n. 4. In the *Clementine Recognitions*, 344 (bk. 7), St. Peter and his followers visit "a certain temple, in which there were very magnificent works of Phidias, on which every one of [the followers] gazed earnestly." Peter, however, was in no way "ravished with the grace of the painting."

9 See no. 17, nn. 4 and 5.

10 The subtitle of G.E. Lessing's *Laokoon* (1766) is *Über die Grenzen der Malerei und Poesie*, "On the Limits of Painting and Poetry."

11 This question appears in the first paragraph of *Alice's Adventures in Wonderland*, in *The Complete Works of Lewis Carroll*, 15 (chap. 1, "Down the Rabbit-Hole").

12 The reference is to the Virgins and Madonnas of Filippo Lippi (1406–69), Piero della Francesca (1410–92), Sandro Botticelli (1445–1512), and Leonardo da Vinci (1452–1519), among others.

13 William Carlos Williams, "Kenneth Burke," in *Selected Essays of William Carlos Williams* (New York: New Directions, 1954), 132.

14 John Ruskin, *Stones of Venice*, ed. Ernest Rhys (London: Dent, 1907), 2:176–7 (chap. 6, secs. 60–1).

15 The painting of grapes so realistic that birds tried to peck them is attributed to Zeuxis, whose legendary rivalry with Parrhasius is recorded by Pliny the Elder in his *Natural History*, bk. 35, chap. 36. Parrhasius painted a curtain that seemed to be covering a canvas; when he showed it to Zeuxis, the latter attempted to draw it open and was thus forced to recognize the superiority of his adversary.

16 George Puttenham, *The Arte of English Poesie*, in *Elizabethan Critical Essays* (no. 2, n. 7), 2:188.

17 "Nature hath made one world, and Art another. In briefe, all things are artificall, for Nature is the Art of God." Sir Thomas Browne, *Religio Medici*, pt. 1, sec. 16 (Keynes, 22).

18 Robert Browning's *Andrea del Sarto* takes as its subject the Florentine painter (1486–1530), whose exemplary composition and craftmanship led to the conventional characterization of his works as "faultless."

19 The painting *La strada entra nella casa* (1911), by Umberto Boccioni (1882–

1916), one of the founders of Futurism, hangs in the Sprengel Museum in Hanover, Germany.

20 See no. 1, n. 126.

21 *Paul Klee on Modern Art* (London: Faber & Faber, 1949), 45: "First, he [the artist] does not attach such intense importance to natural form as do so many realist critics, because, for him, these final forms are not the real stuff of the process of natural creation. For he places more value on the powers which do the forming than on the final forms themselves."

24. The Journey as Metaphor

1 Psalm 12:8 in the AV: "The wicked walk on every side, when the vilest men are exalted."

2 Dante, *Inferno*, canto 1, l. 3: "where the straight way was lost" [trans. John D. Sinclair (New York: Oxford University Press, 1939)].

3 The eightfold path consists of "right views, right intentions, right speech, right conduct, right livelihood, right effort, right mindfulness, right concentration." *Buddhist Scriptures*, ed. and trans. Edward Conze (Harmondsworth: Penguin, 1959), 187; annotated copy in the NFL.

4 John Bunyan, *The Pilgrim's Progress*, ed. Roger Sharrock (Harmondsworth: Penguin, 1965), 289. It is Mr. Great-heart speaking to Christiana, as he acts as a guide through the Valley of Humiliation.

5 Ibid., 370.

6 T.S. Eliot, *Burnt Norton*, ll. 6–10, 46–8: "What might have been is an abstraction / Remaining a perpetual possibility / Only in a world of speculation. / What might have been and what has been / Point to one end, which is always present. / . . . . / Time past and time future / What might have been and what has been / Point to one end, which is always present."

7 See Mircea Eliade, *Shamanism: Archaic Techniques of Ecstasy*, trans. Willard R. Trask (Princeton: Princeton University Press, 1964), 181–214 (chap. 6).

8 See no. 2, n. 19.

9 Ibid.

10 See no. 9, n. 4.

11 The passage actually appears in Xenophon's *The Persian Expedition*, trans. Rex Warner (Harmondsworth: Penguin, 1949), 210–11 (bk. 4, chap. 6).

12 See no. 17, n. 13.

13 *The Book of the Dead* (no. 1, n. 139); and *The Tibetan Book of the Dead*, ed. W.Y. Evans-Wentz, trans. Kazi Dawa-Samdup, 2nd ed. (London: Oxford University Press, 1949); annotated copies in the NFL.

14 See Gertrude Rachel Levy, *The Gate of Horn* (no. 1, n. 126), 147–51.

15 W.F. Jackson Knight, *Vergil: Epic and Anthropology*, ed. John D. Christie (New York: Barnes & Noble, 1967), 226–30 (chap. 7 of *Cumaean Gates*).

16 Ibid., 202–14 (chap. 5 of *Cumaean Gates*).

17 There are annotated copies of two different editions of the work in the NFL: *The Cloud of Unknowing and Other Treatises, by an English Mystic of the Fourteenth Century*, ed. Justin McCann, 6th rev. ed. (London: Burns Oates, 1952), and *The Cloud of Unknowing and The Book of Privy Counselling*, ed. Phyllis Hodgson (London: Oxford University Press, 1958).

18 *The Collected Poems of Theodore Roethke* (Garden City, N.Y.: Doubleday, 1966), 193.

19 Margaret Atwood, *Journey to the Interior*, in *Selected Poems, 1966–1984* (Toronto: Oxford University Press, 1990), 30–1 (from *The Circle Game*).

20 "Haunted by Lack of Ghosts: Some Patterns in Imagery of Canadian Poetry," in *The Canadian Imagination: Dimensions of a Literary Culture*, ed. David Staines (Cambridge: Harvard University Press, 1977), 22–45.

21 Alden Nowlan, *The Genealogy of Morals*, in *The Things Which Are* (Toronto: Contact Press, 1962), 47.

22 "The way up and the way down are one and the same." See *Heraclitus* (no. 1, n. 195), 90 (Fragment 108). T.S. Eliot uses the fragment, in the Greek, as his second epigraph to *Burnt Norton*, a poem which contains the lines, "This is the one way, and the other / Is the same" (pt. 3, ll. 33–4). See also Eliot's *The Dry Salvages*, pt. 3, l. 6: "And the way up is the way down, the way forward is the way back."

23 See no. 1, n. 195.

24 Yeats speaks of the *Hodos Chameliontos* at the beginning and end of *A Vision* (no. 1, n. 92), 5, 299. See also his reference to the Path of the Chameleon in *The Autobiography of William Butler Yeats* (New York: Macmillan, 1938), 232.

25 Gertrude Stein, *Everybody's Autobiography* (London: Heinemann, 1938), 251: "anyway what was the use of my having come from Oakland it was not natural to have come from there yes write about it if I like or anything if I like but not there, there is no there there."

26 "Now faith is the substance of things hoped for, the evidence of things not seen" (Hebrews 11:1).

25. Framework and Assumption

1 See no. 17, n. 18.

2 Jane Austen, *Northanger Abbey*, vol. 5 of *The Novels of Jane Austin* (see no. 1, n. 79), 38 (chap. 5).

3 See James Boswell, *The Life of Samuel Johnson*, ed. George Birkbeck Hill (Oxford: Oxford University Press, 1934), 2:449. The formalist critic is Viktor Shklovsky, whose 1921 essay on Sterne ends with the statement, "*Tristram Shandy* is the most typical novel in world literature." See *Russian Formalist Criticism: Four Essays*, ed. and trans. Lee T. Lemon and Marion J. Reis (Lincoln: University of Nebraska Press, 1965), 57.

4 See no. 23, n. 18.

5 The first of ten annual surveys of Canadian poetry that NF wrote for the *University of Toronto Quarterly*, "Letters in Canada: 1950, Poetry," appeared in April 1951, and the last one, for the year 1959, appeared in July 1960. The entire series has been reprinted in vol. 12 of the Collected Works, *Northrop Frye on Canada* (C, 91–229).

6 In Greek mythology, the Muses were the nine daughters of Mnemosyne (Memory) and Zeus. Calliope was the inspiring spirit associated with heroic poetry, while Clio was the Muse of history.

7 A reference to the closing paragraph of Benjamin's essay "The Work of Art in the Age of Mechanical Reproduction," in *Illuminations*, ed. Hannah Arendt, trans. Harry Zohn (New York: Schocken, 1969), 242.

8 Kenneth Burke, *The Rhetoric of Religion: Studies in Logology* (Berkeley: University of California Press, 1970).

9 NF is playing on Theseus's speech in *A Midsummer Night's Dream*: "The lunatic, the lover and the poet / Are of imagination all compact" (5.1.7–8).

10 See no. 12, n. 27.

11 See no. 12, n. 11, and no. 14, n. 1.

12 See no. 6, n. 9.

13 Gertrude Stein, *Picasso* (London: B.T. Batsford, 1948), 15–16; annotated copy of the original French volume (Paris: Librairie Floury, 1938) in the NFL: "Picasso knows faces as a child knows them and the head and the body. He was then commencing to try to express this consciousness and the struggle was appalling because . . . no one had ever tried to express things seen not as one knows them but as they are when one sees them without remembering having looked at them. . . . Picasso said to me once with a good deal of bitterness, they say I can draw better than Raphael and probably they are right, . . . but if I can draw as well as Raphael I have at least the right to choose my way and they should recognize it, that right, but no, they say no."

14 See Edmund Husserl, "The Thesis of the Natural Standpoint and Its Suspension" and "On Eidetic Reduction," in *Phenomenology: The Philosophy of Edmund Husserl and Its Interpretation*, ed. Joseph J. Kockelmans (Garden City, N.Y.: Doubleday, 1967), 68–79, 105–17; and Quentin Lauer, *Phenomenology: Its Genesis and Prospect* (New York: Harper & Row, 1965), chap. 3; annotated copies in the NFL.

15 William Blake, *Jerusalem*, pl. 48, l. 20 (Erdman, 197).

16 Jonathan Swift, *Gulliver's Travels*, pt. 4, chap. 5.

26. Maps and Territories

1 Lewis Carroll, *The Hunting of the Snark*, in *The Complete Works of Lewis Carroll*, 683.

2 See no. 12, n. 27.
3 Lewis Carroll, *Sylvie and Bruno Concluded*, in *The Complete Works*, 557 (chap. 11, "The Man in the Moon").

27. Epilogo

1 See no. 12, n. 9.
2 Pauline Kogan, *Northrop Frye: The High Priest of Clerical Obscurantism* (Montreal: Progressive Books, 1969).
3 Friedrich Schiller, *On the Aesthetic Education of Man*, an essay published in 1795 in the form of a series of twenty-seven letters. For the significance of "play," see especially letters 14–5 and 26–7.
4 Irving Layton, *Whatever Else Poetry Is Freedom*, in *The Collected Poems of Irving Layton* (Toronto: McClelland & Stewart, 1971), 316–17. It is worth noting that Layton reacted with hostility to NF's criticism of an early book of his poetry (in 1951; see *BG*, 8). NF tried to avoid a personal quarrel, but he remained the subject of Layton's continued attacks over the next decade. See John Ayre, *Northrop Frye: A Biography* (Toronto: Random House, 1989), 235, 277.

28. Auguries of Experience

1 In Shakespeare's *Antony and Cleopatra*, Enobarbus says of Cleopatra: "Age cannot wither her, nor custom stale / Her infinite variety" (2.2.234–5).
2 "If the fool would persist in his folly he would become wise." William Blake, *The Marriage of Heaven and Hell*, pl. 7 (Erdman, 36).
3 See *Kerygma and Myth: A Theological Debate*, ed. Hans-Werner Bartsch, trans. Reginald H. Fuller (London: SPCK, 1972).
4 This phrase echoes Prospero's speech after the masque in *The Tempest*, 4.1.156.

29. Literary and Mechanical Models

1 R.W. Chambers, *Beowulf: An Introduction to the Study of the Poem* (Cambridge: Cambridge University Press, 1921).
2 John Livingston Lowes, *Geoffrey Chaucer and the Development of His Genius* (Boston: Houghton Mifflin, 1934).
3 John Livingston Lowes, *The Road to Xanadu: A Study in the Ways of the Imagination* (Boston: Houghton Mifflin, 1927).
4 F.R. Leavis (1895–1978), author of *The Great Tradition* (1948), was founder and chief editor of the journal *Scrutiny* at Cambridge. William Empson (1906–84), who, like Leavis, was indebted to the practical criticism of I.A.

Richards, championed close reading in his seminal work *Seven Types of Ambiguity* (1930).

5 C.P. Snow's Rede lecture of 1959, *The Two Cultures and the Scientific Revolution* (New York: Cambridge University Press, 1960), 12; annotated copy in the NFL.

6 Ibid.

7 "May not man himself become a sort of parasite upon the machines? An affectionate machine-tickling aphid?" Samuel Butler, *Erewhon*, in *The Shrewsbury Edition of the Works of Samuel Butler*, 2:183 (chap. 24).

8 See C.P. Snow, *The Two Cultures*, 26–7 (chap. 2, "Intellectuals as Natural Luddites").

30. Literature as Therapy

1 Geoffrey Chaucer, "General Prologue," *The Canterbury Tales*, l. 438.

2 Sir Thomas Browne, *Pseudodoxia Epidemica*, in Keynes, 228 ("To the Reader").

3 "The Doctor was more than suspected of having no religion, but somehow Middlemarch tolerated this deficiency in him as if he had been a Lord Chancellor; indeed it is probable that his professional weight was the more believed in, the world-old association of cleverness with the evil principle being still potent in the minds even of lady-patients who had the strictest ideas of frilling and sentiment. . . . At all events, it is certain that if any medical man had come to Middlemarch with the reputation of having very definite religious views, of being given to prayer, and of otherwise showing an active piety, there would have been a general presumption against his medical skill." George Eliot, *Middlemarch* (Harmondsworth: Penguin, 1965), 211 (chap. 18).

4 Geoffrey Chaucer, "General Prologue," *The Canterbury Tales*, l. 333.

5 See no. 2, n. 2.

6 Sir William Osler, "The Library of Robert Burton," in *Robert Burton and the Anatomy of Melancholy*, papers by Sir William Osler, Professor Edward Bensly, et al., ed. F. Madan (Oxford: Oxford University Press, 1926), 183 (vol. 1, pt. 3).

7 James Boswell, *The Life of Samuel Johnson*, 2:121.

8 Robert Burton, *The Anatomy of Melancholy* (London: Dent, 1932), 1:201 (pt. 1, sec. 2, memb. 1, subsec. 2, "A Digression of the Nature of Spirits, Bad Angels, or Devils, and how they cause Melancholy").

9 Jonathan Swift, *A Tale of a Tub and Other Works*, ed. Angus Ross and David Woolley (Oxford: Oxford University Press, 1986), 79 (sec. 9, "A Digression concerning Madness").

10 *The Romeo Error: A Matter of Life and Death* (London: Hodder & Stoughton, 1974), by the biologist Lyall Watson.

11 Aristotle, *Poetics*, chap. 6: "Tragedy is, then, a representation of an action that is heroic and complete and of a certain magnitude—by means of language enriched with all kinds of ornament, each used separately in the different parts of the play: it represents men in action and does not use narrative, and through pity and fear it effects relief to these and similar emotions."

12 See no. 1, n. 143.

13 In Japanese mythology, the sun-goddess Amaterasu Omikami, whose withdrawal to a cave has plunged the world into darkness, is finally drawn out from her hiding place by the raucous dance of a spirit named Uzume. See Joseph Campbell, *The Masks of God: Oriental Mythology* (Harmondsworth: Penguin, 1962), 471.

14 The exact statement has not been found, but for similar observations, see Milan Kundera, "Comedy Is Everywhere," in *They Shoot Writers, Don't They?* ed. George Theiner (London: Faber & Faber, 1984), 153–4; the text of the article is an interview granted to Theiner in 1977. NF, who was speaking only from notes made on file cards, may have improvised on Kundera's ideas slightly to fit the occasion, as there was a member of the audience who kept laughing throughout much of his lecture.

15 The phrase is Coleridge's (see *Table Talk*, vol. 14, pt. 1 of *The Collected Works of Samuel Taylor Coleridge*, 90), an adaptation of Swift's definition of style as "proper words in proper places." See "A Letter to a Young Gentleman," in vol. 9 of *The Prose Works of Jonathan Swift*, ed. Herbert Davis (Oxford: Blackwell, 1948).

31. Response to Papers on "Northrop Frye and Eighteenth-Century Literature"

1 See Henry Fielding, Preface to *Joseph Andrews* (London: Oxford University Press, 1970), 4, and *Tom Jones* (no. 1, n. 80), 159 (bk. 5, chap. 1).

2 NF is referring to Eric Rothstein and Paul Hunter.

3 Eric Rothstein, "Anatomy and Bionomics of Criticism: Eighteenth-Century Cases," *Eighteenth-Century Studies*, 24 (Winter 1990–91): 210: "It is that the anatomical method, especially in support of a textualist system, needs *differential* supplementation to deal with literature in different historical modes."

4 That is, the first chapter or "initial essay" in each of the eighteen books of Henry Fielding's *Tom Jones*.

5 Eric Rothstein, "Anatomy and Bionomics of Criticism," 217.

6 An allusion to the scattered pieces of the body of Orpheus in Greek mythology.

Emendations

page/line

24/38 Better is the sight of the eyes than the wandering of the desire *for* Better is the sight of the eye than the wandering of desire [AV]

55/35–6 I stand for sacrifice *for* I stand here for sacrifice. [Riverside Shakespeare]

58/34 *Leucippe and Clitophon* for *Cleitophon and Leucippe*

63/11 and that of Christianity *for* and of Christianity

68/2 no use *for* no good [Nonesuch edition]

69/32 coats of skins *for* coats of skin [AV]

84/33 hero or heroine is *for* hero or heroine are

94/33, 38 Thyamis *for* Thamyris

107/10, 14 "socialist realism" *for* "social realism"

133/29 Nicholas of Cusa *for* Nicholas of Cusanus

197/32 But trewély *for* And trewély [Riverside Chaucer]

197/36 And wel we weren *for* And whan we weren [Riverside Chaucer]

207/33 bouncing illusions off each other *for* bouncing illusions off against each other

225/18 from deserting the prophetic tradition for a speculative one *for* deserting the prophetic tradition from a speculative one [TS]

258/2 *The Phoenix and Turtle for The Phoenix and the Turtle*

262/17 "socialist realism" *for* "social realism"

296/1 some poetic licence *for* a number of poetic licenses

299/16 poetic licence *for* poetic licences

316/26–7 some poetic licence *for* certain 'poetic licenses'

327/25 As if *for* As though [Johnson edition]

328/17 a symbol, like a metaphor *for* a symbol, like metaphor [TS]

328/32 closer to the *symbolos for* closer to *symbolos* [TS]

329/7 South Korea *for* Southern Korea

332/24 We may take the metaphor, the statement *for* We may take the metaphor, perhaps, the statement

335/17–18 which had previously had the general meaning *for* which previously had usually the general sense [TS]
375/9 extent of influence *for* extent or influence
393/15 of an objective world *for* an objective world
396/24–5 a Chinese jar still *for* a Chinese jar [as in Eliot]
398/34 Verlaine *for* Valéry [*LN*, 215]
399/39 the ones that underlie *for* the one that underlies [to harmonize with NF's revision of 'influence' to 'influences']
402/24 What's the use *for* What's the good [Nonesuch edition]
410/14 Dardanians *for* Dardanides
423/25 detective fiction *for* detection
432/27 Inuit life today *for* Inuit (Eskimo) life today
442/17 a very dangerous quarrel *for* a very dangerous quarrel course
443/24 dedication in my colleagues *for* dedication in my colleagues that I return
453/23 work, there arises *for* work on an assumed level, there arises
463/23 the fruitlesse importunity of Uroscopy *for* the futile portense of uroscopy
471/32 be ironic *for* become ironic
471/37 appeals to and responses of *for* appeals and responses of
473/18–19 does the sick joke *for* is the sick joke
474/8–9 indirect, and there is the strong temptation for many writers *for* indirect for many poets, and there is the strong temptation by many writers
477/15 aspects of being treated *for* aspects being treated [NF's disk]
480/11 story patterns *for* story pattern [NF's disk]
494/28 reliable translations *for* reliable translation

Index